KINSHIP SYSTEMS

KINSHIP SYSTEMS

CHANGE AND RECONSTRUCTION

EDITED BY

Patrick McConvell, Ian Keen, and Rachel Hendery

THE UNIVERSITY OF UTAH PRESS

Salt Lake City

The Defiance House Man colophon is a registered trademark of the University of Utah Press. It is based on a four-foot-tall Ancient Puebloan pictograph (late PIII) near Glen Canyon, Utah.

17 16 15 14 13   1 2 3 4 5

LIBRARY OF CONGRESS CATALOGING-IN-PUBLICATION DATA

Kinship systems : change and reconstruction / edited by Patrick McConvell, Ian Keen, and Rachel Hendery.
pages cm
Includes bibliographical references and index.
ISBN 978-1-60781-244-9 (cloth : alk. paper) — ISBN 978-1-60781-245-6 (ebook)
1. Kinship. 2. Kinship—Terminology. 3. Anthropological linguistics. 4. Comparative linguistics. 5. Language and culture. I. McConvell, Patrick.
GN487.K57 2013
306.83—dc23

2013003841

Printed and bound by Sheridan Books, Inc., Ann Arbor, Michigan.

Contents

Figures

Tables

1

Introduction

Kinship Change in Anthropology and Linguistics

Patrick McConvell

This essay is intended to inform readers about the background to the study of change and reconstruction of kinship in anthropology and linguistics. Most particularly, it aims to introduce linguists to the work in anthropology, anthropologists to the work in linguistics, and all others interested in social change and the history and prehistory of the family to what these disciplines have to offer. First, in section 1, the importance of kinship in social history and prehistory is stressed. Then, in section 2, the engagement of historical linguistics in kinship is introduced, followed in section 3 by the contribution of those areas of anthropology concerned with prehistory and ethnology (comparative anthropology) while remaining alert to the impact of linguistics in these fields. Section 4 deals at some length with a central nexus of theory and method that straddles anthropology and linguistics: semantics and the theory and method of semantic change. This then leads into section 5, on another area to which both linguistics and anthropology/ethnology contribute in their different ways, the reconstruction of past systems, their change, and their evolution, focusing initially on methods that use linguistic forms as a major part of the evidence. Section 6 shifts to looking at approaches in which system transformations are brought to the fore, including both hypotheses involving unilinear evolutionary schemes and those that reject or modify such approaches. Finally, the present book is brought into the spotlight: its origins, its contributions, and its overall significance in the current moment, when kinship studies are experiencing a renaissance in international and interdisciplinary scholarship.

1. Kinship in Human Society and the Human Sciences

Kinship is one of the foundations of human social life and, together with language, is part of the change that made our hominid ancestors human. Kinship in a certain sense was present among these ancestors, as it is among our ape cousins: there is awareness of certain basic family relationships that affect patterns of behavior (such as avoidance of what we would call "incest"). However, other primates do not talk about classes of kinship relationships and give them names, as all humans do—and did, for as far back as we can know.

Kinship is the bedrock of all human societies that we know. All humans recognize fathers and mothers, sons and daughters, brothers and sisters, uncles and aunts, husbands and wives, grandparents, cousins, and often many more complex types of relationships in the terminologies that they use. That is the matrix into which human children are born in the great majority of cases, and their first words are often kinship terms. Our lives from then on are embedded in the families into which we are born, the families we create, and for many societies, much larger extended families in which many people who are not necessarily genealogically connected can be addressed or referred to by kinship terms.

This centrality of kinship to human society has been recognized in anthropology since its beginning as a distinct discipline in the 19th century. From then on a great deal of study went into kinship systems and terminologies, both in ethnography and in comparative ethnology. The comparative tradition initiated by L. H. Morgan was particularly fruitful in allowing us to understand how restricted the types of kinship terminologies are and how these types and underlying principles have functional relationships with other basic structures in society such as marriage, descent, and inheritance.

By the 1980s, however, this tradition had largely been abandoned, and anthropology lost interest in the systematic study of kinship, to the serious detriment of the discipline as a whole. This is not the place to go into the reasons for this (there are some comments on these in Danziger, this volume). The important thing for us now is that we see signs of this negative phase coming to an end and scholars turning once more toward kinship.

This book is part of this turning back to these roots in anthropology: all the chapters here draw on the scientific study of kinship in ethnology as well as the wealth of detail on systems in action recorded in ethnographies. But this is not simply a question of dusting off these old and valuable traditions. We are also building bridges into new areas and with other disciplines that take us beyond where kinship studies had reached. These bridges into linguistics and prehistory were strong in previous eras but have largely collapsed as kinship study has eroded in the core of anthropology. But in rebuilding them we can also develop new methods and new ideas.

2. Historical Linguistics and Kinship

Historical linguistics as a scientific discipline dates back to the early 19th century, earlier than the first systematic anthropology and earlier than the synchronic science of linguistics that has been dominant throughout the 20th century. The rigor of the developing comparative method in linguistics impressed and influenced other emerging sciences such as Darwin's evolutionary biology and Morgan's comparative ethnology, which focused initially on kinship systems.

A key concept of comparative historical linguistics that came to be shared among a number of evolutionary approaches was that of a phylogeny, or family tree. Significantly, the metaphor was borrowed from kinship, and "family trees" were already important as ways of representing genealogy from at least the 11th century on in the Christian tradition, with the "Tree of Jesse" representing the ancestry of Christ.

Historical linguists adopted this phylogenetic approach as an insightful way of representing the relationship between languages. For instance, Latin was the mother of the daughter Romance languages and could be represented as a common higher node from which the daughter languages branched. It became clear that a number of other subgroups existed, like Romance (descended from Latin). Some of the protolanguages (ancestors) of these subgroups were not documented in written form as Latin was. It began to be recognized that these protolanguages and their corresponding subgroups were in turn all related to each other by descent. Linguists began to talk of a Proto-Indo-European language, spoken before any written records existed, which was the common ancestor of all these Indo-European languages.

Nineteenth-century linguists then developed a method for reconstructing this and any other protolanguage, known as the *comparative method* (Clackson 2007). The words in the different languages were collected and compared, and sound correspondences were noted. These were often regular, such that, for example, *p* in certain positions in other Indo-European subgroups corresponded to *f* in Germanic, as, for instance, *pater* 'father' in Latin is a cognate of the English *father.* Linguistics was able to propose and test regular sound correspondences or "sound laws." Sometimes the correspondences were not regular, but the linguists of the Neogrammarian school would not simply concede that regularity did not exist or only existed to a limited extent. The exceptions to regularity themselves constituted another type of regularity to be discovered. This turned out to be an exceptionally productive research strategy.

Importantly, many of the "irregular" correspondences were to be found in loanwords. So, for instance, *padre* 'priest, chaplain' in English retains the *p* because it was borrowed from a Romance language, Spanish or Italian, in the 16th century in the extended meaning of "father" to "priest." *Padre* was not present in the relevant language (Proto-Germanic) when the relevant sound law ($p > f$, part of Grimm's law) applied, at least 1,500 years earlier, so it could not undergo the change. Thus loanwords do not follow regular sound change laws if they arrived after the sound change stopped operating: they are themselves governed by strict rules of the stratigraphy of diffusion and sound change. This framework not only reduced the amount of irregularity but also put an excellent diagnostic tool for discovering lexical diffusion into the hands of the linguists: If a word has not undergone a regular sound change, it is suspect of being a loanword, and work needs to be done on its etymology to ascertain its source and time of borrowing.

What have been stressed above are the sound differences and correspondences between words in different languages. The meaning of the words was also important, but although attention was paid to that, no equivalently rigorous method of dealing with semantic change was devised. I return to this topic below, in sections 4 and 5.

The approach to kinship in anthropology, in contrast, even in the diachronic anthropology of the 19th century, was not oriented to the actual forms of individual kinship terms at all. Rather, it focused on relations within the semantic field of kinship. The forms of words were of interest only inasmuch as they were the same in designating a combination of kin types in a single language or, different, designating a different combination of kin types. If the same term is used, for instance, for mother and mother's sister, then that tells us something about what was known as a kinship pattern or kinship system. In contrast, in a system in another group mother and mother's sister are designated by different terms (as in the English *mother* and *aunt*).

In his mammoth effort of collecting kinship terminologies throughout the world, Morgan was not concerned with whether the forms of the terms were related—the concern of historical linguistics. Instead he focused in his analysis on how the kinship systems differed from each other in terms of semantic structure and constructed a typology of systems. He then showed how particular types of systems correlated with patterns of marriage, descent, and other sociocultural features. In common with his contemporaries he constructed a unilineal scheme of social evolution to explain all these patterns. A great deal of the specifics of the explanations of the roots of kinship terminologies and practices and the grand scheme of evolution as proposed by Morgan has turned out to be mistaken. However, the fundamental method of comparing and typologizing systems of kinship was a great breakthrough and inspired much valuable elaboration over the following hundred years or so. I return to these theoretical developments in anthropological kinship studies below.

Linguistics also studies semantics and semantic fields. Among these, kinship has often been cited as the most studied, probably because of its great interest to anthropology, especially when many linguists were still working in close cooperation with anthropologists or were dual practitioners themselves: anthropological linguists or linguistic anthropologists. A number of the key approaches to lexical semantics, especially those that developed formal rigorous theories and methods (which I will review below in section 4 especially in relation to their relevance to change), cut their teeth on kinship. But kinship is far from the easiest field to encompass with a single approach: the debate about which approach to semantics and semantic change is most useful goes on and is reflected in the different contributions in this book.

The dynamics and histories of kinship have also been subject to some study within linguistics and to some extent in history and sociology. Sometimes the studies are more in the philological tradition, which can give great detail about the changes in kinship semantics and usage within the documented history of a language group. While we do not have a chapter in this book exemplifying this approach, using texts that have a wealth of historical information about kinship, an example is summarized later in this introduction. Such work is not necessarily linked to a particular approach to semantics or semantic change, but in the case of this example of the work on the history of German kinship, it is shown how such research makes valuable contributions to the theory and method of semantic change in general. Such work also broaches topics that are of great importance, such as how kinship terminologies are related to changes in descent, inheritance, and marriage, including the legal frameworks in which these are codified.

3. Prehistory, Ethnology, and Linguistics

This introduction began by pointing to the probable great age of kinship systems roughly coeval with the emergence of humans as we know them, at least 100,000 years ago. The subject of the very earliest development of kinship is one that holds great fascination (Allen 2008; Chapais 2008; Dziebel 2007). It is, however, plagued by speculation, as evidence for kinship behavior in that era is negligible, and evidence for the language of kinship is nonexistent (*pace* those who claim to be able to reconstruct a Proto-Sapiens language, discussed in Hendery and McConvell, this volume).

The chapters in this volume do discuss prehistory, but of a relatively recent period, generally the last few thousand years, for which comparative linguistics and ethnology can provide fairly solid evidence of probable kinship systems at previous stages. More adventurous are the reconstructions of Ehret (e.g., 2008), some of which do reach conclusions about protolanguage communities of up to 15,000 years of age or more. My own preference is for current work to focus on reconstruction in the Holocene period, where it is feasible, perhaps under favorable circumstances back some few millennia into the Pleistocene. On the linguistic side, this is due to the well-recognized fact that vocabulary replacement takes place at a rate that means that a linguo-genetic family relationship cannot be demonstrated for languages once they have been separated for more than around 10,000 years. Similar constraints would operate on attempts to construct phylogenies of great age for kinship systems independent of linguistic forms.[1] Once the task of reconstructing proto-kinship terms and protosystems in the Holocene period has been carried out for a reasonable number of regions of the world, we may attempt to extrapolate a phylogeny that joins up these relatively firmly established reconstructions. However, bridging the yawning gap between around 10,000 years ago and 100,000 or more remains a daunting prospect.

There are a number of approaches that come out of genetics and archaeology that refer to "kinship" but deal with phenomena that are quite distinct from the study of kinship terminologies, or at least the connection has not been made properly. These include the question of postmarital residence, often confused with issues of lineality (e.g., by assumptions that "matrilocal" societies are also matrilineal and so on). Linguists have also encouraged the idea that postmarital residence is correlated with kinship terminology, such as the assumption that the Proto-Indo-European system must have been patrilocal because of the absence of in-law terms for the wife (Clackson 2007: 204–205; Delbrück 1889; for a critique, Goody 1959). Genetics can pick up signs of consistent bias in postmarital residence over time and especially of sex-biased migration on a broader scale (Wilkins and Marlowe 2006). There are no specific links unearthed between these patterns and kinship terminological systems in a strict sense, although making such links cannot be ruled out in future work.

The history of speculative evolutionary schemes involving kinship from Morgan on was mentioned in the previous section. Such work was strongly discouraged in 20th-century anthropology, especially in the "British" school of structural functional social anthropology. But even in American cultural anthropology, where comparative ethnology remained important, large-scale evolutionary schemes were not much in evidence. Hypotheses about the prehistory of regions were more tolerated than in the British school. In France, Durkheim's ideas of mechanical and organic solidarity were reminiscent of an evolutionary scheme, and Lévi-Strauss's (1969) masterly work on kinship also had elements of diachronic evolution in them, such as in the relationship between elementary and complex forms, and restricted as against generalized exchange.

Especially since the 1980s, as I have noted, comparative ethnology of kinship declined everywhere, along with all "grand theories" and attempts to come up with valid concepts and generalizations that were of universal value. However, as this lacuna in sociocultural anthropology widened, people from other disciplines began to interest themselves in how rigorous scientific approaches might be applied to the traditional anthropological subject matter, including eventually kinship. Issues that either lend themselves to having a small array of binary answers or are apparently relatively easily quantifiable, such as postmarital residence and bridewealth/dowry, were among the first to be attended to by those using tree-building software and sophisticated statistical approaches imported from the biological sciences. Kinship terminologies are a thornier field, but where variants of a single parameter, for instance, siblings, can be relatively easily coded, work is proceeding (Jordan, this volume).

The progress of this new phylogenetics in matters related to kinship has been made easier by the fact that there is a great deal of prior work in the tradition of systematic typology in ethnology including Murdock and collaborators (a great tradition beginning with Murdock 1949), Driver and others for North America, and others, including sophisticated mathematical and statistical analyses. Despite the decline in interest in this kind of anthropology in the last quarter of the 20th century, it was maintained by small groups and is now very much back on the agenda (Jones and Milicic 2011).

Within ethnology and anthropology themselves, some scholars began to go against the prevailing orthodoxy and devote themselves to diachronic and evolutionary studies of kinship, which attracted wider attention than such studies normally had done in the period when they were marginalized. Two figures especially merit attention in the context of our book: the late Per Hage, and Nicholas Allen. Their contributions along with those of others in reconstructing kinship in recent years are discussed in section 6.

4. Theories of Semantic Change Applied to Kinship

In this section I will summarize the development of theories of lexical semantics and semantic change and how these have been applied to kinship. In the following sections attention turns to reconstruction: the linguistic, anthropological, and ethnological theories of the evolution of the entire semantic space of kinship, the kinship systems, are reviewed. In the course of this exposition the connections to theories and methods used in the chapters in this volume are drawn out.

Lexical semantics was an active field in the 19th century. Comparative historical linguists were acutely aware that they had developed strong insights into regular sound changes but that semantics, an equally important aspect of reconstruction, lagged behind. There were numbers of theoretical and empirical studies, now largely neglected because they are inaccessible and generally not written in English or translated.

This scholarship led into the theory of *semantic fields* (Lehrer 1974), which has elements of structuralism, promulgated by figures such as Trier (1931, on the field of *knowledge* in the history of German) and later developed by Coseriu and others. The lexical field—such as kinship, for instance—is characterized by paradigmatic contrasts and relationships between words within it. The use of the fields theory, at least in the hands of Trier, was heavily diachronic, describing changes in the relative semantic space occupied by different words within the field over time. Links were made with the sociocultural changes occurring at different historical periods, but there was little rigorous or formal theory.

However, from the matrix of field theory, more attention focused on how the differences between the words within the field could be more systematically described. Here a field like kinship became a playground for the development of the new "componential" approach, since kinship terms seemed especially amenable to decomposition into a small number of semantic features, which were perhaps universal but combined in different ways to form different terms (Allan in press). Terms in different languages with different meanings could be represented by different combinations of the same basic features, at least ideally. This development was almost entirely based on synchronic data, and while a few attempts were made to apply componential semantics to historical change in kinship, they were not notably successful (Frisch and Schutz 1967).

"Structural semantics"—the componential or distinctive feature approach—has been adjudged to be quite inadequate for historical work by some scholars. Fritz (forthcoming: 8) lists several criticisms leveled at the approach: (1) It is weak on *parole* (speech), the use of language; (2) it draws a strict boundary between lexical and encyclopedic knowledge, which makes it difficult to explain innovations due to metaphor and metonym; (3) it is not well equipped to deal with *polysemy*—a key element in meaning change; (4) its definition of features as necessary and sufficient excludes fuzzier mechanisms such as prototypes and "family resemblances." In sum it neglects the context, contextual use, and pragmatics so important for an understanding of change.

Wierzbicka (1987) also points out the inadequacy of componential approaches to kinship in several respects, including lack of a proper account of polysemy. She uses examples from componential analyses of Australian indigenous kinship terms in such works as Burling 1969. While criticizing Scheffler's (1978) use of a componential framework, she (1987:140) applauds his approach to polysemy, which distinguishes the core meanings of such terms as *mother* and *father* from extensions to wider kin.[2] My chapter in this volume adopts a polysemic approach that traces pathways of change with reference to commonly found extensions (equations, polysemies). Danziger's chapter in this volume insists that the componential approach remains viable both for synchronic description and for semantic change in kinship.

In the field of kinship, Coseriu (1964) did use a componential type of approach to analyze the change from what anthropologists would call a Sudanese or lineal system for uncles and aunts in Latin, where mother's sibling is distinguished from father's, to an Eskimo system in descendant languages such as French (for details, see McConvell, chapter 10, this volume; and Kronenfeld, this volume). There is a loss of a distinctive feature, *maternal/paternal*, in this process. Besides yielding a neat description, in this case at least, this kind of approach can make predictions—if, for example, one has a hypothesis that change only occurs where such features are, say, added or dropped—provided the features are well justified, for instance, universal.

Now in this case the maternal/paternal opposition was seen to be the most salient. However, when we approach it from the diachronic viewpoint, another opposition, sometimes called "parity," between parallel (same-sex siblings: MZ and FB) and cross (opposite-sex siblings:

MB and FZ) comes to the fore. This touches on an issue raised by Wierzbicka and others: there are often multiple competing componential analyses and no clear way of deciding between them.

I deal, in the discussion below, with the use of Marking Theory in this case and the ways in which structural approaches were rendered generally more useful to the diachronic enterprise by Marking Theory. Inadequacies in purely componential approaches were also highlighted by phenomena such as skewing in some languages—the equation of kin types in different adjacent generations under one term. This seemed to demand a different, generative rewrite rule approach that gives more weight to the idea that terms have core meanings and extensions (see discussion below and Danziger, this volume, for a different view).

But besides this, the other criticism raised above, of the absence of the social contexts of use in such theories, is telling too in the case of the change in Europe from earlier systems that differentiate maternal and paternal aunts and uncles to later systems that do not make these distinctions in the terminology. What is intriguing about this change in "uncle" and "aunt" terms is not just the simplification of the semantic field but also the reason why it happened. Linguists might object that we are straying from linguistics proper in asking such questions, but anthropologists can surely have no such qualms, and here in this book we are trying to put our methods and theories together. Of course in this case the evidence for how the change occurred might not be detailed enough to resolve such questions, as there is limited documentation of such matters in the "Dark Ages" of Europe, and interpretation of what does exist can be difficult. Such problems are yet more severe where there is no historical documentation, as in Australia or the Amazon of the same period. Nevertheless, if we amass enough examples of such transitions, we can build theories of the probable processes and motivations involved—for instance, Kronenfeld's emphasis on the importance of types of descent and inheritance in such transformations discussed below and in his chapter.

Marking Theory has provided a major impetus to attempts to ground kinship variation and change in a predictive framework This type of theory began in phonology with Trubetzskoy and was further elaborated by Jakobson and others. The explanation of kinship in terms of marking (or "markedness") was an important contribution by Greenberg (1990; see also Kronenfeld 1996 and this volume). While Greenberg hinted at the implications of his marking findings for a diachronic theory of kinship semantic change, it was Hage (1999) especially who drew out the "implicit" diachronic implications from Greenberg's theory and provided empirical evidence.

Among the points Hage (1999:425) derives from Greenberg that are relevant to kinship are the following:

1. *Universal implicational hierarchy.* The presence of the marked term implies the presence of the unmarked term but not necessarily conversely.
2. *Zero expression in the unmarked term.*
3. *Par excellence expression.* The unmarked term may represent the entire category including the marked term. In sibling systems, for instance, if there is a distinction between elder and younger brother, one of these may also be a general word for brother.[3]
4. *Syncretization.* When two sets of categories intersect, distinctions that are present in the unmarked category are absent or neutralized in the marked category. Hage gives the example of the absence of gender distinctions in the English *cousin* but their presence in sibling terms. Another example is the fact that in many systems (including many in Australia) the elder sibling terms (unmarked) have gender distinctions but the younger sibling term does not.
5. *Defectivation.* Certain categories present in the unmarked are absent in the marked, for example, English has *brother-in-law* and *sister-in-law* but no *cousin-in-law.*

Greenberg also had concrete hypotheses about where unmarked and marked divisions would fall in kinship: (1) Genealogically close relations are more unmarked than distant relations, and consanguineal relations are unmarked vis-à-vis marked affines; (2) first ascending generations are unmarked as against all other generations, and ascending generations are unmarked as against the corresponding descending generations. Ehret (2008:205–207) also uses similar kinds of generalizations as a guide for deciding which direction of change is more likely where other evidence is equivocal, which he calls "normative directionalities." One of the principles is that "meaning extension goes from primary to collateral kin." For instance, if a cognate root term has a meaning "father" and elsewhere "father's brother" and/or "mother's brother," this principle points to the meaning "father" being the earliest. A semantic change from FB to F is more or less ruled out. Observations such as those of Matras (2009:130–131) to the effect that close, intimate kinship terms tend to be retained as inheritances, whereas more distant terms are more often borrowed, might be related to this line of thought.

Hage proceeds through an application of the Marking Theory, interpreted diachronically, to the Salishan family of languages in the northwestern United States. He was unusual among contemporary anthropologists in taking very seriously the results of historical linguistics in the reconstruction of forms and the implications of the geographical distribution of cognate forms, and this aspect is taken up below and in my chapter 10. Focusing for the moment on how the marking hypotheses translate into diachronic hypotheses, Hage (1999:433) mentions the following:

1. *Marking and salience.* For instance, sex of relative is more salient than sex of connecting (linking) relative, so systems that neutralize the former and not the latter are more common than those that neutralize the latter and not the former. For instance, systems where MM = MF and/or FF = FM are rare, but systems of MM = FM and FF = MF are common (e.g., the current European system and others in many places). The diachronic interpretation is that systems that distinguish all four of these grandparents (as in the Proto-Salishan system) lose the linking relative sex distinction first, yielding an MM = FM/FF = MF system.[4]
2. *Marking and prototype effects.* Assuming that FF and MM are the best examples or prototypes of grandparents, then if MF and FF are neutralized, it is predicted that the FF term will be the one retained for both and the term for MM will replace that for FM. This is confirmed in Salishan in most cases but not all. In the case of the neutralization of "uncle" terms, the assumption is that MB, the most different from F, is retained, and this is borne out in Salishan. Here Hage cites the Latin case that I have already alluded to, in which *avunculus*, the old term for MB, becomes the term for MB/FB, and in a parallel fashion, *amita*, the old term for FZ, becomes FZ/MZ. I should note though that this is a strong tendency rather than an absolute rule. The reason why the cross aunt/uncle is "prototypical" is not entirely made clear; as noted above, MB and FZ are distinguished by being cross, as against the parallel FB, along the dimension parity, which Hage (1999:435) says should be added to Greenberg's list of important marking relations. The reason why the neutralization/replacement takes place at all is not addressed. As I shall discuss later, it is likely that a transitional period occurs in such changes in which the old distinction of, say, MB and FB is retained in certain contexts while the MB term is used in a broad sense of both in other contexts—an example of what Hage calls syncretization (discussed above).

The combined effect of the marking rules as interpreted diachronically by Hage for Salishan seems to be an evolution toward simpler systems with fewer terms, while some systems in the family remain with more terms reflecting earlier stages. This is a powerful demonstration of this trend, but one has to question if it is in part built into the scheme by the way Marking Theory is put into operation. Marking Theory predicts that the marked members of pairs will be lost first, but there does not appear to be any complementary theory of complexification. In fact no examples of complexification are illustrated for Salishan, which is remarkable. The origins of the simplification emphasis in the diachronic semantics of kinship appear to have been in a reaction to anthropological assumptions of complexification that engendered a controversy in which Hage sided with the linguists on the question of the evolution of Polynesian sibling terms (Blust 1990)—a debate that continues to echo, including in this volume in the chapters by Jordan and Read (see later discussion of the tendency toward polarization of simplifying and complexifying hypotheses).

Certainly there are examples of the addition of terms over time to a kinship system. Classic examples occur in the transition between Dravidian symmetrical and asymmetrical systems, which in the work of Lévi-Strauss and others took on the dimensions of a great watershed between restricted and generalized exchange. Additional terms can be recruited in various ways, such as by borrowing from other languages—indeed the appearance of loanwords can be a signature of complexifying change in the system. In the case of the change from Kariera (Dravidian) to Karadjeri (symmetrical between Cape York Peninsula and northeast Arnhem Land), Omaha-skewed MB and fC terms took over as differentiated MBC and FZC (McConvell and Keen 2011). It is unclear how Marking Theory can help explain such paths of evolution.

Componential analysis was strengthened, as we have seen, by notions of marking and prototype theory, recognizing that there is a core or focal meaning of a lexical item such as a kinship term and that relations exist between items such that one is a more unmarked or prototypical member of a wider category than another. Change of meanings and loss of items can be linked to these properties of systems to some extent.

However, there are limitations to this view of lexical items in general and of kinship terms in particular. The notion of extension once again became important for the semantics of kinship. Kinship terms do not typically have a fuzzy halo around a core meaning like other types of words but, rather, have a specific extended meaning (see Kronenfeld, this volume). So in systems of the classificatory type where, for instance, "father" is the core meaning, the same term also refers to father's brother, a clearly separate and definable kin type. This is an example of polysemy in my view (and Wierzbicka's, as discussed). One could, however, persist with a componential approach and call the focal referent *father* unmarked.

One of the types of kinship systems that troubled those working within the componential approach, including Lounsbury, was *skewing*, which came in two main types, Crow and Omaha. In both kinds, there is an equation between kin types in one generation and a lineally connected kin type in an adjacent generation. So in the Crow variety father's sister and father's sister's daughter (matrilineally connected) can be referred to by the same term—"father's sister"; and in the Omaha variety mother's brother and mother's brother's son (patrilineally connected) can be referred to by the same term—"mother's brother." It is hard to express even these basic equations in a classic componential approach, and this is what led Lounsbury to develop the "rewrite rule" or "reduction rule" approach (Danziger, this volume, takes a different view, claiming that a feature of shared lineage membership can take care of the problem).

The problem is a lot more complicated than that, as it happens. Skewing equations typically ramify throughout the system, such that, for instance, MMBS is also called MMB in an Omaha system. In order to express this kind of extension of meanings, a new way of dealing with formal kinship was needed, and Lounsbury came up with a system of rewrite rules somewhat similar to the new style in generative phonology—or reduction rules as they are commonly called. So MBS can be reduced to MB not just when MB is the actual relative concerned but also where MB is a linking relative in the relative product string. Combining this with other rules, the most complex kin type strings can be reduced to the simpler terms by which they are customarily called.

While this formalism was highly successful in dealing with skewing, it was less so for other problems, such as the variety of Iroquois systems studied by Scheffler (1971). The reduction rules approach was not widely applied to change in kinship terms and systems. Bright and Minnick (1966) propose that Lounsbury's reduction rules should be ordered to capture facts of Fox kinship (again paralleling developments in generative phonology). They (1966: 387) cite Tax as saying that the extension of "father" and "mother" to "father's brother" and "mother's sister," respectively (the parallel sibling rule of Lounsbury or the change from a lineal to a bifurcate pattern), is a recent innovation in Central Algonkian languages such as Fox and suggest that this recency may account for its low priority in rule ordering. This would seem to be opening the door to an exploration of the relationship between rule ordering and diachronic change in kinship as occurred in historical generative phonology and syntax in the late sixties (e.g., King 1969), but there is no evidence that this avenue was explored to any extent.

It has been proposed recently (Jones 2010) that Optimality Theory, which also started life in phonology, in the 1980s, could be applied to kinship. This takes up some of the issues of rule ordering in a different way and also has potential to be utilized in diachronic analysis, not fully realized. Instead of generative rules as in earlier phonology or Lounsbury's approach to kinship, Optimality Theory deals in constraints that are universal or at least widespread but are *ranked* differently in different groups/languages. Working out what these constraints are needs more effort, but one could imagine that a constraint equivalent to the parallel sibling rule might be "treat same-sex siblings alike." This is obviously low in rank in the English and other European systems but high in classificatory systems. The change that Tax suggested had occurred recently in Central Algonkian would promote the rank of this constraint, but not so high that it outranks the Omaha skewing rule (Bright and Minnick's "major lineal rule," which could be restated as a constraint something like "treat people in a patriline alike"; cf. my 2010 critique of Jones in *Behavioral and Brain Sciences*, on the question of using lineage unity in the constraints proposed for Seneca).

Another growing trend in kinship analysis is that of kinship mapping/kinship algebra, triggered by work by Murray Leaf. This trend is also championed by Dwight Read, including in his chapter in this book, which addresses the issue of how this theory approaches change, using as his major example the evolution of Oceanic sibling terminology.

Utilizing literary and legal sources, large amounts of data on kinship terms and their changing meaning and usage have been retrieved in Europe and elsewhere. This is an important area of study since it can provide us with details of the ordering of usage and meaning over hundreds of years, which, as well as illuminating many issues of sociohistorical change in the societies concerned, also provides us with documented evidence of how complex changes proceed, which can serve as models for our reconstruction of prehistoric change where there is no such direct evidence.

For instance, for Germanic languages Jones (1990: 181; cf. Diepeveen 2003) carried out a meticulous study of change in the usage and meaning of kinship terms through the history of German and found abundant evidence for extension of meaning as a prime mechanism of change. The extensions sometimes involved "semantic encroachment" on the domain of other terms, without necessarily any negative impact on the terms that are overlapped, although ultimately such processes did cause upheavals and a reorganization of the field of kinship terminology. A multiplicity of such polysemy and convergence is demonstrated for the term *neve*, a cognate of Proto-Indo-European **nepots*, which was **nefot* in early Germanic. In the 12th–13th centuries, for instance, *neve* overlapped *oeheim* in the meanings MB, MMB, MZS, ZS, and BS and overlapped *veter* in the meanings FB, FBS, and MFB (Jones 1990:183–184). Jones finds asymmetries in *neve*, *oeheim*, and other terms in whether they are used for address and reference or just for reference.

The importance of pragmatic and usage factors is evident and recognized in this study. For instance, *altercentricity* is found.[5] In this case it is the opposite of the filiocentricity mentioned in my chapter 10, where parents adopt the term their children use to call a relative; in this case children adopt the term used by their parents, so *oeheim* is used for MMB as well as MB, and it is possible that in other cases this is the cause of a diachronic change in the meaning of terms. Another type of altercentricity is addressed—inversion, where a speaker calls a relative by the term that person normally calls him or her. This was the pattern of extension first of the FB term *veter* for BS in the late 13th century, followed in succeeding generations by the addition of reversed polarity in this way for other kinship terms (Jones 1990:187–188).

This radical change is roughly contemporaneous with another one in the 13th century, when "downward extension"—the use of a term for a relative and that relative's (sibling's) children—became prevalent. Interestingly the first occurrences of this are the use of *oeheim* MB for MBS and *muome* MZ for MBD. Although Jones does not mention this, these are prime instances of Omaha skewing Type 1 (Lounsbury 1964).[6] Some decades later downward extension was generalized so that *veter* FB began to be used for FBS and *muome* MZ was used for MZD as well as MBD (Jones 1990:190).

Next came the collapse of the bifurcate structure in German, which, like Latin, originally distinguished all four aunts and uncles. This is an example of the loss of the paternal/maternal (or possibly cross/parallel) distinction in "uncle"/"aunt" terms, converting a Sudanese pattern to an Eskimo or lineal one. We have encountered this transformation previously, and it was attributed to marking by Hage.

The MB term *oeheim* was extended to FB also (as predicted by Marking Theory), and other terms also lost their lateral specificity, between the 12th and 14th centuries. However, the other term, *veter* FB, took another path, changing to "FB's son" and "cousin" as described above.[7] Schoof (1900; and following him, Diepeveen 2003) regarded the extension of *Oheim* to FB as a result of the prior change of *veter* to other meanings, thus activating a kind of "drag chain" to fill the gap being created. Neat as this picture seems, the overlaps and variability of these changes as depicted by Jones (1990) probably make this view of strict sequence and causality an oversimplification. What we have is a melee of different types of extension coinciding with and competing with each other during this period of change in the Middle Ages. This should be a lesson to us in reconstructing change processes in prehistory. However, what is important is that the changes are not random but, rather, follow a limited number of patterns that we see time and again throughout the world.

The other change following on the above in German but happening earlier in English and later in Dutch and Scandinavian, between about a.d. 1200 and 1700, is the borrowing of French words for uncle, aunt, cousin, and so on (Diepeveen 2003). There is no straightforward single explanation for this apart from appeal to the political and cultural dominance of the French in Europe in the period.[8] Goody (1983:268, 2000:60) looks at it from the point of view, rather, of what was *not* borrowed—the core nuclear family terms for parents, children, and siblings, which were resistant to the loan tide engulfing the collateral kin types. This may form the basis of a hierarchy of borrowing or perhaps change in general, and I return to similar ideas below. Goody (1983:271) also notes that in England the older Anglo-Saxon terms continued to be used alongside the French loans, and although he calls this a "redundancy," he also illustrates that they had different functions and meanings. These perspectives on the details of transitions are valuable when we come to approach the relationships between polysemy and change.

Empirical studies of historical change in kinship have been undertaken, including by anthropologists, especially dealing with "acculturation" and related issues. Comparative and historical studies of variation and change in kinship terms have used recent ethnography and historical documentation. In North America, Fred Eggan (1937) was early in analyzing change in Native American kinship, followed by Spoehr (1947), Bruner (1955), and others. One of the significant points emerging from these studies is the existence of groups that operated two different systems simultaneously, ostensibly because they were in transition from one system to another. There is a strong possibility that such situations may not be confined to this kind of social change but may be more widespread, where, for instance, groups are in contact and practice more than one system—the equivalent to being bilingual in the kinship realm. The study of earlier change in German kinship also manifests a great deal of variation and overlap of terms, shifting configurations between different generations and probably in different groups.

Recent work on semantic change has been much more oriented toward notions of polysemy and pragmatics (e.g., Geeraerts 2002; Vanhove 2008), which as we have seen are difficult to integrate into a framework of componential semantics, even with the addition of Marking Theory. One view is that semantic change in general is never directly from A to B but must proceed by way of an intermediate polysemy A/B. This idea fits well with the known set of common polysemies (equations) in kinship terms universally and also in regions of the world. This parallelism yields a method of testing the plausibility of a reconstructed change in a kinship term (as illustrated with more references in my chapter 10, this volume). If the change is thought to be from, say, "mother's brother" to "mother's brother's son," then we can fairly confidently say that there must have been an intermediate stage of MB = MBS. We know that such equations exist, and they are known as Omaha skewing. Further tests of the plausibility of the hypothesis include the fact that such equations usually only occur in societies with a patrilineal emphasis. Further examples of actual recent Omaha equations in the region where this is thought to have been the pattern strengthen the case for the hypothesis. A partially similar case is that of the early German FB *veter* (modern *Vetter* 'cousin'), which extended to FBS and then to "cousin" in general.

This is only the first part of testing the change hypothesis A > A/B. The second phase, the loss of A, is harder to deal with. It is not a result of Marking Theory, at least not of the kind used by Hage based on Greenberg. In the example of change via Omaha in northern Australia (McConvell and Alpher 2002; McConvell and Keen 2011), the original MB sense is taken over in Yolngu by a loanword from a neighboring language. In the case of the German *veter*, the extension of *oeheim* from MB to MB + FB eventually removed the original meaning of *veter*, FB. This is more the mechanism than the motivation of the second change, however. In this situation it may be the case that skewing is a highly marked kind of polysemy—and is thought to be so even by groups that have it (Kronenfeld, this volume) and is an "overlay" that can come and go relatively easily in history.

5. Reconstruction of Kinship Change and Evolution: Methods Involving the Linguistic Forms of Terms

In this section I move on from mechanisms of change to review some of the explicit methods for kinship reconstruction that have been proposed. There have been significant attempts at reconstructions of the kinship terms and systems of protolanguages in linguistics since the 19th century for Indo-European and since the 20th century for other language families such as those of Native Americans.

I highlight here a major work that brought together a linguist and an anthropologist to present a well-defined methodology. Dyen and Aberle's (1974) work on the lexical reconstruction of Proto-Athapaskan kinship terminology focuses on the task of reconstructing the prototerminology using lists of terms (related forms, assigned codes) and meanings (also coded). Establishing a subgrouping of the family is important in their (1974:17) method, as the key concept of "retained candidate" is defined using the notion of subgrouping.

The requirements for a retained candidate are that its cognates be in different subgroups (of the highest order) and that it cannot be (according to the evidence) an *innovated candidate*. An innovated candidate results from the

<table>
<tr><td>Ingalik</td><td>Canadian</td><td>Pacific</td><td></td><td>Apachean</td><td></td></tr>
<tr><td>|</td><td>|</td><td>|</td><td></td><td>|</td><td>\</td></tr>
<tr><td>|</td><td>Bear Lake</td><td>Hupic</td><td></td><td>Chiricahua</td><td>Mescalero</td></tr>
<tr><td>.....|</td><td>|</td><td>|</td><td>\</td><td></td><td></td></tr>
<tr><td>.....|</td><td>|</td><td>Tolowa</td><td>Hupa</td><td></td><td></td></tr>
<tr><td>-t'se</td><td>e-tse?</td><td>-t'ceene?</td><td>t'cin</td><td>t'cine</td><td>t'cine</td></tr>
<tr><td>FM=MM</td><td>FM=MM=FF=MF</td><td>FM</td><td>FM</td><td>FM</td><td>FM</td></tr>
</table>

FIGURE 1.1. Proto-Athapaskan **-t'cene* FM.

independent "borrowing" of a word from another list in which it is a retained or innovated candidate. Each such independent borrowing is a *transfer.*

This notion of "transfer" includes, in fact, different meanings in different languages, or meaning change, although the language used by Dyen and Aberle makes this somewhat opaque. They go on to introduce the notion of "inclusion":

> If a candidate *c* appears in a list of subgroups L1 in meaning M1 and also in a different list of subgroups L2 in meaning M2, then if L2 contains all of the subgroups of L1 and at least one subgroup in addition, L2 is said to include L1; our practice is to say that the particular candidate *c* in M2 INCLUDES the candidate *c* in M1.
>
> For example 65 appears in the meaning FM in [Pacific]...and in [Apachean].... Since 65 appears in the meaning SnSn ms...in all subgroups but Tan, SnSn ms includes FM 65.
>
> ...If one candidate includes another and transfers are involved, *the direction of any transfers is probably from the including candidate to the included candidate.* (1974:17–18)

Further heuristics are proposed, including the following, which refers to an example of an etymon that has the meaning MM in some languages and FM in others:[9]

> An included candidate found in two subgroups is immediately regarded as originating from transfers if in the same meaning there is found an unincluded candidate or an included candidate found in at least three subgroups. Thus the candidate MM 3, found in [Ingalik] and [Canadian], is inferred to originate entirely by transfers from FM, found in [Ingalik], [Canadian], [Pacific], and [Apachean]. (Dyen and Aberle 1974:18)

Dyen and Aberle's approach to transfer (meaning change) ingeniously attempts to determine the direction of change entirely by the structure of subgroupings and the numbers of branches with particular forms and meanings. This approach does not delve into the semantics of the terms, including the role of polysemy in change, or the sociocultural embedding of the terms (although the relationship of kinship systems to non-kinship sociocultural features is treated later in the book).

Others (e.g., Blust 1990) have criticized in Dyen and Aberle's method what they see as an overmechanistic approach that denies researchers the opportunity to use relevant sociohistorical evidence that sheds light on the motivations and directions of semantic change. A lot depends on subgrouping in this method, and Campbell (1976) is concerned that this is determined by lexicostatistics, departing from the only reliable method of subgrouping, the comparative method using shared innovations.

Others as well as Blust have criticized what they see as an overmechanistic approach. Whistler writes of

> a basic methodological flaw of Dyen and Aberle's approach to kin classificatory reconstruction.... Thus, for example, they ascribe proto-language status to a reconstructed kinterm and specify its meaning in terms of a mechanical "majority rules" algorithm which counts representations across significant branches in the family. (1980:280)

Whistler's admirable reconstruction of the semantics of Proto-Wintun kinship, drawing on the approach of Lounsbury and Scheffler (1972), "eschews any such formulaic approach; meanings for proto-forms are specified within their specific contexts of equivalence rules, kin super-classes and morphological system" (Whistler 1980:280). Different Wintun subgroups can be characterized by the presence or absence of particular Lounsburian equivalence (reduction) rules. Unfortunately, it seems that this excellent methodology was not followed in succeeding years, probably because of the decline in interest in kinship and particularly the history of kinship systems and attacks on structuralist approaches.

Other studies do allow for a less rigid method, by using cultural data to interpret issues such as direction of change, and a number use the standard comparative method with linguistic data (such as Koch, this volume; Danziger, this volume). Others who draw on linguistic evidence, like Hage, use a less standard method of reconstruction in some cases.

6. Methods Based on System Transformations and Evolution

The history of evolutionary theories of kinship in anthropology and ethnology has already been mentioned. These have profoundly affected reconstruction methods in these disciplines so that in some cases the speculative theories of origin and development dominate and distort the findings. Here is not the place to go into this history in detail from Morgan on. There has, however, been a move away from this way of operating toward approaches that are less directly driven by grand theories and more oriented toward reliable and standardized methods of cultural reconstruction, often regional (such as described in Jordan, this volume), rather than aiming at the reconstruction of proto–world systems.

Nick Allen's research agenda is still operating at the grand theory/proto–world system level, and for me at least, it is hard to connect this to real events and groups that are within the compass of reconstruction from recent and historically available data. None of the authors in this book use his ideas, probably because of their abstractness and conjectural nature. Some of his notions are valuable, such as the "rupturing" of terms—the division of a kinship term into two as an older equation ceases to function. This is a potentially useful way of looking at change in systems and features as part of an approach to the transformation from symmetrical (Dravidian) to asymmetrical kinship and marriage in Australia (see my chapter 10, this volume). This is of course the great watershed that Lévi-Strauss, in one of the most powerful ideas in 20th-century kinship studies, saw dividing restricted from generalized exchange.

Another great tradition in 20th-century kinship studies is that of George P. Murdock (1949), who indeed did present a grand evolutionary scheme but also continued Morgan's other research direction—the compilation and systematic comparison of a large sample of the world's cultures, including their kinship systems. His typology and classification of kinship systems (along with Lowie's, which he built on, and others) provide the framework for much of the diachronic work we are now attempting.

A book has just appeared published by the University of Utah Press celebrating Hage's contribution to kinship and especially to its reinvigoration in recent times (Jones and Milicic 2011). Hage elaborated on ideas from Greenberg to develop a "Marking Theory" of change in kinship terms and systems, discussed above. Beginning with the ideas of abstract transformations between systems, he also saw how historical linguistics made a key contribution to kinship system reconstruction and himself turned toward the use of linguistic reconstruction to establish what kinds of systems existed in protolanguages. One of the main motifs in his work along these lines was the quest for and discovery of Kariera systems in protolanguages in various language families around the world—"Kariera" in a related but different sense from the way the term is used in Australia (cf. McConvell and Hendery 2010).

Hage's research was tending toward a notion that Kariera/Dravidian was the primordial system, at least in many regions of the world in the late Pleistocene. Allen went further in making the proposal that a "tetradic" system was indeed a primordial form of human kinship, from which Kariera/Dravidian developed after some transformations. The trajectory of his work was the inverse of that of Hage, beginning with the reconstruction of systems using historical linguistics in language family branches but later turning to thought experiments about how systems must have started in a hypothetical early stage of human society and how they could have developed into the forms we know today, with little reference to actual times, places, language families, or forms of words (Allen 2004).

One current researcher who also has a broad vision of the sweep of changes from a world primordial system somewhat similar to that of Hage and Allen but different in detail is German Dziebel (2007). While Dziebel does not use linguistic reconstruction methods to any great extent, Christopher Ehret has also been busy reconstructing the kinship systems of African language families going back to the Pleistocene in some cases. He has not made commitments about what lies beyond this in terms of a common ancestor or ancestors, but he (2008) has expressed doubts about whether the kinship varieties he finds at the protolanguage level in Africa can easily be connected to the speculative earlier history of a tetradic system proposed by Allen.

Anthropological and ethnological methods of reconstructing previous systems and pathways of change tend not to engage with linguistic reconstructions to a great extent—among exceptions are Dyen and Aberle, discussed above; Hage; and in earlier work but less so in his later "tetradic" research, Allen. In this respect the ethnologists are in the tradition of Morgan and others who followed him. In another respect, too, they have often tended to follow Morgan in constructing unilinear evolutionary schemes in which one type of kinship system always follows another in a fixed sequence. Of course if this were true, it would provide a reliable method for system reconstruction, but the fact that scholars have proposed radically different unilinear schemes does not inspire confidence. Kryukov (1998) makes the point that such schemes tend to gravitate toward the poles of simplification or complexification—and a battle between proponents of each of these kinds of schemes formed the background to the debate over the direction of change in Polynesian sibling terms (for further contributions on this issue, see Read, this volume; Jordan, this volume).

Kryukov advocates the use of comparative and historical data to arrive at actual transformational sequences between kinship systems (mainly based on Asian data), and when these are revealed, unilinear evolution is no longer an option. However, the conclusion is that while a number of transformations can go in either direction, Dravidian may be at the root of many trees because, according to him, no other system becomes Dravidian. This is compatible with Allen's (1986) "tetradic" scheme, in which Dravidian/"Kariera" is the second stage of kinship evolution. Hage, while finding Dravidian/Kariera at the protostage of many language families, also finds examples of "reversion" to Dravidian after a move to another system in Austronesian—and not only the effects of groups moving into areas where they adopted Dravidian systems from neighbors.

That Dravidian was one of the earliest systems could be suggested also for Amazonia, but Hornborg (this volume) suggests that it may be an effect of depopulation, isolation, and demographic stress. This is interesting, as Dole (1969), cited by Kryukov as a pioneer of more empirically based and realistic research on kinship system change, early suggested that "Hawaiian" or generational systems were a response to these kinds of factors in Amazonia, which led to endogamy.

Mayan is another language family for which Hage claimed the protosystem to be Dravidian (Hage et al. 2004). Danziger (this volume) leaves the question of Proto-Mayan kinship for later research but proposes that the protosystem included patrilateral marriage (for a male), not the bilateral marriage expected in a Dravidian system.

The evidence so far is somewhat fragile, with cultural and to some extent linguistic reconstructions subject to doubt and dispute and far from complete. However, they are suggestive of an ancient background of Dravidian systems in Asia and the Pacific, including the Americas. In Africa and Europe, however, the evidence is not strong. Ehret (2008) cannot find any such systems in the African protolanguages he has reconstructed. One possibility is that those who would see Dravidian or similar systems as primeval on a world scale might propose that it is very early in Africa and Europe, certainly predating what linguistic and probably any variety of ethnological reconstruction can provide evidence for—thus, a pure conjecture. An alternative could be that the Dravidian systems developed in Asia and moved with the expanding human populations into the Americas and the Pacific. If we are talking about the earliest human occupation of Sahul (the joined continent of Australia and New Guinea), this was 50,000 years ago, and no credible evidence could be adduced for such claims.

These new and exciting studies of diachronic kinship, a field that has been woefully neglected, should not be drawn into this morass of speculation. Much more useful at present would be to pursue the kinds of studies presented in this book, validate our methods, and continue the interdisciplinary dialogues. In this way we can clarify how kinship systems have developed in the era for which our methods can reconstruct systems and changes, the Holocene era of the last 10,000 years.

7. This Book

The origins of this book lie in the AustKin project, formally titled "Tracing Change in Family and Social Organization in Indigenous Australia, Using Evidence from Language," a 2008–10 project based at the Australian National University and funded by the Australian Research Council and the Centre de Recherche et de Documentation sur l'Océanie/Centre national de la recherche scientifique. I worked on the AustKin project, and Jeff Marck and I made a submission to run a session at the International Conference on Historical Linguistics in Nijmegen in 2009 with the same title as this book (in the event Marck was unable to attend the conference or contribute to this volume). The following paragraphs outline briefly the content of the papers at the conference session and also serve to introduce the revised essays in the current volume and the additional chapters included.

From the AustKin project, chief investigators Keen and Koch, associate Alpher (paper read by another associate, Claire Bowern), and I gave papers at the conference session, this contingent providing the Australian flavor to the session and to this book, which is commented on further below. Our colleague Rachel Hendery on the project was later invited to contribute her paper on *mama* and *papa* in Australia (coauthored by me), and Jane Simpson was invited to contribute her chapter on historical change in the Warumungu group in Central Australia, neighboring and interacting with the Arandic groups examined by Koch and Alpher.

Kronenfeld gave a keynote talk on some of the main issues in the study of semantic change, and the approaches that he finds most valuable, from the point of view of a leading scholar who has written extensively on both the anthropology of kinship, especially among the Fanti of West Africa, and semantic theory in general. Fiona Jordan's paper represented a contribution from the new phylogenetic methods mentioned above, focusing on postmarital residence and on the evolution of sibling terminology in Oceanic Austronesian languages. Dwight Read's paper (which I presented because he was unable to attend) also engaged with Oceanic systems, especially the role of siblings, and provided an introduction to the "kinship algebra" and "kinship methods" of Read's group and how they can be used to tackle change.

Eve Danziger's paper was on change and reconstruction in Yukatecan Mayan in Central America, broaching issues of borrowing affinal terminology, which seems common in many parts of the world, and as noted earlier in this introduction, advocating the continuing value of the componential approach to meaning in kinship reconstruction. Alf Hornborg's comparative essay on Amazonian kinship systems was invited after the conference and draws on his long-term and authoritative research on this since the 1980s. He advances a typology of systems and outlines various kinds of trends and sequences of kinship systems, with—unusually—Dravidian featuring as a late development, due to the impact of recent historical pressures leading to group endogamy, rather than very early or primordial, as is often proposed.

Dziebel and Ehret, mentioned above, and Antonia Soriente presented papers at the Nijmegen conference session but were not able to contribute them to this volume.

As things turned out, six chapters in the book are on Australia, and six are on other continents and/or on general issues (including this introductory essay). The balance of the book thus rather resembles another book that I edited (with Nick Evans), *Archaeology and Linguistics*, in having both weighty chapters on Australia and a number of others on other regions of the world and general matters of theory.

Some may read into this design a strategy of putting Australia on the map in the field of kinship studies, and this would not be entirely wrong. Great attention was given by world anthropology to Australian indigenous kinship in the past as far back as Morgan and his collaborators Fison and Howitt, the impact of Spencer and Gillen's work on the Arrernte, and Radcliffe-Brown's research. This foundational work fed into diverse streams of anthropology including Lévi-Strauss's seminal work on kinship and componential reanalysis of Kariera and other Australian systems. In recent times, however, interest both within Australia and worldwide has declined, as illustrated by the absence of a chapter dealing substantially with Australia in *Transformations of Kinship*, edited by Godelier et al. in 1998, a turning point in the revival of interest in kinship and especially kinship change (an omission made up for in Godelier 2004).

But there is good reason to pay attention to Australia, apart from this current relative neglect. We can glimpse the important issues and current research in the papers given at the conference and the chapters included in this volume. The strong team of people working on kinship in Australia includes two outstanding scholars in their own fields: Ian Keen in anthropology, a specialist in Australian kinship; and Harold Koch in historical linguistics, a leading practitioner of the comparative method.

Keen further builds models of the development of Yolngu (northeast Arnhem Land) systems in terms of successive transformations of the kinship structures and applies a similar method to another asymmetrical system, that of the Ngarinyin, in the north Kimberley region of Western Australia. Koch applies the comparative method rigorously to the Arandic subgroup of Pama-Nyungan in Central Australia. While complex and phrasal kinship terms are relatively rarely found in Australia, unlike in other parts of the world (e.g., English *great-grandfather, father-in-law*, etc.), Koch unearths examples in the history of Arandic that have been merged into single terms almost beyond recognition and thus opens up for inspection new pathways of change and possibilities of reconstruction.

As we have seen, the position of Dravidianate systems (like "Kariera") at the root of kinship system phylogenies has been a recurring theme in ethnological research both old and recent. Keen's chapter begins with the hypothesis that the Kariera system of kinship usually associated with bilateral cross-cousin marriage was the starting point in kinship evolution, and he focuses attention on the shift to asymmetry in the two areas he examines—one of the key issues that Lévi-Strauss was concerned with but usually approached more abstractly rather than through concrete historical hypotheses. Koch's chapter also bears on this issue, since he is dealing with the type of system—named "Aranda" after the Arrernte languages—that is the counterpoint to Kariera in Radcliffe-Brown's scheme, with a different type of marriage and different patterning of kin terms. Koch has been able to establish by rigorous means that Proto-Arandic in fact had an Aranda kinship system, with marriage to a second cousin rather than a cross-cousin and other features differentiating it from a Kariera system. This is by no means the case for all systems that have been Aranda in type in recent times in Australia—some can be shown to have been probably Kariera or asymmetric at the subgroup protolanguage stage (McConvell 1997).

My chapter is also situated in the same set of issues and is part of a larger effort to understand how grandkin terminologies developed in the Pama-Nyungan family of languages. The Dravidian/Kariera-first hypothesis is reflected here in the proposal that Proto-Pama-Nyungan grandkin terms have a Kariera set of meanings in which parallel grandparents of the same sex are assigned the same term as each other and cross-grandparents of the same sex are similarly assigned the same term as each other. The problem that is in focus here is the fact that on first impressions there appear to be two terms reconstructible for each grandkin slot in the system, and the chapter works through how this comes about with one pair of terms, centered on "mother's father." Rachel Hendery's chapter, which I also coauthored, takes up the issue of the so-called nursery words for parents, *mama* and *papa*, and shows that neither the "baby talk" origin theory nor the reconstruction to some putative "Proto-Sapiens" gets us far when we look at their occurrence in Australia.

Alpher's note, appended to Koch's chapter since it also deals with an Arandic language, takes up an important issue—the apparent transfer of the system of classification of one kinship system, in this case Western Desert ("Aluridja"), to another one, without actual diffusion of the kinship terms from one language to another. This is something that probably happened relatively recently in history as Western Desert speakers moved farther east and exerted their influence on the Arandic speakers of Central Australia. Jane Simpson also focuses on recent change in another group neighboring and influenced by Arandic speakers and shows how careful attention to the historical records of anthropologists and other observers over the last 120 years can give us a more realistic picture of how kinship change proceeds, with overlapping waves of diffusion and accompanying semantic change. In some ways this is parallel to the complexity of the extended example, cited earlier on, of change in German kinship terminology, and as with that example, this is a lesson to us in not oversimplifying the picture. But at the same time it is reassuring that we can recognize the identical patterns of change in these cases and the complexity arising from the ebb and flow of these same patterns and processes as they compete with each other.

The chapters of this book bear witness to a diversity of methods being used by the anthropologists and linguists contributing. This is not just a hubbub of competing voices, however, but the beginnings of an exciting conversation about how to do diachronic study of social institutions like kinship alongside other evidence. In turn, the understandings generated by sociocultural anthropology and ethnology, particularly in the field of lexical semantics, help to fill out areas that are often incomplete or neglected in historical linguistics. The disciplines can be seen as complementary and could be fashioned into an interdisciplinary suite of methods of great power.

Notes

1. Some practitioners of this method, e.g., Dziebel (2007), seem to think that it is possible to reconstruct back a lot further than linguists reconstruct language families.
2. Wierzbicka, however, wishes to restrict this approach to *mother* and *father*, which belong to her set of universal primitives in the theory of Natural Semantic Metalanguage, while assigning wide monosemous meaning to such items as *tjamu* (grandfather and various other relations of that generation; for how this term historically descends by an extension from a narrower "mother's father" term, see McConvell, this volume). The question of semantic change is not addressed in Wierzbicka's article, and it is unclear how the Natural Semantic Metalanguage "natural language definitions" provided in the article might fit into a theory of change.
3. As Hage notes, in the case of siblings, unlike with other kinship terms, one cannot make a universal statement about whether the elder or younger term will be the unmarked term. As noted in the next criterion of syncretization, younger siblings are often marked. It is an empirical question whether these different sources of evidence for marking always point in the same direction in a specific language: they do not seem to in a number of Australian systems.
4. The other possibility is the kind of Kariera system found in Australia or elsewhere, where MM = FF and MF = FM. As in the previous example, parity (cross/parallel) is more important here than either sex of relative or sex of linking relative. For further discussion, see my chapter 10, this volume.
5. This term is used by Merlan (1982) primarily to refer to cases where a plain kinship term, e.g., *mother*, is used to mean "your mother" rather than "my mother," but it is argued that this is the basis of a type of meaning change also in teknocentricity or filiocentricity, when a term used from the point of view of a person's child is adopted, causing changes such as F(B) > B; see Hendery and McConvell, this volume.
6. Jones mentions Omaha skewing only at a different place in the book, with reference to remarks by Lounsbury about Latin and early Germanic having an Omaha system that equates MB with MF (a Type 3 variant).
7. It is not clear whether a specific step in the sequence between FB and FBS—the addition of the BS meaning to FB—is justified by historical evidence. FB = BS is an unusual equation in kinship terms.
8. The general trend away from bifurcate-collateral to lineal terminologies in Europe has been linked to the replacement of the patrilineal extended family by the conjugal family as the basic unit of society (Jones 1990:192). Kronenfeld (this volume) suggests that inheritance systems could have been implicated in this change, in line with his more general idea that inheritance has a role in molding kinship systems. Certainly there were important trends in inheritance in this period: in Germany, for instance, principalities and family properties became increasingly fragmented due to the fact that all sons inherited shares of the territory or property (Spiess 2007). It has been argued that this change in systems took place in Germanic languages before the borrowing of the French terms, but this was due to the influence of French and other Romance languages. Here the notion comes into play that a change to a neighboring system without formal loanwords prepares the ground for subsequent loan of forms.
9. This is similar to the case examined in McConvell (2013), of **kami* in Pama-Nyungan, except that in the Australian case the change is apparently in the opposite direction, from MM to FM via the polysemy FM = MM.

References Cited

Allan, K. In press. Semantics and Pragmatics in the Late 20th Century. In *Cambridge History of Linguistics*. L. R. Waugh, J. Joseph, and M. Monville-Burston, eds. Cambridge: Cambridge University Press. Electronic document, http://users.monash.edu.au/~kallan/papers/SemPragCHL.pdf.

Allen, N. 1986. Tetradic Theory: An Approach to Kinship. *Journal of the Anthropological Society of Oxford* 17(2):89–109.

Allen, N. J. 2004. Tetradic Theory: An Approach to Kinship. In *Kinship and Family: An Anthropological Reader*. R. Parkin and L. Stone, eds. Pp. 221-235. Oxford: Blackwell.

Allen, N. J. 2008. Tetradic Theory and the Origin of Human Kinship Systems. In *Early Human Kinship: From Sex to Social Reproduction*. N. Allen, H. Callan, R. Dunbar, and W. James, eds. Pp. 96–112. Oxford: Wiley-Blackwell.

Blust, R. 1990. Language and Culture History. *Asian Perspectives* 27(2):205–227.

Bright, W., and J. Minnick. 1966. Reduction Rules in Fox Kinship. *Southwestern Journal of Anthropology* 22(4):381–388.

Bruner, E. M. 1955. Two Processes of Change in Mandan-Hidatsa Kinship Terminology. *American Anthropologist* 57(4):840–850.

Burling, R. 1969. Cognition and Componential Analysis: God's Truth or Hocus-Pocus? In *Cognitive Anthropology*. S. Tyler, ed. Pp. 419–428. New York: Holt, Rinehart and Winston.

Campbell, L. 1976. Review of I. Dyen and D. Aberle, *Lexical Reconstruction: The Case of the Proto-Athapaskan Kinship System*. *American Anthropologist* 78(2):454–455.

Chapais, B. 2008. *Primeval Kinship: How Pair-Bonding Gave Birth to Human Society*. Cambridge: Harvard University Press.

Clackson, J. 2007. *Indo-European Linguistics: An Introduction*. Cambridge: Cambridge University Press.

Coseriu, E. 1964. Pour une sémantique diachronique structurale. *Travaux de Linguistique et de Littérature* 2(1):139–186.

Delbrück, B. 1889. *Die indogermanischen verwandtschaftsnamen: Ein beitrag zur vergleichenden alterthumskunde*. Leipzig: S. Hirzel.

Diepeveen, A. 2003. Verwantschapstermen in de Germaanse Talen. Ph.D. dissertation, University of Antwerp.

Dole, G. 1969. Generation Kinship Nomenclature as an Adaptation to Endogamy. *Southwestern Journal of Anthropology* 25(2):105–123.

Dyen, I., and D. F. Aberle. 1974. *Lexical Reconstruction: The Case of the Proto-Athapaskan Kinship System*. London: Cambridge University Press.

Dziebel, G. V. 2007. *The Genius of Kinship: The Phenomenon of Human Kinship and the Global Diversity of Kinship Terminologies*. Youngstown, N.Y.: Cambria Press.

Eggan, F. 1937. Historical Changes in the Choctaw Kinship System. *American Anthropologist* 39(1):34–52.

Ehret, C. 2008. Reconstructing Ancient Kinship in Africa. In *Early Human Kinship: From Sex to Social Reproduction*. N. J. Allen, H. Callan, R. Dunbar, and W. James, eds. Pp. 200–236. Oxford: Blackwell.

Frisch, J. A., and N. W. Schutz. 1967. Componential Analysis and Semantic Reconstruction: The Proto Central Yuman Kinship System. *Ethnology* 6(3):272–293.

Fritz, G. Forthcoming. Theories of Meaning Change: An Overview. In *Semantics: An International Handbook of Natural Language Meaning*, vol. 3. C. Maienborn, K. von Heusinger, and P. Portner, eds. Berlin: Mouton de Gruyter.

Geeraerts, D. 2002. The Theoretical and Descriptive Development of Lexical Semantics. In *The Lexicon in Focus: Competition and Convergence in Current Lexicology*. L. Behrens and D. Zaefferer, eds. Pp. 23–42. Frankfurt am Main: Peter Lang Publishing.

Godelier, M. 2004. *Métamorphoses de la parenté*. Paris: Fayard.

Godelier, M., T. B. Trautmann, and F. E. Tjon Sie Fat, eds. *Transformations of Kinship*. Washington, DC: Smithsonian.

Goody, J. 1959. Indo-European Kinship. In *Comparative Studies in Kinship*. J. Goody, ed. Pp. 235–239. London: Routledge.

Goody, J. 1983. *The Development of the Family and Marriage in Europe*. Cambridge: Cambridge University Press.

Goody, J. 2000. *The European Family: An Historico-anthropological Essay*. Oxford: Wiley-Blackwell.

Greenberg, J. 1990[1980]. Universals of Kinship Terminology. In *On Language: Selected Writings of Joseph H. Greenberg*. K. Denning and S. Kemmer, eds. Pp. 310–327. Stanford: Stanford University Press.

Hage, P. 1999. Marking Universals and the Structure and Evolution of Kinship Terminologies: Evidence from Salish. *Journal of the Royal Anthropological Institute* 5(3):423–441.

Hage, P., B. Milicic, M. Mixco, and M. J. P. Nichols. 2004. The Proto-Numic Kinship System. *Journal of Anthropological Research* 60(3):359–377.

Jones, D. 2010. Human Kinship, from Conceptual Structure to Grammar. *Behavioral and Brain Sciences* 33:367–404.

Jones, D., and B. Milicic, eds. 2011. *Kinship, Language, and Prehistory: Per Hage and the Renaissance in Kinship Studies*. Salt Lake City: University of Utah Press.

Jones, W. J. 1990. *German Kinship Terms, 750–1500: Documentation and Analysis*. Berlin: Walter de Gruyter.

King, R. D. 1969. *Historical Linguistics and Generative Grammar*. 1st edition. Englewood Cliffs, NJ: Prentice Hall.

Kronenfeld, D. B. 1996. *Plastic Glasses and Church Fathers: Semantic Extension from the Ethnoscience Tradition*. Oxford: Oxford University Press.

Kryukov, M. V. 1998. The Synchro-diachronic Method and the Multidirectionality of Kinship Transformations. In *Transformations of Kinship*. M. Godelier, T. B. Trautmann, and F. E. Tjon Sie Fat, eds. Pp. 294–313. Washington, DC: Smithsonian.

Lehrer, A. 1974. *Semantic Fields and Lexical Structure*. Amsterdam: American Elsevier.

Lévi-Strauss, C. 1969. *The Elementary Structures of Kinship*. Boston: Beacon Press.

Lounsbury, F. G. 1964. The Formal Analysis of Crow- and Omaha-Type Kinship Terminologies. In *Explorations in Cultural Anthropology: Essays in Honor of George Peter Murdock*. W. H. Goodenough, ed. Pp. 351–393. New York: McGraw-Hill Book Co.

Matras, Y. 2009. *Language Contact*. Cambridge: Cambridge University Press.

McConvell, P. 1997. Long-Lost Relations: Pama-Nyungan and Northern Kinship. In *Archaeology and Linguistics: Aboriginal Australia in Global Perspective*. P. McConvell and N. Evans, eds. Pp. 207–235. Melbourne: Oxford University Press.

McConvell, P. 2010. Getting the Constraints Right. *Behavioral and Brain Sciences* 33:394–395.

McConvell, P. 2013. "Granny Got Cross": Semantic Change of *Kami* 'Mother's Mother' to 'Father's Mother' in Pama-Nyungan. In *Lexical and Structural Etymology: Beyond Word Histories*. R. Mailhammer, ed. Studies in Language Change. Pp. 147–184. Berlin: de Gruyter Mouton.

McConvell, P., and B. Alpher. 2002. On the Omaha Trail in Australia: Tracking Skewing from East to West. *Anthropological Forum* 12(2):159–75.

McConvell, P., and R. Hendery. 2010. Investigating the Multiple Meanings of "Kariera System" with AUSTKIN Database Queries. Unpublished MS, Australian National University.

McConvell, P., and I. Keen. 2011. The Transition from Kariera to an Asymmetrical System: Cape York Peninsula to North-East Arnhem Land. In *Kinship, Language, and Prehistory: Per Hage and the Renaissance in Kinship Studies*. D. Jones and B. Milicic, eds. Pp. 99–132. Salt Lake City: University of Utah Press.

Merlan, F. 1982. Egocentric and Altercentric Kinterms. In *Languages of Kinship in Australia*. F. Merlan, J. Heath, and A. Rumsey, eds. Pp. 107–124. Oceania Monograph, 24. Sydney: University of Sydney.

Murdock, G. P. 1949. *Social Structure*. New York: Macmillan.

Scheffler, H. W. 1971. Dravidian-Iroquois: The Melanesian Evidence. In *Anthropology in Oceania: Essays Presented to Ian Hogbin*. L. R. Hiatt and E. Jayawardena, eds. Pp. 231–254. Sydney: Angus and Robertson.

Scheffler, H. W. 1972. Kinship Semantics. *Annual Review of Anthropology* 1(1):309–328.

Scheffler, H. W. 1978. *Australian Kin Classification*. Cambridge: Cambridge University Press.

Schoof, W. 1900. *Die deutschen Verwandtschaftsnamen. Zeitschrift für hochdeutsche Mundarten herausgegeben von Otto Heilig und Philipp Lenz*. Marburg.

Spiess, K-H. 2007. Lordship, Kinship and Inheritance among the German High Nobility in the Middle Ages and Early Modern Ages. In *Kinship in Europe: Approaches to Long-Term Development (1300–1900)*. D. W. Sabean, S. Teuscher, and J. Mathieu, eds. Pp. 57–75. New York: Berghahan Books.

Spoehr, A. 1947. *Changing Kinship Systems: A Study in the Acculturation of the Creeks, Cherokee, and Choctaw*. Chicago: Field Museum of Natural History. Electronic document, http://www.archive.org/details/changingkinships334spoe, accessed October 12, 2010.

Trier, J. 1931. Der deutsche Wortschatz im Sinnbezirk des Verstandes. Ph.D. dissertation, Bonn.

Vanhove, Martine, ed. 2008. *From Polysemy to Semantic Change: Towards a Typology of Lexical Semantic Associations*. Amsterdam: John Benjamins.

Whistler, Kenneth. 1980. Proto-Wintun Kin Classification: A Case-Study in the Reconstruction of a Complex Semantic System. Ph.D. dissertation, University of California, Berkeley.

Wierzbicka, A. 1987. Kinship Semantics: Lexical Universals as a Key to Psychological Reality. *Anthropological Linguistics* 29(2):131–156.

Wilkins, J. F., and F. W. Marlowe. 2006. Sex-Biased Migration in Humans: What Should We Expect from Genetic Data? *BioEssays: News and Reviews in Molecular, Cellular and Developmental Biology* 28(3):290–300.

2

Kinship Terms

Typology and History

David B. Kronenfeld

I will be exploring the theoretical and analytic context within which the kinship aspects of the present collection might best be understood. That is, each contributor has made choices concerning data, analytic approach, typological system for classification, and so forth. I want to provide some idea of what they have not chosen and of what analytic considerations are implied by one versus another choice.

Different kinship analyses or analytical systems are not *necessarily* mutually contradictory—although some anthropological thinking has tended to see them as such. Rather, different analytical systems may reveal different aspects of kinship systems, and the wider kinship systems may not be as rigidly unified—and thus their different aspects may not be as tightly tied together as has been sometimes thought. And, in turn, each of these different aspects tells us different things about the history, sociology, and cognitive systems of those who use the terminologies. In what follows I will try to spell out what I mean.

This chapter will be a little encyclopedic—partially because of the task and partially (importantly) because I am a theoretic and methodological omnivore. That is, I am in favor of whatever approach best does any given job—even while insistent that each analytic game should be played in a logically and empirically rigorous way.

General Background Understanding

Kin terms are words in one or another language. Thus the normal analytic and usage perspectives that apply to the semantics of words apply to them too, along with any special systemic properties peculiar to them or to wider categories to which they belong. These normal perspectives include the following:

a. Semantics, which traditionally includes sense relations of contrast and inclusion among terms and the referential relations by which the terms are related to the "objects" in the world that they are understood to label. For example, think of living rooms versus dining rooms as kinds of rooms, tables versus chairs as kinds of furniture, dining chairs versus easy chairs as kinds of chairs, and end tables versus coffee tables versus dining tables as kinds of tables—and think of how to tell them apart.
b. Pragmatics, which refers to the nonlinguistic relations among terms' referents, which are presumed in usage: for example, our knowledge that dining chairs and dining tables go together in dining rooms, while easy chairs, end tables, and coffee tables all go in living rooms.
c. The wider cultural structuring of the interrelationships of their referents that comes from general social relations, conceptual organization, social and geographic distribution, cultural instantiations of economics, and so forth: for example, our knowledge of what styles, materials, price, and so on imply about the social class, economic standing, aesthetics, occupation, and so forth of the residents of the house.

In addition to these general perspectives come whatever special properties and constraints that characterize kinship terminological systems of one type or another (see Simpson, this volume).

In understanding what is specific about kin terms, we first need to think about what they do. A person's initial ascribed social location—defining who is responsible for the person and what specific ascribed rights and privileges the person has—accounts (as F. K. Lehman has noted [see Kronenfeld 2001a:166–167 n. 16]) for the universality of kinship terminological systems, for their core focal relations, and for their binary nature. That is, we always start with *mommy*, *daddy*, and those who share *mommy* and *daddy* (and, later, their reciprocals).

Kinds of Analytic Perspectives with Attendant Contrasts

At issue here are the analytic approaches we use to understand what is meant by a kin term that appears in one or another context and what other information might aid our understanding. Contexts can range from word lists, through reports of examples of usage, to appearance in texts and so forth. Information can include context of use, relevant semantic paradigms, relevant pragmatic contexts, social conventions, and so forth.

Treatment of the Kinship Terminological System vis-à-vis Other Uses of the Same Terms

One perspective approach issue concerns how one treats the kinship terminological system vis-à-vis other uses of the same terms. The common choice is a separate formal analysis of kin terms from analysis of other uses (which are often treated as some form of figurative extension). The other alternative is a direct analysis of the whole range of reference of the terms that include kin referents. Leach's (1958) analysis of *tabu* in Trobriand is the major example, and see responses by Lounsbury (1965) and Scheffler (1972b). Such whole-category approaches seem not to have panned out—in the sense that few since Leach seem seriously to have tried one; but Danziger (2001) has further explored the issue in interesting and sophisticated ways.

Semantic Distinctive Features versus Pragmatic Algebraic Relations

An important distinction is that between analyses based on semantic "distinctive features" and ones based on pragmatic algebraic relations (see Kronenfeld 1996:133, 2009:7–9, for my understanding of the semantics/pragmatics distinction). Semantic relations concern contrast (e.g., a "brother" as opposed to what?—a "sister," a "father," etc.), inclusion (e.g., a "brother" is a kind of "sibling," which is, in turn, a kind of kinsperson), and the attributes that structure these (e.g., sex, generation, lineality [see Danziger, this volume]). Pragmatic relations represent what we know or presume about the world to which words (lexemes) refer and, in particular in the present context, what knowledge about the world is implicit in (or presumed by) our use of kin terms (e.g., each of us has a mother and a father, who themselves each have a mother and a father and who, in many cases, have other children, and so on; each person's mother and father are presumed—in the absence of other information—to be married to each other and living in a household with that person and with their other children, and so forth).

The general linguistic distinction between semantics and pragmatics, joined with the role of each, gives us a way of understanding why two very different and not easily commensurate analytic approaches can both strike many analysts as useful and important—and thus why one has not given way to the other. In particular, algebraic approaches represent the relative product logic by which relationship categories are calculated from other relationship categories—as in, for English, my "mother's brother" is my "uncle."[1] On the other hand, semantic feature approaches are based on the analytic features or attributes on which native terms contrast with one another—as, in English, *father* differs from *mother* on sex of relative and from *uncle* on lineality.

Semantic features were initially seen as providing the distinctive features that distinguished all of the members of one terminological category from the members of another—as in the classic early componential analyses of Lounsbury, Goodenough, and Wallace and Atkins. More recently, triggered by Lounsbury's work on Crow- and Omaha-type systems, distinctive features that define relations among kin terms have only been applied *necessarily* to focal referents of those terms. The connection of other referents to the terms was seen as a secondary one whereby they were first related to the focal referents and then, via those focal referents, to the appropriate terminological categories. For example, in Fanti, a mother's sister falls into the *na* 'mother' category via some form of an equivalence-of-same-sex-siblings extension rule. The secondary connection has sometimes been taken as simply a wider application of the initial distinctive features, sometimes as a feature neutralization rules (Scheffler's [1972a: 359–362] approach [and see Scheffler and Lounsbury 1971:51]), and sometimes as separate rewrite equivalence rules (my approach [see Kronenfeld 1973, 1980a]).

One approach to studying change, as seen, for example, in Per Hage's (e.g., 1999, 2001) use of Marking Theory, makes use of distinctive semantic features. See the characterization of Marking Theory below.

Pragmatic algebraic relations refer to the system of

interrelationships among the referents of kin terms as natives conceptualize them or as seems implicit in the terminology itself—and to the relationship of these referents to terminological categories. Read's (2001 and this volume) formal algebraic approach emphasizes the ethnographic details of particular systems along with a formalized distillation of native speaker operations on native language categories. Read's system is embedded in a computer program, which should aid its use by others.

Gould's algebraic analytic system is ethnologically oriented and so is based on analytic relationship categories (at root, "mother," "father," and "spouse"). It thus ignores some of the detail of some specific systems—that is, detail systemically irrelevant to that structure—such as, for Fanti, the fact that any "father's sister" is called by the "mother" term. This detail is "irrelevant" because the structural relations of M, which all apply to any "mother's sister" (e.g., the equation of "*mother*'s brother" with "uncle" does not apply to any "father's sister," even though she is a "mother"). Gould's system includes a new way of formally representing the reciprocals of father and mother categories and a system of graphic representation of the algebraic relations that allows easy visualization of systems' structures and easy tracing of terminological relationships within systems. I will say more about Gould's system a little later.

Ethnography and Ethnology

In general, a comparative ethnological approach works best with categories that do not build in the specific differentiating details of particular systems but which rely on common elements that run across classes or types of systems—that is, an external analytically or comparatively based etic approach. On the other hand, ethnographic accuracy can sometimes best be served by approaches (categories and operations) that are more or less unique to the given system—and hence emic. The tension between the two perspectives or approaches has run through the history of our discipline at least since the invention of ethnography. See my Goodenough versus Fischer article (Kronenfeld 1992) for a fuller discussion of this problem.

Emic versus Etic Approaches

I use the terms *emic* and *etic* in their linguistic-based sense of representing a distinction between the native speaker categories and operations that are arrived at analytically by a linguist or anthropologist and categories and operations that the analyst brings in from the outside (whether based on theory, science, prejudice—or abstractions from some set of emic characterizations). This is *not* Marvin Harris's construction of the distinction as between native folk theories and outside scientific ones.

Emic-based analyses are constructed within a given culture's categories and operations and are geared toward an ethnographic account. They can be used to compare emic rules across systems, to study cognitive operations, or to work out the logic of the system. Read's algebraic approach seems particularly aimed at these goals. Keen's (1985) approach was aimed at more specifically portraying how native speakers actually calculated within the system.

Etic-based analyses are usually applied across cultural systems and are geared toward an ethnological account. One can aim at structural regularities across systems and the typology that comes out of these (see Hornborg's example, this volume), as has Gould. This perspective is implicit in traditional typologies of kin term systems, such as those of Morgan (1871), Lowie (e.g., 1948:60–67), and Murdock (1949).

In my own work I have found that this approach, rather than a more emic one, allowed the cleanest analysis of the relationship between Fanti kin terms and Fanti social relations and social groups. That is, an etic-based and feature-based terminological analysis—structured for cross-system comparison—turned out also to be useful for intrasystem comparisons of kin terminological patterns with patterns of behavior among kin. This perhaps surprising result was the effect of differences between how Fanti people calculated kin term category membership and how they calculated kin group membership and social or behavioral relations. These differences included differing metrics for category extension (relative products for kin term categories versus specifically relevant distinctive features for behavioral relations) and also behavioral recognition of conceptual entities that were not coded in the terminology—such as a "parent" category (see immediately below). Thus, a good etic analysis can capture something that is ethnographically important that does not show up in an emic analysis of native speaker calculations.

My Fanti experience has shown regularities (e.g., conjunctivities) in their kinship relations that Fanti seem clearly aware of but which they clearly avoid recognizing in their terminological system. The reasons seem to be, in some sense, ideological; that is, they have a way of constructing a balanced contrast between one's nuclear family and one's matrilineage that might be undermined by any overt privileging of the mother's relationship to her nuclear family as opposed to her lineage. Such privileging might be implied by any overt recognition of a "parent" category (i.e., classing lineage-member mother with non-lineage-member father) that contrasted with the lineage-member maternal uncle in the absence of any kin term category that included "mother" and "mother's brother" but not "father."[2] The similarity between parents is recognized elsewhere in the terminology—through reciprocals—where there is a parentally shared "child" category that contrasts with a man's "nibling," and in various behavioral and economic responsibilities (i.e., in their behavior and implicitly in conversations they recognized a "parent" category even though no such category was in any way coded in the terminology).

Connotation and Metaphor

I turn now to the problem of linking technically proper denotative kin term usage with connotative and figurative extensions. Such usage does *not* relate in any direct fashion to algebraic representations but nonetheless is productive and systematic. It uses attributes that are mapped off of feature attributes of categories in the denotative system proper. I am talking about the range of application issues that an analysis might speak to:

a. Narrow denotatively correct usage can be indicated by hedges such as "Joe *really* is my uncle." (For a few close direct relations in classificatory systems, the hedges split: Molly *really* is my "mother," but Edna still is my *real* mother.) Most anthropological work on kinship terms focuses on this denotative level of usage, though often with asides relating to b and c below.
b. A little wider range includes connotative usage, such as "Frank is not technically my 'uncle,' but he is like an uncle to me." See the Fanti courtesy pattern, as described in Kronenfeld 1973, 1980a, 2009: chs. 1–2.
c. An even wider net includes figurative usage. For example, "Milton Berle became known to many TV watchers as 'Uncle Miltie' on the basis of more or less avuncular behavior in some of his idiot skits." Other examples include "Uncle Sam is trying to tax every cent I earn" and "Will you say 'uncle,' or should I keep twisting until your arm breaks?"

This perspective differs from that of Leach's Trobriand *tabu* above because Leach did not accord any primacy to what I am calling "narrow denotatively correct usage."[3]

Systems of Classification of Types of Kin Terminologies

To start, we have the traditional Murdock type of kin terminology system based on central cousin equivalences and central uncle/aunt equivalences. There are some problems with it. First, it does not deal with whole actual systems and thus can be misled where there are inconsistencies among those central terms—as in Fanti, where "father's sister" is called by the "mother" term, while "mother's brother" has a separate term from the "father" term. And second, it thus is oblivious to type distinctions that are based on alternative extension patterns (as Dravidian- versus Iroquois-type systems). Dole (1972) extensively uses, discusses, criticizes, and works on this approach.

Then we have the common modern approach, based on Morgan and Lowie, of classifying systems based on general patterns of equivalences often recognized through diagnostic equations—our system of Hawaiian, Iroquois-Dravidian, Cheyenne, Omaha, Crow, and Eskimo types (see Hornborg, this volume). (Some anthropologists seem not to attend to Lounsbury's [1969b] distinguishing of Dravidian type from Iroquois type.) Problems include the fuzziness of actual definitions and lack of any understanding of the systematic relations that generate the systems. Dole's (1972) discussion is also relevant here.

Lounsbury's (1969a) expansion/reduction rule equivalences suggested another classificatory possibility, but one that has never really been followed up on. It seemed particularly useful for delimiting skewed systems and for capturing the differences between Crow and Omaha types but did not seem to apply so cleanly elsewhere. And while it was based on formal equivalences, it did not embody any formal (mathematical) system.

Note that Lounsbury's rewrite rules do not work to distinguish types of cross/parallel in Dravidian- and Iroquois-type systems. He used a whole-category componential analysis for Iroquois. To the best of my knowledge he provided no analysis of any Dravidian-type system.[4] It seems possible that Lounsbury's awareness of this difference in how the two types of systems seemed best handled explains why he never moved to put the two approaches together into any general analytic system.

Gould (2000) introduced a formal classification of types of systems that is based on his new analytic system. That system is a combination of a notational scheme and a formal algebraic analytic model.[5] Gould's notational system is designed both to accurately represent genealogical strings and to facilitate the application of his new and powerful algebraic analysis to those strings. The algebraic analysis in turn produces formal definitions of the traditional types of kin term systems.

To understand Gould's classification we first need a definition of his notational system—provided in Table 2.1. His algebraic analysis depends on symmetric equivalences such that either of the equivalent expressions can be substituted for the other in any expression without changing that expression's kin term structural class (the actual kin term category will depend on the descriptive features such as sex of alter that subdivide the class). Some examples are provided in Table 2.2. The basic traditional types are defined by different equivalence rule sets. The rule sets for these types are provided in Table 2.3. Note that there is, in that table, an initial rule set that applies to all classificatory systems (that is, types of systems in which collateral relatives consistently fall in the same categories as lineal relatives); following that rule are the rules that define—and thus distinguish—the major types of classificatory systems. In Table 2.4 I offer equivalent rules for variant versions of the Eskimo-type system that is represented by English (Kronenfeld 2001b). Note that the rules for the "maximal" system there are the same as the specific rules (in Table 2.3) for generating Hawaiian-type systems; the difference is that the general classificatory system rule applies to Hawaiian-type systems but *not* to Eskimo-type ones like English.

Appendix A offers a brief English example of the Gould system treatment of affines. That example also illustrates how deductive calculations work in the system.

One of Gould's major innovations—one that is simple and powerful and seems to "cut nature at a joint"—is his introduction of $\overline{M}$ (motherling) and $\overline{F}$ (fatherling) as the strict reciprocals of M (mother) and F (father) rather than the hitherto normal D (daughter) and S (son) partial reciprocals that were used whenever anyone tried to break apart the sexes in P,C (parent, child)-based formal analyses. The lack of clean reciprocals kept analysts away from a sex-marked F,M approach and pushed them to the P,C one, but taking P and C as logical primaries made the handling of many sex-based distinctions (such as cross versus parallel) very awkward.

Gould also introduces a very clear and simple graphic representation for his algebraic system, "kin graphs," which allow a quick discernment of the patterns produced by the various equivalence-rule systems and also allow the kin term categories of kin types to be quickly and easily traced out. In it the boxes represent the sets of structurally equivalent genealogical (and terminological) positions produced by the defining equations;[6] different boxes represent structurally distinct sets; and the lines connecting them (solid for father/child, dashed for mother/child) represent the links among these.

TABLE 2.1. Gould's notational system.

Notation	Meaning
F	Someone's father
M	Someone's mother
P	Someone's parent
$\overline{F}$	'fatherling', the inverse of 'father', F, referring to a man's child of either sex
$\overline{M}$	'motherling', the inverse of 'mother', M, referring to a woman's child of either sex
$\overline{P}$	Someone's child
I	The identity relation, refers to self
J	Sibling ($F\overline{F}$, $M\overline{M}$)
X	Focal cross-cousin ($FJ\overline{M}$, $MJ\overline{F}$ written $F\overline{M}$, $M\overline{F}$)
μ	In kin-type strings, male ego (if initial on the string) or alter (if terminal)
φ	In kin-type strings, female ego (if initial) or alter (if terminal)
XY	Example of a relative product, referring to "X's Y"
↔	Structural equivalence where in any expression either of the equivalent elements can be replaced by the other
≈	A concurrence; a local, structurally irrelevant equivalence between the item to the left of the sign and the item to the right, as in X » Y

In a kin graph one can determine a terminological assignment of a kin type by tracing that kin type through the boxes by following the lines that connect them. Lines with arrowpoints are unidirectional; ones without points can be followed in either direction. The labels outside the boxes indicate the structural elements of the boxes, and those inside represent the included kin terms; lines inside the boxes represent features (such as sex in English) that are not structurally relevant.

The two kin graphs in Figures 2.1–2.2 are adapted from Kronenfeld 2001b (also Kronenfeld 2009: ch. 11) and Gould 2000. Figure 2.1 shows the full English system(s), while Figure 2.2 shows the minimal English system one gets if one ignores intracategory modifiers (cf. Simpson, this volume). The graphs in Figures 2.3–2.4 are

TABLE 2.2. Equivalence rules in Gould's system.

Example	Equivalence Rules
1. English	A terminological equivalence, such as $M \leftrightarrow F$ in English, means that in any other expression, such as MFF (mother's father's father), either expression can be substituted for the other without changing the structural class of the expression. Thus, MMF, for instance, falls in the same category as the original MFF, as does MFM. (Remember, the actual kin term category will depend on the descriptive features such as sex of alter that subdivide the class, as in Figures 2.1 and 2.2.) Therefore MFF = MMF = MFM
2. Fanti (Unskewed)	Let us take father's mother's sister's son as the kin type whose terminological category we seek. We first translate it into Gould's notation: $\mathrm{FMJ\overline{F}}\mu$. We next apply the equivalence rules for the unskewed Fanti system, the Cheyenne type in Table 2.3. The rules are unordered; whatever fits can be applied.
Expression	Rule that reduces it to the next expression
$\mathrm{FMJ\overline{F}}\mu$	$I \leftrightarrow J$
$\mathrm{FMI\overline{F}}\mu$	Definition of I—as the identity operator
$\mathrm{FM\overline{F}}\mu$	$FM \leftrightarrow FF$
$\mathrm{FF\overline{F}}\mu$	Definition of J: $\mathrm{F\overline{F}}$
$\mathrm{FJ}\mu$	$I \leftrightarrow J$, and definition of I
$\mathrm{F}\mu$	The resulting expression is a male member of the FATHER structural category (as opposed to $\mathrm{F}\varphi$, which would be a female member, i.e., father's sister who is a "mother" in Fanti). Thus we see that the analytic system allows the deduction of the appropriate structural category, which contains structurally equivalent kin terms. Components such as sex of alter, sex of ego, relative age, etc. then are used to arrive at the precise kin term assignment. See Figures 2.1 and 2.2 for a graphic version for English of the subdivision of structural categories by features.
3. Fanti (Skewed)	Let us take a man's mother's mother's father's sister's son's daughter as the kin type whose terminological category we seek. We first translate it into Gould's notation: $\mathrm{mMMFJ\overline{M}\overline{F}f}$. We next apply the equivalence rules for the skewed Fanti system, the Crow type in Table 2.3. The rules are unordered; whatever fits can be applied.
Expression	Rule that reduces it to the next expression
$\mu\mathrm{MMFJ\overline{M}\overline{F}}\varphi$	$I \leftrightarrow J$, and definition of I
$\mu\mathrm{MMF\overline{M}\overline{F}}\varphi$	$\mathrm{F\overline{M}} \leftrightarrow F$
$\mu\mathrm{MMF\overline{F}}\varphi$	Definition of J: $\mathrm{F\overline{F}}$
$\mu\mathrm{MMJ}\varphi$	$I \leftrightarrow J$, and definition of I
$\mu\mathrm{MM}\varphi$	By definition of "grandrelative" in Fanti
MM	The resulting expression is a "grandrelative" (the single term in Fanti that covers grandfather, grandmother, grandson, and granddaughter). The lead male ego and the final female alter both turn out to be terminologically irrelevant as well as structurally irrelevant. But note that in Crow-type skewed systems, the kind of grandrelative does matter: that is, $MM \neq MF \neq FF \neq FM$.

adapted from Gould 2000. Figure 2.3 shows a generic Dravidian-type system. By way of contrast with Dravidian, Figure 2.4 shows a generic Iroquois-type system.

Aranda (Arrernte) Kin Term System and Sections

Gould's kin graph of Aranda (i.e., Arrernte) is presented in Figure 2.5, along with matching kin graphs of the section and subsection systems (Figures 2.6–2.7). These figures are offered by way of illustrating another application of kin graphs. They are not intended as the latest word on the specifics of these systems (see Keen, this volume; Koch, this volume; Alpher, this volume). Instead they demonstrate how kin graphs can aid our understanding of section and subsection systems and how they can illustrate the relationship between kin term systems and section systems and between related four- and eight-section systems. Gould (2000) offers similar treatments of some other types of section systems.

TABLE 2.3. Equivalences that define and generate the basic traditional types.

Type	Equation(s)	Reference
All Classificatory Systems	$I \leftrightarrow J \leftrightarrow \overline{M}M \leftrightarrow \overline{F}F$	Gould 2000:137
Particular Classificatory Systems		
Generational (Hawaiian Type)	$M \leftrightarrow F$	Gould 2000:137
Reciprocal Hawaiian Type	$\overline{M} \leftrightarrow \overline{F}$	
Cheyenne Type	$X \leftrightarrow J$; $MF \leftrightarrow MM$; $FM \leftrightarrow FF$	Gould 2000:266
Reciprocal Cheyenne Type	$\overline{F}\overline{M} \leftrightarrow \overline{M}\overline{M}$ $\overline{M}\overline{F} \leftrightarrow \overline{F}\overline{F}$	
Iroquois Type (or Seneca)	$MF \leftrightarrow MM$; $FM \leftrightarrow FF$	Gould 2000:251
Reciprocal Iroquois Type	$\overline{F}\overline{M} \leftrightarrow \overline{M}\overline{M}$ $\overline{M}\overline{F} \leftrightarrow \overline{F}\overline{F}$	
Dravidian Type (or Tamil)	$FF \leftrightarrow MM$; $FM \leftrightarrow MF$	Gould 2000:156
Reciprocal Dravidian Type	$\overline{F}\overline{F} \leftrightarrow \overline{M}\overline{M}$ $\overline{M}\overline{F} \leftrightarrow \overline{F}\overline{M}$	
Omaha Type	$F\overline{M} \leftrightarrow \overline{M}$	Gould 2000:297, 309
Reciprocal Omaha Type	$M\overline{M} \leftrightarrow M$	
Crow Type	$M\overline{F} \leftrightarrow \overline{F}$	Gould 2000:321
Reciprocal Crow Type	$F\overline{M} \leftrightarrow F$	

Note: Expressions such as MM should not be seen as grandparents per se but only as kin types that can be substituted for the indicated equivalent kin types.

TABLE 2.4. Nonclassificatory, English, in Gould's system.

Type of System	Equation(s)
Eskimo Type (as in the Maximal English System with Cousin Types)	$M \leftrightarrow F$
Reciprocal Eskimo Type	$\overline{M} \leftrightarrow \overline{F}$
Core (Minimal English System, Limited to Unmodified Lexemes)	$M \leftrightarrow F$; $PPP \leftrightarrow PP$
Reciprocal Core	$\overline{M} \leftrightarrow \overline{F}$; $\overline{P}\overline{P}\overline{P} \leftrightarrow \overline{P}\overline{P}$

Note: I have added these expressions for the nonclassificatory, i.e., descriptive system. The classificatory equivalences do *not* apply, and this absence is what defines the difference between the Hawaiian type and English (Eskimo type).

TABLE 2.5. Aranda sections with subsections.

Section	Code
A. Panunga	
Panunga	A_1
Uknaria	A_2
B. Purula	
Purula	B_1
Ungalla	B_2
C. Kumara	
Kumara	C_1
Umbitchana	C_2
D. Bultara	
Bultara	D_1
Appungerta	D_2

Source: Adapted from Gould 2000:248.

Figure 2.5 shows Gould's (2000:213) representation of Aranda. In it one can see how this more complex type of system relates to the generic Dravidian-type system of Figure 2.3. Figures 2.6 and 2.7, keyed to the labels and component arrangement of Table 2.5, give us Gould's (2000:248–249) kin graph representations of Aranda sections and subsections. Gould's suggestion is that the sections and subsections map directly onto the structural classes (or superclasses) of the terminology—and thus, given additional observational information, can be used to identify kin terms for people whose actual genealogical connections were unknown (or nonexistent)—apart from whatever other social or aesthetic uses the section system might have.

A comparison of algebraic analytic approaches such as Gould's or Read's with feature-based approaches (whether monosemic whole-kin-term-category componential ones such as Lounsbury's [1969b] Iroquois article or polysemic extension [from a kernel componential paradigm] ones such as Lounsbury's [1969a] analysis of Crow- and

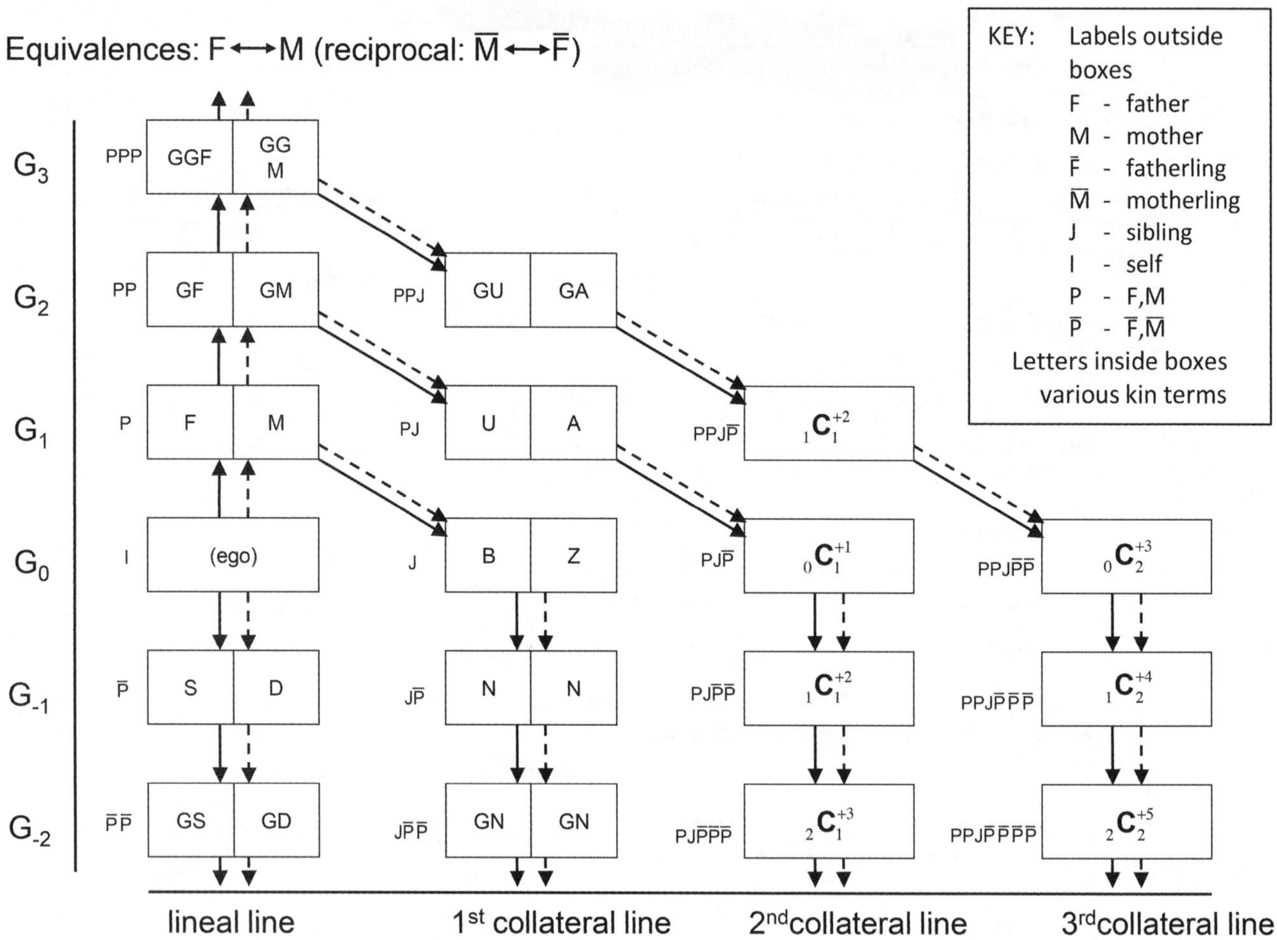

FIGURE 2.1. Maximal English system. From Kronenfeld 2001b:176.

Omaha-type systems) points to some important differences. The algebraic approaches can model native speaker decision processes regarding terminological assignments and thus changes in these processes over time (see Read, this volume), while the feature approaches cannot—because a number of the features depend on already knowing the links from ego to the relative. The features, on the other hand, do seem to capture a way of thinking about categories of relatives (including their functional relationship to social categories) that the algebraic approach seems unable to speak to. Additionally, certain kinds of regional patterns are more easily perceived via a feature approach. Since our major terminological types are based on intercategory relations (even if this does not always seem obvious!), these types and their interrelations are easily represented algebraically—and much harder to represent componentially or via component-based extension rules.

My own comparison of the two kinds of approach (Kronenfeld 1980b), as well as the comparison by Gould (implicit in his parallel presentation of both approaches to all of the many systems he analyzes), make clear a kind of deep incommensurability of the two systems (and see Chit Hlaing 2011). That is, while one can link the categories or operations of the one to the language of the other, the actual categories and operations as well as some of the analytic concepts of the one do not at all match those of the other. For example, in componential approaches it is often important to distinguish linking relatives from terminal ones (i.e., ego or alter); but in algebraic approaches the distinction seems irrelevant and not part of the normal analytic machinery. I also note that a single algebraic approach (whether Gould's or Read's) seems quite capable of dealing consistently with the full range of types of kin terminologies, while this seems not to be the case for feature-based approaches. That is, for example, the kind of feature approach that Lounsbury (1969b) uses for Iroquois does not work for Dravidian-type systems, and the extension-rule approach that he (1969a) uses for Crow- and Omaha-type systems works for neither Iroquois-type

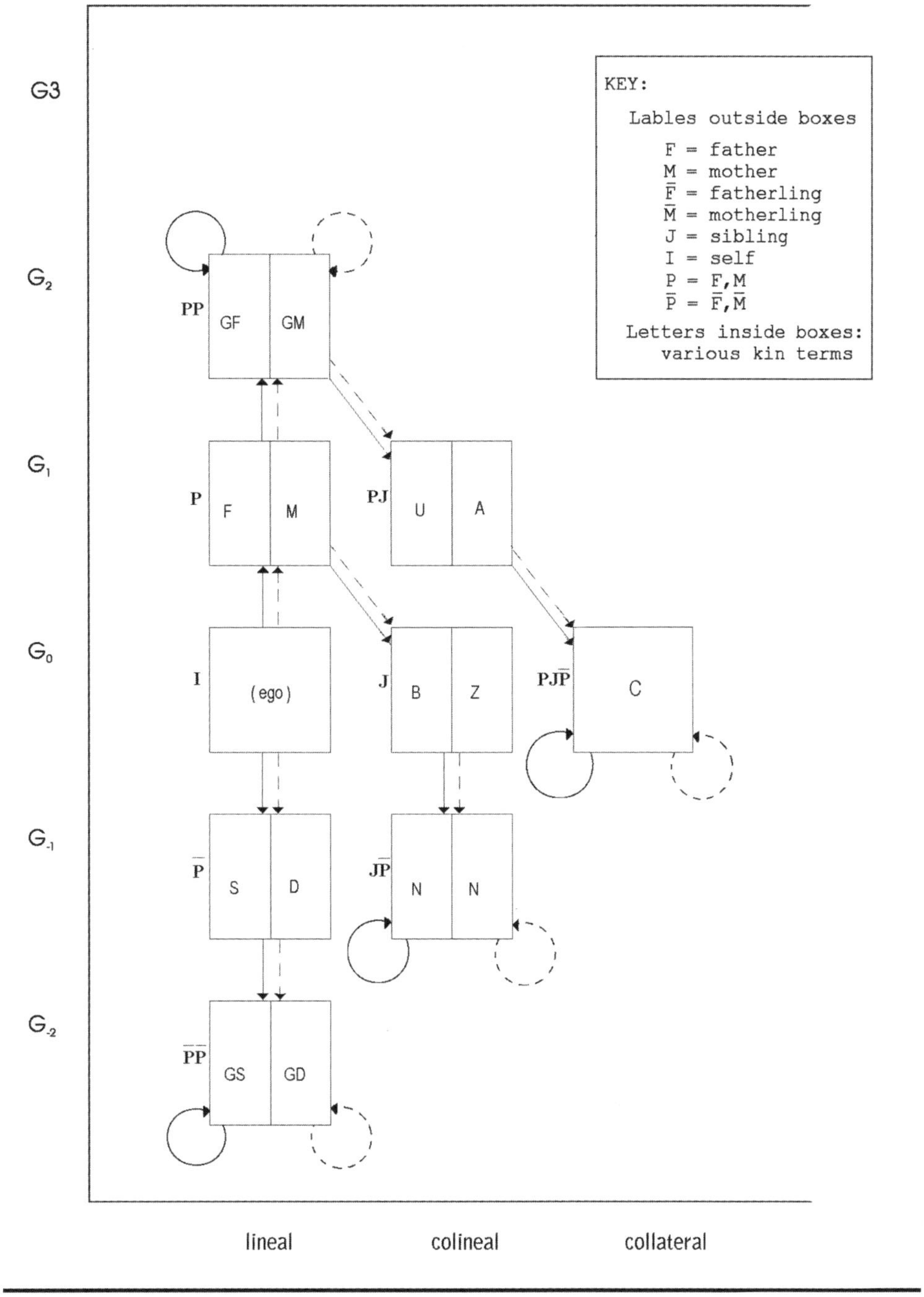

Equivalences: M ↔ F (and reciprocally $\overline{F}$ ↔ $\overline{M}$)
PPP ↔ PP (and reciprocally $\overline{PPP}$ ↔ $\overline{PP}$)

FIGURE 2.2. Minimal English system. From Kronenfeld 2001b:178.

nor Dravidian-type systems. Gould, in the componential part of his book, does design kinds of components (sometimes quite complex) that enable componential-extension analyses of all the systems he considers, but his (2000: app. H) total list of componential-extension complexes is quite lengthy and contains a great variety of features.

Distinction between Central and Peripheral Referents

Consistent across most of these alternative approaches is some version of a distinction between central (whether core, kernel, prototypic, primary, or focal) referents or exemplars and peripheral (extended, secondary) ones. Different analytic and theoretic approaches define the

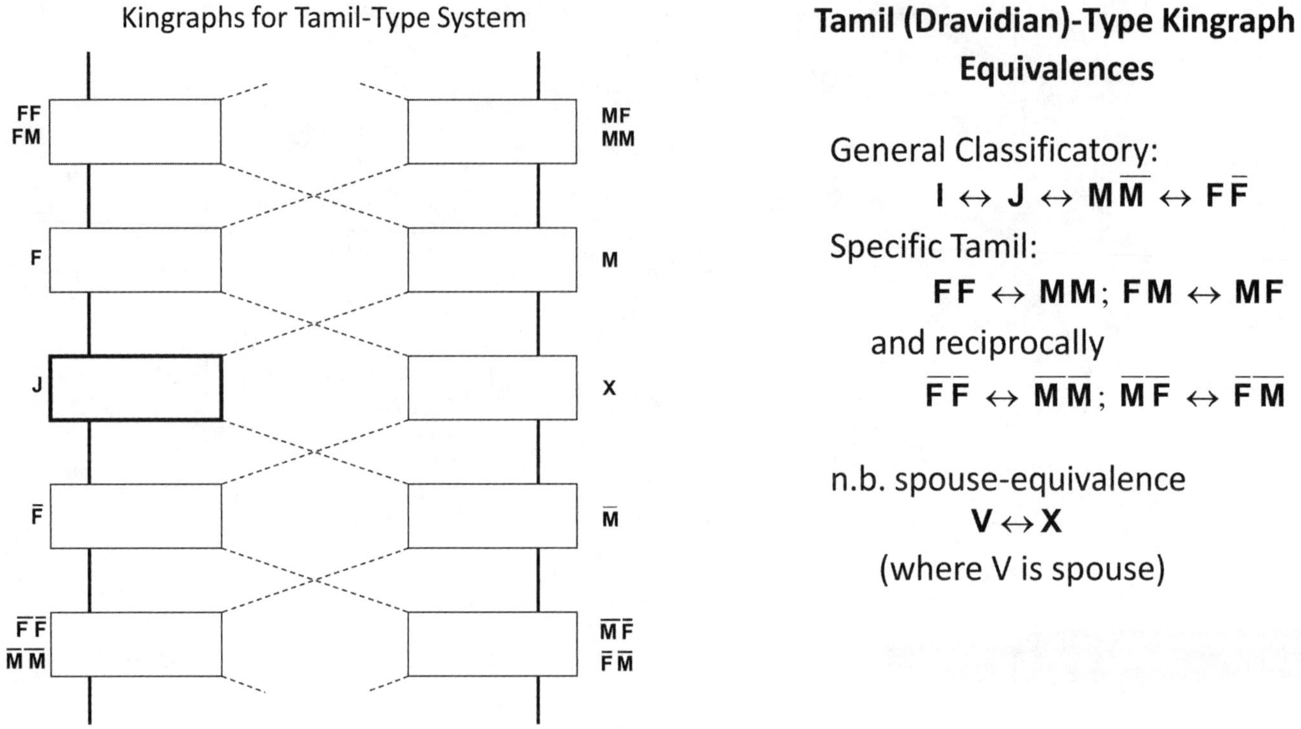

FIGURE 2.3. Tamil (Dravidian)-type kin graph. From Kronenfeld 2001b:188.

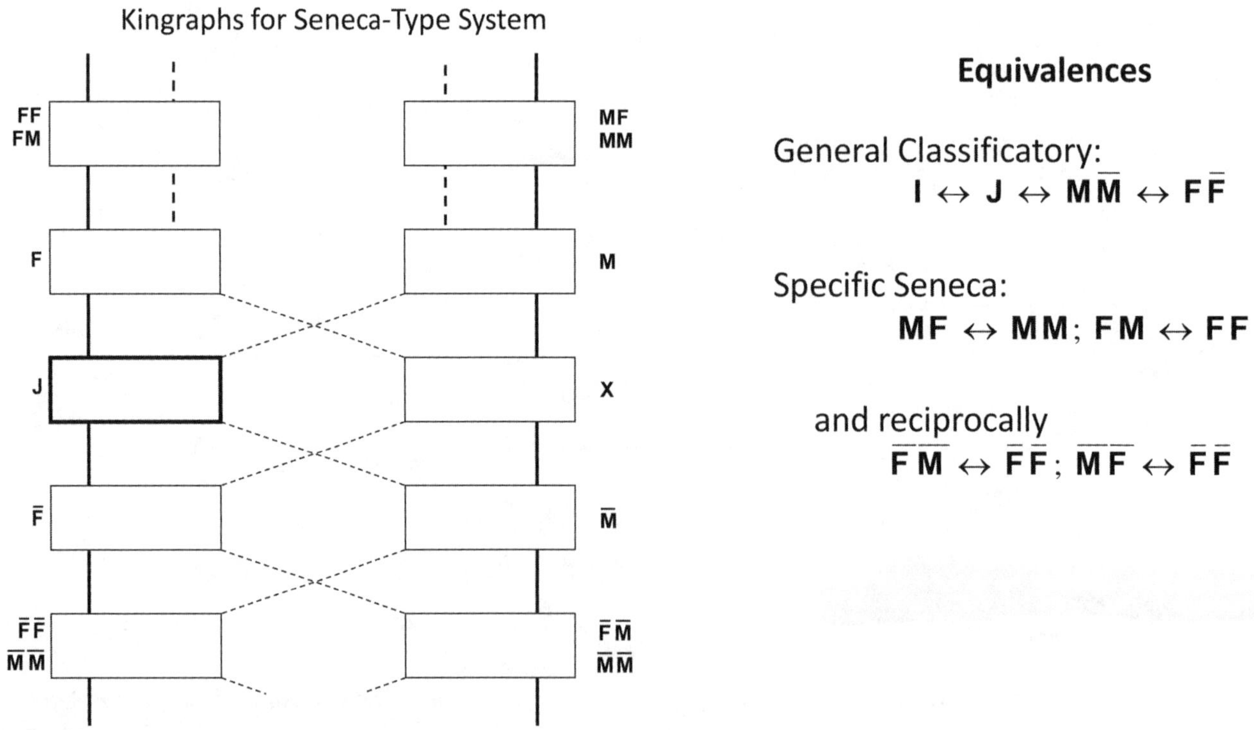

FIGURE 2.4. Seneca (Iroquois)-type kin graph. From Kronenfeld 2001b:187.

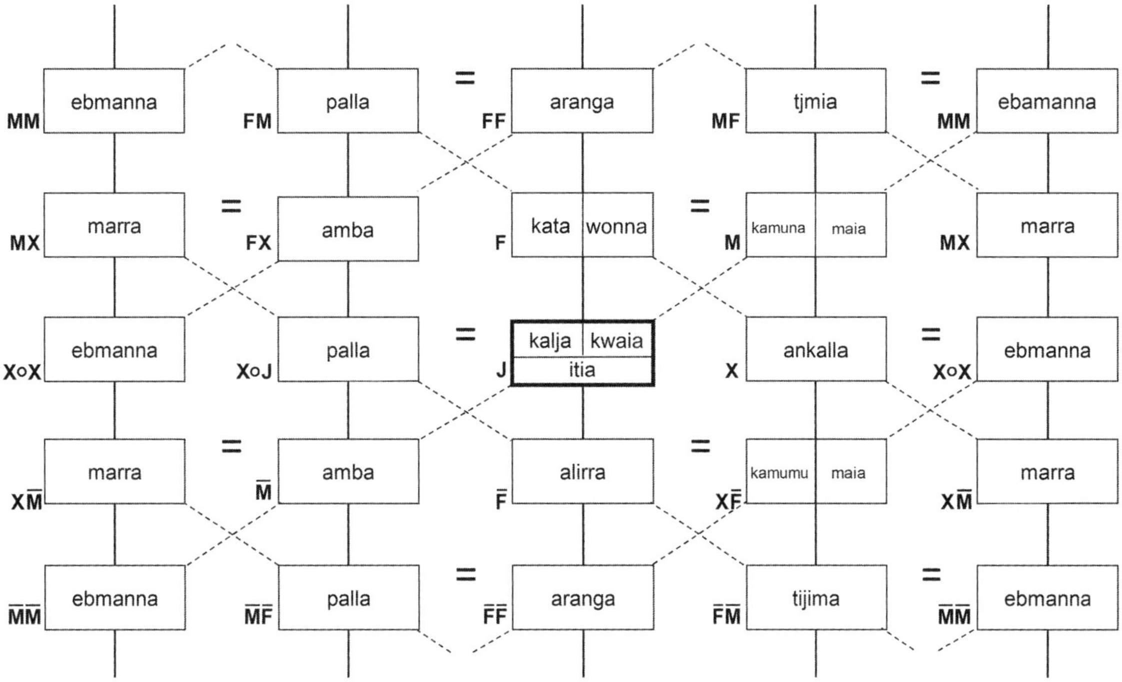

FIGURE 2.5. Aranda kinship terminology kin graph. Equivalences: FFF ↔ MFM, MMM ↔ FMF; reciprocals: $\overline{F}\,\overline{F}\,\overline{F} \leftrightarrow \overline{M}\,\overline{F}\,\overline{M}$, $\overline{M}\,\overline{M}\,\overline{M} \leftrightarrow \overline{F}\,\overline{M}\,\overline{F}$. *Note:* Spouse equivalence: V ↔ X ○ J (where V is spouse). From Gould 2000:213.

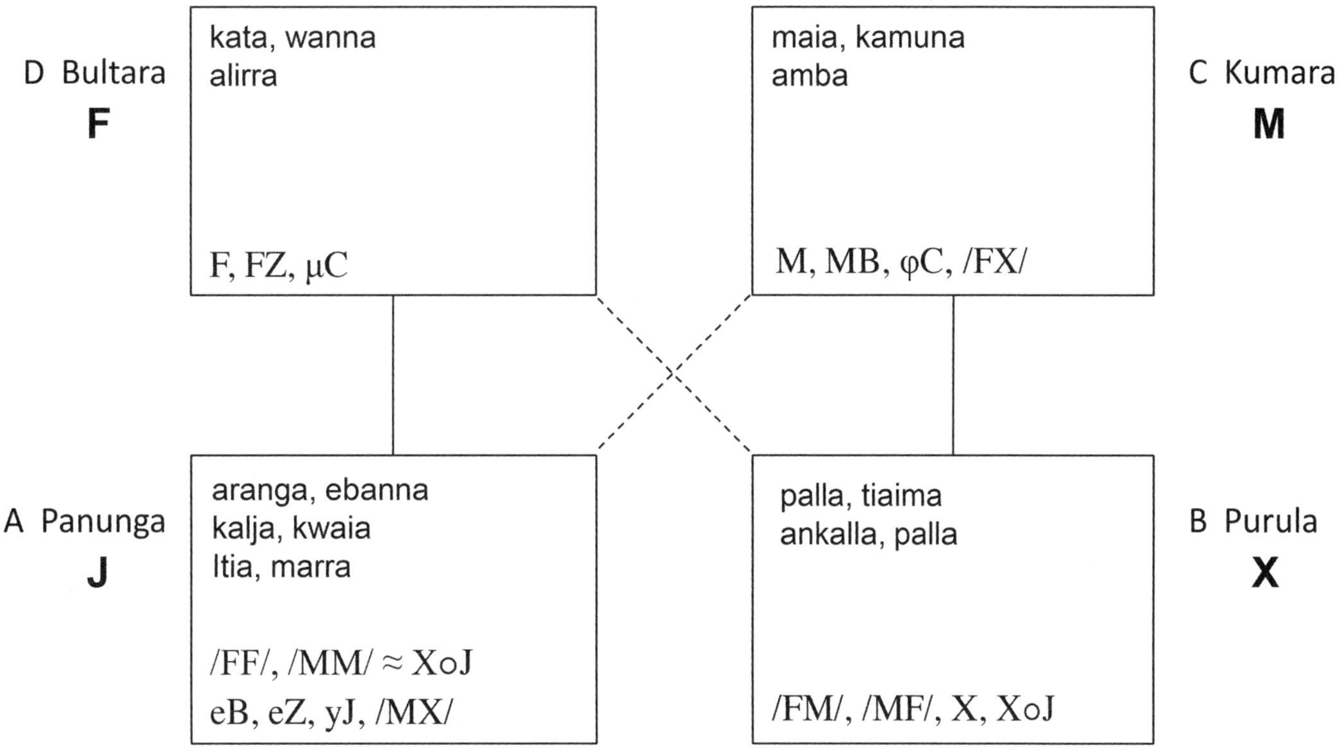

FIGURE 2.6. Aranda section kin graph. Interior kin types are examples of included relatives; interior words are included kin term categories. From Gould 2000:248.

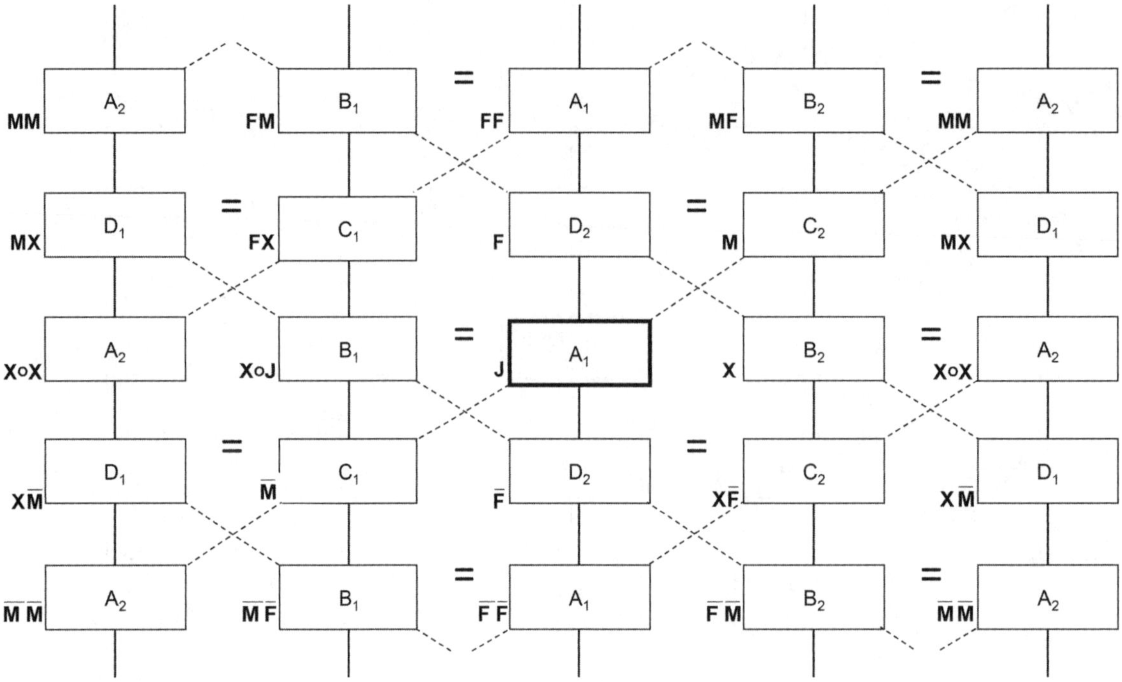

FIGURE 2.7. Aranda subsection kin graph. From Gould 2000:249.

contrast somewhat differently, so analytic examples of the use of either central referents alone or the full range of central plus peripheral referents depend on which approach is being used. I give examples elsewhere in this chapter of how the contrast applies within my approach.

Relationship of Marriage Patterns to Kin Term Analysis

An alternative analytic approach to analyzing kin terminologies has been to see kin term systems as relating to marriage rules or patterns (see Danziger, this volume).[7]

Marriages as Intrinsic versus Correlative versus Indifferent to the Terminological Pattern

Serious attention to the role of marriage in Dravidian forces some reconsideration of our general understanding of the relationships among Iroquois and Dravidian types. One feature, a traditionally taken marker of Dravidian-type (and similar) systems, is whether a system of cross-cousin marriage is built into the terminological system or not (see Hornborg, this volume). My added second feature would be whether or not the cross/parallel distinction is made in a socially consistent manner (which means whether the full genealogical string connecting ego to alter is relevant or not).

Iroquois-type systems lack the socially consistent form of cross/parallel and so cannot include any coding of any cross-cousin marriage pattern. Dravidian-type systems have been traditionally taken as including both the socially consistent form of cross/parallel and the coding of a cross-cousin marriage pattern.

I, among many others, have in the past bought into the notion that both features were necessarily intrinsic to Dravidian-type systems. My reasoning had to do with the cognitive load required to keep track of the train of specific genealogical links if one were to want or need to calculate kin terms directly from genealogical information (as opposed to the simple calculations needed for the Iroquois type)—as in, for example, the kind of situation described by Keen (this volume). But recently, in an attempt to explain my views to a colleague, I decided to work out for a generic Dravidian-type system the kind of relative-product Cayley table that I had come up with to formalize my understanding of Fanti kin term calculations. That table is reproduced in appendix B, along with the comparable table for an Iroquois-type system. The point of the table is that the kin term assignment calculations for Dravidian, while genealogically complex, are quite simple and easy to process if calculated directly from the terms themselves without recourse to genealogy (and see Read, this volume).

This in turn raises the possibility of the existence of a Dravidian-type system with*out* built-in marriage relations. It seems possible, from the above reasoning, that we might want to add a third, say, the Erehwonian, type to our Dravidian and Iroquois set. (If subsequent empirical research were to turn up such a system, then it could be given a more traditional name!)

Presumably the "goal" of an Erehwonian-type system would be sociologically consistent and coherent kin term categories of the sort lacking in Iroquois-type systems. Empirically, the marker of such a system would be the presence of separate affinal terms—as opposed to the systematic use of consanguineal terms for affines (as in classic Dravidian systems).[8] This marker, applied to Dravidian-type systems, opens the possibility of a new area for diachronic research concerning, first, the presence of Erehwonian—and, if empirically present, then the kinds of transitions that it participated in.

Dravidian-type systems (as usually understood) build in logically necessary—intrinsic—marriage relations among classes of relatives, often labeled as groups, such as moieties or sections. Some kinds of systems where the marriage relationship is not logically built in are seen as normally going with a particular kind of marriage relationship; this correlative connection can be a statistical one or some kind of structural one. Some anthropological analysts have seen some Crow- and/or Omaha-type systems as falling here; but Fanti, the Crow-type system I know best, clearly does not exhibit any such connection with marriage.

In general, kinship terminologies do not necessarily tell us much about marriage biases. Again, the Fanti can marry cross-cousins, who fall into either the "sibling" category or one of the "father/mother" or "child" categories.

Alliance Systems

If we are concerned with some sort of alliance system to which kin terminologies might be related, we need to consider the following:

> How many marriages in what temporal period are needed to maintain an existing alliance or to initiate a new one?
>
> What are the effective alliance units—lineages, clans, or clusters of clans? (For examples, see Brudner and White 1997; Houseman and White 1998; Romney 1971; Strauss and Romney 1982.) And if clusters, how stable are the clusters?

An issue that comes out of White's work (see Brudner and White 1997; Houseman and White 1998) concerns whether or not the units in a marriage system need be explicit—versus only implicit (as seen in the patterning of actual marriages).

If we are talking about any system in which marriages by members of a kin group are restricted to members of some particular kin group (whether endogamously within their own group or exogamously [by alliance] to members of some other group), what do people do when, because of demographic variation, there are no available spouses in the given target group? And how is such a situation to be "scored" analytically? (See Romney 1971; Strauss and Romney 1982; White and Denham 2008.)

Perspectives on the Nature of Given Changes

The nature of some given change (what is actually changing and how it might best be described)—versus the reasons for it (i.e., what changes in people's lives—physical, economic, aesthetic, or whatever—that impels them to make the given change)—provides two important perspectives on change. Both perspectives can represent an "explanation," but they are different, and it is important to be clear on which is which.

Kinds of Change in a Kin Term System

An understanding of how kin terms relate to history—both in the sense of historical changes themselves and in the sense of the ways in which we infer patterns of change—requires some consideration of how kin term systems change. Some kinds of changes are systematic or "evolutionary" (maybe adaptive) changes within one of the relevant systems (see Read, this volume), while others seem to be deeper changes in/of the system itself—where the "systems" describe real empirical data patterns but are themselves always to some degree artifacts of the analytic approach taken (see Danziger, this volume).[9] The gradual acquisition by English of *sibling* as an alternative kin term to *brother* and *sister* is an example of an adaptive change within a system (cf. Simpson, this volume, for some comparable changes). The general European transition from an older presumed Omaha-type system to the Eskimo-type ones we now see would be a change of the system.

Change in the Algebraic Rule System

One kind of change involves changes in the algebraic rule system—in which the new version can be seen as some modification of an old-version rule. What counts as a “modification” depends on the system. One nicely worked-out example of possible changes—and thus a kind of motivated typology—is Dwight Read’s (2007, 2009, this volume). It would be nice to know what kinds of changes elsewhere in people’s lives lead to such changes in rule systems. Alternatively, from a different perspective, it would be nice to know what changes in the rule system would be forced by what changes in focal distinctive features.

Change in the Distinctive Features of Semantic Contrast

A second kind involves changes in the distinctive features of semantic contrast. Ideally—to my mind—this should be semantic contrast tied to the paradigm of categories defined by contrasts among focal referents as opposed to that tied to features that distinguish extended ranges, but for some types of systems such as Hawaiian and Eskimo (i.e., English!) the difference does not matter. These contrasts, often if perhaps not always, seem fairly deep-seated and heavily constrained by some combination of history and the basic relations of the algebraic system that generates them. (Where the algebraic system is only minimally affected, and where social conditions change, change can possibly be easy—see the case of the English *sibling* below.)

Marking Theory was first developed by Trubetzkoy (1969); he applied it to “privative oppositions in phonology.”[10] Greenberg (1966) importantly generalized the definition and extended the application to morphology, syntax, and semantics. I (1996: ch. 7, especially 110–111 n. 3; also see Kronenfeld 2009; and McConvell, chapter 1, this volume) give a general overview and discussion; I have extended the idea to alternative systems for kin term expansion from a common focal paradigm. Hage (e.g., 1999, 2001), following on notions from Greenberg, applied Marking Theory to diachronic change in kinship terminological systems (especially in the paradigm of focal oppositions).

Marking (Marking Theory, marking relations) refers to an asymmetric opposition of members of a contrast set or opposition such that one of the opposed elements is considered the default member. Not all oppositions in language exhibit marking, but where marking is found, an impressive bundle of correlative phenomena shows up. The default member is the one that represents the whole set when the opposition that structures the set is neutralized; it is the member that comes to mind when a member of the set is evoked in the absence of any specification of which member is meant;[11] and it is normally the most commonly used member of the set: if one member of the opposition has more internal subdivision or variety of forms than the other, that more frequently subdivided member will be the unmarked one. Comparing etic oppositions across systems, where there exists a marking relationship, the unmarked member can occur in one or another system without the marked member but the marked member can never occur without the presence of the unmarked member. This aspect of the asymmetry has important diachronic implications. Since the marked member can only occur in a system that already contains the unmarked member, it means that systems acquire the unmarked member before they acquire the marked member and that if there is a loss, it is the marked member that is lost before the unmarked member. Marking relations do not produce change, but they do constrain it—identifying certain transitions as impossible or improbable.

As Greenberg first suggested and as Per Hage has shown, one can sometimes find chains of marking relations among kin terminology feature sets that have clear implications regarding possible paths of diachronic change. These paths, as Hage (1997, 1999, 2001) has shown, when joined with some relevant concrete historical or comparative data, can imply specific historical sequences of kin terminologies. Allen has used such features to speculate about a more basic and general developmental sequence for kin terminologies.

I (1991, 2009: ch. 13), in part following Lounsbury (1969a), have speculated that these basic distinctive feature sets result from the intersection of a universal pattern of default (or presumptive) nuclear family roles (mother, father, child) with culturally specific patterns representing rules of succession and inheritance. Since these rules are typically (if apparently not absolutely or universally) associated with characteristic kinds of kin groups, information about terminologies can suggest useful hypotheses about social organization and history (see Danziger, this volume; Hornborg, this volume). Kin terminologies do not directly reflect kin groups, but kin groups do seem to be based, if independently, on the same property rights that help structure kin terminologies. Thus Crow- and Omaha-type terminologies do seem, respectively, to go with matrilineal and patrilineal inheritance—and, more strongly, often go with corporate descent groups based on this inheritance.[12] If kin terminologies in part (along with kin groups) track major patterns of inheritance and succession, one would expect that as these change (whether shifts in emphasis or the introduction of new patterns), the kin terminology should change accordingly.

Where the terminological changes seem gradual and incremental, perhaps like those described by Hage (1997, 1999, 2001), the question of what drives the changes again arises (also relevant are Allen 1998; Dole 1972). Sometimes it seems like a version of "linguistic drift" (e.g., see Sapir 1921). One suspects that these changes entail only minimal concomitant changes in the underlying algebraic system. But there sometimes occur abrupt major changes, where the basic set of contrasts is changed (necessitating major changes in the algebraic system)—such as what seems to have happened in English and other Western European systems (regarding collateral relatives) in about the 14th century: one guesses that there was some significant/radical change in social/property relations and thus in inheritance patterns (who had what stake in what property). Large-scale systematic borrowing of terms can provide historical evidence of such a change (as well, perhaps, of whence the relevant social changes came)—as one sees in English, where the direct terms (*mother, father, sister, brother, son, daughter*) are directly descended from (and all recognizably close to) their Proto-Indo-European sources (see McConvell, chapter 10, this volume), while the collateral terms (*uncle, aunt, nephew, niece, cousin*) seem all to be circa 14th-century borrowings from French. This pattern seems replicated in many northwestern European or Germanic systems.

Such major borrowing raises the question of whether there was simply a borrowing of a (perhaps higher-status) terminological system or whether there was some borrowing of economic and/or legal relations that then led to changes in the terminology—in a situation in which the source of the borrowed cultural changes also had available (for linguistic borrowing) the new terms and terminological system that went with the economic and/or legal changes. The role of English loanwords in Fanti (see Kronenfeld 1991, 2009: ch. 13; McConvell, chapter 10, this volume, discusses another version of this analytic problem) perhaps represents such a change—caught in mid-process. The issue concerns how tightly terminological system features of one sort or another are or are not tied to changes in the wider cultural system.

In the English loanword example, Fanti speakers were very consistently using English lexemes for kernel and near-kernel members of their "mother" and "father" categories and using Fanti lexemes for more distant ones. At the same time they repeatedly, without exception, insisted that the English and Fanti lexemes were totally interchangeable—that is, carried (for them) no difference in meaning. The apparently relevant economic condition was a move from a traditional adelphic matrilineal inheritance pattern (laterally through siblings and cousins before moving down to the next generation) toward modern Ghana's more direct parent–child emphasis relative to both fathers and mothers.

Relatedly, the history of the "uncle" term within the Latin/French tradition is of interest (see also McConvell, chapter 10, this volume). In Latin, the "grandfather" term (*avus*) is extended via a diminutive (*avunculus*) to "mother's brother"—in contrast to the "father's brother" term (*patruus*), which is derived from the term for "father" (*pater*). This extension seems consistent with known Latin patrilineal groups. Then later, presumably with the demise of the patrilineal groups in favor of more recent bilateral ones, the maternal versus paternal uncle distinction disappears, and it is the maternal one that replaces both—since the paternal one was basically an extended version of the "father" term, where in the new system the need was to keep both kinds of uncle distinct from father. (I would love to find out more about Latin kinship, since I had always been given to understand that early Rome had an Omaha-type system and since the *avus/avunculus* relationship suggests an original sense of "maternal grandfather" for *avus*, with it becoming the cover term for the same kind of reason that *avunculus* [later?] became the "uncle" term.[13])

A mundane non-kinship illustrative example of extension leading to semantic change as cultural conditions change can be seen in the movement of the word *corn* from being a general word for grain—as in the English "corn exchange" and in extension to "corned beef" (cured with rock salt)—to its modern narrowed meaning of maize via "Indian corn." The shift reflects not just the encounter with a new grain but also the subsequent economic importance of that grain. And it would appear that the new focus of *corn* led to some broadening of *grain*, from *small* granular stuff to granular stuff in general.

Shifts in the Extension Rules: Patterns by which Contrasts Are Applied to Nonfocal Referents

Extension from core (prototypic, focal, kernel) referents can be of several sorts:

a. simple generational extension—either without regard to mother's versus father's side or with distinguishing by side. This seems maybe a kind of simplest default—where there exist no "reasons" based on property or succession rights for making further distinctions. Examples include traditional Hawaiian and Eskimo types, as well as Cheyenne type.

b. extension by cross versus parallel categories. This feature is what traditionally distinguishes Iroquois and Dravidian types from those listed just above. It also provides the now traditional basis for distinguishing Iroquois-type systems from Dravidian-type ones. The distinction was already noticed by Morgan but was considered inconsequential—until Lounsbury pointed out that Dravidian-type extension entails the kind of marriage/affinal relations associated with moieties while Iroquois-type extension is absolutely incompatible with such relations. Both Tyler (1966) and Tjon Sie Fat (1998) have proposed the consideration of additional versions of cross/parallel extension, but nothing so far seems to have followed from these suggestions.

c. extension by skewing (with merging)—producing the set of variants of Crow- and Omaha-type systems described by Lounsbury.

The major diachronic implication is that extension patterns seem much more historically volatile than do the basic patterns of core categories themselves. At least, in Morgan's large compendium of North American systems, among closely related languages in his Dakota family (our Sioux family), some were unskewed, some were Crow-type skewed, and some were Omaha-type skewed—in a situation where both the core distinctive features and the actual kin term lexemes (the kinds of elements Koch examines in this volume) were quite consistent across the whole family. Conversely, those Dakota Crow-type terminologies look quite different from the Crow-type Fanti terminology, other than their sharing of Crow-type skewing.

This situation suggests that these extension pattern changes are very fast, easy, and shallow. The inference follows that these extension patterns do *not* define established kinship complexes (as has sometimes been suggested in the literature) but, instead, represent fairly superficial overlays on the underlying pattern of core referent contrasts. My suggestion here is that in these situations the underlying way in which kin groups and kin terms relate to property and ecology remains constant and that what changes (or varies) is simply which specific ecological/property relations emerge as most salient in a given local context.

A second, related comparative hypothesis is that skewed systems when present always (within any given language/culture community) represent a marked variant of an unmarked (default) unskewed variant (see Kronenfeld 2006)—as I (1973, 1980a) have described for the Fanti case. Such cases of alternative variants do not show up in the literature. My suggestion is that this results from a combination of factors: (1) a strong presupposition in the discipline for many years that there had to exist only one correct system for any given culture and that any apparent variation had to be the result of informant error, acculturation, or cultural disintegration; and (2) the linked presupposition that where contrasting variants were noticed, the one more like English (or other Western European languages) had to be the result of acculturation—and hence not really part of the given culture. David Schneider did once tell me that he was strongly pressured as a graduate student not to find terminological variation.

Stability of Polymorphism

There is always the interpretation question regarding any polymorphism—such as the alternative patterns of extension for Fanti kin terms—of whether it represents a stable condition or represents diachronic change caught in the process. In cases of internal variability where there seems to be a lack of knowledge and/or consensus within the community regarding some terminological feature, the variability may signal a process of loss or change. That is, at the minimum, it means that the social factors that drove the aspects at issue must have weakened or otherwise changed. A prime example is the English system for sorting out types of cousins ("first," "second," "third," etc., with the alternative ways of counting that go with the presence or absence of "once removed," "twice removed," etc. [cf. Simpson, this volume]). This English variability is different from that I have described for alternative Fanti extension patterns because all three of the Fanti variants were known and used by all members of the community I worked in. In the specific Fanti case, thus, I do believe the variability to be stable. The Fanti use of English loanwords was not self-conscious (I tried probing it) but was common and consistent across the community. Thus, the difference between it and English cousins seems to be that between an emerging pattern and a disappearing one.

Relevance of Learning

Learning and Change

How kinship systems are learned is very important for any consideration of possible/impossible or likely/unlikely change. Kin terms are (among other things) a part of language and are learned and organized accordingly.

Children are not taught the "rules" of their native language but, instead, hear messages, repeat these messages, and then try to adapt the messages to their communicative aims. In doing so they guess at regularities (patterns or what linguists would come to call "rules") and use feedback from those around them to adjust their representation of these regularities. A variety of psychological considerations, including conjunctivity, marking, and other cognitive ease considerations (see Kronenfeld 1996: chs. 6–8), constrain the constructions that emerge from this process.

Systemic change comes when the conditions of frequent and salient adult usage change (as ad hoc special usage rather than as implementation of any actually perceived or operated on system change), which leads to changes in the patterns to which learners are exposed. The kids of the adults thus are exposed to a pattern that has changed from what their parents were exposed to as kids and so come up with a shifted algebraic representation. Change in a system only comes when new learners have built the change into their internal representations of the system.

Each learner re-creates the rules; communicative and interactive constraints keep the created rules of different individuals adequately similar to one another. Children base their creation upon what language they experience; thus a large shift in some aspect of conversation (say, the loss or addition of salient concepts or constructions) will produce a corresponding change in the model of the language that these new learners pull out. My sense is that changed cultural conditions work directly on feature contrasts (and maybe subsequently on extension patterns) and then only indirectly on the generating algebraic system.

Thus, kin terms behave like other words in a language but with this additional downstream algebraic constraint. That is, what comes first is experienced usage (the terms, their referents, their usage) and only afterward the formal system by which the terms are organized. The form of learning means that linguistic systems, including kinship terminologies, can, over time, "leap" in a way that they could not if, alternatively, change had to come only via modification of the axioms of the existing formal system.

I see change in language—whether simple linguistic "drift" or more driven change—as a result of what kids learn and how they learn it. I have elsewhere suggested that semantic extension and change have to be seen and understood as a matter of whole contrast sets versus simply individual items (see McConvell's discussion of semantic fields, chapter 10, this volume). The insight follows directly from Saussure's pathbreaking conclusion regarding Proto-Indo-European phonology. Rundblad and I offer a worked-out semantic example involving English terms for watercourses (Kronenfeld and Rundblad 2003). This focus on the full contrast set ("lexical field" there) and its structure seems even more necessary for a domain such as kinship, where terms also have to form a productive generative pragmatic system.[14]

Learning Kin Terminologies

The learning process seems to involve something like the following steps:

- The learner learns words as pertaining to particular referents—which become tentative focal (core, kernel, prototypic) referents.
- From that knowledge, the learner pulls out basic apparent (visible) contrastive attributes.
- Then the learner uses the apparent contrasting attributes to begin extending the terms to other referents.
- Feedback from other people narrows the application, clarifies focality, and begins introducing the learner to the relative products of kin terms.
- From relative products, the system begins to be abstracted.
- "Decentering" (Piaget's term) allows this knowledge to be applied to other reference points (egos) and allows the self to be seen as simply one particular reference point.
- Relative products and decentering allow relationships to be concatenated and so allow the learner to infer the algebraic system—the pragmatic system of relations among kinfolk.
- Meanwhile, the basic apparent (visible) contrastive referents become part of the basis for connotative and figurative extension, along with the social attributes that initially seem to the learner to apply to referents. The relationship of social attributes to features is refined through feedback.

- Inferred features (such as generation) are then mapped off of the relative product system and come to serve as the basis for the semantic classification of kinfolk.

This is an area where more good, careful research is needed across different kinds of systems. One impressive example of such research is Danziger's (2001) study of Mopan Mayan.

Practical Issues

Classification of Systems

My general sense is that assignment to types should be by overall structure—that is, by system rules or generative equivalences, not by incidental concurrences. I like Gould's term *concurrences* for this—because it clarifies the difference between them and more systematically important "equivalences." In Fanti an example of concurrence is the fact that one's father's sister falls in the *na* (mother) category, even though her structural relations, as seen in relative product calculations, are totally different from those of one's mother. *Mother* and *father* in English are two separate terms that are structurally equivalent, in that, in any consanguineal calculation, one can be substituted for the other without changing the outcome. But sometimes concurrences (these incidental equivalences) are informative and so should be noted.

For clarity, given the existence of more than one system for classifying (at least those of Lounsbury, Gould, and Read), one should indicate which system is being utilized in any given analytic discussion. This is important because the various classificatory systems in use (as well as notational and analytic systems) are often quite different in what they foreground or emphasize and sometimes are even simply incommensurable. The issue is not that everyone should be functionally adept in all systems but, rather, one should always be aware of which system one is using, including what it does well and what it does badly and what it emphasizes or de-emphasizes. Ideally one should have a reason for one's choice of classificatory system and should briefly provide that reason.

Role of Ethnographic Evidence in Support of One or Another Analytic Approach

Kinship, including kin terms, is an overdetermined domain. Natives have a lot of knowledge from a variety of perspectives. Different uses or functions can imply different ways of coding the system—as long as they all come out with more or less the same terminological assignments (the "more or less" hedge means that, while core assignments have to be consistent, fringe ones can vary a little; the relevant scope—range of application—ascribed to a given query can be part of the basis for that variation).

So, depending on the queries and measures used, a variety of alternative analytic approaches can be supported. Analytic alternatives do *not* strike me as presenting an "either/or" proposition.

What Is Relevant to a Given Social or Cultural Question or Issue

The relevant factor may not be the word (term, whether morpheme or lexeme) itself but, rather, some larger, culturally implicit construction. For example, my comparison of English *brother/sister,* Spanish *hermano/hermana,* and Fanti *nua* suggests that the matter is complicated (Kronenfeld 1991). English uses different morphemes for the brother/sister contrast, whereas Spanish constructs its lexemes out of a single sibling morpheme and grammatically obligatory gender endings (but note that Spanish, when it "wants to," can have separate gendered lexemes, such as for *padre* versus *madre*). Fanti has the single term (morpheme, lexeme) but typically in conversation, except when the information is clear from context, distinguishes same-sex siblings by a general senior/junior (*panyin/kakraba*) modifier and opposite-sex siblings by a general male/female (*banyin/besia*) modifier. The Fanti modifiers are general and in no way tied to kin relations—for example, a rooster is a "chicken *banyin*" and so forth. This Fanti usage is perhaps similar to Koch's "phrasal kin terms" (this volume), except that informants gave me only the kin word (*nua*) as a kin term, not the whole phrase.

One could try to argue some social significance from the specific morphemes, but that would miss the ethnographic observation that Spanish-speaking countries have in general traditionally seemed as hung up on sex differences as English-speaking ones; which language expressed this concern with dedicated morphemes was perhaps just an accidental by-product of the nature of the wider grammatical system. Fanti does, in a lot of ways, seem egalitarian. But seniority is generally recognized between members of all dyads—and thus across the local community. The seniority system often seems separate and distinct for men and women. Hence the grammatically optional modifiers may be as socially important to Fanti speakers as are the morphemic and lexemic distinctions made, respectively, by English and Spanish speakers.

The bottom line seems to be that, ethnographically, one wants/needs all of the above kinds of information and that any of them could be relevant to a given classification, depending on the goal of the classification. This issue was highlighted by Paul Kay's (1975) critique of Lounsbury's Iroquois analysis, based on the fact that Lounsbury's terms contained syntactic information—of the "you mother me" versus "I mother you" type—where Kay said that only the word *mother* should have been used in the kin term analysis, since the rest is covered by the general Iroquois syntax rules. How tied in to the general description of the language should the kin term list and analysis be? That is, does one only look at primary morphemes or lexemes or at larger constructions? Does one analyze dedicated specific kin lexemes or the larger expressions that Lounsbury used for Iroquois? Lounsbury, to the best of my knowledge, did not reply to Kay and did not explain his choice. But since Iroquois culture and linguistics were one of the major continuing thrusts of his career, one must presume that he was aware of the kinds of terms he was using and that he had good ethnographic reasons for his choice. The choice depends on what you are after: kin term manipulations, historical processes, representations of socially important differences, standard conceptual processes, or whatever.

Essential Properties

Where kin terms are held by members of the studied culture to have behavioral or kin group associations and/or where there exist strong analytic reasons for claiming such an association (cf. the "essential properties" that philosophers sometimes speak of),

- these may only *necessarily* apply to prototypic members of the kin term category;
- they may only be found to apply actually/empirically to a subset of the wider membership of the given kin term category; or
- they may be particularly important for connotative usage—where, if connotative extension exists, such associated attributes are likely to be the determiners of which terms are extended to whom.

Conclusion

I think it benefits us periodically to step back and review the range of perspectives and questions, theories, classifications, findings, and tools that inform our empirical work. In a field as old, as rich, and as central to anthropology as kinship, these objects of review—as well as others that I have not had the space (or the knowledge) to cover—represent a complex and growing multistranded body of knowledge. My goal in this chapter has been to provide such an analytic overview of kinship—but one focused particularly on issues related to typology and its relevance to history. I have tried to be broad and catholic in my coverage, but nonetheless such an overview is always through some particular author's eyes, and I am aware that others might have done the job somewhat differently. The goal is not to make everyone ask the same questions or do the same job. It is instead to provide a framework that will enable researchers doing different jobs to understand and communicate with each other and, hopefully, to help each of them widen the relevance and resonance of their own particular work.

Appendix A

Spousal Connections in English in the Gould System

V is spouse. No formal constraint on sex, but the presupposition is that the two are opposite.

VP and its reciprocal CV are "-in-law."

Hence VP and CV specifically are *father-* or *mother-in-law* and *son-* or *daughter-in-law*, respectively.

Since VC ↔ C ("spouse's child" is "own child")

and, reciprocally, PV ↔ P ("parent's spouse" is "own parent"),

and since by definition, *brother-in-law* or *sister-in-law* in English is reciprocally "spouse's sibling" or "sibling's spouse," i.e., JV ↔ VJ,

then PJV is terminologically equivalent to PVJ.

Substituting P for PV makes PVJ equivalent to PJ and both equivalent to PJV,

which gives us PJV equivalent to PJ,

which accounts for why parents' siblings' spouses are uncles or aunts versus in-laws.

Abnormal, Nondefault Relations

VC when ≠ C defines the "step-" set (i.e., when "spouse's child" is not "own child").

PV…when ≠ P defines the "half-" set (i.e., when "parent's spouse" is not "own parent").

Appendix B

Dravidian Type without Built-In Marriage

I would now like to turn to a consideration of how a Dravidian-type system lacking built-in moiety-like marriage relations would work as a lexemic system for members of the community in question. This consideration will be based on a systematic treatment of relative products of the "my UNCLE's SON is my COUSIN" sort. The systematicity comes from organizing these relations into a complete table of permissible products. Note that these Cayley tables portray relations among the terms that make up each kin term system and make no reference to genealogy, to any metalanguage (such as Gould algebra, Romney notation, or English), or to any classification scheme or type. And, for the moment, I am limiting the picture to consanguine terms; I will address affinal categories below; but I want to note that taking, say, UNCLE, AUNT, COUSIN*, and COUSIN* to include affinal referents will in no way affect the relevance or operation of the tables.

Note, by the way, that this approach allows consistent deduction of the appropriate kin term to use regarding some person, even in the absence of knowledge of the precise genealogical connection, as long as one knows the kin term for the person's parent and maybe a little about kin terms for some other close relatives.

I use COUSIN* to refer to a female member of a cross-cousin category and COUSIN* to refer to a male member, where a parallel cousin is referred to as BROTHER or SISTER:

Terms.

Term	Kin Gloss
Mother	M
Father	F
Uncle	U
Aunt	A
Brother	B
Sister	Z
Cousin (f.)	Cf
Cousin (m.)	Cm
Son	S
Daughter	D
Nephew	Np
Niece	Nc
Grandfather	GF
Grandmother	GM
Grandson	GS
Granddaughter	GD
Wife	WI
Husband	HU
In-Law	L

Actual "emic" usage would be based on something like the following multiplication tables.

Let us first examine a generic Iroquois-type terminology, as analyzed by Lounsbury from Morgan's data, and then a generic Dravidian type. After the two tables (kept together to facilitate comparison) I shall make some observations about each. In the tables below, the only differences are in bold:

Lounsbury's Iroquois type.

	M	F	U	A	B	Z	Cm	Cf	S	D	Np	Nc
M	GM	GF	*	*	**U**	**M**	**U**	**M**	B	Z	Cm	C
F	GM	GF	*	*	**F**	**A**	**F**	**A**	B	Z	Cm	C
U	*	*	*	*	*	*	*	*	Cm	Cf	B	Z
A	*	*	*	*	*	*	*	*	Cm	Cf	B	Z
*B	*	*	*	*	*	*	*	*	S	D	*	*
*B	*	*	*	*	*	*	*	*	Np	Nc	*	*
*Z	*	*	*	*	*	*	*	*	Np	Nc	*	*
*Z	*	*	*	*	*	*	*	*	S	D	*	*
*Cm	*	*	*	*	*	*	*	*	S	D	*	*
*Cm	*	*	*	*	*	*	*	*	Cm	Cf	*	*
*Cf	*	*	*	*	*	*	*	*	Np	Nc	*	*
*Cf	*	*	*	*	*	*	*	*	S	D	*	*
S	*	*	*	*	*	*	*	*	GS	GD	*	*
D	*	*	*	*	*	*	*	*	GS	GD	*	*
Np	*	*	*	*	*	*	*	*	◊	◊	*	*
Nc	*	*	*	*	*	*	*	*	◊	◊	*	*

◊ refers to ones that are, I think, irrelevant.

Generic Dravidian type.

	M	F	U	A	B	Z	Cm	Cf	S	D	Np	Nc
M	GM	GF	*	*	**U**	**M**	**F**	**A**	B	Z	Cm	C
F	GM	GF	*	*	**F**	**A**	**U**	**M**	B	Z	Cm	C

	M	F	U	A	B	Z	Cm	Cf	S	D	Np	Nc
U	*	*	*	*	*	*	*	*	Cm	Cf	B	Z
A	*	*	*	*	*	*	*	*	Cm	Cf	B	Z
*B	*	*	*	*	*	*	*	*	S	D	*	*
*B	*	*	*	*	*	*	*	*	Np	Nc	*	*
*Z	*	*	*	*	*	*	*	*	Np	Nc	*	*
*Z	*	*	*	*	*	*	*	*	S	D	*	*
*Cm	*	*	*	*	*	*	*	*	S	D	*	*
*Cm	*	*	*	*	*	*	*	*	Cm	Cf	*	*
*Cf	*	*	*	*	*	*	*	*	Np	Nc	*	*
*Cf	*	*	*	*	*	*	*	*	S	D	*	*
S	*	*	*	*	*	*	*	*	GS	GD	*	*
D	*	*	*	*	*	*	*	*	GS	GD	*	*
Np	*	*	*	*	*	*	*	*	◊	◊	*	*
Nc	*	*	*	*	*	*	*	*	◊	◊	*	*

In both tables, * refers to a redundant expression, which would normally be evaluated through a more direct route. And, yes, the NEPHEWs and NIECEs of MOTHERs, FATHERs, UNCLEs, and AUNTs are redundant; I have included them as a cross-check on my calculations.

◊ refers to ones that are, I think, irrelevant.

The tables are read/used by taking the row entry (X) times the column entry (Y) as equal to Z, the XY position in the matrix. E.g., $M \times B = U$; that is, M times B equals U, or MOTHER's BROTHER is UNCLE. Note that these relationships work without any reference to marriage or affines.

Lounsbury Iroquois Type

Cross versus parallel determinations are inconsistent. The ambiguity is that ego's categorizations of G+1 relatives are inconsistent with the categorizations of those relatives made by ego's parents. That is, ego's FATHER's BROTHERs and COUSIN*s (i.e., parallel and cross same-generation relatives) both fall into ego's FATHER term (i.e., are parallel relatives); ego's FATHER's SISTERs and COUSIN*s both fall into ego's AUNT term (i.e., are cross-relatives). And it works similarly for MOTHER's same-generation relatives.

The children (SON, DAUGHTER) of ego's cross-relatives (UNCLE, AUNT, COUSIN*, COUSIN*) fall into the same cross or parallel categories (COUSIN* or COUSIN*, BROTHER or SISTER, NEPHEW or NIECE, SON or DAUGHTER, respectively) as do the children of ego's parallel relatives (FATHER, MOTHER, BROTHER, SISTER, respectively).

Such a system would, of course, have separate affinal terms. That is, WIFE [1] COUSIN*.

It maps badly onto lineages. The categorical inconsistency regarding cross and parallel kin term categories would seem to make any transition into a Crow- or Omaha-type system complicated and difficult.

Generic Dravidian Type

Cross versus parallel determinations are consistent. If this really works, it means that I have been wrong in claiming that Dravidian would not work without the moiety mental crutch.

This system as I describe it could have separate affinal terms, that is, WIFE [1] COUSIN*, though it would also be consistent with the common Dravidian-type classifying of affines with cross-relatives.

It maps well onto lineages. It could easily shift to a skewed system, by changing $U \times S$, $U \times D$, $A \times S$, and $A \times D$ from kinds of C to appropriate G+1 terms. The cross/parallel calculation required for skewing would be consistent with that present in this unskewed system.

In this case my explanation of one kind of way in which Iroquois-type systems might arise (e.g., in Kronenfeld 1989), the collapse of moieties resulting in calculation problems in maintaining a Dravidian-type system, would be badly undercut. Instead I would offer an alternative hypothesis. This Dravidian-type system still requires a reasonable awareness of actual genealogical links, and it depends on children (learners) having enough experience with enough kinds of relatives (close and distant) to learn not just the categories but the specific relations among them. Thus a fallback from Dravidian type to Iroquois type would still seem a reasonable response to a major population collapse (as was experienced by the Iroquois themselves between the arrival of the Europeans and the ethnography of L. H. Morgan).

I want to note that such an approach is not inconsistent with Trautmann and Barnes's (1998) idea that social features drive transitions, as increasing social complexity takes their Type B into Type A and then into skewed systems. In my terms, that sequence would be recast as Dravidian type (without built-in affinals) into Dravidian type (with built-in affinals) into skewed. A second, different sequence would be Dravidian type into Iroquois type, driven by large-scale social collapse.

Affines

For affines we can add to our relative product kin lexeme multiplication table something like the following rows and columns:

Consanguine terms used for affines.

	F	M	U	A	B	Z	Cm	Cf
WI	U	A	F	M	Cm	Cf	B	Z
HU	U	A	F	M	Cm	Cf	B	Z

WI stands for wife. HU stands for husband. This would be for a system with affinal cross-equations (in Gould, something like V ↔ X).

For a system without affinal cross-equations, the table would be something like the following:

Consanguine terms not used for affines.

	F	M	U	A	B	Z	Cm	Cf
WI	FL	ML	?	?	BL	ZL	?	?
HU	FL	ML	?	?	BL	ZL	?	?

I am using L to mark some equivalent of our English IN-LAW lexeme. As Gould says, affinal information in the literature, especially in the absence of affinal equations with consanguines, is awfully thin and awfully variable.

Notes

Many thanks go to Jerrold E. Kronenfeld for help with the graphics and to Jerrold E. Kronenfeld, Judy Z. Kronenfeld, and Patrick McConvell for helpful advice on the chapter itself.

1. The relevant mathematics of equivalence relations is laid out in appendix A of Gould 2000; the relevant mathematics of monoids and groups appears in appendix B.
2. There is no corresponding "paternal aunt" term in Fanti.
3. Sometimes an item that is "like an X" is taken to be a member of a superclass based on X. My sense is that superclasses are defined by shared structural relations, such as having a joint reciprocal or producing equivalent relative products.
4. Components such as what Lounsbury used for Iroquois seem hard to come up with for Dravidian, unless one introduces a new *kind* of component that involves counting the number of sex changes in the genealogical string relating ego to alter or counting the number of males and females in the string connecting ego to alter. Such a detailed consideration of the whole string is inconsistent with the componential approaches that one sees in the literature.

   Similarly, the rewrite rule approach does not work for Dravidian-type systems. The merging rule works for apical same-sex sibling pairs (as one encounters them in the sequence of rewrites), but the successive application of rules that the approach depends on is blocked by the first apical cross-sex sibling pair that one encounters (or reduces down to). One might invent a whole new *kind* of rule, but—since it has nothing to reduce to—such a rule would have to insert some sort of marker, which would radically change (and complicate) the approach. A different, but similar, problem would obtain in any attempt to come up with a rewrite rule approach for Iroquois-type systems.
5. I should note that Gould (2000) also provides a tight formal version of Lounsbury's componential and componential-with-rewrite-rules approaches, which he applies to all the included terminological systems, including Iroquois type and Dravidian type. He briefly considers whole-category components (in chapter 7) before opting (in chapter 8) for componential definitions of only focal (core or kernel) sets and then using his algebraic rules to account for extensions of these.

   He leaves the two types of approaches as apparently incommensurable; that is, he makes no move to translate either into the other. He seems to consider both important (and, thus, presumably useful) but does not discuss the issue. In Kronenfeld 1980b (and see Kronenfeld 2006) I offer one view of what these different uses might be. Since Gould restricts his algebraic system to structurally relevant equivalence classes (what we might see as superclasses), he does use simple, basic components (such as sex of ego, sex of alter, relative age) to define the members of the separate terms that fall within his equivalence classes. In this context it is important to note that Gould uses his algebraic approach, not his componential one, to define the major types.
6. The terminological relations can be traced even in the absence of actual genealogical knowledge—in the manner spoken of by Read (this volume) and Keen (this volume).
7. Following Lounsbury, I see other social structural factors such as the presence/nature of descent groups as relating to terminologies via their common dependence on rights of succession and inheritance. Some of this is discussed later.
8. This marker is a familiar one, having long been unnecessarily applied to Iroquois-type systems.
9. For example, Gould's (2000:287, 325) algebraic characterization of the two Fanti systems ignores the concurrence between "father's sister" and "mother's sister"—because of its structural irrelevance—while my formalization of Fanti reasoning (Kronenfeld 1980b), as well as Gould's (2000:288, 326) and my (1973, 1980a) componential/rewrite analyses, did deal with the concurrence.
10. The term *marking* was coined by Trubetzkoy in recognition of the fact that in his phonological examples, the marked member of the opposition (say, /d/ versus /t/) was

distinguished from the unmarked (/t/) by an added definitional "mark" or phonic substance (that is, /d/ in German or English can be seen as a /t/ to which voicing has been added). The criterial role of added substantive substance was subsequently shown by Greenberg (1966) not to obtain outside of phonology; this difference flows from the linguistic function of phonemes—to distinguish one morpheme (Saussurean sign) from another—where that function is dependent on substantive physical differences among phonemes. Morphology, syntax, and semantics deal with the concepts delineated by phonemes and contrast conceptually (versus physically) even if morphological marking often exhibits some added item—as in English, where the past tense is marked in opposition to the unmarked present tense and where the normal form of that marking is the addition of *-ed*, as in *walked* versus *walk*, but where other forms such as *sung* versus *sing* are frequent (especially for frequently used words!).

11. Thus we can see the unmarked member as representing a kind of "default option." The reasons for the development of default options for parameter values in "canned" computer programs include simplifying data entry and allowing users who had no specific preference or values in mind to go with generic values. The effectiveness of such defaults depends on there being some significant bias in user needs for the one value over others; the more likely that values for some given parameter are variable, the more likely that one will actually have to enter one's specific parameter value. The computer version may provide some insight into what may be one functional basis for marking in language.
12. It is tempting to speculate, as others have, that classificatory terminologies in general go with some sort of unilineal kin groups—often, maybe, corporate in the sense of collectively controlling some (possibly intangible) property.
13. I am curious (do not know) whether the fact that the "maternal grandfather" term (*avus*) became the main term had to do with the relative salience of maternal grandparents versus paternal ones in a situation in which there was normally a substantial difference in the age of marriage for women versus men (say, maybe, 20 versus 40?). In this case paternal grandparents, especially grandfathers, would commonly be dead by the time most of their grandchildren were old enough to talk with or about them and thus would mostly be part of the collection of agnatic ancestors. On the other hand, maternal grandparents would be much more likely to be around (even if, still, less so for grandfathers than for grandmothers)—and thus to be talked enough to or about to generate and maintain a dedicated kin term. This is purely speculative—but is at least a kind of hypothesis that I would like to explore.
14. However, there can exist complications—as in the overlap (versus contrast) between the Fanti male-speaking "sister" term (*akyereba*) and the general "sibling" term (*nua*)—see Kronenfeld 1980a, 1980b, 2009: chs. 2–3. And see McConvell, chapter 10, this volume.

References Cited

Allen, N. J. 1998. The Prehistory of Dravidian-Type Terminologies. In *Transformations of Kinship*. M. Godelier, T. R. Trautmann, and F. F. Tjon Sie Fat, eds. Pp. 324–331. Washington, DC: Smithsonian Institution Press.

Brudner, L. A., and D. White. 1997. Class, Property, and Structural Endogamy: Visualizing Networked Histories. *Theory and Society* 25(2):161–208. Electronic document, http://repositories.cdlib.org/postprints/3/.

Chit Hlaing, F. K. L. (F. K. Lehman). 2011. Kinship Theory and Cognitive Theory in Anthropology. In *A Companion to Cognitive Anthropology*. D. B. Kronenfeld, Giovanni Bennardo, Victor C. de Munck, and Michael D. Fischer, eds. Pp. 254–269. Malden, MA: Blackwell.

Danziger, E. 2001. *Relatively Speaking: Language, Thought, and Kinship among the Mopan Maya*. Oxford: Oxford University Press.

Dole, G. E. 1972. Developmental Sequences of Kinship Patterns. In *Kinship Studies in the Morgan Centennial Year*. P. Reining, ed. Pp. 134–166. Washington, DC: Anthropological Society of Washington.

Gould, Sydney H. 2000. *A New System for the Formal Analysis of Kinship*. D. B. Kronenfeld, ed. Lanham, MD: University Press of America.

Greenberg, J. H. 1966. *Language Universals with Special Reference to Feature Hierarchies*. Janua Linguarum, 59. The Hague: Mouton.

Hage, P. 1997. Unthinkable Categories and the Fundamental Laws of Kinship. *American Ethnologist* 24:652–667.

Hage, P. 1999. Marking Universals and the Structure and Evolution of Kinship Terminologies: Evidence from Salish. *Journal of the Royal Anthropological Institute* 5:423–441.

Hage, P. 2001. Marking Theory and Kinship Analysis: Cross-Cultural and Historical Applications. Theme issue, "Kinship," D. Kronenfeld, ed., *Anthropological Theory* 1: 197–211.

Houseman, M., and D. White. 1998. Network Mediation of Exchange Structures: Ambilateral Sidedness and Property Flows in Pul Eliya. In *Kinship, Networks and Exchange*. T. Schweizer and Douglas R. White, eds. Pp. 58–88. Cambridge: Cambridge University Press. Electronic document, http://eclectic.ss.uci.edu/~drwhite/pub/PUL-CAMB1a.pdf.

Kay, P. 1975. The Generative Analysis of Kinship Semantics: A Reanalysis of the Seneca Data. *Foundations of Language* 13:201–214.

Keen, I. 1985. Definitions of Kin. *Journal of Anthropological Research* 41:62–90.

Kronenfeld, D. B. 1973. Fanti Kinship: The Structure of Terminology and Behavior. *American Anthropologist* 75:1577–1595.

Kronenfeld, D. B. 1980a. A Formal Analysis of Fanti Kinship Terminology (Ghana). *Anthropos* 75:586–608.

Kronenfeld, D. B. 1980b. Particularistic or Universalistic Analysis of Fanti Kin-terminology: The Alternative Goals of Terminological Analysis. *Man* 15(1):151–169.

Kronenfeld, D. B. 1989. Morgan vs. Dorsey on the Omaha Cross–Parallel Contrast: Theoretical Implications. *L'Homme* 19:78–101.

Kronenfeld, D. B. 1991. Fanti Kinship: Language, Inheritance, and Kin Groups. *Anthropos* 86:19–31.

Kronenfeld, D. B. 1992. Goodenough vs. Fischer on Residence: A Generation Later. *Journal of Quantitative Anthropology* 4:1–21.

Kronenfeld, D. B. 1996. *Plastic Glasses and Church Fathers: Semantic Extension from the Ethnoscience Tradition*. New York: Oxford University Press.

Kronenfeld, D. B. 2001a. Introduction: The Uses of Formal Analysis Re Cognitive and Social Issues. Theme issue, "Kinship," D. B. Kronenfeld, ed., *Anthropological Theory* 1(2):1–172.

Kronenfeld, D. B. 2001b. Using Sydney H. Gould's Formalization of Kin Terminologies: Social Information, Skewing, and Structural Types. Theme issue, "Kinship," David B. Kronenfeld, ed., *Anthropological Theory* 1(2):173–196.

Kronenfeld, D. B. 2006. Issues in the Classification of Kinship Terminologies: Toward a New Typology. *Anthropos* 101: 203–219.

Kronenfeld, D. B. 2009. *Fanti Kinship and the Analysis of Kinship Terminologies*. Urbana: University of Illinois Press.

Kronenfeld, D. B., and G. Rundblad. 2003. The Semantic Structure of Lexical Fields: Variation and Change. In *Words in Time: Diachronic Semantics from Different Points of View*. R. Eckardt, K. von Heusinger, and C. Schwarze, eds. Pp. 67–114. Berlin: Mouton de Gruyter.

Leach, E. 1958. Concerning Trobriand Clans and the Kinship Category *Tabu*. In *The Developmental Cycle in Domestic Groups*. J. Goody, ed. Pp. 120–145. Cambridge: Cambridge University Press.

Lounsbury, F. G. 1965. Another View of the Trobriand Kinship Categories. Theme issue, "Formal Semantic Analysis," E. H. Hammel, ed., *American Anthropologist* 67(5), pt. 2: 142–185.

Lounsbury, F. G. 1969a[1964]. A Formal Account of the Crow- and Omaha-Type Kinship Terminologies. Reprint. In *Cognitive Anthropology*. S. A. Tyler, ed. Pp. 212–255. New York: Holt, Rinehart and Winston.

Lounsbury, F. G. 1969b[1964]. The Structural Analysis of Kinship Semantics. Reprint. In *Cognitive Anthropology*. S. A. Tyler, ed. Pp. 193–212. New York: Holt, Rinehart and Winston.

Lowie, R. H. 1948. *Social Organization*. New York: Holt, Rinehart and Winston.

Morgan, L. H. 1871. *Systems of Consanguinity and Affinity of the Human Family*. Smithsonian Contributions to Knowledge, 218. Washington, DC: Smithsonian Institution.

Murdock, G. P. 1949. *Social Structure*. New York: Free Press.

Read, D. W. 2001. Formal Analysis of Kinship Terminologies and Its Relationship to What Constitutes Kinship. Theme issue, "Kinship," D. B. Kronenfeld, ed., *Anthropological Theory* 1:239–287.

Read, D. W. 2007. From Anthropological Reasoning to Mathematical Reasoning and Back. Paper presented at the Society for Anthropological Sciences Meetings, San Antonio, February 22.

Read, D. W. 2009. From Empirical Networks to Cultural Concept Formation: The Case of Kinship Systems. Paper presented at the International Network for Social Network Analysis Annual Conference.

Romney, A. K. 1971. A Model for the Analysis of Endogamy. In *Explorations in Mathematical Anthropology*. Paul Kay, ed. Pp. 191–213. Cambridge: MIT Press.

Sapir, E. 1921. *Language: An Introduction to the Study of Speech*. New York: Harcourt.

Scheffler, H. W. 1972a. Baniata Kin Classification: The Case for Extensions. *Southwestern Journal of Anthropology* 28:350–381.

Scheffler, H. W. 1972b. Kinship Semantics. *Annual Review of Anthropology* 1:309–328.

Scheffler, H. W., and F. G. Lounsbury. 1971. *A Study in Structural Semantics: The Siriono Kinship System*. Englewood Cliffs, NJ: Prentice Hall.

Strauss, D. J., and A. K. Romney. 1982. Log-Linear Multiplicative Models for the Analysis of Endogamy. *Ethnology* 21: 79–99.

Tjon Sie Fat, F. 1998. On the Formal Analysis of "Dravidian," "Iroquois," and "Generational" Varieties as Nearly Associative Combinations. In *Transformations of Kinship*. M. Godelier, T. R. Trautmann, and F. E. Tjon Sie Fat, eds. Pp. 59–93. Washington, DC: Smithsonian Institution Press.

Trautmann, Thomas R., and R. H. Barnes. 1998. "Dravidian," "Iroquois," and "Crow Omaha" in North American Perspective. In *Transformations of Kinship*. M. Godelier, T. R. Trautmann, and F. E. Tjon Sie Fat, eds. Pp. 27–58. Washington, DC: Smithsonian Institution Press.

Trubetzkoy, N. S. 1969[1939]. *Principles of Phonology*. Berkeley: University of California Press.

Tyler, S. A. 1966. Parallel/Cross: An Evaluation of Definitions. *Southwestern Journal of Anthropology* 22:416–432.

White, D. R., and W. W. Denham. 2008. The Indigenous Australian Marriage Paradox: Small-World Dynamics on a Continental Scale. Electronic document, http://intersci.ss.uci.edu/wiki/pub/Paradox07b.pdf.

3

Comparative Phylogenetic Methods and the Study of Pattern and Process in Kinship

Fiona M. Jordan

If we ask how it is that a society has the social institutions that it does have at a particular time the answer can only be supplied by history.
(Radcliffe-Brown 1950:1)

Phylogenies can be used to infer the historical evolutionary processes that must have existed in the past, given the patterns of diversity seen in the present.
(Pagel 1997:331)

Anthropology began by comparing aspects of kinship across cultures, while linguists interested in semantic domains such as kinship necessarily compare across languages. In this chapter I show how phylogenetic comparative methods from evolutionary biology can be used to study evolutionary processes relating to kinship and kinship terminologies across language and culture. To properly study cultural evolution across populations, we need to account for the effect that shared ancestry may have in creating relationships and patterns in the traits we examine, a problem recognized in anthropology since Galton (Tylor 1889). To combat what is essentially the same difficulty—the hierarchical relatedness of species—evolutionary biologists employ phylogenies (family trees) of species as population histories and use a set of statistical techniques called comparative methods to control for evolutionary history in trait evolution (Felsenstein 1985; Harvey and Pagel 1991). Anthropologists, like biologists, are most often interested in evolutionary processes beyond reconstructing "the tree," so phylogenies and comparative methods are not meant as a replacement for existing approaches but are simply another tool for the scientific tool kit.

Kinship terminologies constituted the raw material for the earliest scientific (i.e., comparative) anthropology (Morgan 1871). While the postmodern turn in anthropology saw the abandonment of the scientific approach in many aspects (D'Andrade 2000), anthropological scholarship has turned toward deeply contextual descriptions of social life (Geertz 1973), including kinship (Colleran and Mace 2011). Ethnology—the comparative study of culture—could be poised to have a renaissance because scientific comparison is now tractable and it can shed light on history. Pattern is an outcome of process, and one can be used to understand the other, as both Radcliffe-Brown and Pagel note above.

Unlike material aspects of culture, social behavior does not fossilize, so in order to gain an understanding of the historical processes that produced current cultural diversity in kinship we have to make inferences on the basis of scarce and sometimes problematic data. These include material culture correlates of social structure and demographic estimates from archaeology, historical records for societies with written traditions, and more recently, genetic narratives that interpret patterns of sex-specific markers as indicative of past marriage and dispersal behavior (Wilkins and Marlowe 2006). Taken together, these data help us triangulate our inferences about the past, but none make much use of the primary data at hand, that is, the comparative ethnographic record. Linguistic approaches to kinship in contrast *do* have a long tradition of diachronic inference. The linguistic comparative method has the capability of reconstructing protoforms for the vocabulary of ancestral speech communities. In this way, linguistics has provided a substantial contribution to our understanding of society in prehistory (e.g., Mallory and Adams 2006; Pawley et al. 2003). However, such "linguistic paleontology" has its limits—words can be reconstructed, but their meanings may be extremely fuzzy, and reconstruction in itself is not a guarantee that the meaning (be it an item or a concept) was present in the ancestral speech community (McMahon and McMahon 2005).

Some of the long-standing questions in anthropology are to do with the evolution of kinship systems over the time scale of human history (Allen et al. 2008; Chapais 2008). What, if anything, can we say about hominid family structure? Once modern humans had language, how did we start to refer to kin? And how, over tens of thousands of years and the dispersal of humans to vastly different ecological environments around the globe, did our kin terminologies diversify into the variation we see today—albeit a restricted diversity that is remarkable for its boundedness and logical structure (Nerlove and Romney 1967)? Why do different language families contain instances of the same structural patterns in terminology, albeit with different linguistic forms? Are there rules that govern the transformation of one sort of terminological system into another? Can we derive those processes simply from an analysis of the synchronic data we have available through the ethnographic record? In the introduction to their important volume, Godelier et al. (1998) echo Morgan in stressing three of these questions: the correlated evolution of terminologies and aspects of social structure, the restricted diversity of systems worldwide, and the dynamics that govern the transformation of kin term systems; and these still remain some of the most intriguing and important questions in the study of human cultural diversity.

In the past 25 years evolutionary biologists have developed a suite of tools to investigate diversity, correlated evolution, and character transformation across species while controlling for historical relatedness (Felsenstein 1985; Ord and Martins 2010). These tools have been adopted by a small number of anthropologists and linguists interested in the same sorts of questions as above, and a burgeoning literature on their application exists (Forster and Renfrew 2006; Gray et al. 2007; Lipo et al. 2006; Mace 2005; Mace and Pagel 1994; Mace et al. 2005; Shennan 2009). Much of this work has focused on phylogenetic tree-building, but in what follows I provide a nontechnical introduction to phylogenetic comparative approaches, discuss the components of an analysis, and detail how these methods have been applied to cultural phenomena. I then discuss in some detail two kinship case studies, one concerned with reconstructing ancestral states of postmarital residence and the other aimed at elucidating the dynamics of change in sibling terminologies. The chapter concludes with remarks for the future study of kinship terminologies with these evolutionary methods.

Phylogenetic Comparative Methods

Phylogenetic comparative methods (PCMs) are a class of statistical procedures developed in evolutionary biology to analyze the historical processes that have shaped diversity among species—or, more broadly defined, taxa of some sort. These methods work by statistically reconstructing the evolutionary pathways that are likely to have produced the observed distribution of a trait across a group of related taxa. PCMs comprise a diachronic aspect, in that they recognize the descent relationships of taxa through time, for example, the diversification of the class Mammalia in the last 100,000,000 years. They also comprise a synchronic aspect, in that they are concerned with the expression of some type of feature across a number of contemporaneous taxa—for example, different mammalian adaptations for locomotion such as forelimbs or flippers. Both are crucial, because the synchronic variation cannot be properly understood without the control for evolutionary relatedness that is provided by the ancestor–descendant relationships of the diachronic phylogenetic tree. Put simply, we cannot count lions and tigers and bears as three independent data points in a study of carnivores. We should rather count their carnivorous common ancestor as a single data point. In biology, PCMs were initially developed to overcome the problem of hierarchical relatedness in order to answer comparative questions about adaptation and coevolution (Harvey and Pagel 1991; Pagel 1999a): Are changes in one feature of an organism (or its environment) correlated with changes in other features? Besides coevolution, four other main types of evolutionary questions can be approached with PCMs: (1) assessing the amount of historical signal in the data, (2) characterizing the ancestral states of features, (3) determining the timing of evolutionary events, and (4) investigating the mode of evolutionary change (Ord and Martins 2010; Pagel 1999b)—see Figure 3.1 for more detail.

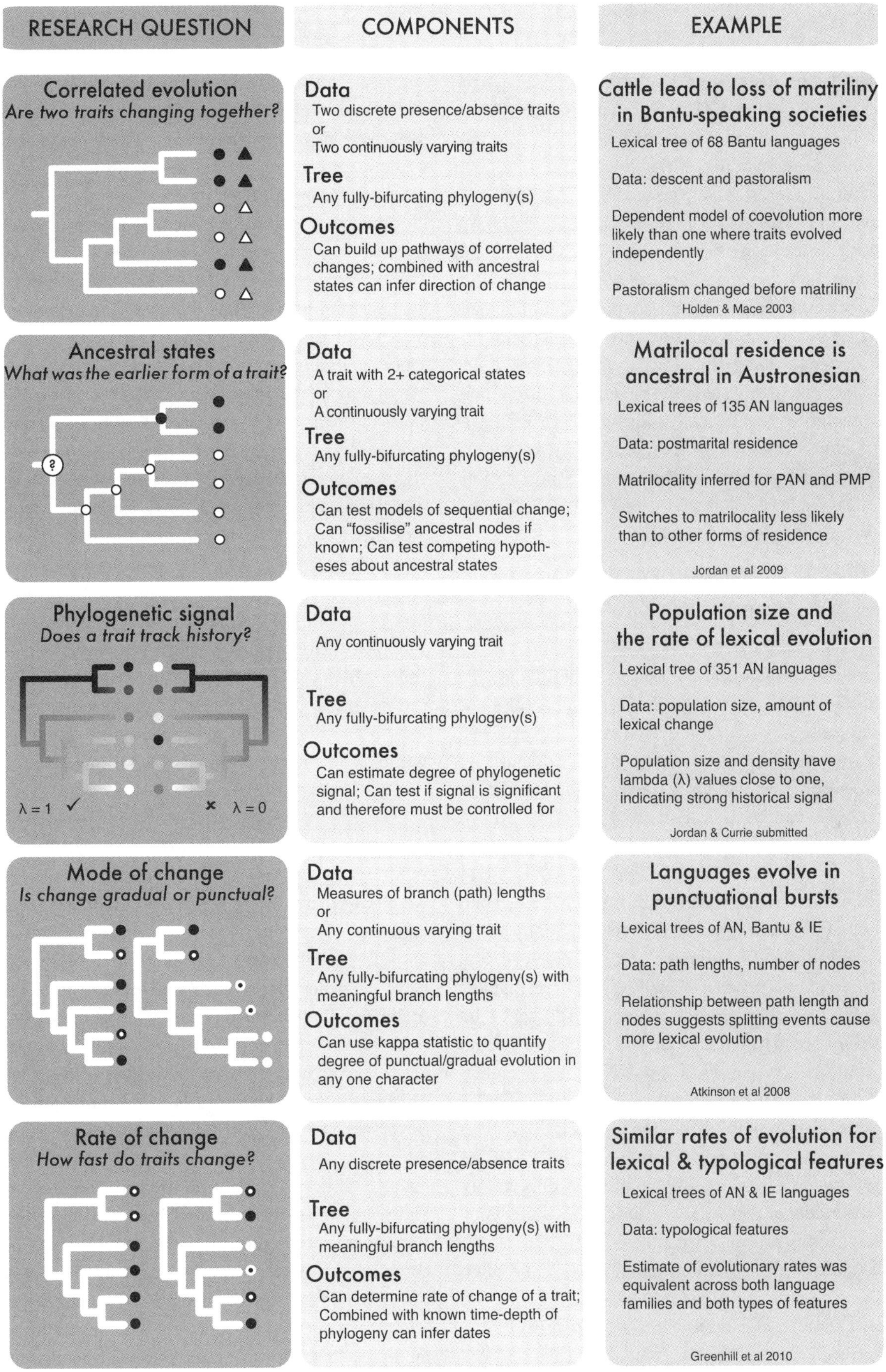

FIGURE 3.1. Overview of five types of evolutionary questions that can be answered using phylogenetic comparative methods. The left box for each question is presented with a schematic diagram representing the approach. The middle box details the practical components (type of data, type of phylogeny, and outcomes of the procedures), and the right box describes a recent empirical example. AN = Austronesian; IE = Indo-European; PAN = Proto-Austronesian; PMP = Proto-Malayo-Polynesian.

These types of statistical explorations require three components in common: (1) a phylogenetic tree or trees representing hypotheses about the historical relationships among the taxa, (2) observations for each taxa on some trait of interest, and (3) a model of how the traits have evolved through time (Felsenstein 1985; Harvey and Pagel 1991). From there, the details of software and algorithms vary, but the principles remain the same. In a cross-cultural or cross-linguistic framework, phylogenetic trees of human populations are derived from linguistic or genetic data; comparative ethnographic or linguistic data are mapped onto the phylogeny, and a model of trait evolution is statistically inferred (Mace and Pagel 1994). Below I describe each of these steps; interested readers are referred to further literature for more technical details (see Felsenstein 2004; Lemey et al. 2009; Ord and Martins 2010; Ronquist 2004).

Components of a Phylogenetic Comparative Analysis

Phylogenetic Trees

It is important to stress at the outset that PCMs are *not* tree-building methods, though they rely on having some sort of evolutionary tree (phylogeny) as input to proceed. In this way they differ from the linguistic comparative method, which is essentially a tree-building method. In theory, PCMs can be used with any type of hypothesis about hierarchical relatedness and could take input as varied as a traditional historical linguistics tree, a tree of human populations based on features such as skull morphology or blood groups, or a set of equally likely phylogenies derived by analysis of DNA sequence data from different populations. What is important is that any phylogeny is simply a hypothesis about the descent relationships between different taxa, and in questions about human culture, a phylogeny is normally some representation of population history. Thus, because any particular tree is most likely *not* the "true tree" (especially with respect to human populations—where one "true tree" does not exist), we prefer methods that address uncertainty about the model of population history. This can be done by incorporating probability estimates of particular subgroups (clades) and by summarizing multiple and often conflicting lineages with a representative sample of trees. In recent years, a class of approaches known as Bayesian likelihood approaches has come to be the preferred method of phylogenetic inference because they do a good job of quantifying uncertainty in precisely these desired ways. They also provide phylogenies that have meaningful estimates of evolutionary divergence, that is, branch lengths that quantify the change in a set of features since some shared common ancestor (Huelsenbeck et al. 2001; Yang and Rannala 1997).

Biologists wishing to infer the phylogenetic relationships of a set of species (to "draw a tree") usually proceed by obtaining some set of DNA sequences, aligning those sequences to compare like with like, and then employing a phylogenetic software package to build evolutionary trees according to some optimization criterion such as parsimony or maximum likelihood. For a linguist using these methods, cognate-coded lexical items on standardized word lists are the usual input to software packages, though any codable set of characters with a structured evolutionary history may be used. Space does not permit a detailed description of the computational phylogenetic tree-inference procedures common in evolutionary biology and now being employed in evolutionary anthropology and linguistics (Dunn 2009; Gray et al. 2007). In-depth introductions to phylogeny construction are contained in Felsenstein 2004 and Lemey et al. 2009. For the remainder of this chapter, I take the existence of phylogenies as a given, but in the case studies more details will be given on the particular phylogenies used in each analysis.

Observations: Comparative Data

PCMs derive their name from the comparative data about which we wish to infer some evolutionary process. In biological analyses these data can be morphological (e.g., body size), behavioral (e.g., territorial defense strategies), physiological, or chemical—in fact, any feature of organisms that varies between populations. Likewise in cultural evolution, comparative data can be the biological characteristics of populations, such as the proportion of lactose-tolerant individuals (Holden and Mace 1997) or the sex ratio at birth (Mace and Jordan 2005). Ethnographic data are common; for example, researchers have investigated the coevolution of marriage systems and payments (Fortunato and Mace 2009), subsistence and inheritance systems (Holden and Mace 2003), or a combination of ethnographic and ecological information, for example, latitude and political complexity. Comparative linguistic data can also be analyzed with these methods: dependencies in the structural features of language (Dunn et al. 2011), the frequency of word use and rates of evolution (Pagel et al. 2007), and the relationship between population size and the rate of lexical evolution (Jordan and Currie n.d.) have all been studied.

While the sorts of analyses undertaken will depend on the research question, there exists a small number of restrictions on the form of the comparative data. First, the data must be codable in some meaningful form, so categorical data must be expressed in a small number of meaningful classes, either as binary presence/absence or as "multistate" characters. Continuous data are frequent in biological analyses (e.g., body size) but are less common in cultural features; continuous variables may be more appropriately clustered as ordinal features, for example, percentage dependence on some type of subsistence as high/medium/low. Second, the comparative data must not be the same as those used to construct the phylogeny. Independence is important, so, for example, an analysis of grammatical features should preferably use a phylogeny built from lexical data. Third, there must be sufficient variation in the data to answer the research question, and relatedly, there must be sufficient data for the statistical models to work. A rule of thumb is that an order of magnitude more taxa are needed than characters, so for a binary feature, 20 is a desirable number of taxa for any analysis, and for two binary features we should have ~40 taxa.

Coding comparative cultural and linguistic data is a task fraught with the difficult reduction decisions familiar to all scientifically minded anthropologists. It should be noted, however, that biologists face similar decisions in their attempts to understand biological diversity. The structure of a complex ecological community in a rain forest, with mutualistic and context-dependent interactions among plants, fungi, microorganisms, insects, and vertebrates, is not a simple thing to untangle, yet biologists get on and do what they can. The use of PCMs forces us to be explicit about what hypothesis we are testing and to justify how we distill the (for example) complex behaviors of a speech community to manageable variation.

Models of Evolution

Thus far, the combination of "comparative data + population history" should be familiar and somewhat obvious to historical linguists and comparative anthropologists—for an example, see Kirch and Green's (2001) reconstruction of ancestral Polynesian society. PCMs depart from the familiar with the introduction of a (1) quantitatively expressed and (2) statistically inferred model of change. These two features require a computational approach for the simple fact that keeping track of, and comparing and assessing all permutations of, Trees + Data + Models is beyond the capability of a single human brain for any data sets beyond the most trivially small.

A word should be said about the definition of *model*. In the terminology of computational phylogenetics, a model specifies the assumptions we have about the process of evolutionary change, and it does so by imposing some sort of criterion on the data. A simple example is that of parsimony: we should prefer explanations for the data that minimize the amount of evolutionary change that takes place. Another model may specify that rates of change are equally likely in both directions: a trait may be gained or lost with the same probability. Models are contentious, as we only have some ideas about the proper expectations for evolutionary change. For example, in molecular evolution, elucidation of the chemical structure of DNA molecules means biologists know that certain types of mutational changes (transitions, between two purine or two pyrimidine bases) are more likely than others (transversions, between a purine and a pyrimidine) and so can weight models accordingly (Li and Graur 1991). But we have very little analogous knowledge with respect to cultural and linguistic change, and our models need to be built from the ground up with as few assumptions as possible (cf. the problem of inferring the direction of change between "Dravidian" and other kin types, as discussed in McConvell, chapter 1, this volume; and Hornborg, this volume).

The sorts of evolutionary models implemented in PCMs for organismal change, particularly behavioral change, tend to be simple maximization algorithms that either (1) maximize parsimony by preferring the least number of historical changes to explain the current data or (2) maximize the likelihood of the current data, given the phylogeny and some specifications about how to judge the likelihood of change in the character. This specification will state something like "A change from 0 to 1 is x times as likely as a change from 1 to 0," and the algorithm will explore a number of possible values of x, returning a likelihood score for each and summing over all characters. More complex models will introduce specifications like "Allow different characters to vary their likelihood of change" or "Allow different taxa to vary their rate of evolution," drawing values for these variable quantities from probability distributions specified by the researcher. A burgeoning literature exists on maximum likelihood, models, and their Bayesian implementation (e.g., Lewis 2001; Pagel 1999a; Ronquist 2004; Schmidt and von

Haeseler 2009). It is fairly easy to see that calculating likelihoods is not a trivial task and that computational power is necessary. Thus, for example, the "inclusion criteria" proposed by Dyen and Aberle (1974; discussed in McConvell, chapter 1, this volume) actually resemble a type of likelihood-based inference, but in their case this is based on an *a priori* belief that optimization will correctly characterize the process of lexico-semantic evolution. More desirable is the statistical comparison of the proposed solution to other alternatives across the data set as a whole, something implemented as routine in phylogenetic comparative inference.

Much cultural phylogenetic work has taken advantage of the probabilistic approach afforded by what are known as Bayesian Markov-chain Monte Carlo (MCMC) methods and has employed PCM software that implements this framework (Pagel and Meade 2006; Pagel et al. 2004). Say we are interested in estimating the ancestral state (presence/absence) of matrilateral cross-cousin marriage in a particular group of related societies. While some PCMs will return a simple yes/no/equivocal value that is dependent on the particular phylogeny being used, Bayesian methods will estimate something called a *posterior probability distribution* for the presence of cross-cousin marriage in the common ancestor. The methods will also return a probability distribution of the rates of change in the marriage character, that is, how frequently the character changes through time. The posterior probability of a parameter value is a quantity proportional to its likelihood of having produced the observed data and represents the probability of the parameter value given the data and model of trait evolution (Huelsenbeck et al. 2001; Lewis 2001). Because posterior probabilities cannot feasibly be computed analytically, posterior probability distributions are inferred instead using an MCMC sampling algorithm. This distributional approach provides information about the degree of statistical uncertainty in the cultural trait reconstructions. Relatedly, this approach makes it possible to account for the effect of uncertainty in the phylogenetic tree model representing population history, a nontrivial consideration in the study of cultural traits, as a single branching tree is unlikely to accurately represent human population history (Boyd et al. 1997). The estimation of parameters over a probability sample of trees yields estimates that are not dependent on any specific phylogenetic hypothesis. Finally, parameters can be estimated over different models of trait evolution, and this yields estimates that are not dependent on any specific model of how the cultural traits have evolved.

All PCMs, Bayesian or not, offer the ability to quantify and test theoretical predictions with empirical data by using hypothesis tests or model comparisons. The boxes in Figure 3.1 describe five types of evolutionary questions that PCMs can be used for, giving a cultural/linguistic example of each and demonstrating an appropriate hypothesis test. Gray, Greenhill, and Ross (2007) give some further examples of how phylogenetic methods can answer questions about cultural evolution. They show how phylogenies can be built and dated using independent calibration of known events (for an Indo-European example, see Gray and Atkinson 2003) and how reticulate signal in the data, such as the borrowing of elements of languages (such as words) or dialect continua, can be explored and represented with network models (for an example using Chinese dialects, see Ben Hamed 2005). Here I elaborate on two case studies where PCMs have been used to study kinship: the reconstruction of ancestral states of postmarital residence in Indo-European and Austronesian and the comparison of sequential models of change in sibling terminologies in Austronesian and Bantu.

Case Studies

Case Study 1: Postmarital Residence in Proto-Austronesian and Proto-Indo-European

Marital residence norms are an important part of human social organization. Accurately inferring past patterns of postmarital residence is a challenge to our understanding of population history (Wilkins and Marlowe 2006) because these norms shape the patterns of genetic variation within and between populations by regulating the movement of people. Indo-European and Austronesian are two large-scale language families that are thought to represent Neolithic expansions associated with new domestication technologies. Their population histories have been inferred through a combination of archaeology, linguistics, genetics, and comparative anthropology (e.g., Bellwood and Renfrew 2002; Clackson 2007; Diamond and Bellwood 2003; Forster and Renfrew 2006; Hurles et al. 2003; Renfrew 1992; Zerjal et al. 2001). However, ancestral kinship patterns in these two families have mostly been inferred through reconstructions of kin terminologies in ancestral protolanguages using the linguistic comparative method and/or through geographic or distributional arguments based on patterns of kin terms and ethnographic observations. These approaches have produced detailed and valuable hypotheses about kinship prehistory, but in Fortunato and Jordan (2010) we argue that in many respects the processes through which conclusions have been drawn from the data fail to provide explicit criteria for systematic testing of alternative hypotheses. To address this, we used PCMs on Indo-European (IE) and Austronesian (AN) lexical trees, and ethnographic data on postmarital residence, to infer the likely states of residence in the ancestors of these language families.

Analysis

We used the following posterior probability samples of language trees: (1) 27 IE ethnolinguistic groups, 750 trees published in Pagel et al. 2007; and (2) 135 AN groups, 1,000 trees published in Jordan et al. 2009. For hypothetical ancestral speech communities or groups of languages, we abbreviated Proto-Indo-Hittite (PIH; IE languages and their Hittite sister group), Proto-Indo-European (PIE), Proto-Austronesian (PAN), and Proto-Malayo-Polynesian (PMP; the hypothetical ancestor of all non-Formosan AN languages). We matched each language to ethnographic data on marital residence from a variety of sources including Murdock's *Ethnographic Atlas* (1967; for details, see Fortunato and Jordan 2010; Jordan et al. 2009). We coded societies according to both prevailing and alternative modes of residence as practicing neolocality (i.e., residence apart from the kin of either spouse as neolocal; state N), uxorilocality (i.e., residence with or near the wife's kin; state U), or virilocality (i.e., residence with or near the husband's kin; state V). Ambilocal societies, where married couples take residence optionally with (or near) the kin of either spouse, and with approximately equal frequency, were assigned the dual state UV.

We used the PCM BayesMultistate, available as part of the BayesTraits package (Pagel and Meade 2006; Pagel et al. 2004). Given the comparative data and tree sample, BayesMultistate uses a continuous-time Markov model to describe the evolution of the trait of interest along the branches of a phylogeny. Under this model, the trait "residence" can switch repeatedly among its three states, N, U, and V, in any of the branches of a tree. Three states require six rate parameters quantifying the possible transitions (switches)—in this case, q_{NU}, q_{NV}, q_{UN}, q_{UV}, q_{VN}, and q_{VU}. Rate parameters are used to define (1) the probabilities of these changes, (2) the character states at internal nodes on a tree, and (3) the likelihood of the data (Pagel 1994, 1999b). The Bayesian MCMC implementation of Multistate estimates the posterior probability distributions of these three quantities (Pagel et al. 2004). The MCMC chain explores "parameter space" widely, randomly modifying the parameters and trying them out on the sample of trees over consecutive iterations. While the chain attempts to maximize the likelihood, it also accepts less likely combinations of parameters at a frequency proportional to their likelihood into the posterior probability distributions. This distribution then contains combinations of parameters such that those with higher support are sampled to a greater extent. A "reversible-jump" procedure that reduces the complexities of the underlying model of evolution to tractable dimensions was employed (Pagel and Meade 2006; see Fortunato and Jordan 2010).

The means of the posterior probability distribution of character states at ancestral nodes, for example, $p(V)$, $p(U)$, and $p(N)$, are combined with the posterior probability of each node existing in the tree, which represents the probability that the node exists (Lewis 2001). For PIH, PIE, PAN, and PMP this probability was 1, but when there is phylogenetic uncertainty (i.e., the node probability is less than 1), this information is combined with the estimate of the character state to give a conservative "combined probability." Once we estimated the ancestral state reconstructions for the four basal nodes, we then tested how much support we had for alternative reconstructions by fixing, or "fossilizing," each node to be one of the three possible states (N, V, U), in turn. We determined which fossilized state had relatively higher support at a given node by comparing the likelihoods using a measure called the Bayes factor (Raftery 1996).

Results for Indo-European showed that PCMs could reconstruct virilocality for PIH at $p(V) = .64 \pm .14$ and for PIE at $p(V) = .90 \pm .12$ (see Figure 3.2a). Virilocality reconstructed with high posterior probabilities within the Indo-Iranian (node F) and Balto-Slavic (node E) clades, but for the Italic, Germanic, and Celtic clade (node D) $p(V)$ dropped to .40, with the probability of neolocality inferred as equally likely. Using the fossilization test, we showed that there was strong or positive evidence for virilocality for PIE over the alternatives, but for PIH, the evidence was weaker, and none of the residence patterns had positive support. The reconstruction of early IE virilocality is in line with a popular scenario derived from the linguistic evidence, including kinship terminology

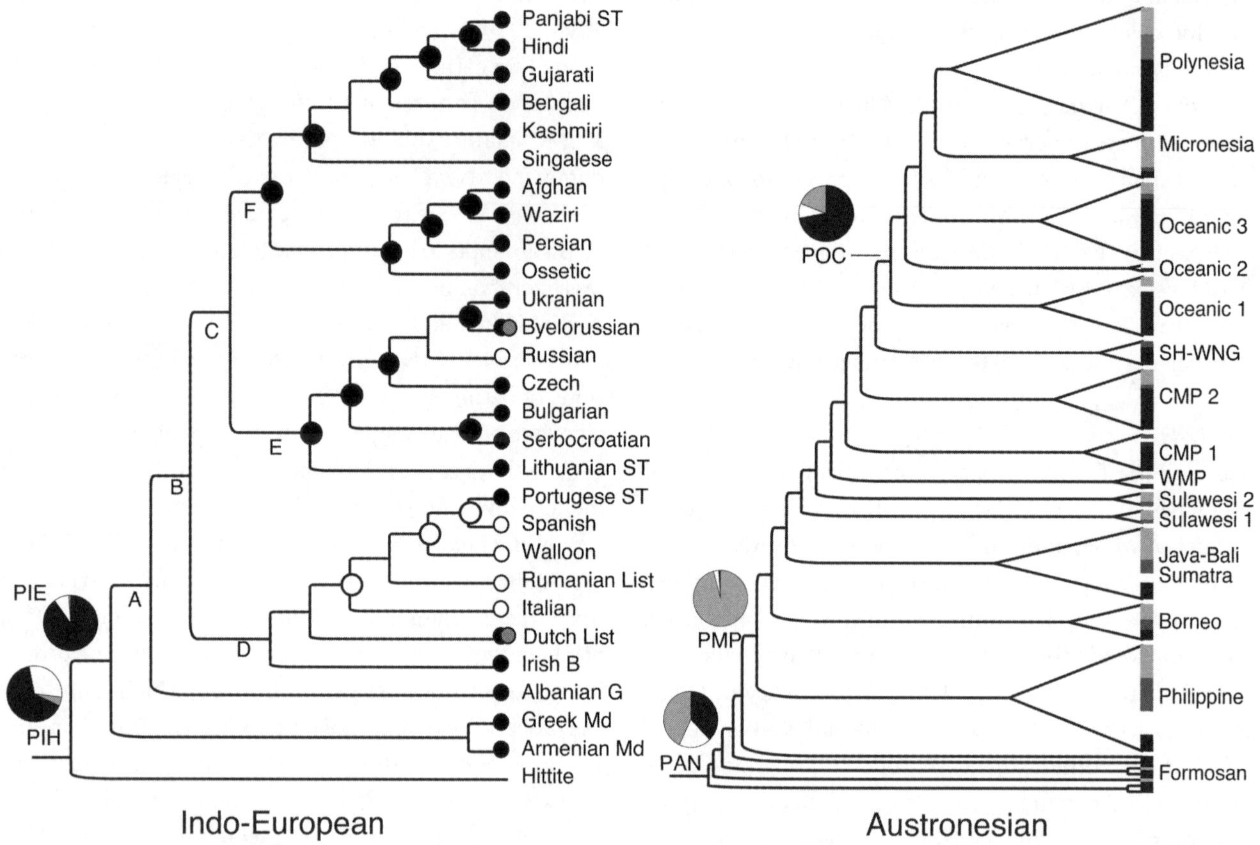

FIGURE 3.2. Trees (50 percent majority rule consensus) summarizing the sample of 1,000 phylogenies for (a) Indo-European and (b) Austronesian languages, including compatible groupings. Residence data are plotted by color: white = neolocality; light gray = uxorilocality; black = virilocality; dark gray = ambilocality. Reconstructed nodes are shown colored according to the ancestral state reconstruction. In (a) node labels are discussed in the text: PIE = Proto-Indo-European; PIH = Proto-Indo-Hittite. In (b) collapsed groups are proportional in size to number of languages and terminate in a bar shaded proportional to residence patterns within that group: PAN = Proto-Austronesian; PMP = Proto-Malayo-Polynesian; POC = Proto-Oceanic.

(Delbruck 1889; Friedrich 1966; Mallory and Adams 2006), though Goody (1959) was critical of this scenario and its faulty interpretation of ethnological data. More strongly, we noted that Clackson (2007) has described several equally plausible alternatives for early IE peoples. Uncertainty for PIH attests to this, and these methods can progress the debate by providing rigorous quantitative tests of the evidence in integrative studies of prehistory.

In Austronesian, uxorilocality was robustly reconstructed for PMP at $p(\mathrm{U}) = .96 \pm .06$ (Figure 3.2b). PAN was not reconstructed to any state with certainty, in comparison to results from Jordan et al. (2009) that reconstructed uxorilocality with $p(\mathrm{U}) = .70$. However, that earlier work does not consider alternative modes of residence. When testing using the fossilization procedure, there was positive evidence in favor of PAN uxorilocality over viri- and neolocality and very strong evidence for PMP uxorilocality over the alternatives. This is in line with some interpretations of PAN and PMP kinship terminologies (Blust 1980), although not all scholars agree (e.g., Chowning 1981). As with Indo-European, here we provide an independent confirmation from cross-cultural data. More recent work attempting to reconcile the different patterns of uniparental genetic markers seen in the Pacific (mtDNA and Y chromosome data) has suggested that uxorilocality was a later development in Austronesian, that is, Proto-Oceanic, cultures (Hage and Marck 2003; Harvey and Pagel 1991; Kayser et al. 2008).

We also used the transition-rate parameters to characterize the dynamics of change and compare these between the two language families. Results suggested that in both Indo-European and Austronesian the loss of virilocality is a rare event, indicated by low relative values of the rate parameters capturing these transitions (q_{VU} and q_{VN}).

Further, changes from uxori- toward virilocality (q_{UV}) occur at a higher rate than the reverse transition (q_{VU}): q_{UV} is over 30 times more likely than q_{VU} in IE and one and a half times more likely in AN. This may reflect the instability of "matricentric" systems (e.g., systems involving matrilineal descent) as observed by Richards (1950) for African societies (Holden and Mace 2005; Holden et al. 2003). We further suggest that explanations for variation in residence could plausibly be linked to variation in subsistence and ecological niche in both Indo-European and Austronesian.

Implications

In Fortunato and Jordan (2010), we not only show that it is possible to reconstruct the states of kinship norms in hypothetical ancestral speech communities that existed more than 6,000 years ago but also demonstrate that it is possible to statistically test those inferences by comparing them against the alternatives. We suggest avenues for quantifying the dynamics of change in societal norms of residence, finding commonalities between the two families that support the idea that human social life is not infinitely varied but, rather, is constrained by local environments. Moreover, we propose that by asking the same questions in different ethnographic regions we can start to infer the general mechanisms of cultural evolutionary change, that is, the identification of lineage-specific processes within global domains (cf. Dunn et al. 2011; Evans and Levinson 2009). In relation to kinship terminology, our analyses demonstrate that PCMs can both confirm previous historical linguistic work (as demonstrated for Indo-European) and disagree with it. These conflicts are important, as they demand a reexamination of both our data and our theoretical framework and suggest avenues for further investigation. In the Austronesian analysis, we found (as do Jordan et al. [2009]) that Proto-Oceanic was either ambiguous or patrilocal. This is in contrast to Hage and Marck (2003), who suggest that Proto-Oceanic was matrilineal and uxorilocal, basing these inferences on both reconstructed and synchronic kinship terminologies. PCMs may be unable to reconstruct uxorilocal residence for Proto-Oceanic because many daughter societies have, while retaining an uxorilocal option, since switched to virilocality as the prevailing mode—perhaps due to cultural contact with nearby non-Austronesian societies (Jordan et al. 2009). However, aspects of the theoretical framework employed by Hage and colleagues demand reanalysis, as they rely on mid-20th-century statistical associations between types of kinship terminology and types of social structure that themselves do not control for historical relatedness. I return to this point in the conclusion.

Case Study 2: The Evolution of Sibling Terminologies in Austronesian and Bantu

In this case study I describe some recent cross-linguistic analyses of evolutionary processes in kin terminologies. These results come from a wider project aimed at addressing the extensional semantics of complete sets of individual kin terms (see also Jordan 2011). Sibling terminologies are a useful partial set of all possible kin with which to strategically investigate evolutionary processes, and their general suitability as kin term test cases has long been established (Kronenfeld 1974; Nerlove and Romney 1967). Sibling terms are limited to a single generation, that of ego's own; they have a limited set of parameters (such as sex or age) on which they can be distinguished; and they concern immediate lineal kin, and thus, unlike cousin terminologies, they are not heavily impacted by considerations of marriageability.

Context

The sibling terminologies analyzed here are drawn from data on the Austronesian and Bantu language families collected together by Dziebel (2009). Both Austronesian and Bantu societies vary in ways representative of worldwide diversity in kinship (Fox 1994; Murdock 1968), and this diversity, combined with available models of population history provided by lexical phylogenies, provides two useful regional cases to test hypotheses about the nature of change in kinship terms. In Austronesian, sibling terms in particular have received attention from a number of scholars (Blust 1980, 1994; Epling et al. 1973; Firth 1936; Fox 1995; Marshall 1983, 1984). Like Austronesian, Bantu is thought to be the result of a recent dispersal (ca. 5,000–2,000 kya) of peoples and farming technologies throughout sub-Saharan Africa, although this is a matter of some debate (Huffman 1982; Phillipson 1993; Vansina 1990). The kinship terminologies of the Bantu languages have received comparatively less attention (for some recent work on East Bantu, see Marck and Bostoen 2010; Marck et al. 2010). As with cousins and other subsets of kin terms, many studies have used typological schemes to classify patterns of sibling terms (Epling et al. 1973; Kronenfeld 1974; Marshall 1984; Murdock 1968; Nerlove and Romney 1967), sometimes regardless of historical relationship, often raising the ire of historical linguists (e.g., see replies by Blust and Chowning to Marshall 1984). Sequential, or stepwise, change processes in these structural patterns are often seen as explaining the current diversity across languages, such that appropriate models are those in which binary distinctions in meaning (e.g., male|female) were added or removed to a pattern (e.g., older sibling| younger sibling) to create the next pattern in the sequence (e.g., older brother|older sister|younger sibling). That is, these models are based on parsimony, and stepwise transformations are applied to the patterns themselves rather than the distinctions separately. However, by using statistical inference techniques to reconstruct the evolution of the semantic distinctions themselves, we need not rely on any particular typology of schemes to understand these processes. I note here also that the analyses concentrated on the distinctions in meaning: the investigation of *coevolution* in linguistic forms and meanings (the traditional purvey of historical linguistics) is a future study.

Here I show how Bayesian PCMs can specifically test the idea of sequential models of change in kin terms. A fuller account of the Austronesian study is in Jordan (2011): this case study examines the elaboration and reduction of the "same-sex|opposite-sex" distinction in Austronesian compared with Bantu. To do this, I derive evolutionary models of the transitions (gains and losses) between different meaning distinctions. Single-step changes are implicit or explicit in most lattice models (Epling et al. 1973; Hage 2001; Marshall 1984; see also Danziger, this volume). Thus the prediction is that an opposite-sex distinction (i.e., having one term for opposite-sex siblings and another for same-sex siblings) could evolve from a situation where the distinction was absent. Further, the opposite-sex term could then be elaborated by the sex of speaker, that is, it could be split into a term for "woman's brother" and "man's sister." However, how often languages then collapse this elaboration back into the single term, or skip straight from absence of the distinction to a two-term system, is unknown. Read (this volume) has qualms with a research framework that investigates the addition or removal of distinctions to terms or meanings in isolation; I view these qualms as a distinction between pattern and process and return to the point in the discussion. With respect to the case at hand, we can use PCMs to address this question quantitatively.

Sibling term data from Dziebel (2009) were coded for Austronesian and Bantu languages according to the meaning distinctions that were expressed in each language's terminology. I matched these languages to 208 Austronesian languages in the Gray et al. (2009) 400-language phylogenies and to 73 Bantu languages from the Atkinson et al. (2008) 96-language phylogenies. Languages were coded under the multistate scheme: 0 = language has no same/opposite distinction; 1 = language has a single term for opposite-sex sibling, used by both sexes; 2 = language has separate terms denoting the opposite-sex sibling for each sex (e.g., woman's brother, man's sister). Languages with intermediate distinctions (e.g., a term for "woman's brother" only) were not used in this analysis because models with four or five states failed to converge on consistent likelihood estimates; these will be explored in the future. The final set of taxa with appropriate data thus comprised 180 Austronesian and 68 Bantu languages.

To analyze the evolution of the opposite-sex distinctions I used the PCM Multistate implemented in the BayesTraits package (Pagel 1999b; Pagel et al. 2004). The approach is the same as in Case Study 1: given the comparative data and a set of trees, we model the evolution of the trait of interest among its three states (0, 1, 2) along the branches of a phylogeny. Rate parameters specifying the six possible transitions ($q01$, $q10$, $q12$, $q21$, $q02$, and $q20$) measure the instantaneous rates of change from one state to another and are used to define the probabilities of these changes, the character states at internal nodes on a tree, and the likelihood of the data (Pagel 1994, 1999b). Again, I used a "reversible-jump" procedure to reduce the complexities of the underlying model of evolution to tractable dimensions. To give directionality for the models, an estimation of ancestral states for relative-age and relative-sex distinctions in Austronesian was obtained from earlier analyses (Jordan 2011). There, a relative-age distinction was robustly inferred for PAN and PMP, but the relative-sex distinction was not. In Bantu, the three character states directly pertaining to the opposite-sex distinction were directly inferred and found to be ambiguous at the root: $p(0) = .36$, $p(1) = .32$, $p(2) = .32$. However, these suggest that Proto-Bantu was more likely to have some form of opposite-sex distinction than none, because $p(1,2) = .64$.

Models of Change in the Elaboration of Opposite-Sex Sibling Terms

The flow diagrams in Figure 3.3 show the summaries of the most popular models found by reversible-jump Bayesian MCMC for (a) Austronesian and (b) Bantu. These diagrams compare the relative transition rates of the top three models, which account for 70 percent of all models

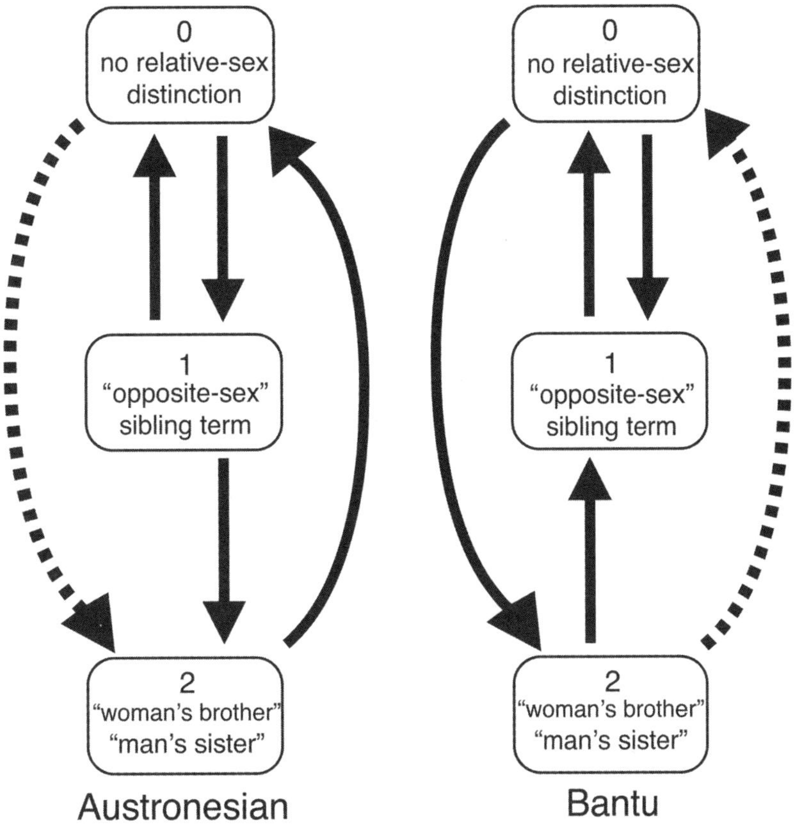

FIGURE 3.3. Models of evolution describing the elaboration of the "opposite-sex sibling" term in (a) Austronesian and (b) Bantu. Flow diagrams summarize transitions that accounted for over 70 percent of all models visited by the reversible-jump procedure. The absence of an arrow means that transition is set to 0. Dotted arrows mean that the transition includes zero values. Solid arrows are equivalent rates, i.e., those transitions happen with equal frequency.

found in both language families. The reversible-jump procedure integrates out the specific numerical parameters of the transition rates, giving models in terms of relative rate classes: rates are either zero (no arrow), infrequent (dotted arrows), or otherwise equivalent (solid arrows). This technique allows us to succinctly summarize a diverse and complex set of parameter estimates.

Figure 3.3a suggests that the most likely evolutionary pathway in Austronesian (starting at state 0: no opposite-sex distinction) was a gain of the single-term "opposite-sex sibling"; this was then elaborated into two terms—"woman's brother"/"man's sister"—in a number of linguistic subgroups. Jumps from the absence of the distinction to the two-term situation ($q02$) were rare and often zero; collapses of "woman's brother"/"man's sister" back to the single "opposite-sex sibling" term ($q21$) were all zero. The loss of the distinction overall occurred at a high rate (i.e., $q20$ and $q10$). When all models are considered, those where $q21$ is in the zero bin have a higher likelihood than those where it has a nonzero rate, providing support for the hypothesis that collapses of an elaborated term are rare.

A different dynamic exists in the Bantu languages. Again, the analysis shows that some transitions are set at zero, that some are infrequent, and that all others may be set equivalent. In common with Austronesian, the gains and losses of a single-term "opposite-sex sibling" from the state without the distinction are equivalent and frequent ($q01 = q10$). However, the dynamics governing the gain and loss of the two-term "woman's brother"/"man's sister" state are exactly opposite to those found in Austronesian. Here, once the two-term state is gained it rarely collapses to a complete absence (i.e., $q20$ is infrequent), but it seems to be gained from the no-distinction state frequently, and languages do not switch from a single term to a two-term system (i.e., $q12 = 0$). Given that the ancestral state reconstruction suggests that early Bantu speech communities had some form of opposite-sex distinction in place already, it may be that pressures external to the sibling terminologies (perhaps considerations of marking lineal group membership, for example) act to drive these dynamics (Marck et al. 2010).

These findings are preliminary, but for the purposes of this chapter the point is, I hope, conveyed that PCMs are useful methods with which to test ideas about evolutionary transformations in kinship terminologies. Further work will combine this approach with the rich theoretical and empirical resources of historical linguistics. Because convergence (independent innovation) of the same meanings with the same linguistic forms in unrelated (or in contact) languages is vastly improbable, we shall be able to use linguistic reconstructions to "fossilize" known forms in ancestral nodes. This will give directionality to language change, and we will be able to identify when independent gains of a distinction in different languages should be invoked as explanation or when there is a shift in meaning in some daughter languages but not others. One of the most promising applications will be in testing the implicational hierarchies of change in kin terms formulated by Hage (1998), including incorporating information on markedness to test that aspect of Hage's work. Meaning–meaning coevolution can be tested as well. For example, these analyses only trace the presence of a relative-age distinction in the sibling terminology as a whole, whereas a more fine-grained analysis will test the coevolution of an age distinction with sex of referent versus sex of speaker, as occurs in Austronesian. When combined with their evolving lexical forms, these coupled meaning–meaning changes will fully characterize the system, and from that point, testing how processes ramify through the entire terminological system will be possible (cf. Read, this volume). But even with these simple examples, it is possible to see how commonalities and divergences in kin term evolution across different language families can be discovered.

Conclusions

In this chapter, I have attempted to give an overview of phylogenetic comparative methods and their potential applications in cultural evolutionary work generally and, with the presentation of the two case studies, in the study of kinship more specifically. PCMs are tools for asking questions about evolutionary change, and many of the outstanding questions in the study of kinship and kinship terminology are, at basis, questions of evolution: Why are human kinship systems the way they are, that is, variable yet restricted? Do historical explanations suffice, or are there regularities of the human mind, and/or of the human niche, that make some forms of kinship-directed norms more adaptive? What regularities, if any, can be found in the transformations of kinship systems cross-culturally? Such questions are the everyday investigations of comparative biologists, and to the extent to which we can accept the linguistic relatedness of cultural groups as a model of their population history, anthropologists and linguists can co-opt PCMs to answer the above questions in a statistical framework that allows for quantitative testing of hypotheses.

Objections exist. By necessity, these approaches require complex cultural and linguistic features to be assigned to a small number of abstract categories. It is not my purpose here to deal with the broader issue of opposition to scientific hypothesis testing and cultural categorizing/reification in anthropology (Colleran and Mace 2011). The field of cultural phylogenetics has been relentlessly reviewed and subject to critique throughout its short history: both the tree-building enterprises and the use of PCMs have attracted skepticism. Some critiques have been methodological, or misunderstandings thereof, but in many respects these misgivings have been ameliorated by the adoption of (1) the newer, probabilistic Bayesian methods as used here; (2) simulation techniques to determine the conditions under which phylogenetic methods are inappropriate for cultural data, such as widespread borrowing and high rates of change (Atkinson et al. 2005; Greenhill et al. 2008); and (3) a plurality of techniques that do not require a branching tree structure and instead can represent noncongruent data, such as those produced by cultural contact, in a network (Gray et al. 2007). There remain two issues that force a serious critical engagement, and these are (1) the effects of cultural contact and "horizontal transmission" and (2) the multiplicity of trait lineages with different evolutionary histories within any one ethnolinguistic population (but see Mathews et al. 2011). Scholars using phylogenetic techniques are motivated to acknowledge, control for, and incorporate these concerns into their analyses, but to some extents we are simply limited by a lack of appropriate techniques: in evolutionary biology the analogous concerns are that of horizontal gene transfer at the root of the tree of life and the incongruence of individual gene trees with both each other and so-called species trees. These two topics constitute cutting-edge research in biology, attracting the serious attention of hundreds of scholars worldwide, but they are hard problems. It may be some time before we can deal with similar, and perhaps more complex, issues in human culture.

There are some ways in which we can progress our theoretical and methodological tool kit without waiting for the biologists: here I suggest a few. First and foremost, anthropologists and linguists need to engage in digital data-sharing. The genomic revolution only took off once a critical amount of genetic information was made easily available to all. New analytic methods were developed, and geneticists are beginning to use these data for a new theoretical understanding of biological inheritance. A similar revolution, both technical and theoretical, could happen for our understanding of human social structure if databases and repositories could collate and make accessible the ephemeral but vast "ethnographic record." Second, we need to revisit the mid-20th-century efforts of Murdock and associates, who began the task of searching for statistical regularities and associations in the ethnographic and comparative linguistic record. Many of these so-called regularities are used by scholars to draw inferences from reconstructed kin term systems to hypothetical ancestral social norms (Ehret 2008; Hage 1998, 2001). The area-sampling approach offered by (for instance) the Standard Cross-Cultural Sample acknowledged Galton's Problem, but the implementations were rudimentary, and new approaches offer more sophisticated control for historical relatedness (Mace and Pagel 1994).

Third, and more positively, there exists a grand opportunity for the separate phylogenetic and linguistic comparative methods to be brought together in the study of kinship terminology. PCMs offer a wide range of algorithms designed to explicitly test and infer correlated evolution, where two traits change together through time in a coupled fashion. The linguistic comparative method in historical linguistics deals with the implicit coupling of form (of cognate lexical items, for example) and meaning (the semantic fields over which those forms are distributed). How form drifts over meaning and vice versa are major questions in cognitive semantics that are beginning to be considered in an evolutionary framework (Jones 2010; Jordan and Dunn 2010). As well, the relatively restricted set of referents given by kin terms (as compared with, for example, the continuous spectra of colors), as well as the empirically rich and cross-linguistically comparable data that exist, make this a tractable place to start, and efforts toward this end are obvious in other chapters in this volume (McConvell, chapter 1, this volume; Read, this volume). Read's chapter in particular shows how the identification of a small number of kin concepts, and the ways that human societies have of combining those together, can produce the apparent diversity of terminologies seen cross-culturally. His case study of Polynesian kin terms shows that contextualizing terminology change against the background of linguistic phylogeny is an important part of the analytic process. Read is, however, skeptical that examining term or meaning changes in isolation hides "a culturally unidentified process" (this volume), because a change in a subset of terms will of necessity have knock-on effects through the full terminological system. On this point I agree, but I think that we are coming from different angles with (I hope) complementary approaches. The phylogenetic approach takes the pattern of current diversity and infers the evolutionary process that happened in the past to produce that diversity, given some knowledge of history and a model of change. What Read is doing is specifying different (and highly specific) versions of the model of change itself—something often underspecified in a phylogenetic comparative analysis due to lack of cultural information. An exciting next step would thus be the combination of Read's models for change with the apparatus of the comparative phylogenetic approach, across different language families and their kinship terminologies. There is a potential then to arbitrate various macrolevel hypotheses about kinship terminologies, as in Allen et al. (2008).

Finally, to return to evolution once more. The variation in how we classify kin by using language is nonrandom worldwide: not all combinations and distinctions exist. Our terms for kin do a specific job of work: They tell us who is kin and who is not, and they make equivalences and differentiations across a small number of consistent social and biological distinctions, such as age and sex, generation, lineage or descent group, and marriageability. Linguistically, kin terms can be understood from a perspective of semantic variation, but in contrast to other domains such as color and space, they are unique because of the onerous and vital tasks they mediate: communicating and coordinating kin-directed behaviors such as altruism, parental care and investment, grandparental care, sibling competition, marriage, and alliance. Jones (2003) postulates that the constrained set of considerations implicit in any kinship terms include group membership (e.g., male|female, in-group|out-group), genealogical distance (e.g., older|younger, levels of generation), and social rank—all candidates for a species-typical, flexibly generative psychology of kinship. Though these ideas are largely untested, theoretically they derive from evolutionarily relevant considerations such as kin selection, the likelihood of altruistic behavior, and aspects of our primate heritage. Kinship terms are thus the most directly Darwinian of all lexemes, and the study of how and why they evolve across languages can contribute much to our understanding of human social behavior.

Acknowledgments

Thanks go to Laura Fortunato for graciously allowing the reproduction of our joint work on postmarital residence, to German Dziebel for discussion and making his database available, and to Ger Reesink, Clare Bowern, Ian Keen, and Pat McConvell for their useful comments on the manuscript. I also thank my former colleagues in the Evolutionary Processes in Language and Culture Group at the Max Planck Institute for Psycholinguistics for their encouragement during the writing of this chapter.

References Cited

Allen, N. J., H. Callan, R. Dunbar, and W. James, eds. 2008. *Early Human Kinship: From Sex to Social Reproduction.* Oxford: Blackwell.

Atkinson, Q., A. Meade, C. Venditti, S. J. Greenhill, and M. Pagel. 2008. Languages Evolve in Punctuational Bursts. *Science* 319(5863):588.

Atkinson, Q., G. Nicholls, D. Welch, and R. Gray. 2005. From Words to Dates: Water into Wine, Mathemagic or Phylogenetic Inference? *Transactions of the Philological Society* 103(2):193–219.

Bellwood, P. B., and C. Renfrew, eds. 2002. *Examining the Farming/Language Dispersal Hypothesis.* Cambridge: McDonald Institute for Archaeological Research.

Ben Hamed, M. 2005. Neighbour-Nets Portray the Chinese Dialect Continuum and the Linguistic Legacy of China's Demic History. *Proceedings of the Royal Society of London B—Biological Sciences* 272(1567):1015–1022.

Blust, R. 1980. Early Austronesian Social Organization: The Evidence of Language. *Current Anthropology* 21(2):205–247.

Blust, R. 1994. Austronesian Sibling Terms and Culture History. In *Austronesian Terminologies: Continuity and Change.* A. Pawley and M. D. Ross, eds. Pp. 71–72. Canberra: ANU Press.

Boyd, R., M. Borgerhoff Mulder, W. H. Durham, and P. J. Richerson. 1997. Are Cultural Phylogenies Possible? In *Human by Nature: Between Biology and the Social Sciences.* P. Weingart, P. J. Richerson, S. D. Mitchell, and S. Maasen, eds. Pp. 355–386. Mahwah, NJ: Lawrence Erlbaum.

Chapais, B. 2008. *How Pair-Bonding Gave Birth to Human Society.* Cambridge: Harvard University Press.

Chowning, A. 1981. More on Early Austronesian Social-Organization. *Current Anthropology* 22(2):184–185.

Clackson, J. 2007. *Indo-European Linguistics: An Introduction.* Cambridge Textbooks in Linguistics. Cambridge: Cambridge University Press.

Colleran, H., and R. Mace. 2011. Contrasts and Conflicts in Anthropology and Archaeology: The Evolutionary/Interpretive Dichotomy in Human Behavioural Research. In *Darwinian Archaeologies: A Discussion.* E. Cochrane and A. Gardner, eds.

D'Andrade, R. 2000. The Sad Story of Anthropology 1950–1999. *Cross-Cultural Research* 34(3):219–232.

Delbruck, B. 1889. *Die indogermanischen verwandtschaftsnamen: Ein beitrag zur vergleichenden alterthumskunde.* Leipzig: S. Hirzel.

Diamond, J., and P. Bellwood. 2003. Farmers and Their Languages: The First Expansions. *Science* 300(5619):597–603.

Dunn, M. 2009. Contact and Phylogeny in Island Melanesia. *Lingua* 119(11):1664–1678.

Dunn, M., S. J. Greenhill, S. C. Levinson, and R. D. Gray. 2011. Evolved Structure of Language Shows Lineage-Specific Terms in Word-Order Universals. *Nature* 473:79–82.

Dyen, I., and D. Aberle. 1974. *Lexical Reconstruction: The Case of the Proto-Athapaskan Kinship System.* New York: Oxford University Press.

Dziebel, G. V. 2009. *Kinship Studies.* Electronic document, http://kinshipstudies.org, accessed July 4, 2009.

Ehret, C. 2008. Reconstructing Ancient Kinship in Africa. In *Early Human Kinship: From Sex to Social Reproduction.* N. J. Allen, H. Callan, R. Dunbar, and W. James, eds. Pp. 200–231. Oxford: Blackwell.

Epling, P., J. Kirk, and J. Boyd. 1973. Genetic Relations of Polynesian Sibling Terminologies. *American Anthropologist* 75: 1596–1625.

Evans, N., and S. C. Levinson. 2009. The Myth of Language Universals: Language Diversity and Its Importance for Cognitive Science. *Behavioral and Brain Sciences* 32(5):429–448.

Felsenstein, J. 1985. Phylogenies and the Comparative Method. *American Naturalist* 125(1):1–15.

Felsenstein, J. 2004. *Inferring Phylogenies.* Sunderland, MA: Sinauer Associates.

Firth, R. 1936. *We, the Tikopia.* London: Allen and Unwin.

Forster, P., and C. Renfrew. 2006. *Phylogenetic Methods and the Prehistory of Languages.* Cambridge: McDonald Institute for Archaeological Research.

Fortunato, L., and F. M. Jordan. 2010. Your Place or Mine? A Phylogenetic Comparative Analysis of Postmarital Residence in Indo-European and Austronesian Societies. *Philosophical Transactions of the Royal Society of London B—Biological Sciences* 365:3913–3922.

Fortunato, L., and R. Mace. 2009. Testing Functional Hypotheses about Cross-Cultural Variation: A Maximum-Likelihood Comparative Analysis of Indo-European Marriage Practices. In *Pattern and Process in Cultural Evolution.* S. J. Shennan, ed. Pp. 235–250. Berkeley: University of California Press.

Fox, J. J. 1994. Who's Who in Ego's Generation: Probing the Semantics of Malayo-Polynesian Kinship Classification. In *Austronesian Terminologies: Continuity and Change*. A. Pawley and M. Ross, eds. Pp. 127–140. Canberra: ANU Press.

Fox, J. J. 1995. Austronesian Societies and Their Transformations. In *The Austronesians: Historical and Comparative Perspectives*. P. Bellwood, J. J. Fox, and D. Tryon, eds. Pp. 229–240. Canberra: ANU E Press.

Friedrich, P. 1966. Proto-Indo-European Kinship. *Ethnology* 5(1):1–36.

Geertz, C. 1973. *The Interpretation of Cultures*. New York: Basic Books.

Godelier, M., T. Trautmann, and F. E. Tjon Sie Fat. 1998. Introduction. In *Transformations of Kinship*. M. Godelier, T. Trautmann, and F. E. Tjon Sie Fat, eds. Pp. 1–26. Washington, DC: Smithsonian.

Goody, J. 1959. Indo-European Society. *Past and Present* 16(1): 88–92.

Gray, R. D., and Q. D. Atkinson. 2003. Language-Tree Divergence Times Support the Anatolian Theory of Indo-European Origin. *Nature* 426(6965):435–439.

Gray, R. D., A. J. Drummond, and S. J. Greenhill. 2009. Language Phylogenies Reveal Expansion Pulses and Pauses in Pacific Settlement. *Science* 323(5913):479–483.

Gray, R. D., S. J. Greenhill, and R. M. Ross. 2007. The Pleasures and Perils of Darwinizing Culture (with Phylogenies). *Biological Theory* 2(4):360–375.

Greenhill, S. J., T. E. Currie, and R. D. Gray. 2008. Does Horizontal Transmission Invalidate Cultural Phylogenies? *Proceedings of the Royal Society B* 276(1665):2299–2306.

Hage, P. 1998. Was Proto-Oceanic Society Matrilineal? *Journal of the Polynesian Society* 107(4):365–379.

Hage, P. 2001. Marking Theory and Kinship Analysis: Cross-Cultural and Historical Applications. *Anthropological Theory* 1(2):197–211.

Hage, P., and J. Marck. 2003. Matrilineality and the Melanesian Origin of Polynesian Y Chromosomes. *Current Anthropology* 44:S121–S127.

Harvey, P. H., and M. D. Pagel. 1991. *The Comparative Method in Evolutionary Biology*. New York: Oxford University Press.

Holden, C., and R. Mace. 1997. Phylogenetic Analysis of the Evolution of Lactose Digestion in Adults. *Human Biology* 69(5):605–628.

Holden, C. J., and R. Mace. 2003. Spread of Cattle Led to the Loss of Matrilineal Descent in Africa: A Coevolutionary Analysis. *Proceedings of the Royal Society of London B—Biological Sciences* 270(1532):2425–2433.

Holden, C. J., and R. Mace. 2005. "The Cow Is the Enemy of Matriliny": Using Phylogenetic Methods to Investigate Cultural Diversity in Africa. In *The Evolution of Cultural Diversity: A Phylogenetic Approach*. R. Mace, C. J. Holden, and S. Shennan, eds. Pp. 217–234. London: UCL Press.

Holden, C. J., R. Sear, and R. Mace. 2003. Matriliny as Daughter-Biased Investment. *Evolution and Human Behavior* 24(2): 99–112.

Huelsenbeck, J. P., F. Ronquist, R. Nielsen, and J. P. Bollback. 2001. Bayesian Inference of Phylogeny and Its Impact on Evolutionary Biology. *Science* 294(5550):2310–2314.

Huffman, J. C. 1982. Archaeology and Ethnohistory of the African Iron Age. *Annual Review of Anthropology* 11:133–150.

Hurles, M. E., E. Matisoo-Smith, R. D. Gray, and D. Penny. 2003. Untangling Oceanic Settlement: The Edge of the Knowable. *Trends in Ecology and Evolution* 18(10):531–540.

Jones, D. 2003. The Generative Psychology of Kinship—Pt. 1. Cognitive Universals and Evolutionary Psychology. *Evolution and Human Behavior* 24(5):303–319.

Jones, D. 2010. Human Kinship, from Conceptual Structure to Grammar. *Behavioral and Brain Sciences* 33:367–416.

Jordan, F. M. 2011. A Phylogenetic Analysis of the Evolution of Austronesian Sibling Terminologies. *Human Biology* 83(2): 297–321.

Jordan, F. M., and T. E. Currie. N.d. Population Size Affects the Rate of Lexical Evolution.

Jordan, F. M., and M. Dunn. 2010. Kin Term Diversity Is the Result of Multilevel, Historical Processes. *Behavioral and Brain Sciences* 33:388.

Jordan, F. M., R. D. Gray, S. J. Greenhill, and R. Mace. 2009. Matrilocal Residence Is Ancestral in Austronesian Societies. *Proceedings of the Royal Society of London B—Biological Sciences* 276(1664):1957–1964.

Kayser, M., O. Lao, K. Saar, S. Brauer, X. Wang, P. Nürnberg, R. J. Trent, and M. Stoneking. 2008. Genome-Wide Analysis Indicates More Asian than Melanesian Ancestry of Polynesians. *American Journal of Human Genetics* 82(1):194–198.

Kirch, P. V., and R. C. Green. 2001. *Hawaiiki, Ancestral Polynesia: An Essay in Historical Reconstruction*. Cambridge: Cambridge University Press.

Kronenfeld, D. 1974. Sibling typology: beyond Nerlove and Romney. *American Ethnologist* 1(3):489–506.

Lemey, P., M. Salemi, and A. M. Vandamme, eds. 2009. *The Phylogenetic Handbook: A Practical Approach to Phylogenetic Analysis and Hypothesis Testing*. 2nd edition. Cambridge: Cambridge University Press.

Lewis, P. O. 2001. Phylogenetic Systematics Turns Over a New Leaf. *Trends in Ecology and Evolution* 16(1):30–37.

Li, W. H., and D. Graur. 1991. *Fundamentals of Molecular Evolution*. Sunderland, MA: Sinauer Associates.

Lipo, C. P., M. J. O'Brien, M. Collard, and S. Shennan, eds. 2006. *Mapping Our Ancestors: Phylogenetic Approaches in Anthropology and Prehistory*. New York: Aldine.

Mace, R. 2005. Introduction: A Phylogenetic Approach to the Evolution of Cultural Diversity. In *The Evolution of Cultural Diversity: A Phylogenetic Approach*. R. Mace, C. J. Holden, and S. Shennan, eds. Pp. 1–10. London: UCL Press.

Mace, R., C. J. Holden, and S. Shennan, eds. 2005. *The Evolution of Cultural Diversity: A Phylogenetic Approach*. London: Left Coast Press and Berg.

Mace, R., and F. M. Jordan. 2005. The Evolution of Human Sex-Ratio at Birth: A Bio-cultural Analysis. In *The Evolution of Cultural Diversity: A Phylogenetic Approach*. R. Mace,

C. J. Holden, and S. Shennan, eds. Pp. 207–216. London: UCL Press.

Mace, R., and M. Pagel. 1994. The Comparative Method in Anthropology. *Current Anthropology* 35(5):549–564.

Mallory, J. P., and D. Q. Adams. 2006. *The Oxford Introduction to Proto-Indo-European and the Proto-Indo-European World*. Oxford: Oxford University Press.

Marck, J., and K. Bostoen. 2010. Proto-Oceanic (Austronesian) and Proto–East Bantu (Niger-Congo) Residence, Descent, and Kin Terms ca. 1000 BC. In *Kinship, Language and Prehistory: Per Hage and the Renaissance in Kinship Studies*. D. Jones and B. Milicic, eds. Pp. 83–94. Salt Lake City: University of Utah Press.

Marck, J., P. Hage, K. Bostoen, and J.-G. K. Muzenga. 2010. Kin Terms in the East Bantu Proto Languages: Initial Findings. In *Kinship, Language and Prehistory: Per Hage and the Renaissance in Kinship Studies*. D. Jones and B. Milicic, eds. Pp. 79–82. Salt Lake City: University of Utah Press.

Marshall, M. 1983. *Siblingship in Oceania: Studies in the Meaning of Kin Relations*. ASAO Monograph. Lanham, MD: University Press of America.

Marshall, M. 1984. Structural Patterns of Sibling Classification in Island Oceania—Implications for Culture History. *Current Anthropology* 25(5):597–637.

Matthews, L. J., J. J. Tehrani, F. M. Jordan, M. Collard, and C. L. Nunn. 2011. Testing for Divergent Transmission Histories Among Cultural Characters: A Study Using Bayesian Phylogenetic Methods and Iranian Tribal Textile Data. *PLoS ONE* 6 (4): e14810.

McMahon, A., and R. McMahon. 2005. *Language Classification by Numbers*. Oxford: Oxford University Press.

Morgan, L. H. 1871. *Systems of Consanguinity and Affinity in the Human Family*. Contributions to Knowledge. Washington, DC: Smithsonian Institution.

Murdock, G. P. 1967. *Ethnographic Atlas*. Pittsburg: University of Pittsburg Press.

Murdock, G. P. 1968. Patterns of Sibling Terminology. *Ethnology* 7(1):1–24.

Nerlove, S., and A. K. Romney. 1967. Sibling Terminology and Cross-Sex Behavior. *American Anthropologist* 69:179–187.

Ord, T. J., and E. P. Martins. 2010. Evolution of Behavior: Phylogeny and the Origin of Present-Day Diversity. In *Evolutionary Behavioral Ecology*. D. F. Westneat and C. Fox, eds. Pp. 108–128. Oxford: Oxford University Press.

Pagel, M. 1994. Detecting Correlated Evolution on Phylogenies—A General Method for the Comparative Analysis of Discrete Characters. *Proceedings of the Royal Society of London B—Biological Sciences* 255(1342):37–45.

Pagel, M. 1997. Inferring Evolutionary Processes from Phylogenies. *Zoologica Scripta* 26(4):331–348.

Pagel, M. 1999a. Inferring the Historical Patterns of Biological Evolution. *Nature* 401(6756):877–884.

Pagel, M. 1999b. The Maximum Likelihood Approach to Reconstructing Ancestral Character States of Discrete Characters on Phylogenies. *Systematic Biology* 48(3):612–622.

Pagel, M., Q. D. Atkinson, and A. Meade. 2007. Frequency of Word-Use Predicts Rates of Lexical Evolution throughout Indo-European History. *Nature* 449(7163):717–720.

Pagel, M., and A. Meade. 2006. Bayesian Analysis of Correlated Evolution of Discrete Characters by Reversible-Jump Markov Chain Monte Carlo. *American Naturalist* 167:808–825.

Pagel, M., A. Meade, and D. Barker. 2004. Bayesian Estimation of Ancestral Character States on Phylogenies. *Systematic Biology* 53(5):673–684.

Pawley, A., M. Ross, and M. K. Osmond, eds. 2003. *The Lexicon of Proto Oceanic: The Culture and Environment of Ancestral Oceanic Society, 2: The Physical World*. Canberra: Pacific Linguistics.

Phillipson, D. W. 1993. *African Archaeology*. 2nd edition. Cambridge: Cambridge University Press.

Radcliffe-Brown, A. R. 1950. Introduction. In *African Systems of Kinship and Marriage*. A. R. Radcliffe-Brown and C. D. Forde, eds. Pp. 1–85. London: Oxford University Press.

Raftery, A. E. 1996. Hypothesis Testing and Model Selection. In *Markov Chain Monte Carlo in Practice*. W. R. Gilks, S. Richardson, and D. J. Spiegelhalter, eds. Pp. 163–188. London: Chapman and Hall.

Renfrew, C. 1992. Archaeology, Genetics and Linguistic Diversity. *Man* 27(3):445–478.

Richards, A. R. 1950. Some Types of Family Structure amongst the Central Bantu. In *African Systems of Kinship and Marriage*. A. R. Radcliffe-Brown and C. D. Forde, eds. Pp. 207–251. London: Oxford University Press.

Ronquist, F. 2004. Bayesian Inference of Character Evolution. *Trends in Ecology and Evolution* 19(9):475–481.

Schmidt, H. A., and A. von Haeseler. 2009. Phylogenetic Inference Using Maximum Likelihood Methods. In *The Phylogenetic Handbook: A Practical Approach to Phylogenetic Analysis and Hypothesis Testing*. 2nd edition. P. Lemey, M. Salemi, and A. M. Vandamme, eds. Pp. 181–209. Cambridge: Cambridge University Press.

Shennan, S. J., ed. 2009. *Pattern and Process in Cultural Evolution*. Berkeley: University of California Press.

Tylor, E. B. 1889. On a Method of Investigating the Development of Institutions Applied to Laws of Marriage and Descent. *Journal of the Royal Anthropological Institute* 18:245–386.

Vansina, J. 1990. *Paths in the Rainforests: Toward a History of Political Tradition in Equatorial Africa*. London: Currey.

Wilkins, J. F., and F. Marlowe. 2006. Sex-Biased Migration in Humans: What Should We Expect from Genetic Data. *BioEssays* 28(3):290–300.

Yang, Z. H., and B. Rannala. 1997. Bayesian Phylogenetic Inference Using DNA Sequences: A Markov Chain Monte Carlo Method. *Molecular Biology and Evolution* 14(7):717–724.

Zerjal, T., L. Beckman, G. Beckman, A. V. Mikelsaar, A. Krumina, V. Kucinskas, M. E. Hurles, and C. Tyler-Smith. 2001. Geographical, Linguistic, and Cultural Influences on Genetic Diversity: Y-Chromosomal Distribution in Northern European Populations. *Molecular Biology and Evolution* 18(6):1077–1087.

4

Reconstructing the Proto-Polynesian Terminology

Kinship Terminologies as Evolving Logical Structures

Dwight Read

In his 1991 Marett Memorial Lecture at Exeter College, Thomas Trautmann observed that even though "anthropology has something quite distinctive to say about human history," nonetheless "social anthropology has drawn back from active construction of schemata of human social development over very long duration," even though it has not rejected the "developmental concepts... that gave anthropology its start in life." He went on to observe that a culturally grounded theory of the evolution and development of kinship systems is a way to "synthesize the contents of ethnological time" and "is wanted... for in inventing the study of kinship, anthropology invented itself" (1992:392–393). In this chapter, kinship terminologies will be taken as an appropriate domain for exploring the developmental aspect of kinship systems identified by Trautmann. The focus will be on kinship terminologies, as these are integral to what we mean by kinship due to the fact that "kinship terminologies are a system of cultural ideas that formalize an 'intuition' of kinship" (M. Leaf, e-mail communication, 2010). By *kinship*, it should be noted, is not meant a single, specific aspect of a human society but, rather, the range of concepts, ideas, and behavior that, to one degree or another, reflect and relate to the social relations individuals have with one another. As culture-bearers, we have an intuitive understanding of kinship, and "this intuition is not just the recognition of one kind of fact, but rather the recognition of complex ongoing situations that include the facts of reproduction and associated emotional bonding and dependencies, but are not limited to them" (Leaf, e-mail communication, 2010).

I will consider the developmental aspect of kinship systems by focusing on a single region in which we can identify time-based structural changes in the formal aspects of kinship terminologies for the populations in that region. Terminologies from the Polynesian region will be used for this purpose since the broad pattern of prehistoric populations moving into this region, as well as the genetic relations among the Polynesian languages, have already been worked out from archaeological, genetic, and linguistic data. Methodologically, I will first delineate the formal structure of Polynesian kinship terminologies in the ethnographic present. Then I will identify an implied, temporal pattern of structural changes from the ethnographic past that accounts for the differences in present-day terminology structures. Next, following a suggestion by Ilia Peiros, I will construct a *kinship tree* of genetic relations among these kinship terminologies in analogy with a language tree.[1] To do this, I will use methods analogous to those employed in historical linguistics for developing a language tree depicting genetic relations among related languages. I can then compare the kinship tree with a language tree for the same populations so as to assess whether the cultural systems of language and kinship change in parallel.[2] If not, then our understanding of kinship terminology structure cannot simply be subsumed under the study of linguistic structures (*pace* Jones 2010). I will conclude with a comparison of changes in the structural and linguistic aspects of the same terminologies so as to enrich our understanding of the factors influencing the development of kinship terminologies through time. This will increase our understanding of the time-based development of kinship systems.

The research reported in this chapter is not the first to consider changes in the structure of kinship terminologies in the Polynesian region. Murdock (1968, 1970) included the Polynesian region in his study of the relationship among patterns for the classification of sibling terms in kinship terminologies and language boundaries. Epling et al. (1973) developed a classification of Polynesian sibling kin terms based on binary dimensions such as sex, parity, and relative age and worked out an evolutionary sequence for changes in the sibling terms, assuming that changes take place one character state at a time. For example, a terminology that currently has a relative age difference for same-sex siblings could drop the age difference in one evolutionary step regardless of the character states for the other dimensions for the kin terms. Marshall (1984) expanded the database to include what he referred to as "Oceanic Island" populations, mainly Melanesian, Micronesian, and Polynesian populations. Like Epling et al. (1973), he assumed that terminologies are a sum of independent traits, with evolutionary change constrained only by a single change in character state at each step in the evolutionary sequence. However, terminologies are systems of interconnected, not independent, kin terms, and both the character states for the terminology and change in those states are constrained by the generative logic underlying the structure of the kinship terminology. Thus to identify the temporal pattern for structural changes in Polynesian terminologies we must begin by making evident their generative logic and the differences therein.

Generative Logic of Terminologies

I will identify the generative logic of Polynesian terminologies by viewing a terminology as a system of conceptually interconnected kinship terms (Leaf and Read 2012; Read 1984, 2001a, 2007). The system of interconnections constitutes a *kin term space* whose form is determined by the structural logic embedded within a terminology. A kin term space and the more familiar *genealogical space* jointly form a *kinship space* of kin relations upon which a kinship system is based. As Robert Parkin has noted, when kin terms are viewed as defining categories, it follows that "category and genealogy represent different forms of knowledge about kinship.... [I]f there is any universal here... all speech communities use both category and genealogy... in explaining kinship to themselves and to others, depending on the context" (2009:164–165; emphasis added; see also Parkin 1996; Read 2001b).

Formally, we can display the structure of a terminology in the kinship space through a kin term map based on the interconnections among the kin terms using natural language representations (Kronenfeld 2006b). These representations can be expressed directly using algebraic formalism; thus the algebraic formalism derives from the cultural knowledge embedded in the terminology rather than being imposed. This differs from unconstrained formalisms such as componential analysis and rewrite rule analysis that impose formalisms over an assumed kinship terminology structure and so only provide descriptive accounts (Keen 1985; Leaf and Read 2012; Read 2000, 2001a). In this way, the algebra formalism makes it possible to deconstruct the terminology structure using cultural knowledge embedded in the terminology in order to determine whether, and in what way, the structure has an underlying generative logic. If so, we can then identify the primary kinship concepts from which we may generate the terminology structure through the computations that are part of the generative logic embedded in that structure.

The cultural knowledge is made evident through the kin term computations invoked when two persons compute their kin relation to each other by the kin terms they use to refer to a third person. For example, consider three native English speakers. If the first of these three persons (properly) refers to the third person by the kin term *uncle* and that person (properly) refers to the second person by the kin term *child*, then the first person will recognize that he or she would (properly) use the kin term *cousin* for the second person; that is, we have, as part of cultural knowledge, the kinship term computation "child of uncle is cousin." This cultural knowledge is formally embedded in a kinship terminology through the interconnections among the kin terms in the kin term space and is not derived from the properties of a genealogical space. A genealogical space, by itself, does not serve as a singular foundation for uncovering the structural logic of a kinship terminology. Instead, we must consider the conceptual foundations for genealogy in what I will refer to as a family space.

Family Space

The two forms of kinship knowledge identified by Parkin reflect the fact that kinship relations are conceptualized in two different ways using the cultural concepts of parenthood, childhood, and siblinghood (possibly with sex marking) derived from (but not necessarily equivalent to) the facts of reproduction, along with the cultural concepts of husband and wife derived from marriage as a cultural institution. These concepts are logically prior to kinship relation concepts (Keen 1985) and make up what we can refer to as a *family space* (see Figure 4.1). Within the

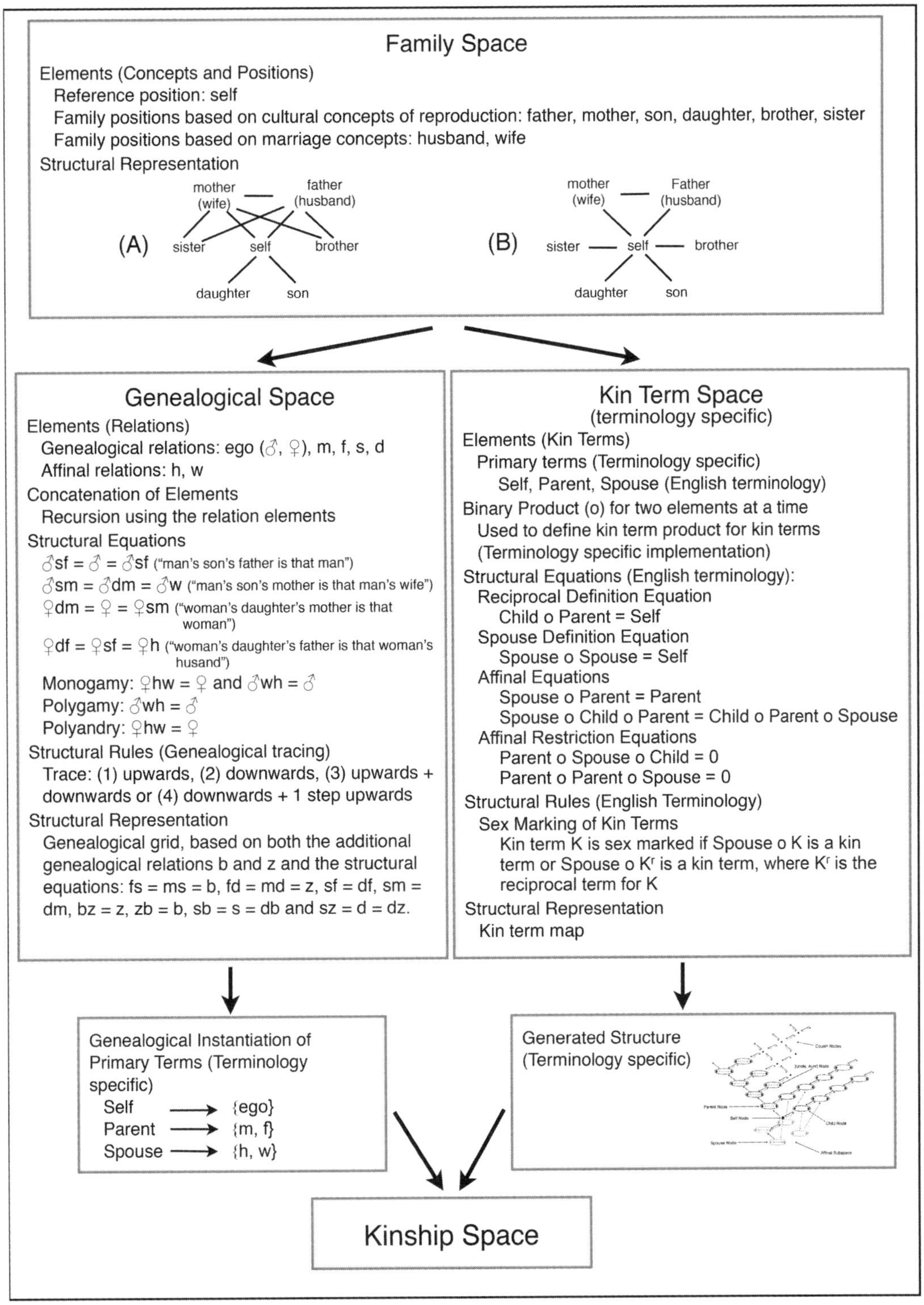

FIGURE 4.1. Relationship of family space to genealogical space and kin term space and the relationship of these two spaces to kinship space. The family space consists of positions determined by the cultural concepts of father, mother, son, daughter, brother, and sister grounded in biological reproduction and the concepts of wife and husband grounded in the cultural construct of marriage. Two ways, labeled (A) and (B), that the brother and sister positions are embedded in the family space are shown (lines indicate parent/child or spouse relations). The genealogical space is based on the interpretation of the concepts of the family space as genealogical relations and is constructed through recursive use of the parent/child relations. The kin term space is based on the interpretation of the concepts of the family space as primary kin terms over which a kin term product is culturally defined and through which new terminological positions are constructed, subject to structural equations that determine the form of a particular terminology structure. The structure of the kinship terminology, as elicited from culture-bearers (Leaf 2006; Leaf and Read 2012), can be expressed using a kin term map (see Figures 4.3–4.5). The genealogical space and the kin term space jointly form the kinship space through (1) cultural instantiation of the primary kin terms as categories of genealogical relations and (2) instantiation of all other kin terms through products of the categories of genealogical relations corresponding to the representation of a kin term as a product of primary kin terms. The kinship space encompasses the family space, the genealogical space, and the kin term space as an integrated system that provides the conceptual basis for the culturally defined kin relations upon which kinship in human societies is based.

family space, the concept of self acts as a "center point" for structurally defining parent/child, wife/husband, brother/brother, sister/sister, and brother/sister as pairs of reciprocal, relational concepts. The concepts of brother and sister, though, unlike the other concepts, are structurally incorporated in the family space in one way in some societies and in a different way in other societies. This difference will be critical, as we will see below, for making a formal distinction between Lewis Henry Morgan's categories of descriptive and classificatory terminologies, with the latter characterizing Polynesian terminologies.

The first way in which the brother and sister concepts are embedded in the family space—and a way familiar to English speakers—is with the brother and sister positions being linked directly to the mother and father positions by the son and daughter concepts (see Figure 4.1A, Family Space), thus making brother and sister into second-order concepts in contrast to the first-order mother and father concepts (Keen 1985).[3] Under this embedding, brother and sister are indirectly linked to self through brother conceptualized as son of mother (or father) of self and sister conceptualized as daughter of mother (or father) of self.

In the second embedding, brother and sister are concepts directly linked to self (see Figure 4.1B, Family Space). That ego and alter are siblings under this embedding implies that they share the usage of the concept of "parent," or more precisely, ego conceptualizes the genealogical parent of alter as "parent" and alter conceptualizes the genealogical parent of ego as "parent" even if a genealogical parent of ego is not the same person as a genealogical parent of alter. For example, the Kaluli of New Guinea, with this embedding of brother and sister concepts in the family space, say, "I call so-and-so brother (*nao*) because my father called his father brother" (Schieffelin 1976:53). For the Kaluli, the male speaker calls both his father and his father's brother by the same term, *nawa* (father), hence he refers both to the father of his patrilateral parallel cousin—a (genealogical) cousin he refers to as *nao* (brother)—and to his father by the term *nawa* even though the two fathers are not the same person. Consequently, in contrast to the sequence from *self* to *father* to *brother* for the first embedding, which makes *brother* a second-order term, this sequence of conceptual relations from *self* to *brother* to *father* makes *brother* a first-order term (*pace* Keen 1985; Radcliffe-Brown 1950).[4] Ethnographically, we have extensive evidence for brother and sister concepts being embedded in this second way in the family space in Polynesian societies through the primacy of the brother/sister relationship (see ethnographic reports in Marshall 1983).[5]

Genealogical Space

Two spaces can be constructed from the relations making up the family space (see the middle part of Figure 4.1), each involving a different computational logic. The first is the *genealogical space* of genealogical pathways, or lines of ascent and descent, using the mother/father (or parent) and son/daughter (or child) positions, each interpreted as defining a genealogical relation.[6] For example, a genealogical mother relation is defined between ego and person A when A is in the mother position with respect to ego in the instantiation of the family space that includes ego. We may denote this genealogical pathway by the statement "A is ego's (genealogical) mother."

A genealogical pathway, P, formed in this manner from ego to person A can be extended recursively by taking A, the output of the genealogical pathway from ego, as the new input for forming a genealogical pathway and then forming a genealogical pathway from A to a person, B, linked to A through a position in the family space for A. For example, when A is ego's mother and B is A's father, we can form the genealogical pathway from ego to B by first going from ego to A and then from A to B. We denote this pathway, in this example, by the statement "B is ego's mother's father." The extension of genealogical pathways through recursion can also be viewed as a *concatenation* of genealogical pathways. From the time of W.H.R. Rivers, the pathways in genealogical space have been used to etically define kin terms from a kinship terminology by linking a genealogical pathway from one person to a second person with the kin term that would be used by the first person to refer to the second person and then grouping together all those genealogical pathways linked with the same kin term as the definition of that kin term. However, it is not always possible to make kin term definitions in this manner. Consider the terminology used by the !Kung San, a hunter-gatherer group in the northwestern part of Botswana. In their terminology, the kin term reference by ego for a person A outside of the scope of the family relations depends on the genealogical relation of A to the name-giver for ego (Marshall 1976). This dependency of the kin term relation on the name-giver relation highlights the problem with trying to reduce kinship knowledge to properties expressed using genealogical relations. It is not with genealogical relations and the concatenation of genealogical relations where we find the cultural kinship knowledge embedded in a kinship terminology but, rather, with computations using kin terms, making up a kin term space (see the middle right side of Figure 4.1).

Kin Term Space

The *kin term space* is determined by the structural logic underlying the computations that users of a terminology make with kin terms without necessary reference to genealogy. Consider my previous example for the relations among the English kin terms *uncle*, *child*, and *cousin* expressed using the product "child of uncle is cousin." The product for the kin terms *child* and *uncle* that results in the kin term *cousin* expresses the cultural knowledge English-speaking users have of their kinship terminology system as a system of interconnected concepts.

The ethnographic literature is replete with ethnographic examples showing how kin term relations are computed in this manner using products of kin terms (see references in Read 2007). For example, Levinson makes the computation explicit for Rossel Island in Papua New Guinea:

> Kinship reckoning on Rossel does not rely on knowledge of kin-type strings. . . . What is essential in order to apply a kin term to an individual X, is to know how someone else, of a determinate kinship type to oneself, refers to X. From that knowledge alone, a correct appellation can be deduced. For example, suppose someone I call *a tîdê* "sister" calls X *a tp:ee* "my child," then I can call X *a chênê* "my nephew," without having the faintest idea of my genealogical connection to X. (2002:18)

Dousset observes, for Aboriginal Australia, that this kind of reckoning by one person enables kin relations to all community members to be worked out: "When two foreigners can both trace their classificatory relationships towards a third person, the remaining relationships among all other members of the community can be deduced from this set" (2005:22).[7]

I will refer to culturally salient computations made in this manner as *kin term products* (first defined in Read 1984).[8] Kin term products provide a means through which new kin term concepts are generated, such as the English kin term concept "cousin," generated (as noted above) by the kin term product of the kin term concepts "child"

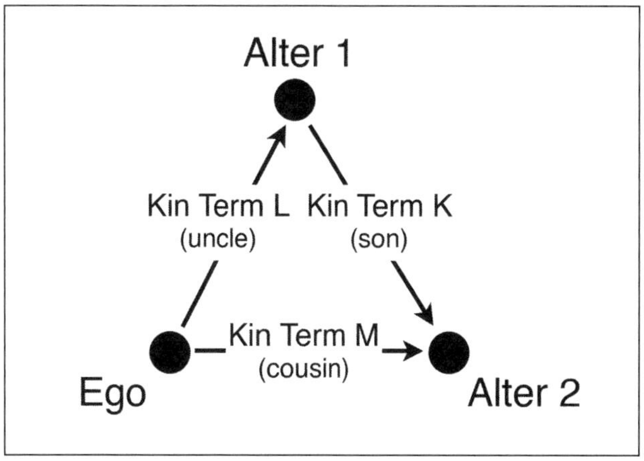

FIGURE 4.2. Graphical illustration of a kin term product. The product of the kin terms K (e.g., English *son*) and L (e.g., English *uncle*) is the kin term ego properly uses for alter 2 (in this case, *cousin*, for English speakers). Modified from Read and Behrens 1990.

and "uncle" in the English kinship terminology: "child of uncle is cousin." We can define formally a kin term product for the kin terms in a kinship terminology as follows: If ego (properly) refers to alter 1 by the kin term L and alter 1 (properly) refers to alter 2 by the kin term K, then the kin term M used (properly) by ego to refer to alter 2 is the *kin term product* of K and L, written "K of L is M" or, more formally, K o L = M, where o stands for the binary product that connects K and L to M. (By a *binary product* over a set of elements [e.g., the terms in a kinship terminology] is meant a computation acting on two elements [e.g., two kin terms] at a time from that set of elements and yielding an element in that set of elements as the outcome of the computation. For example, multiplication is a binary product over the natural numbers since for any two natural numbers, we may compute another natural number by forming the multiplicative product of the two natural numbers.) The definition for *kin term product* expresses the way people on the ground compute kin relations (Kronenfeld 2006a) without reference to, and even without knowledge of, the genealogical relations involved.

The definition can be graphically represented as in Figure 4.2.[9] In Figure 4.2, ego refers to alter 1 by the kin term L (e.g., *uncle* for users of the American kinship terminology), alter 1 refers to alter 2 by the kin term K (e.g., *child*), and ego refers to alter 2 by the kin term M (e.g., *cousin*), so, as a product of kin terms, K o L = M (e.g., *child* of *uncle* = *cousin*). Whereas the genealogical space has to do with relations among persons determined through recursively defined computations based on the positions making up the family space, the kin term space has to do with relations among kin terms derived from the family space and based on kin term products. I have made explicit the cultural knowledge and systematicity underlying the kin term products: "The kin term product... depends upon informant knowledge for its calculation. Kin term products are thus culturally specific and convey cultural concepts about how the kinship relations identified by the terms in the terminology may form a system of relationships" (2001b:95).

Kinship Space

The *kinship space* for the users of a kinship terminology is formed by integrating together the kin term space and the genealogical space through the genealogical definitions of kin terms (bottom part of Figure 4.1) derived from the logic of the kin term space (for details on deducing the genealogical definition of kin terms from the kin term space, see Bennardo and Read 2005, 2007; Leaf and Read 2012; Read 2001a). Within the kinship space, relationships between pairs of individuals can be expressed, for English speakers, either by a kin term expression such as "He is my uncle" or by a genealogical pathway such as "He is my father's brother," which makes explicit the distinction between category and genealogy referred to by Parkin.

The kinship space, then, consists of both a conceptual system based on the logic and properties of a genealogical space generated through genealogical tracing and a conceptual system having to do with the logic and properties of a kin term space generated through computations with kin terms using the kin term product. Neither of these (left and right sides of the middle portion of Figure 4.1) can be reduced to, or derived from, the other.

Terminology Structure and Kin Term Maps

Now consider the terminology structure expressed by a kin term map constructed using kin term products. In the kin term map, each kin term is a node, and nodes are connected in accordance with kin term products as follows. We begin the kin term map with a node labeled self that acts as the "center" of the kinship terminology structure. Self is a concept common across all terminologies (either in neutral or in sex-marked form), and its instantiation is the person taken as the reference person—for example, ego for the purposes of abstracted genealogical tracing. Next, primary kin terms are identified for the relations within the family space, such as the kin terms *parent*, *child*, and *spouse* in English. Beginning with self, products are formed with each primary kin term.[10] Each time a kin term is identified through a kin term product, such as "parent of self is parent" in English, a node labeled with the resulting kin term (in this case, *parent*) is entered in the kin term map. Also entered in the map is an arrow (with a distinctive arrow for each primary kin term) pointing from the initial kin term to the kin term resulting from the kin term product of the initial term with the primary kin term represented by the arrow. To continue the "parent of self" example, an arrow specific to the *parent* kin term will point from the self node to the parent node, indicating that "parent of self is parent." From the parent node the same kind of arrow points to the grandparent node, indicating that "parent of parent is grandparent."

This procedure is continued until one of four kinds of conceptual boundaries (contra Good 1996: n. 18) is reached: (1) kin term products continue indefinitely in a fixed pattern (e.g., *parent, grandparent, great-grandparent*, etc. in English), (2) the product does not give rise to a kin term (e.g., there is no kin term for parent of parent-in-law in English), (3) the product maps back to a kin term already in the structure (e.g., child of cousin is *cousin* in English), or (4) the product maps around to make the structure circular (e.g., "father" of ["father" of "father"] is "son" of "son" in the Australian Kariera terminology [Radcliffe-Brown 1913]). Figure 4.3 shows a kin term map for the American kinship terminology, and Figure 4.4 shows a contrasting kin term map for the Shipibo terminology (the Shipibo are a horticultural group in the eastern part of Peru). Just from the kin term maps alone, structural differences in the kinship terminologies are immediately apparent.

Kin Term Map for the *Proto-Polynesian Terminology

Both the American and the Shipibo terminologies are from societies with the family space as shown in Figure 4.1A, and both societies have what Morgan referred to as descriptive terminologies. Descriptive terminologies are those in which the sibling concepts are computed from the parent and child concepts; namely, in the English/American terminology, brother is "son of parent" and sister is "daughter of parent." Contrasting with descriptive terminologies are classificatory terminologies in which there are no collateral distinctions in the terminology, and so a kin term product such as "son of grandfather" would be

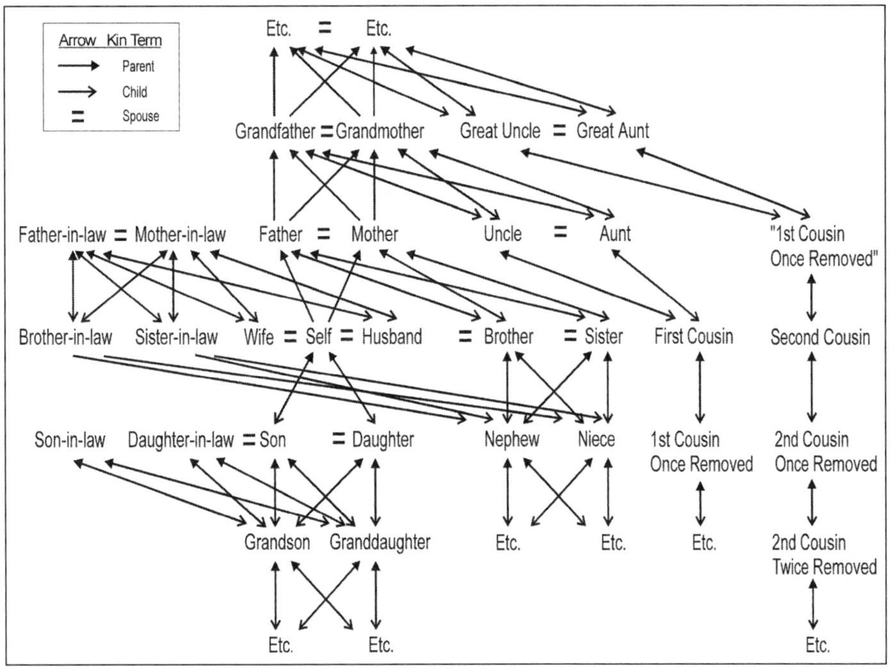

FIGURE 4.3. Kin term map for American kinship terminology based on the generating kin terms *parent*, *child*, and *spouse*.

father and not *uncle*, for example, if the American/English terminology were a classificatory terminology. Classificatory terminologies such as Polynesian terminologies correspond to the second family space (see Figure 4.1B) in which "sibling" is also a core concept (in addition to parent and reciprocally child, each possibly sex marked) connected directly to "self," thus the terminology has irreducible, first-order sibling terms. This implies that sibling concepts are primary kin terms (along with parent terms) from which other kin terms are constructed (Bennardo and Read 2005, 2007; Leaf and Read 2012; Read 2007; Read and Behrens 1990).

The distinction I am making here is between terminologies such as the American and Shipibo terminologies in which parent terms are primary and sibling terms are derivative and classificatory terminologies in which sibling terms are primary in addition to parent terms. Accordingly, we expect that the kin term map for a classificatory terminology such as the reconstructed Proto-Polynesian (*PPN) terminology will have a substantially different topology, or *blauplan*, than is the case for a descriptive terminology.

The linguistically reconstructed *PPN classificatory terminology is given in Table 4.1, and its kin term map is shown in Figure 4.5. As expected, the structure of this kin term map has a completely different *blauplan* than the kin

TABLE 4.1. Proto-Polynesian kin terms.

Term	Gloss
**tupuna*	'grandparent'
**tama(na)*	'father', 'brother of father'
**tina(na)*	'mother', 'sister of mother'
**tuʔa-tina*	'brother of mother'
**masaki-tanga*	'sister of father'
**tuaka(na)*	'elder same-sex sibling'
**tahina*	'younger same-sex sibling'
**tua-ŋaʔane*	♀ 'brother'
**tua-fafine*	♂ 'sister'
**tama*	♀ 'son'
***fosa*	♂ 'son'
**tama-ʔa-fine*	♀ 'daughter'
**ʔo-fafine*	♂ 'daughter'
***faka-fotu*	♀ 'child of brother'
**ʔilamutu*	♂ 'child of sister'
**makupuna*	'grandchild'

Note: Sex symbols indicate the sex of the speaker for a kin term. * = reconstructed Proto-Polynesian linguistic form; ** = uncertain if the linguistic form is Proto-Polynesian (Marck 1996a).
Source: Data from Hage and Marck 2001; Marck 1996a (affinal terms not included).

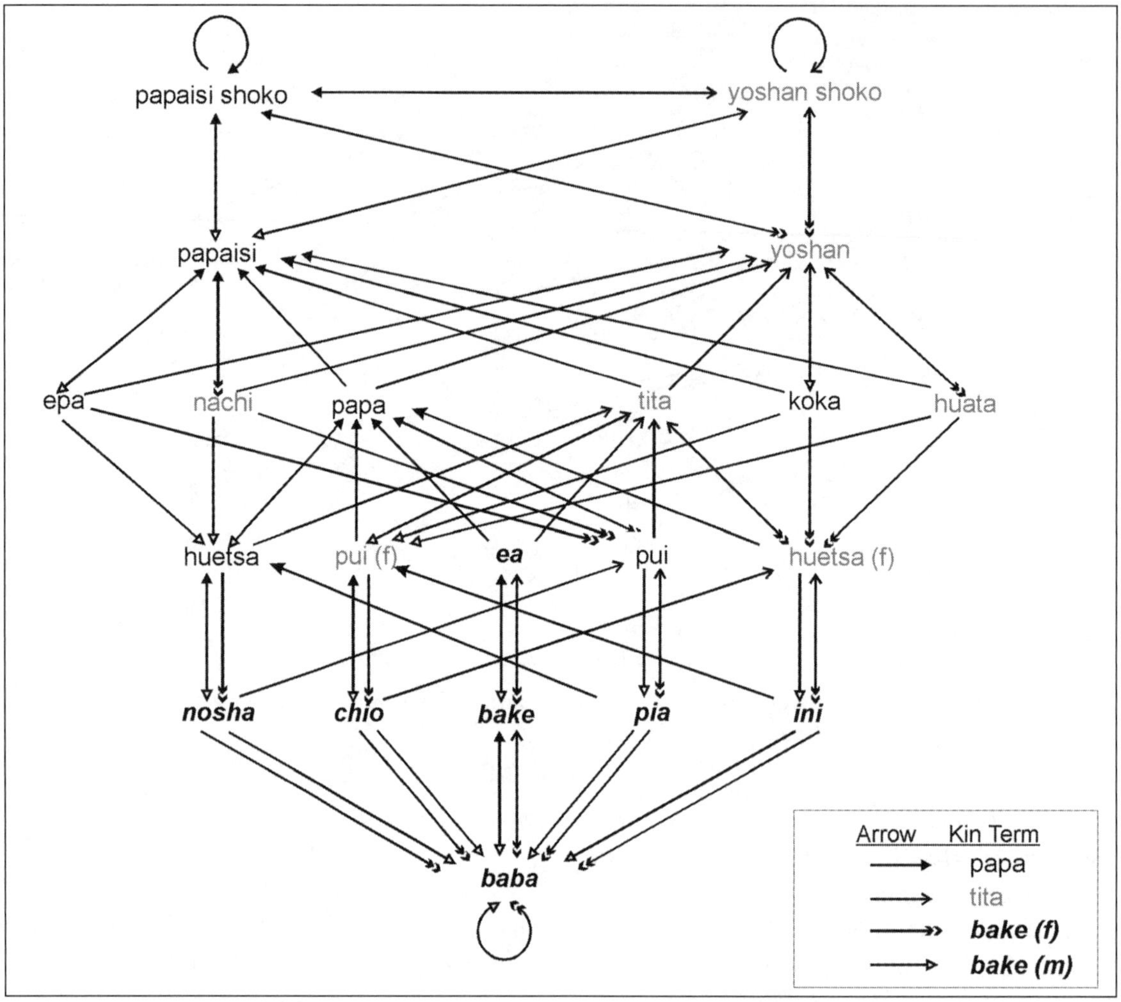

FIGURE 4.4. Kin term map for Shipibo kinship terminology based on the generating kin terms *papa* (father), *tita* (mother), and *bake* (child), with implicit sex marking for *bake* (f; daughter) and *bake* (m; son). The kin terms are *papaisi shoko* (great-grandfather), *yosan shoko* (great-grandmother), *papaisi* (grandfather), *yoshan* (grandmother), *epa* (paternal uncle), *nachi* (paternal aunt), *papa* (father), *tita* (mother), *koka* (maternal uncle), *huata* (maternal aunt), *huetsa* (brother or male paternal cousin [ms]), *pui* (f; brother or male maternal cousin [ws]), *ea* (self), *pui* (sister or female paternal cousin [ms]), *huetsa* (f; sister or female maternal cousin [ws]), *nosha* (child of brother [ms]), *chio* (child of brother [ws]), *pia* (child of sister [ms]), *ini* (child of sister [ws]), and *baba* (grandchild). Terms in black are male-marked terms, terms in gray are female-marked terms, and terms in bold italic are neutral terms.

term maps for the American and Shipibo terminologies. The division of the kin term map into a set of male-marked (and neutral) kin terms and a set of female-marked (and neutral) kin terms connected via the male self and the female self nodes is characteristic of classificatory terminologies (see Bennardo and Read 2005, 2007; Read 2007). Elsewhere, I have demonstrated that genealogically framed classificatory equations such as f = fb ≠ mb and m = mz ≠ fz, the equations used to define bifurcate merging (classificatory) terminologies, derive logically from having a sibling term as one of the primary, generating terms, along with a general procedure for the generation of a kinship terminology from its generating terms and structural equations (for details, see Bennardo and Read 2005, 2007; Leaf and Read 2012; Read 2007; Read and Behrens 1990). Due to the importance of having a sibling generating term (hereafter, *sibling generator*) as one of the generating terms for a classificatory terminology, the focus will now be on structural properties that are the consequence of having a sibling generator in a kin term map.

Elsewhere I have detailed the general procedure for generating a kinship terminology structure from the generating terms for a kinship terminology (in Bennardo and

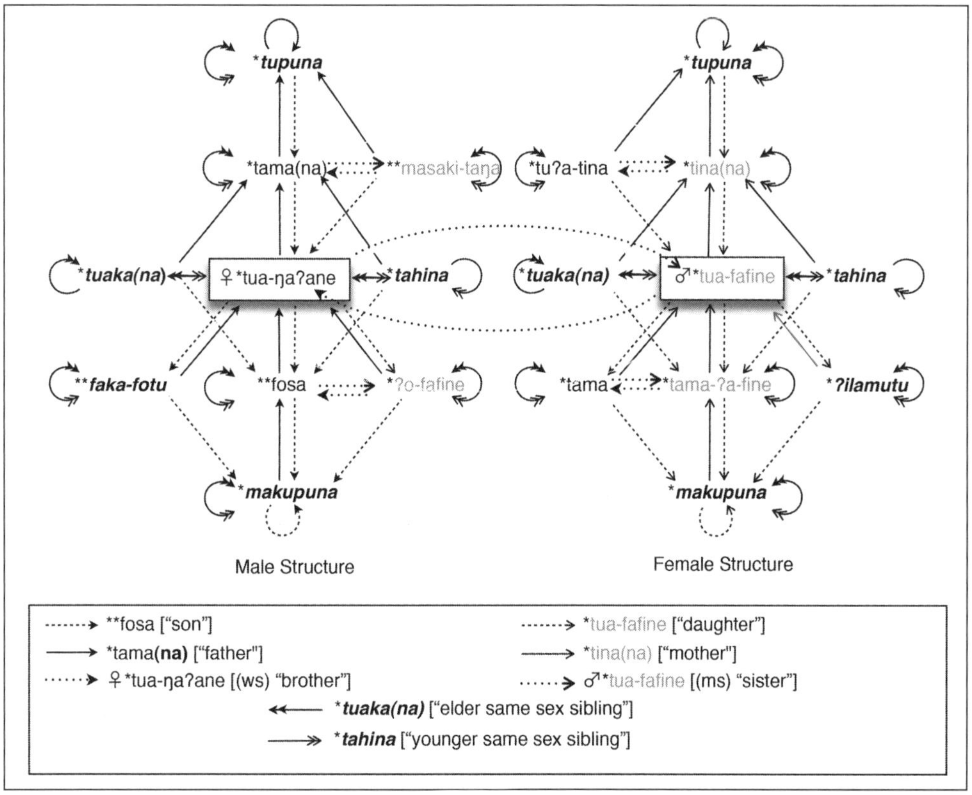

FIGURE 4.5. Kin term map for *Proto-Polynesian kinship terminology. There is a hidden male self position beneath the box in the male structure and a hidden female self position beneath the box in the female structure. Except for the two long, curved, dotted arrows in the center of the figure, all arrows pointing to or originating at the center position for each of the two structures are with respect to the male self and the female self position. For example, in the male structure, the horizontal, double-headed arrow pointing to *tahina* originates at the male self position (i.e., **tahina* of male self = **tahina*), and the horizontal, double-headed arrow originating at **tahina* points to male self (i.e., **tuaka[na]* of **tahina* is male self). Terms in boxes show the connection between the male structure and the female structure via the male self becoming **tua-ŋaʔane* (brother) with respect to the female self position and the female self becoming **tua-fafine* (sister) with respect to the male self position.

Read 2005, 2007; Leaf and Read 2012; Read 2007); for our purposes here, only the first part of the procedure is needed. The generation of a terminology structure begins by identifying the term (or terms) that generates a structure of ascending kin terms of a single sex (including neutral terms) such as *self, parent, grandparent,* and so on in the American kinship terminology. For the consanguineal terms in the *PPN terminology, the generating terms for the structure of ascending male (including neutral) terms are "male self," **tama(na)* (father), and **tuaka(na)* (elder same-sex sibling). Note the inclusion of **tuaka(na)* as an ascending term since a person referred to as **tuaka(na)* by ego is reproductively prior to ego, hence **tuaka(na)* identifies an ascending position with respect to the male self. Its reciprocal, **tahina*, will be a descending term.

From the term **tama(na)*, we generate the ascending sequence "male self," **tama(na)* (father), and **tupuna* (grandparent) = **tama(na)* of **tama(na)*, which is structurally analogous to the English sequence *self, parent,* and *grandparent* = "parent of parent" and so on, except that further extension of the sequence for the Proto-Polynesian terminology simply repeats the term **tupuna* due to the kin term product **tama(na)* of **tupuna* is **tupuna*. The ascending term **tuaka(na)* (elder same-sex sibling) only generates the sequence male self and **tuaka(na)* due to the kin term product **tuaka(na)* of **tuaka(na)* is **tuaka(na)*. Altogether, the ascending structure of male terms for the kin term map of male terms for the *PPN (see the left side of Figure 4.5) is generated by **tama(na)* (father) and **tuaka(na)* (elder same-sex sibling), along with the following structural equations:

(1) **tama(na)* of **tuaka(na)* = **tama(na)* ("father" of "elder same-sex sibling" is "father")

(2) *tuaka(na) of *tuaka(na) = *tuaka(na) (“elder same-sex sibling” of “elder same-sex sibling” is “elder same-sex sibling”)
(3) *tama(na) of *tama(na) of *tama(na) = *tama(na) of *tama(na) (“father” of “father” of “father” is “father” of “father”)

Note that equation (1) expresses the second way for embedding a sibling term in the family space discussed above (see Figure 4.1B), and equation (2) structurally defines *tuaka(na)* to have the sibling term property of being self-reflexive. Together, these two equations structurally define *tama(na)* to be a sibling term. Equation (3) provides an upper bound for generating new ascending terms.

Next, a descending structure isomorphic to the ascending structure is constructed by forming a set of generators and structural equations isomorphic to the generators and structural equations for the ascending structure. For the *PPN, the isomorphic generating set consists of “male self,” **fosa* (son [ms]), and *tahina* (younger same-sex sibling); and the isomorphic structural equations for equations (1)–(3), respectively, are

(4) **fosa* of *tahina* = **fosa* (“son” of “younger same-sex sibling” is “son”)
(5) *tahina* of *tahina* = *tahina* (“younger same-sex sibling” of “younger same-sex sibling” is “younger same-sex sibling”)
(6) **fosa* of **fosa* of **fosa* = **fosa* of **fosa* (“son” of “son” of “son” is “son” of “son”)

Note that equation (4) lays the foundation for the classificatory aspect of the Proto-Polynesian terminology since whenever an equation is part of the terminology structure, then the reciprocal of that equation is also part of the terminology structure (Read 1984, 2007; Read and Behrens 1990). This means that since equation (4) is part of the descending structure, its reciprocal equation, namely, *tuaka(na)* of *tama(na)* = *tama(na)* (“elder brother” of “father” = “father”), is also part of the terminology structure, and this latter equation is one of the defining equations for classificatory kinship terminologies (for details, see Bennardo and Read 2005, 2007; Leaf and Read 2012; Read 2007; Read and Behrens 1990). Equation (5) defines *tahina* to be self-reciprocal, and equation (6) provides a lower bound for generating new descending terms.

The construction continues by introducing a structural equation that structurally makes *tama(na)* and **fosa* into reciprocal terms. Note that properties such as the reciprocity of kin terms must be structurally defined, for the usage definition of kin term reciprocity, namely, K is the reciprocal of the kin term L when ego (properly) refers to alter by L and alter (properly) refers to ego by K, must be expressed structurally because the kin term space is based on relations among kin terms and not relations among persons and usage of kin terms by persons. In general, an ascending generating term L and a descending generating term K are reciprocal terms when they satisfy the equation “L of K = self,” since this equation implies (see Figure 4.2) that if ego (properly) refers to alter 1 by the kin term K and alter 1 (properly) refers to alter 2 by the kin term L, then ego refers to alter 2 by the term *self*; that is, alter 2 is ego. But if alter 2 is ego, then L must be the reciprocal of K through kin term usage, since “L of K = self” now implies that when ego refers to alter (= alter 1 in the definition of a kin term product) by the kin term K, then alter refers to ego by the kin term L, and so K and L are reciprocal kin terms. For example, if K = *child* and L = *parent*, then “parent of child = self” is the equation structurally defining *child* and *parent* to be reciprocal English kin terms.

I now apply this structural definition of kin term reciprocity and include the following equation in order to define the ascending and descending generating kin terms *tama(na)* (father) and **fosa* (son) as reciprocal terms:

(7) *tama(na)* of **fosa* = male self (“father” of “son” is male self)

I will also include the equation

(7') **fosa* of *tama(na)* = male self (“son” of “father” is male self)

for the following three reasons. First, note that equation (7') is from the perspective of the male self since it is part of the structure of male terms and identifies structurally the fact that the “same-sex sibling” terms *tuaka(na)* and *tahina* are generating terms and not compounds constructed from “son” of “father” as is the case for *brother* in the American kinship terminology. Second, from a female perspective, **fosa* of *tama(na)* becomes “brother” (ws) since the male structure of kin terms and the female structure of kin terms (see below) are joined through interpreting the male self in the male structure as "brother" (ws) and the female self in the female structure as "sister" (ms), as shown in Figure 4.5. Third, the structural equation ***fosa* of **tama(na)* = male self is consistent with the fact that ***fosa* of **tama(na)* is not a distinct kin term for a male speaker (since ***fosa* of **tama(na)* = male self and male self is not distinguished as a kin term by having a kin term label) and ***fosa* of **tama(na)* = "brother" (ws) (since ***fosa* of **tama(na)* = male self and male self is "brother" from a female's perspective).[11] The structure of male terms determined by equations (1)–(7') is shown on the left side of Figure 4.5 (for details, see Bennardo and Read 2005, 2007; Leaf and Read 2012; Read 2007).

Next, the structure of female terms is constructed isomorphic to the structure of male terms in the following manner. First, a set of female-marked generating terms—{female self, **tina(na)* (mother), and **tuaka(na)* (elder same-sex sibling)}—is selected corresponding to the set of male-marked generating terms given by {male self, **tama(na)* (father), and **tuaka(na)* (elder same-sex sibling)}. (Note that **tuaka[na]* can appear in both sets since it is a neutral term and so is both male marked and female marked.) Next, equations (1)–(7') are included as structural equations for the structure of female-marked terms, but with any male-marked generating term in an equation replaced by its corresponding (that is, isomorphic) female-marked generating term. For example, equation (1) becomes the equation **tina(na)* of **tuaka(na)* = **tina(na)* ("mother" of "elder same-sex sibling" is "mother") in the structure of female-marked terms, and so on for the other equations. The structure of female-marked terms generated in this manner is isomorphic to the structure of male-marked terms and is shown on the right side of Figure 4.5.

These two structures are then joined, as indicated in Figure 4.5 by the long, curved arrows between the *male self* and *female self* positions, with male self becoming **tua-ŋaʔane* (brother) with respect to the female self position and female self becoming **tua-fafine* (sister) with respect to the male self position. In other words, from the viewpoint of a female, A, the male self position is instantiated with a male, B, such that if A refers to person C by the kin term **tina(na)* or **tama(na)*, then B refers to C by the same kin term and vice versa. This implements the concept of the sibling relation being determined by having a genealogical parent in common. An analogous statement applies to a male, A, and a female, B, who is the instantiation of the female self position from A's perspective (for more details, see Bennardo and Read 2005, 2007; Leaf and Read 2012; Read 2007).

The reciprocals for the sibling generators, however, are more complex. How the sibling terms **tuaka(na)* and **tahina* are made structurally into reciprocal terms, which justifies their respective translations as "elder same-sex sibling" and "younger same-sex sibling," is central to identifying structural differences among Polynesian terminologies, as I will now show. First, though, we need to determine the pattern for the sibling generators in Polynesian terminologies by categorizing the terminologies according to the structural properties of the sibling terms.

Categorization of Polynesian Terminologies

Epling et al. (1973) categorized Polynesian terminologies according to five structural patterns among the sibling terms by using attribute differences (including the absence of an attribute) among these terms. The attribute differences are the polar extremes for three dichotomous dimensions: relative age (older versus younger), parity of sibling with respect to speaker (same sex versus cross sex), and sex of sibling with respect to speaker (male versus female). Marshall (1984) expanded the list to 11 patterns so as to accommodate variation in sibling terms throughout the oceanic area. Marshall's numbering system for the patterns will be followed here.

Four patterns, with two variants on one of the patterns, can be distinguished among Polynesian terminologies. I first distinguish Pattern 10, the most common pattern among Polynesian terminologies. Pattern 10 is determined by having terms for "elder same-sex sibling" versus "younger same-sex sibling" and for "cross-sex sibling" bifurcated into male and female terms based on sex of sibling with respect to the speaker. Next I distinguish the pattern for Tongan and other similar terminologies. While the Tongan terminology has four sibling terms matching Pattern 10, it differs by having a covering term, *tokoua* (same-sex sibling), for *tao-kete* (elder same-sex sibling) and *tehina* (younger same-sex sibling [Bennardo and Read 2005, 2007]). This pattern does not occur in Marshall's list and will be called Pattern 12. The third pattern I distinguish is Pattern 3, which has terms expressing the parity difference, "same-sex sibling" versus "cross-sex sibling," and has two variants: (1) neither "same-sex sibling" nor "cross-sex sibling" is sex-marked, which characterizes all of the Pattern 3 terminologies except Pileni and Pukapuka, and (2) "cross-sex sibling" is sex-marked but "same-sex sibling" is not (Pileni and Pukapuka). Last, I distinguish Pattern 1, which has a single "sibling" term and occurs in two Polynesian societies, Kapingamarangi and Nukuoro.

Of these patterns, Patterns 10, 3A, 3B, and 1 correspond to the four patterns identified by Clark (1975) and Marshall (1984) for Polynesia and to four of the five patterns identified by Epling et al. (1973). Epling et al. identified Samoa as having a fifth pattern, but both Clark (1975) and Marshall (1984) disagree with their assessment of Samoa. Other sources (e.g., Ministry of Education 2009) show that Samoa has Pattern 3B. Neither Epling et al. (1973), nor Marshall (1984), nor Clark (1975) identified Pattern 12 as a distinct pattern; instead, all included it under Pattern 10. The Polynesian terminologies reported in the literature and categorized by sibling pattern are shown in Table 4.2.

The presence of four structural patterns for the sibling terms raises the question of what constitutes the relationship among them. As we will now see, the answer lies in the different structural ways the reciprocal term for the "elder sibling" generating term is constructed. To show this, it will be easier to use symbols rather than actual kin terms. For the ascending generators, let I be a symbol corresponding to male self. Let F be a symbol representing the ascending generating term (e.g., **tama[na]* [father] in *PPN), and let G be a symbol representing the (neutral) sibling term in the ascending structure.[12] The set of male-marked, ascending generating terms, in symbolic form, is given by

A = {I, F, G}

and the structural equations identified above can be written symbolically as follows:

FFF = FF,
FG = F, and
GG = G.

When we generate the structure of ascending female-marked terms, the ascending generating set will be {i, M, G}, where i is a symbol corresponding to female self; M is a symbol representing the ascending, female-marked generating term; and the same symbol, G, is used for the sibling term in the ascending structure of female-marked terms. The structural equations will be the equivalent of equations (8)–(10) with male-marked generating terms replaced by female-marked terms.

Generative Basis for Sibling Term Patterns

Reciprocal Sibling Generators and Pattern 1

When the descending structure of male-marked terms is constructed isomorphic to the ascending structure, one possibility is that a new symbol, call it g, isomorphic to G, is used in the generating set for the descending structure along with a symbol, S, isomorphic to F, so that the generating set for the descending structure is given by D = {I, S, g}, with structural equations as follows:

SSS = SS,
Sg = S, and
gg = g.

The elements F and S in D become reciprocal elements to each other through the structural equation FS = I; that is, "father" of "son" is male self. Then G and g become reciprocal elements via the equation Gg = I = gG; that is, "elder sibling" of "younger sibling" is male self is "younger sibling" of "elder sibling" in the structure of male terms. This gives rise to Pattern 10 in Table 4.2 and includes the *PPN terminology, where G = **tuaka(na)* and g = **tahina*, along with most of the other Polynesian terminologies.

Reciprocal Sibling Generators and Pattern 2

A second way to form the descending structure of male-marked terms and the reciprocity of the sibling term is to also use the symbol G (same-sex sibling) as an element in the set of generators for the descending structure:

D = {I, S, G}.

In this case, the single sibling element G cannot be made into a self-reciprocal element via the equation GG = I without losing its distinctiveness as a kin term, for then we would have I = GG = G (but see the next section for a disjunctive definition interpretation of I = G). Instead, reciprocity for the sibling element G arises in the terminologies in these societies by a conceptual elaboration in which G is also bifurcated into the elements G+ and G–, along with the equation G+G– = I = G–G+, which defines G+ and G– to be reciprocal elements. As a result, G (same-sex sibling) becomes a cover term for G+ (elder same-sex sibling) and G– (younger same-sex sibling)—analogous to *parent* as a cover term in the American

TABLE 4.2. Sibling terms for Polynesian societies.

Society	Elder Same-Sex Sibling	Younger Same-Sex Sibling	Same-Sex Sibling	♂ Sister	♀ Brother	Cross-Sex Sibling	Sibling	Geographical Area
Pattern 10: "Elder Same-Sex Sibling" Generator								
Reciprocal Equation: "elder same-sex sibling" of "younger same-sex sibling" = self								
*Proto-Polynesian	**tuaka(na)*	**tahina*		**tua-fafine*	**tua-ŋaʔane*			
Aitutaki	*tuakana*	*teina*		*tungane*	*tuaine*			E
Atiu	*tuakana*	*teina*		*tungane*	*tuaine*			E
Hawai'i	*kai-kua-'ana*	*kai-kaina*		*kai-kua-hine*	*kai-kunaane*			E
Mangaia	*tuakana*	*teina*		*tungane*	*tua'ine*			E
Mangareva	*tuakana*	*teina*		*tue'ine*	*tugane*			E
Manihiki and Rakahanga	*tua-kana*	*teina*		*tua-hine*	*tua-ngane*			E
Maori	*tuakana*	*teina*		*tua-hine*	*tungane*			E
Marquesas	*tua'ana*	*teina*		*tuehine*	*tunane*			E
Pukarua	*tuakana*	*teina*		*tugane*	*tuahiine*			E
Rangiroa	*tua-'ana*	*teina*		*tua-hine*	*tu'ane*			E
Rapa	*tua'ana*	*teina*		*tua-hine*	*tu'aane*			E
Rapanui	*tua-kana*	*taina* (same sex??)		*tama'aror*	*tuahine*			E
Raroia	*tuakana*	*teina*		*tuogane*	*tuahine*			E
Rarotonga	*tua-kana*	*teina*		*tua-'ine*	*tu-ngane*			E
Rennell	*tau-kete*	*taina*		*tua-hine*	*tua-nga'ane*			W
Tahiti	*tua'ana*	*teina*		*tua-hine*	*tua'ane*			E
Taumako	*tokana*	*teina*		*tahini*	*tungane*			W
Tongareva	*tua-kana*	*teina*		*tua-hine*	*tua-ngane*			E
Tubuai	*tua-ana*	*teina*		*tua-hine*	*tuane*	*tae'ae*		E
Pattern 12: "Same-Sex Sibling" Generator								
Reciprocal Equation: "elder same-sex sibling" of "younger same-sex sibling" = self								
Bellona	*ta'okete*	*taina*	*hai hanau*	*tu-hahine*	*tu-nga'ane*			W
East Uvea	*tao-kete*	*tehina*	*toko-lua*	*tua-fafine*	*tua-ngaane* ??	*tua-ngaane* ??		W
Niue	*taokete*	*tehina*	*matakain-aanga*	*mahakitaga*, *tuahine*	*tugane*			W
Tokelau	*kimaua*, *faka-mua* (oldest)	*kimuli* (youngest)	*taina*	*tua-fafine*	*tua-gane*			W
Tonga	*tao-kete*	*tehina*	*tokoua*	*tuo-fefine*	*tuongaane*			W

TABLE 4.2. (cont'd.) Sibling terms for Polynesian societies.

Society	Elder Same-Sex Sibling	Younger Same-Sex Sibling	Same-Sex Sibling	♂ Sister	♀ Brother	Cross-Sex Sibling	Sibling	Geographical Area
Pattern 3: "Same-Sex Sibling" Generator								
Reciprocal Equation: "sibling" of "sibling" = self								
A								
Anuta			*taina*			*kave*		W
Luangiua			*hangau, kainga*			*'ave*		W
Tikopia			*taina*			*kave*		W
West Futuna			*soa*			*kave*		W
East Futuna	♂ *ta'o-kete* (oldest)		*taina*			*tua-nga'ane*		W
Nanumea			*taina, takete*			*tua-gane*		W
Takuu			*taina*			*kave*		W
Tuvalu			*taina*			*tua-ngane*		W
B								
Pileni, Reef Islands			*toga/ toka/ togaku*	*tukutungani*	*tukutuahine*			W
Pukapuka			*taina*	*tua-wawine*	*tua-tane*	*kainga*		W
Samoa		*tei* (either sex)	*uso* (*tua'aa*)	*tua-fafine*	*tua-gane*	*tau-soga* (recent??)		W
Pattern 1: "Sibling" Generator								
Reciprocal Equation: "child" of "parent" = "sibling"								
Kapinga-marangi							*tuahin(a)*	W
Nukuoro							*teina*	W
Uncertain Pattern								
Aniwa			♂ *tuku sò* (brother), ♀ *ta kawe* (sister)	*tuku kawe*	*tuku sò*			W

Note: E = East Polynesia; W = West Polynesia; ?? = either an uncertain kin term or an uncertain attribute for a kin term. Pattern 12 is a new pattern identified as Pattern 2 in Read 2010. Pattern numbers 1, 2, and 4 used in Read 2010 have been changed here to match pattern numbers 10, 6, and 1, respectively, in Marshall 1984: app. Patterns 3A and 3B, here and in Read 2010, correspond to Patterns 3 and 5, respectively, in Marshall 1984.

Source: Kin terms compiled from Marck 1996b, except Nukuoro (Epling et al. 1973); Aitutaki, Atiu, Mangaia, Pileni, Raroia, and Takuu (Marshall 1984); and Bellona "elder/younger same-sex sibling" and "sibling" (Elbert and Monberg 1965).

kinship terminology for the terms *mother* and *father.* This bifurcation procedure accounts for Pattern 12 terminologies, which includes the Tongan terminology.

For the Tongan terminology, G = *tokoua*, G+ = *tao-kete*, and G– = *tehina*. The same pattern occurs in East Uvea, with G = *toko-loua* (a cognate of *tokoua*), G+ = *tao-kete*, and G– = *tehina*. In Niue G = *matakainaanga*, G+ = *taokete*, and G– = *tehina*. The Tokelau society follows the same pattern but with the modification that the "elder/younger same-sex sibling" terms have become "eldest/youngest same-sex sibling" terms.

The construction outlined here for the Tongan terminology has ethnographic corroboration through the fact that in Tonga the *tao-kete* and *tehina* terms are used for "son of a man's elder brother" and "son of a man's younger brother," respectively, despite the lack of a terminological distinction among "father," "elder same-sex sibling" of "father," and "younger same-sex sibling" of "father" (Biersack 1982). The above construction accounts for this kin term usage (see Bennardo and Read 2005, 2007, for details). Niue, which is linguistically closely related to Tonga, has the same pattern, with the term *mata-kainaga* having the translation "a man's elder brother; man's father's elder brother's son" (Marck 1996b:5).

Reciprocal Sibling Generators and Pattern 3

A third way to form the descending structure of male-marked terms and the reciprocity of the generating sibling terms is through the equation GG = I. This equation, in conjunction with the equation GG = G, implies G = GG = I, as has already been noted. As a consequence, the structure for the male-marked terms will have a single term in the 0 generation (rather than the three terms shown in Figure 4.5), hence the identity element I (in the symbolic model for the male structure) plays a dual role: its instantiation refers either to the focal male person or to those who are "brother" to a male focal person. Thus the symbol I has disjunctive meaning, for it can be instantiated either as the focal person or as the "same-sex sibling" of the focal person due to the equation I = G. I will denote this disjunction by the symbol [I, G], thus indicating that there is an (unnamed) covering concept for I and G.

When a female structure is formed isomorphic to this structure and the two structures are joined through the male self having the interpretation "cross-sex sibling" for a female focal person and the female self having the interpretation "cross-sex sibling" for a male focal person, there are two ways that the two structures may be combined together. When [I, G] replaces I and [i, G] replaces i in the male and female structures, respectively, then these two nodes in the combined structure will be labeled either "same-sex sibling" (from within a structure) or "cross-sex sibling" (between the two structures; see Figure 4.6A), which gives rise to Pattern 3A. If, however, the elements I and i, along with the mapping from G to these two elements, are kept distinct in the male and female structures, then the combined structure will have three kinds of sibling nodes, the first of which corresponds to "same-sex sibling"; the second, to "male cross-sex sibling"; and the third, to "female cross-sex sibling" (see Figure 4.6B)—precisely as is the case for the two Polynesian groups, Pileni and Pukapuka, listed under Pattern 3B. Clark (1975) considered Tokelau to also have Pattern 3B, but this ignores the "oldest/youngest same-sex sibling" terms in the Tokelau terminology, and so it is included under Pattern 12 here.

Reciprocal Sibling Generators and Pattern 4

The fourth pattern arises by using (1) self (that is, a neutral self element) in place of male self and female self; (2) *parent* (P) in place of *father* as the ascending generating term, along with *child* (C) as its reciprocal; and (3) *sibling* (G; without sex marking), which becomes self-reciprocal through the equation CP = G—that is, "child" of "parent" is "sibling." That the equation CP = G implies that the reciprocal of G is just G can be seen by computing the reciprocal of the kin term product CP. The kin term product CP has the reciprocal $(CP)^r = P^rC^r = CP = G$, since $P^r = C$ and $C^r = P$, hence $G^r = (CP)^r = CP = G$, and so G is self-reciprocal because $G^r = G$.

This kin term product equation also occurs in the American kinship terminology where the kin terms (not kin types) *brother* or *sister* are compounds constructed via sex marking of the kin term product "child of parent." Here, though, G is not a compound term because it is a generating term (and must be a generating term for the terminology to be a classificatory terminology). The equation does not construct the sibling term G but, rather, identifies a relation that holds among C, P, and G from which it follows that the reciprocal of G must be G; that is, G must be self-reciprocal. Altogether, there will just be a "sibling" term and no "same-sex sibling" or "cross-sex sibling" terms under this construction due to the absence of sex-marked self nodes.

This is precisely the kin term pattern for Kapingamarangi and Nukuoro, the only Polynesian societies with a

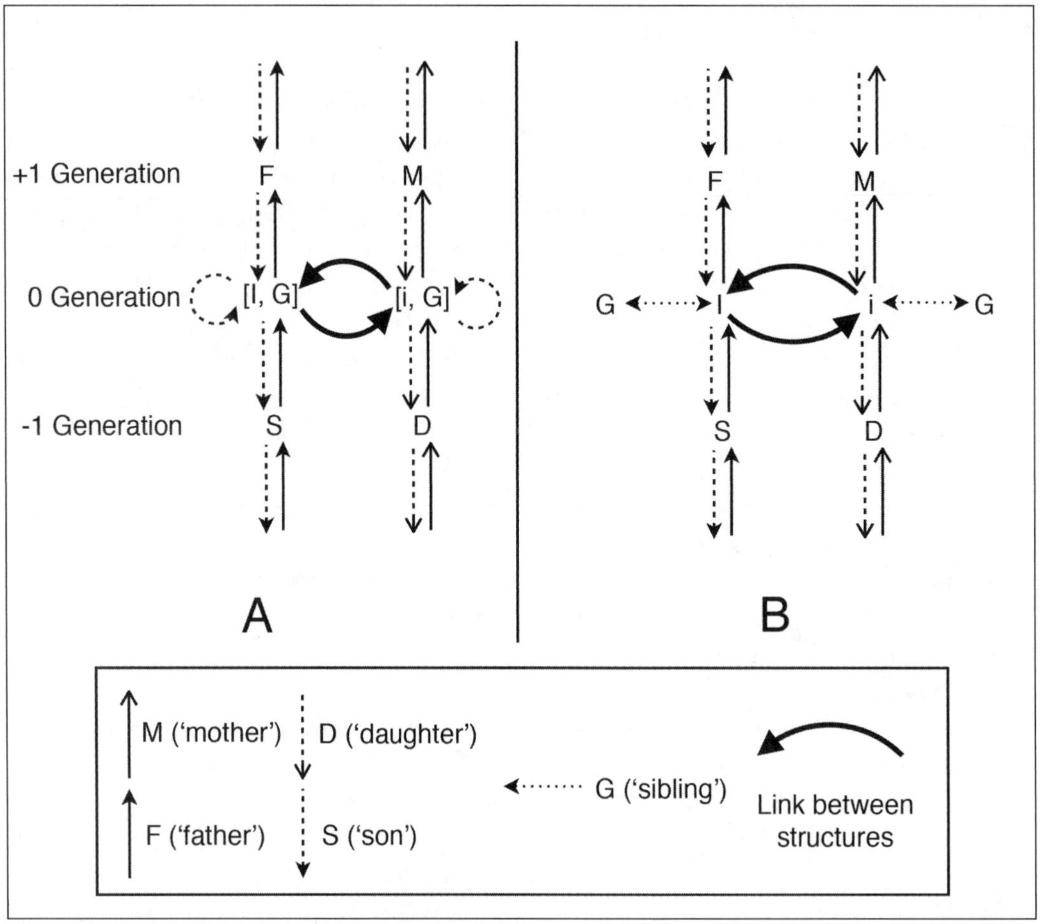

FIGURE 4.6. Two ways to link isomorphic male and female structures. Symbols are used instead of kin terms and only the middle three generations are shown for clarity. (A) Denote I = G (male self = "sibling") by the neutral covering term (I, G) and i = G (female self = "sibling") by the neutral covering term (i, G). The covering term is used in place of the identity elements I (male self) and i (female self), so the link between I and i in Figure 4.5 becomes a link between (I, G) and (i, G). There are just two 0-generation sibling terms: (1) "same sex sibling" (the [reflexive] arrow from I or i to G) and (2) "cross sex sibling" (the link between [I, G] and [i, G]). (B) Link the identity elements I and i as in Figure 4.5. There are three 0-generation sibling terms: (1) "same sex sibling" (same reasons as for A[1]), (2) "male cross sex sibling" (the arrow from the I node to the I node and (3) "female cross sex sibling" (the arrow from the I node to the I node).

Pattern 1 terminology. First, unlike all of the other Polynesian terminologies, the Kapingamarangi terminology has the neutral generating term *matua* (parent), with the reciprocal term *tama* (child), and the term *matumatua* (grandparent), with the reciprocal *tama-tama* (grandchild), a pattern that follows from using P as a generating element (see Figure 4.3). Sex distinctions only apply to *matua*, which is bifurcated by sex marking into *taman(a)* (father) and *tinan(a)* (mother). ("Grandmother" is expressed via the kin term product *tina-na matua*; and "grandfather," via the kin term product *tamana matua*.) Second, it has a single "sibling" term, *tuahin(a)*. Finally, the term *taman(a)* "may be extended to parents' brothers and husbands of parent's sisters," which simply expresses the classificatory aspect of the terminology, namely, GP = P, "but commonly the relationship is simply described 'brother of my father' *tuahin toku tamana*" (Marck 1996b: 35). The latter reflects the way that the equation CP = G implies (CP)P = GP ("sibling" of "parent"); that is, the expression "sibling of parent" (or "sibling of father") is derived from CP = G, and so "sibling of parent" is appropriate as a distinguishable relation under the logic of the equation CP = G. Hence the genealogical position "my father's brother" comes under both (1) the kin term *taman(a)* according to the classificatory equation GP = P derived from sibling as a generating term and (2) the kin term given by the kin term product *tuahin toku tamana* according to the equation CP = G introduced as a means to structurally make the sibling generator into a self-reciprocal term. Similar comments apply to the kin term *tinan(a)*. Marck's comment, which otherwise might be seen just as expressing an oddity of the Kapingamarangi terminology, reflects in fact the generative logic giving rise to its terminology structure.

Uncertain Pattern

Last, the data on Aniwa (Guiart 1961) have, according to Marck (1996b), incomplete specification and analysis. The pattern for Aniwa is uncertain.

Results

Typology for Kinship Terminologies

I will form a typology for these terminologies based on the structural logic leading to the four patterns for the sibling terms in order to show the generative logic underlying each of these patterns and how the patterns diverge from one another through that generative logic. The typology (see Figure 4.7) starts with an ascending generating set that includes a male parent element (F) and a sibling element (G) for generating the ascending structure. (The generating set could, equivalently, be based on a female parent and a sibling element.) The inclusion of the sibling element identifies the four Polynesian patterns as sharing commonality with other classificatory terminologies but not with descriptive terminologies.

The first split in the typology, Descending Generating Set, uses a contrast between including an isomorphic sibling element in the set of descending generators distinct from its corresponding element in the set of ascending generators (viz., g in the set of descending generators in lieu of G in the set of ascending generators) and using the same ascending sibling generating element in the set of descending generators. Next there is a split, Bifurcation, based on the element G being bifurcated into two elements, call them G+ and G–. The bifurcation, when it occurs, happens only when G is both an ascending and a descending generating element.

Following this is the split, Reciprocal Sibling Term Equations, based on the reciprocal equations for the sibling generators. With G as an ascending generating element and g as the isomorphic descending generating element, the structural equation for defining G and g to be reciprocal elements is Gg = I = gG. When G is bifurcated into G+ and G–, the equation G+G– = I = G–G+ makes G+ and G– into structurally reciprocal elements. The remaining terminologies use the equation GG = I to make G into a self-reciprocal element.

The next split, Sibling/Self Distinction, is based on the equation G = I (G = i in the structure of female-marked terms), derived from the reciprocal equation GG = I (GG = i in the structure of female-marked terms). The opposition expressed in the split is between replacing I and i with G (see Figure 4.6A) and including both I and G (and i and G) in the structure (see Figure 4.6B). The last split in the typology, Parent, Child Equation, is an opposition based on whether the reciprocal equations GG = I and GG = i for male-marked and female-marked terms, respectively, are replaced by the single equation CP = G.

The societies corresponding to each branch of the typology are shown at the bottom of Figure 4.7. With but two exceptions, all of the societies under Pattern 10, which corresponds to the left branch of the typology diagram, are geographically and linguistically East Polynesia societies. All other patterns correspond to the geographical (but linguistically diverse) West Polynesia societies. The exceptions are Rennell and Taumako. The pattern may actually be without exceptions, as these two societies may fit under Pattern 12 rather than Pattern 10 for the following reasons (but see below for an alternative interpretation).

Consider Rennell first. Though Marck (1996b) does not list a "same-sex sibling" term for Rennell, it has the term *ma* (same-sex sibling-in-law), and the only other societies with this term are Anuta and Tikopia, each with a "same-sex sibling" term. In addition, Rennell has the term *haihaanau* (classificatory siblings [Marck 1996b:112]), suggesting a concept of "same-sex sibling" without an older/younger distinction. Immediately adjacent to Rennell is the island of Bellona, and the Bellona have a similar term, *hai hanau*, which is used for all siblings. Altogether, these data suggest that "same-sex sibling" is a sibling term concept in Rennell society, which would make it a Pattern 12 society.

Taumako, the other exception, also has the term "ma 'HuSi, WiBr, man's BrWi, woman's SiHu'" (Marck 1996b:26), and the last two expressions in this gloss have the same form as the gloss for the *ma* term in the Rennell terminology. In addition, as in Tonga and Niue, the "older/younger same-sex sibling" terms are also applied to the son of ego's parent's older and younger siblings. Marck (1996a) gives "man's father's younger brother's son, man's mother's younger sister's son" for *teina* and "man's elder

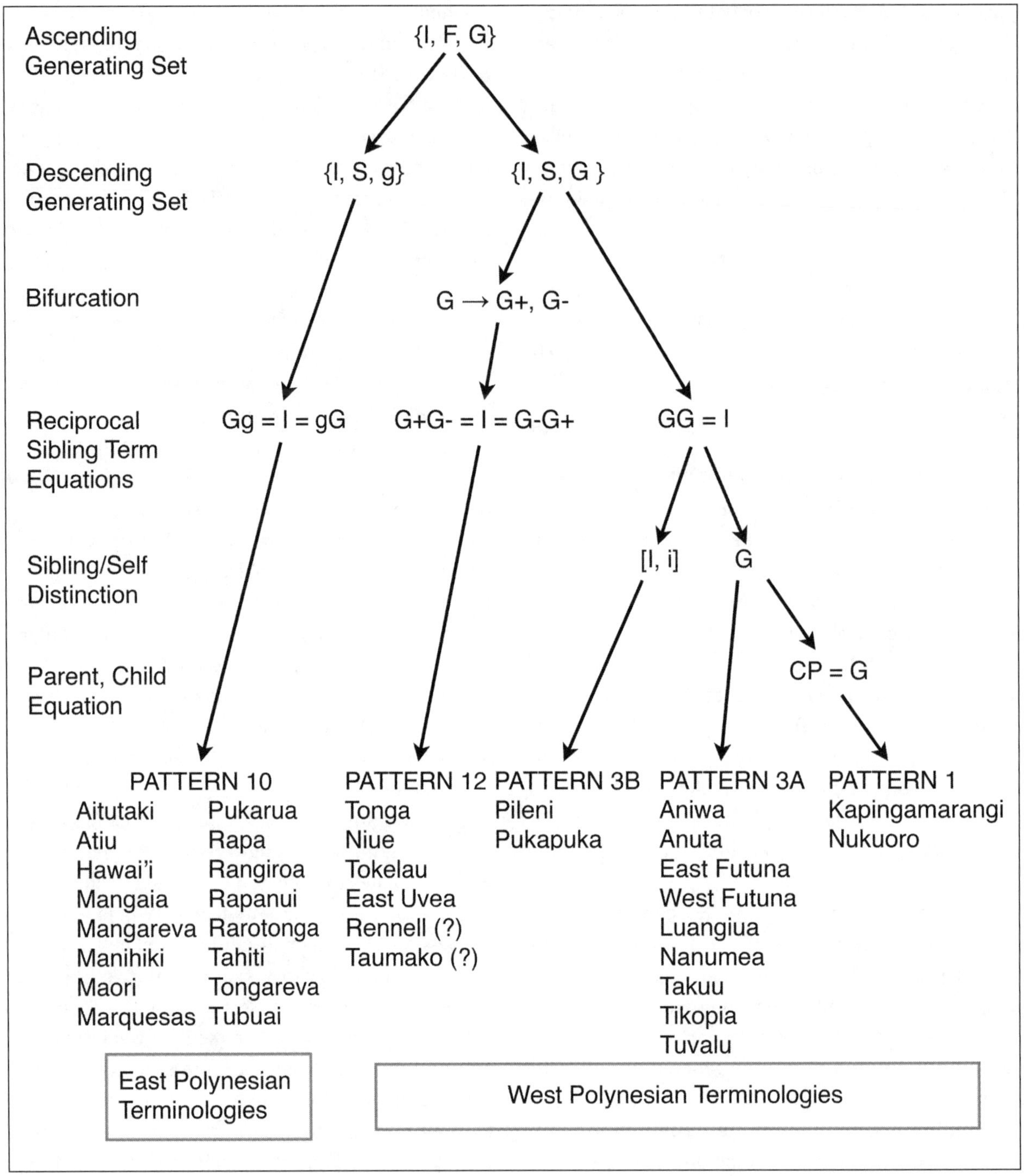

FIGURE 4.7. Typology of Polynesian terminologies using a contrast on a single dimension for each split in the typology. All of the East Polynesia terminologies have a Pattern 1 sibling structure and are grouped together as a single type. Rennell and Taumako are West Polynesia societies with Pattern 1 terminologies but also have features suggesting that they should be included with the Pattern 2 terminologies (see text for details). All patterns other than Pattern 1 correspond to West Polynesia terminologies.

brother's son, mother's elder sister's son" for *tokana*. Thus the terminologies for both Rennell and Taumako have kin term properties that occur only in those societies with a "same-sex sibling" term. Consequently, both societies are listed under Pattern 12 in Figure 4.6 with a question mark. If, in fact, Rennell and Taumako are societies with Pattern 12 terminologies, then we would have a perfect correspondence between Pattern 10 and East Polynesia, with all other patterns corresponding to geographical West Polynesia societies.

Some of the societies grouped together reflect their close linguistic affinity: For example, Tonga and Niue (Pattern 12) both have Tongic languages; Anuta, Tikopia, and West Futunan (Pattern 3A) are grouped as "Futunic" Outliers; Luangiua and Tuvalu (Pattern 3A) are grouped under Outlier Ellicean (Marck 1996b); Hawaii, Mangareva, and Marquesas (Pattern 10) are grouped under Proto-Marquesic (Marck 2000: fig. 1); and Kapingamarangi and Nukuoro (Pattern 4) have languages with a common origin, though today they have distinct languages (Clark 1994). However, there are also exceptions to the correspondence between societies grouped together in the typology diagram and language affinity. East Futuna is under Pattern 3A but linguistically associated with East Uvea, listed under Pattern 12, and Tokelau is under Pattern 12 but associated linguistically with Tuvalu, listed under Pattern 3A (Marck 1999). Thus for the West Polynesian societies, there is only partial agreement between the language affinity and structural affinity of kinship terminologies, in keeping with the conclusions drawn by Epling et al. (1973) and Marshall (1984), despite the use of different ways for characterizing the relationships among sibling kin patterns.

Structural Changes in Sibling Term Patterns

I now construct a plausible, historical sequence for change in the structural patterns for the sibling terms (see Figure 4.8). I start with a root structure having all of the structural features shared across the Polynesian terminologies and the sibling term pattern(s) corresponding to this root structure. Then I identify structural transformations that give rise to the other sibling term patterns, with the constraint that a transformation should only make simple structural changes. The sequence of structural changes provides a historical ordering for the terminology types as presented in Figure 4.7.

All Polynesian terminologies have (1) a set of sex-marked generating elements for an ascending structure that includes a sex-marked sibling element, (2) a set of sex-marked generating elements for a descending structure isomorphic to the set of ascending generating elements, and (3) structural equations that define an ascending element and its isomorphic descending element to be a reciprocal pair of elements. The simplest implementation of the generating sets for this common structure is one in which the ascending and descending generating sets differ only with respect to the ascending, generating element (F) and its reciprocal, descending generating element (S). Accordingly, both ascending and descending sets of generators in the root structure will have the same sibling generating element, G, along with the reciprocal structural equations GG = I and GG = i that make G a self-reciprocal element (see the top part of Figure 4.8).

This structure may be implemented in two ways when a structure of male terms is joined with a structure of female terms, with the latter a structural property common to classificatory terminologies in general. One implementation leads to Pattern 3A when the two structures are joined using the elements [I, G] and [i, G] (see Figure 4.6A). The other implementation leads to Pattern 3B when the two structures are joined using the male self (I) and the female self (i) elements along with the element G structurally linked to I and i, respectively (see Figure 4.6B). Neither of these two sibling structure patterns need be structurally prior to the other, and both are alternative ways to join the male term and female term structures into a single structure, so Patterns 3A and 3B will both be considered to be root sibling structures as shown in Figure 4.8.

As noted previously, the equation GG = I, in conjunction with the equation GG = G, implies the potential contradiction that G = I, in which case there is no structural distinction between "(male) sibling" and "male self." As discussed above, the potential contradiction can be resolved through a disjunctive interpretation of I as either "male self" or "(male) sibling." Alternatively, the equation I = G that is the source for the disjunctive interpretation may be removed by Transformation 1 of kin terms as shown in Figure 4.8. There are two ways Transformation 1 may be implemented: (1) replace GG = I with the equation CP = G ("child" of "parent" is "sibling"; see the left middle part of Figure 4.8), which corresponds to Pattern 1 terminologies (see Figure 4.7), or (2) bifurcate G into G+ and G– and replace GG = I with the structural

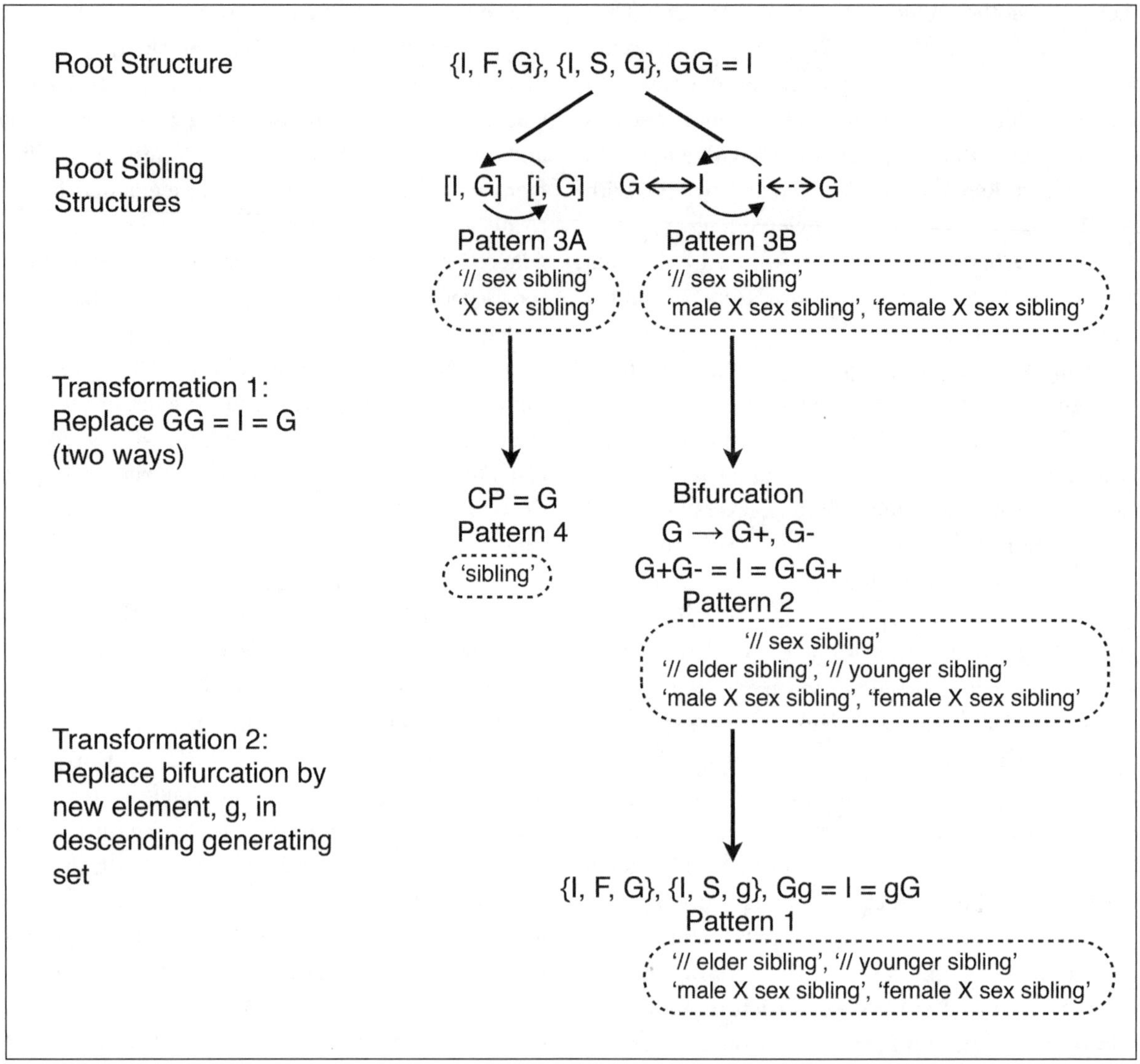

FIGURE 4.8. Structural changes for Polynesian terminologies. The root structure has properties shared across all of the terminologies. The root structure leads to two root sibling structures (Pattern 3A and Pattern 3B), depending on how the structures of male terms and of female terms are joined. Transformation 1 and Transformation 2 indicate hypothesized evolutionary changes in the root sibling structures. Transformation 1 either replaces the reciprocal equation BB = I with the structural equation CP = G (which gives rise to Pattern 4) or introduces a bifurcated form of B (which gives rise to Pattern 2). Transformation 2 simplifies the bifurcation structure in Pattern 2 by introducing a new element in the set of generating elements, thereby giving rise to Pattern 1.

equation G+G– = I = G–G+ (right middle part of Figure 4.8), which corresponds to the structure for Pattern 12 terminologies (see Figure 4.7).

Consider the first way to realize Transformation 1 by replacing GG = I with CP = G. This transformation can be implemented, beginning with Pattern 3A, in a straightforward way by overlapping the vertical male and female structures in Figure 4.6A so as to remove the sex distinction between the left and right vertical structures and then replacing M and F with a single, neutral element, P, and replacing S and D with a single, neutral element, C (the reciprocal element for P). In this modified structure, CP = G. As with the English/American terminology based on generating elements P and C, sex marking can now be reintroduced through bifurcating P into F and M. This method for implementing Transformation 1 leads to the Kapingamarangi terminology, an exemplar of Pattern 1, as a transformation of Pattern 3A.

The second way that Transformation 1 is realized is by bifurcating G into G+ and G–. This is a simple way to transform Pattern 3B into Pattern 12, since the only structural change for the sibling terms that is involved in going from Pattern 3B to Pattern 12 lies in the bifurcation of the G term. The structure of male elements and the structure of female elements are already made into a single structure in the same way in Pattern 3B and Pattern 12. In both patterns, the I and i elements are linked to join the structure of male terms with the structure of female terms (see Figure 4.6B and Figure 4.8 for the way I and i are linked in Pattern 3B; see Bennardo and Read 2005, 2007, for the way I and i are linked in the same way in the Tongan terminology as an exemplar of Pattern 12). In either case, Transformation 1 only involves a simple structural transformation, either from Pattern 3A to Pattern 4 or from Pattern 3B to Pattern 12. Note that directionality is implicit in Transformation 1, as there is no straightforward structural basis for transforming Pattern 10 into Pattern 3A or Pattern 12 into Pattern 3B.

Transformation 2, in which a new element, g, is introduced in the descending generating set (rather than carrying forward the element G from the set of ascending generators and then bifurcating G into two elements, G+ and G–), is a simple transformation from Pattern 12 to Pattern 10 due to the fact that Pattern 12 already has the structural form of "elder/younger same-sex sibling" terms that is part of Pattern 10. Thus the transformation maintains the structure of Pattern 12 sex-marked sibling terms but results in the "same-sex sibling" term dropping out of the terminology, thereby going from the Pattern 12 to the Pattern 10 sibling term structure. This transformation also has directionality, since a transformation from Pattern 10 to Pattern 12 would require reforming the generating set for the descending terms so as to replace the generating element g with the ascending generating element G and then bifurcating G into G+ and G–.

Kinship Tree for Polynesian Terminologies

I can now use the pattern of structural changes shown in Figure 4.8 to construct a kinship tree. To do this, I first form a prototerminology structure for each set of terminologies that share the same sibling structure. I will refer to a root prototerminology structure as *Proto-Pattern n* when all the terminologies in a set have Pattern n, where n = 1, 3, 10, or 12. Then I connect each Proto-Pattern n in accordance with Figure 4.8 until I reach the root terminology structure. This procedure leads to the kinship tree shown in Figure 4.9.

Discussion

The kinship tree does not establish relationships among Polynesian languages but, rather, shows how terminology structures are distributed among the Polynesian languages corresponding to the societies listed in Figure 4.9. The kinship tree groups Tokelau and East Uvea with Tonga and Niue, for example, whereas the Tongan and Niuean languages are grouped under Proto-Tongic, but the East Uvean and Tokelauan languages are included under Proto–Nuclear Polynesian (see Figure 4.10). This difference in the two trees implies that changes in the structural properties and the linguistic properties of kinship terminologies involve different, though to some extent interrelated, processes. (The processes are interrelated if only because each node in a terminology structure has a kin term label and each kin term label corresponds to a node in that structure.) In brief, language divergence is not the same as kinship terminology structure divergence. The kinship terminology structure for a protolanguage can be maintained when the parent protolanguage diverges into daughter languages; hence different, present-day languages may share the same kinship terminology structure. Or divergence in terminology structure can occur between different groups with the same languages, and so on.

There is, however, an inconsistency that arises when the two trees are given historical interpretations. To see the inconsistency, we must first observe that the *Proto-Polynesian kinship terminology given in Table 4.1 has a Pattern 10 structure but the kinship tree implies that it should have a Pattern 3A or 3B structure, a conclusion comparable to that reached by Marshall (1984). From both a geographic location and a date of colonization perspective, Patterns 3A and 3B would be the earliest patterns (see Figure 4.11), followed by Pattern 12, then Pattern 10, and last Pattern 1, which is consistent with the proposed sequences of structural changes shown in Figure 4.8. We, of course, do not know the extent to which terminology structures have been conservative within a single society, and for some islands the original population may have died out and then been replaced by a new population without any connection with the earlier population, possibly bringing with it a different kinship terminology system and structure. Nonetheless, positing Pattern 10 unequivocally as the root structure (e.g., Blust 1984) is problematic, as it requires that somehow changes in terminology structure within a society are also patterned between societies in such a manner as to

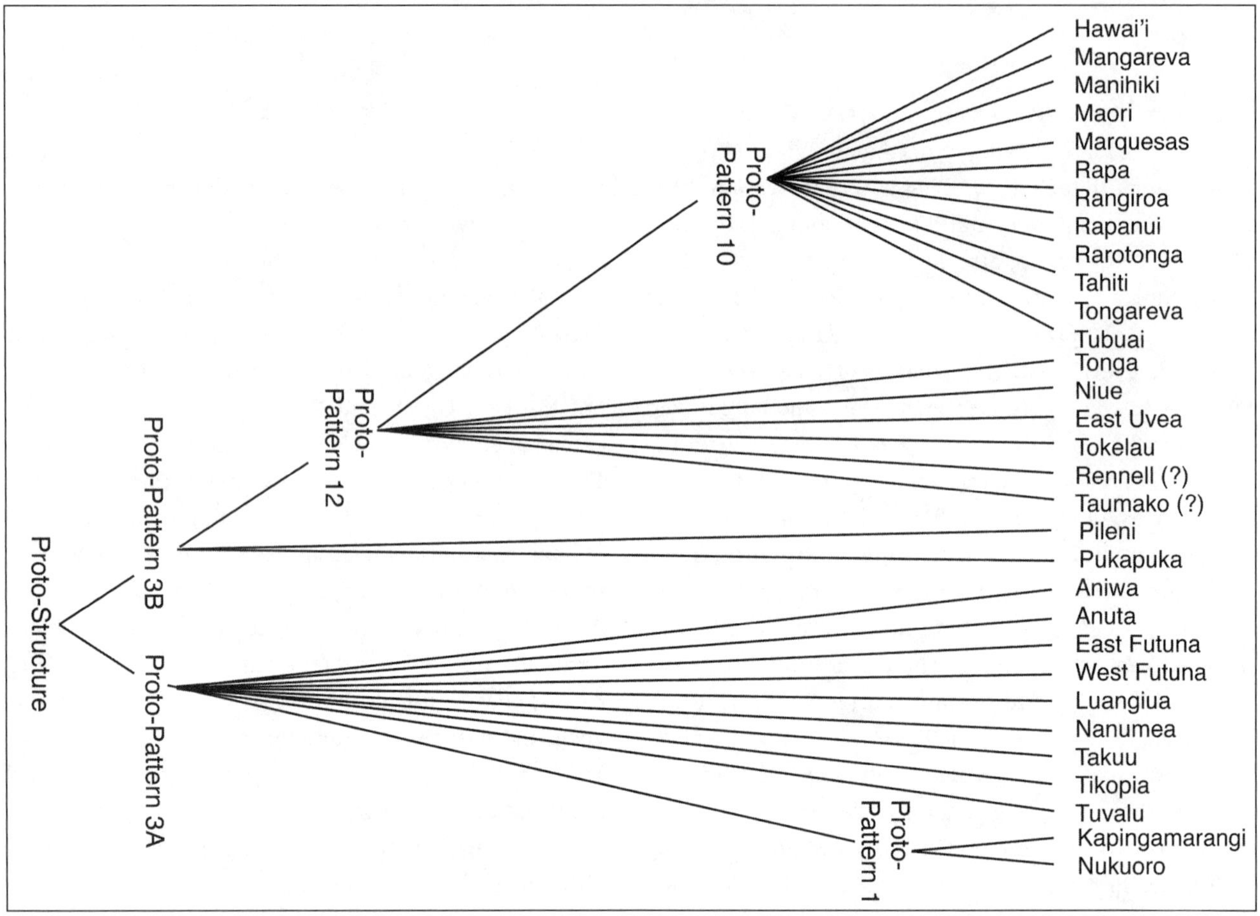

FIGURE 4.9. Kinship tree for Polynesian societies based on structural patterns for sibling terms. The patterns for sibling terms are discussed in the text. Connections between proto-patterns are based on Figure 4.8, and the relative time-sequence location from left (older event) to right (younger event) is based on colonization dates in Figure 4.11.

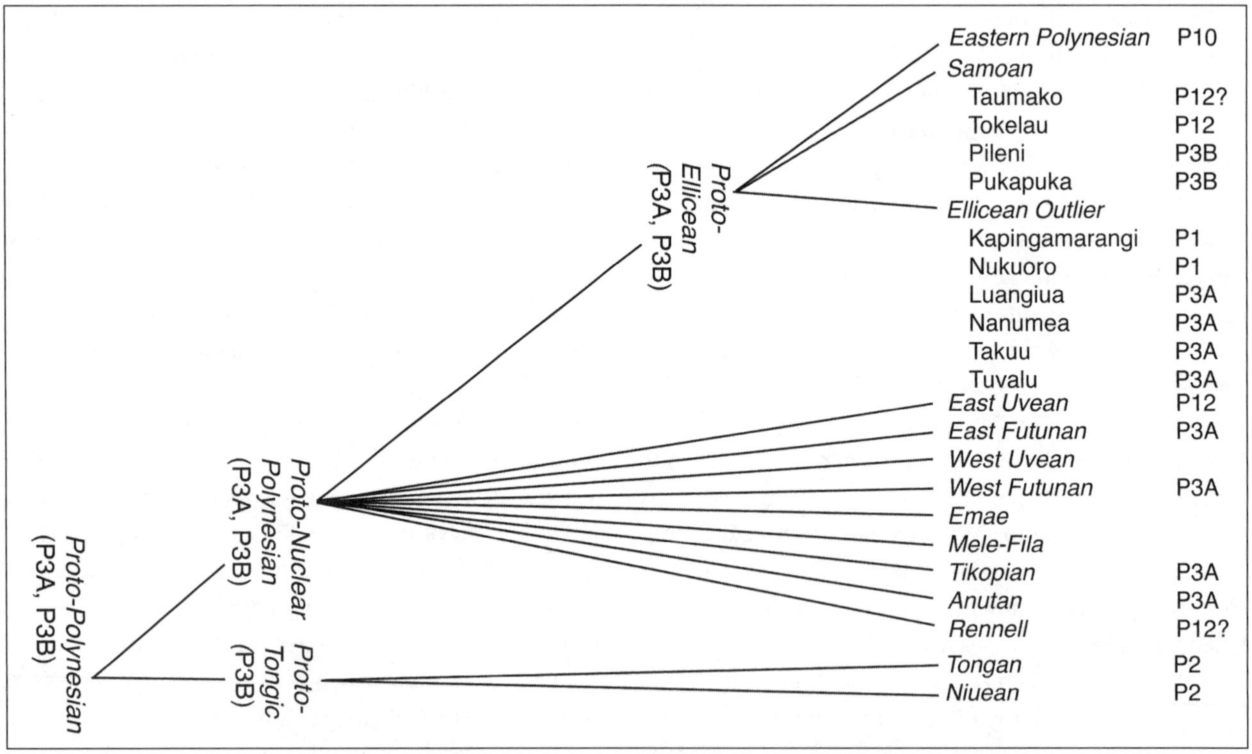

FIGURE 4.10. Language tree for Polynesian languages. Language names are in italics. Individual societies are listed when the language includes several societies with different sibling term patterns. The patterns listed under each protolanguage make up the minimal set of patterns needed to account for the structural changes leading to present-day terminologies from that protolanguage. Language tree based on Marck 1996a: fig. 2.

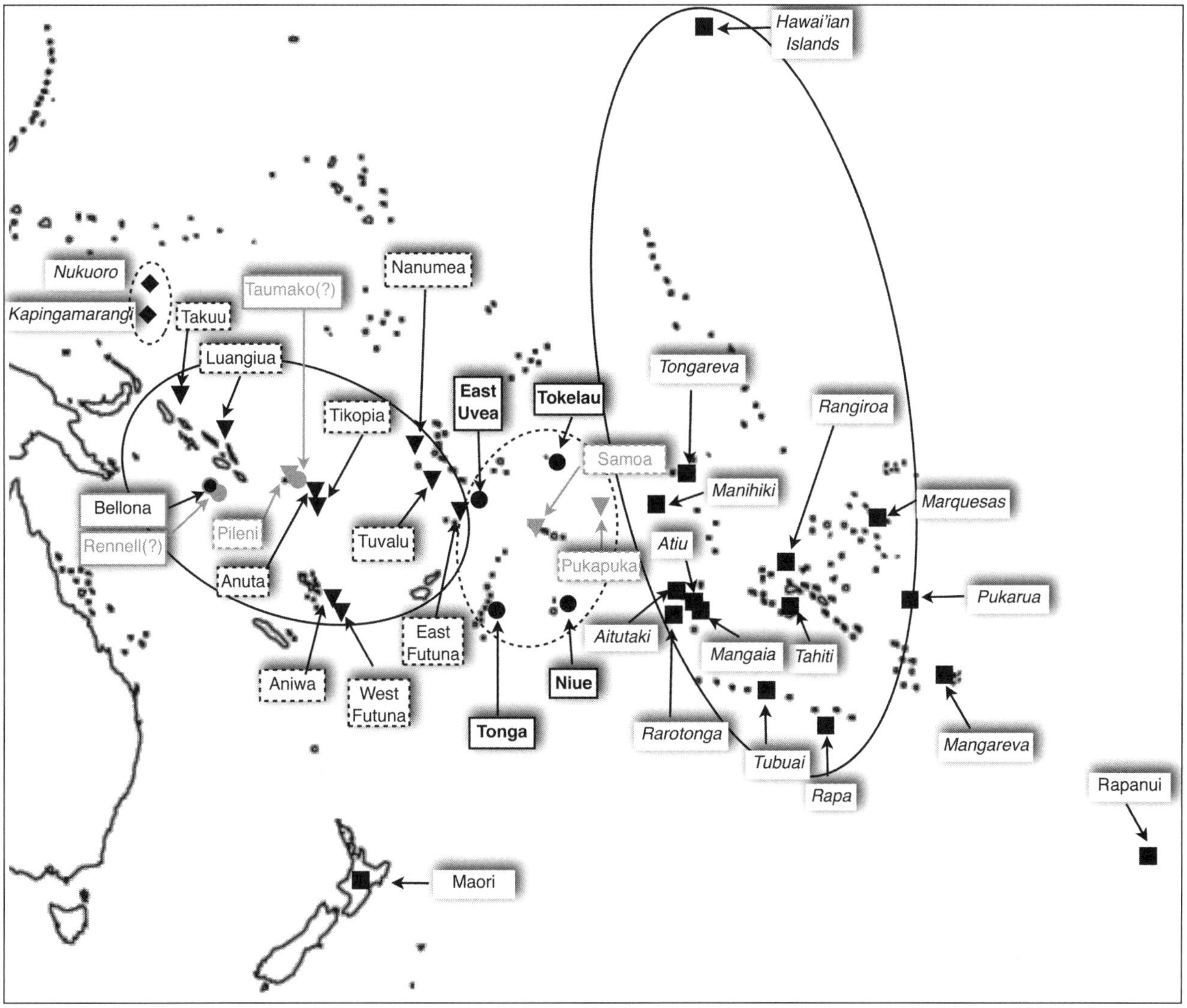

FIGURE 4.11. Geographic distribution of sibling term patterns. ■ = Pattern 10; ● = Pattern 12; ● = questionable assignment (see text for details); ▼ = Pattern 3A; ▼ = Pattern 3B; ♦ = Pattern 1. Each pattern (except 3B) corresponds to a distinct geographical subregion as shown by the ellipses. These regions also correspond to the colonization pattern for the western and eastern parts of Polynesia. Colonization in the region (Near Oceanic) for Pattern 3 (solid ellipse, left side of figure, names in regular font) began around 3500–3300 BP with the spread of the Lapita cultural complex (Kirch 2001; Spriggs 1999). Colonization and further spread of the Lapita cultural complex reached the region (Far Oceanic) for Pattern 12 (dashed ellipse, center of figure, names in bold) around 3100 BP (Kirch 2000) or 2800 BP (Spriggs 1999). After a hiatus, the region for Pattern 10 (solid ellipse, right side of figure, names in italics) started to be colonized around 2500–2000 BP (Kirch 2000). The region for Pattern 1 (dashed ellipse, left side of figure, names in italics) corresponds to a back migration, possibly from Samoa, dating to around 1000 BP (Kirch 2000).

coincidentally yield the clear correspondence between the hypothesized pattern for structural change and its geographical and temporal distribution shown in Figure 4.11. While this possibility cannot be ruled out given our incomplete understanding of the processes leading to structural changes in kinship terminologies, it is worth exploring the assumptions that have led to assigning Pattern 10 historically as the root structure. It should be noted that this assignment does not derive directly from the linguistic tree, as "the Comparative Method [of historical linguistics] *as such* is not, in fact, historical; it provides evidence of linguistic relationships to which we may give a historical interpretation" (Fox 1995:141; emphasis in original).

Assigning Pattern 10 as the root structure for the terminologies, hence historically the earliest, has the problem, noted by Marshall (1984), of this pattern being found primarily in the eastern parts of Polynesia that were colonized last (see Figure 4.11). In addition, it does not occur in any of the 11 Micronesian societies in Marshall's database of 237 societies (except possibly in the Marshall Islands [Hage 1999:368 n. 3]), and Pattern 10 only occurs 17 times out of 137 Melanesian societies listed by Marshall (1984). Of these 17 occurrences, it is only found in societies on islands around the Bismarck Sea (six times) or in the Vanuatu Islands (11 times). Despite this limited occurrence, Pattern 10 is said to characterize the reconstructed Proto-Oceanic terminology with sibling terms **taqa(ka)* (same-sex elder sibling), **taci* (same-sex younger sibling), **mwaqane* (female cross-sex sibling), and **papine* (male cross-sex sibling [Blust 1980; Milke 1938; Pawley 1981]); hence the Melanesian and Micronesian terminologies must also have Pattern 10 for their root structure despite the pattern's limited or nonoccurrence therein.

We need to consider in more detail, then, the evidence for the historical interpretation that Pattern 10 is the root structure for all of the Oceanic terminologies as well as the Polynesian terminologies. I first consider the evidence for making this assignment for the Polynesian terminologies and then, more broadly, the evidence for the Oceanic terminologies.

In his authoritative work on Polynesian kin terms, Marck comments:

> Clark (1975) reconstructed PPn *tuakana 'elder same-sex sibling', *tahina 'younger same-sex sibling', *tua-r)a?ane 'woman's brother' and *tuafafine 'man's sister', but then goes on to say, "Here we reconstruct PPn *ta?o-kete 'same-sex sibling' and *kawe 'cross-sex sibling'." (1996a:218)

This creates the anomaly, noted by Marck, of having terms both with and without an "older"/"younger" marking for cross-sex siblings: "It seems that PPn had words for cross-sex siblings in general, the male cross-sex sibling, and the female cross-sex sibling, but this terminological situation may have been inherently unstable, a little redundant perhaps" (1996a:223).[13] Attributing the anomaly to "redundancy" with consequent instability does not resolve the matter, as his argument does not account for why there should be redundancy in the first place, especially if redundancy is inherently unstable. In addition, attributing Pattern 10 to Proto-Polynesian (and not just to Proto–East Polynesian) required Clark to argue for the "replacement of terms" and "elimination of semantic distinctions" (1975:86) to account for the sibling patterns in modern-day Polynesian languages, but Clark provides no basis for these changes other than as a way to match what is required when Pattern 10 is assigned to Proto-Polynesian.

Clark's reason for assigning Pattern 10 to be historically the root terminology structure for Polynesian terminologies is not a strong argument. Essentially, Clark relies on a statistical observation coupled with finding cognates between Polynesian and Melanesian terms. Statistically, he argues, "the system is reflected intact in all the Eastern languages except Easter Island, and in the Taumako outlier dialect.... The same set of semantic distinctions, but with an unrelated form for term (1) (*tuakana), is found in Rennellese, Tongan, Niue, and East Uvea" (1975:86). But the East Polynesian languages are late developments in the colonization of this region (see Figure 4.11) and by themselves do not establish the antiquity of Pattern 10. The comparison with the Tonga, Niue, and East Uvea terminologies does not take into account the "same-sex sibling" term that appears in these terminologies, which is the basis for Pattern 12 (and possibly includes Rennell, as discussed above). Finally, simply asserting that "terms (1) (*tuakana) and (2) (*tahina) have widespread cognates in Melanesia with the same meanings" (Clark 1975:86) without working out the pattern of sibling terms in the Melanesian area first does not establish the antiquity of Pattern 10.

J. Marck attributes the antiquity of Pattern 10 not to the reconstructed terminology based on East Polynesian terminologies, which he refers to as Proto–Eastern Polynesian, but to the same structural form apparently being the pattern for Proto-Oceanic, which is ancestral to Proto-Polynesian: "Most of the living languages of Eastern Polynesia today have directly and continuously inherited the Pattern 10 system from Proto Oceanic" (e-mail communication, March 2011). According to Marck, then, the antiquity of Pattern 10 for Polynesian terminologies is shown by it being a pattern carried forward from Proto-Oceanic to the East Polynesian terminologies. In other words, assigning Pattern 10 as the root terminology structure rests on that pattern characterizing the reconstructed Proto-Oceanic terminology. However, expanding the database to include the Oceanic-language Melanesian and Micronesian terminologies listed by Marshall (1984) makes the picture more, not less, complicated.

As can be seen in Figure 4.12, Pattern 10 occurs in the terminologies for either the western or the eastern oceanic societies but not in between, despite a west-to-east spread of oceanic languages across Melanesia, Micronesia, and Polynesia. Melanesia also has a sibling terminology pattern, Pattern 6, that does not occur in any of

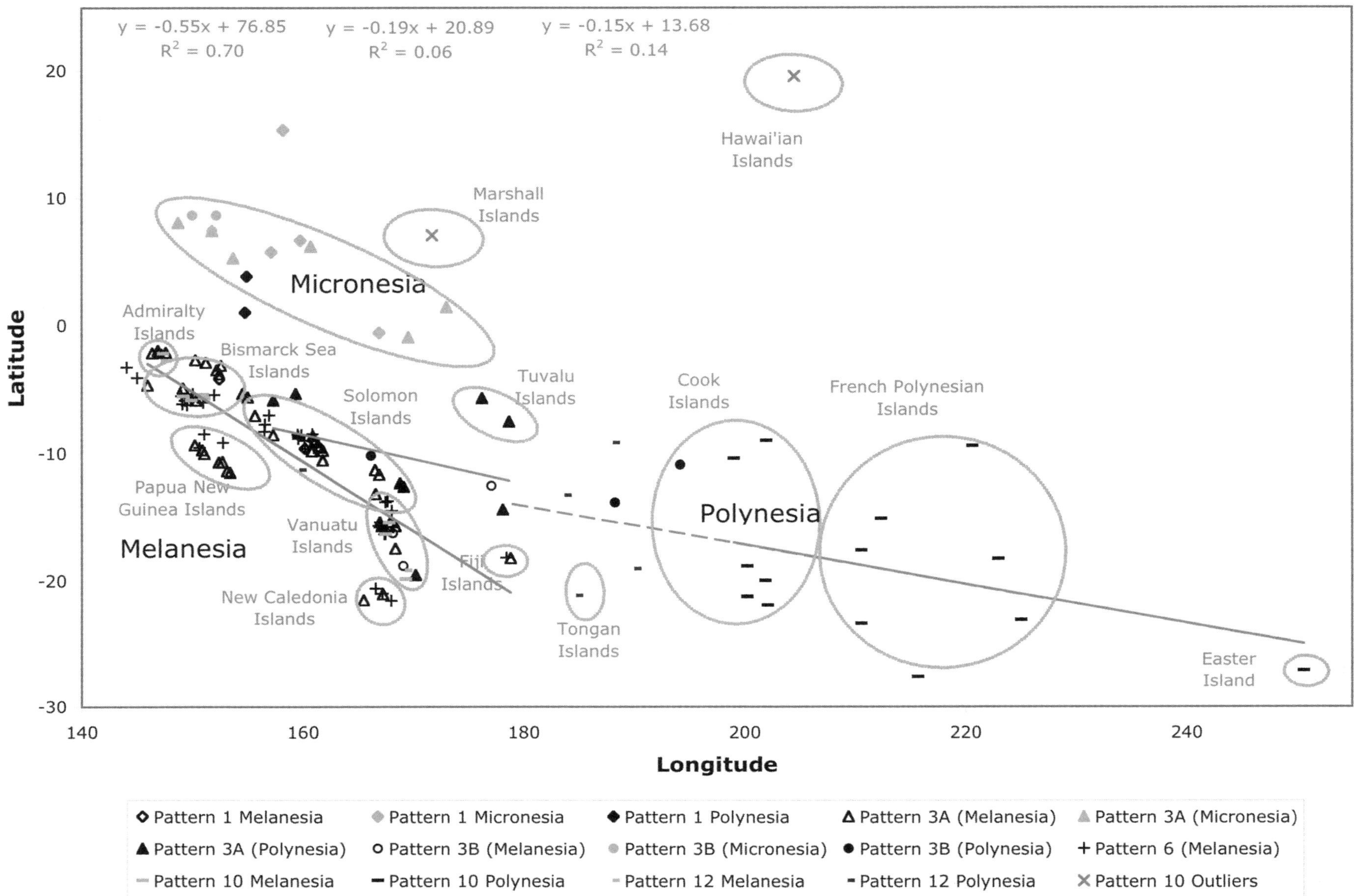

FIGURE 4.12. Geographic distribution of the sibling kin term patterns for Melanesian, Micronesian, and Polynesian kinship terminologies. The three regression lines are based on latitude versus longitude. The three equations correspond to the left, middle, and right regression lines, respectively. The dashed line is an extension of the right regression line. The societies and associated patterns are from Marshall 1984, except that Patterns 3A and 3b correspond to his Patterns 3 and 5, respectively (see text for details). Except for Pattern 6, only patterns that appear among the Polynesian kinship terminologies have been included.

the Polynesian terminologies. Pattern 6 has three sibling terms: "same-sex elder sibling," "same-sex younger sibling," and "cross-sex sibling." Ann Chowning (1984) has noted that this sibling term pattern occurs on the offshore islands along the north coast of Papua New Guinea and extends into the northwestern part of New Britain on the eastern edge of the Bismarck Sea, thus making it a candidate for being a pattern that occurs early on in terminologies in the Melanesian area. Her suggestion highlights the need to consider the geographic distribution not just of Pattern 10 but also of Pattern 6 and Pattern 3A, the two most common patterns in the Melanesian area.

These types are primarily distributed along an axis (see the leftmost regression line in Figure 4.12) extending southeast from the Admiralty to the Vanuatu islands, reflecting the geographic fact that the Melanesian region consists of a generally linear pattern of islands extending southeast from the north coast of Papua New Guinea. The axis can also be seen in the same west-to-southeast geographic locations for the Admiralties, St. Matthias, Western Oceanic and Meso-Melanesian, Southeast Solomons, Temotu, and Southern Oceanic languages. Both Pattern 3A for the Melanesian terminologies and Pattern 6 have similar distributions along this line, except that the Pattern 3A locations are statistically ($p < .05$) more prevalent above than below this axis. Pattern 10 for the Melanesian societies is also distributed along this axis, but only in societies located at its beginning and ending segments. Broadly speaking, the distribution patterns for Patterns 3A and 6 are consistent with these terminology structures being part of the colonization of this region by Austronesian/Oceanic-speaking peoples coming from Southeast Asia and Taiwan. In contrast to the wide dispersal of these two patterns, the limitation of Pattern 10 to just two localities suggests that it arose for localized reasons rather than as part of the overall, geographic pattern for the colonization of this region by Oceanic-language speakers.

The Polynesian terminologies have a very different distribution pattern. For the Pattern 3A Polynesian terminologies, the regression line for latitude versus longitude is close to horizontal, indicating an approximately west-to-east migration pattern (see the short solid line in Figure 4.12). For these terminologies, Pattern 10 does not co-occur with Pattern 3A and instead only occurs in the eastern part of the Polynesian region. If we regress latitude on longitude for the societies with a Pattern 10 terminology, we obtain an axis (long solid line in Figure 4.12), and when it is extended westward (dashed line in Figure 4.12) toward the locality where the Polynesian Pattern 3A terminologies are located, the two regression lines almost meet perfectly, thus showing the very different axis along which Polynesian colonization took place. Polynesian groups migrated easterly to the northern part of the Solomon Islands and then continued their eastward colonization along an axis heading toward Samoa (including Fiji and Tonga to the south and Tokelau to the north of this axis) rather than the more southeasterly axis that leads to the Vanuatu Islands. This easterly axis continued to the Cook Islands, French Polynesia, and Easter Island, as well as north to Hawaii. In sum, the distribution patterns for Oceanic terminologies argue against Pattern 10 being the root terminology structure.

Suppose we do not assume that Pattern 10 characterizes the reconstructed Proto-Polynesian terminology and also that there may be more than a single root terminology among Proto-Polynesian speakers. Consider what happens if Pattern 3A and Pattern 3B are both sibling patterns for root terminologies among the societies speaking Proto-Polynesian. This leads to a simple and consistent way to account for the geographical location and temporal changes in the structure of the sibling terms that is also in accord with the well-substantiated linguistic changes in the terminologies. First, Marck's reconstruction of "*kawe 'cross-sex sibling'" (1996a:218) would apply to Pattern 3A only. Second, of the two reconstructed terms, **tahina* and **tuakana*, only **tahina*, with the meaning "same-sex sibling" (rather than its "younger same-sex sibling" meaning when it is paired with **tuakana*), would be the reconstructed term for Proto-Polynesian due to its apparent time depth and stability (Marck 1996a). Third, **tahina* would occur in both Pattern 3A and Pattern 3B, as we find reflexes of **tahina* in present-day Pattern 3A and 3B terminologies (see Table 4.2). This would also account for the fact that the single term for "sibling" in Nukuoro is a reflex of **tahina* (Clark 1975; see Figure 4.9), since the structural argument implies that Pattern 1 is a transformation of Pattern 3A. Fourth, although Patterns 3A and 3B both have a "same-sex sibling" structural position, there is no reason why the linguistic expression for the "same-sex sibling" term cannot differ between Pattern 3A and Pattern 3B, just as not all present-day terminologies with Pattern 3A have terms for "same-sex sibling" that are cognates. Some Proto-Polynesian-speaking societies with Pattern 3B may have had the term **taʔo-kete*, in keeping with Marck's reconstruction of "PPn *taʔo-kete 'same-sex sibling'" (1996a:218). This would account for reflexes of

**ta?o-kete* in the Pattern 12 terminologies (see Table 4.2) as a transformation of Pattern 3B. Fifth, the "male cross-sex sibling" and "female cross-sex sibling" terms in Pattern 3B would be **tuanga'ane* and **tuafafine*, respectively, as suggested by Clark (1975) and discussed in detail in Marck 1996a.

With Patterns 3A and 3B as separate beginning points, all of the current-day terminologies are consistent with both the kinship tree and the language tree once we also include the fact that changes in terminology structure can occur independently of changes in languages. For example, as part of the Proto-Tongic and Proto–Nuclear Polynesian divergence, the ancestral societies for Tonga and Niuea would initially have been societies with Pattern 3B, which then transformed into Pattern 12. This transformation from Pattern 3B to Pattern 12 would also have occurred in the ancestral societies of East Uvea and Tokelau during their transition to Proto–Nuclear Polynesian speakers and possibly for Rennell and Taumako as well. Tonga, Niuea, East Uvea, and Tokelau would then have continued with the same terminology structure, though the ancestral society for Tokelau underwent additional linguistic change and linguistically diverged from Proto–Nuclear Polynesia to Outer Ellicean (but without any change in terminology structure).

The pattern of some societies speaking the same (or closely related) languages having Pattern 3A terminologies and others having Pattern 3B terminologies would also apply to Proto–Nuclear Polynesian speakers and to Ellicean Outlier speakers. The disappearance of Pattern 3B in present-day societies with languages that are part of Proto–Nuclear Polynesian suggests that Pattern 3B was not conservative, since there is a simple transformation from Pattern 3B to Pattern 12. Similarly, the relative paucity of Pattern 12 among current-day societies suggests that Pattern 12 was also not conservative, as there is a simple transformation from Pattern 12 to Pattern 10. As can be seen from Figure 4.10, Pattern 3A, however, appears empirically to be stable, as the only transformation is a relatively late change from Pattern 3A to Pattern 1. On the face of it, though, Pattern 1 is not a likely pattern for sibling terms because it must integrate together both a primary sibling generating term, G, and an equation, CP = G, that, by itself, implies that the sibling term is derivative and not primary. Interestingly, both examples of Pattern 1 are in the Ellicean Outlier language group, and all other societies in this group have Pattern 3A, the precursor to Pattern 1. It appears, based on the features of the kinship structure that ensued (discussed above), that this was not as simple a transformation as that from Pattern 3B to Pattern 12 or from Pattern 12 to Pattern 10, hence its relative infrequency. Finally, the ambiguity of Taumako and Rennell may reflect a recent structural transformation from Pattern 12 to Pattern 10 (assuming that the absence of a "same-sex sibling" term in these two terminologies is correct), and some aspects of Pattern 12 were carried forward in this transformation.

In sum, assigning Patterns 3A and 3B as distinct root structures for the sibling terms is consistent with all features of the current Proto-Polynesian reconstructions of the sibling terms except that of the older/younger distinction for "same-sex sibling." But the latter reconstruction leads both to an anomaly in the reconstructed Proto-Polynesian terminology as noted by Marck and to complex patterns of addition and removal of terms and change in attributes that has little motivation other than what is required for assigning the "older same-sex sibling"/"younger same-sex sibling" distinction to the Proto-Polynesian terminology. If, instead, there are two root Polynesian terminologies based on sibling term Patterns 3A and 3B due to the two structural forms being variants on the generative logic shown in Figure 4.6A and 4.6B, then we have a far simpler reconstruction that accounts for the distribution of kin terms across present-day terminologies without anomalies or positing multiple changes motivated primarily as a way to accommodate the data on the terminologies to the purported reconstruction. The two root terminologies would not need to operate simultaneously within a single society; instead, some of the early Polynesian societies would have sibling Pattern 3A, and other societies in the same time period would have sibling Pattern 3B.

There remains, however, Milke's (1938) reconstruction of Proto-Oceanic (*POC) as a Pattern 10 terminology. If that reconstruction is correct, then Pattern 10 must be the root terminology. Other authors (e.g., Blust 1980; Pawley 1981) defer to Milke (1938), so we only need to consider his reconstruction of the Proto-Oceanic sibling terms. The matter of concern here is not the historical-linguistic methods, per se, but what appears to be Milke's assumption of a single, reconstructed Proto-Oceanic terminology. Consider the patterning of the sibling terms in the terminologies used by Milke to reconstruct Proto-Oceania. Milke compiled 125 terminologies from groups from the northeastern part of Papua New Guinea extending eastward through the oceanic islands. His database consisted of the terms for either same-sex sibling, cross-sex sibling, or both. Of his 125 sets of sibling terms, 27 either are listed with some uncertain kin terms or did not have a term for both same-sex and cross-sex siblings. These sets of sibling terms will not be considered further here. Of the remaining 98 groups, 61 had a single "cross-sex sibling" term, regardless of the sex of speaker. Of these, 36 are Pattern 3A, and 25 are Pattern 6. Another 12 are Pattern 3B, with a single "same-sex sibling" term and cross-sex terms distinguished by sex of speaker. One group is Pattern 1. Finally, 24 are Pattern 10; and of these, one is actually Pattern 6 (Marshall 1984 and references therein), and two are Pattern 12, leaving 21 with Pattern 10. Of these ten are East Polynesian, and 11 are non-Polynesian. Since the ten Polynesian groups are from the most recent migration, they do not provide evidence for the antiquity of Pattern 10. Of the remaining 11 non-Polynesian groups, geographically, nine of them are from the Vanuatu Islands region, one is from the Huon Gulf near New Britain, and the last is from the Marshall Islands.

Altogether, 46 of these terminologies (Pattern 6 plus Pattern 10) have an "elder same-sex sibling"/"younger same-sex sibling" pair of terms, and 33 (Pattern 3B plus Pattern 10) have a pair of male-speaking/female-speaking "cross-sex sibling" terms. From these data Milke reconstructed *POC with the pair **taqa(ka)* (same-sex elder sibling) and **taci* (same-sex younger sibling) and the pair **mwaqane* (female cross-sex sibling) and **papine* (male cross-sex sibling). But putting these two pairs together to form a single terminology requires the assumption that all *POC speakers had a single terminology structure despite the relative rarity of Pattern 10 among the non-Polynesian groups in Milke's data set. In addition, like Pattern 10 for the Melanesian groups in Marshall's (1984) data set (which only partially overlaps with Milke's data set), these terminologies are from groups in the Vanuatu Islands, again suggesting that Pattern 10 arose as a later development and was not the pattern for the terminologies brought into the oceanic region by the colonizing Austronesian/Oceanic-speaking peoples. In contrast, and without the problems that arise with assuming that *POC is Pattern 10, positing Patterns 3A and 3B as the root structures for the Polynesian terminologies accounts for their temporal, geographic, and structural patterns. In addition, Pattern 3B accounts for the pair of cross-sex sibling terms. Pattern 6, which traces back to eastern New Guinea and has been suggested by Chowning (1984) as a possible root terminology structure, would account for the pair of parallel-sex sibling terms. Thus, allowing for *POC speakers to have had more than a single terminology structure accommodates both the linguistic data on the morphological form of kin terms and the data on the structure of the kinship terminologies.

Conclusion

Other formal analyses of kinship terminology systems, ranging from componential analysis and reduction rules to the application of Optimality Theory from phonetics, begin by assuming the terminology as a given, and consequently "questions about why kinship structures took the forms they did were ignored" (D'Andrade 2003:311). Answering these questions has been central to the argument presented here and provides the basis for constructing a kinship tree. I began the task of forming answers to these questions by distinguishing between a genealogical space and a kinship term space. This allows us to identify the cultural knowledge of kin term computations through which the structural logic of a kinship terminology is expressed. The cultural knowledge is made evident with a graphic representation of the kinship terminology structure based on the way the users of terminologies compute kin relations directly from kin terms. The structural properties of the graph help us to identify the generative logic—hence the cultural knowledge—underlying the kinship terminology that makes it possible for users of the terminology to do such computations. That generative logic is made explicit through the formal analysis of the kinship terminology structure. Not surprisingly, we find reflections of cultural knowledge embedded in the kinship terminology structure in other cultural domains. As I previously noted, the concept of brothers and sisters as alter egos in the Gilbert Islands mirrors the way a structure of male terms and a structure of female terms are joined to make a single terminology (see Figure 4.5) through the male self and the female self being interpreted as a "cross-sex sibling" and in the meaning—male and female—of the terms used as labels for the male self and female self positions.

To make the logic apparent, it has been necessary to cast it formally, which makes for difficult reading. But behind the formalism, relatively simple ideas are being examined. Stripping it to its core, I am asking: What are the basic concepts of a terminology, and how are these organized together as a system of ideas? Not surprisingly, the basic concepts are that of a parent, the reciprocal concept of a child, the self-reciprocal concept of a sibling, and the concept of spouse—concepts fundamental to what is meant by a family based on reproduction and marriage. The formalism makes it evident how a kinship terminology is generated from these basic concepts. The generative process is not fixed, in the sense that there may be alternative ways that a structure can be generated, such as whether, in some societies, sibling is conceptualized as a primary concept and used in the generation of a terminology or, in other societies, is derived from other primary concepts, such as "brother (sister)" is "son (daughter)" of "parent" in the English/American kinship terminology. Or as shown in Figure 4.6, there may be alternative ways to achieve the same end, for example, alternative ways to link together a structure of male-marked terms and a structure of female-marked terms to form a single terminology. These alternatives give rise to differences in kinship terminology structures.

Rather than seeing differences between kinship terminologies as arising from a culturally unidentified process of adding or removing terms, attributes, or equations—the assumption underlying the analyses by Epling et al. (1973) and Marshall (1984) of change in the patterns of sibling terms in the Polynesian and Oceanic terminologies, the argument of Allen (2008) for a tetradic origin of kinship terminologies, or the use of phylogenetic comparative methods borrowed from evolutionary biology (Jordan, this volume)—the structural analysis presented here identifies the generative logic behind those changes in their terms, attributes, or equations, hence what structural changes in a kinship terminology would be needed to effect the observed changes in kin terms. From a cultural perspective, one does not transform a classificatory terminology into a descriptive terminology merely by removing equations such as fb = f and mz = m, for example, since these equations derive from the logic entailed by having a sibling generating term, hence from the cultural knowledge embedded in a kinship terminology. Nor do we transform a terminology merely by users of a terminology promoting or demoting supposedly universal rules, as has been suggested by Jones (2010) as a way to apply Optimality Theory borrowed from phonetics to kinship terminologies. For the transformation from a classificatory to a descriptive terminology to take place, there would need to be, on the part of the users of the terminology, minimally a reformulation of the concept of a sibling term as a derivative and not a primary concept. Similarly, one does not change a terminology with a "same-sex sibling"/"cross-sex sibling" distinction into a terminology with a single "sibling" term merely by erasing the same-sex/cross-sex distinction. There must also be structural changes so that the generative logic now leads to a single "sibling" term rather than a pair of sibling terms.

The formalism also makes it possible to separate analytically the structural logic of the terminology from linguistic principles that relate to the morphological form of kin terms, changes in those forms, and instances where a kin term may be added to a terminology for reasons outside the generative logic of a terminology, such as the older/younger distinction for "brother of mother" in the Tongan terminology (discussed in Bennardo and Read 2005, 2007). These two kinds of analysis must ultimately be integrated together for us to have a more complete understanding of what we mean by kinship systems and kinship terminologies and how changes in the domain of kinship relate to linguistic changes, in general, and vice versa. The structural argument presented here regarding the generative logic behind the patterns for sibling terms makes it possible to work out a plausible sequence for changes in those patterns, which in turn raises questions about some aspects of the linguistic reconstruction of a Proto-Polynesian kinship terminology and the sequence of changes in kinship terminologies through time implied by that reconstruction.

One cannot just assert that *PPN first becomes, say, a terminology like Anuta by erasing the elder/younger attribute from the "same-sex sibling" terms and the sex distinction from the "cross-sex sibling" terms and then this Anuta-like terminology becomes the Kapingamarangi terminology by erasing the sex distinction and the parallel/cross distinction for sibling terms. The posited changes have to take into account the structural changes that are involved for the proposed modification of the sibling terms. Going from *PPN to a terminology such as Anuta implies that the way the ascending/descending terms are generated has to be changed from the generating sets {male self, "father," "elder sibling"}/{male self, "son," "younger sibling"}, along with the equation "elder sibling" of "younger sibling" = male self = "younger sibling" of "older sibling," into sets of generating ascending/descending terms given by {male self, "father," "sibling"}/{male self, "son," "sibling"}, along with the equation "sibling" of "sibling" = male self (for male terms). Then to go from the sibling structure of a terminology like Anuta to Kapingamarangi, another change has to take place in the ascending and descending generators from sex-marked ascending generating terms to non-sex-marked ascending generating terms, and the equation "child" of "parent" is "sibling" has to be introduced. On the face of it, this appears to be an implausible sequence of structural changes. Rather than implausible changes, the combination of the structural analysis and the linguistic analysis presented here leads to a reconstruction in which all of the posited changes are consistent with what we understand about both linguistic aspects of kin terms and structural aspects of kinship terminologies.

The kinship tree and the language tree provide us with different kinds of information about kinship terminologies. The kinship tree takes into account what structural changes are feasible, whereas the language tree integrates the structure with the linguistic domain through changes in the morphological forms of kin terms among related languages. Integrating these two kinds of analyses will lead to a richer and deeper understanding of kinship and kinship terminologies.

Notes

Murray Leaf and Kris Lehman provided useful comments on an earlier draft of the first part of this chapter on kinship space. Their comments led to a number of revisions in my discussion about family space, genealogical space, and kin term space. Critical comments and questions from editors Ian Keen and Patrick McConvell helped me to iron out some of the rough places in an earlier version of this chapter. E-mail correspondence with Jeff Marck highlighted the need to ensure that the structural analysis is not contradicted by what has already been established by historical linguists working with the Polynesian languages. His comments led to my discovery that Patterns 3A and 3B are both root structures, and that has been the key to integrating together the historical linguistic research with the structural analysis research. Any errors in the argument, though, are my responsibility.

1. The idea of constructing a kinship tree analogous to a linguistic tree was suggested by Ilia Peiros as an application of the method for the algebraic, structural analysis of kinship terminology structures that I presented at a meeting with Murray Gell-Mann at the Santa Fe Institute in Santa Fe, New Mexico, in summer 2004. Further discussions with Peiros led to focusing on the Polynesian terminologies to work out empirically the idea of a kinship tree.
2. The idea of comparing kin term changes with linguistic changes is not new (e.g., Murdock 1968). A comparison of changes in Polynesian sibling terms with language change was made by Epling et al. (1973) based on the assumption that evolutionary change in sibling terminology structure could be expressed through step changes in the binary dimensions older/younger, cross/parallel, and male/female for sibling terms. For example, in their argument a terminology with a single, neutral sibling term could change in one step to a pair of neutral parallel and cross-sibling terms or in one step to a pair of neutral older and younger sibling terms. The approach presented here differs by focusing on changes in the underlying structural logic that accounts for the patterning among the sibling terms.
3. Radcliffe-Brown (1950) considered all the relations in the family space, including sibling relations, to be first-order relations. This is consistent with a sibling relation conceptualized as a direct relation (see Figure 4.1B) and not one traced through another person (see Figure 4.1A) as assumed by Keen (1985).
4. Other authors have also noted that "sibling" appears to be conceptualized in two ways. For example, Stanley Witowski comments:

   > I considered eliminating the notion of Sb [sibling] and deriving it from underlying PC [parent's child]. With this analysis, however, I was never able to achieve a simple weighting solution to account for the [Guttman] scale ordering effects.... [S]chemes which attempt to reduce the number of semantic primitives prove unworkable.... [T]he notions of Sp, P, C, and Sb are culturally universal notions, regardless of how they are specifically defined from society to society.... [T]hese notions are universal because the relationships that they are predicated on, namely marriage (Sp), parenthood (P/C), and shared parenthood (Sb) are themselves culturally universal. (1972:181–182)

   By "shared parenthood" he is referring to the equation "parent of sibling" = "parent of self." In a similar vein, German Dziebel distinguishes terminologies where, he suggests, "ego prefers to think that he shares...common ascent with his siblings" from those he takes to be a latter stage in the evolution of kinship terminologies, when "siblings begin to be defined genealogically as parents' children" (2007:233).
5. The distinction between the two ways that brother and sister may be embedded in the family space is supported by experimental results showing decreased accuracy and longer time for informants from a culture with the first family structure (American college students) to respond to kinship terminology questions involving siblings versus parents in comparison with informants from Tonga, a culture with the second family structure (details in Bennardo and Read 2010).
6. A related construct is that of the *genealogical grid,* defined as an idealized genealogy and used methodologically for presenting genealogical definitions of kin terms.
7. Though Dousset does not make the connection, the deductions are based on the kin term product of kin terms defined in Read 1984.

8. Note also that the notion of a "relative product" has not been used consistently by different authors. Sometimes it is used to refer to products of kin types; other times, to the mathematical product of relations when kin terms are interpreted through the formalism of mathematical relations; and yet other times, with a meaning similar to the definition of a kin term product (Read 2010).
9. Dousset (2008) diagrams the kin term calculations in the form of what he refers to as a relational triangle, using the same graph structure (compare his figure 3 with Figure 4.2 in this chapter) that was introduced in Read and Behrens 1990 for diagrammatically representing a kin term product and which I have subsequently used in numerous publications.
10. Kin term products may be elicited directly from informants in the manner discussed by Murray Leaf (2006; see also Leaf and Read 2012) for the Punjabi terminology or inferred from published information on kinship terminologies.
11. The interpretation of male self as "brother" (ws) and female self as "sister" (ms) is supported by Robert Blust's observation regarding "the use of terms meaning 'male,' 'female' for the cross-siblings" (1984:627). Blust attributes the use of such terms to "drift," but that is tantamount to saying that he has no way to account for this meaning of the cross-sex sibling terms. His additional comment that "the terms for 'male,' 'female' served as classificatory labels for social groups that were conceptually individualized (or concretized) *through the cross-sibling relationship*" (1984:627; emphasis added) reinforces the structural argument presented here for the interpretation of male self as "brother" (ws) and female self as "sister" (ms). Additional support comes from the Gilbert Islands, where "brothers and sisters *are alter egos*" (Lambert 1981:190; emphasis added).
12. I use a neutral term since the Polynesian terminologies do not make a sex distinction for the same-sex parity difference. In other terminologies, including some of the Melanesian terminologies listed in Marshall 1984: app., "same-sex sibling" may be differentiated into "male same-sex sibling" and "female same-sex sibling."
13. Marck goes on to comment, "Similarly, no example comes to mind of a contemporary Polynesian language that has a term for 'same-sex' sibling and also distinguishes same-sex siblings by relative age" (1996a:223); however, the societies listed under Pattern 12 in Table 4.2 have this combination of sibling terms.

References Cited

Allen, N. J. 2008. Tetradic Theory and the Origin of Human Kinship Systems. In *Early Human Kinship: From Sex to Social Reproduction*. N. J. Allen, H. Callan, R. Dunbar, and W. James, eds. Pp. 96–112. Oxford: Blackwell Publishing.

Bennardo, G., and D. Read. 2005. The Tongan Kinship Terminology: Insights from an Algebraic Analysis. *Mathematical Anthropology and Cultural Theory* 2. Electronic document, http://www.mathematicalanthropology.org/?PG=TOC.

Bennardo, G., and D. Read. 2007. Cognition, Algebra, and Culture in the Tongan Kinship Terminology. *Journal of Cognition and Culture* 7:49–88.

Bennardo, G., and D. Read. 2010. Salience of Verticality and Horizontality in American and Tongan Kinship Terminologies. In *Kinship, Language, and Prehistory: Per Hage and the Renaissance in Kinship Studies*. D. Jones and B. Milicic, eds. Pp. 173–191. Salt Lake City: University of Utah Press.

Biersack, A. 1982. Tongan Exchange Structures: Beyond Descent and Alliance. *Journal of the Polynesian Society* 91: 181–212.

Blust, R. 1980. Early Austronesian Social Organization. *Current Anthropology* 21:205–247.

Blust, R. 1984. Comment. *Current Anthropology* 25:626–628.

Chowning, A. 1984. Comment. *Current Anthropology* 25:628.

Clark, R. 1975. Comment on Polynesian Sibling Terms. *American Anthropologist* 77:85–88.

Clark, R. 1994. The Polynesian Outliers as a Locus of Language Contact. In *Language Contact and Change in the Austronesian World*. T. Dutton and D. T. Tryon, eds. Pp. 109–139. Berlin: Mouton de Gruyter.

D'Andrade, R. 2003. Why Not Cheer? *Journal of Cognition and Culture* 4:310–314.

Dousset, L. 2005. Structure and Substance: Combining "Classic" and "Modern" Kinship Studies in the Australian Western Desert. *Australian Journal of Anthropology* 16:18–30.

Dousset, L. 2008. The "Global" versus the "Local": Cognitive Processes of Kin Determination in Aboriginal Australia. *Oceania* 78:260–279.

Dziebel, G. 2007. *The Genius of Kinship: The Phenomenon of Human Kinship and the Global Diversity of Kinship Terminologies*. Youngstown, N.Y.: Cambria Press.

Elbert, S. H., and T. Monberg. 1965. *From the Two Canoes: Oral Traditions of Rennell and Bellona Islands*. Honolulu: University of Hawaii Press.

Epling, P. J., J. Kirk, and J. P. Boyd. 1973. Genetic Relations of Polynesian Sibling Terminologies. *American Anthropologist* 75:1596–1625.

Fox, A. 1995. *Linguistic Reconstruction: An Introduction to Theory and Method*. Oxford: Oxford University Press.

Good, A. 1996. *On the Non-existence of "Dravidian Kinship."* Edinburgh: Centre for South Asian Studies, University of Edinburgh.

Guiart, J. 1961. The Social Anthropology of Aniwa, Southern New Hebrides. *Oceania* 32:34–53.

Hage, P. 1999. Linguistic Evidence for Primogeniture and Ranking in Proto-Oceanic Society. *Oceanic Linguistics* 38: 366–375.

Hage, P., and J. Marck. 2001. The Marking of Sex Distinctions in Polynesian Kinship Terminologies. *Oceanic Linguistics* 40:156–166.

Jones, D. 2010. Human Kinship, from Conceptual Structure to Grammar. *Behavioral and Brain Sciences* 33:367–381.

Keen, I. 1985. Definitions of Kin. *Journal of Anthropological Research* 41:62–90.

Kirch, P. V. 2000. *On the Road of the Winds: An Archaeological History of the Pacific Islands before European Contact.* Berkeley: University of California Press.

Kirch, P. V. 2001. A Radiocarbon Chronology for the Mussau Islands. In *Lapita and Its Transformations in Near Oceania: Archaeological Investigations in the Mussau Islands, Papua New Guinea, 1985–88*. P. V. Kirsch, ed. Pp. 196–222. Archaeological Research Facility Contribution, 59. Berkeley: University of California Press.

Kronenfeld, D. 2006a. Formal Rules, Cognitive Representations and Learning in Language and Other Cultural Systems. *Language Sciences* 28:424–435.

Kronenfeld, D. 2006b. Issues in the Classification of Kinship Terminologies: Toward a New Typology. *Anthropos* 101: 203–221.

Lambert, B. 1981. Equivalence, Authority, and Complementarity in Butaritari-Makin Sibling Relationships (Northern Gilbert Islands). In *Siblingship in Oceania*. M. Marshall, ed. Pp. 149–200. Ann Arbor: University of Michigan Press.

Leaf, M. 2006. Experimental Analysis of Kinship. *Ethnology* 45: 305–330.

Leaf, M., and D. Read. 2012. *The Conceptual Foundation of Human Society and Thought: Anthropolgy on a New Plane*. Lanham, MD: Lexington Books.

Levinson, S. C. 2002. Matrilineal Clans and Kin Terms on Rossel Island. *Linguistics* 48:1–43.

Marck, J. 1996a. Kin Terms in the Polynesian Proto-Languages. *Oceanic Linguistics* 35:195–257.

Marck, J. 1996b. *Polynesian Language and Culture: Polynesian Kinship Appendix*. Canberra: Australian National University.

Marck, J. 1999. Revising Polynesian Linguistic Subgrouping and Its Culture History Implications. In *Language Change and Cultural Transformation*. R. Blench and M. Spriggs, eds. Pp. 95–122. London: Routledge.

Marck, J. 2000. *Topics in Polynesian Language and Culture*. Canberra: Pacific Linguistics.

Marshall, L. 1976. *The !Kung of Nyae Nyae*. Cambridge: Harvard University Press.

Marshall, M. 1984. Structural Patterns of Sibling Classification in Island Oceania: Implications for Culture History. *Current Anthropology* 25:597–637.

Marshall, M., ed. 1983. *Siblingship in Oceania*. ASAO Monograph, 8. Lanham, MD: University Press of America.

Milke, W. 1938. Die Benennungen der Geschwister in den austronesischen Sprachen ozeaniens. *Zeitschrift für Ethnologie* 70:51–66.

Ministry of Education. 2009. *Mua Ō! An Introduction to Gagana Sāmoa*. Auckland: Teuila Consultancy and Ethnic Communications.

Murdock, G. P. 1968. Patterns of Sibling Terminology. *Ethnology* 7:1–24.

Murdock, G. P. 1970. Kin Term Patterns and Their Distribution. *Ethnology* 9:165–207.

Parkin, R. 1996. Genealogy and Category: An Operational View. *L'Homme* 139:87–108.

Parkin, R. 2009. What Shapiro and McKinnon Are All About, and Why Kinship Still Needs Anthropologists. *Social Anthropology* 17:158–170.

Pawley, A. 1981. Melanesian Diversity and Polynesian Homogeneity. In *Studies in Pacific Languages and Cultures in Honour of Bruce Biggs*. J. Hollyman and A. Pawley, eds. Pp. 269–309. Auckland: Linguistic Society of New Zealand.

Radcliffe-Brown, A. 1913. Three Tribes of Western Australia. *Journal of the Royal Anthropological Institute* (n.s.) 43:143–194.

Radcliffe-Brown, A. R. 1950. Introduction. In *African Systems of Kinship and Marriage*. A. R. Radcliffe-Brown and D. Forde, eds. Pp. 1–85. Oxford: Oxford University Press.

Read, D. 1984. An Algebraic Account of the American Kinship Terminology. *Current Anthropology* 25:417–449.

Read, D. 2000. Formal Analysis of Kinship Terminologies and Its Relationship to What Constitutes Kinship (Complete Text). *Mathematical Anthropology and Culture Theory* 1:1–46.

Read, D. 2001a. Formal Analysis of Kinship Terminologies and Its Relationship to What Constitutes Kinship. *Anthropological Theory* 1:239–267.

Read, D. 2001b. What Is Kinship? In *The Cultural Analysis of Kinship: The Legacy of David Schneider and Its Implications for Anthropological Relativism*. R. Feinberg and M. Ottenheimer, eds. Pp. 78–117. Urbana: University of Illinois Press.

Read, D. 2007. Kinship Theory: A Paradigm Shift. *Ethnology* 46:329–364.

Read, D. 2010. The Logic and Structure of Kinship Terminologies: Implications for Theory and Historical Reconstructions. In *Kinship, Language, and Prehistory: Per Hage and the Renaissance in Kinship Studies*. D. Jones and B. Milicic, eds. Pp. 152–172. Salt Lake City: University of Utah Press.

Read, D., and C. Behrens. 1990. KAES: An Expert System for the Algebraic Analysis of Kinship Terminologies. *Journal of Quantitative Anthropology* 2:353–393.

Schieffelin, E. L. 1976. *The Sorrow of the Lonely and the Burning of the Dancers*. New York: St. Martin's Press.

Spriggs, M. 1999. Archaeological Dates and Linguistic Subgroups in the Settlements of the Island Southeast Asian–Pacific Region. *Bulletin of the Indo-Pacific Prehistory Association* 18:17–24.

Trautmann, T. R. 1992. The Revolution in Ethnological Time. *Man* (n.s.) 27:379–397.

Witowski, S. 1972. Guttman Scaling of Semantic Distinctions. In *Kinship Studies in the Morgan Centennial Year*. P. Reining, ed. Pp. 167–188. Washington, DC: Smithsonian Institution.

5

On Husband-Borrowing

The Linguistic Reconstruction of Ancient Yukatekan Marriage Practices

Eve Danziger

The ruins of a sophisticated and literate society lie scattered in the rain forests and plains of Guatemala, Belize, and southern Mexico. These ruins are found over a wide variety of ecological terrains, from the snowcapped Highlands of the Pacific to the hot, dry, low-lying plains of the Yucatán Peninsula that juts into the Caribbean and in the rain forests of the more modestly mountained Petén area in between. The ruins, and the inscribed texts that are found in them, testify to the history and prehistory of the Maya peoples who have for the past several millennia occupied this area (Coe 2005). The ancient Maya, as they are popularly known, are justly famous for their monumental architecture, their writing system (Coe 1999), and their elaboration of astronomy, cosmology, and mathematics (Schele and Freidel 1992).

Prehistorians agree that we would like to know more about the social organization, and particularly the marriage practices, of the preconquest peoples of the modern Maya area (Gillespie 2000:467). Based on ethnographic comparison with the modern Mayan groups and on the accounts of the Spanish, there is general agreement that patrilineal descent—which today characterizes all of the modern groups—was one foundation of social organization throughout Mayan prehistory.[1] A consensus that cousin marriage of some kind was a prominent feature is also notable (cf. Eggan 1934; Fox and Justeson 1986; Hopkins 1988), but there is little agreement on the question of the precise marriage type(s) that might have been the norm in this area over the long period of precontact fluorescence.

The content of the stone inscriptions is largely historical and tells of kings and their conquests (cf. Schele and Freidel 1992). The content of the few surviving bark books of the immediately precolonial period concerns astronomy and prophecy (Wald 2004). In neither case are there extant indigenous accounts of local social organization, although kin relations are mentioned from time to time (Coe and Van Stone 2001; Stuart 1997). Therefore, despite the pre-European tradition of literacy in the Maya area, for an understanding of the kinship and marriage practices of the ancient Maya we are dependent on the accounts of Terminal Postclassic practices left by Spanish friars from the 16th century on, and on the traditional techniques of the prehistorian—that is, on ethnographic analogy, archaeological extrapolation, and linguistic reconstruction.

In what follows, I pursue the question from the point of view of historical linguistics, examining in particular the probable historical semantics of kin and affine terminology in Proto-Yukatekan, one subfamily of the large Mayan family. Drawing evidence most particularly from terms for "husband" and "wife," in the context of a full reconstruction of the Proto-Yukatekan terminological system, and with reference to neighboring groups with whom contact is already attested, I propose that the Proto-Yukatekans practiced patrilateral cross-cousin marriage (prescribed marriage of a man to his classificatory father's sister's daughter) during the first millennium BCE (mid- to late Preclassic). I propose these ideas based on a method of kin term reconstruction that exploits fully the existing analogy between the synchronic analysis of kinship terms as bundles of semantic features and the analysis of speech sounds as bundles of phonological features. Exploitation of this analogy allows me to "piggyback" my reconstruction of kin term meanings on the very successful methods of phonological reconstruction in historical linguistics first pioneered by the Neogrammarians in the 19th century and still the textbook basis of phonological reconstruction today (Campbell 1998; Hock and Joseph 1996).

Kin Term Semantics and Phonological Reconstruction

Feature-Based Approaches

In the study of kin term semantics, an important breakthrough was achieved with the insight (Goodenough 1956; Lounsbury 1956) that contrasting values of the same recurring semantic dimensions, or semantic "features," are in use across the various terms of the domain within any given language and to some extent across languages as well. For example, the point was made that, in English, the semantic difference between the two terms *aunt* and *uncle* is reducible to their different values (female and male, respectively) on the single dimension "sex of referent," whereas the difference between the two terms *aunt* and *niece* is reducible to their different values (senior and junior, respectively) on another dimension—that of seniority. The difference between the two terms *aunt* and *nephew* could then be seen as a difference in semantic value on both of these dimensions at once. The contrasting values on dimensions that distinguish one kin term from another within a system in this way are often specified as "features" of a term. So the English *aunt* bears the features "plus senior," "plus female," and so on.

Many of the dimensions that have been identified as semantically contrastive in the kinship vocabularies of the world's languages are less intuitively labeled than these by the untrained analyst—for example, the difference between *mother* and *aunt* in English is traceable to their different values on a dimension we can call collaterality.[2] And many, of course, do not apply in English at all (Kroeber 1909). An area of debate within the field of feature-based kinship semantics at the time of its heyday in the 1960s and 1970s was the question of whether analysts could expect to find new dimensions of contrast—some perhaps startlingly unfamiliar to Europeanists—as they explored kin term systems in more and more languages or whether a small and finite set of such dimensions existed, which could be assumed by the mid–20th century to have been fully discovered (Leach 1958; Lounsbury 1964). The latter is of course the more universalizing position; the former recognizes more relativistic possibilities (cf. Danziger 2001 and discussion below).

Under either philosophical umbrella, the approach to kinship semantics in terms of feature values on dimensions of contrast is undoubtedly helpful in bringing order to lists of terms that otherwise appear as mere jumbles of disjunct extensions. So, for example, Boremanse writes of the kin term system of the Northern Lacandon (Lakantun) Maya that

> a man classifies his father and son in the same category (*yum*) whereas a woman classifies her father in one category (*yum*) and her son in another category (*äkän*). On the other hand a man classifies his mother in one category (*na'*) and his daughter in another (*ixkit*), whereas a woman classifies her mother and her daughter in the same category. (1977–78:142)[3]

Elsewhere in Boremanse's (1977–78:134–135) description, we discover that the term *ixkit* also refers, for both men and women, to a father's sister (FZ) and to a brother's daughter (BD), while the term *äkän* also refers, for both men and women, to a mother's brother (MB) and to a sister's son (ZS).[4] We also learn that *na'* applies to a man's or a woman's mother's sister (MZ) and is used by both men and women to refer to a sister's daughter (ZD). In analogous fashion, *yum* applies to a man's or a woman's father's brother (FB) and is used by both men and women to refer to a brother's son (BS).

We can apply an analysis in terms of semantic features to bring clarity to the set of meanings of these four terms. Each term refers to kin who are separated by a single generation, and we can describe the differences among them as those that result from realizing all possibilities at the intersection of two semantic dimensions that have two possible values each. The two dimensions and their values are as follows: (1) the sex of the referent (male or female) and (2) the sex of the relative who links referent to relatum in the position immediately adjacent to the referent (male or female).[5] Thus, all four terms can be defined as applying to one member of a pair of kin who are separated by a single generation:

> Northern Lakantun:
> *na'*: The referent is female, and the link between referent and relatum passes through a female in the position immediately adjacent to the referent. This person is referenced in her capacity as a mother or as the daughter or sister of a woman.
> *yum*: The referent is male, and the link between

referent and relatum passes through a male in the position immediately adjacent to the referent. This person is referenced in his capacity as a father or as the son or brother of a man.

äkän: The referent is male, and the link between referent and relatum passes through a female in the position immediately adjacent to the referent. This person is referenced in his capacity as the son or brother of a woman.

ixkit: The referent is female, and the link between referent and relatum passes through a male in the position immediately adjacent to the referent. This person is referenced in her capacity as the daughter or sister of a man.

The interest of this semantic approach for historical reconstruction lies in the fact that it was developed explicitly on the model of feature-based analysis in the study of speech sounds. In traditional phonology, the different phonemes of a given language are understood to differ from one another as a consequence of their realization of a unique combination of features on each of the several phonological dimensions (e.g., voicing, fricativity, nasality) that are relevant to that language. Speech sounds, like kin term meanings under dimensional analysis, can readily be described as the instantiation of a set of contrasting values on a set of common dimensions.

While newer approaches to synchronic analysis in phonology have come and gone, the approach based on phonological features remains the uncontested leader when it comes to the reconstruction of protophonologies in past language systems. This feature-based approach to phonology underpins the solid success of the comparative method in phonological reconstruction and is uniformly recognized in pedagogical texts as the sine qua non of historical-linguistic method (Campbell 1998; Hock and Joseph 1996).

In this method, recurring correspondences of the same sounds in similar words are compared across languages, and if the correspondences are regular, a protosound is proposed ("reconstructed") for each such correspondence set. Each reconstructed protosound is expected to instantiate an ancestral sound for all of the daughters in the correspondence set. Where the sounds in the correspondence set are not all identical, the reconstruction of any particular ancestral sound is ipso facto also the postulation of some specific sound change(s) that must have taken place in order to derive the modified daughter(s) from the proposed ancestor. Ancestral sounds ("protosounds") are therefore best reconstructed such that they would require the fewest and most probable sound changes in order to have produced their daughter sound(s). Probable sound changes are identified from known cases in other languages and families. Meanwhile, the calculation of fewest necessary changes is made in terms of preservation in the protolanguage of those phonological dimensions shown in the greatest possible number of daughter languages and, similarly, preservation of the most common values on each such dimension. If reconstructed protosounds must vary from what is actually found in one or more of the daughters, they should vary in as few features as possible. Finally, it is desirable that the full inventory of reconstructed protosounds should reproduce the relative systematicity of known phonological inventories. Newly reconstructed sounds should make use of phonological dimensions already in play elsewhere in the already reconstructed inventory. To the extent possible, proliferation of special-purpose, one-time-use dimensions is to be avoided, and all possible values on already postulated dimensions should be exploited. In applying this method, an inventory of specific changes can be built up and can itself in the future be examined for evidence about the nature, direction, and likelihood of change in other language contexts.

I propose that the analogy between the feature-based approach to phonological analysis and the feature-based approach to kin term semantics can be used to address the historical reconstruction of kin term systems (cf. Frisch and Schutz 1967). Using the analogy, it should be possible to apply feature-based reconstruction to terms of the kinship domain within related languages. I will defend my proposal by undertaking a reconstruction of the kinship terms of Proto-Yukatekan, a protolanguage ancestral to the several extant languages of the Yukatekan subfamily of the Mayan language family. While principles of historical phonology have been used to add various terms with kinship-related glosses to the relatively extensive lists of reconstructed vocabulary for both Proto-Yukatekan and its ancestor, Proto-Mayan (Dienhart 1989; Fox and Justeson 1986; Kaufman and Justeson 2003), these terms are not integrated into the kinds of interlocking semantic paradigms that we know to be characteristic of living kin term systems throughout the world (cf. McConvell, chapter 10, this volume). Conversely, several attempts to reconstruct the full system of Proto-Yukatekan kinship (Eggan 1934; Hage 2003) do not fully exploit the resources of historical-linguistic and archaeological knowledge that exist today for the Maya area.

Semantic change is an area of historical linguistics that—unlike sound change, for example—offers little in the way of predictable regularity. The best that students of semantic change are ordinarily able to do is to create typologies of known changes (widening, narrowing, etc.) after they have occurred. Semantic change is perhaps best understood at the most general level as the outcome of a process of recurrent reanalysis in some consistent direction (Fortson 2005) that is itself facilitated by a frequently recurring "bridging context" (Evans and Wilkins 2000) of use. Change of this kind, in short, often takes place through unrecognized misunderstanding, in contexts that allow the same misunderstanding to occur frequently and to go more or less unrecognized over the long term. The semantic changes that result may endure in the language long after the sociological bridging contexts that fostered them have disappeared (for example, it is often repeated that the origins of the English word *salary* lie in the fact that Roman soldiers were at one time paid partly in salt). With respect to kin term usage, one way in which bridging contexts could arise that would repeatedly favor unrecognized reanalysis in a consistent direction is through the operation of prescribed or preferred marriage and residence rules. While recognizing that such efforts are merely statements of hypotheses, I follow the exposition of the Proto-Yukatekan reconstruction proper with some speculations about the social organization(s) that might have provided communicative bridging contexts favorable to the origins of the semantic arrangements that the reconstruction proposes. I conclude that during the middle (1000–250 BCE) and late Preclassic (250 BCE–CE 250), ordinary Proto-Yukatekans practiced patrilateral cross-cousin marriage. The study thus raises new questions for linguistic, sociocultural, and archaeological reflection in the Maya area while at the same time demonstrating a method for the reconstruction of kinship terms that is in principle applicable to all areas of the world.

Rewrite Rules and Other Challenges to Feature-Based Analyses

The demonstration that feature-based semantic analyses were applicable to terminological domains such as that of kinship caused great excitement in anthropology, even engendering a new subfield: "cognitive anthropology" (D'Andrade 1995). But dimensional analyses based on formal semantics are no longer the norm in ethnographic studies of kinship. Several factors were responsible for the decline of the approach. None of these, I maintain, is sufficient to warrant its rejection as an aid to the reconstruction of historical semantics.

A major factor in the abandonment of the feature-based approach to kinship in anthropology was a cataclysmic shift in paradigm (the "Rethinking Anthropology" movement [Needham 1971]) in which it was maintained that comparison across cultures was in general a pointless exercise, since no third terms existed or could be created that would allow such comparison. The study of kinship terminology was held up as a central example, with citation of the fact that the actual application of such terminology showed both emergent and, especially, non-genealogical uses in many cases. The radical conclusion was drawn that "there is no such thing as kinship, and it follows that there can be no such thing as kinship theory" (Needham 1971:5). While the argument may (or may not) be persuasive that "there is no such thing as kinship," it is in fact in the face of the evidence not at all persuasive that there is no such thing across languages as semantic structuring in terms of an interlocking set of contrastive dimensions (not necessarily the same ones across all languages, but remarkable in showing a high degree of recurrence nonetheless) of a set of terms for two-placed predications of relationships among social beings. In certain cases, if the content of one or more dimensions is not genealogical (Leach 1958), we might engage in debate as to whether we should properly use the word *kinship*. Such debate is of little import for the question of whether the reconstruction of domains so structured can be pursued using the analogy with feature-based phonology that their structuring suggests.

This defense of the existence of "kinship terminology" (if not of "kinship" itself) means that the method for the reconstruction of kin term systems here demonstrated has much in common with accepted approaches to the reconstruction of morphological paradigms—themselves often implicitly or explicitly analyzed in terms of contrastive values on crosscutting semantic dimensions. By the same token, this method of kin term reconstruction probably does not, as was at one time claimed (Frisch and Schutz 1967), have wider applicability to the amorphous field of semantic reconstruction in general.

From the point of view of the formal issues involved, a more serious challenge to feature-based approaches to kinship analysis came from one of its own founders

(Lounsbury 1964). In what came to be called Crow-Omaha systems of kin term application, terminologies confounded Europeanist observers by classifying relatives in the parents' generation together with their own children. So, under the variant of Omaha classification practiced by the Tzeltal Maya of the Spanish colonial period (Tenner 1978), for example, a man calls his mother's brother by the same term (*ichan*, reciprocal *ichak*) that he uses for that same mother's brother's child.[6] In complementary fashion, the original man classifies his father's sister's and his own (elder) sister's children (FZC, eZC) together (*ichak*, reciprocal *ichan*), although one set of children (FZC) are members of his own generation (his patrilateral cross-cousins) and the other (eZC) are members of a generation junior to his own.[7] This kind of terminological practice has given rise to the expression "generational skewing" often used by analysts to characterize Crow-Omaha kinship terminologies.

The Kroeberian (1909) repertoire of genealogical dimensions available to discriminate among kinship terms did not include anything that could handle such a phenomenon. Lounsbury's (1964) solution, explicitly modeled on the new ideas of the Transformational Generative linguists who were then coming into popularity, was to analyze "generational skewing" precisely as such—in terms of "rewrite rules" that reduced the complicated "skewed" classifications to simpler ones that could be handled in Kroeberian terms.[8] Thus, for the Colonial Tzeltal example above, the relationship MBC could undergo a stipulated "rewrite," to specify that this relationship should be considered formally equivalent to that of MB. Then, the full analysis could go forward taking MB alone (minus the awkward inclusion of MBC) as notionally the only denotatum of *ichan*, the lexeme that includes both MB and MBC among its kin type extensions (see Hopkins 1969).

For analysts willing to part company with Kroeber (1909), however, and to propose the existence of new and sometimes culturally particular dimensions of "kinship" contrast where the evidence suggested them, a feature-based approach to "generational skewing" was, on the other hand, quite possible. For example, commonalities of tribute obligations (Leach 1958) or of inheritance (Lounsbury 1956), often tied to lineage affiliation, might unite certain kin across the generation boundary. A feature-based approach to Omaha usage therefore deals with the fact that MB is classified with MBC, despite the fact that they belong to different generations, simply by proposing that the dimension of "generation" is not relevant to making this particular contrast.

Even at the time, many of those involved (W. H. Goodenough, personal communication, 1991) took the view that unless one was proposing to investigate issues of individual psychology (cf. Danziger 2001; Kronenfeld 2006), the feature-based and the rewrite approach could be taken simply to be notational variants of one another. If one took the trouble to motivate one's rewrite rules at all (as many analysts do [cf. McConvell n.d.]), one was likely to end up with a motivating principle (albeit a novel one with respect to the Kroeberian list) that could be used by the adventurous feature-analyst as a primary dimension of contrast. Conversely, we could propose, the existence of terminologically skewed systems in the historical record may license the hypothesis that an even earlier "bridging context" of frequent social practice once constituted a motivation for the semantic merger that is now seen as "skewing."

Not all practitioners of kinship analysis were willing, however, to abandon their Europeanist intuitions sufficiently to allow this kind of comfortable coexistence. Many were uneasy with the idea that new semantic dimensions for kinship analysis could be admitted at will (Lounsbury 1969) and insisted upon the primacy of basic and universal nuclear family categories.[9] Rewrite rules in kinship analysis, then, like the syntactic devices of the transformationalists on which they were based, had as one of their strongest motivations an overriding desire to achieve universality in the basic architectures being proposed and an aversion to the idea that culturally particular features or dimensions of analysis, perhaps very distant from those that could be seen to operate in English, might otherwise have to be proposed in order to do justice to systems of linguistic usage newly coming under analysis.[10]

Whatever its merits in preserving the possibility of comparison across cultures, there is little to be gained in proposing that an approach based on rewrite rules could be a fruitful avenue into the reconstruction of past kinship systems. In historical reconstruction, such an approach would be pointless if applied to the basic categories to which rewrite rules and their equivalents reduce all variation (since by definition these are always the same—prehistoric kinship systems were all based on the same universal nuclear family referents as are those of today) and redundant with a feature-based approach if applied to the rewrite rules themselves (since we have seen that well-motivated rewrite rules are largely equivalent in content to semantically unifying features). What was radical in the rewrite approach with respect to the feature-based one, in short, was precisely that which will not translate into an interesting plan for tackling diachronic change—namely, a proposal that all kin term systems are ultimately alike.

Proto-Mayan and Its Descendants

The indigenous inhabitants of the entire region over which ancient Mayan ruins are found are speakers of languages that are related to one another by descent from a common ancestor ("Proto-Mayan") that began to break up about 4,000 years ago (Swadesh 1961). It will be useful for what follows to be roughly familiar with the three successive chronological periods into which archaeologists divide the long pre-Columbian era of social complexity in the Maya region. The Classic era of Mayan civilization (roughly CE 250–900) flourished in the geographically central Petén area of the region and has as its diagnostic criterion the use of "Long Count" calendar dates in inscriptions in this area.[11] The earlier Preclassic era (roughly 2000 BCE to CE 250) covers the immediately preceding period, which, although already marked by monumental architecture and elaborate iconography, predates the introduction of the Long Count into the Maya area (for recent updates to this characterization, see Tedlock 2010). The Postclassic era, meanwhile, began during the tenth century CE, when Long Count dates ceased to be used at the—still monumental, still literate—sites of the region. The loss of the Long Count is a major diagnostic of the famous demographic and ecological "collapse" in pre-Columbian Maya history, which occurred at the transition between the Classic and Postclassic eras. At the time of the collapse as well, the focus of monumental architecture and written history shifted from the Petén rain forest to the Yucatán Peninsula. The Postclassic era is considered to terminate with the arrival of the Spanish in 1524.

The sound correspondences and sound changes that characterize the relatedness of the 30-odd languages of the large Mayan family are well worked out (Campbell 1984), and the grand lines of subclassification within the family are also well understood (Campbell and Kaufman 1985; McQuown 1956). The Wastekan ("Huaxtecan" or "Tenek"), the Yukatekan ("Yucatecan"), the Eastern Mayan, and the Greater Cholan subfamilies are generally recognized as high-level subgroupings identified by shared phonological innovations.[12] The association of the Classic period monuments with speakers of (Greater) Cholan is now largely accepted (Houston et al. 2000), as is the association of Postclassic society in the Yucatán with Yukatekan speakers. It is with these two Mayan subfamilies that we will be most concerned.

Figure 5.1 provides a reference graphic for the Mayan language family. The subdivision of Greater Cholan into the lower-level subfamilies of Cholan proper (which includes the postconquest languages Chol, Chontal, Ch'orti, and Ch'olti) and of Tzeltalan (which includes the two modern languages Tzeltal and Tzotzil) is well accepted. Yukatekan meanwhile subdivides relatively recently into a number of modern languages: Mopan, Itza, Lakantun, and Yukatek. While there is some difference of opinion as to the exact subclassification of the different Yukatekan languages among themselves (Hofling 2004), they share many features of grammar and lexicon (Danziger 1996) and are mutually intelligible. Estimates of the date of the breakup of the Yukatekan subfamily conventionally place this event about 1,000 years ago, or roughly at the time of the Classic–Postclassic transition (Swadesh 1961). The prehistory of the Proto-Yukatekan subfamily is therefore a long one: Proto-Yukatekan is imagined to have diverged from Proto-Mayan very early on and subsequently to have maintained itself as a single speech community for perhaps three millennia. In the geographic environment of the flat, easily traveled Yucatán Peninsula, this is not impossible to imagine.

The language spoken in the Yucatán Peninsula during the 16th century was an immediate ancestor of modern Yukatek known as "Colonial Yukatek."[13] Spanish missionary policies of the time made documentation of the indigenous languages a priority, and the earliest dictionary of Colonial Yukatek bears a publication date of 1577 (Martinez Hernandez 1930[1577]). Spanish documentation also informs us that speakers of a Yukatekan language were, in 16th-century Yucatán, the builders and inhabitants of great cities and that the Mayan inscriptions and codices of the time could be read—and written—in Colonial Yukatek (Landa 1941[1566]). Knowledge of the writing system was, however, deliberately eradicated in very short order by the Spanish and had to be painstakingly pieced together over the course of the 19th and 20th centuries to reach the point where today, a large portion of the texts can again be read (Coe 1999).

Yukatekan speakers, however, were not the primary initiators and bearers of cultural complexity in the Maya area. The archaeological indexes of social complexity

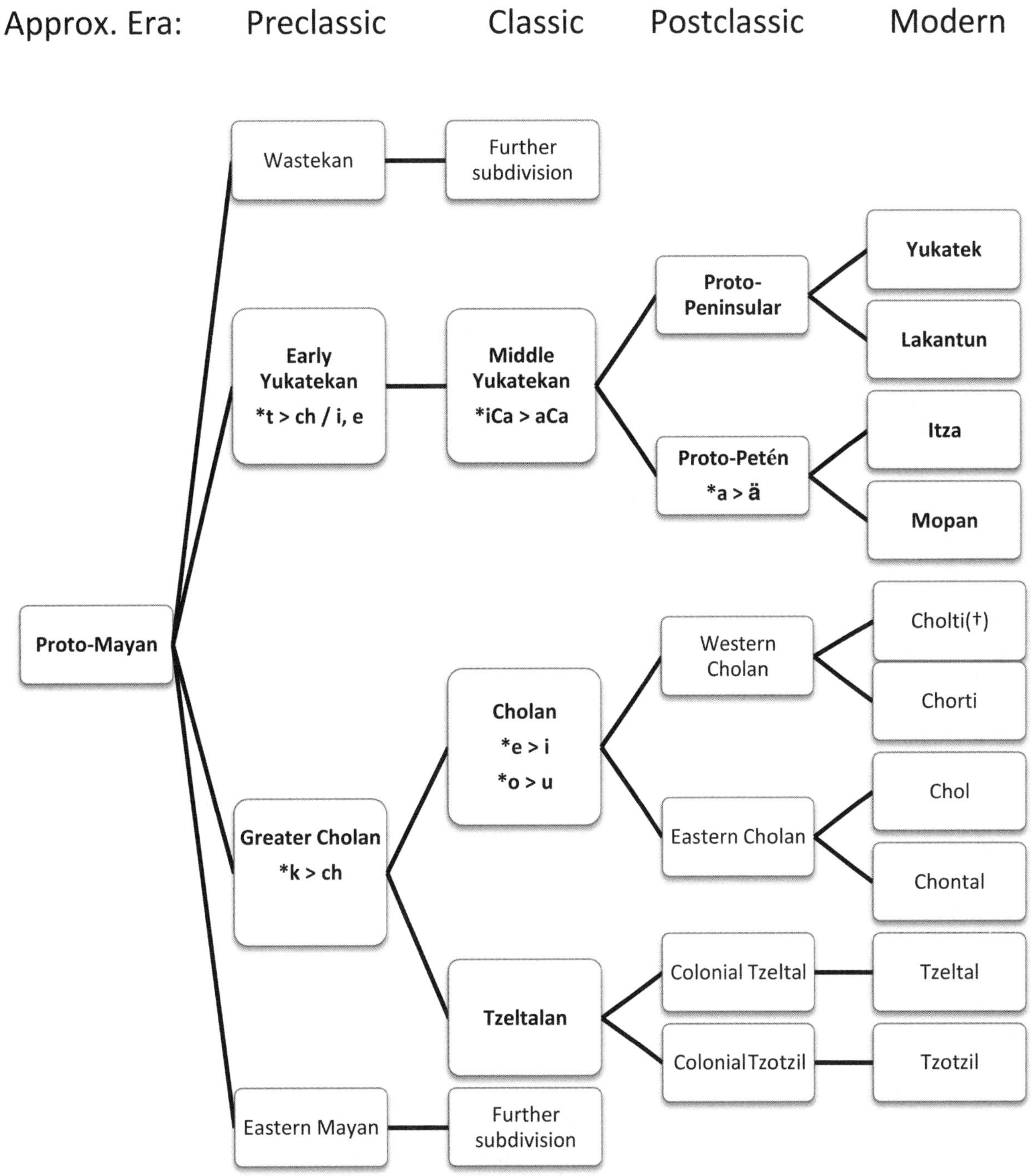

FIGURE 5.1. Mayan language family. Families and languages of interest to the argument are shown in bold, with some diagnostic sound changes. Figure draws on Kaufman 1990; Law 2009:219.

are earliest in the Pacific Highlands area, where they are associated with earlier, non-Mayan civilizations already flourishing farther north in other regions of what is now Mexico (Coe and Koontz 2008). The new ideas traveled slowly west through the Petén area and eventually into the Yucatán, where evidence of complex society is discernible only by the mid-Preclassic. On archaeological and geographic evidence, Greater Cholan is associated with the bearers of complex society during the later Preclassic period. After the breakup of Greater Cholan, Cholan speakers alone are credited with the Classic-era production of Long Count dates and their associated inscriptions.[14] Yukatekan is the subfamily most closely associated with the developments of the Postclassic era.[15]

TABLE 5.1. Archaeological, geographic, and linguistic correlates in the Maya area.

Archaeological Period	Dates	Geographic Area	Language Subfamily
Preclassic			
Early	2000–1000 BCE	Highlands	Non-Mayan
Mid	1000–250 BCE	Highlands	Non-Mayan/(Greater) Cholan
Late	250 BCE–250 CE	Highlands/Petén	Non-Mayan/(Greater) Cholan
Classic			
Early	250–600 CE	Petén	Cholan
Late	600–900 CE	Petén/Yucatán	Cholan/Yukatekan
Postclassic			
Early	900–1200 CE	Yucatán	Yukatekan
Late	1200–1500 CE	Yucatán	Yukatekan

Table 5.1 gives a rough summary of archaeological, geographic, and linguistic associations in the Maya area (cf. Kaufman 1976).[16]

There is good linguistic evidence of extensive and sustained contact between Proto-Yukatekan and Greater Cholan. Such contact has reflexes that are visible in Yukatekan, Cholan, and Tzeltalan languages of today, and borrowings in both directions between the two subfamilies, which include grammatical influences, can be identified (Justeson et al. 1985). Certain innovated vocabulary of this period is shared across Yukatekan and Greater Cholan languages (Greater Lowland Mayan, or GLM, vocabulary). The evidence suggests, however, that after the breakup of Greater Cholan, contact with Proto-Yukatekan was limited to speakers of Cholan proper; the new Tzeltalan subfamily lost contact with Proto-Yukatekan (Justeson et al. 1985). A corpus of innovated vocabulary shared only between Yukatekan and Cholan languages is known as the Lowland Mayan (LM) vocabulary. Of particular relevance to the present argument, certain borrowings from (Greater) Cholan into Yukatekan can be identified because they show evidence of the hallmark sound change **k(')* > *ch(')*, which characterizes Greater Cholan but which did not occur in Yukatekan (Kaufman and Norman 1984). This Greater Cholan sound change, and the concomitant separation of Greater Cholan from its sister subfamilies, must have been complete by the final centuries of the pre-Christian era. We know this because the sound change did not affect the [k] sounds in the Greater Cholan word for "chocolate." It is clear from archaeological evidence that cacao arrived in the Greater Cholan area only in the middle Preclassic—evidently too late for the newly arrived term to undergo the change. In some cases, lexical doublets appear in Yukatekan: one member of the pair is native Yukatekan and shows [k] in the positions where the Cholan borrowing shows [ch]. As we would expect, there is usually a slight difference in meaning between the two members of the pair. Some but not all elements of GLM vocabulary show this doubling. All relevant elements of LM vocabulary show it.

Meanwhile, in the Yukatekan subfamily, a conditioned sound change took place that did not affect the Greater Cholan languages (Justeson et al. 1985): In Yukatekan **iCa* > *aCa*, if the first vowel is short, and C is not [h].[17] There is good evidence (for example, in the fact that the GLM word **kitaam* 'peccary' did not undergo this Yukatekan change [cf. Mopan *kitam*]) that this change was complete by the time that the lexical innovations of even the earliest episodes of Yukatekan contact with Greater Cholan began to be made. We know that the Greater Cholan change **k* > *ch* was ongoing during the GLM contact era, and that this consonant change was complete by the time of the arrival of chocolate in the mid-Preclassic. Since the Yukatekan vowel change was earlier, it must have taken place in the early or perhaps early middle Preclassic (i.e., no later than about 500 BCE).

Yukatekan Kinship

Among the Yukatekan languages, it is possible to prepare a full analysis of the indigenous kin term systems only of Northern Lakantun (Boremanse 1977–78), Mopan (Danziger 2001; Thompson 1930), and, thanks to the

1577 Motul dictionary, to a great extent Colonial Yukatek (Martinez Hernandez 1930[1577]). The kinship system of Southern Lakantun is undocumented. In Modern Yukatek and in Itza, usage has largely switched to Spanish terminology. Happily, the three languages for which good information is available span the subfamily.

A system of kin terminology in which kin terms recur in alternate generations (so that a brother and a father's father are, for example, called by the same term), coupled with a strong preference for cross-cousin marriage, was documented in the late 20th century among Northern Lakantun speakers (Boremanse 1977–78). Traces of such a system, including probable cross-cousin marriage, are also discernible in Colonial Yukatek records (Eggan 1934). On these grounds, it has recently been proposed (Hage 2003) that Proto-Yukatekans practiced social arrangements such that exactly two lineage groups simply "exchanged sisters" in a marriage type known as "bilateral cross-cousin marriage," in which one's spouse is normally the child both of one's mother's brother and of one's father's sister. Hage (2003) uses the term *Kariera*—perhaps nonstandardly (cf. Hornborg, this volume, on "Dravidian" marriage)—to describe this marriage type.

Using the method of comparative reconstruction of kin term features already described, I undertake here a full reconstruction of Proto-Yukatekan kinship terms, enumerate the semantic changes that this reconstruction entails, and propose some possible "bridging contexts" in past social arrangements that could have produced those changes. Along the way, I also identify two terms that appear to have been borrowed into Proto-Yukatekan, perhaps from (Greater) Cholan, and I discuss the significance of these borrowings—particularly the possible borrowing of a term for "husband"—for the reconstruction of past social organization in the Yucatán. I conclude that, despite their alternating-generation terminology, the earliest Proto-Yukatekans did not practice bilateral cross-cousin marriage, and—more speculatively—I further propose that they prescribed patrilateral cross-cousin marriage (marriage of a man to his father's sister's daughter) up to and perhaps after the late Preclassic period (250 BCE–CE 250).

Reconstructing Kinship

It is an axiom of historical linguistics that in large language families where subclassification based on sound correspondences has already been accomplished, attempted reconstructions of vocabulary should be conducted first within subfamilies (cf. Campbell 1988). Proto-forms ancestral to each subfamily may then be compared widely across the larger family. Accordingly, I will be concerned here with the reconstruction of Proto-Yukatekan kinship alone. The method I demonstrate is applicable to the reconstruction of Proto-Cholan and of Greater Cholan kinship too of course, and a full reconstruction of the kinship semantics of (Greater) Cholan and ultimately of Proto-Mayan as a whole would naturally be of enormous interest. But such an undertaking is too large to attempt at present. In the course of the Proto-Yukatekan demonstration, a sideways glance will be cast at Greater Cholan by virtue of kinship borrowings between the subfamilies. But in general, the reconstruction of kin term systems in other Mayan subfamilies, and in Proto-Mayan as a whole, must wait for another opportunity.

Again, since the method involves systematically working back through subfamilies from the earliest documentation, the initial results will apply primarily to the Postclassic period and to the Classic–Postclassic transition (ca. CE 900),[18] with additional postulations perhaps leading back sufficiently far to allow us to make proposals relevant to the Classic or Preclassic periods. Finally, I have made use of all linguistic and archaeological information to which I have access, including a practice of checking back with the larger family as appropriate. If a term is known from other subfamilies to go back to Proto-Mayan, then I assume that it existed in Proto-Yukatekan even if the Yukatekan evidence is scant ("forward reconstruction"). It will be important at all times to be clear about the linguistic affiliation(s), geographic territory, and time periods that are implicated in the various proposals that will be made. Assumptions, for example, that reconstructed Proto-Yukatekan kin practices can be projected back to the earliest moments of human social existence (contra Hage 2003) will certainly not be made.

In preparing the synchronic analyses of kinship terminology in Northern Lakantun, Colonial Yukatek, and Mopan, I have followed these guidelines:

1. Use the earliest documents as uniquely as possible. Refer to later varieties for confirmation, cross-checking, and hypothesis-formation only.
2. If using a historically documented variety, stay synchronic with respect to it. In other words, for Colonial Yukatek consult only the Motul dictionary of 1577 or others more or less contemporary with it. Do not merge a 16th-century system with, say, a 19th-century one (contra Álvarez 1997; Eggan 1934).

3. Prepare the analysis for the earliest possible system that is plausible in the language. That is, begin by conducting a form of internal reconstruction within each language. At the least, this means eliminating known European borrowings and stripping off any transparent diminutives or other modifiers from terms (Frisch and Schutz's [1967] pioneering attempt suffers from a failure to carry out this desideratum).
4. Separate consanguineal from affinal extensions, if both are given for a single term. Analyze the consanguineal extensions primarily, and use any overlapping affinal extensions to suggest likely marriage patterns based on these. This methodological step formalizes the idea (often implicit in earlier treatments) that marriage rules provide a fertile "bridging context" for the recurrent reanalyses that ultimately result in semantic change. Put differently, it proposes to understand homonymy as evidence of reanalysis-in-progress, presupposing the existence of a bridging context that supports the reanalysis (cf. McConvell, chapter 10, this volume).
5. To the extent possible, avoid polysemy. Where possible, propose semantic dimensions that include as many as possible of the different documented extensions of a term. It is this assumption that dictates the rejection of analyses in terms of universal prototypes and rewrite rules (see discussion above) and is what makes possible the reconstruction of kin terms with reference to the very successful paradigm of phonological reconstruction based on distinctive features.
6. Analysis should be conducted over reciprocal pairs of terms, not over single terms. The final dimensional value for any pair distinguishes the two reciprocal members from one another (Goodenough 1956).

Tables 5.2–5.12 present the results of the analysis. Columns 2, 3, and 4 of each table give the initial dimensional analysis of the terms for Northern Lakantun, Colonial Yukatek, and Mopan, respectively. Column 5 represents the reconstructed values on each dimension for the corresponding term in Proto-Yukatekan. Because the languages are so closely related, and because sound changes in this language family are relatively well understood, we can recognize cognate terms across the first three languages without difficulty. These may vary slightly in phonological form across the languages, but that is not the focus of the present investigation. I therefore regularize each phonological string to a virtual lemma, rendered in modified International Phonetic Alphabet orthography and preceded by an asterisk to indicate its reconstructed nature, which appears in the leftmost column (column 1) for each entry.[19] An entry for each lemma is then made for each of the three languages, using kin type notation to indicate some of its characteristic extensions. The values for this term on a common set of dimensions that distinguish it from all the other terms in the same language are then noted. Where the value for a particular dimension is not contrastive in a particular language or for a particular term, it is noted as "unspecified." Because reconstruction is the ultimate goal, dimensions that apply to any term in any one of the languages may be listed as well for other terms in other languages. This means that in some cases, a dimension is listed for one of the languages that is never actually contrastive in it. For ease of presentation, the row dedicated to a dimension that plays no contrastive role for a particular term in one language is at times used to specify instead the value on a different, similar dimension that has contrastive value only in that language. For example, dimension (2) appears most often as "Sex of Senior," but in lemmas (k) and (l) as "Sex of Relatum." Such cases yield the hypothesis that the nature of the dimension itself has changed over time. An alternative would be to list both dimensions exhaustively and to specify the proposed changes as the loss and/or innovation of dimensions, rather than the mutation of one dimension into another. The modern term, in the original orthography for each language, is listed with its reciprocal as the last column entry for each language.

In preparing this reconstruction, I have made full use of the analogy between the crosscutting semantic features that distinguish kinship terms within the same language from one another and the crosscutting phonological features that distinguish speech sounds within the same language from one another. At every point in the kin term reconstruction, I have endeavored to exploit the phonological analogy by using insights and techniques from the well worked-out domain of phonological reconstruction to guide the semantic reconstruction. I therefore reconstruct protomeanings feature by feature, preserving any semantic features that are common across the modern languages and reconstructing those that occur most frequently. When reconstructing features that are not common to all of the modern languages, I endeavor to remain aware that such reconstruction implies a proposed semantic change between the reconstructed protolanguage and at least one of the modern languages. I keep

TABLE 5.2. Term attested in all three languages, with full correspondence of semantic features.

Dimensions by Lemma	Northern Lakantun	Colonial Yukatek	Mopan	Proto-Yukatekan
a. *mu’*				
Kin Gloss	e.g., WZ, BW, ZH, HB	e.g., WZ, BW, ZH, HB	e.g., WZ, BW, ZH, HB	e.g., WZ, BW, ZH, HB
1. Generation	0	0	0	0/(±2)
2. Sex of Senior	Unspecified	Unspecified	Unspecified	Unspecified
3. Seniority	Unspecified	Unspecified	Unspecified	Unspecified
4. Affine/Consanguine	Affine	Affine	Affine	Affine
5. Collateral/Lineal	Collateral	Collateral	Collateral	Collateral
6. Cross/Parallel	Cross	Cross	Cross	Cross
7. Laterality	Unspecified	Unspecified	Unspecified	Unspecified
8. Sex of Referent	Opposite from relatum	Opposite from relatum	Opposite from relatum	Opposite from relatum
Term and Reciprocal	*mu; mu*	*mu’; mu’*	*mu’; mu’*	**mu’*; **mu’*

TABLE 5.3. Terms attested in two languages, with full correspondence of semantic features.

Dimensions by Lemma	Northern Lakantun	Colonial Yukatek	Mopan	Proto-Yukatekan
b. *ha’an*				
Kin Gloss	minimally attested: DH	e.g., DH, WM, WF, WMB, MB	e.g., DH, WM, WF	e.g., DH, WM, WF
1. Generation		±1	±1	±1
2. Sex of Senior		Unspecified	Unspecified	Unspecified
3. Seniority		Unspecified	Unspecified	Unspecified
4. Affine/Consanguine		Affine	Affine	Affine
5. Collateral/Lineal		Unspecified	Unspecified	Unspecified
6. Cross/Parallel		Affinal link is through female	Affinal link is through female	Affinal link is through female
7. Laterality		Unspecified	Unspecified	Unspecified
8. Sex of Referent		Unspecified	Unspecified	Unspecified
Term and Reciprocal		*ha’n; ha’n*	*ha’an; ha’an*	**ha’an*; **ha’an*
c. *alib				
Kin Gloss	Unattested	e.g., SW, WBD, HM, HF	e.g., SW, HM, HF	e.g., SW, HM, HF
1. Generation		±1	±1	±1
2. Sex of Senior		Unspecified	Unspecified	Unspecified
3. Seniority		Unspecified	Unspecified	Unspecified
4. Affine/Consanguine		Affine	Affine	Affine
5. Collateral/Lineal		Unspecified	Unspecified	Unspecified
6. Cross/Parallel		Affinal link is through male	Affinal link is through male	Affinal link is through male
7. Laterality		Unspecified	Unspecified	Unspecified
8. Sex of Referent		Unspecified	Unspecified	Unspecified
Term and Reciprocal		*ilib; ilib*	*əli’; əli’*	**alib*; **alib*

TABLE 5.3. (cont'd.) Terms attested in two languages, with full correspondence of semantic features.

Dimensions by Lemma	Northern Lakantun	Colonial Yukatek	Mopan	Proto-Yukatekan
d. *ataan				
Kin Gloss	Unattested	W	W	W
8. Sex of Referent		Female	Female	Female
9. Marriage		Referent is married to relatum	Referent is married to relatum	Referent is married to relatum
Term(s) and Reciprocal		*atan; icham*	*ətan; icham*	**ataan; *ichaam*
e. *ichaam				
Kin Gloss	Unattested	H	H	Late Proto-Yukatekan only, H
8. Sex of Referent		Male	Male	Male
9. Marriage		Referent is married to relatum	Referent is married to relatum	Referent is married to relatum
Term and Reciprocal(s)		*icham; atan*	*icham; ətan*	**ichaam; *ataan*
f. *laak'				
Kin Gloss	Minimally attested: H	Possibly *la(a)k'* 'other, next'	Possibly *lak'* 'other, next'	'other'

TABLE 5.4. Partial correspondence set: brothers.

Dimensions by Lemma	Northern Lakantun	Colonial Yukatek	Mopan	Proto-Yukatekan
g. *suku'n				
Kin Gloss	oB, oFBS, oMZS, FF, FFB	oB, oFBS, oMZS, FF	oB, oFBS, oMZS, oMBS	oB, oFBS, oMZS, FF, FFB
1. Generation	0/±2	0/±2	0	0/±2
2. Sex of Senior	Male	Male	Male	Male
3. Seniority	Senior	Senior	Senior	Senior
4. Affine/Consanguine	Consanguine	Consanguine	Consanguine	Consanguine
5. Collateral/Lineal	Unspecified	Unspecified	Unspecified	Unspecified
6. Cross/Parallel	Parallel	Parallel	Unspecified	Parallel
7. Laterality	Unspecified	Unspecified	Unspecified	Unspecified
8. Sex of Referent	Redundantly male	Redundantly male	Redundantly male	Redundantly male
Term and Reciprocal	*sukun; itsin*	*suku'n; its'in*	*suku'un; its'iin*	**suku'n; *its'in*
h. *its'in				
Kin Gloss	yB, yZ, yFBD, yFBS, yMZD, yMZS, mSS, mSD	yB, yZ, yFBD, yFBS, yMZD, yMZS, mSS, mSD	yB, yZ, yFBD, yFBS, yMZD, yMZS, yFZS, yFZD, yMBS, yMBD	yB, yZ, yFBD, yFBS, yMZD, yMZS, mSS, mSD, wDD, wDS
1. Generation	0/±2	0/±2	0	0/±2
2. Sex of Senior	Unspecified	Unspecified	Unspecified	Unspecified
3. Seniority	Junior	Junior	Junior	Junior
4. Affine/Consanguine	Consanguine	Consanguine	Consanguine	Consanguine

TABLE 5.4. (cont'd.) Partial correspondence set: brothers.

Dimensions by Lemma	Northern Lakantun	Colonial Yukatek	Mopan	Proto-Yukatekan
5. Collateral/Lineal	Unspecified	Unspecified	Unspecified	Unspecified
6. Cross/Parallel	Parallel	Parallel	Unspecified	Parallel
7. Laterality	Unspecified	Unspecified	Unspecified	Unspecified
8. Sex of Referent	Unspecified	Unspecified	Unspecified	Unspecified
Term and Reciprocals	*itsin*; *kik/sukun/chiich*	*its'in*; *kik/suku'n*	*its'iin*; *kik/suku'un*	**its'in*; **kik/*suku'n*

TABLE 5.5. Partial correspondence set: sisters.

Dimensions by Lemma	Northern Lakantun	Colonial Yukatek	Mopan	Proto-Yukatekan
i. *kik				
Kin Gloss	oZ, oFBD, oMZD	oZ, MM, mSWM	oZ, oFBD, oMZD, oFZD, oMBD	oZ, oFBD, oMZD, MM, MMZ
1. Generation	0	0; ±2	0	0/±2
2. Sex of Senior	Female	Female	Female	Female
3. Seniority	Senior	Senior	Senior	Senior
4. Affine/Consanguine	Consanguine	Consanguine	Consanguine	Consanguine
5. Collateral/Lineal	Unspecified	Unspecified	Unspecified	Unspecified
6. Cross/Parallel	Parallel	Parallel	Unspecified	Parallel
7. Laterality	Unspecified	Redundantly ascends matrilaterally	Unspecified	Redundantly ascends matrilaterally
8. Sex of Referent	Redundantly female	Redundantly female	Redundantly female	Redundantly female
Term and Reciprocal	*kik*; *itsin*	*kik*; *its'in*	*kik*; *its'in*	**kik*; **its'in*
j. *chich				
Kin Gloss	MM, MMZ, wDS, wDD	MM, mSSW, WBW	MM, MMZ, FM, wDS, wDD, wSD, wSS	Introduced as borrowing from (Greater) Cholan. Initially, semantically redundant with **kik* above
1. Generation	±2	0; ±2	±2	0/±2
2. Sex of Senior	Female	Female	Female	Female
3. Seniority	Senior	Senior	Unspecified	Senior
4. Affine/Consanguine	Consanguine	Consanguine	Consanguine	Consanguine
5. Collateral/Lineal	Unspecified	Unspecified	Unspecified	Unspecified
6. Cross/Parallel	Parallel	Parallel	Unspecified	Parallel
7. Laterality	Redundantly ascends matrilaterally	Redundantly ascends matrilaterally	Unspecified	Redundantly ascends matrilaterally
8. Sex of Referent	Unspecified	Redundantly female	Unspecified	Redundantly female
Term and Reciprocal	*chiich*; *itsin*	*chich*; reciprocal undocumented	*chich*; *chich*	**chich*; **its'in*

TABLE 5.6. Partial correspondence set: siblings-in-law.

Dimensions by Lemma	Northern Lakantun	Colonial Yukatek	Mopan	Proto-Yukatekan
k. *baal*				
Kin Gloss	Unattested	WB, WFF, mSWF, mDHF	WB, mZH	WB, WFF
1. Generation		0/±2	0	0/±2
2. Sex of Relatum		Male	Male	Male; senior is male
3. Seniority		Unspecified	Unspecified	Unspecified
4. Affine/Consanguine		Affine	Affine	Affine
5. Collateral/Lineal		Unspecified	Unspecified	Unspecified
6. Cross/Parallel		Unspecified	Unspecified	Unspecified
7. Laterality		Unspecified	Unspecified	Unspecified
8. Sex of Referent		Same as relatum	Same as relatum	Same as relatum
Term and Reciprocal		*bal*; *bal*	*bal*; *bal*	**baal*; **baal*
l. *haawan*				
Kin Gloss	wMBD, wFZD	HZ, wBW, wDHM, wSWM	HZ, wBW	HZ, wBW
1. Generation	0	0	0	0/±2
2. Sex of Relatum	Female	Female	Female	Female
3. Seniority	Unspecified	Unspecified	Unspecified	Unspecified
4. Affine/Consanguine	Consanguine	Affine	Affine	Affine
5. Collateral/Lineal	Collateral	Unspecified	Unspecified	Unspecified
6. Cross/Parallel	Cross	Unspecified	Unspecified	Unspecified
7. Laterality	Unspecified	Unspecified	Unspecified	Unspecified
8. Sex of Referent	Same as relatum	Same as relatum	Same as relatum	Same as relatum
Term and Reciprocal	*hawan*; *hawan*	*hawan*; *hawan*	*habən*; *habən*	**haawan*; **haawan*

TABLE 5.7. Partial correspondence set: cross-grandfathers.

Dimensions by Lemma	Northern Lakantun	Colonial Yukatek	Mopan	Proto-Yukatekan
m. *maam*				
Kin Gloss	MF, mDS, mDD, mMBD, FZD, FZS, MBS	MF, FMF, FBS, FBD, MZS, MZD	MF, FF, mSS, mSD, mDD, mDS	MF, mDS, mDD, MBS, myMBD
1. Generation	0/±2	0/±2	±2	0/±2
2. Sex of Senior	Unspecified	Unspecified	Male	Male
3. Seniority	Unspecified	Unspecified	Unspecified	Senior
4. Affine/Consanguine	Consanguine	Consanguine	Consanguine	Consanguine
5. Collateral/Lineal	Unspecified	Unspecified	Lineal	Lineal
6. Cross/Parallel	Cross	Unspecified	Unspecified	Cross
7. Laterality	Unspecified	Unspecified	Unspecified	Unspecified
8. Sex of Referent	Unspecified	Unspecified	Unspecified	Unspecified
Term and Reciprocal	*mam*; *mam*	*mam*; reciprocal undocumented	*mam*; *mam*	**maam*; **i'*

TABLE 5.8. Partial correspondence set: cross-grandmothers.

Dimensions by Lemma	Northern Lakantun	Colonial Yukatek	Mopan	Proto-Yukatekan
n. *mim				
Kin Gloss	FM, wSS, wSD	FM, MFM (MMM?)	Unattested	FM, wSS, wSD, oFZD, wFZS
1. Generation	±2	+2 and higher		0/±2
2. Sex of Senior	Female	Female		Female
3. Seniority	Unspecified	Senior		Senior
4. Affine/Consanguine	Consanguine	Consanguine		Consanguine
5. Collateral/Lineal	Lineal or unspecified	Lineal or unspecified		Unspecified
6. Cross/Parallel	Cross	Cross		Cross
7. Laterality	Ascends patrilaterally	Ascends patrilaterally		Unspecified
8. Sex of Referent	Unspecified	Redundantly female		Unspecified
Term and Reciprocal	*mim*; *mim*	*mim*; *i'*		**mim*; **i'*
o. *i'				
Kin Gloss	Unattested	wSS, wSD	Unattested	wSS, wSD, yFZD, yFZS
1. Generation		–2		±2
2. Sex of Senior		Female		Unspecified
3. Seniority		Junior		Junior
4. Affine/ Consanguine		Consanguine		Consanguine
5. Collateral/ Lineal		Lineal or unspecified		Unspecified
6. Cross/Parallel		Cross		Cross
7. Laterality		Redundantly ascends patrilaterally		Unspecified
8. Sex of Referent		Unspecified		Unspecified
Term and Reciprocal		*i'*; *mim*		**i'*; **mim/*maam*

TABLE 5.9. Partial correspondence set: mother and children.

Dimensions by Lemma	Northern Lakantun	Colonial Yukatek	Mopan	Proto-Yukatekan
p. *naa'				
Kin Gloss	M, MZ, wD, ZD	M, MZ	M, MZ, FZ	M, MZ
1. Generation	±1	+1	+1	+1
2. Sex of Senior	Unspecified	Female	Female	Female
3. Seniority	Unspecified	Senior	Senior	Senior
4. Affine/Consanguine	Consanguine	Consanguine	Consanguine	Consanguine
5. Collateral/Lineal	Unspecified	Unspecified	Unspecified	Unspecified
6. Cross/Parallel	Adjacent link is through female	Parallel	Unspecified	Parallel
7. Laterality	Ascends matrilaterally	Ascends matrilaterally	Unspecified	Ascends matrilaterally

TABLE 5.9. (cont'd.) Partial correspondence set: mother and children.

Dimensions by Lemma	Northern Lakantun	Colonial Yukatek	Mopan	Proto-Yukatekan
8. Sex of Referent	Female	Redundantly female	Redundantly female	Redundantly female
Term and Reciprocal(s)	*(ts'e) na'*; *ts'e na'/äkän, tet*	*na'*; *al*	*na'*; *al*	**naa'*; **aal*
q. ****aal*				
Kin Gloss	Unattested	wS, wD, wZS, wZD	wS, wD, wZS, wZD, wBS, wBD	wS, wD, wZS, wZD
1. Generation		+1	+1	+1
2. Sex of Senior		Female	Female	Female
3. Seniority		Junior	Junior	Junior
4. Affine/Consanguine		Consanguine	Consanguine	Consanguine
5. Collateral/Lineal		Unspecified	Unspecified	Unspecified
6. Cross/Parallel		Parallel	Unspecified	Parallel
7. Laterality		Ascends matrilaterally	Ascends matrilaterally	Ascends matrilaterally
8. Sex of Referent		Unspecified	Unspecified	Unspecified
Term and Reciprocal		*al*; *na'*	*al*; *na'*	**aal*; **naa'*

TABLE 5.10. Partial correspondence set: mother's brother.

Dimensions by Lemma	Northern Lakantun	Colonial Yukatek	Mopan	Proto-Yukatekan
r. ****ikaan*				
Kin Gloss	MB, ZS, wS	MB, MFF, MMF, FZH	Unattested	MB
1. Generation	±1/3	±1/3		±1/3
2. Sex of Senior	Unspecified	Male		Male
3. Seniority	Unspecified	Senior		Senior
4. Affine/Consanguine	Consanguine	Consanguine		Consanguine
5. Collateral/Lineal	Unspecified	Collateral		Collateral
6. Cross/Parallel	Adjacent link is through female	Cross		Cross
7. Laterality	Ascends matrilaterally	Ascends matrilaterally		Ascends matrilaterally.
8. Sex of Referent	Male	Redundantly male		Redundantly male
Term and Reciprocal(s)	*äkän*; *äkän/(ts'e) na'*	*akan*; *achak'*		**ikaan*; *†*ikaaq'/*ichaak'*
s. †**ikaaq'/*ichaak'***				
Kin Gloss	Unattested	mZS, mZD	Unattested	Introduced from (Greater) Cholan in middle Proto-Yukatekan. Originally redundant with native *†*ikaak'*. mZS, mZD

TABLE 5.10. (cont'd.) Partial correspondence set: mother's brother.

Dimensions by Lemma	Northern Lakantun	Colonial Yukatek	Mopan	Proto-Yukatekan
1. Generation		+1		+1
2. Sex of Senior		Male		Male
3. Seniority		Junior		Junior
4. Affine/Consanguine		Consanguine		Consanguine
5. Collateral/Lineal		Collateral		Collateral
6. Cross/Parallel		Cross		Cross
7. Laterality		Ascends matrilaterally		Ascends matrilaterally
8. Sex of Referent		Unspecified		Unspecified
Term(s) and Reciprocal		*achak'*; *akan*		†**ikaaq'/*ichaak'*; **ikaan*

TABLE 5.11. Partial correspondence set: father.

Dimensions by Lemma	Northern Lakantun	Colonial Yukatek	Mopan	Proto-Yukatekan
t. **yum*				
Kin Gloss	F, FB, mS, BS	F, FB	F, FB, MB	F, FB
1. Generation	±1	+1	+1	+1
2. Sex of Senior	Unspecified	Male	Male	Male
3. Seniority	Unspecified	Senior	Senior	Senior
4. Affine/Consanguine	Consanguine	Consanguine	Consanguine	Consanguine
5. Collateral/Lineal	Unspecified	Unspecified	Unspecified	Unspecified
6. Cross/Parallel	Adjacent link is through male	Parallel	Unspecified	Parallel
7. Laterality	Redundantly ascends patrilaterally	Redundantly ascends patrilaterally	Unspecified	Redundantly ascends patrilaterally
8. Sex of Referent	Male	Redundantly male	Redundantly male	Redundantly male
Term and Reciprocal(s)	*yum*; *yum/ixkit*, *tet*	*yum*; *mehen*	Archaic	**yum*; **mehen*
u. **taat*				
Kin Gloss	F	Unattested	F, FB, MB	Introduced in F
1. Generation	±1		+1	
2. Sex of Senior	Male		Male	
3. Seniority	Senior		Senior	
4. Affine/Consanguine	Consanguine		Consanguine	
5. Collateral/Lineal	Lineal		Unspecified	
6. Cross/Parallel	Parallel		Unspecified	
7. Laterality	Redundantly ascends patrilaterally		Redundantly ascends patrilaterally	
8. Sex of Referent	Redundantly male		Redundantly male	
Term and Reciprocal(s)	*tet*; *yum/ixkit*		*tat*; *mehen*	**taat*; **mehen*

TABLE 5.12. Partial correspondence set: women and children of ego's patriline.

Dimensions by Lemma	Northern Lakantun	Colonial Yukatek	Mopan	Proto-Yukatekan
v. *mehen				
Kin Gloss	Unattested	mS, mD, BS, BD, child of ego's patriline	mS, mD, mBS, mBD, mZS, mZD	mS, mD, mBS, mBD
1. Generation		+1	+1	+1
2. Sex of Senior		Unspecified	Male	Unspecified
3. Seniority		Junior	Junior	Junior
4. Affine/Consanguine		Consanguine	Consanguine	Consanguine
5. Collateral/Lineal		Unspecified	Unspecified	Unspecified
6. Cross/Parallel		Unspecified	Unspecified	Parallel
7. Laterality		Ascends patrilaterally	Ascends patrilaterally	Ascends patrilaterally
8. Sex of Referent		Unspecified	Unspecified	Unspecified
Term and Reciprocal(s)		*mehen*; *yum/ixkit*	*mehen*; *tat*	**mehen*; **yum/*(ix) kit*
w. *(ix)kit				
Kin Gloss	FZ, BD, mD	FZ, older w of ego's patriline	Unattested	FZ, older w of ego's patriline
1. Generation	±1	+1		+1
2. Sex of Senior	Unspecified	Female		Female
3. Seniority	Unspecified	Senior		Senior
4. Affine/Consanguine	Consanguine	Consanguine		Consanguine
5. Collateral/Lineal	Unspecified	Unspecified		Unspecified
6. Cross/Parallel	Adjacent link is through male	Cross		Cross
7. Laterality	Ascends patrilaterally	Ascends patrilaterally		Ascends patrilaterally
8. Sex of Referent	Female	Redundantly female		Female
Term and Reciprocal(s)	*ixkit*; *yum/ixkit, tet*	*ixkit*; *mehen*		**(ix)kit*; **mehen*

the number of proposed changes to the minimum. This means, to the extent possible, that I reconstruct in the protolanguage semantic features that are still extant in at least one of the languages rather than inventing new ones and that I make use of dimensions and features that have already been reconstructed elsewhere in the system rather than inventing new ones. I have also attempted to pay some attention to the "naturalness" (likelihood, based on the types of semantic changes that are known to occur in other languages and language families) of the changes that are implied by a particular reconstruction and to consider the systematicity of the reconstructed proto-inventory. Ideally, the same dimensions of contrast should recur to distinguish among different terms of the protosystem, and the extensions covered by one reconstructed term should not leave gaps when viewed from the perspective of the full set of reconstructed dimensions.

Proto-Yukatekan Kin Term System

Having laid out in tabular form each term with its semantic cognates, along with a specification of the different semantic features that distinguish each term from its fellows in each language, I am in a position to begin my semantic reconstruction. In phonological reconstruction, it is expedient to reconstruct first those protosounds for which all daughter sounds are identical and which differ in no feature. In such cases, the principles of parsimony in reconstruction dictate the reconstruction of that same sound in the protolanguage. Subsequent reconstructions are ordered with respect to the amount of similarity in the daughters. Such ordering is expected to correspond more or less to the amount of change that must be proposed, although it is not ruled out that adherence to principles of systematicity in the proto-inventory will require some modification of this expectation (cf. Campbell 1998; Hock and Joseph 1996). I follow the same principle in my semantic reconstruction of Yukatekan kinship terms.

Total Correspondences

A single term in my inventory that is fully identical in all of its features across all three languages (Table 5.2):

> **mu'* (reciprocal **mu'*): a relative of the same generation as the relatum, acquired through a marriage, and of the opposite sex to the relatum—but not the marriage partner him- or herself; for example, mBW, WZ, wZH, HB

Almost as obvious in their reconstruction are the following four terms, which are identical in the two languages in which they are attested and which have presumably simply been lost as terms in the third (Table 5.3):

> **ha'an* (reciprocal **ha'an*):[20] a relative one generation distant from the relatum, acquired through a woman's marriage in the junior generation; for example, DH, WF, WM
> **alib* (reciprocal **alib*): a relative one generation distant from the relatum, acquired through a man's marriage in the junior generation; for example, SW, HF, HM
> **ataan* (reciprocal **ichaam*): wife
> **ichaam* (reciprocal **ataan*): husband

I have thus already reconstructed an interlocking grid of affines for Proto-Yukatekan, in which terms for an ego's spouse and for the spouse's parents, all differentiated by the sex of the spouse, are delineated. No semantic changes have yet been postulated, although the use of the Northern Lakantun term *lak* with reference to husband is now recognizable as a lexical innovation in that language. Northern Lakantun is also understood to have lost the term **alib* (self-reciprocal; SW, HM, HF) as well as full use of the term **ha'an*.[21]

Before moving on, it is worth noting, first, that there is no reason to see **ataan* 'wife' as other than an ancestral Proto-Yukatekan form, either in its semantics or in its phonology. This is relevant to an extant proposal (Fox 1985; Fox and Justeson 1986) that Yukatekan **ataan* 'wife' may be related via borrowing to a phonologically similar (Greater) Cholan form meaning "sister," "sibling," or "sibling's spouse" in that subfamily. If so, the direction of borrowing is more likely to be from Proto-Yukatekan into (Greater) Cholan than the reverse (Danziger n.d.).[22]

On the contrary, meanwhile, the late Proto-Yukatekan form **ichaam* 'husband' is clearly not an original form in the subfamily. If it were, it would have undergone the early Preclassic sound change **iCa > aCa*. Instead, this term has been borrowed or was innovated in Proto-Yukatekan at some later period. I will have more to say about this later.

Partial Correspondences

I should now in principle proceed to a consideration of terms that are attested in all three languages but which are different from one another only in one feature, in just one of the languages. This kind of correspondence set would suggest a clear semantic reconstruction, involving just one semantic change in one language. No such cases are found.

Moving forward, I now consider terms that are attested in all three languages but for which there is a difference in more than one semantic feature among the attested usages. Consider term (g) in Table 5.4: **suku'n*. The term is found in all three of the languages being compared, and in every case it is found with the reciprocal *its'in*. But in each case the set of kin type extensions to which the term applies is slightly different. This means that the particular values accorded to this term on certain of the eight basic semantic dimensions are also different across the languages. The tabular view allows me, for each dimension and each term, to propose a reconstructed value in the protolanguage and ultimately to propose a full semantic position for the reconstructed term within a set of reconstructed dimensions. To do so, I look for reconstructions that propose the minimum amount of semantic change to reach the observed situation in each daughter language while at the same time creating a coherent protosystem. To achieve this for **suku'n*, I leave dimensions 2–5 and 7–8 unchanged in the protolanguage. For these dimensions, all three languages retain the same values. No semantic change therefore need be or should be proposed for these dimensions. Dimension 6 (cross/parallel) shows an unspecified value in Mopan (this dimension is never contrastive in that language) and shows the identical value—parallel—in Northern Lakantun and in Colonial Yukatek. I therefore appeal to parsimony and reconstruct "parallel" as the value for this dimension in Proto-Yukatekan as well. Finally, dimension 1, generation, also shows the same value for Northern Lakantun and for the Colonial variety, so I choose this value to reconstruct the protolanguage as well. The reconstructed meaning of **suku'n* (oB, reciprocal **its'in*) in Proto-Yukatekan is complete (Table 5.4):

> **suku'n* (reciprocal **its'in*): senior male consanguine, whose links to the relatum are through the same sex ("parallel") and who belongs to a generation that is "harmonic" (same generation or two generations removed) with the relatum's own; for example, oB, oFBS, oMZS, FF, FFB

In making this proposal, I have also proposed two semantic changes in the development of Mopan since the breakup of the protolanguage: I propose that the pair **suku'n/*its'in* lost reference to harmonic generation and began to refer only to ego's own generation, and I propose that the cross/parallel distinction became neutralized for this term in the development of Mopan from Proto-Yukatekan. In its usage as reciprocal to **suku'n*, the term **its'in* can be said to have undergone these same changes in Mopan.

Consider now the term **kik* (reciprocal **its'in*), reflexes of which are used in all three languages to denote an older sister and also an older female parallel cousin (Table 5.5). Neither in Northern Lakantun nor in Mopan is grandparent usage attested, but in Colonial Yukatek a granddaughter could address her mother's mother as *kaa' kik* 'second/recurrent *kik*' (Barrera Vasquez 1980:292), although grandparent usage is not one of the glosses included under the bare form *cic* in the Motul dictionary (Martinez Hernandez 1930[1577]:182).[23] By analogy with its already reconstructed masculine alternate, therefore, and in order to regularize the semantic reconstruction of their shared reciprocal term **its'in* without recourse to polysemy, I propose the following on this basis (Tables 5.4 and 5.5):

> **kik* (reciprocal **its'in*): senior female consanguine, whose links to the relatum are through the same sex ("parallel") and who belongs to a generation that is harmonic (same generation or two generations removed) with the relatum's own; for example, oZ, oFBD, oMZD, MM, MMZ
>
> **its'in* (reciprocal **suku'n*, **kik*): junior consanguine whose links to the relatum are through the same sex ("parallel") and who belongs to a generation that is harmonic (same generation or two generations removed) with the relatum's own; for example, yB, yZ, yFBS, yMZS, yFBD, mSS, mSD, mBSS, mBSD, wDS, wZDS, wZDD

This reconstruction of **suku'n/*kik/*its'in* exhausts the semantic space at the intersection of harmonic generation and parallel connection. To a large extent the reconstruction of these three terms on the analogy of feature-based phonological reconstruction merely formalizes the kind of comparative inspection of individual terms across languages that has underpinned earlier treatments of Proto-Yukatekan kinship semantics (cf. Fox and Justeson 1986; Hage 2003; Kaufman and Justeson 2003) and which long ago (Eggan 1934) had already led to the conclusion that Proto-Yukatekan used alternate-generation terminology. However, if we continue in this vein of analysis, we will be led to further discoveries, on the one hand, about the nature of the Proto-Yukatekan system and, on the other, about the events and arrangements in prehistory that may have shaped its development.

Intriguingly, a term exists in all three languages that competes with the reflexes of **kik* (reciprocal **its'in*) in that it also makes reference to the parallel grandmother (MM). The term is **chich* (reciprocal *itsin* in Northern Lakantun, reciprocal undocumented in Colonial Yukatek, self-reciprocal in Mopan). There is in addition evidence from the Motul dictionary that *chich* (reciprocal undocumented) could also apply to women of ego's own generation. For example (Martinez Hernandez 1930[1577]:307), *chich* appears in the Motul dictionary as a man's sister-in-law—specified as his wife's brother's wife.[24] In 16th-century Colonial Yukatek, then, there appears to have existed a lexical doublet *kik/chich* covering the semantic terrain of the senior female parallel consanguine in the harmonic generation.[25]

Recall that substantial borrowing from Greater Cholan languages into Yukatekan occurred throughout the Classic period and earlier and that where the native Yukatekan shows a [k] sound, these borrowings are often recognizable for showing [ch] instead. It appears plausible that the Yukatekan *kik/chich* is such a doublet and that **chich* (reciprocal **its'in*) is the Greater Cholan cognate of *kik (reciprocal its'in), appearing in Yukatekan as a borrowing. Indeed, a term chich (reciprocal its'in or ih) appears in five of the six Greater Cholan languages, with reference to senior females in the kin domain.[26] I propose that the following term existed in Proto-Yukatekan as an imported borrowing from (Greater) Cholan (Table 5.5):[27]

> *chich (reciprocal *its'in): senior female consanguine, whose links to the relatum are through the same sex ("parallel") and who belongs to a generation that is harmonic (same generation or two generations removed) with the relatum's own; for example, oZ, oFBD, oMZD, MM, MMZ

As in many cases of cognate borrowing, the lexical doublet of native and borrowed term split the original semantic territory so that each term came to have a unique meaning. In Yukatekan, *chich* took over the "generation +/–2" ("grandmother") territory, leaving *kik* with the "zero generation" ("older sister") part of the original meaning. The resulting semantic division of the original "harmonic/disharmonic generation" dimension into one that instead simply distinguishes the different degrees of generational distance from ego is profound for the system and may have been the initial impetus for the breakdown of alternating usage.[28]

Harmonic Generations in Affine Terms

At this point it is appropriate to proceed to a consideration of the term reconstructed as *baal* (self-reciprocal; e.g., WB, mZH), which is attested in only two of the documented languages and which does not have quite the same meaning in each (Table 5.6). The guiding principle "propose fewest changes" cannot help us in cases of only two attestations, since we know that whichever way we decide to reconstruct, we will be proposing a change in exactly one of the modern forms. But we can use the reconstructions so far accomplished as a guide to parsimony in another way. A few notes in the Motul dictionary (Barrera Vasquez 1980:31) inform us that the term *bal* (self-reciprocal) could refer in Colonial Yukatek not only to a man's sister's husband or to his wife's brother (zero generation) but also to his wife's father's father (generation +2). Having now postulated harmonic generation as a recurring feature of the protolanguage, and having therefore also postulated a recurrent change from harmonic generation to zero-generation reference in Mopan in several different terms, it is reasonable to propose that the same value, and the same semantic change, recurs again elsewhere in the system. I accept Eggan's (1934) proposal that uses of *bal* by a man to the father of his own child's spouse (mSWF, mDHF) in Colonial Yukatek arose incidentally, in the context of a sustained practice of cross-cousin marriage.[29] The Proto-Yukatekan **baal*, I conclude, referred simply to a man's male affines in the harmonic generations (Table 5.6):

> *baal (self-reciprocal): a man's relative of harmonic generation of the same sex as himself, acquired through a marriage; for example, WB, mZH, WFF, mSDH

By analogy with **baal*, and on the gender-alternate model of **suku'n* and **kik*, I reconstruct a corresponding harmonic-generation meaning for the term **mu* and also for **haawan* (self-reciprocal; e.g., HZ, wBW)—this time a term for which documentation of alternate-generation usage is not present in any of the modern languages. In this case, I must postulate the loss of generation +2 usage in Colonial Yukatek as well as in Mopan and also significant semantic change rather than actual loss of the term in Northern Lakantun (Table 5.6):[30]

> *haawan (self-reciprocal): a woman's relative of harmonic generation of the same sex as herself, acquired through a marriage; for example, HZ, wBW, HMM

Harmonic Generations and Nonparallel Grandparents

To complete the set of harmonic-generation relationships in Proto-Yukatekan, we are now ready to consider the puzzling usages of the term *mam* (self-reciprocal) across the chart of languages (Table 5.7). In all of the languages, this term refers at least to the cross-grandfather—the mother's father. In Northern Lakantun, it refers also to the matrilateral cross-cousins, and in Colonial Yukatek, apparently to the parallel cousins.[31] By analogy with the terms that I have already considered, and adhering to the principles to avoid polysemy where possible and to use dimensions of the protosystem that have already been postulated, I propose that the term **maam* existed in the protolanguage in reference to matrilaterally related cross-relatives of the harmonic generation, in which the senior party was (necessarily, by the intersection of "cross" and "matrilateral") male.[32]

This allows us also (Table 5.8) to reconstruct **mim* and the reciprocal **i'* as the pair occupying a symmetrical space to **maam* on the patrilateral side (patrilaterally related cross-relatives of the harmonic generation, in which the senior party is necessarily female). Again by analogy with the terms for parallel relatives in the harmonic generation, I might propose that the term **i'* was once the reciprocal for **maam* as well as for **mim*, meaning that specifications of sex of senior were neutralized when reference was to a junior. The **mim/*i'* pair would have included a younger person's reference to his or her older FZD and her return of reference to that person (i.e., a woman to the younger children of her mother's brother). The **maam/*i'* pair would have included a younger person's reference to his or her older MBS and his return of reference to that person (i.e., a man to the younger children of his father's sister).

An alternative to the reconstruction of **i'* as reciprocal to both **maam* and **mim* would be to propose that **i'* is an innovation (it appears in only one language of the three) and that in earlier times, again by analogy (but this time in the opposite direction), **mim*, like **maam*, was self-reciprocal but neutral as to junior's gender. In that case, **mim* would have covered oFZD, wyMBS, and wyMBD, while **maam* would have covered oMBS, myFZD, and myFZS. Note, however, that **i'* recurs as a term in other Mayan languages beyond the Yukatekan subfamily and may in fact be a very old term (Kaufman and Justeson [2003] reconstruct **'i'h*, frequently glossed as "grandchild," to Proto-Mayan), providing the root on which other terms (e.g., **its'in*) were built through ancient modifications, no longer transparent to current speakers (Fox and Justeson 1986). I therefore prefer the first solution.[33]

The reconstruction of **maam*, **mim*, and **i'* ought now in principle to be complete. Note, however, that this combination of reconstructed feature values allows the terms to cover only certain of the cross-cousins (oFZD, oMBS, wyMBS, wyMBD, myFZD, myFZS) and leaves certain others terminologically unaccounted for (oFZS and oMBD and their reciprocals myMBS, myMBD, wyFZS, wyFZD). In the absence of any candidate terms in any of the languages for these other cousins, I choose to neutralize one of the features in the existing reconstruction in order to cover all of the cross-cousins with these three terms. To do so, I must neutralize either sex of senior or laterality. Relatively arbitrarily (but taking into account the evidence from the three languages that laterality is more often unspecified than is sex of senior for reflexes of **maam* and **mim*), I choose to preserve sex of senior and sacrifice laterality,[34] yielding the following (Tables 5.7 and 5.8):

> **mim* (reciprocal **i'*): senior female consanguine, whose links to the relatum are through the opposite sex ("cross") and who belongs to a generation that is harmonic (same generation or two generations removed) with the relatum's own; for example, FM, oFZD, oMBD
>
> **maam* (reciprocal **i'*): senior male consanguine, whose links to the relatum are through the opposite sex ("cross") and who belongs to a generation that is harmonic (same generation or two generations removed) with the relatum's own; for example, MF, oMBS, oFZS
>
> **i'* (reciprocal **maam*, **mim*): junior consanguine who is linked to a senior relatum through the opposite sex ("cross") and who belongs to a generation that is harmonic (same generation or two generations removed) with the relatum's own; for example, yMBS, yMBD, yFZD, yFZS

Disharmonic Generations

We now come to consider terms that are used for relatives one generation above and below that of ego (parent and parent's sibling terms and terms for one's own children). In their reflexes of the term that includes one's "mother" (**naa'*, reciprocal **aal*), Colonial Yukatek and Mopan are similar to one another (Table 5.9). No semantic changes other than those already postulated to have taken place elsewhere in the system (loss of the cross/parallel distinction and a concomitant loss of the distinction of laterality) are necessary to derive Mopan usage from one very similar to that of Colonial Yukatek. The similarity of these two leads to the following reconstruction (Table 5.9):

> **naa'* (reciprocal **aal*): a senior female consanguine, whose links to the relatum are through the same sex ("parallel") and who belongs to a generation that is disharmonic (one generation removed) with the relatum's own; for example, M, MZ
>
> **aal* (reciprocal **naa'*): a junior consanguine, linked to a senior female relatum, whose links to the relatum are through the same sex ("parallel") and who belongs to a generation that is disharmonic (one generation removed) with the relatum's own; for example, wS, wD, wZS, wZD

This reconstruction leads me to interpret the very different usage of *na'* (reciprocal *äkän*, *yum*, *ixkit*) in Northern Lakantun as the product of an elaborate set of innovations that are applied also to the use of the terms *äkän*, *yum*, and *ixkit*. The changes in Northern Lakantun involve the loss of the sex-of-senior dimension for these four terms, loss of the dimension that identifies the senior party in the relationship, and innovation of the two features sex of referent (not contrastive anywhere else in the languages) and sex of adjacent link (bearing some resemblance to sex of linking relative as used for the affinal one-generation terms **haan* and **aalib*). In Northern Lakantun also, the reflex of the term **aal* (reciprocal **naa'*) is lost, as is that of the term **mehen* (reciprocal *tat* or *yum*; see below).

The Lakantun form *äkän* and the Colonial Yukatek *akan* (reciprocal *achak'*) are recognizable (Fox 1985) as regular reflexes of the Proto-Mayan **ikaan* 'mother's brother' (see Kaufman and Justeson 2003:119). In Proto-Yukatekan, this term would have undergone the regular Yukatekan sound change **iCa > aCa* to yield the documented forms. Although the reciprocal *achak'* (mZC) is attested only in Colonial Yukatek, we know that the Proto-Mayan term **ikaaq'* (Kaufman and Justeson 2003: 120), often glossed as "nephew" or "cousin," is likely to have existed. It is noteworthy, however, that the regular Yukatekan reflex of that protoform should be **akaak'* but that no such form is attested in any documented Yukatekan language. Once again, we may have to do with a (Greater) Cholan borrowing into Yukatekan, to which the doublet [k]/[ch] bears witness.[35] In this case, the borrowed form appears simply to have replaced the native Yukatekan reflex. Since the Yukatekan change **iCa > aCa* affected this borrowing, the borrowing must have been in place by the early Preclassic, before that change took effect. For later Proto-Yukatekan I reconstruct the following (Table 5.10):[36]

> **ikaan* (reciprocal †**ikaaq'*, **ichaak'*): a senior male consanguine, whose links to the relatum are through the opposite sex ("cross") and who belongs to a generation that is disharmonic (one generation removed) with the relatum's own; for example, MB
>
> **ichaak'*/†**ikaaq'* (reciprocal **ikaan*): a junior consanguine, linked to a senior male relatum, whose links to the relatum are through the opposite sex ("cross") and who belongs to a generation that is disharmonic (one generation removed) with the relatum's own; for example, mZS, mZD

The pair **yum*/**mehen* (F/mC) appears to operate largely similarly to the *naa'*/*aal* (M/wC) pair above. Here, however, some complication is introduced by the fact that in Colonial Yukatek *mehen* is also the reciprocal of *ixkit* (see below) and by the fact that an additional term (*tet*) appears to compete for the semantic space of *yum* (Table 5.11). The **taat*/**yum* doublet is well documented across the Mayan family. Some have opined that **taat* goes back to a Nahua borrowing (Wisdom 1940); others, that it is actually a Spanish form. In either case, as it is a relatively late borrowing, I do not reconstruct **taat* as a component of Proto-Yukatekan. Kaufman and Justeson (2003:110) also see **yum* as a borrowing, this time from the non-Mayan Mesoamerican family Zoquean. The term is common to Yukatekan and to Cholan languages only. Even if originally borrowed, therefore, the reconstructed term **yum* probably merits a place in the terminological system for much of the later history of Proto-Yukatekan.

We would now expect a senior female pair to fill out the analogy with **akaan*/**achaak'* (MB/mZC), designating the father's sister and her reciprocals. The obvious term to choose for the senior member of this pair is *ixkit*, used in exactly this way in Colonial Yukatek and also as the gender alternate to *äkän* in Northern Lakantun. Here, however, we encounter a problem. By analogy with the other harmonic-generation terms, I expect a dedicated reciprocal for this term, but none appears in the data (Table 5.12). In Northern Lakantun, the form participates in a four-way intersection with *na'*, *yum*, and *äkän*, which I have already reconstructed as an innovation. In Colonial Yukatek, the reciprocal of *ixkit* is *mehen*, already reconstructed above as "child of a parallel man"—the reciprocal of *yum*. Scrutiny across the language family is this time of no help. Across the Mayan languages, there is wide variability in terms for the father's sister and her children (Dienhart 1989). No form emerges as a plausible cognate for *ixkit*, which we might interrogate for its reciprocal. In addition, it now seems relevant to examine the fact that the form *ixkit* itself is transparently equipped with the feminizing prefix *-ix*, so that the bare form for reconstruction is properly simply *kit*. The Motul dictionary has no entry for the term *kit*, however, and we must wait until Roys's dictionary of the mid–20th century for a listing. The listing gives the gloss "término reverencial para padre, respectful term for father" (Roys 1940, cited in Barrera Vasquez 1980:362).

Given the relatively late date of this entry with respect to the 16th-century variety I am considering, it should be

	Parallel		**Cross**		**Affine**				
					Collateral			**Lineal**	
					same sex		**opposite sex**		
Generation	**Senior is female**	**Senior is male**	**Senior is female**	**Senior is male**	**Alter is female**	**Alter is male**		**Link is female**	**Link is male**
+3	**naa'*	**yum*	**(ix)kit*	**akaan*				**ha'an*	**alib*
+2	**kik*	**suku'un*	**mim*	**maam*	**haawan*	**baal*	**mu'*	**ataan*	**ichaam*
+1	**naa'*	**yum*	**(ix)kit*	**akaan*				**ha'an*	**alib*
older	**kik*	**suku'un*	**mim*	**maam*	**haawan*	**baal*	**mu'*	**ataan*	**ichaam*
0	*EGO*	*EGO*	*EGO*	*EGO*	*EGO*	*EGO*	*EGO*		
younger	**its'in*	**its'in*	**i'* or **maam*	**i'* or **maam*	**haawan*	**baal*	**mu'*	**ataan*	**ichaam*
-1	**aal*	**mehen*	**mehen*	**akaaq'*				**ha'an*	**alib*
-2	**its'in*	**its'in*	**i'* or **maam*	**i'* or **maam*	**haawan*	**baal*	**mu'*	**ataan*	**ichaam*
-3	**aal*	**mehen*	**mehen*	**akaaq'*				**ha'an*	**alib*

FIGURE 5.2. Full reconstructed set of Proto-Yukatekan kinship terms, with semantic components.

treated with some caution. But certainly an understanding of *ixkit* that considers it more or less as a "feminine father" makes it easy to accept that its original reciprocal could indeed be the same as the reciprocal of the term for "father," exactly as documented in the Motul dictionary—namely, *mehen*.

This reconstruction leads me to propose a reconstructed meaning of **mehen* (reciprocal **[ix]kit, *yum*) as "disharmonic-generation child of ego's patriline." Its reciprocals **yum* and **[ix]kit* are also modified to read "disharmonic senior man of ego's (father's) patrilineage" and "disharmonic senior woman of ego's (father's) patrilineage," respectively (Tables 5.11 and 5.12):[37]

> **mehen* (reciprocal **yum*): a junior consanguine who belongs to the relatum's patriline and to a generation that is disharmonic with (an odd number of generations removed from) the relatum's own; for example, mS, mD, BS, BD
>
> **(ix)kit* (reciprocal **mehen*): a senior female consanguine who belongs to the relatum's patriline and to a generation that is disharmonic with (an odd number of generations removed from) the relatum's own; for example, FZ
>
> **yum* (reciprocal **mehen*): a senior male consanguine who belongs to the relatum's patriline and to a generation that is disharmonic with (an odd number of generations removed from) the relatum's own; for example, F, FB

Support for this reconstruction is to be found in the otherwise extremely complicated set of semantic changes that would be needed to account for the meanings of the terms *na'*, *yum*, *äkän*, and *ixkit* in Northern Lakantun today. A gloss in terms of patrilineage affiliation (coupled with the relatively simple substitution of a sex-of-referent distinction for the older sex-of-senior distinction) accounts well for the uses of *yum* and *ixkit* in Northern Lakantun as I have understood them above. By analogy, the current Northern Lakantun meanings of *na'* and *äkän* could readily be derived from these. This scenario provides a motivation for the innovation of the otherwise rather surprising "sex of linking relative closest to referent" as a contrastive feature in Northern Lakantun.

Conclusions from the Reconstruction

Figure 5.2 summarizes the reconstructed kinship terminology of Proto-Yukatekan that I have produced. This exhaustive reconstruction of the Proto-Yukatekan relationship terms allows us to confirm with some confidence the existing claim (Eggan 1934; Hage 2003) that at the moment immediately before the breakup of Proto-Yukatekan (perhaps during the Terminal Classic era, around CE 900), a system of kin terminology that was characterized by alternating-generation usage was to be found across the Yucatán Peninsula. The system also had a well-developed set of dedicated terms for affines and placed considerable weight on the issue of patrilineage affiliation. In the course of the Postclassic, this usage began to break apart. During the colonial and modern periods, it has almost completely disappeared, in favor of a Hawaiian-type system in Mopan (Danziger 2001) and of Spanish kin term usage in Modern Yukatek.

Despite its use of alternating-generation terminology, however, the Proto-Yukatekan kinship system was not a Kariera one (contra Hage 2003), nor were the accompanying marriage arrangements of the Kariera type (where this is understood as "sister exchange" between exactly two corporate groups). This can be deduced from the simple fact that the Proto-Yukatekan set of affinal terms is among the clearest and most easily reconstructed elements of the entire system. Criterially, terminological systems that accompany "Kariera" marriage arrangements have no terms for affines (Radcliffe-Brown 1953, cited in Dumont 1983a), or if they do (Dumont 1983b), they are indistinguishable from terms for the cross-relations. That is, under the type of multigenerational bilateral cross-cousin marriage often described as Kariera and reconstructed by Hage (2003) as the prevailing Proto-Yukatekan marriage type, there is no need to distinguish the mother's brother (Proto-Yukatekan **ikaan*) from the wife's father (Proto-Yukatekan **ha'an*), and no coherence in doing so, because these roles are always played by the same man. In Colonial Yukatek, there is indeed some evidence of overlapping usage, taken by Eggan (1934) with some justification as evidence for a cross-cousin marriage preference—even possibly for bilateral cross-cousin marriage—at the time of documentation. But the mere fact that overlap in usage can be detected means that the terminology in use was not one that developed under such a marriage system. It is worth noting that many of the affinal terms that I have reconstructed for Proto-Yukatekan also have reflexes distributed widely across the entire Mayan language family and can therefore be proposed as elements of Proto-Mayan itself (Kaufman and Justeson 2003). They cannot be dismissed as recent innovations within Proto-Yukatekan. The distinction between collaterals and affines was made from the earliest Proto-Yukatekan times and was presumably motivated by marriage arrangements in which these two categories of relative were, at least some of the time, distinct.

Proto-Yukatekan Marriage

The prehistorian is always doomed to attempt or accept leaps of faith that the synchronic analyst has the luxury of eschewing. Accordingly, in what follows I make free use of speculations about social arrangements that might have provided the bridging contexts for certain of the semantic changes that my reconstruction proposes. If alternating-generation terminology is not motivated by a Kariera marriage system of generational sections ("direct exchange"), then it may be motivated by a marriage preference for "indirect exchange," in which members of the generations called by the same sets of terms marry "in the same direction" (Fox 1983). That is, a man marries into the same group in which his father's father found his wife (thus motivating the terminological similarity between the male ego and his father's father), and a woman marries into the group from which her mother's mother found a husband. Meanwhile, parents and their same-sex children (a man and his father, a woman and her mother) do not marry people from the same group. This form of marriage results in "the return of women" to the original group after the passage of one generation. The cross-cousin marriage rule that will bring this about is patrilateral cross-cousin marriage—a rule that men must marry their fathers' sisters' daughters, and women, their mothers' brothers' sons.[38] Figure 5.3 shows a schematic of how this works. While it is well known that the use of alternating-generation terminology does not reliably correlate with the practice of indirect-exchange marriage practices in synchronic analysis, nevertheless some account of the kind of "bridging context" (Evans and Wilkins 2000) that would have at some moment in the past motivated the terminological equivalence of members of harmonic and disharmonic generations is, for a prehistorian, better than none. I propose that in early Proto-Yukatekan times, the alternating-generation motif in Proto-Yukatekan kinship terminology was motivated and sustained by a FZD marriage rule.

In this connection, it is worth noting that the Colonial Yukatek terms *icham* 'husband' and *atan* 'wife' apparently participated in the alternating-generation schema when (as with other alternating-generation usages of Colonial Yukatek) these words were modified with the term *kaa'* 'second, recurrent' (Barrera Vasquez 1980). A woman's

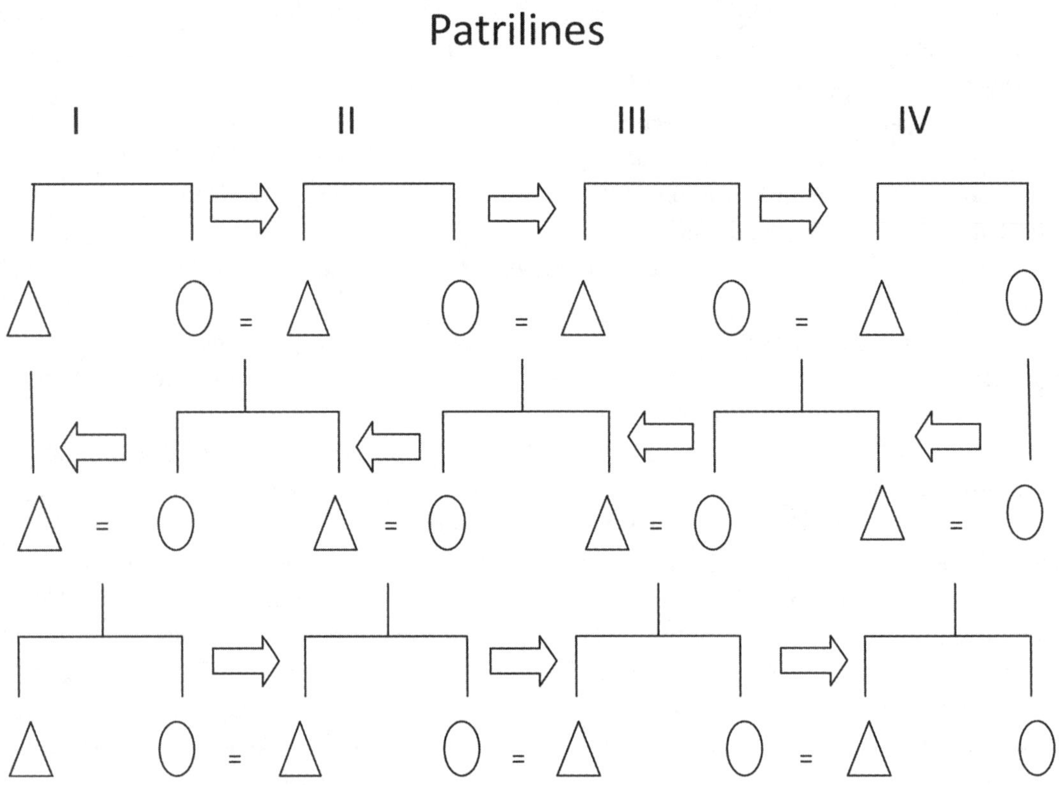

FIGURE 5.3. FZD Marriage. Direction of marriage is the same in alternating generations. Direction of women's marriage is shown with arrows (cf. Fox 1983:205).

kaa' icham 'recurring husband' is said to have included her CDH and her PF. A man's *kaa' atan* 'recurring wife' included his CSW and his MM.[39] While there are difficulties in fully interpreting these entries, they certainly show that alternating-generation kin term usage extended, at least in Colonial Yukatek and perhaps earlier, to the categorization of opposite-sex members of generations harmonic with ego's own with the terminological "marriage partners" of ego.

The range of marriage preferences and proscriptions among the documented Yukatekan groups is wide, but none actually practice FZD marriage. In Mopan, marriage with any cousin is taboo (Danziger 2001). In Colonial Yukatek, the friars tell us that men could not marry their parallel cousins (Landa 1941[1566]), and an inspection of terminological usage in cases where a single term was used both for consanguines and for affines has revealed that cross-cousin marriage was apparently frequently—perhaps preferentially—practiced (Eggan 1934). Among the Northern Lakantun, marriage with a cross-cousin is strongly preferred.

The fact that even those postcontact groups that retain vestiges of alternating-generation terminology do not practice the associated patrilateral marriage rule is not, however, all that surprising. If the terminological system was already beginning to disintegrate during the Postclassic, then we can assume that the marriage system that lay behind the terminology was already long gone by that point. I conclude, then, that the full indirect-exchange arrangements were present in the Yucatán only at some time prior to the middle or late Postclassic (the last moment at which Proto-Yukatekan was a single entity). At that earlier time, men preferentially (and perhaps prescriptively) married their father's sister's daughters; and women, their mother's brother's sons.

Proto-Yukatekan "Husband"

Recall that the readily reconstructible late Proto-Yukatekan term **ichaam* 'husband' (reciprocal **ataan*) cannot in fact be native to Proto-Yukatekan, since if it were, it would have undergone the early Preclassic sound change **iCa* > *aCa*. The term can only be a lexical innovation of some kind. I suggest that this form is a borrowed reflection of the Greater Cholan **ichan* (MB, reciprocal **ichak'*), itself cognate (Fox 1985) with the native Yukatekan term **ikaan* (MB).[40] The phonological forms for

Proto-Yukatekan "husband" and Greater Cholan "mother's brother" are persuasively similar, although the irregular labialization of the final consonant in Yukatekan remains to be accounted for.[41]

There is, however, on the face of things a significant semantic difficulty. Under patrilateral cross-cousin marriage, any Proto-Yukatekan term for "husband" that originated in a term for a consanguine should be one that in its original meaning indicated MBS. But the term I am considering apparently indicates the mother's brother himself. Practitioners of indirect exchange and users of alternating-generation terminology, of all people, should not be inclined to wink at matters of generational distinction, so this might seem to be a significant difficulty for the proposal. Recall, however, that in at least one branch of the Greater Cholan subfamily (the Tzeltalan), Omaha "generational skewing" characteristics are documented. In Colonial Tzeltal (Tenner 1978), the term *ichan* (reciprocal *ichak'*) follows typical Omaha practice in referring both to the mother's brother and to the mother's brother's children.[42] The Proto-Yukatekan term for "husband," in short, is a very plausible borrowing from Greater Cholan, on both phonological and semantic grounds—if we accept that the donor language followed Omaha kin term conventions and that the speakers of the recipient language preferentially practiced FZD marriage (I do not attempt to reconstruct the marriage practices of the Omaha speakers, although see Danziger n.d.).

When did this borrowing take place? The only documented users of an Omaha system in the Mayan family belong to the Tzeltalan branch of the Greater Cholan subfamily. No speakers of languages in the Cholan subbranch of Greater Cholan are known historically to have been Omaha users (although see Hopkins 1988). On the other hand, the weight of linguistic evidence (Justeson et al. 1985) indicates that there was no independent Proto-Yukatekan contact with the Omaha-using Tzeltalans after the breakup of Greater Cholan. One version of the borrowing scenario therefore proposes that it occurred before the breakup of Greater Cholan. This version allows us to imagine that Omaha usage disappeared in the Cholan line after the breakup, but it does entail that we attribute such usage to the common ancestors of the Tzeltalans and the Cholans and that we therefore project Omaha kin terminology in the Greater Cholan line back into Preclassic times and perhaps further.[43]

Meanwhile, the borrowing does show the Greater Cholan sound change **k* > *ch*, which we know to have been completed by the time that chocolate appeared in the Maya area in the mid-Preclassic. Since it applies to both branches of Greater Cholan, this change must have been complete before the subfamily split. This change was ongoing during the period of GLM contact between Proto-Yukatekan and Greater Cholan. This therefore places the borrowing moment—and the last moment at which we can be reasonably sure that Proto-Yukatekans were still living under indirect-exchange arrangements—to a temporal window in the mid- to late Preclassic, between the completion of the Proto-Yukatekan vowel harmonic change (which the borrowing did not undergo) and the mid-Preclassic completion of the Greater Cholan **k* > *ch* change (which it did undergo) that closely predates the breakup of the Greater Cholan subfamily.

Conclusions

I have proposed that contemplation of prototerminologies in the kinship domain is facilitated by a system-wide vision rather than by consideration of each term in isolation. Analysis in terms of semantic dimensions (Goodenough 1956) offers a parallel to feature-based analyses of phonology that can be carried into the realm of historical reconstruction and which is fruitful in pointing the way forward in kin term reconstruction in this and other areas of the world. Such reconstruction in turn points the way to new ideas about past systems of social organization and social life. In this particular case, the feature-based reconstruction of the full Proto-Yukatekan kin term system has paved the way for the following proposals:

New theses of interest to Mayan historical linguistics

1. Since **iCa* > *aCa* did not affect GLM **kitaam* 'peccary' or LM **sik'ab* 'cane', this change was completed before the end of the GLM contact episode. That episode came to an end in the late Preclassic, with the breakup of Greater Cholan.
2. The Proto-Yukatekan **ataan* 'wife' shows no semantic or phonological anomalies that would lead us to propose that it derives from Greater Cholan. (The reverse derivation of the Proto-Cholan **ihtaan* from this Yukatekan form remains a possibility.)
3. The Proto-Yukatekan **ichaam* 'husband' is not native Yukatekan but a relatively late borrowing or innovation. It may be a borrowing from

(Greater) Cholan or from an Eastern Mayan language.

4. The Proto-Yukatekan **chich* 'senior female of harmonic generation/grandmother' is a borrowing from (Greater) Cholan.

New theses on ancient Maya social organization

1. Proto-Yukatekans used alternating-generation terminology during the Postclassic and before (Eggan 1934) but did not at any time practice sister exchange ("Kariera" marriage) as a general rule. Rather, alternating-generation terminology was motivated by marriage practices of indirect exchange (FZD marriage), which were in place by the late Preclassic (by semantic possibility of in-borrowing a term for "husband" that meant MBS in the donor language).
2. The Greater Cholans of the late Preclassic (donors of the Proto-Yukatekan "husband" borrowing) used an Omaha-type kin terminology. Omaha usage is thus not an innovation in the Tzeltalan line but goes back to Greater Cholan. The Cholan speakers of the early Classic may also therefore have been Omaha users (cf. Hopkins 1988).

Notes

I am grateful to the Mopan Maya speakers of San Antonio, Belize, who first introduced me to issues of Mayan kinship. Thanks are also due to the editors of and contributors to this volume, particularly Patrick McConvell and David Kronenfeld, and to the anonymous reviewers who helped to make this a better chapter.

1. A proposal that matrilineal descent was also a factor (Roys 1940) has been persuasively debunked (Hopkins 1988). Evidence in the inscriptions for some attention to rulers' matrilineal descent is perhaps best explained as strategic maneuvering on the part of a royal house (Gillespie 2000; Schele and Freidel 1992) when the required patrilineal pedigree was wanting.
2. The different values of collaterality that distinguish *mother* from *aunt* are, in the case of *mother*, being related only through "vertical" links of direct lineality and, in the case of *aunt*, being related (also) through "horizontal" links of common descent from the same lineal ancestor.
3. The original orthography is retained; here and below [ä] represents a mid-central vowel, the apostrophe denotes glottalization (glottal stop or glottalization of the preceding consonant), and [x] represents a voiceless alveopalatal fricative.
4. The abbreviations used for kin type glosses are as follows: B = brother, C = child (i.e., offspring of either sex), D = daughter, F = father, H = husband, M = mother, P = parent (of either sex), S = son, Z = sister, W = wife. Juxtaposition of two or more of these characters should be read as possession of each right-hand kin type by the kin type to its immediate left: e.g., FBWZ = father's brother's wife's sister. Modifications not supplied by this adaptation of the English terms to metalanguage are added in lowercase preceding the modified kin type as follows: m = man's, o = older, w = woman's, y = younger. Possession skips the "older" and "younger" indicators. So, moBWyZ reads "man's older brother's wife's younger sister."
5. Where there is no linking relative—if, for example, referent and relatum are related at only one remove, as in the case of parents and children—then the senior party counts as the link for the purpose of finding a value for this feature. So the mother of a male child is called *na'* (female, related through female) and not *ixkit* (female, related through male), and the child himself is called *äkän* (male, related through female) and not *yum* (male, related through male).
6. Tzeltal is a Mayan language, but it is not a member of the Yukatekan Mayan subfamily. There is no attested case of Crow-Omaha usage in Yukatekan. Here and below, [ch] represents the voiceless alveopalatal affricate.
7. The illustration is drawn from a patrilineal group. "Crow" systems, practiced in matrilineal societies, show analogous terminological patterns but reversed as to laterality (Fox 1983).
8. Like the feature-based model, the rewrite-rules approach to kin term semantics was explicitly extrapolated from the linguistic models of the time. In the case of rewrite rules, however, it was an analogy from syntax, not one from phonology, that was used. It is significant that the later-developed field of generative phonology (Chomsky and Halle 1991)—whatever its merits for capturing the nature of synchronic systems—has not proved fruitful for diachronic reconstruction of past systems of speech sounds themselves.
9. This unease was not without warrant—as we have seen, a rampant refusal of universalism in comparative analysis was at that time leading toward a wholesale rejection of all comparative endeavor that, arguably, still confounds the discipline of anthropology in our own day.
10. Newer offshoots of the same paradigm include proposals for "radial structure" in the lexicon (Lakoff 1987). See Danziger 2001, 2005, for further discussion, especially of the question of the "psychological reality" of the various proposals.
11. Dates given in the Long Count are absolute in time. They can, with some calibration, be located with respect to other absolute calendars, such as that of the Christian church.
12. Debates over the existence of "Western Mayan" and of

various proposed lower-level groupings in each subfamily need not concern us here.

13. The variety, like its descendants and immediate sister languages, was known to its speakers simply as "Maya." Scholars and others carried the name "Maya(n)" across Chiapas, Belize, and Guatemala to cover the entire family of 30-odd languages to which Yukatek belongs, although most of these more distant sister languages are not traditionally called "Maya" by their own speakers.
14. The Classic inscriptions phonetically represent the vowel raising that characterizes Cholan proper only (Houston et al. 2000; Justeson et al. 1985). The breakup of Greater Cholan into its constituent subgroups, including Cholan proper, was therefore complete by the early Classic period.
15. While it is therefore important in pre-Columbian Mayan history, Yukatekan is certainly not (contra Hage 2003) the only "ancient Mayan" language subfamily.
16. Naturally, the level of oversimplification in Table 5.1 is extreme.
17. C stands for any consonant.
18. Roughly the last moment at which Proto-Yukatekan was a single linguistic entity.
19. Original documentation cannot always be completely trusted for phonetic accuracy, but phonological reconstruction is attempted for each Proto-Yukatekan lemma. For example, protoforms that result in reflexes with [a] in Mopan must have had [aa] in Proto-Yukatekan (Fisher 1973). Mayanist conventions depart from those of the International Phonetic Alphabet in using [ch] to represent the voiceless alveopalatal affricate and [x] to represent the voiceless alveopalatal fricative.
20. The glottal fricative ([h]) is represented in some orthographies as [j].
21. Boremanse (1977–78) tells us that the Lakantun term *äkän* (MB) can also be used for WF. It is not difficult to see how this extension came about, in the context of the strong preference for cross-cousin marriage, which Boremanse also documents.
22. Alternatively, Kaufman and Justeson (2003) propose that the Yukatekan form is derived by metathesis from a pre-Proto-Yukatekan form, **'anat*, apparently with the primary meaning "old woman," which is attested in two of the Q'anjob'alan languages (a Tzeltal word, *'antz* 'woman', is also proposed as relevant). While it is not to be rejected out of hand, the data in support of this proposal are scanty and are therefore compatible with the possibility of chance resemblance. Closer analysis of the vowels in the various proposed related forms provides further clues: in order to give the Modern Yukatekan reflexes (especially Mopan *ətan*), the first syllable of the Proto-Yukatekan form must have had a short vowel and cannot have been of the form *VhC* or *V'C* (as some of the proposed Cholan forms apparently are). The vowel in the second syllable cannot have been short (as the Q'anjob'alan vowel apparently is).
23. Apparently due to scribal error, the Motul entry for *cic* [kik] (Martinez Hernandez 1930[1577]:182) was not included in the *Diccionario Maya Cordemex* (Barrera Vasquez 1980), the great concordance of Yukatekan dictionaries.
24. Under some types of cousin marriage, this woman would also be the man's own parallel cousin.
25. In Northern Lakantun and in Mopan, there is no such sharing of semantic space today: *kik* (reciprocal *its'in*) designates senior parallel women of the zero generation only, and *chich* designates those of the grandparent generation only. Nevertheless, note that in Northern Lakantun the reciprocal of *chich* is, tellingly, the same as that of *kik*, namely, *itsin*. (In Mopan the term is self-reciprocal and designates a woman's grandchildren as well as the grandmother herself.)
26. Across the six Greater Cholan languages, *chich* appears sometimes as "grandmother" (Colonial Tzeltal—reciprocal *ih* [Tenner 1978]; Cholti—reciprocal *ytzin* [Gates 1935]) and sometimes as "older sister" (Chontal—reciprocal *its'in* [Keller and Placido 1997]; Chol—reciprocal *its'in* [Aulie and Aulie 2009; L. Rodriguez, personal communication, 2010]). In Tzotzil (Hopkins 1969), *chich* (reciprocal *chich'ol*) refers to the mother's brother's wife. In Modern Tzeltal (Kaufman and Justeson 2003) the term (reciprocal not supplied) is glossed simply as *pariente hembra* or "female relative." In addition, a term **chiich* 'grandmother' is also noted in Chuj, Q'anjob'al, and Mocho (Kaufman and Justeson 2003). Other lexical borrowings from Cholan into Mayan languages other than Yukatekan are known to have occurred (Campbell 1984).
27. I assign an asterisk to the form to indicate that I reconstructed its presence in (later) Proto-Yukatekan. Note, however, that the asterisk should not be taken to indicate that this is a native Proto-Yukatekan form—I explicitly envisage early stages of Proto-Yukatekan before the borrowing took place in which the form **chich* would not have been present.
28. An alternative hypothesis is that *chich* is native Yukatekan, derived by regular phonological changes from the Proto-Mayan *(a)tit* 'grandmother' (Dienhart 1989) and widely borrowed—with meanings of either zero or +2 generation—into the Greater Cholan (and other) Mayan languages from Yukatekan. There are two difficulties with this account, although the phonology is compelling: (1) It has no explanation for the existence of **kik* (reciprocal **its'in*) within Yukatekan, and (2) the relevant sound changes (especially the change of final *[t] to [ch]) would not have been complete in Proto-Yukatekan until the mid-Postclassic or later (Justeson et al. 1985), arguably leaving little time for the many episodes of borrowing and semantic change required to produce the present distribution of this form across the language family.
29. And perhaps under pressure to name certain relationships newly recognized under colonial arrangements, namely, those of Spanish compadrazgo (cf. analogous colonial-era uses of *cic* in Martinez Hernandez 1930[1577]:182).
30. In the context of the significant pressure for cross-cousin marriage documented in Northern Lakantun (Boremanse

1977–78), the affinal relationship of a woman to her brother's wife became regularized to that of a woman's female cross-cousin.

31. This has understandably sometimes been considered a mistranscription or a misunderstanding on the part of the original documenters, since the *suku'n/kik/its'in* set is also recorded for Colonial Yukatek in reference to the parallel cousins and no Colonial Yukatek terms are recorded for the cross-cousins.
32. Original and sustained reference of this phonological form to male ancestors is, incidentally, a counterexample to the famous generalization that [mam] is a universally preferred phonological form for referring to the mother (cf. Hendery and McConvell, this volume).
33. A third solution reconstructs a Proto-Yukatekan system in which usage from senior females (who used **i'* to their juniors and received **mim*) was not analogous to that from senior males (for whom **maam* was self-reciprocal).
34. Noting also the fact that in the corresponding parallel series (**suku'n/*kik/*its'in*), all children of a parent's parallel sibling are grouped together, without regard for laterality.
35. Justeson et al. (1985:15) propose a Yukatekan sound change in which **k(') > ch(')/__aq(')*. If such a change took place, it would account for the Colonial form *achak'* without proposing borrowing and lexical replacement. In the later stages of both Proto-Yukatekan and Greater Cholan, **q(') > k(')*.
36. Once again on the understanding that the asterisk preceding **ichaak'* here indicates a licensed presumption of its presence in late Proto-Yukatekan but not necessarily a reconstruction to the earliest stages of the protolanguage.
37. The Motul dictionary gives additional glosses for the word *mehen* in addition to that of "man's child." The word could also mean "something small" or, quite simply, "semen."
38. Marriage to the mother's brother's daughter does not result in this pattern of indirect exchange but, rather, in the "circulating connubium" pattern of generalized exchange (Fox 1983:209; Lévi-Strauss 1949).
39. As they stand, these entries fail to make the two terms reciprocals of one another. It is also not clear whether certain of the masculine-gendered Spanish terms should be read as gender neutral.
40. Proto-Mayan **ikaan > ichan* in Greater Cholan and Proto-Mayan **ikaan > akan* in Yukatekan by regular sound change in each subfamily.
41. Other possibilities include that of a borrowing from some reflex of the Eastern Mayan term **'ehtyaam* 'woman's brother-in-law' (Kaufman and Justeson 2003:134) or perhaps of the term **'iitaam* 'old man', 'man', whose reflexes are found exclusively in a diffusion zone around the Guatemalan town of Huehuetenango (a considerable distance from the Yucatán Peninsula) that normally includes certain Q'anjob'alan and Mamean languages but not Yukatekan ones (Kaufman and Justeson 2003:135). Both of these proposals account well for that final labial consonant (but introduce phonological anomalies of their own) and presume only relatively plausible degrees of semantic shift. Both, however, also require a proposal of long-distance borrowing from an unusual source.
42. In 20th-century Tzotzil, also Omaha with respect to its kin term system (Hopkins 1969), the term *ichan* does not appear, but a different term (*wom*, reciprocal *ichok'*) designates both the mother's brother and his children.
43. The alternative is to propose that the borrowing scenario occurred much later, and with speakers of Cholan proper alone. In that case, I would be proposing that the Cholans of the Classic Maya era were themselves users of an Omaha-type kin term system—and therefore, once again, that such usage goes back to the Greater Cholans. I would also be proposing that Proto-Yukatekans preserved patrilateral cross-cousin marriage preferences (not just alternating-generation terminology) into a much later time period. The first alternative is therefore on more than one count the more conservative, and it is the one that I prefer.

References Cited

Álvarez, C. 1997. *Diccionario etnolingüístico del idioma maya yucateco colonial.* Mexico City: UNAM.

Aulie, H. W., and E. W. D. Aulie. 2009. *Diccionario Ch'ol de Tumbalá, Chiapas, con Variaciones Dialectales de Tila y Sabanilla.* Mexico City: Instituto Lingüístico de Verano.

Barrera Vásquez, Alfredo. 1980. *Diccionario Maya Cordemex.* Merida: Ediciones Cordemex.

Boremanse, D. 1977–78. Northern Lacandon Relationship Terminology. *Folk* 19–20:133–149.

Campbell, L. 1984. The Implications of Mayan Historical Linguistics for Glyphic Research. In *Phoneticism in Mayan Hieroglyphic Writing.* J. S. Justeson and L. Campbell, eds. Pp. 1–11. Albany: State University of New York Institute for Mesoamerican Studies.

Campbell, L. 1988. Review of *Language in the Americas* by Joseph Greenberg. *Language* 64(3):591–615.

Campbell, L. 1998. *Historical Linguistics: An Introduction.* Edinburgh: Edinburgh University Press.

Campbell, L., and T. Kaufman. 1985. Mayan Linguistics: Where Are We Now? *Annual Review of Anthropology* 14(1):187–198.

Chomsky, N., and M. Halle. 1991. *The Sound Pattern of English.* Cambridge: MIT Press.

Coe, M. D. 1999. *Breaking the Maya Code.* Rev. edition. New York: Thames and Hudson.

Coe, M. D. 2005. *The Maya.* 7th edition. New York: Thames and Hudson.

Coe, M. D., and R. Koontz. 2008. *Mexico: From the Olmecs to the Aztecs.* 6th edition. New York: Thames and Hudson.

Coe, M. D., and M. Van Stone. 2001. Relationships. In *Reading the Maya Glyphs.* Pp. 86–88. London: Thames and Hudson.

D'Andrade, R. G. 1995. Toward an Analysis of Meaning. In *The Development of Cognitive Anthropology.* Pp. 16–30. Cambridge: Cambridge University Press.

Danziger, E. 1996. Split Intransitivity and Active–Inactive Patterning in Mopan Maya. *International Journal of American Linguistics* 62(4):379–414.

Danziger, E. 2001. *Relatively Speaking: Language, Thought, and Kinship among the Mopan Maya*. New York: Oxford University Press.

Danziger, E. 2005. The Eye of the Beholder: How Linguistic Categorization Affects "Natural" Experience. In *Complexities: Beyond Nature and Nurture*. S. McKinnon and S. Silverman, eds. Pp. 64–80. Chicago: University of Chicago Press.

Danziger, E. N.d. Good Wives: Non-elite Kinship and Marriage Practices of the Classic Maya.

Dienhart, J. M. 1989. *The Mayan Languages: A Comparative Vocabulary*. Odense: University Press of Southern Denmark.

Dumont, L. 1983a[1953]. The Dravidian Kinship Vocabulary as an Expression of Marriage. In *Affinity as a Value: Marriage Alliance in South India, with Comparative Essays on Australia*. Pp. 3–35. Chicago: University of Chicago Press.

Dumont, L. 1983b[1953]. The Kariera Kinship Vocabulary: An Analysis. In *Affinity as a Value: Marriage Alliance in South India, with Comparative Essays on Australia*. Pp. 175–191. Chicago: University of Chicago Press.

Eggan, F. 1934. The Maya Kinship System and Cross-Cousin Marriage. *American Anthropologist* 36(2):188–202.

Evans, N., and D. Wilkins. 2000. In the Mind's Ear: The Semantic Extensions of Perception Verbs in Australian Languages. *Language* 76(3):546–592.

Fisher, W. M. 1973. Toward a Reconstruction of Proto-Yucatec. Ph.D. dissertation, Department of Linguistics, University of Chicago.

Fortson, B. W. I. 2005[2003]. An Approach to Semantic Change. In *The Handbook of Historical Linguistics*. B. Joseph and R. Janda, eds. Pp. 648–666. Oxford: Wiley-Blackwell.

Fox, J. A. 1985. Kinship Terminology and Social Process: Two Mayan Etymologies. *International Journal of American Linguistics* 51(4):405–407.

Fox, J. A., and J. S. Justeson. 1986. Classic Maya Dynastic Alliance and Succession. In *Supplement to the Handbook of Middle American Indians, vol. 4: Ethnohistory*. R. Spores and P. A. Andrews, eds. Pp. 7–34. Austin: University of Texas Press.

Fox, R. 1983. *Kinship and Marriage: An Anthropological Perspective*. Cambridge: Cambridge University Press.

Frisch, J. A., and N. W. Schutz. 1967. Componential Analysis and Semantic Reconstruction: The Proto Central Yuman Kinship System. *Ethnology* 6(3):272–293.

Gates, W. 1935. *Arte y Diccionario en Lengua Cholti*. Baltimore: Maya Society.

Gillespie, S. D. 2000. Rethinking Ancient Maya Social Organization: Replacing "Lineage" with "House." *American Anthropologist* 102(3):467–484.

Goodenough, W. H. 1956. Componential Analysis and the Study of Meaning. *Language* 32(1):195–216.

Hage, P. 2003. The Ancient Maya Kinship System. *Journal of Anthropological Research* 59(1):5–21.

Hock, H. H., and B. D. Joseph. 1996. *Language History, Language Change, and Language Relationship: An Introduction to Historical and Comparative Linguistics*. 1st edition. Berlin: Mouton de Gruyter.

Hofling, C. A. 2004. Language and Cultural Contacts among Yukatekan Mayans. *Collegium Antropologicum* 28(suppl. 1): 241–248.

Hopkins, N. A. 1969. A Formal Account of Chalchihuitan Tzotzil Kinship Terminology. *Ethnology* 8:85–102.

Hopkins, N. A. 1988. Classic Mayan Kinship Systems: Epigraphic and Ethnographic Evidence for Patrilineality. *Estudios de Cultura Maya* 17:87–121.

Houston, S., J. Robertson, and D. Stuart. 2000. The Language of Classic Maya Inscriptions. *Current Anthropology* 41(3):321–356.

Justeson, J. S., W. M. Norman, and T. Kaufman. 1985. The Lowland Mayan Language Area. In *The Foreign Impact on Lowland Mayan Language and Script*. J. S. Justeson, ed. Pp. 9–20. Middle American Research Institute, 53. New Orleans: Middle American Research Institute, Tulane University.

Kaufman, T. 1976. Archaeological and Linguistic Correlations in Mayaland and Associated Areas of Meso-America. *World Archaeology* 8(1):101–118.

Kaufman, T. 1990. Algunos rasgos estructurales de los idiomas Mayances con referencia especial al K'iche. In *Lecturas sobre la lingüística Maya*. N. C. England and S. R. Elliott, eds. Pp. 59–114. Antigua Guatemala: CIRMA.

Kaufman, T., and J. Justeson. 2003. *A Preliminary Mayan Etymological Dictionary*. FAMSI. Electronic document, http://www.famsi.org/reports/01051/index.html.

Kaufman, T., and W. Norman. 1984. An Outline of Proto-Cholan Phonology, Morphology, and Vocabulary. In *Phoneticism in Mayan Hieroglyphic Writing*. J. S. Justeson and L. Campbell, eds. Pp. 77–166. Albany: State University of New York Institute for Mesoamerican Studies.

Keller, K. C., and P. L. G. Plácido. 1997. *Diccionario chontal de Tabasco (Mayense)*. 1st edition. Serie de vocabularios y diccionarios indigenas "Mariano Silva y Aceves" 36. Guatemala City: Instituto Lingüístico de Verano.

Kroeber, A. L. 1909. Classificatory Systems of Relationship. *Journal of the Royal Anthropological Institute of Great Britain and Ireland* 39:77–84.

Kronenfeld, D. 2006. Formal Rules, Cognitive Representations, and Learning in Language and Other Cultural Systems. *Language Sciences* 28:424–435.

Lakoff, G. 1987. *Women, Fire, and Dangerous Things: What Categories Reveal about the Mind*. Chicago: University of Chicago Press.

Landa, D. D. 1941[1566]. *Landa's Relación de las Cosas de Yucatán: A Translation*. A. M. Tozzer, ed. Cambridge: Kraus Reprint Corp.

Law, D. 2009. Pronominal Borrowing among the Maya. *Diachronica* 26(2):214–252.

Leach, E. 1958. Concerning Trobriand Clans and the Kinship Category *Tabu*. In *The Developmental Cycle of Domestic Groups*. J. Goody, ed. Pp. 120–145. Cambridge Papers in Social Anthropology. Cambridge: Cambridge University Press.

Lévi-Strauss, C. 1949. *Les Structures élémentaires de la parenté*. Paris: Presses Universitaires de France.

Lounsbury, F. G. 1956. A Semantic Analysis of the Pawnee Kinship Usage. *Language* 32(1):158–194.

Lounsbury, F. G. 1964. The Formal Analysis of Crow- and Omaha-Type Kinship Terminologies. In *Explorations in Cultural Anthropology: Essays in Honor of George Peter Murdock*. W. H. Goodenough, ed. Pp. 351–393. New York: McGraw-Hill Book Co.

Lounsbury, F. G. 1969. Language and Culture. In *Language and Philosophy*. S. Hook, ed. Pp. 3–29. New York: New York University Press.

Martínez Hernández, J., ed. 1930[1577]. *Diccionario de Motul, Maya–Español, Atribuido a Fray Antonio de Ciudad Real, y Arte de Lengua Maya, por Fray Juan Coronel*. Merida: Talleres de la compañía Tipográfica Yucateca.

McConvell, P. N.d. Omaha Skewing in Australia: Overlays, Dynamism and Change.

McQuown, N. A. 1956. The Classification of the Mayan Languages. *International Journal of American Linguistics* 22(3): 191–195.

Needham, R. 1971. Remarks on the Analysis of Kinship and Marriage. In *Rethinking Kinship and Marriage*. R. Needham, ed. Pp. 1–34. ASA Monographs, 11. London: Tavistock Publications.

Radcliffe-Brown, A. R. 1953. Dravidian Kinship Terminology. *Man* 53:112.

Roys, R. L. 1940. *Personal Names of the Maya of Yucatan*. Washington, DC: Carnegie Institution of Washington.

Schele, L., and D. Freidel. 1992. *A Forest of Kings: The Untold Story of the Ancient Maya*. New York: Quill/W. Morrow.

Stuart, D. 1997. Kinship Terms in Maya Inscriptions. In *The Language of Maya Hieroglyphs*. M. J. Macri and A. Ford, eds. Pp. 1–11. San Francisco: PreColumbian Art Research Institute.

Swadesh, M. 1961. Interrelaciones de las Lenguas Mayas. *Anales del INAH* 13:231–267.

Tedlock, D. 2010. Early Mayan Writing. In *2000 Years of Mayan Literature*. Pp. 25–30. Berkeley: University of California Press.

Tenner, M. P. 1978. A Problem of Pre-Columbian Tzeltal Kinship. In *Papers in Mayan Linguistics*. N. C. England, ed. Pp. 254–289. University of Missouri Publications in Anthropology. Columbia: Department of Anthropology, University of Missouri.

Thompson, J. E. S. 1930. *Ethnology of the Mayas of Southern and Central British Honduras*. Chicago: Field Museum of Natural History.

Wald, R. F. 2004. The Languages of the Dresden Codex: Legacy of the Classic Maya. In *Linguistics of Maya Writing*. S. Wichmann, ed. Pp. 27–58. Salt Lake City: University of Utah Press.

Wisdom, C. 1940. *The Chorti Indians of Guatemala*. Chicago: University of Chicago Press.

6

Kin Terminologies as Linguistic Imprints of Regional Processes

The Socioecological Contexts of Close versus Distant Marriage Patterns in Indigenous Amazonia

Alf Hornborg

Through Lewis Henry Morgan, the study of kin nomenclatures among premodern societies became the point of departure for the discipline of anthropology (Parkin and Stone 2004; Trautmann 1987). For over a century, the significance of the structural regularities and variation that he discovered has been the subject of extensive discussion. Although global comparisons of kinship systems can generate insights about the limited number of options open to kin-organized societies, studies of structural variation within single regions are more likely to yield feasible interpretations of the causes of such variation. This chapter reviews the ethnographic record of kin terminologies in indigenous Amazonia during the late 20th century and offers a framework for interpreting their variation in terms of the positions of studied communities within regional systems of exchange. By juxtaposing 20th-century ethnography with reconstructions of the nature of intercommunity relations, I hope to show that ethnolinguistic groups that emphasize (and linguistically codify) locally endogamous marriage (e.g., through Dravidian kin terminologies) tend to have a history of socioeconomic fragmentation, whereas groups that incline toward (and linguistically codify) more distant marriages tend to have been more involved in long-distance exchange. This correlation, first suggested many years ago in my doctoral thesis (Hornborg 1988), could help us understand the specific characteristics of kinship systems among ethnolinguistic families such as Carib, Tukano, Pano, and Arawak, not in terms of essentialist cultural traditions but as expressions of a wider historical dynamic that has left linguistic imprints among its constituent subsystems.

Thirty years ago, I was attracted to the anthropological study of "kinship" because it offered unusually distinct data for cross-cultural comparison and modeling (Hornborg 1988). It was the apparent exactness of various types of kin terminologies that made the classification of different kinship systems (Dravidian, Crow, Omaha, etc.) seem legitimate and intellectually challenging. Like other students of kinship since Morgan, I sensed that there must be a way of logically explaining the regularities and contrasts between systems of kin classification in terms of other features of social organization. At that time, I was especially interested in the widespread significance of Dravidian-type kin terminologies in Amazonia. Using data from a sample of 48 indigenous groups in Amazonia, I correlated types of kin terminologies with a set of other factors, including the nature of external relations, suggesting, among other things, that Dravidian terminologies were correlated with the relative isolation and endogamy of local groups. I also argued that "Hawaiianization" (the inclusion of all cousins in the category of siblings) was associated with exogamy rather than endogamy, as previously argued by Dole (1969). Isolation and exogamy, I noted, were conditions largely determined by the extent of regional integration into systems of supralocal exchange. Ten years later, using a smaller sample, Henley (1996) offered a similar interpretation, adding important observations on some of the cultural correlates of this variation.

In my 1986 thesis, I showed how, in some groups, various principles more or less implicitly inherent in Dravidian terminologies had been transformed into other, more explicit features of kin classification (cf. Hornborg 1993, 1998). From a Dravidian universe of categories-cum-relationships, I suggested, a number of implicit regularities had been objectified and codified into new expressions that often transcended the limits of that universe:

1. Its focus on male ego's marriage to the daughter of his father's brother-in-law suggested the embryo of matrilateral cross-cousin marriage (Txicào, Sirionó).
2. Its implicit principles of parallel transmission (the coexistence of complementary, male and female perspectives on succession) provided matrices for unilocal residence and unilineal descent (Gé, Tukano).
3. Its encouragement of specific kinds of oblique marriage could generate Crow-Omaha systems (Sherente, Bororo).
4. The alternative emphasis on the equivalence of alternating generations was conducive to Kariera-like systems of marriage sections (Pano).
5. Its pervasive emphasis on reciprocity and dualism laid the foundation for dual organization (Gé, Tupí, Pano).
6. Finally, the various "Iroquois" attempts at reproducing its logic of "cross" and "parallel" threatened to muddle it to oblivion.

Such transformations, I argued, were like the overlapping of several fibers in a thread and what the structural analysis of serial redundancies in kinship systems was all about.

Although some of my comparative conclusions on indigenous social organization in Amazonia were widely off the mark, this fundamental argument still seems valid. The very activity of continuously reformulating extant regularities in social organization may contribute to its transformation. My early approach to Dravidian-type terminologies in Amazonia built on an implicit if ambiguous assumption that they represented the point of departure for other systems of kin classification over time. This unidirectional evolutionist bias, which accompanies much of the study of kinship since Morgan, can certainly be questioned. I am not convinced that we are justified in postulating hypothetical, antecedent prototypes to account for the existence of nomenclatures documented by ethnography (cf. Henley 1996; Viveiros de Castro 1998). Rather than viewing transformations as always being unidirectional, I believe that terminological variation reflects a spectrum of structural possibilities, the realization of which may in part be reversible (Hornborg 1998). In the current context, as I return to the data on Amazonian kin terminologies, I shall be more careful about postulating trajectories of succession of kinship systems, instead focusing more consistently on actual correlations between terminological features and the nature of recent intercommunity relations. Although such correlations were important to me even in my earliest studies (Hornborg 1988), other theoretical concerns prevented me from focusing specifically on these aspects. Since then, my understanding of indigenous Amazonian social organization over the long term has been significantly elaborated (Hornborg 2005; Hornborg and Hill 2011), providing a foundation for renewed attempts to account for regularities and contrasts in kin classification.

The empirical point of departure for this renewed analysis is summarized in Table 6.1. Building largely on the data compiled in my previous studies (Hornborg 1988) but with the addition of some more recent ethnographical monographs (Chernela 1993; Gow 1991; Johnson 2003; Kensinger 1995; McCallum 2001; Picchi 2000; Rival 2002; Santos-Granero 1991; Viveiros de Castro 1992), Table 6.1 lists 53 indigenous groups, their linguistic affiliations, kin terminologies as defined by certain diagnostic equations, and the genealogical correlates of explicit marriage preferences reported in the ethnographies.

A central problem, of course, is the typology of kin terminologies applied to the Amazonian data. After some deliberation, I decided to use a simplified, quadripartite typology based on specific equations and distinctions as diagnostic criteria. Thus, first, a "Dravidian" terminology is here defined as a system of kin classification where MBD and FZD are generally equated and denominated with the same term as is used for W or BW (male ego) and where all of ego's relatives in the three medial generations are categorized as "kin" or "affines" in consequence with their positions as "parallel" versus "cross"-relatives (see Figure 6.1 and Figure 6.2). Second, a "Hawaiian" terminology is identified where cross-cousins are generally equated with parallel cousins and siblings. Third, the "Crow-Omaha" label is here used for systems where MBD is terminologically distinguished from FZD and one or both of these kinswomen are equated with kinswomen of adjacent generations. Such cross-generational skewing is further subdivided into "Crow," where the predominant tendency is toward matrilineal equations (MBD = D, FZ = FZD), and "Omaha," where equations are generally patrilineal (M = MBD, FZD = ZD). Finally, the term "Iroquois" is reserved for those systems that resemble Dravidian systems by distinguishing cross-cousins from parallel

TABLE 6.1. Kin terminologies and marriage preferences in 53 indigenous groups in Amazonia.

Indigenous Group	Linguistic Affiliation	Kin Terms (Defined by Diagnostic Equations)	Marriage (Genealogical Correlates)
Krahó	N. Gé (E. Timbira)	3a	MBD, FZD
Ramkokamekra	N. Gé (E. Timbira)	3a	Not first cousins
Krikatí	N. Gé (E. Timbira)	3	Not first cousins
Apinayé	N. Gé (W. Timbira)	3	FZD, but not first cousins
Kayapó	N. Gé	3b	No information
Suyá	N. Gé	3b	MBD, FZD
Shavante	C. Gé	4	FZD, but not first cousins
Sherente	C. Gé	3b	FZD
Caingang	S. Gé	2	MBD, FZD, ZD, FZ
Bororo	Macro-Gé	3a	MBD, FZD, FZ
Karajá	Macro-Gé	2	MBD, FZD, ZD
Nambikwara	Macro-Gé	1	MBD, FZD, ZD
Machiguenga	Arawak	4	MBD, FZD, ZD, FZ
Mehinacu	Arawak	4	Not first cousins
Amuesha	Arawak	1	MBD, FZD
Piro	Arawak	4	MBD, FZD in the past, but not first cousins now
Trio	Carib	3	MBD, FZD, ZD, FZ
Kalapalo	Carib	1	MBD, FZD
Kuikuru	Carib	2	MBD, FZD
Karinya	Carib	1	MBD, FZD, ZD
Barama River Carib	Carib	1	MBD, FZD, ZD
Pemon	Carib	1	MBD, FZD, ZD
Waiwai	Carib	1	MBD, FZD, ZD, FZ
Txicáo	Carib	3a	MBD
Bakairí	Carib	4	MBD, FZD
Tapirapé	Tupí	2	Not first cousins
Mundurucú	Tupí	3	MBD, FZD, ZD
Parintintin	Tupí	1	MBD, FZD, ZD
Sirionó	Tupí	3a	MBD
Araweté	Tupí	4	MBD, FZD, ZD, FZ
Amahuaca	Pano	1	MBD, FZD, ZD, FZ
Mayoruna	Pano	1	MBD, FZD
Sharanahua	Pano	1	MBD, FZD
Cashinahua	Pano	1	MBD, FZD
Cubeo	Tukano	4	MBD, FZD
Barasana	Tukano	4	MBD, FZD, ZD
Bará	Tukano	4	MBD, FZD
Makuna	Tukano	1	MBD, FZD, ZD
Wanano	Tukano	4	FZD, MBD

TABLE 6.1. (cont'd.) Kin terminologies and marriage preferences in 53 indigenous groups in Amazonia.

Indigenous Group	Linguistic Affiliation	Kin Terms (Defined by Diagnostic Equations)	Marriage (Genealogical Correlates)
Yanomamö	Yanoama	1	MBD, FZD
Yanomam	Yanoama	1	MBD, FZD
Sanumá	Yanoama	1	MBD, FZD, ZD
Jívaro	Jívaroan	1	MBD, FZD
Achuar	Jívaroan	4	MBD, FZD
Aguaruna	Jívaroan	1	MBD, FZD
Piaroa	Salivan	1	MBD, FZD, ZD
Witoto	Witoto	2	Not first cousins
Bora	Witoto	2	Not first cousins
Trumaí	Trumaí	4	MBD, FZD
Warao	Warao	2	MBD, FZD, ZD, FZ
Kadiwéu	Guaycurú	2	Not first cousins
Cuiva	Guahibo	1	MBD, FZD
Waorani	Waorani	4	MBD, FZD

Note: 1 = Dravidian; 2 = Hawaiian; 3 = Crow-Omaha (3a = Crow; 3b = Omaha); 4 = Iroquois. See Hornborg 1988 for main sources.

Gen +2	**FF = MF**		*FM = MM*	
Gen +1	**F = FB = MZH**	*M = MZ = FBW*	**WF = MB = FZH**	*WM = FZ = MBW*
Gen 0	**B = FBS = MZS = WZH**	*Z = FBD = MZD = WBW*	**WB = MBS = FZS = ZH**	*W = MBD = FZD = BW*
Gen –1	**S = BS = ZDH**	*D = BD = ZSW*	**DH = ZS = WBS**	*SW = ZD = WBD*
Gen –2	**SS = DS**		*SD = DD*	

FIGURE 6.1. Categorical alignments of kin and affines in a Dravidian system of kin classification. Male relatives are in bold, and female relatives are in italics.

cousins and siblings (bifurcate merging) but do not equate cross-cousins with actual spouses and affines (such as W or BW) and where "cross" versus "parallel" kinship does not consistently coincide with a distinction between affines and kin among more distant cousins.

Marriage preferences also represent a tricky kind of data for comparative analysis. In most of the ethnographies, however, there are reports of explicit preferences that are presented in terms of the genealogical correlates of the relevant kin categories. The indigenous kin categories are of course central for understanding how these systems of classification operate, but the possibility of translating them into focal genealogical positions, attested to by most of the ethnographers, offers anthropology a common ground for comparison, much like the color spectrum does for the comparative study of color terms or the Linnaean taxonomy does for the comparative study of ethnobotany. Although contested (for an overview of this debate, see Parkin and Stone 2004), this approach to kinship continues to make it a favorite field for comparativists, as it was for Morgan and the other "inventors" of anthropology. The genealogical bias may nevertheless be responsible for instances where such data are contradictory (Apinayé, Shavante) or simply missing (Kayapó).

Before I proceed to discuss the correlations in Table 6.1, I should pause to consider in more detail the structure of a so-called Dravidian system (cf. Trautmann 1981). This type of kinship terminology is unequivocally present in 20 of the groups in my sample and has been attributed by ethnographers to several of the additional 13 cases that are here classified as "Iroquois." It has served as a point of departure for a number of comparative attempts to characterize indigenous social organization in Amazonia (Århem 1981; Balée 1985; Dreyfus 1977; Henley

FF	isawpigi			FM	initsu		
MF	isawpigi			MM	initsu		
F	isuwi	M	isi	WF	ijogu	WM	itsigi
FB	isuwi	MZ	isi	MB	ijogu	FZ	itsigi
MZH	isuwi	FBW	isi	FZH	ijogu	MBW	itsigi
B	efiñano/efisu	Z	ifasu/ikene	WB	ifandaw	W	ifandaw
FBS	efiñano/efisu	FBD	ifasu/ikene	MBS	ifandaw	MBD	ifandaw
MZS	efiñano/efisu	MZD	ifasu/ikene	FZS	ifandaw	FZD	ifandaw
WZH	efiñano/efisu	WBW	ifasu/ikene	ZH	ifandaw	BW	ifandaw
S	mukugu	D	ndisi	DH	ifatuwi	SW	ifati
BS	mukugu	BD	ndisi	ZS	ifatuwi	ZD	ifati
SS	ifijaw			SD	ifijaw		
DS	ifijaw			DD	ifijaw		

FIGURE 6.2. Kin terminology of the Kalapalo (male ego, terms of reference). From Basso 1973:78–80.

1982, 1996; Hornborg 1988; Houseman and White 1998; Kensinger 1979; Overing Kaplan 1973; Rivière 1973; Schwerin 1982; Shapiro 1984; Viveiros de Castro 1998). The fundamental structure of a Dravidian kin terminology can be represented as in Figure 6.1, indicating the consistent equation of "parallel" relatives with kin and "cross"-relatives with affines in the three medial generations. A perfect ethnographic example is the kin terminology of the Carib-speaking Kalapalo of the Upper Xingú (Figure 6.2). In a Dravidian system, "affines" are same-sex relatives in the three medial generations classified as related to ego through marriage alliances rather than consanguinity.

The line between a "Dravidian" and an "Iroquois" system is difficult to draw, the reason being—at least in my view (Hornborg 1998)—that the two are structurally and historically related. Iroquois systems may be former Dravidian systems that have been transformed by various attempts to replace their automatic generation of kin/affine dualism with explicit principles for kin classification. The "automatism" of Dravidian dualism is inherent in the widespread practice of sister exchange, also described as symmetric alliance or bilateral cross-cousin marriage, whereby cross-relatives automatically end up in the marriageable category (affines) while parallel relatives remain kin. When this automatism for some reason, such as growth in community size or a higher frequency of local exogamy, is replaced with reflexive explication of traditional principles of kin classification, the result would be the inconsistent application of "cross" versus "parallel" that has been identified as characteristic of Iroquois systems (Lounsbury 1964:1079 n. 4; Scheffler 1971:233–252; Trautmann 1981:82–89). An Iroquois system cannot be consistent in its delineation of a kin/affine dichotomy when it classifies as cross all children of paternal aunts and maternal uncles and of all opposite-sex members of ego's own generation, irrespective of whether these relatives themselves are cross or parallel (Hornborg 1998). Often, however, an Iroquois terminology is combined with a preference for marrying a bilateral cross-cousin (for instance, among Tukano speakers, the Bakairí, the Araweté, and the Waorani), indicating that it is appropriate to consider Iroquois terminologies as "Dravidianate" or even "ex-Dravidian." The introduction of separate affinal terms and the difficulties of keeping track of cross- and parallel relatives in Iroquois systems suggest a transition to larger communities and a higher frequency of distant marriages. However, the actual history of Amazonia suggests that the inverse trajectory is equally plausible. The widespread reduction of large communities and dissolution of regional exchange networks following European conquest, leaving only small and isolated groups over much of Amazonia, offer a historical explanation for the predominance of Dravidian systems in the region in the 20th century. The transition between Dravidian and Iroquois thus seems to be reversible. Where Iroquois terminologies occur today, they may be interpreted as reflecting more integrated systems of indigenous social organization.

Another way of linguistically codifying a preference for more distant marriages is represented by Hawaiian systems. Although Dole (1969) presented a contrary interpretation, the Hawaiian inclusion of all same-generation relatives in the category of siblings is evidently geared to a preference for marrying nonrelatives (cf. Hornborg 1998). Crow-Omaha systems, finally, codify unilateral skewing and oblique marriages with FZ or ZD, respectively. The Crow-Omaha extension of cross-cousin categories to specific positions in adjacent generations seems geared to other kinds of genealogically close (here oblique) marriages in the context of a strong cultural emphasis on unilineal principles such as unilocal postmarital residence. As I have argued elsewhere (Hornborg 1998:177, fig. 7.1), the logic of Crow-Omaha skewing identifies FZ as the prototypical oblique marriage from a matrilineal, male perspective and ZD as the prototypical oblique marriage from a patrilineal, male perspective.

Let us now turn to an interpretation of the data in Table 6.1. I begin with some straightforward statistical observations:

1. In the sample of 53, 20 have been classified as Dravidian terminologies, eight as Hawaiian, 12 as Crow-Omaha, and 13 as Iroquois.
2. Out of 12 groups affiliated to the Gé linguistic family, eight have terminologies classified as Crow-Omaha. Conversely, out of 12 terminologies classified as Crow-Omaha, eight are found among groups speaking Macro-Gé languages.
3. Three out of four Arawak-speaking groups have terminologies classified as Iroquois.
4. Five out of nine Carib-speaking groups have terminologies classified as Dravidian.
5. All four Pano-speaking groups have terminologies classified as Dravidian.
6. Four out of five Tukano-speaking groups have terminologies classified as Iroquois.
7. All three Yanoama-speaking groups have terminologies classified as Dravidian.
8. Two out of three Jívaroan-speaking groups have terminologies classified as Dravidian.
9. In the sample of 53, no fewer than 40 groups express a preference for bilateral cross-cousin marriage, while three express a preference for FZD marriage, and two, for MBD marriage.
10. In the sample of 53, 19 groups include oblique marriages (ZD and/or FZ) among preferred options, while ten groups express preferences for marrying more distantly than first cousins.
11. A preference for bilateral cross-cousin marriage is reported from three out of four Arawak-speaking groups (albeit one only in the past), eight out of nine Carib-speaking groups, three out of four Tupí-speaking groups, and all 15 Pano-, Tukano-, Yanoama- and Jívaroan-speaking groups.
12. All three groups expressing preferences for FZD marriage are speakers of Macro-Gé.
13. Preferences for oblique marriages occur in five out of nine Carib-speaking groups, in three out of five Tupí-speaking groups, and in all four groups classified either as Southern Gé or as Macro-Gé.
14. Of the ten groups expressing preferences for marrying more distantly than first cousins, four are speakers of Macro-Gé, and two are Arawak speakers. Thus, two out of four Arawak-speaking groups express this preference.
15. All of the 20 terminologies classified as Dravidian occur in groups expressing a preference for bilateral cross-cousin marriage, and ten of them occur in groups expressing a preference for oblique marriage.
16. Of the ten groups expressing preferences for marrying more distantly than first cousins, four have terminologies classified as Hawaiian; three, Iroquois; and three, Crow-Omaha.
17. Four of the five groups expressing a unilateral cross-cousin marriage preference have terminologies classified as Crow-Omaha.

These observations lend support to several general conclusions. As anticipated, a majority of groups in the sample have a preference for bilateral cross-cousin marriage and either Dravidian or Iroquois ("Dravidianate")

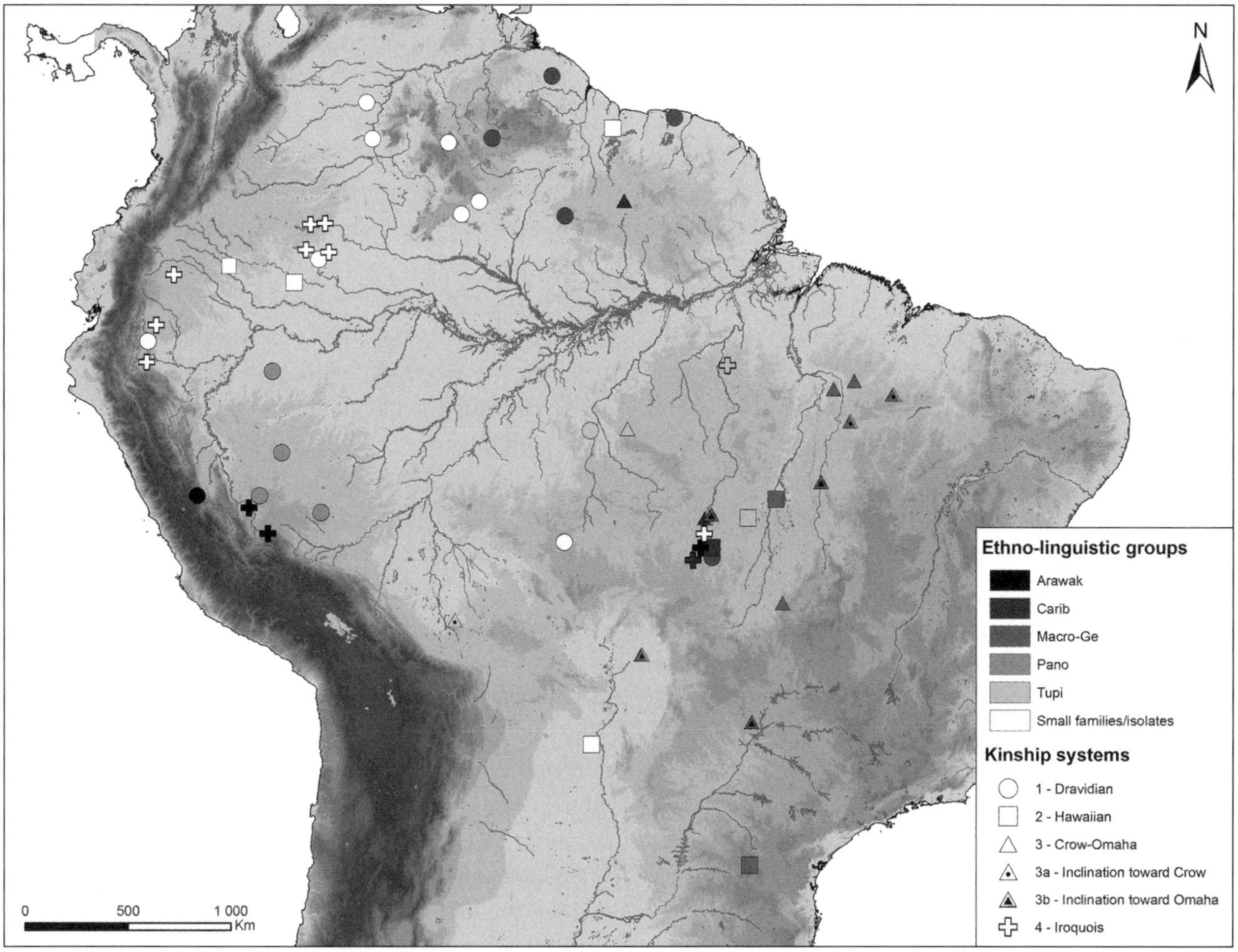

FIGURE 6.3. Geographical distribution of occurrences of kin terminologies in the sample. Map compiled by Love Eriksen.

terminologies. This marriage preference is universal among the Pano-, Tukano-, Yanoama-, and Jívaroan-speaking groups in the sample and next to universal among Carib speakers. Dravidian terminologies are predominant among Pano, Yanoama, Jívaroan, and Carib speakers, while Iroquois terminologies are predominant among Arawak and Tukano speakers. Speakers of Macro-Gé are instead inclined toward Crow-Omaha terminologies and unilateral cross-cousin marriage preferences. Hawaiian terminologies occur in several language families (Gé, Carib, Tupí, Witoto, Warao, Guaycurú), often in conjunction with a preference to marry more distantly than first cousins (Tapirapé, Witoto, Bora, Kadiwéu). Other instances of this preference occur in conjunction with terminologies classified as Iroquois (Shavante, Mehinacu, Piro) or Crow-Omaha (Ramkokamekra, Krikatí, Apinayé). Preferences for oblique marriage occur in most language families (Gé, Arawak, Carib, Tupí, Pano, Tukano, Yanoama, Salivan, Warao) irrespective of kin terminology.

In order to pursue the hypothesis presented at the outset of this chapter—namely, that ethnolinguistic groups that emphasize locally endogamous marriage tend to have a history of socioeconomic fragmentation, whereas groups that express preferences for distant marriages tend to have been more involved in long-distance exchange—I need to examine the geographical location of each group in the sample (Figure 6.3). When plotted onto a map, the distribution of different types of terminologies reveals some significant patterns. Most evidently, and not surprisingly, the occurrence of Crow-Omaha terminologies is more or less completely restricted to eastern Brazil, the area occupied by speakers of Macro-Gé. More interesting for my purposes, however, is the concentration of Iroquois terminologies in the Vaupés, the Upper Xingú, and the Andean foothills of Ecuador and Peru. These are areas where indigenous exchange relations between communities have remained unusually intact through history, compared with most other parts of Amazonia. Largely because of their geographical isolation, these areas have been home to indigenous societies that managed to survive much of the colonial holocaust, epidemics, and slave raids. While most other indigenous groups in Amazonia have contracted into isolated and locally endogamous communities, several groups in the Vaupés, the Upper Xingú, and the Andean foothills have been able to sustain denser populations and more intensive intercommunity exchange. It is reasonable to suggest that this may be the reason why Iroquois terminologies are largely concentrated in these areas. It simultaneously gives us reasons to believe that Iroquois terminologies were more widespread in Amazonia in the past, before demographic fragmentation reduced most indigenous groups to small, atomized, and largely endogamous communities. This probably also applies to Hawaiian terminologies, which, although in this sample they are too few to lend themselves to significant geographical distribution patterns, similarly indicate an inclination toward distant marriage.

This comparative analysis of the relation between kin terminologies and social organization in indigenous Amazonia rests on some admittedly traditional assumptions of kinship studies that have an ancestry going back to Lewis Henry Morgan. First, one such assumption is that "kinship" *is* a real phenomenon that deserves continued attention particularly from anthropologists concerned with the comparative study of nonmodern forms of social organization. Second, it is valid to examine the relation between systems of kin classification and actual social relations, including predominant patterns of marriage alliance. Third, kin terminologies labeled "Dravidian" and "Iroquois" undoubtedly have a structural or historical relation to so-called cross-cousin marriage. Finally, for a comparative study of kinship systems to be feasible, it must permit itself to apply a genealogical lens to the translation of kin categories and marriage preferences.

Given these assumptions, the correlations among marriage preferences, kin terminologies, and the geography of Amazonia presented in this chapter suggest that systems of kin classification may represent linguistic imprints of regional historical processes. In most of Amazonia over the past three centuries, such processes have favored community isolation and local endogamy, while in a few areas such as the Vaupés and Upper Xingú, more distant intercommunity alliances have been maintained. The contemporary predominance of Dravidian terminologies and preferences for bilateral cross-cousin marriage in indigenous Amazonia should not be interpreted as an archaic and primeval form of social organization in the region but, rather, as a result of historical processes of community contraction following European contact. No more than contemporary community size, population density, or agricultural practices should the kinship systems documented by 20th-century ethnographers be taken as representative of precolonial conditions. Rather than essentializing the kin terminologies now considered typical of different language families as elements of their specific cultural traditions, variation between language families should be understood in terms of their geographical positions within a region unevenly affected by the traumas of European encroachment. Such considerations would no doubt help us explain why Dravidian terminologies are almost ubiquitous among Carib and Yanoama speakers of Guayana and hinterland Pano speakers of eastern Peru, while Iroquois, Hawaiian, and other non-Dravidian systems of kin classification are predominant among Tukano, Arawak, Tupí, and Carib speakers in the Vaupés and Xingú.

Given the historical role of Arawak-speaking groups as riverine traders occupying large and complex social formations (Hornborg 2005; Hornborg and Hill 2011), considerations of regional socioecological contexts may also help explain why three of the four Arawak-speaking groups in the sample have applied an Iroquois system of kin classification and why at least half of them express a preference for distant marriage.

References Cited

Århem, K. 1981. *Makuna Social Organization: A Study in Descent, Alliance, and the Formation of Corporate Groups in the North-Western Amazon*. Uppsala Studies in Cultural Anthropology 4. Stockholm: Almqvist och Wiksell.

Balée, W. H. 1985. Review of K. M. Kensinger, ed., *Marriage Practices in Lowland South America*. *American Anthropologist* 87:419–420.

Basso, E. B. 1973. *The Kalapalo Indians of Central Brazil*. New York: Holt, Rinehart and Winston.

Chernela, J. M. 1993. *The Wanano Indians of the Brazilian Amazon: A Sense of Space*. Austin: University of Texas Press.

Dole, G. E. 1969. Generation Kinship Nomenclature as an Adaptation to Endogamy. *Southwestern Journal of Anthropology* 25:105–123.

Dreyfus, S. 1977. Propositions pour un modèle Sud-Américain de l'alliance symétrique. In *Actes du XLIIe Congrès International des Américanistes*, vol. 2. Pp. 379–385. Paris: Société des Américanistes.

Gow, P. 1991. *Of Mixed Blood: Kinship and History in Peruvian Amazonia*. Oxford: Clarendon Press.

Henley, P. 1982. *The Panare: Tradition and Change on the Amazonian Frontier*. New Haven: Yale University Press.

Henley, P. 1996. *South Indian Models in the Amazonian Lowlands*. Manchester Papers in Social Anthropology, 1. Manchester: Department of Social Anthropology, University of Manchester.

Hornborg, A. 1988[1986]. *Dualism and Hierarchy in Lowland South America: Trajectories of Indigenous Social Organization*. Uppsala Studies in Cultural Anthropology, 9. Stockholm: Almqvist och Wiksell.

Hornborg, A. 1993. Panoan Marriage Sections: A Comparative Perspective. *Ethnology* 32:101–108.

Hornborg, A. 1998. Serial Redundancy in Amazonian Social Structure: Is There a Method for Poststructuralist Comparison? In *Transformations of Kinship*. M. Godelier, T. R. Trautmann, and F. E. Tjon Sie Fat, eds. Pp. 168–186. Washington, DC: Smithsonian Institution Press.

Hornborg, A. 2005. Ethnogenesis, Regional Integration, and Ecology in Prehistoric Amazonia: Toward a System Perspective. *Current Anthropology* 46(4):589–620.

Hornborg, A., and J. D. Hill, eds. 2011. *Ethnicity in Ancient Amazonia: Reconstructing Past Identities from Archaeology, Linguistics, and Ethnohistory*. Boulder: University Press of Colorado.

Houseman, M., and D. R. White. 1998. Taking Sides: Marriage Networks and Dravidian Kinship in Lowland South America. In *Transformations of Kinship*. M. Godelier, T. R. Trautmann, and F. E. Tjon Sie Fat, eds. Pp. 214–243. Washington, DC: Smithsonian Institution Press.

Johnson, A. 2003. *Families of the Forest: The Matsigenka Indians of the Peruvian Amazon*. Berkeley: University of California Press.

Kensinger, K. M. 1995. *How Real People Ought to Live: The Cashinahua of Eastern Peru*. Prospect Heights, IL: Waveland Press.

Kensinger, K. M., ed. 1979. *Social Correlates of Kin Terminology*. Working Papers on South American Indians, 1. Bennington, VT: Bennington College.

Lounsbury, F. G. 1964. The Structural Analysis of Kinship Semantics. In *Proceedings of the Ninth International Congress of Linguists*. H. G. Lunt, ed. Pp. 1073–1093. The Hague: Mouton.

McCallum, C. 2001. *Gender and Sociality in Amazonia: How Real People Are Made*. Oxford: Berg.

Overing Kaplan, J. 1973. Endogamy and the Marriage Alliance: A Note on Continuity in Kindred-Based Groups. *Man* 8: 555–570.

Parkin, R., and L. Stone. 2004. General Introduction. In *Kinship and Family: An Anthropological Reader*. Robert Parkin and Linda Stone, eds. Pp. 1–23. Oxford: Blackwell.

Picchi, D. 2000. *The Bakairí Indians of Brazil: Politics, Ecology, and Change*. Prospect Heights, IL: Waveland Press.

Rival, L. 2002. *Trekking through History: The Huaorani of Amazonian Ecuador*. New York: Columbia University Press.

Rivière, P. G. 1973. The Lowland South America Culture Area: Towards a Structural Definition. Paper presented at the 72nd Annual Meeting of the American Anthropological Association, New Orleans.

Santos-Granero, F. 1991. *The Power of Love: The Moral Use of Knowledge amongst the Amuesha of Central Peru*. London: Athlone Press.

Scheffler, H. W. 1971. Dravidian-Iroquois: The Melanesian Evidence. In *Anthropology in Oceania: Essays Presented to Ian Hogbin*. C. Jayawardena and L. Hiatt, eds. Pp. 231–254. Sydney: Angus and Robertson.

Schwerin, K. H. 1982. The Kin Integration System among Caribs. Paper presented at the 44th International Congress of Americanists, Manchester.

Shapiro, J. R. 1984. Marriage Rules, Marriage Exchange, and the Definition of Marriage in Lowland South American Societies. In *Marriage Practices in Lowland South America*. K. M. Kensinger, ed. Pp. 1–30. Illinois Studies in Anthropology, 14. Urbana: University of Illinois Press.

Trautmann, T. R. 1981. *Dravidian Kinship*. Cambridge: Cambridge University Press.

Trautmann, T. R. 1987. *Lewis Henry Morgan and the Invention of Kinship*. Berkeley: University of California Press.

Viveiros de Castro, E. 1992. *From the Enemy's Point of View: Humanity and Divinity in an Amazonian Society*. Chicago: University of Chicago Press.

Viveiros de Castro, E. 1998. Dravidian and Related Kinship Systems. In *Transformations of Kinship*. M. Godelier, T. R. Trautmann, and F. E. Tjon Sie Fat, eds. Pp. 332–385. Washington, DC: Smithsonian Institution Press.

7

The Evolution of Yolngu and Ngarinyin Kinship Terminologies

Models of Cumulative Transformations

Ian Keen

We are thus justified, I think, in regarding the Kariera and the Aranda systems as two terms in an evolutionary process, for evolution, as the term is used here, is a process by which stable integrations at a higher level are substituted for or replace integrations at a lower level. This does not involve the assumption that the Aranda system is derived historically from one identical with the existing Kariera system.
(Radcliffe-Brown 1931:426)

Radcliffe-Brown thought that Aboriginal kinship systems of the Aranda type, characterized by four "lines of descent," provide a "wider integration" than Kariera systems, characterized by two lines of descent, and bring "a single individual into social relations with a wider circle" (1931:426). As the epigraph shows, he went on to suggest that these types of systems represent stages in an evolutionary process, although he did not see the Kariera-type system itself as temporally prior. Radcliffe-Brown was almost certainly wrong in suggesting that Aranda-type systems link individuals in a broader network of relations, for Kariera and Aranda systems of kin categories are iterated through a population in similar ways, through "classificatory" and inherited kin relations (Keen 2004). In the case of inherited kinship a person is related to another person, such as his or her mother's "sister," through an intermediary, but the genealogical connection between the intermediary and that person is not precisely known. In "mediated kinship" two people may compute a relationship on the basis of a common relative, but again the precise genealogical connections may not be known (see Dousset 2008 on the relational triangle).

Elkin (1970) surmised, more boldly than Radcliffe-Brown, that Kariera-type systems were the original structures from which the more complex terminologies developed. Citing Elkin, McConvell and I (2011) posit an evolutionary trajectory from a Kariera system to the asymmetrical Yolngu ("Murngin") terminology. This chapter expands on that suggestion and presents models of the evolution of two distinct types of Australian Aboriginal kinship terminology, the first associated with Yolngu languages of northeast Arnhem Land and classified as Murngin type by Radcliffe-Brown (1931) and the second associated with the Ngarinyin language of the northwest Kimberley and its Worrorra and Wunambal neighbors, classified as similar to the Aranda type by Radcliffe-Brown (1931) but distinguished by Omaha skewing, although he did not use that expression (see also Elkin 1931–32; Turner 1980). Although the Ngarinyin terminology has been classified as of the Aranda type, it differs in many respects from such terminologies and is best regarded as an asymmetrical terminology (Keen 2004), though different in form from the asymmetrical Yolngu terminology. The chapter proposes that the two terminologies developed along distinct trajectories of changes from similar foundations, namely, terminologies broadly of the Kariera type in Radcliffe-Brown's (1931) typology.[1]

There are several reasons for suggesting that the

Yolngu terminology may have evolved from a Kariera-like one. First, it is Kariera-like in generations +3 and –3 in classifying kin into parallel and cross-great-grandkin. Second, there is an unexpectedly high number of cognate forms linking Yolngu kin categories to those of eastern Cape York Peninsula, which are predominantly Kariera in type (McConvell and Keen 2011). Third, Yir-Yoront people of western Cape York Peninsula have a Murngin-type terminology similar in form to the Yolngu terminology, though less elaborate, while their neighbors have Kariera-type terminologies. It is possible that the Yir-Yoront terminology also developed from a system similar to neighboring ones. (At the present stage of research the relationship between the Yir-Yoront and Yolngu kinship lexicons has not been systematically explored.) There are also good reasons for suggesting that the form of kinship terminology characteristic of Ngarinyin speakers and their neighbors (Worrorra and Wunambal) developed out of a Kariera form of terminology. First, the terminologies of certain of their neighbors are Kariera-like, and second, the Ngarinyin terminology is readily derived from a Kariera terminology by means of a series of changes, in particular Omaha skewing.

The Ngarinyin terminology, previously classified as Aranda type (Radcliffe-Brown 1931; Turner 1980; Warner 1933) but with Omaha skewing, is in fact quite different from Aranda systems and is associated with asymmetrical marriage patterns not unlike those of the Yolngu (Blundell and Layton 1978; Keen 1982, 2004). The preferred marriage in the Ngarinyin system is between a man and his "FM," including FMBSD and FMBSSD. This is also a matrilateral marriage (from the man's point of view), for the preferred wife category is of the father's mother's patriline. The Marra terminology may be similar in structure to the Ngarinyin one: Heath (1981) records an asymmetrical terminology, although Warner (1933) represents the Marra terminology as of the Aranda type.

Asymmetrical terminologies and marriage systems appear to be local and rather rare elaborations of the widespread Kariera type. Aranda-type terminologies may also be posited as elaborations of the Kariera type, but they are more numerous and more widely dispersed than the asymmetrical ones, being found in regions including arid and semiarid zones and the tropical north, but more restricted in distribution than Kariera-type terminologies. Moreover, the asymmetrical terminologies may readily be derived from Kariera ones by ordered series of differentiations and equivalences (see below). It is cumbersome, however, to derive formally the asymmetrical terminologies from Aranda-type terminologies. In effect such a terminology would have to be simplified to a Kariera-type terminology before being converted to an asymmetrical one.

An analysis of terminologies in the AUSTKIN database (Keen 2010) shows that many systems of kin classification are intermediate between the Kariera type and the Aranda type. Some are Kariera-like but with either a parent's cross-cousin or a person's second cross-cousin as a distinct category or both (e.g., Murrinh-patha). Others are Aranda-like but with some horizontal merging (e.g., Ngan'gikurunggurr).

The known asymmetrical terminologies are all located in the tropical north among societies inhabiting country on or near the coast in an area endowed with relatively rich resources (relatively rich, that is, in the context of the overall aridity of the Australian environment [Keen 2004, 2006]). The exemplars of each type are widely separated in space, with Murngin-type terminologies located in northeast Arnhem Land (Yolngu people) and western Cape York Peninsula (Yir-Yoront people) and the Ngarinyin type of terminology located in the northwest Kimberley (Ngarinyin, Worrorra, and Wunambal languages) and perhaps the western Gulf of Carpentaria (Marra language). A feature that links the two types indirectly is Omaha skewing. The Ngarinyin and similar terminologies include Omaha skewing, and it seems likely that the precursors of the Yolngu terminology were also skewed (McConvell and Keen 2011).

The cultural geographies within which Yolngu and Ngarinyin systems are or were embedded are very different. The Yolngu region forms an enclave of suffixing Pama-Nyungan language varieties, with speakers of prefixing non-Pama-Nyungan languages living to the west and south and bounded by the sea to the north and east. The kinship terminologies of neighboring groups are of contrasting types, with, for example, the Aranda-type terminologies of Gijingarli (Hiatt 1965) and Ngalagkan speakers (Merlan 1983) to the northwest and southwest of the Yolngu region, respectively. The neighbors of Ngarinyin, Worrorra, and Wunambal people, whose languages are of a non-Pama-Nyungan family, have Kariera-type kinship terminologies in which MM, MMZ, and MMB are distinguished from FF, FFB, and FFZ, and the preferred marriage is to a distant cross-cousin (see below). Among the neighboring languages of the Marra of the western Gulf of Carpentaria, Yukulta (Keen 1983) appears to have a Kariera-type kinship terminology (and belongs to a different language family), and Warner classifies Yanyula as Aranda type. (It too belongs to a different language family from Marra.) As mentioned, the terminology of Ngalagkan people to the west is Aranda type.

McConvell and I (2011) show that the Yolngu terminology shares an unexpected number of cognates with terminologies of eastern Cape York Peninsula. Data for terminologies of the intervening region of the Gulf of Carpentaria south coast are rather scanty, but Marra and Yanyula in the western gulf appear to have only two or three obvious cognates with Yolngu kin terms, and terminologies of the western gulf such as those of Mayi-Kulan and Mayi-Thakurr people share perhaps three cognate forms. Kin terminologies of the Simpson and Tanami deserts such as Yarluyandi and Bilinara share perhaps five cognate terms with the Yolngu terminology. On Cape York Peninsula, Kuku-Yalanji and Kuuku-Ya'u terminologies (Hershberger and Hershberger 1982; Thompson 1998) both have six or more terms that are likely cognates of Yolngu terms, though with some shifts in meaning (McConvell and Keen 2011). The relationship between the Yolngu kinship vocabulary and that of Yir-Yoront people of the west coast of Cape York Peninsula, whose kinship terminology has a similar form, is as yet unclear, although they share perhaps four cognates.

McConvell and I (2011) posit historical links between the Yolngu terminology and the Kariera-type terminologies of eastern Cape York Peninsula, although the location of the original Yolngu homeland (assuming that they migrated to their present location) is unclear, and it is not known how ancestors of Yolngu peoples might have arrived in northeast Arnhem Land. Migration around the coast by a founder group is one possibility; displacement by the gradual flooding of the gulf following the end of the Pleistocene is another. The gulf appears to have reached its present level by 6000 BP (Faulkner 2008; Faulkner and Clarke 2004; Smart 1977), and the coastal wetland ecology developed after 4000 BP.

The main purpose of this chapter is to model two series of transformations from Kariera-type systems toward the asymmetric forms of the Yolngu and Ngarinyin terminologies, with implications for the evolution of Yir-Yoront and perhaps Marra terminologies. The resulting models are offered as heuristics, to be tested against possible historical linguistic evidence for protoforms and for genetic relations between languages and kinship terminologies. (See Read, this volume, for an alternative approach to structural change in kin terminologies.)

Kariera Terminologies

Prototypically, Kariera-type terminologies sort relatives into parallel and cross categories at each generation except for the parents' generation, which sorts them into matrilateral and patrilateral kin (McConvell and Keen 2011; Radcliffe-Brown 1931:47). In generation +2 parallel grandparents (MM and FF) are distinguished from cross-grandparent (MF and FM), and in the type case as described by Radcliffe-Brown the terms for grandparents' opposite-sex siblings are merged with the grandparent of the same gender, matching parallel and cross: FFZ with MM, MMB with FF, FMB with MF, and MFZ with FM. Grandparental terminologies vary, but the terminology in the parents' generation is bifurcate merging, with FZ differentiated from M and MZ, which are merged, and from F and FB, which are also merged. In a similar way MB is differentiated from F/FB and M/MZ. In ego's generation parallel cousins are classified with siblings and distinguished from cross-cousins, who may be differentiated by gender. In the child's generation the categories of a man's children and a person's brother's children are merged and distinguished from categories for a woman's children and a person's sister's children, which are also merged. In the type case, categories in the grandchild's generation are the same as in generation +2, denoting wDC/ZDC, mSC/BSC, wSC/ZSC, and mDC/BDC. The terminology can be sorted into two "lines" (and Kariera terminologies are sometimes referred to as "two-line" systems), through either patrifiliation, consistent with patri-moieties, or matrifiliation, consistent with matri-moieties. The terms also map onto four-section systems so that kin categories in alternate generations of each line appear in the same section. Kariera terminologies are assumed to correlate with bilateral cross-cousin marriage, often in practice between the somewhat distantly related "classificatory" cross-cousins. (See McConvell, chapter 10, this volume, on the relationship between Kariera and Dravidian terminologies.)

Current research on materials in the AUSTKIN database (Dousset et al. 2010) reveals a good deal of variation in so-called Kariera-type terminologies, so that rather few kinship terminologies in the database conform closely to the prototypical form. The simplest, such as Kariyarra ("Kariera" [Radcliffe-Brown 1913]) and Maringarr (Scheffler 1978), have two or four categories in generations +2 and –2. Wati-wati (Morey 2008) has distinct terms for an opposite-sex sibling's child, different for men and women, which are differentiated from terms for "man's child" and "woman's child." The Nyamal terminology (Epling 1961) has a general "child" term and an "opposite-sex sibling's child" term. Some such as Bandjalang (Crowley 1978) mark the relative age of one or both parents' siblings in generation +1. Some Kariera-type terminologies are augmented with distinct "second cross-cousin" and/or "parent's cross-cousin" terms. A number of Kariera terminologies have alternate-generations agnatic (AGA) and/or alternate-generations uterine equivalences (Scheffler 1978): Parnkalla (Elkin 1938–39), for example, equates FM/B with FZC and wSC, and MB with ZC. A number, particularly on Cape York Peninsula, exhibit Omaha skewing as well as the marking of parents' older and younger siblings (McConvell 2010).[2]

This degree of variation raises the question of what particular "Kariera" features should be taken as the baseline of a transition to a Murngin type or Ngarinyin type of terminology. Given the possible links between Yolngu and eastern Cape York Peninsula terminologies, the features of the latter are pertinent. Among eastern Cape York Peninsula terminologies the Umpila and Kuuku-Ya'u system (Thomson 1972) conforms to the prototype in generation +2. It distinguishes cross-cousins from siblings and parallel cousins, which are merged, and mC/BC from wC/ZC. Unlike the Kariera prototype, relative age differences marked in the parents' generation carry down to ego's generation. Thus the children of one's father's elder brother are all "elder brother" and "elder sister," while the children of one's father's younger brother are all one's "younger brother" and "younger sister." The senior/junior distinction also applies to cross-cousins and parallel cousins classified as siblings. Ideally, the various kinds of relatives can be sorted into those of one's own (and one's father's) patri-moiety and those of one's mother's father and father's mother.

The Umpila/Kuuku-Ya'u terminology also exhibits Omaha skewing. People regard a person's close female cross-cousin (*ngami*, senior; and *thaatha*, junior) as "like a mother" and consequently not marriageable. Conversely, one's close father's sister's child is classified as "woman's child." This feature does not apply to more distant or "outside" cross-cousins, who are potential spouses. These skewing features appear to be secondary, in that their application is limited and their potential consequences for other kin relations are not followed through (Scheffler 1972, 1978:150–151, 169; Thomson 1972). McConvell and I (2011) show that a skewing terminology of this kind has implications for changes in meaning between terms in eastern Cape York Peninsula and Yolngu kin classifications. For the purposes of the model, however, we took a simpler Kariera form as the starting point, without age differences marked in generation +1 and without Omaha skewing, for these would have to be neutralized in any case (Figures 7.1–7.16).

Yolngu Terminology

Kariera terminologies have two "lines of descent" in Radcliffe-Brown's analysis. The Yolngu terminology ("Murngin" type) has seven lines of descent in his (1931: 53) analysis (see also Warner 1937) and so differentiates many more categories of kin than Kariera terminologies (Keen 1994; Morphy 1984; Shapiro 1981; Warner 1937). Beginning with ego's generation, siblings are classified by gender and relative age; parallel cousins (FBC, MZC, FFFBSC, etc.) are merged with siblings, but matrilineal cross-cousins are differentiated from patrilateral cross-cousins. In Kariera systems cross-cousins of cross-cousins are classified as siblings; but in the Yolngu terminology the patri-cross-cousin of a matri-cross cousin and the matri-cross-cousin of a patri-cross-cousin are classified as siblings, while the matri-cross-cousin of a matri-cross-cousin is classified as MM/MMZ or MMB (through AGA equivalences), and reciprocally the patri-cross-cousin of a patri-cross-cousin is classified as wDC/ZDC.

In the parents' generation the terminology includes a bifurcate-merging component as in Kariera-type terminologies (and other Australian types of kinship terminologies), but not all kin of this generation are so classified. Ego's mother's matri-cross-cousins are not "F/FB" or "FZ" but, rather, constitute distinct WM/WMZ and WMB categories. Ego's father's patri-cross-cousins are classified not as "M/MZ" or "MB" but as "wC/ZC" through AGA equivalences. A similar number of distinctions are made in the generation of ego's children.

In ego's grandparents' generation FM/FMZ and MFZ are classified together, as are MF/MFB and FMB. The parallel grandkin are differentiated, however. MM/MMZ and MMB are merged (as *ma:ri*) and distinguished from FF/FFB and FFZ (*mari'mu*), though not in the Ritharrngu dialect (Heath 1980). The FF/FFB category is formed from the MM/MMB category with a suffix added. Not all cross-grandkin are classified together, however. Ego's MMMBD and MMMBS (WMM and WMMB) are not classified as FM/FMZ/MFZ (*momu*) and MF/MFB/FMB (*ngathi*) but, instead, distinguished as *mumalkur* and *ngathiwalkur*, although not in the Ritharrngu dialect. These are the matrilateral cross-cousins of *ma:ri* (MM/MMZ/MMB) and the mother and mother's brother of male ego's potential WM (*mukul rumaru*) and WMB (*maralkur*). The reciprocals are also differentiated. These categories are repeated by AGA equivalence two generations lower. In generations +3 and –3, however, the form of the terminology is Kariera-like in distinguishing only two kinds of kin, "mC/BC" (*ga:thu*) and "wC/ZC" (*waku*).

These differences between Kariera-type terminologies and the Yolngu terminology are associated with profound differences in marriage systems and affinal networks. In Kariera systems marriage takes place between bilaterally defined cross-cousins, although often restricted to relatively distant cross-cousins (forced, for example, by Omaha skewing of close matri-kin categories). The associated marriage network is typically one of "dispersed affinal alliance" (Keen 2004) in which the affinal network shifts at each generation. Marriage in the Yolngu system is asymmetrical: a man marries his matrilateral cross-cousin ("MBD" or "MMBDD," which are equivalent), and sometimes MBSD or MBSSD, with a preference for quite close cross-cousins as spouses. This pattern of marriage is reproduced in successive generations of the same patrilineages. The resulting network is of multiple asymmetrical links between lineages, linked in chains of asymmetrical marriages. At the patrigroup ("clan") level, however, marriage relations are often reciprocal, although these sort into asymmetrical relations at the lineage level (Keen 1978, 1982).

Kariera-type systems are associated with low to moderate levels of polygyny (Keen 1982, 2004, 2006). Matrilateral cross-cousin marriage, in contrast, enables high levels of polygyny in Australian systems, affecting inter-patrigroup competition and demography. Elsewhere (Keen 1982) I have suggested that high polygyny is made possible by the tendency in systems with matrilateral cross-cousin marriage for the appropriate age difference between potential spouses to be reproduced in each generation and by the prerogative of the oldest in a set of male siblings, who have rights in the same women as wives, to marry these women.

Posited Transformations from a Kariera-Type to the Yolngu Murngin-Type Terminology

The main process posited here is cumulative terminological differentiation; the model derives the Yolngu terminology from a Kariera type through an ordered and cumulative series of differentiations, some engendered by AGA equivalences. (See Kronenfeld, this volume, on changes in extension rules.) I illustrate the posited changes with a series of diagrams (Figures 7.1–7.25), in which kin terms and glosses in vertical columns represent patrifilial relations, while terms and glosses in diagonal alignment are related by matrifiliation. I describe the posited transformations here (see McConvell and Keen 2011). Kryukov's (1998) model of drift in kinship transformations suggests that the differentiation of categories begins at the first ascending generation, whereas any fusion of kin terms begins with ego's generation; the following model requires differentiation to begin with generation 0.

The first posited change is differentiation between matri- and patrilateral cross-cousins (the key step), equated in Kariera terminologies—the prescribed wife category is MBD, and the prescribed H/HB category is FZS (Figures 7.2–7.3):

MBC/MMBDC (*galay*) ≠ FZC/MFZDC (*dhuway*)

In the second posited change (Figures 7.4–7.5) WM is distinguished from FZ (the type WM category in the prototypical Kariera system), and WMB is distinguished from F/FB. Reciprocally, wDH and wDHZ are differentiated from mC/BC:

WM (*mukul rumaru*) ≠ FZ (*mukul ba:pa*)
WMB (*maralkur*) ≠ F/FB (*ba:pa*)
and reciprocally:
wDH/FZDC (*gurrung*) ≠ mSC (*ga:thu*)

The logic of matrilateral cross-cousin marriage implies that the father of WM is MMB. The third posited change (Figures 7.6–7.7) is that MMB is differentiated from FF and MM is differentiated from FFZ. Reciprocally, wDC/ZDC is differentiated from mSC:

	ga:thu	waku	
	ma:ri	momu ngathi	
	ba:pa mukul ba:pa	ngandi gawal, ngapipi	
	wa:wa eB yapa mZ, weZ yokuyuku- myB, wySb **EGO**	galay	
	ga:thu	waku	
	gutharra	gaminyarr	
	ba:pa mukul ba:pa	ngandi gawal, ngapipi	

FIGURE 7.1. Posited transformations from a Kariera-type terminology to the Yolngu terminology. Yolngu terminology as Kariera-type terminology.

MMB (WMF) and MM (WMFZ) (*ma:ri*) ≠ FF/FFZ (*mari'mu*)
and reciprocally:
mDDH/BDDH = wDC/ZDC (*gutharra*) ≠ mSC (*marratja*)

In the fourth set of changes (Figures 7.8–7.9) AGA equivalences come into play. The terms for M/MZ and MB and for MBC are extended down two generations to denote MBSD, MBSS, and MBSSC, respectively:

MBSD = M/MZ (*nga:ṉḏi*)
MBSS = MB (*ngapipi, gawal*) ≠ wC/ZC (*waku*)
MBSSC = MBC (*galay*) ≠ wSC/ZSC/mDC/BDC (*gaminyarr*)

It follows from these extensions that these kin are differentiated from wC/ZC and from wSC/ZSC/mDC/BDC, with which they are equated in Kariera-type terminologies. Reciprocally, wC and FZC terms are extended two generations up to differentiated children of women in the FF patriline from kin in the MF/FM patriline:

FFFZC => FZC ≠ FM/FMZ (*momu*) and MF/FMB (*ngathi*)
FFZC = wC/ZC (*waku*) ≠ M (*nga:ṉḏi*) and MB (*ngapipi*)

			'mC/BC' FFF FFFZ MMF MMFZ FMMB FMM etc.	'wC/ZC' FFM MFF MMM MMMB MFFZ FFMB etc.		
			FF FFZ MMB MM	FM MF MFZ FMB		
			F/FB FZ SpMB SpM	M /MZ MB SpFZ SpF etc.		
		FZC H/HB/ HZ ZH/ZH B/ ZHZ	← eB mZ, myB weZ ySb wyZ **EGO**	→ MBC/FZC MMBDC FFZSC W/WB/BW/ BWB etc.		
			mC/BC MBDC FZDC etc.	wC/ZC MBSC FZSC etc.		
			mSC, wDC/ZDC etc.	wSC/ZSC/ mDC/BDC MBSSC FZSSC etc.		
			'F/FB' 'FZ' mSSC, wDSC etc.	'M' 'MB' wSSC, mSDC etc.		

FIGURE 7.2. First differentiation.

In the fifth set of changes (Figures 7.10–7.11), AGA equivalences are applied to MM/MMB and to MMBD and MMBS (now distinguished from FF and FFZ and from F and FZ). The patrilineal descendants of MMB are thus further differentiated from kin in the FF patriline:

MMBSC = MM/MMB (WMF/WMFZ) (*ma:ri*) ≠ eB (*wa:wa*), eZ (*yapa*), ySb (*yokuyuku, gutha*)

and reciprocally:

FFZDC (*gutharra*) ≠ eB (*wa:wa*), eZ (*yapa*), ySb (*yokuyuku, gutha*)

MMBSSD = MMBD/WM (*mukul rumaru*)

MMBSSS = MMBS/WMB (*maralkur*) ≠ mC/BC (*ga:thu*)

and reciprocally:

FFFZDC = FZDC/wDH/wDHZ (*gurrung*) ≠ F/FB (*ba:pa*) and FZ (*mukul ba:pa*)

FFZDC = wdC/ZDC

FIGURE 7.3. First differentiation, Yolngu terms.

The result is the repetition of the WM category two generations down, enabling male ego to make claims on women of that generation as wives' mothers. The Yir-Yoront terminology leaves the process of differentiation there, but the Yolngu terminology goes further.

In the sixth change (Figures 7.12–7.13) the mother and mother's brother of WM and WMB (MMMBD and MMMBS) are differentiated from FM/MFZ and MF/FMB, and reciprocally FZDDC is differentiated from wSC/ZDC. The W/WZ of MMB becomes "WMM" (MMMBD), and the H/HB (FZS) of wDC becomes FZDDS:

WMM = MMMBD (*mumalkur*) ≠ FM/MFZ (*momu*)
WMMB ≠ MF/FMB (*ngathi*) = MMMBS (*ngathiwalkur*)
and reciprocally:
FZDDC ≠ wSC/ZDC (*gaminyarr*) = wDDH/ZDDH (*dhumun.gur*)

Seventh, terms in the generations +3 and –3 reproduce Kariera-type terms, distinguishing the parents of parallel and cross-grandparents and their reciprocals (Figures 7.14–7.15). For example, the term for FFF/FFZ is *ga:thu*, "mC/BC," and for MFF/MFFZ the term is *waku*, "wC/ZC."

In the eighth change (Figures 7.16–7.17) *dhumun.gur* (FZDDC) is equated with its reciprocals *ngathiwalkur* and *mumalkur* (MMMBS, MMMBD) in being specified as the M and MB of "wife's mother" and "wife's mother's brother" (*mukul rumaru* and *maralkur*), so closing the circle and enabling the exchange of sister's daughter's daughters (Shapiro 1981):

FZDDDD = MMBD/WM (*mukul rumaru*)
FZDDDS = MMBS/WMB (*maralkur*) ≠ wDSD (*mukul ba:pa*, "FZ") and wDSS (*ba:pa*, "F/FB")

			'mC/BC' FFF FFFZ MMF MMFZ FMMB FMM etc.	'wC/ZC' FFM MFF MMM MMMB MFFZ FFMB etc.		
		(FM MF)	FF FFZ MMB MM	FM MF MFZ FMB		
		(M MB)	F/FB FZ HMB HM	M /MZ MB SpFZ SpF etc.	WM WMB MBW MBWB	
		FZC H/HB/HZ ZH/ZHB/ ZHZ	eB mZ, myB weZ ySb wyZ **EGO**	MBC/FZC MMBDC FFZSC W/WB BW etc.		
	FZDC wDH/wDHZ ZDH/ZDHZ	wC/ZC mDH, mDHZ	mC/BC MBDC etc.	MBSC FZSC mSW, mSWB		
		(wSC/ZSC/ mDC/BDC)	mSC, wDC/ZDC etc.	wSC/ZSC/ mDC/BDC MBSSC FZSSC etc.		
		('M' 'MB' wSSC, mSDC etc.)	'F/FB' 'FZ' mSSC, wDSC etc.	'M' 'MB' wSSC, mSDC 'M' 'MB' etc.		

FIGURE 7.4. Second differentiation.

By these means the chain of affinal relations is able to close the circle among six patrilineages (Morphy 1984).

McConvell and I (2011) suggest what the linguistic resources needed for the expanding terminology might have been. These include the combination of two terms into a single term (e.g., *ngathi* + *walkur*), borrowings from neighboring non-Pama-Nyungan languages (e.g., *gurrung*), and the conversion of non-kin terms into kin terms (e.g., *marratja* from *marra* 'head hair'). Certain core Yolngu terms may have been inherited from the earlier Kariera-like terminology, and some may have been derived from skewed terms.

The proposed sequence of changes makes sense from a cognitive point of view when seen as the extension of the distinction between matri- and patri-cross-cousins through the whole terminology (except for generations +3 and −3). For example, *mukul rumaru* (MMBD) and *maralkur* (MMBS) are the matri-cross-cousins of *ngaṉḏi* (M/MZ) and *ngapipi* (MB) and are distinguished from *mukul ba:pa* (FZ) and *ba:pa* (F/FB), their patri-cross-cousins. The extension of this pattern through the terminology does not seem necessary for the organization of marriage, provided that a person's potential spouse category is specified, perhaps with the addition of distinct WM and WF categories. The global extension of the distinction between matri- and patri-cross-cousins is linked

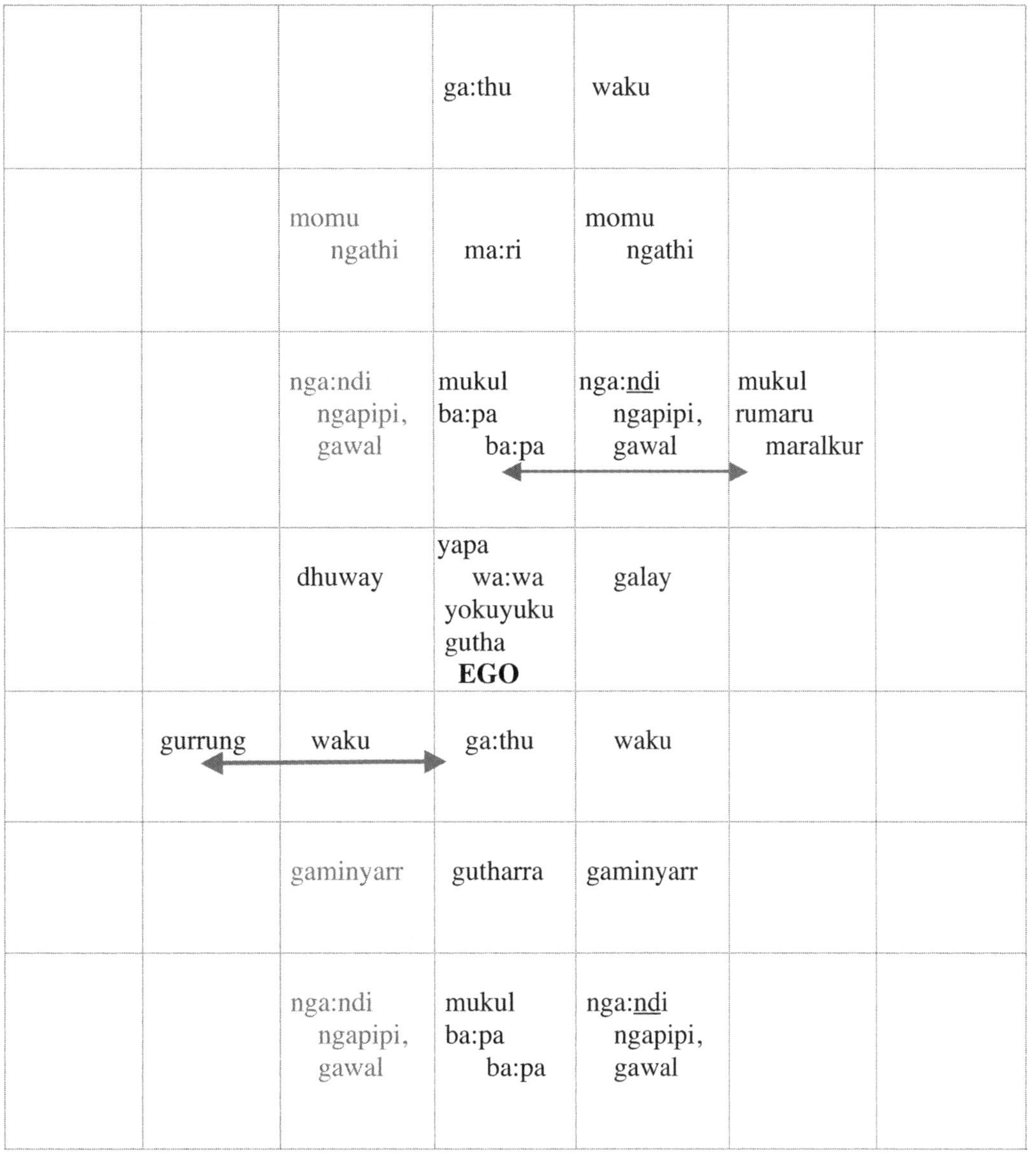

FIGURE 7.5. Second differentiation, Yolngu terms.

to the widening of the field of potential marriage claims and of relations involved in bestowal. WMM and WMMB are distinguished from FM/MFZ and MF/FMB as the M and MB of a potential WM, involving long-term contracts and the possibility of ZDD exchange (Shapiro 1968, 1981). The AGA extensions have to do with the potential marriage claims of a man to his MBSSD, whose mother is his MMBSSD, and whose father (MBSS) is also *ngapipi* ("MB").

Ngarinyin Terminology

The transformation of a Kariera-type terminology into the Ngarinyin form takes a different path. The Ngarinyin kinship terminology appears to be Aranda-like in distinguishing four kinds of relatives in the grandparental generation. It differentiates MFZ (*mamingi, ngaji*) from FM (*marringi*), and FMB (*wayingi*) from MF (*mamingi, garndingi*), and it distinguishes first from second cross-cousins. The terminology is different from Aranda terminologies, however, in that by being equated with FMBSSD and FMBSSS (*marringi, wayingi*), the wC/ZC term (*marlangi*) does not map onto the FM/FMB patriline of terms, and by being equated with MMBSSC (*gayingi*), the wDC/ZDC term (*marlangi*) does not map onto the MM/MMB patriline of terms (see Keen 2004).

The skewing of terms in ego's mother's and father's mother's lines, combined with a preference for marriage of a man to his classificatory "father's mother" (including FMBSD), transforms the system into an asymmetrical one. A man should not marry a person of his own mother's

			'mC/BC' FFF FFFZ MMF MMFZ FMMB FMM etc.	'wC/ZC' FFM MFF MMM MMMB MFFZ FFMB etc.		
		(FM MF)	**FF** **FFZ**	FM MF MFZ FMB	**MM/MMB** WMF/WMFZ	
	(F/FB FZ)	(M MB)	F/FB FZ HMB HM	M/MZ MB SpFZ SpF etc.	WM WMB MMMD MMBS MBW MBWB	
	(eB mZ, myB weZ ySb wyZ)	FZC FFZDC H/HB/HZ	eB mZ, myB weZ ySb wyZ **EGO**	MBC/ MMBDC W/WB BW etc.	(eB mZ, myB weZ ySb wyZ)	
	FZDC wDH/wDHZ ZDH/ZDHZ	wC/ZC mDH, mDHZ	mC/BC MBDC etc.	MBSC FZSC mSW, mSWB	(mC/BC MBDC etc.)	
	wDC/ZDC mDDH/BD DH	(wSC/ZSC/ mDC/BDC)	mSC etc.	wSC/ZSC/ mDC/BDC MBSSC FZSSC etc.		
		('M/MZ' 'MB' wSSC, mSDC etc.)	'F/FB' 'FZ' mSSC, wDSC etc.	'M/MZ' 'MB' wSSD wSSS etc.		

FIGURE 7.6. Third differentiation.

patrigroup, although marriage to a distant "mother" (*ngaji*) attracted only mild sanctions, as did marriage between first cross-cousins (FZS and MBD) and between distant "mother's brother" and "sister's daughter" (Lucich 1968). In spite of these alternative marriages, in practice marriage relations between patrigroups are predominantly asymmetrical (Blundell and Layton 1978). Consistent with the asymmetry, Ngarinyin and their neighbors discouraged sister exchange on the part of men. The Ngarinyin marriage system thus comes to resemble the Yolngu system in the asymmetry of exchange between groups. Unlike in the Yolngu marriage system, however, a man cannot legitimately marry into his mother's lineage (although he can marry into his mother's patrigroup if a "father's mother's" lineage is distinct from other lineages within the group). Thus, unlike in the Yolngu system, marriages between two lineages are not repeated in successive generations, although they can be repeated in alternate generations. (Since a man cannot marry into his own mother's group, his son's FM must be in a different lineage to the man's father's FM.) Men of a given patrigroup must therefore obtain wives from two or more patrilineages of the opposite moiety. Due to the skewing rule, however, its women can marry men of the same patrigroup each

			ga:thu	waku	ga:thu 'mC/BC'	
		momu ngathi	ma:ri'mu	momu ngathi	ma:ri	
	mukul ba:pa ba:pa	nga:ndi ngapipi, gawal	mukul ba:pa ba:pa	nga:ndi ngapipi, gawal	mukul rumaru maralkur	
	yapa wa:wa yokuyuku gutha	dhuway	yapa wa:wa yokuyuku gutha **EGO**	galay	yapa wa:wa yokuyuku gutha	
	gurrung	waku	ga:thu	waku	ga:thu	
	gutharra	gaminyarr	marratja	gaminyarr		
	mukul ba:pa ba:pa	nga:ndi ngapipi, gawal	mukul ba:pa ba:pa			

FIGURE 7.7. Third differentiation, Yolngu terms.

generation, although their husbands would be from alternate generations of each patrigroup. This marriage preference gives the Ngarinyin/Worrorra/Wunambal marriage network a particular character, with chains of asymmetrical marriage exchange linking patrigroups but with men of each patrigroup marrying women from at least two other groups (Blundell and Layton 1978).

It is therefore Omaha skewing that converts a Kariera system into the Ngarinyin terminology and gives it its particular character. As Rumsey (1981) points out, skewing is up to a point context-dependent, particularly in the MF patriline where terms are skewed in contexts of discourse about interclan relations, including marriage. Terms in the FM/FMB and MM/MMB patrilines are skewed in all contexts, however.

Neighboring Kariera Terminologies

Elkin's (1931–32) survey shows that certain terminologies of the west and north Kimberley and its southwestern neighbors are Kariera-like, but with MM and MMB distinguished from FF and FFZ (merged in the Kariera prototype; e.g., Martuthunira) and with a strong preference in the region for marriage between distant "FZS" and "MBD." Within that general picture there are significant

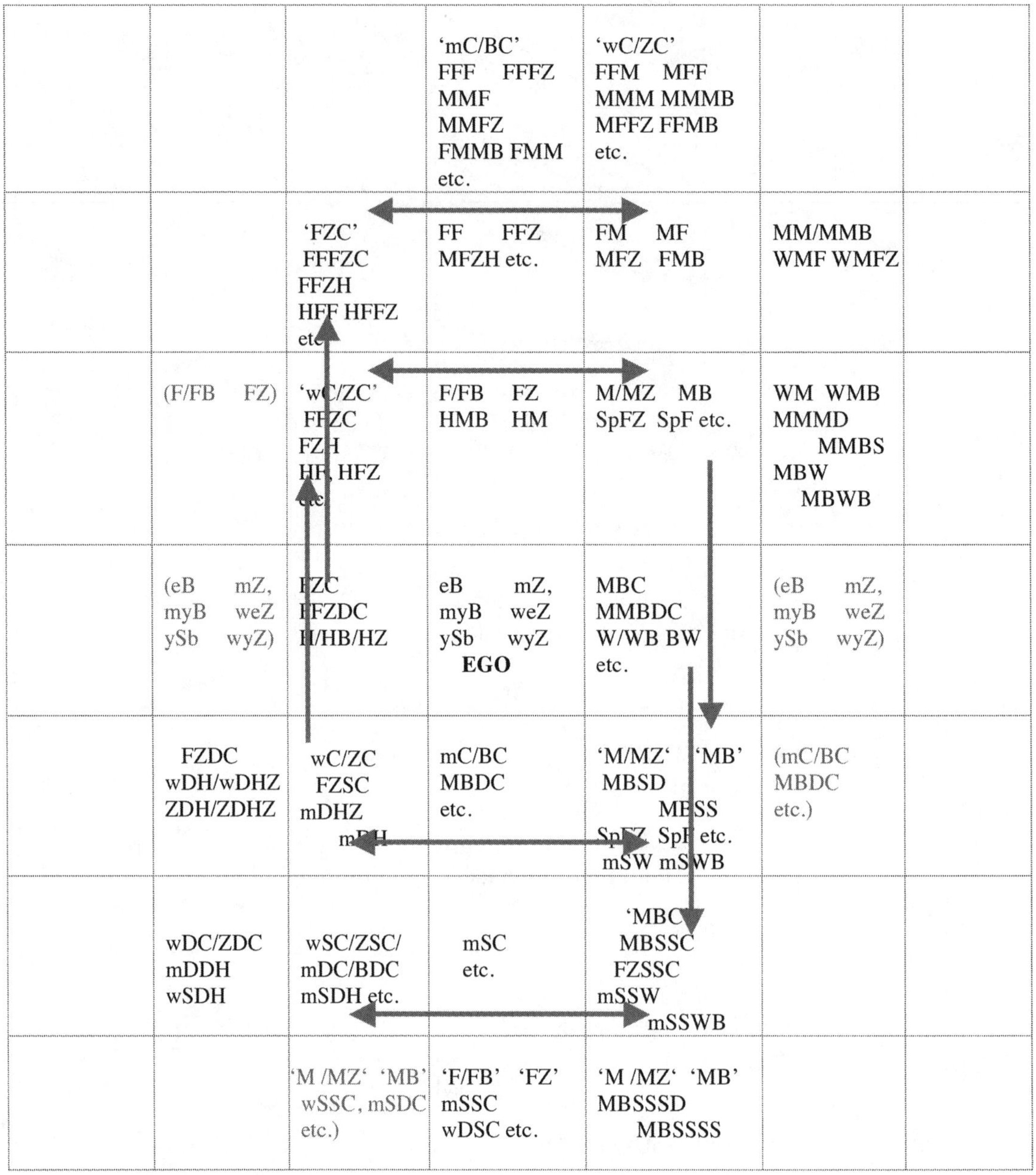

FIGURE 7.8. Fourth set of differentiations.

variations. The Karrajarri ("Karadjeri") system is of the Kariera type and is not asymmetrical, for, contrary to Radcliffe-Brown (1931) and Elkin (1931–32), sister exchange was not prohibited (Scheffler 1978:219). However, MM and MMB are distinguished from FF and FFZ, rather than FFZ being merged with MM/MMZ and MMB being merged with FF/FFB. The preferred marriage is between a man and a somewhat distant MBD; the WF can be a close MB, however, provided the WM is a distant relative (Elkin 1931–32). The preferred marriage reported for Bardi (which has a Kariera-type terminology), who have no moieties, sections, or subsections, is between a man and his classificatory "MMBSD"; alternative marriages include that between a man and his "MFZ" or "mDD." A close cross-cousin is thought of as sibling-like (as in the Western Desert).

In a northeast Kimberley variant, Forrest River people (Yiiji and Gwini languages) again have a Kariera-type terminology, with separate terms for MM/MMB and a preference for marriage between rather distantly related people in an FZS–MBD relationship. Elkin (1931–32) reports "ZSD" marriage (two generations down from MBD),

			ga:thu	waku	ga:thu		
		dhuway	ma:ri'mu	momu ngathi	ma:ri		
	mukul ba:pa ba:pa	waku	muul ba:pa ba:pa	nga:ndi ngapipi, gawal	mukul rumaru maralkur		
	yapa wa:wa yokuyuku gutha	dhuway	yapa wa:wa yokuyuku gutha **EGO**	galay	yapa wa:wa yokuyuku gutha		
	gurrung	waku	ga:thu	nga:ndi ngapipi, gawal	ga:thu		
	gutharra	gaminyarr	marratja	galay			
	mukul ba:pa ba:pa	nga:ndi ngapipi, gawal	mukul ba:pa ba:pa				

FIGURE 7.9. Fourth set of differentiations, Yolngu terms.

also represented as the exchange of sisters' daughters. A man bestows his sister's daughter on his "son," who in turn gives his sister's daughter (the first man's "daughter's daughter") in return. This type of terminology may be a forerunner of the Ngarinyin type as represented in the Worrorran language, since Yiiji and Gwini are also of the Worrorran language family. It may be the case that the type developed in Worrorran and was taken up by neighboring Ngarinyin and Wunambal people.

			'mC/BC' FFF FFFZ MMF MMFZ FMMB FMM etc.	'wC/ZC' FFM MFF MMM MMMB MFFZ FFMB etc.		
		'FZC' FFFZC FFZH HFF HFFZ etc.	FF Z FF/FFB MFZH etc.	FM MF MFZ FMB	MM/MMB WMF WMRZ	
	'FZDC' FFFZDC	'wC/ZC' FFZC FZH HF, HFZ etc/	FZ F/FB HM HMB	M /MZ MB SpFZ SpF etc.	WM WMB MMMD MMBS MBW MBWB	
	'wDC/ZDC' FFZDC	FZC FFZDC H/HB/HZ	mZ eB, weZ myB wyZ ySb **EGO**	MBC MMBDC W/WB BW etc.	'MM/MMB' MMBSC WMF WMRZ	
	FZDC wDH/wDHZ ZDH/ZDHZ	wC/ZC FZSC mDHZ mDH	mC/BC MBDC etc.	'M/MZ ' 'MB' MBSC SpFZ SpF etc. mSW mSWB	'WM' 'WMB' MMBSSD MMBSSS	
	wDC/ZDC mDDH wSDH	wSC/ZSC/ mDC/BDC mSDH etc.	mSC etc.	'MBC' MBSSC FZSSC mSSW mSSWB		
		'M/MZ ''MB' wSSC, mSDC etc.	'FZ' 'F/FB' mSSC wDSC etc.			

FIGURE 7.10. Fifth set of differentiations.

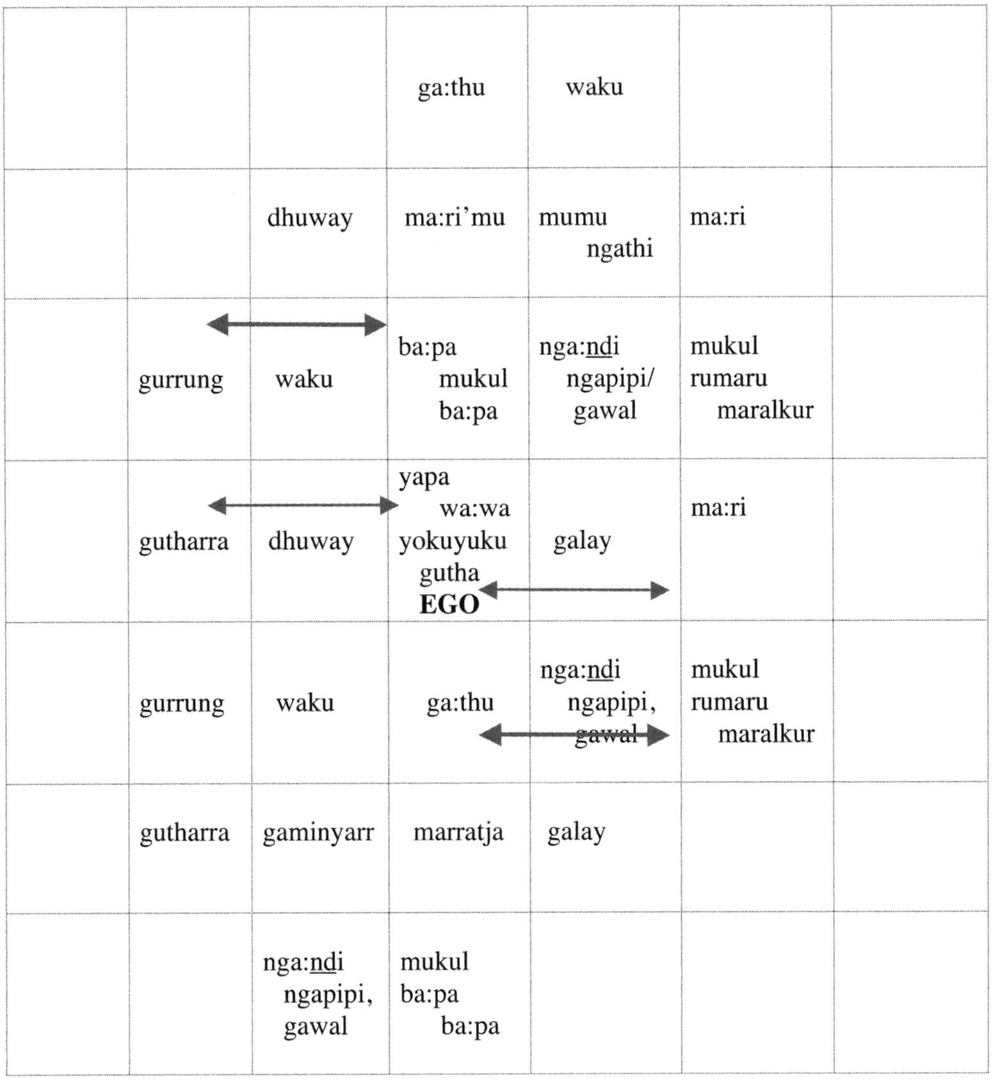

FIGURE 7.11. Fifth set of differentiations, Yolngu terms.

			‘mC/BC’ FFFZ FFF/FFFB MMFZ MMF FMM FMMB etc.	‘wC/ZC’ FFM MFF MMM MMMB MFFZ FFMB etc.		
		‘FZC’ FFFZC FFZH HFF HFFZ etc.	FFZ FF/FFB MFZH etc.	FM MF MFZ FMB	MM/MMB WMF WMRZ	MMMBD MMMBS WMM WMMB
	‘FZDC’ FFFZDC	‘wC/ZC’ FFZC FZH HF, HFZ etc/	FZ F/FB HM HMB	M/MZ MB SpFZ SpF etc.	WM WMB MMMD MMBS MBW MBWB	
	‘wDC/ZDC’ FFZDC	FZC FFZDC H/HB/HZ	eB mZ, myB weZ ySb wyZ **EGO**	MBC MMBDC W/WB BW etc.	‘MM/MMB’ MMBSS/D WMF WMRZ	
	FZDC wDH/wDHZ ZDH/ZDHZ	wC/ZC FZSC mDHZ mDH	mC/BC MBDC etc.	‘M/MZ’ ‘MB’ MBSC SpFZ SpF etc. mSW mSWB	WM WMB MMBSSS MMBSSD	
FZDDC wDDH/ZDDH wDDHZ/ ZDDHZ	wDC/ZDC mDDH wSDH	wSC/ZSC/ mDC/BDC mSDH etc.	mSC etc.	‘MBC’ MBSSC FZSSC mSSW mSSWB		
		‘M/MZ ‘ ‘MB’ wSSC, mSDC etc.	‘FZ’ ‘F/FB’ mSSC wDSC etc.			

FIGURE 7.12. Sixth differentiation.

			ga:thu	waku		
		dhuway	ma:ri'mu	momu ngathi	ma:ri	mumalkur ngathi- walkur
	gurrung	waku	mukul ba:pa ba:pa	nga:ndi ngapipi, gawal	mukul rumaru maralkur	
	gutharra	dhuway	wa:wa yokuyuku gutha **EGO**	galay	ma:ri	
	gurrung	waku	ga:thu	nga:ndi ngapipi, gawal	mukul rumaru maralkur	
dhumun.gur	gutharra	gaminyarr	marratja	galay		
		nga:ndi ngapipi, gawal	mukul ba:pa ba:pa			

FIGURE 7.13. Sixth differentiation, Yolngu terms.

<table>
<tr><td></td><td></td><td></td><td>‘mC/BC’
FFFZ FFF/FFFB
MMFZ MMF
FMM FMMB
etc.</td><td>‘wC/ZC’
FFM MFF
MMM MMMB
MFFZ FFMB
etc.</td><td>‘mC/BC’
FMM/FMMB
MMFZ MMF</td><td>‘wC/ZC’
MMM
MMMB</td></tr>
<tr><td></td><td></td><td>‘FZC’
FFFZC
FFZH
HFF HFFZ
etc.</td><td>FFZ FF/FFB
MFZH etc.</td><td>FM MF
MFZ FMB</td><td>MM/MMB
WMF
WMRZ</td><td>MMMBD
MMMBS
WMM
WMMB</td></tr>
<tr><td></td><td>‘FZDC’
FFFZDC</td><td>‘wC/ZC’
FFZC
FZH
HF, HFZ
etc/</td><td>FZ F/FB
HM HMB</td><td>M /MZ MB
SpFZ SpF etc.</td><td>WM WMB
MMMD
MMBS
MBW
MBWB</td><td>‘/MZ’ ‘MB’
MMMBSD
MMMBSS</td></tr>
<tr><td>‘FZC’
FFFZDDC</td><td>wDC/ZDC
FFZDC</td><td>FZC
FFZDC
H/HB/HZ</td><td>eB mZ,
myB weZ
ySb wyZ
EGO</td><td>MBC
MMBDC
W/WB BW
etc.</td><td>‘MM/MMB’
MMBSS/D
WMF
WMRZ</td><td>‘MBC’
MMMBSSD
MMMBSSS</td></tr>
<tr><td>wC/ZC
FFZDDD
FFZDDDS</td><td>FZDC
wDH/wDHZ
ZDH/ZDHZ</td><td>wC/ZC
FZSC
mDHZ
mDH</td><td>mC/BC
MBDC
etc.</td><td>‘M/MZ‘ ‘MB’
MBSC
SpFZ SpF etc.
mSW mSWB</td><td>WM WMB
MMBSSS
MMBSSD</td><td></td></tr>
<tr><td>FZDDC
wDDH/ZDDH
wDDHZ/
ZDDHZ</td><td>wDC/ZDC
mDDH
wSDH</td><td>wSC/ZSC/
mDC/BDC
mSDH etc.</td><td>mSC
etc.</td><td>‘MBC’
MBSSC
FZSSC
mSSW
mSSWB</td><td></td><td></td></tr>
<tr><td>M /MZ‘ ‘MB’
wDDC/ZDDC</td><td>‘FZ’ ‘F/FB’
mSDC,
wDSC</td><td>‘M /MZ‘ ‘MB’
wSSC,
mSDC etc.</td><td>‘FZ’ ‘F/FB’
mSSC
wDSC etc.</td><td></td><td></td><td></td></tr>
</table>

FIGURE 7.14. Seventh change; addition of categories at the periphery.

			ga:thu	waku	ga:thu	waku
		dhuway	ma:ri'mu	momu ngathi	ma:ri	mumalkur ngathi- walkur
	gurrung	waku	mukul ba:pa ba:pa	nga:ndi ngapipi, gawal	mukul rumaru maralkur	nga:ndi ngapipi/ gawal
dhuway	gutharra	dhuway	yapa wa:wa yokuyuku gutha **EGO**	galay	ma:ri	galay
waku	gurrung	waku	ga:thu	nga:ndi ngapipi, gawal	mukul rumaru maralkur	
dhumun.gur	gutharra	gaminyarr	marratja	galay		
nga:ndi ngapipi, gawal	mukul ba:pa ba:pa	nga:ndi ngapipi, gawal	mukul ba:pa ba:pa			

FIGURE 7.15. Addition of categories at the periphery, Yolngu terms.

				‘mC/BC’ FFFZ FFF MMFZ MMF FMM FMMB etc.	‘wC/ZC’ FFM MFF MMM MMMB MFFZ FFMB etc.	‘mC/BC’ FMM/FMMB MMFZ MMF	‘wC/ZC’ MMM MMMB
			‘FZC’ FFFZC FFZH HFF HFFZ etc.	FFZ FF/FFB MFZH etc.	FM MF MFZ FMB	MM/MMB WMF WMRZ	MMMBD MMMBS WMM WMMB
		‘FZDC’ FFFZDC	‘wC/ZC’ FFZC FZH HF, HFZ etc/	FZ F/FB HM HMB	M /MZ MB SpFZ SpF etc.	WM WMB MMMD MMBS MBW MBWB	‘M/MZ’ ‘MB’ MMMBSD MMMBSS
	‘FZC’ FFFZDDC	wDC/ZDC FFZDC	FZC FFZDC H/HB/HZ	eB mZ, myB weZ ySb wyZ **EGO**	MBC MMBDC W/WB BW etc.	‘MM/MMB’ MMBSS/DWM F WMRZ	‘MBC’ MMMBSSD MMMBSSS
	wC/ZC FFZDDD FFZDDDS	FZDC wDH/wDHZ ZDH/ZDHZ	wC/ZC FZSC mDHZ mDH	mC/BC MBDC etc.	‘M /MZ‘ ‘MB’ MBSC SpFZ SpF. mSW mSWB	WM WMB MMBSSS MMBSSD	
	FZDDC wDDH/ZDDH wDDHZ/ ZDDHZ	wDC/ZDC mDDH wSDH	wSC/ZSC/ mDC/BDC mSDH etc.	mSC etc.	‘MBC’ MBSSC FZSSC mSSW mSSWB		
WM WMB FZDDDD FZDDDS	M/MZ‘ ‘MB’ wDDC/ ZDDC	‘FZ’ ‘F/FB’ mSDC, wDSC	‘M /MZ‘ ‘MB’ wSSC, mSDC etc.	‘FZ’ ‘F/FB’ mSSC wDSC etc.			

FIGURE 7.16. Eighth change; closing the circle: Specification of FZDDDD as “WM” and FZDDDS as “WMB.”

<table>
<tr><td></td><td></td><td></td><td></td><td>ga:thu</td><td>waku</td><td>ga:thu</td><td>waku</td></tr>
<tr><td></td><td></td><td></td><td>dhuway</td><td>ma:ri'mu</td><td>momu
ngathi</td><td>ma:ri</td><td>mumalkur
ngathi-
walkur</td></tr>
<tr><td></td><td></td><td>gurrung</td><td>waku</td><td>ba:pa
mukul
ba:pa</td><td>nga:ndi
ngapipi/
gawal</td><td>mukul
rumaru
maralkur</td><td>nga:ndi
ngapipi/
gawal</td></tr>
<tr><td></td><td></td><td>gutharra</td><td>dhuway</td><td>wa:wa
yokuyuku
gutha
EGO</td><td>galay</td><td>ma:ri</td><td>galay</td></tr>
<tr><td></td><td>dhuway</td><td>gurrung</td><td>waku</td><td>ga:thu</td><td>nga:ndi
ngapipi,
gawal</td><td>mukul
rumaru
maralkur</td><td></td></tr>
<tr><td></td><td>dhumun.gur</td><td>gutharra</td><td>gaminyarr</td><td>marratja</td><td>galay</td><td></td><td></td></tr>
<tr><td>mukul
rumaru
maralkur</td><td>nga:ndi
ngapipi,
gawal</td><td>ba:pa
mukul
ba:pa</td><td>nga:ndi
ngapipi</td><td>ba:pa
mukul
ba:pa</td><td></td><td></td><td></td></tr>
</table>

FIGURE 7.17. Eighth change: closing the circle, specification of FZDDDD as "WM" and FZDDDS as "WMB," Yolngu terms.

FFZ FF/FFB lalingi ngolingi ('eZ') ('eB')	FM/MFZ MF/FMB mamingi
FZ F/FB amalngi idja	M MB ngaji garndingi
eZ lalingi eB ngolingi ySb margingi	MBD/FZD MBS/FZS mamingi
mD mS amalngi idja	wS wD ngaji garndingi
mSC margingi (ySB) mSD lalingi	wSS wSD mamingi

FIGURE 7.18. Posited transformations from a Kariera-type terminology to the Ngarinyin terminology. The Ngarinyin terminology as a Kariera-type terminology.

Model of Transformations from Kariera to Ngarinyin

How might a Kariera-type terminology typical of the west and north Kimberley (Figure 7.18) have changed into the asymmetrical terminology characteristic of Ngarinyin, Worrorra, and Wunambal languages? A series of four key changes from a Kariera system is posited (Figures 7.19–7.24). A preliminary condition is that MMBD is the preferred WM (*rambarr*), and hence FZDS is the preferred DH. Consistent with this condition is the differentiation of MM/MMZ and MMB from FFZ and FF/FFB, already present in terminologies of the region. (It is for this reason that I call it a preliminary condition and not the first posited transformation from a Kariera-like system.)

The first posited change (Figure 7.19) is the differentiation of MM/MMZ and MMB from FF/FFB and FFZ, merged in the Kariera terminologies of the region, and of their reciprocals:

MM/MMZ ≠ FFZ
MMB ≠ FF/FFB
and reciprocally:
wDC/ZDC ≠ mSC/BSC
MMBD is the preferred WM (*rambarr*), and hence FZDS is the preferred DH.

The second posited change (Figure 7.20) is the differentiation of FM/FMZ and FMB from MF/MFB and FMZ, merged in the Kariera terminologies of the region, and of their reciprocals:

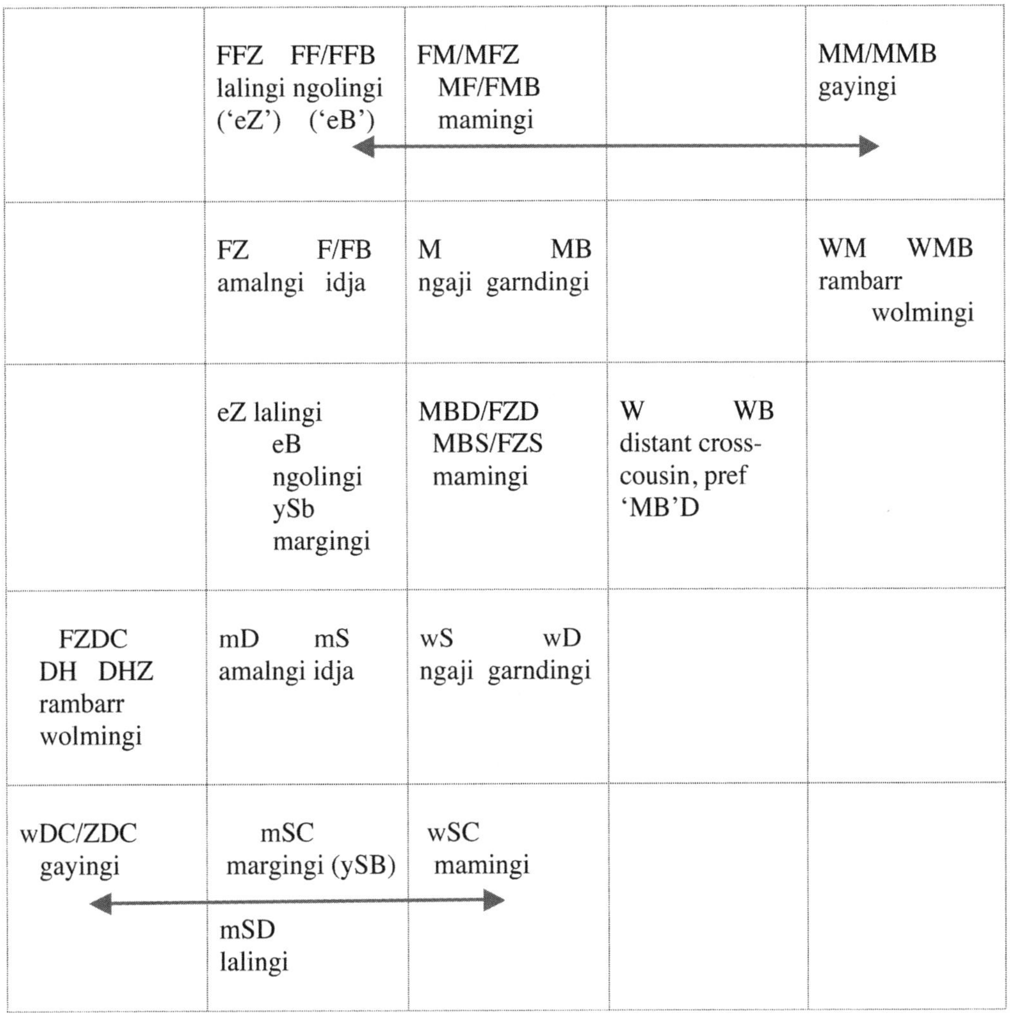

FIGURE 7.19. First differentiation.

FM ≠ MFZ
MF ≠ FMB
and reciprocally:
wSC ≠ mDC

W and WB are identified as "FM" and "FMB"; and H and HZ, as "wSC."

The third set of changes (Figure 7.21) comes about through skewing in the FM/FMB patri-sequence of terms; the FM and FMB terms are extended to all descending agnatic kin (regardless of context):

FMBD = FM
FMBS = FMB (differentiated from M and MB)
FMBSD = FM
FMBSS = FMB (differentiated from cross-cousin)
FMBSSD = FM
FMBSSS = FMB (differentiated from wC/ZC)
and reciprocally:
FZSC = wSC (differentiated from wC)
FFZSC = wSC (differentiated from cross-cousin)
FFFZSC = wSC (differentiated from M and MB)

It follows that WF ≠ MB. These reciprocal categories appear in different patrilines, under the assumption that alternate generations of women of ego's patriline "marry" into different lines.

The fourth set of changes comes about through skewing in the MF/MFZ patri-sequence of terms (Figure 7.22). The M and MB terms are extended to agnatic descendants in contexts where interclan relations are discussed:

			FFZ FF /FFB lalingi, ngolingi	MFZ MF mamingi	FM FMB marringi wayingi	MM/MMB gayingi (also wDC/ZDC)
			FZ F/FB amalngi idja	M MB ngaji garndingi		WM WMB rambarr wolmingi
			eB eZ ngolingi lalingi ySb margingi	MBD/FZD MBS/FZS mamingi	W WB distant cross- cousin, pref 'MB'D FMBSD	
DH DHZ rambarr wolmingi			mD mS amalngi idja	wD wS ngaji garndingi		
wDC/ZDC gayingi	mDC marlangi	wSC wurningi	mSC margingi('ySb') mSD lalingi	wSC mamingi		

FIGURE 7.20. Second differentiation.

MFZ = M
MF = MB
MBD = M
MBS = MB
MBSSD = M
MBSSS = MB
and reciprocally:
mDC/BDC = wC ≠ MBSSC
FZC = wC ≠ MBC
FFFZC = wC ≠ MFZ, MF

The reciprocals are thus differentiated from terms in the MF patriline (and are the reciprocals of the unskewed terms as well).

In the fifth set of changes (Figure 7.23) the term for MM/MMB is extended through Omaha skewing to each succeeding generation in the patriline (in all contexts):

MMBC = MM/MMB ≠ FZ/F/FB
MMBSC = MM/MMB ≠ eB, yB, Z

Reciprocally, the term for wDC/ZDC is extended two generations up the patriline:

FZDC = wDC/ZDC ≠ mD, mS
FFZDC = wDC/ZDC ≠ eB, yB, Z

There are separate terms for WM, WMB, wDH, and wDHZ. This final skewing operation completes the terminology (Figure 7.24).

There are some complications, however. Lucich (1968) records many alternative terms for most kin types, some of which can be explained as the result of skewing, as well as a combination of reference and vocative terms. Others may be explained by alternative marriages, for example, between people related as cross-cousins.

How might the Ngarinyin marriage system and kinship terminology have evolved from a Kariera one? Let us imagine a language group with the Kariera-like terminology typical of the west and north Kimberley, with MM/MMB recognized as distinct from FF/FFB and FFZ,

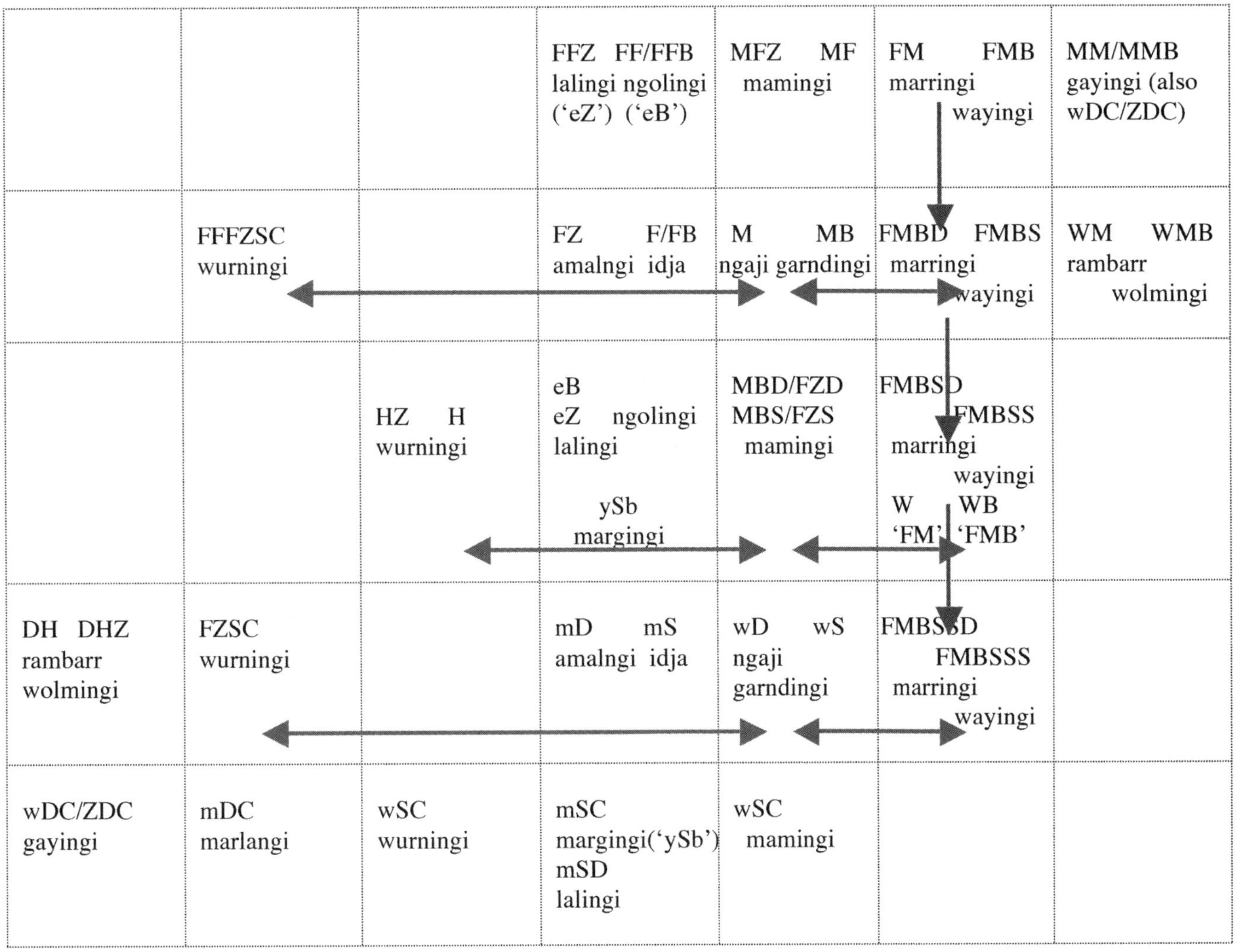

FIGURE 7.21. Third set of differentiations.

distinct affinal terms, and a preference for marriage with a distant MBD rather than an FZD. This matrilateral bias may have led to regular asymmetrical exchanges between patrigroups. (A similar condition may have been instrumental in the transformation of the Yolngu terminology.) A de facto relation of asymmetrical marriages between patrigroups may have been formalized into a preference for marriage to a FMBSD or FMBSSD, a second cross-cousin—that is, the father's male matrilateral cross-cousin's daughter. This marriage can be repeated between two patrigroups in alternate generations. A man marries his "FMBSD" or any woman of the "FM" category (although not his own FM of course), but women in the next generation of his wife's patrigroup are his son's MBDs and so not preferred as wives. But the next generation of women in that patrigroup (the man's FMB group) are potential wives for the man's son's sons, being their FMBSDs in turn. Thus marriage relations between two patrigroups can be repeated asymmetrically in alternate generations (the Ngarinyin pattern). Intermediate generations (ego's father, son, and SSS) have married and may marry women of ego's mother's patrigroup. The marriage preference thus requires that men of a lineage marry women of at least two patrigroups (or at least lineages), one for generation +2, 0, and –2; one for generation +1 and –1; and so on.

This pattern can be institutionalized by women of the FM's patrigroup being classified together as "father's mothers" (and wives) and those of the M's patrigroup being classified as "mothers," leading to a skewed terminology. The "FM" and "FMB" terms are skewed, and a preference for marriage by a man to his "FM" is specified. The M and MB terms are also skewed, and so women in the mother's group are not potential wives (or at least, not preferred as spouses). The features of the rest of the Ngarinyin terminology follow from adding the reciprocals.

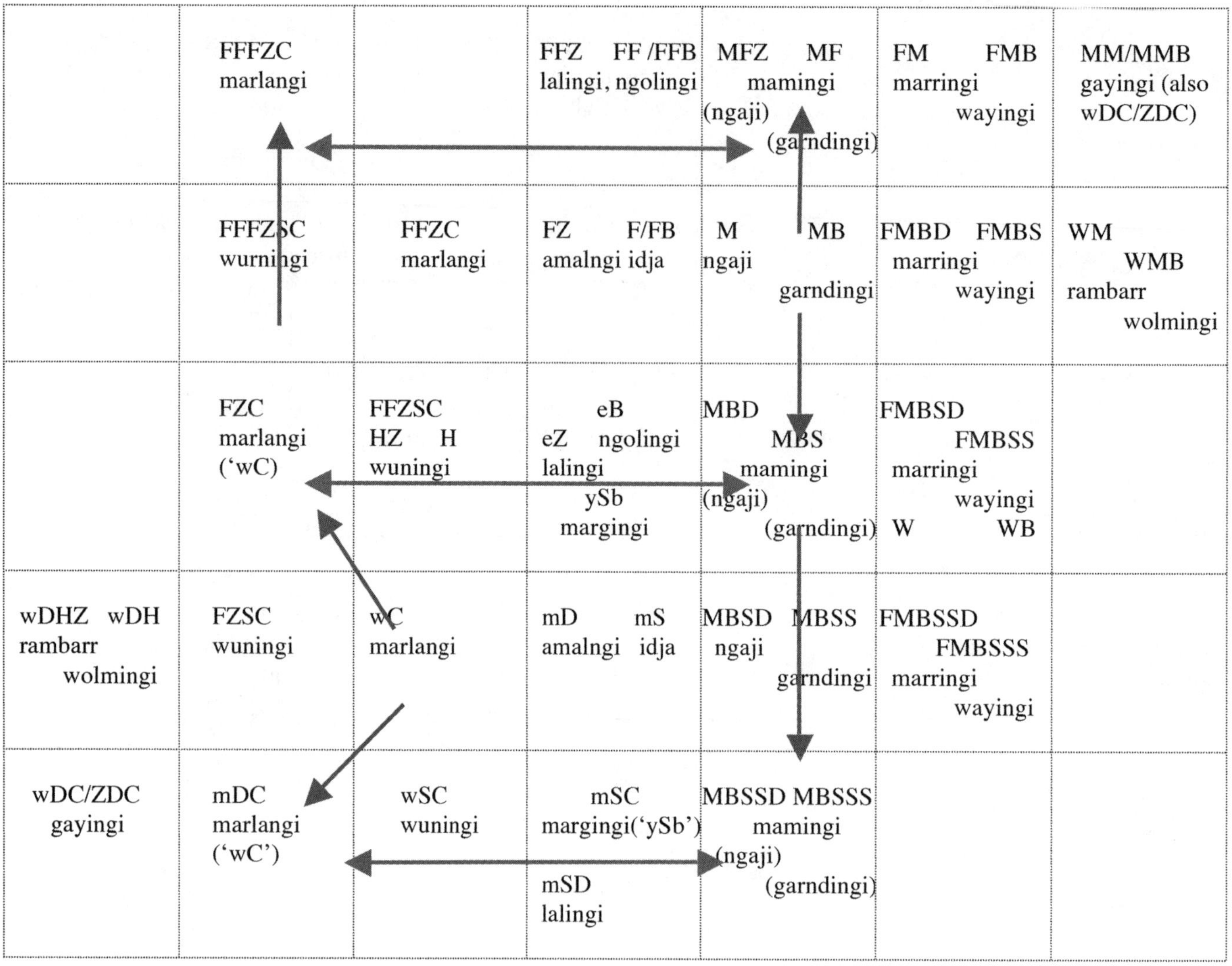

FIGURE 7.22. Fourth set of differentiations.

Discussion

The second model shows that the Ngarinyin terminology comes about by the differentiation of parallel and cross-grandkin into an Aranda-type pattern, as in the Nyul-nyul system, but then instead of differentiating parallel and cross-cousins in the Aranda way, the Ngarinyin terminology is generated through skewing of the FM/FMB and MF/MFZ terms and by the AGA extension of the MM/MMB term. The transformations posited for the Yolngu system involve a similar start, namely, the differentiation of WM and WMB from F and FZ (taken as given in Ngarinyin) and the differentiation of MM/MMB from FF/FFZ (as in Ngarinyin). Unlike the Ngarinyin system, the Yolngu terminology retains equivalences in cross-grandparental terms and adds AGA extensions of M, MB, and MBC terms. Like the Ngarinyin system the Yolngu terminology adds AGA extensions of MM/MMB, MMBS, and MMBD (WM) terms. Unlike the Ngarinyin one, however, the Yolngu system makes a further differentiation of WMM and WMMB from cross-grandkin. The direction of change suggested here contrasts with Walker's (2009) recent account of change in the Amazon, which posits the "Hawaiianization" of kin terms in generation 0, related to a trend away from prescriptive cross-cousin marriage toward a negative rule excluding close relatives as spouses (see Hornborg, this volume).

How plausible are the transformations posited here as models of evolutionary change? One way in which they can in principle be tested is through historical linguistic reconstructions of prototerminologies and through further research on links between Yolngu and eastern Cape York Peninsula terminologies and those of other

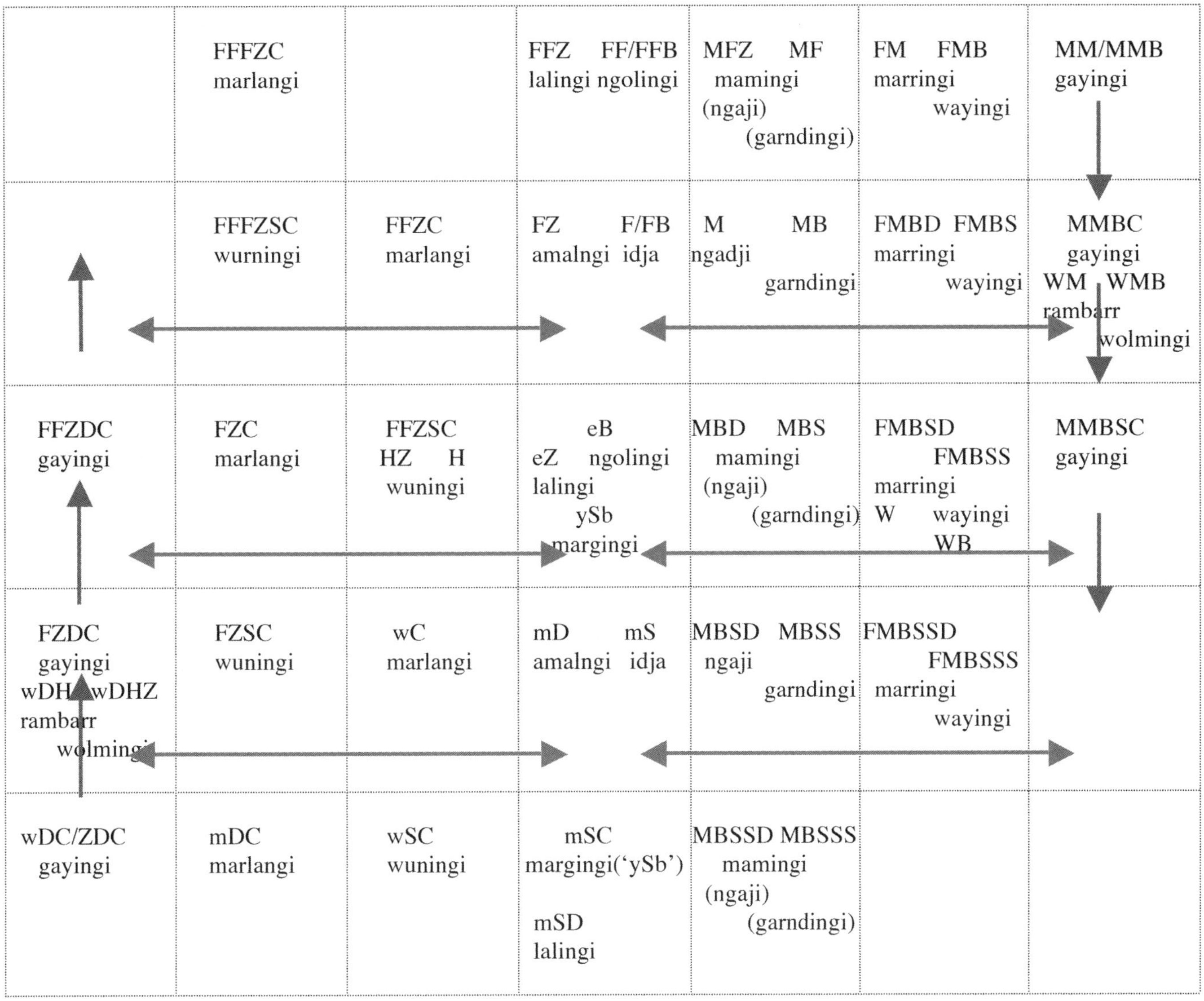

FIGURE 7.23. Fifth differentiation.

languages, as essayed in McConvell and Keen 2011. Another way in which the models could be tested would be through the existence of intermediate types of terminologies. The form of the Yir-Yoront terminology can be seen as representing the penultimate stage of the evolution of the Yolngu form from a Kariera-type base, as can some variants in northeast Arnhem Land such as Ritharrngu (Heath 1980), which, like Yir-Yoront, appears to lack distinct WMM/WMMZ (*mumalkur*) and WMMB (*ngathiwalkur*) categories. The discovery of forms representative of earlier stages in the transition is unlikely, however.

The hypothesis that these terminologies evolved from Kariera-type systems receives some support from the variety and distribution of types of kinship terminologies in Australia, as revealed by the AUSTKIN database (Dousset et al. 2010). This database brings together material on more than 500 terminologies, of which about 80 appear to be reasonably complete sets of reference terms and about 40 are deemed the most reliable. Some 59 percent of the most reliable sets are broadly of the Kariera type, about 31 percent are of the Aranda type, 13 percent are Western Desert terminologies (Aluridja type in Elkin's typology), 8 percent are of the Murngin type in Radcliffe-Brown's (1931) typology, and 5 percent are of the Ngarinyin type. (See Alpher, this volume, and Koch, this volume, on Arandic terminologies.) The asymmetric Yir-Yoront and Yolngu terminologies are the only exemplars of the Murngin type in the database (although there are several Yolngu variants), and Ngarinyin and possibly Marra are the only examples of that asymmetric form (although

wDC/ZDC line **wDH line**	**mDC/BDC line**	**wC/ZC line**	**own, F, FF etc. line**	**M/MB line**	**FM FMB, W, WB line**	**MM, MMB line** **WM line**
	FFFZC marlangi		FFZ FF /FFB lalingi, ngolingi	MFZ MF mamingi (ngaji) (garndingi)	FM FMB marringi wayingi	MM/MMB gayingi
	FFFZSC wurningi	FFZC marlangi	FZ F/FB amalngi idja	M MB ngadji garndingi	FMBD FMBS marringi wayingi	MMBC gayingi WM WMB rambarr wolmingi
FFZDC gayingi	FZC marlangi	FFZSC HZ H wurningi	eB eZ ngolingi lalingi ySb margingi	MBD MBS mamingi (ngaji) (garndingi)	FMBSD FMBSS marringi wayingi W WB	MMBSC gayingi
FZDC gayingi wDH wDHZ rambarr wolmingi	FZSC wurningi	wC marlangi	mD mS amalngi idja	MBSD MBSS ngaji garndingi	FMBSSD FMBSSS marringi wayingi	
wDC/ZDC gayingi	mDC marlangi	wSC wurningi	mSC ('ySb') margingi mSD lalingi	MBSSD MBSSS mamingi (ngaji) (garndingi)		

FIGURE 7.24. The complete terminology. The FM, FMB line and reciprocals are shown in green and M, MB line and reciprocals in red.

Worrorra and Wunambal could be added). These asymmetric types of terminologies thus appear to be unusual and localized developments in the Australian scene. Kariera-type terminologies are numerically dominant.

The plausibility of these posited evolutionary trajectories is also supported by recent developments in Australian prehistory. Both types of terminologies are instruments of high levels of polygyny (Keen 2003, 2004, 2006), a precondition for which appears to be the relatively rich resources of the tropical coasts and hinterland and relatively high population densities. The rich ecologies of these coastal regions developed during the later Holocene, providing the conditions for these developments (Brockwell et al. 2009; Faulkner 2008; Faulkner and Clarke 2004). Relatively high population densities appear to have been a precondition for high-polygyny regimes, enabled also (for demographic reasons) by asymmetrical marriage (Keen 1982). It is likely that ecological changes on the coasts of the tropical north provided the rich resources enabling higher population densities, putting in place the conditions for the development of forms of kinship terminology and asymmetrical marriage that foster consistently high levels of polygyny. These in turn had profound effects on social dynamics, fostering fast-growing and larger patrigroups and marked differences in power between the large and small patrigroups. The distribution of language varieties in northeast Arnhem Land, such as the wide distribution of Dhuwal and Dhuwal language varieties from east to west (Morphy 1983), suggests that successful patrigroups in the past were able to expand territorially, leaving swathes of country associated with the same language variety. (The spread of the Nhangu language variety along the north coast and between islands is another example, but this may also have been fostered by relative ease of communication along the coast.) A similar set of conditions may be posited for Yir-Yoront of the very rich environment of the Mitchell and Coleman rivers of western Cape York Peninsula on the eastern side of the Gulf of Carpentaria.

The Ngarinyin terminology was also associated with high levels of polygyny, though lower than Yolngu levels (Keen 2004). The western Kimberley environment is very different from that of the Yolngu, but the many inlets and islands provided enormously rich estuarine and marine resources. Marra country lies across the rich estuary and coastal plains of the Limmen Bight; data on levels of polygyny for Marra have not yet been located, however. The models proposed here provide possible pathways for the evolution of the symbolic instruments that enabled these late Holocene developments in marriage and related social dynamics.

Notes

1. In the view of Dousset (2003), Western Desert terminologies, classified by Elkin (1938–39) as "Aluridja" (Luritja) type, are similar to Kariera-type terminologies in being Dravidian in form but in which socially close (co-resident) cross-cousins are assimilated to sibling categories. The Kanai (Kûrnai) terminology (Gippsland, Victoria [see Howitt 1904]), which has been classified as an Aluridja-type terminology (Dousset 2003), is distinctive in apparently classifying cross-cousins as well as parallel cousins as siblings.
2. Aranda-type terminologies also vary, for example, in the presence and variety of alternate-generations agnatic and alternate-generations uterine equivalences (Scheffler 1978) and in merging certain categories "horizontally," e.g., eliminating the distinction between MMBDC and sibling categories, as in the Wangkangurru terminology (Hercus 1994), but retaining other distinctions.

References Cited

Blundell, V., and R. H. Layton. 1978. Marriage, Myth and Models of Exchange in the West Kimberley. *Mankind* 11(3): 231–245.

Brockwell, S., P. Faulkner, P. Bourke, A. Clarke, C. Crassweller, D. Guse, B. Meehan, and R. Sim. 2009. Radiocarbon Dates from the Top End: A Cultural Chronology for the Northern Territory Coastal Plains. *Australian Aboriginal Studies* 1:54–76.

Crowley, T. 1978. *The Middle Clarence Dialects of Bandjalang.* Canberra: Australian Institute of Aboriginal Studies.

Dousset, L. 2003. On the Misinterpretation of the Aluridja Kinship System Type (Australian Western Desert). *Social Anthropology* 11(1):43–61.

Dousset, L. 2008. The "Global" versus the "Local": Cognitive Processes of Kin Determination in Aboriginal Australia. *Oceania* 78(3):260–277.

Dousset, L., R. Hendery, C. Bowern, H. Koch, and P. McConvell. 2010. Developing a Database for Australian Indigenous Kinship Terminology: The AustKin Project. *Australian Aboriginal Studies* 1:42–56.

Elkin, A. P. 1931–32. Social Organisation in the Kimberley Division, North-Western Australia. *Oceania* 2(3):296–333.

Elkin, A. P. 1938–39. Kinship in South Australia. *Oceania* 9: 341–349.

Elkin, A. P. 1970. The Aborigines of Australia: "One in Thought, Word and Deed." In *Pacific Linguistic Studies in Honour of Arthur Capell.* S. A. Wurm and D. C. Laycock, eds. Pp. 697–716. Pacific Linguistics Series C, 13. Canberra: Australian National University.

Epling, P. J. 1961. A Note on Nyamal Kin-Terms. *Man* 61:152–159.

Faulkner, P. 2008. Patterns of Chronological Variability in Occupation on the Coastal Margin of Blue Mud Bay [Online]. *Archaeology in Oceania* 43(2):81–88.

Faulkner, P., and A. Clarke. 2004. Late Holocene Coastal Economy in Blue Mud Bay, Northeast Arnhem Land: Preliminary Archaeological Findings. *Australian Archaeology* 59:23–30.

Heath, J. 1980. *Basic Materials in Ritharrngu: Grammar, Texts and Dictionary.* Pacific Linguistics Series C, 62. Canberra: Department of Linguistics, Research School of Pacific Studies, Australian National University.

Heath, J. 1981. *Basic Materials in Mara: Grammar, Texts and Dictionary.* Pacific Linguistics Series C, 60. Canberra: Department of Linguistics, Research School of Pacific Studies, Australian National University.

Hercus, L. A. 1994. *A Grammar of the Arabana-Wangkangurru Language, Lake Eyre Basin, South Australia*. Pacific Linguistics Series C, 28. Canberra: Department of Linguistics, Research School of Pacific Studies, Australian National University.

Hershberger, H. D., and R. Hershberger. 1982. *Kuku–Yalanji Dictionary*. Work Papers of SIL-AAB, Series B, vol. 7. Darwin: SIL.

Hiatt, L. R. 1965. *Kinship and Conflict: A Study of an Aboriginal Community in Northern Arnhem Land*. Canberra: Australian National University Press.

Howitt, A. W. 1904. *The Native Tribes of South-East Australia*. Melbourne: Macmillan.

Keen, I. 1978. An Economy of Religious Knowledge: Yolngu of Northeast Arnhem Land. Ph.D. dissertation, Australian National University.

Keen, I. 1982. How Some Murngin Men Marry Ten Wives: The Marital Implications of Matrilateral Cross-Cousin Structures. *Man* 17(4):620–642.

Keen, I. 1994. *Knowledge and Secrecy in an Aboriginal Religion: Yolngu of Northeast Arnhem Land*. Oxford: Clarendon Press.

Keen, I. 2003. Aboriginal Economy and Society at the Threshold of Colonisation: A Comparative Study. *Before Farming* 3(2):1–29.

Keen, I. 2004. *Aboriginal Economy and Society: Australia at the Threshold of Colonisation*. Melbourne: Oxford University Press.

Keen, I. 2006. Constraints on the Development of Enduring Inequalities in Late Holocene Australia. *Current Anthropology* 47(1):7–38.

Keen, I. 2010. A New Typology of Australian Aboriginal Kinship Systems. Paper presented at the AustKin Project Workshop, Canberra, October 26.

Keen, S. 1983. Yukulta. In *Handbook of Australian Languages*, vol. 3. R. M. W. Dixon and Barry J. Blake, eds. Pp. 190–304. Canberra: Australian National University Press.

Kryukov, M. V. 1998. The Synchro-diachronic Method and the Multidirectionality of Kinship Transformations. In *Transformations of Kinship*. M. Godelier, T. R. Trautmann, and F. E. Tjon Sie Fat, eds. Pp. 294–313. Washington, DC: Smithsonian Institution Press.

Lucich, P. 1968. *The Development of Omaha Kinship Terminologies in Three Australian Tribes of the Kimberley Division, Western Australia*. Canberra: Australian Institute of Aboriginal Studies.

McConvell, P. 2010. Omaha Skewing in Australia and New Guinea: Overlays, Dynamism and Change [2010 version]. Paper presented at the Crow-Omaha Seminar, Amerind Centre, Tucson, February 27–March 1, 2009.

McConvell, P., and I. Keen. 2011. Cape York Peninsula Kariera to North-East Arnhem Land Karadjeri Kinship and Marriage: Unfolding Systems and Rupturing Terminologies. In *Kinship, Language, and Prehistory: Per Hage and the Renaissance in Kinship Studies*. D. Jones and B. Milicic, eds. Pp. 99–132. Salt Lake City: University of Utah Press.

Merlan, F. 1983. *Ngalakan Grammar, Texts and Vocabulary*. Pacific Linguistics B, 89. Canberra: Research School of Pacific Studies, Australian National University.

Morey, S. 2008. Kinship Terms in Wathi Wathi: Compiled from MS 8006, Series 7 Folder 3b. R. H. Mathews. Pp. 20–25. Unpublished MS.

Morphy, F. 1983. Djapu, a Yolngu Dialect. In *Handbook of Australian Languages*, vol. 3. R. M. W. Dixon and B. J. Blake, eds. Pp. 1–188. Canberra: Australian National University Press.

Morphy, H. 1984. *Journey to the Crocodile's Nest: An Accompanying Monograph to the Film "Madarrpa Funeral at Gurka'wuy."* Canberra: Australian Institute of Aboriginal Studies.

Radcliffe-Brown, A. R. 1913. Three Tribes of Western Australia. *Journal of the Royal Anthropological Institute* 43:175–190.

Radcliffe-Brown, A. R. 1931. The Social Organization of Australian Tribes. *Oceania* 1:34–63, 206–256, 322–341, 426–456.

Rumsey, A. 1981. Kinship and Context among the Ngarinyin. *Oceania* 51(3):181–192.

Scheffler, H. W. 1972. Afterword. In *Kinship and Behaviour in North Queensland: A Preliminary Account of Kinship and Social Organisation on Cape York Peninsula*. D. F. Thomson, ed. Australian Aboriginal Studies, 51. Canberra: Australian Institute of Aboriginal Studies.

Scheffler, H. W. 1978. *Australian Kin Classification*. Cambridge: Cambridge University Press.

Shapiro, W. 1968. The Exchange of Sister's Daughter's Daughters in Northeast Arnhem Land. *Southwestern Journal of Anthropology* 14:346–353.

Shapiro, W. 1981. *Miwuyt Marriage: The Cultural Anthropology of Affinity in Northeast Arnhem Land*. Philadelphia: Institute for the Study of Human Issues.

Smart, J. 1977. Late Quaternary Sea-Level Changes, Gulf of Carpentaria, Australia. *Geology* 5(12):755–759.

Thompson, D. A. 1998. *Lockhart River "Sand Beach" Language: An Outline of Kuuku Ya'u and Umpila*. Work Papers of SIL-AAIB, Series A, vol. 11. Darwin: Summer Institute of Linguistics Australian Aborigines and Islanders Branch.

Thomson, D. F., ed. 1972. *Kinship and Behaviour in North Queensland: A Preliminary Account of Kinship and Social Organisation on Cape York Peninsula*. Australian Aboriginal Studies, 51. Canberra: Australian Institute of Aboriginal Studies.

Turner, D. H. 1980. *Australian Aboriginal Social Organization*. Atlantic Highlands, NJ: Humanities Press International.

Walker, H. 2009. Transformations of Urarina Kinship. *JASO-Online* 1(1):52–69.

Warner, W. L. 1933. Kinship Morphology of Forty-One North Australian Tribes. *American Anthropologist* 35(1): 63–86.

Warner, W. L. 1937. *A Black Civilization: A Social Study of an Australian Tribe*. New York: Harper New York.

8

The Reconstruction of Kinship Terminology in the Arandic Languages of Australia

Harold Koch

1. Aims and Overview

This chapter aims to reconstruct the forms and basic meanings of principal kin terms in the Arandic subgroup of the Pama-Nyungan language family of Australia. It provides strong evidence that the Proto-Arandic kinship system belonged to the "Aranda" type in Radcliffe-Brown's Australian kinship classification—whose terminology distinguishes four grandparental terms and presupposes marriage between people classed as second cousins (cf. Scheffler 1978:42). This reconstruction demonstrates the antiquity of this system among the Arandic-speaking peoples, which is an important finding within the Australian context. How do I arrive at such a claim? By comparing the forms of the kin terms in all the languages of the Arandic subgroup and applying to them the methods of historical-comparative linguistic reconstruction. The chapter serves as a demonstration of these methods as well as a study that produces substantive results concerning the linguistic past.

The focus is on the forms rather than on the details of kinship semantics. The chapter is not intended to be a comprehensive account of the historical aspects of Arandic kinship terminology. Rather, it serves as an illustration of what is involved in reconstructing earlier stages of linguistic forms (here applied to kin terms). This involves identifying cognate forms, observing the phonological correspondences that account for their differences, determining what level of protolanguage they can be attributed to, identifying borrowing across languages, and reconstructing simpler stems in cases where forms have been expanded through the accretion of inflections, reduplication, and compounding. The role of chronology in the documents of a language will also be addressed. For languages with little recorded history, reconstruction is necessary in order to make inferences about changes in forms or meanings. In fact, positing changes is an integral part of doing linguistic reconstruction, since every reconstruction involves hypotheses about both an earlier form and changes that it has undergone over time.

The basis of all reconstruction is etymology, that is, establishing that different words are historically related to one another and then working out in detail what the nature of this history consists of. But when historical linguists (and lexicographers) talk about "the etymology" of a particular word, it is a question of the origin and history of that word. Historical explanations of words can involve three kinds of origins. Etymological study (1) traces word histories back to earlier stages of the language or to an ancestral protolanguage (justified by cognates in related languages), (2) finds that words have been borrowed from another language, or (3) explains that they have been constructed out of preexisting elements in their own language. The discussion in section 3 involves all of these kinds of explanations.

This chapter constitutes an explicit demonstration of how the methods of historical-comparative linguistics are successfully applied in Australia. While these methods should be widely understood, their application to the languages of Australia has been contested (see Bowern and Koch 2004; Campbell and Poser 2008; Dixon 1997, 2001, 2002; Sutton and Koch 2008). This chapter can also be seen as a contribution to the discussion of historical linguistic methodology, consistent with the recent observation that

> just as studies of Indo-European languages have long dominated discussion of theories of language change and methods of comparative reconstruction, so studies of Australian languages are coming to be equally important within such

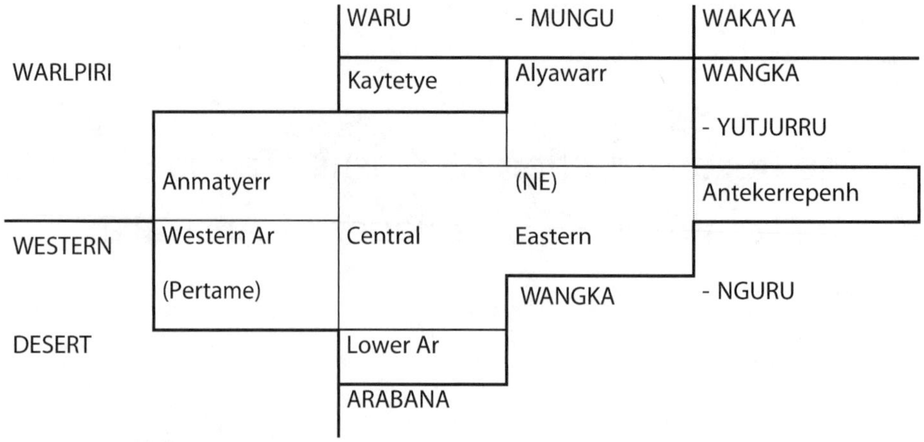

FIGURE 8.1. Arandic languages: geographical distribution and neighbors (schematic). Ar = Arrernte.

> discussions as Australianists rigorously apply traditional methods of historical linguistics, and present data which challenges some of the traditional notions within the discipline. (Bowern et al. 2008:6)

Some of my findings can be foreshadowed here. Perhaps more than in most Australian languages, many of the Arandic kin terms are here shown to consist etymologically of compounds or reduplicated forms. Unraveling this structure constitutes a large part of the argumentation. As a prelude to this analysis, I show that transparent compounds and phrasal kinship expressions are commonly used synchronically, which strengthens the claim that compounding was also used prehistorically. A further finding is that a number of kin terms that are widely distributed within the subgroup can nevertheless be shown to have been borrowed from outside languages. Separating inherited terms from borrowed terms is important in reconstructing the terminological system of earlier stages of the languages. Finally, I establish that for the oldest level considered here, Proto-Arandic, it is possible to reconstruct an array of kin terms that manifest Radcliffe-Brown's so-called Aranda kinship system. This will be important in sorting out the historical development of different kinship types within Australia.

1.1. Geographical Distribution of the Arandic Languages

The Arandic languages are located in Central Australia. The relative geographical distribution of the seven lects that will be discussed is shown schematically in Figure 8.1. Here the thickness of the lines within the Arandic group indicates the distinctiveness of the lects. Figure 8.1 also indicates (in capital letters) the surrounding languages.

1.2. Genetic Relations of the Arandic Languages

The Arandic languages form a subgroup of the Pama-Nyungan family of Australian languages. This subgroup has long been assumed, but its unity was challenged by Dixon (2001, 2002). Elsewhere I (Koch 2004) provide a considerable body of the evidence—phonological, morphological, lexical—that justifies Arandic as a subgroup defined by common innovations.

The internal relationships, as proposed by Hale (1962)—based on a lexicostatistical comparison of a 100-word list and confirmed by later work—are shown in Figure 8.2. Note that (1) Kaytetye (Kay) is the most divergent lect, (2) Lower Arrernte (LAr) is somewhat separate from the rest, and (3) the remaining lects were treated by Hale as forming a dialect chain, which he labeled "Upper Arrernte." Contemporary usage recognizes as separate languages Alyawarr (Aly), Anmatyerr (Anm), Western Arrernte (WAr; and its subdialect Pertame), Eastern and Central Arrernte (ECAr; often described together, plus the subdialect Northeastern Arrernte), and the extinct Antekerrepenh (Ant).[1] For the purposes of my reconstruction I will be using the term *Proto-Arandic* (pArc) for the highest node, *Proto-Arrernte* (pAr) for the ancestor of all lects except Kaytetye, and *Proto–Upper Arrernte* for the ancestor of all but Lower Arrernte and Kaytetye.

1.3. Phonology and Orthography

The Arandic phonological system is somewhat more complex than is the norm for Australian languages—as the result of historic sound changes that drastically altered the pronunciation. The main vowel phonemes are just

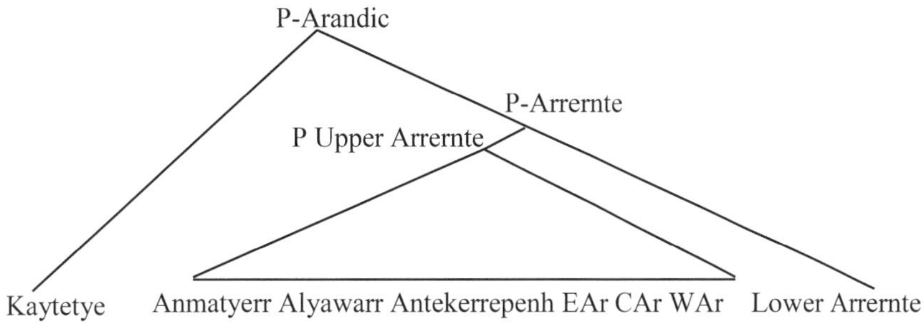

FIGURE 8.2. Arandic linguistic relationships. P = Proto; EAr = Eastern Arrernte; CAr = Central Arrernte; WAr = Western Arrernte.

TABLE 8.1. Arandic consonants.

Consonant	Labial	Lamino-dental	Apico-alveolar	Apico-post-alveolar	Prepalatized Apical	Laminal Palatal	Dorsal
Stop	*p*	*th*	*t*	*rt*	*yt*	*ty*	*k*
Prestopped Nasal	*pm*	*tnh*	*tn*	*rtn*	*ytn*	*tny*	*kng*
Nasal	*m*	*nh*	*n*	*rn*	*yn*	*ny*	*ng*
Lateral		*lh*	*l*	*rl*	*yl*	*ly*	
Tap/Trill			*rr*				
Approximant	*w*			*r*		*y*	*h*

/a/ and the central vowel schwa /ə/, which is spelled e in the orthographies. There is some use of an /i/ vowel, but /u/ is recognized only in some lects. Rounding has rather become largely a feature of consonants; rounded consonants are indicated orthographically by a w after the consonant symbol. The maximal system of unrounded consonants (plus *w*) is displayed in Table 8.1. The symbol *h* is used for a velar-uvular approximant—much like an unrounded *w*—which tends to disappear in the modern lects. The prepalatized apicals have been lost from the central and western lects, in most instances having merged with the laminal palatals.

1.4. Historical-Comparative Issues

Because of the drastic sound changes affecting the prehistory of the Arandic language, the reconstruction of vocabulary, including kin terms, is more complicated than for most other Australian languages. The historical sound changes had the effect of making the Arandic reflexes of Pama-Nyungan words almost unrecognizable. Major changes include the loss of initial consonants, shifting of stress to the second syllable, reduction of all vowels in noninitial syllables to schwa (spelled *e*), change of plain nasals to prestopped nasals when the word-initial consonant was not nasal, reduction of homorganic nasal-stop clusters (like *mp*) to just the nasal (*m*), and change of the *u* vowel in the first syllable to the rounding of the next consonant. The major sound changes are justified in Koch (1997b) and summarized in Koch (2004), with a few details added in Koch (2007). As a result of these changes most words begin with a vowel (cf. Breen and Pensalfini 1999)—although even these tend to disappear in some lects—and all words end in *e*.[2] Words that once had a structure CVCV (where C stands for any consonant [cluster], and V, for any vowel) have been reduced to *VCe*; for example, *ngama* > *ame* M, *ngatyi* > *atye* MF, and *kaka* > *ake* eB. The shortness and potential ambiguity of words have often been compensated for by processes that lengthen the words, as we shall see in the discussion of some kin term etymologies. Some of the morphological changes in the Arandic languages have been discussed in Koch (1995), (1996), (2003). The lexical reconstruction of 50 basic vocabulary items is discussed in Koch (2001). An analysis of Arandic loanwords into and from Warlpiri is presented in Koch (1997a).

1.5. Sources

The main sources for lexical data that have been used are indicated in Table 8.2, which also includes the abbreviations used for the various lects. A number of early sources on LAr are included within Curr (1886–87) and Taplin's (1879) works.[3]

TABLE 8.2. Lexical data sources for Arandic languages.

Language	Abbreviation	Reference(s)
Kaytetye	Kay	Turpin and Ross 2012; Hale, field notes; Koch, field notes
Alyawarr	Aly	Green 1992
Anmatyerr	Anm	Green 2009
Antekerrepenh	Ant	Breen 2002
Eastern and Central Arrernte	ECAr	Henderson and Dobson 1994
Northeastern Arrernte	NEAr	Henderson and Dobson 1994
Western Arrernte	WAr	Breen 2000; Strehlow n.d.
Pertame	Pert	Swan and Cousins 1993
Lower Arrernte	LAr	Breen 1997; Curr 1886–87; Taplin 1879

2. Synchronic Morphological Aspects of Arandic Kin Terms

This section examines general issues in the formation of Arandic kin terms, as a prelude to the etymological study of individual forms in the next section.

2.1. Inflectional Morphology of Arandic Kin Terms

Arandic kin terms inflect for the person of the propositus, that is, the person from whose perspective the kin relation is reckoned. All the lects of Aranda use suffixes to mark person—except for Western Arrernte, which has given up this inflection.[4] Kaytetye, on the other hand, uses prefixes to mark the second and third person but a suffix to mark the first person. All Arandic lects use the suffix *-nhenge* to mark dyads, that is, two or more people in a relationship (mother and child, grandparent and grandchild, etc.).[5] Table 8.3 indicates the normal inflections added to the stem *arrenge* 'father's father'.

TABLE 8.3. Arandic kin term inflection, using the example of *arrenge* FF.

Inflection	Arrernte (except Western)	Kaytetye
My	*arreng-**atye***	*arrenge-**ye***
Your	*arreng-**ungkwe***	***ngk**-arrenge*
His/Her	*arreng-**ikwe***	***kw**-arrenge*
Dyad	*arrenge-**nhenge***	*arrenge-**nhenge***

Note: Inflectional suffix/prefix is indicated in bold.

From Table 8.3 it can be seen that the Kaytetye prefixes for second and third person are cognate with the functionally equivalent suffixes of Arrernte. These Arrernte suffixes and the first-person marker *-atye* are reflexes of clitic dative forms of personal pronouns, which have come to be positioned as suffixes in the Arrernte and prefixes in Kaytetye (except that *-atye* is not found in Kaytetye). The likely pre-Arandic forms are **ngatyu* (1SgDAT), **nyungku* (2SgDAT), and **nguku* (3SgDAT). The Kaytetye 1Sg suffix *-ye* corresponds to a removable part of the stem of kin terms in Arrernte. I reconstruct it as a 1Sg suffix in Proto-Arandic and hypothesize that its ultimate origin was probably an enclitic from **-tyu* of the Proto-Pama-Nyungan 1SgDAT pronoun **ngatyu*—ultimately the same form that provided the (later) Arrernte 1Sg marker *-atye* (see Koch 1996, 2003, 2004, 2007, for justification of these etymologies). The person markers, which originated as singular pronouns, are sometimes used to mark more than one propositus; for example, *-atye* may signal "our" as well as "my."

Forms inflected with the dyadic suffix may be further inflected by means of a suffix marking dual or plural number. Some lects use reduplication of the dyadic suffix, *-nhengenhenge*, to indicate a set of three or more people in a dyadic relationship (e.g., mother and two children, or child and two "mothers"). Many of the lects of Arrernte (but not Kaytetye) have a further suffix, *-ntyerre*, that marks a set of people involved in a dyadic relationship and is synonymous with the reduplicated dyadic suffix.

2.2. Stem Formation of Arandic Kin Terms

This section discusses the formal aspects of lexical stems that denote kin relations. The methodological approach is to first describe the synchronic patterns of word formation—for kin terms that are complex—and then use the results to justify the reconstruction of formerly complex forms, which will help us discover the etymology of the terms. In other words, it is argued that since some kin terms are synchronically multimorphemic, other terms that are no longer synchronically complex may nevertheless be multimorphemic etymologically. Synchronically complex kin terms include phrasal terms, reduplicated terms, compound terms, and terms manifesting truncated stems. These are discussed in turn. More complete lists of examples of each are given in the appendix.

2.2.1. Phrasal Kin Terms

A number of Arandic kin terms occur as two-word phrases. The second term is to be taken as the modifier, which indicates what specific kind of kin relation is involved. Several patterns emerge. In the first place, *kngerre* 'big' and *kweke* 'little' are used to indicate an elder or younger sibling,[6] for example, ECAr *yaye akngerre* 'sister big' (eZ) and *yaye akweke* 'sister little' (yZ). These modifiers are also used for the siblings of one's father (WAr *karte kngerre* 'father big' FeB), one's mother (WAr *meye kweke* 'mother little' MyZ), one's father's sister (WAr *wenhe kweke* 'auntie little' FyZ),[7] and one's spouse (WAr *newe kngerre* 'spouse big' WeZ/HeB).[8] In Strehlow's (n.d.) WAr, *lere* is used in this function of *little*, although its independent meaning is "man's child" (*meye lere* 'mother *little' MyZ, *mparne lere* 'brother-in-law *little' yZH). Further examples are given in Table 8.A1 in the appendix.

A second pattern uses *boy* and *girl* as modifiers to indicate the sex of a child. In ECAr the non-kin expressions *ampe urreye* 'boy' and *ampe marle* 'girl' show this use of gender-marking modifiers, where *ampe* is "child" and *urreye* and *marle* are "boy/male" and "girl/woman/female," respectively (Henderson and Dobson 1994:118). In WAr as described by Breen (2000) *ketyeye* means "child" in a non-kin sense or female's (or sister's) child as a kin term.[9] When modified by terms for "girl" or "boy" it designates "daughter" and "son," respectively. Although Breen does not specify that this is only a female's or sister's offspring, this can probably be inferred from the fact that *ketyeye* modified by *lere* denotes a "woman's brother's child"—here *lere* 'man's/brother's child' provides the paternal link. In this case the modifier is itself a kin term. These examples are set out in Table 8.A2 in the appendix.

In the Arandic lects there are sporadic instances of phrases where the first element has a classifying function and the second element may be a kin term (as well as non-kin words). ECAr *artwe* 'man', for example, is used in this way; one of its uses is described thus: "goes before other words that only refer to a man: *artwe anewe* 'husband' (*anewe* 'wife, husband'); *artwe ngangkere* 'traditional magic man'; *artwe ampwe* 'older man' (*ampwe* 'older person')" (Henderson and Dobson 1994:286). The term for "woman," *arelhe*, has a similar function, and examples are given as *arelhe anewe* 'wife, girlfriend', *arelhe ngangkere* 'woman traditional healer', and *arelhe ampwe* 'mature woman' (Henderson and Dobson 1994:195). Phrases of this kind applied to kin enjoy a special elaboration in WAr.

From forms given in Strehlow's (n.d.) dictionary we can infer a number of classificatory first elements that specify sex and seniority. How these operate can be seen most easily from their use with the four grandkin terms that are known in other varieties of Arrernte to designate each type of grandparent—*ipmenhe* MM, *perle* FM, *arrenge* FF, and *tyemeye* MF—and the siblings of each, along with the reciprocal grandchildren, grandnephews, and grandnieces of each. The term *lyurre*, which by itself means "grandmother," as a classifier of senior females occurs with grandkin terms to designate grandparents and their siblings, provided they are female, for example, *lyurre ipmenhe* MM and *lyurre perle* FM. Corresponding senior males are indicated by the use of *kngeye* or *kngerretye*, which by themselves mean "father" (e.g., *kngeye perle* or *kngerretye perle* FMB), or by *kelye*, which by itself means "elder brother" (e.g., *kelye ipmenhe* MMB). Members of the descending generation, that is, grandchildren, -nephews, and -nieces, use *kweye* 'girl' (e.g., *kweye ipmenhe* [f]DD)[10] as a "junior female" classifier and *werre* or *weye* 'boy' (e.g., *werre ipmenhe* [f]DS, *weye perle* [f]SS) as a "junior male" classifier. For a fuller list, see Table 8.A3 in the appendix.

2.2.2. Compound Kin Terms

Another kind of kin term is found that resembles phrasal kin expressions except that the two elements occur within a single word. Examples from Strehlow's (n.d.) WAr are *wey-alere*, apparently "man's son"; *wey-ampe*, apparently "woman's son"; and *kely-iteye* yB.[11] This last form consists obviously of the elements *kelye* eB and *iteye* yB, both of which occur independently. The same form is attested as *akely-irteye* in LAr, where this kind of kin term is especially prevalent. In LAr *akelye* by itself denotes either "boy" or "elder brother," and *irteye* by itself means "junior sibling." That *akely-* in compounds is not just "brother" is indicated by the fact that it recurs in a term for "man's son." It should therefore rather be considered a kind of classifier for "male" terms (cf. the combination of *kelye* with a MM term in WAr above).

A couple of terms denoting a female relative have as their first element *kweye* 'girl', which by itself means "girl." A shorter variant of this same element is apparent in the form *kw(e)*,[12] which occurs in a number of terms. One of these, *kw-ampe*, co-occurs with a synonymous form, *ampe*, that lacks the first element: both mean "female's child." This pattern of optional *kw(e)* allows us to interpret the WAr and Pertame form *kwaye* eZ as historically including the "junior female" classifier *kw(e)-* combined with an earlier term, **aye*, for eZ (see section 3.6.2). The LAr term given as *kungkere* eZ can likewise be interpreted as *kw(e)* plus *ungkwere*, the expected LAr reflex of the general Arrernte term *angkwere* eZ (see section 3.5).

Several terms for "brother's child" or "male's child" include the first element *(a)weye* (e.g., *wey-alere* mS, *awey-irteye* yB): by itself *weye* means "boy." The parallel between the compounding forms *kwey(e)-* and *kw(e)-* allows us to interpret forms beginning with *w-* that refer to male relatives (*w-alere* fBS, *w-irteye* yB) as short variants of the "boy" classifier *wey(e)*. A couple of forms with (apparently) *werre* as the first element occur in Curr's (1886–87) Wychinga (LAr) word list—spelled as *ueele-idea* and *ueele-ucca*. These may be phrases or compounds involving the term *werre* 'boy',[13] attested in WAr as a variant of *weye*, combined with *irteye* yB/yZ and *ake*, which I reconstruct as an earlier form for eB (see section 3.6.2).

Several terms denoting male relatives are found with the first element *aknge-*: these relatives are of the grandparental generation (*akng-arrenge* FF, *aknge-rtarte* MF, *akng-ipmenhe* MMB) but include one instance of a brother-in-law (*aknge-mperne* WB). This *akng(e)* must be a short form of *akngeye* F—note the parallel with phrasal expressions including *kngeye* F (and *kngerretye*) in WAr.[14] Finally, there is one compound, *alywe-rtarte*, that denotes a female relative of the grandparental generation and includes as its first element *alywe-*, which must surely be a short form of **alywerre* that would correspond to the WAr kin term *lyurre* 'grandmother', which occurs as a "senior female" classifier in phrasal kin expressions.

The full set of attested LAr compound kin terms is given in Table 8.A4 in the appendix. This section has highlighted the tricky nature of discovering the elements in these merged compounds. It is primarily the existence of phrasal kin terms and transparent compounds, in WAr in particular, that has permitted me to interpret the odd-looking LAr kin terms as being formed from elements that are found elsewhere in the kinship terminology of the Arrernte lects. Some of these principles of kin term structure will be drawn upon to reconstruct the etymologies of even more obscure Arandic kin terms in subsequent sections.

2.2.3. Reduplicated Kin Terms

Reduplication of kin terms is common in some lects, especially in the Baby Talk register. Thus the dictionary defines ECAr *arrenge-arrenge* as "an affectionate and casual form of *arrenge*" (Henderson and Dobson 1994:246); by itself *arrenge* means "father's father" and his siblings and the reciprocal of any of these. Similarly *alere-alere* is glossed simply as "= *alere*," which is "a man's child" or "brother's child" (Henderson and Dobson 1994:84). Sometimes reduplication involves further changes to the phonological structure, as for the "man's mother-in-law" term *mweye-mweye*: "a more casual form of *mwere*, probably from the 'baby talk' style of pronunciation used with babies and young children" (Henderson and Dobson 1994:487); here *r* has been replaced by *y*. Since reduplicated forms occur synchronically, one can posit earlier reduplicated forms to explain some of the longer stems that co-occur with short stems (see section 3.6.2 below)—again using attested patterns of kin term structure to help unlock the etymology of more obscure terms.

2.2.4. Kin Terms with Short Stem Variants

For a number of kin terms, one or more inflections and/or derivatives are based on a shorter stem than the citation stem. There are at least three patterns here, which are illustrated in Table 8.4 by representative forms. The first pattern, seen in WAr *meye* and Anm *ameye*, involves a long stem that includes the erstwhile 1Sg suffix *-ye*, which disappears in inflected forms. In the second pattern, the long stem appears to involve reduplication; thus in WAr the short stem of eB, *ke-* (< **ake-*), appears to have a reduplicated form in *kake* < **ak(e)-ake*. In other lects this longer stem is further suffixed with the suffix *-ye*, which originally indicated first-person singular. In the third pattern, the long stem appears to be a compound; thus Anm *atye-meye* appears to consist of the short stem *atye-* combined with *meye* M. The historical interpretation of these three kinds of lengthened stems is discussed in section 3.6.

2.2.5. Kin Terms with Suppletive Stem Variants

It is worth noting that not all stem alternation involves related long and short stems. Sometimes alternative stems are suppletive, that is, unrelated in form. For example, WAr for F is either *kngeye* or *karte*, but the dyadic form

TABLE 8.4. Long and short kin term stems.

Lect	Stem Gloss	Long Stem	Short Stem	Suffix Gloss
WAr	M	*meye*	*me-nhenge*	Dyadic
Anm	M	*ameye*	*am-atye*	1st
			amwengke[a]	2nd
			am-ikwe	3rd
WAr	eB	*kake*	*ke-nhenge*	Dyadic
Anm	eB	*kake(ye)*	*ke-ngkwe*	2nd
			k-ikw	3rd
			ke-nhenge	Dyadic
			ke-paretye	Respectful
Ant	eB	*kakeye*	*k-atye*	1Sg
			k-angkwe	2Sg
			ke-yekwe[b]	3Sg
Anm	MF	*atyemeye*	*atye-ngkwe*	2nd
			aty-ikwe	3rd
			atye-nhenge	Dyadic
Ant	MF	*atyemenye*[c]	*aty-atye*	1Sg
			atye-nhenge	Dyadic

Note: Anm = Anmatyerr; Ant = Antekerrepenh; WAr = Western Arrernte.

[a] This is historically from *amengkwe*, with anticipatory transfer of the rounding from *k* to the *m*.

[b] The form *-yekwe* is a variant of *-ikwe*.

[c] The form *-menye* is isolated within Arandic and unexplained.

nye-nhenge involves the unrelated stem *nye-*, which recurs elsewhere in Arandic as *(a)nye* or *ayne-* (see section 3.3). In the same lect the normal term for eB is *kelye*, but *kake* is used for address, and the dyadic form is *ke-nhenge*, building on the short stem *ke-*.

3. Reconstruction of Kin Terms

The most common method of reconstruction consists of comparing cognate words, that is, words that are so similar in both form and meaning that the most likely explanation for this agreement is that they are all reflexes of a common source word that existed in a language ancestral to all the lects in which they occur. This antecedent word is called a proto-word, the related words are called cognates, and each is said to be a reflex of the source word or etymon. Reconstructed words are preceded by an asterisk to emphasize the lack of direct attestation. Words can be reconstructed to different levels of protolanguages, according to how they are distributed across the related lects. In the following subsections I give the cognate sets that justify reconstruction to the levels of Proto-Arandic, Proto-Arrernte, and Proto–Upper Arrernte. I then discuss (in section 3.4) some forms that have a localized distribution that does not correspond to a genetic grouping of lects. Some of these result from borrowing. This leads to the question of how loanwords are recognized. Terms borrowed from outside of the Arandic languages are discussed in section 3.5. In section 3.6 I discuss cases where an earlier shorter stem form can be reconstructed on the basis that it occurs in longer stems that result from the incorporation of an inflection, reduplication, compounding, or the possible absorption of an incremental syllable of uncertain origin. This discussion is informed by the findings of section 2 on the synchronic structure of Arandic kin terms. Finally, in section 3.7 I discuss the importance of paying attention to the internal chronology of the documentation of the languages for a proper evaluation of the historical significance of forms.

3.1. Terms Reconstructible to Proto-Arandic

The kin terms discussed here are attested in all the Arandic lects. This distribution is assumed to reflect the fact that they were already present in Proto-Arandic, the language ancestral to all these lects. We begin with the ones that are easiest to reconstruct (see Table 8.5).

The FF term *arrenge* is attested in all lects and so is reconstructible to Proto-Arandic. In LAr it has been compounded with *aknge*, which is "father" elsewhere in Arrernte, possibly to designate only FF and FFB, excluding FFZ. The term *arrenge* has no known cognates outside of the Arandic languages. But the term *arrengeye* ("my FF" in Kaytetye but just "FF" in Arrernte) has been borrowed as *warringiyi* into Warlpiri, which adjoins the Arandic languages on the northwest, where it has the same range of meanings as in Arandic.

The FM term *(a)perle* is likewise reconstructible to Proto-Arandic, being attested in all lects.[15] The absence of the initial *a* in WAr is characteristic of this dialect (Breen 2001:65). The FM's sibling sense is not attested in LAr and Ant nor the grandchild sense in LAr (both with limited sources). The Arandic term is surely a reflex of the widely distributed term *kaparli*, which occurs in many languages to the west of Arandic—for example, in Nyangumarta, Kariyarra, Nyamal, Panyjima as FM and in Western Desert, Ngadjumaya, and Wirangu as FM or MM. The Arandic term has been borrowed as *yaparla* into Warlpiri, where it has the same range of senses as in Arandic.

TABLE 8.5. Kin terms reconstructible to Proto-Arandic: consanguineal.

Language	FF	FM	MM	mMBS/mFZS	fMBD/fFZD
Lower Arrernte	*akngarrenge*	*perle-*	*ipmenhe*	*ankele*	*kweltyele*
Western Arrernte	*arrenge*	*perle*	*ipmenhe*	*ankele*	*ltyele, altyele*
Eastern and Central Arrernte	*arrenge*	*aperle*	*ipmenhe*	*ankele*	*altyele*
Anmatyerr	*arrenge*	*aperle*	*ipmenhe, aypmenhe, aylpmenhe*	*ankele*	*altyele*
Antekerrepenh	*arrenge*	*perle-*	*aylpmenhe*	*ankele*	*altyele*
Alyawarr	*arrenge*	*aperle*	*aypmenhe*	*ankele*	*altyele*
Kaytetye	*arrenge*	*aperle*	*aytnmenhe, aytnmerre*	*atnkele*	*altyele*
Proto-Arandic	**arrenge*	**aperle*	**aylpmenhe*	**atnkele*	**altyele*
Cognates	**kaparli*			**parnku*	

The MM terms involve more complexities than most cognate sets. I reconstruct for pArc the form **aylpmenhe*—with a complex consonant cluster consisting of a prepalatized lateral *yl* followed by a prestopped nasal *pm*. This form is preserved only in Ant and Eastern Anmatyerr (EAnm). In Kaytetye the sequence of lateral and nasal has changed (regularly) to nasal plus nasal, with prestopping on the first one.[16] In Aly *yl* has simplified to *y* in *aypmenhe*, which is also a variant in Anm. In the other lects (as in many words) the initial *a* has been dropped, and the result is the vocalization of *y* to *i*.[17] A fourth grandparental term, **atye* MF (from the earlier **ngatyi*), is probably also reconstructible, but discussion will be deferred until section 3.6.3 because of the complexities involved.

Cross-cousin terms can also be reconstructed to Proto-Arandic. The languages distinguish between a term used when one cousin is male and another term used when both cousins are female; that is, *altyele* is used only between female cross-cousins, while *ankele* is used between all other cross-cousins. The male term is slightly different in Kaytetye—having a prestopped nasal before the next consonant—but is obviously the same term in origin. In LAr a specifically male cousin is indicated by *akelyankele*, where *ankele* is compounded with the male marker *akelye*, and a female cousin is indicated by *kweltyele*, where the cousin term *ltyele* is compounded with the female marker *kwe-*. The Arandic word *a(t)nkele* appears to be cognate with the Ngumpin "cousin" term *parnku*, which is sometimes extended to *parnkurti* (in various languages).[18] The Arandic form would represent the extension *pankulV* (where V denotes a vowel whose quality is unknown). The Arandic term has been borrowed as *wankili* into the western neighbor Warlpiri, where it denotes a male cross-cousin as in Arandic, and the northern neighbor Warumungu (and its western neighbor Warlmanpa), where it has an extended sense of any cross-cousin.

We turn now to affinal terms (see Table 8.6). The "brother-in-law" term is attested in all lects. In Alyawarr it also means "husband," and in Kaytetye, "husband" or "wife" as well. LAr lacks the rounding, as does WAr, which also has lowered the vowel from *e* to *a*.[19] The rounding in *mpwerne* reflects an earlier *u* in the first syllable, so the pre-Arandic form was **umperne*, from an earlier form, **ngumparna*, that is attested as 'brother-in-law' or 'husband' in the Ngumpin-Yapa languages to the west and northwest. The "sister-in-law" term, *arntenge*, sometimes restricted to "woman's sister-in-law," is likewise found in all lects. In LAr it is combined with the female marker *kwe-*. The initial vowel is sometimes omitted, and in WAr it has been phonemicized with an initial *i*. The term is not attested in Ant. No external cognates are known.[20]

The reciprocal term *anherre* HM/fSW is attested in all lects except Ant. It has cognates outside of Arandic: *ngunharri* in Warluwarra and *ngunyarri* in Western Desert, the Ngumpin-Yapa languages, and Warumungu (languages that do not distinguish *nh* from *ny*).[21]

The term for "wife's father" (and often also "husband's father") and its converse mDH is reconstructible to pArc as **ahenterre* (with some alteration to the initial vowel). The sound *h* is unstable; it tends to lower the following

TABLE 8.6. Kin terms reconstructible to Proto-Arandic: affinal.

Language	WB	HZ	HM/fSW	WF/mDH[a]
Lower Arrernte	*mperne*	*kwarntenge*	*anherre*	*ihenterre*
Western Arrernte	*mparne*	*irntenge*	*nherre*	*henterre, anterre*
Eastern and Central Arrernte	*mpwerne*	*arntenge*	*anherre*	*ahenterre*
Anmatyerr	*mpwerne*	*arntenge*	*anherre*	*ahenterre*
Antekerrepenh	*mpwerne*	—	—	*henterre*
Alyawarr	*mpwerne*	*arntenge*	*anherre*	*ahenterre*
Kaytetye	*mpwerne*	*arntenge*	*anherre*	*ahanterre*
Proto-Arandic	**mpwerne*	**arntenge*	**anherre*	**ahenterre*
Pre-Arandic	**ngumparna*		**ngunharri*	

[a] The meaning given for WAr and ECAr is HF, "woman's father-in-law."

TABLE 8.7. Proto-Arrernte kin terms and Kaytetye equivalents.

Language	FZ	F	m/BC	f/ZC	yB/yZ
Lower Arrernte	*awenhe*	*akngeye*	*lere*	*ampe*	*irteye*
Western Arrernte	*wenhe*	*kngeye*	*lere*	*ampe*	*tyeye*
Eastern and Central Arrernte	*awenhe*	*akngeye*	*alere*	*ampe*	*atyeye*
Anmatyerr	*awenhe*	*a(k)ngeye*	*alere*	*ampe*	*ayteye, atyeye*
Antekerrepenh	*awenhe*	*akngeye*	*alere*	*ampe*	*ayteye, atyeye*
Alyawarr	*awenhe*	*akngeye*	*alere*	*ampe*	*ayteye*
Proto-Arrernte	**awenhe*	**akngeye*	**alere*	**ampe*	**ayteye*
Kaytetye	*akele*	*arlweye*	*artemperre*	*artewaleye*	*atyerre*

vowel to *a* and to disappear itself. The Arandic form *hanterre* or *henterre* has been borrowed into Warlpiri as *wantirri*, with the glide *h* adapted as *w*, as is normal (Koch 1997a).[22] (It will be argued in section 3.6.3 below that **ahenterre* has a complex structure historically.)

Other terms that can probably be reconstructed back to pArc include **ame* M (from the earlier **ngama*) and **atye* MF (from the earlier **ngatyi*). Since these involve other issues, however, they will be deferred until sections 3.6.1 and 3.6.2–3, respectively.

3.2. Terms Reconstructible to Proto-Arrernte

A considerable number of kin terms are reconstructible to Proto-Arrernte on the basis of cognates attested in all (or most) lects other than Kaytetye (see Table 8.7). These could have been innovations in Proto-Arrernte, or, if the Kaytetye terms are innovations, they may have descended from Proto-Arandic or earlier. Methodologically, however, we cannot reconstruct them beyond Proto-Arrernte.

FZ is universally *awenhe* (with the regular loss of the initial *a* in WAr), which has no obvious external cognates. The corresponding term in Kaytetye is *akele*, which also lacks an etymology.[23]

A term for "father," *akngeye*, is found in all lects. (WAr lacks the initial *a*, and Western Anmatyerr has [regularly] simplified the prestopped nasal *kng* to just *ng*.) This form does not inflect; in Upper Arrernte lects the inflecting stem is, rather, a stem that reflects **ayne-* (see section 3.3). It is argued in section 3.6.1 below that *akngeye* consists etymologically of the stem *aknge* with an absorbed inflectional suffix *-ye*. Kaytetye lacks this form but has the form *arlweye*.

Terms for "male's child" and "female's child" are also reconstructible to Proto-Arrernte. "A man's child" or "brother's child" (the converse of F, FB, or FZ) is *alere*, with loss of the initial *a* in WAr and LAr. No certain external cognates are known.[24] The corresponding term for "woman's child" or "sister's child" is *ampe* in all varieties of Arrernte. This term can also be used for just "child" in a non-kinship sense. The corresponding Kaytetye terms for "man's child" and "woman's child" are *artemperre* and *artewaleye*.

The Arrernte terms for "younger sibling" are cognate, although they differ somewhat phonologically. There is a conservative form, *ayteye*, attested in Aly, Ant, and Anm and a form that reflects the change of the prepalatalized *yt* to the palatal *ty* in ECAr, WAr, Ant (beside *ayteye*), and parts of Anm. I interpret the *rt* of LAr as being another instance of the original *yt*. The initial *a* has been lost in WAr and is replaced by *i* in LAr. In LAr the kin term occurs by itself, as well as in combination with *akelye*, *we-*, and *werre* to designate a male ("younger brother") and with *kweye* and *kwe-* to designate a female ("younger sister"). There are no known external cognates of **ayteye*. The Kaytetye term for "younger sibling" is *atyerre*, which cannot be cognate, since *ty* does not come from *yt* in Kaytetye.

Other terms that can probably be reconstructed back to pAr include **ameye* M, **kamerne* MB, **ake* eB, **aye* eZ, and **mwere* 'mother-in-law'. Since these involve other issues, however, they will be deferred until later.

3.3. Terms Reconstructible to Proto–Upper Arrernte

Given the subgrouping diagrammed in Figure 8.2, we might expect some terms to reflect innovations in Proto–Upper Arrernte. A candidate is a term for "father" that reconstructs as **ayne*. The uninflected term is supplied by another term such as *(a)kngeye* (or in WAr, *karte*). The forms that support this reconstruction are given in Table 8.8, where a dash at the end of a form indicates that it is attested only with inflectional suffixes. The prepalatalized *yn* has been changed (as is normal) to *ny* in a number of lects. The lack of prestopping in the nasal indicates that the original word-initial consonant must have been a nasal (Koch 1997b). Possible external cognates are *ngarnidya* F (assuming that the *-dya* is a historical increment) in Wangkumara, an eastern Karnic language, and *ngarni* eB (with different semantics) in Kalkatungu.[25]

3.4. Terms with Regional Distribution

Certain kin terms occur only in a part of the Arandic area. These can usually be interpreted as innovations that took place, after the lects had already diversified, in one particular region. In origin they may have been borrowed from a non-Arandic language, and they may have spread subsequently to adjacent Arandic lects.

TABLE 8.8. Forms reconstructible to the Proto–Upper Arrernte kin term **ayne* F.

Language	Form
Western Arrernte	*anye, nye-*
Eastern and Central Arrernte	*anye-*
Western Anmatyerr	*anye*
Eastern Anmatyerr	*ayne*
Antekerrepenh	*ayne-*
Alyawarr	*ayne-*
Proto–Upper Arrernte	**ayne-*

A term for "child" is found in the western area of Arandic, as *akatyeye* in LAr and *ketyeye* in WAr and Western Anmatyerr. In the first two lects it has become a kin term denoting "son" or "daughter" (cf. section 2.2.1).[26] In origin this may have been an adapted form of Western Desert *katya* 'child', which is also used as a kin term for "son"/"daughter"/"nephew"/"niece."

The term *karte* F occurs only in WAr. The term *arrengkwe* occurs in Kaytetye as "mother," and a minimally different form, *arrwengke*, is found in the adjacent Alyawarr in the sense fDDD, which must be related, since great-grandchildren are typically called by the same terms as parents.[27] Since these two languages are in different subgroups of Arandic, the innovation of *arrengkwe/arrwengke* must have been relatively recent and must have taken place only in the northeastern part of the Arandic domain.

The historical interpretation of regional distribution can be uncertain. For instance, *nyanye* or *anyanye* occurs in all the lects except WAr and LAr as a term for MM (see next section). Does this represent a post-Proto-Arandic innovation that spread from the east but failed to reach the most southerly and westerly lects, or could it, rather, have been a feature of pArc that was inherited into all lects but replaced in WAr and LAr? It is difficult to tell.

It can be helpful to plot the areal distribution of terms on a map. This kind of display can reveal, better than a vertical word list, the contiguous nature of the distribution of forms across lects and suggest hypotheses about where an innovation may have originated (cf. Koch 2001). Figure 8.3 shows a west–south versus northeastern distribution of terms for "elder brother," *(a)kelye* and *awaye*, in the Arrernte subgroup, as well as Kaytetye *alkere*. Hence the origin of *awaye* should be sought in the northeast, and that of *(a)kelye*, in the southwest.

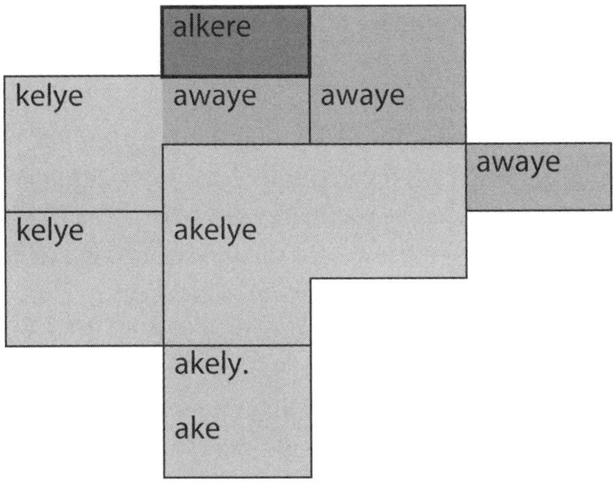

FIGURE 8.3. Areal distribution for eB terms.

3.5. Terms Borrowed from Outside the Arandic Subgroup

Terms that have been borrowed from neighboring languages can be identified by a number of means, including their geographical distribution, distinctive phonological correspondences, the existence of synonyms, and aspects of their semantics (see Koch 1997a for examples of loanwords between Kaytetye and Warlpiri). Several terms are given in Table 8.9.

The term *arrwempe* has the complex semantics of denoting an opposite-sex sibling or parallel cousin. Both of these correspond to the term *nyarrumpa* of identical semantics in the Western Desert language. I conclude that its variants have been borrowed with the following phonological adaptations: The initial consonant has been deleted (in imitation of correspondences that result from the Arandic sound changes applying to genuine cognates); the final vowel has been replaced by the vowel *e*, which is found on all words in Arandic languages; and stress has been shifted from the first syllable normal in Western Desert to the second syllable (if the word begins in a vowel), as is the norm in Arandic. A word-internal *u* vowel has been interpreted as *e* preceded by a rounded consonant. This contrasts with the development of word-internal vowels in inherited Arandic words, which all become *e*. The preservation of *mp* in *arrwempe* also shows that this cannot be an inherited word, since *mp* would have been reduced to *m* in this environment. Furthermore, the word-initial sequence *nya* in an inherited word would be expected to become *i* in Arrernte, according to a sound change established in Koch 2007. Thus a pAr **nyarrumpa* would have become, by the regular sound changes, **irreme*. In LAr the initial *a* has been dropped, and rounding has reverted to the initial syllable, yielding *urrempe*, by further developments discussed in Breen 2001:67.

The Arrernte term for eZ is suspected of being a loanword, since there is a synonym, *yaye*, in several lects.[28] The form is *angkwere*, except for WAr *ngkwere*, where the initial *a* has been lost (as is usual), and in LAr where the rounding has turned into a rounded initial vowel and the resultant (unattested) **ungkere* has been combined with the "girl" classifying element *kw(e)-* to form *kw-ungkere* (cf. section 2.2.2), which I interpret to be the underlying phonology of *kungkere*.[29] I assume that Western Desert *kangkuru* was borrowed into an Arrernte lect, being adapted to *angkwere* in the same manner as *nyarrumpa* was adapted to *arrwempe*, and then spread to all other lects of Arrernte (except Aly).

TABLE 8.9. Arandic kin terms borrowed from western languages.

Language	mZ/fB	eZ	WB	W/H	WM/fDH
Lower Arrernte	*urrempe*	*kungkere*		*irrkare*	*urtaltye*
Western Arrernte	*(a)rrwempe*	*ngkwere*		*arrkare*	*twaltye*
Eastern and Central Arrernte	*arrwempe*	*angkwere*		*arrkare*	*urtaltye*
Anmatyerr	*arrwempe*	*angkwere*		*arrkare*	*rtwaltye*
Antekerrepenh	*arrwempe*[a]	*angkwere*		—	—
Alyawarr	—	*angkwere*	*akwente*	*arrkare*	*rtwaltye*
Kaytetye	*arrwempe*[b]		*makwernte*	*arrkare*	*rtwaltye*
Source Form	*nyarrumpa*	*kangkuru*	*makurnta*	*marrkari*	*tyurtaltya*
Source Language	Western Desert	Western Desert	Warlpiri	Western Desert/Warlpiri	Warlpiri

[a] Gloss given is yZ.

[b] Only in Modern Kaytetye.

Phonological adaptation similar to that in the two words above can be seen in Aly *akwente* 'man's brother-in-law', which appears to be a loanword (without the retroflexion in the *nt* cluster) from the Western Desert *makurnta* WB/mZH. The same term was apparently borrowed, without the loss of the initial *m*, as Kay *makwernte* WB.[30] More recent loanwords in Kaytetye may be borrowed without the truncation of the initial consonant (see Koch 1997a, where these two patterns of borrowing are established). A plausible scenario, which takes into account the fact that Alyawarr is separated from Warlpiri by Kaytetye, is that *makurnta* was first borrowed into Kaytetye and adapted to *akwernte* and was then transmitted farther east to Alyawarr from Kaytetye (with the retroflexion missing), and that the Kaytetye later upgraded their *akwernte* to *makwernte* to better conform with the Warlpiri model.

Words with an *a* vowel in the internal syllable are also suspected of being loanwords, since the *a* vowel changed to *e* by regular sound change in inherited Arandic words. Most Arandic lects have a form for "spouse," *arrkare* (*irrkare* in LAr, with loss of the initial *a* and substitution of *i*). This is not the normal word for "spouse" but, rather, has been defined as "the husband or wife of someone who is in the same generation moiety as oneself" (Green 2009:220); for example, it is used to refer to the spouse of one's sibling, cross-cousin, or grandparent when speaking to that relative. It is what is called a "trirelational" kin term, since its interpretation depends on relations among the speaker, addressee, and referent (Laughren 1982). The form *marrkari*, with a similar meaning, is found in Warlpiri and Walmanpa (David Nash, personal communication, September 20, 2010) and in Pintupi/Luritja. It is assumed that the Arandic form has been borrowed from Pintupi/Luritja or Warlpiri, with the normal adaptations—loss of the initial consonant and change of the final vowel to *e*.

The widespread Arandic term *rtwaltye* (with its variants) also has the hallmarks of a loanword: internal vowel *a* and in-law semantics (in-law terms appear to be more liable to borrowing than other kin terms). The term refers to "wife's mother" and her siblings, as well as a "woman's daughter's husband." In LAr it includes WF, WB, and WZ as well as WM. The external source seems to be Warlpiri, where *jurdalja* (Meggitt 1962: *tyurdaltya* in our standardized orthography) denotes any member of one's wife's matriline (Hale 1995:4). Warlmanpa has *tyurtattya* (< *tyurtaltya*) for WM/fDH (Nash 1979).[31] In this word the *u* vowel of the first syllable has been adapted as rounding on the following consonant in Arandic.

Kay *ayletye* WM corresponds to *mwere* in the other Arandic languages. It appears to have been borrowed ultimately from the form *mali* that occurs in the Ngumpin-Yapa languages to the northwest. In Warlpiri, the closest of these languages to Kaytetye, the current form is *malirdi*, which includes the increment *-rdi*, which recurs in other kin terms and is relatively widespread in Pama-Nyungan languages (Nash 1992). Another increment, **-tyi* or **tyu* (for which, see McConvell 2008), is attested for this term in Ngumpin languages indirectly by lenited forms like the Jaru *maliyi* (< **malityi*); forms with the bare stem *mali* also occur in Ngumpin languages. The Kaytetye form can be derived from the earlier **malityi* or **malityu*, if such a form was borrowed before the sound changes took place that reduced it to *ayletye*.[32] What is particularly interesting about this loanword is that it presupposes the form **malityi* in the lending language that no longer survives. The linguistic stratigraphy that I posit involves these stages for Warlpiri: (1) *mali* WM and *mali-tyi* 'my WM'; (2) Kaytetye (or pre-Kaytetye) borrows *malityi* as just WM; (3) Warlpiri discontinues *malityi* and replaces *mali* with *malirdi*.

The loanwords discussed so far have all been borrowed from languages to the west (Western Desert and Warlpiri). There are also at least two kin terms that can be explained as loanwords from the Karnic languages, which adjoin Arandic on the east and south (see Table 8.10). All lects of Arrernte, but not Kaytetye, have a term for "spouse" of the form *newe*, sometimes *anewe*, as well as LAr *unewe*.[33] This form is surely related somehow to the widespread Pama-Nyungan term *nhupa*.[34] But if such a form had gone through the Arandic sound changes, it would have ended up as **pwe*. In the nearby Karnic languages it is found as Arabana and Wangkangurru *nhupa* and Wangka-Yutjurru and Pitta-Pitta *nhupu*. Farther to the southeast, it is attested as *nhuwa* in Diyari. I propose that the form **nhuwa* or **nhuwu* occurred earlier in a language close to pAr, that it was copied as *newe* (with an alveolar instead of a lamino-dental nasal),[35] and that it subsequently acquired a variable initial vowel (since many other words varied in this way). The borrowing may have been as early as Proto-Arrernte. Kaytetye did not participate in this borrowing but, rather, continued to use *mpwerne* for "spouse" as well as "brother-in-law."

TABLE 8.10. Arandic kin terms borrowed from eastern languages.

Language	Spouse	MF_1	MF_2	MF_3
Lower Arrernte	*unewe*	*aknge.rtarte, alywe.rtarte*		
Western Arrernte	*newe*			*tartarte*
Eastern and Central Arrernte	*(a)newe*			*(r)tartarte*
Anmatyerr	*anewe*		*artartetye, artarteye*	*(r)tartarte*
Antekerrepenh	*(a)newe*		*(a)rtartetye*	
Alyawarr	*anewe*		*artartetye, artarteye*	
Source Form	**nhuwa*	*(ng)artarta*		
Source Language	Karnic	Karnic		

Another kin term that appears to have been borrowed from Karnic languages is an MF term synonymous with *atye(-meye)*. The form *artarte* can serve as the starting point of discussion. A form without the initial vowel occurs in LAr, combined with *aknge-* and *alywe-* to designate MF and MFZ, respectively. The form *artarte* serves as the inflected stem for EAnm second- and third-person forms *artartengkwe* and *artartikwe*. There is another form with an extra initial consonant *rt* (or *t*) attested in Anm, (modern only) WAr, and (parts of) ECAr. I suggest that this *rtartarte* (or *tartarte*) may have originated as a Baby Talk modification of *artarte*, parallel to the terms for FM: ECAr *(a) papape*, "'Baby talk' version of *aperle-aperle*" (Henderson and Dobson 1994:183); Anm *papape*; and *mamame*, meaning "grandmother" in WAr and MM for some speakers of ECAr.[36] The form *tartarte* has apparently been borrowed from WAr as *tartarta* into Pintupi/Luritja, where it denotes a grandfather or grandson. More difficult to explain are forms with the extra syllable *-tye* or (apparently its lenited version) *-ye* at the end of the stem, which occur in Ant, Aly, and EAnm. The forms *artartetye* and *artarteye* also serve as bases for inflection, but EAnm *artartetye* is indicated as the first-person form. These forms do not show the usual *-atye* inflection for the first person.

I suggest that *artarte* was borrowed into the Arrernte lects from Karnic languages to the east. The relevant Karnic terms are Wangkangurru *artarta* MF, Pitta-Pitta and Wangka-Yutjurru *ngartarta* FF, Diyari *ngardarda* MF, and Yarluyandi *ngatarta* MF/FF. If the Arrernte lects have borrowed the term *ngartarta*, they have adapted it by the truncation of the first consonant and neutralization of the final vowel to *e*, as with loanwords from languages to the west (but unlike the short term *newe*).[37] Given the possible ambiguity of the referent of the grandparental term in the neighboring Karnic languages (FF in Wangka-Yutjurru but MF in Wangkangurru),[38] it is conceivable that Arrernte speakers clarified the kind of grandparent by compounding *artarte* with their inherited term for MF, **atye/*itye* (see section 3.6.2–3), and that this accounts for the extended form *artartetye*—which then combines two historically different terms for MF, **ngartarta* and **ngatyi*.

3.6. Shorter Kin Terms Reconstructible from Complex Terms

Where some inflections are added to a stem that is shorter than the citation stem, this can be taken as evidence that the normal stem has been elaborated historically by one of three mechanisms: (1) reduplication, (2) compounding, or (3) absorption of an erstwhile inflection. Generally Arandic kin terms that ended up with a VCV structure (as a result of the regular loss of initial consonants from a CVCV form) are attested in a longer form—the stem being extended with an inflectional suffix that adds at least one syllable, or the extension *-ye*, or reduplication, or a compounding element.

3.6.1. *Stems Incorporating* -ye

The term for M is *(a)meye* in most lects of Arrernte: *meye* in LAr, ECAr, and War and *ameye* in Aly, Anm, and Modern Kaytetye.[39] The inflected forms, however, omit the *ye* syllable and are based on the stem *(a)me-*: for example, Ant *m-atye*, *m-angkwe*, *me-yekwe*, and *me-nhenge*. The short stem is also found in the ECAr compound verb *meakeme/makeme* 'call someone mother's brother'. Here the stem has the extended meaning of MB that is an informal usage of *meye*; MB can also be referred to as *artwe meye* (lit. "man mother"; for these usages, see Henderson and

Dobson 1994:475). A short form also occurs in Kay, *ame-nhenge*, the dyadic form corresponding to MB—which indicates the same extension from M to MB.

I interpret the *-ye* as an absorbed 1Sg marker. I assume that it is cognate with the Kay 1Sg marker *-ye*, which was a feature of pArc, but that its place was later taken in pAr by a new 1Sg marker, *-atye*. This absorption was facilitated by the fact that the 1Sg form can sometimes be used as the general term for the kin relation, with the propositus being indicated if necessary by a separate possessive pronoun. Thus the ECAr dictionary gives for *m-atye*, beside the first meaning "my mother, our mother," a second sense: "mother (not necessarily mine/ours)" (Henderson and Dobson 1994:473). The tendency for Australian kin terms that are explicitly marked for the 1Sg propositus to absorb this marker into the stem is discussed in Koch 1995. McConvell (2008) discusses the tendency of Pama-Nyungan languages to incorporate into their stems the 1Sg marker *-tyu* in particular (being in origin an enclitic form of the 1Sg dative pronoun **ngatyu*). From the comparison of the extended forms discussed here and the relic form *(a)me-*, I can safely reconstruct back to pArc the form **ame* M. This is a reflex of an earlier form, **ngama* M, which is widely attested in the Pama-Nyungan languages.

All lects of Arrernte have *(a)kngeye* as one of their terms for "father." In WAr *karte* is more common. Inflectional forms are typically supplied by the suppletive stem **ayne-* (cf. section 2.2.5). The stem *(a)kngeye* does not take inflections, nor are any inflections added to the shorter stem *(a)knge-*. Nevertheless, the short stem *aknge-* occurs in LAr compounds, where it functions as a classifier for senior males (section 2.2.2). This shows that *akngeye* is likely to consist of the same short form followed by the *-ye* suffix. Both *aknge-* and *akngeye* appear to be etymologically related to the Arrernte forms for "big" or "senior," *(a)kngerre* and *(a)kngerretye* (*akngerrtye* in LAr). The former is used as the modifier "elder" in WAr and ECAr; *kngerretye* occurs in WAr as a term for "father" and as a classifier for senior males; and *akngerretye* in Anm is used as "a respectful word for mother's brother (used by men)" (Green 2009:99). A common term for an older or senior person in ECAr is the derivative *akngerrepate* (Henderson and Dobson 1994:72). The case is thus strong for interpreting *(a)kngeye* F as an erstwhile inflected form of **aknge*, which in turn, with the related forms **akngerre* and **akngerretye*, derives ultimately from a stem that indicated "big," "senior," and so on.

Kay *arlweye* F has been claimed to be another kin term that has historically absorbed the 1Sg suffix *-ye*. The pre-Kaytetye form would then have been **urle*, which has a plausible cognate in Kalkatungu **kurla* (Koch 1995).

There is a strong tendency for Arrernte kin terms with a short stem of the structure VCV, when not occurring with an inflectional suffix, to occur as the longer stem *VCVye*—*ameye*, *akngeye*, and so on—rather than just **ame*, **aknge*, and so forth. An exception is *ampe* 'female's child', also "child" in the non-kin sense, which occurs with the suffix *-atye* but never *-ye*. This may be explained by a hypothesis that *ampe* did not become a kin term until after *-ye* ceased to be used productively in the Arrernte branch of the Arandic subgroup.

3.6.2. Reduplicated Stems

There are a number of kin terms that have the structure *CaCe*, where the two consonants are identical: *kake* eB, *yaye* eZ, *tyatye* MF, *nyanye* MM. Such a structure can hardly descend from a pre-Arandic trisyllabic word that has lost its first syllable by sound change, that is, **CVCaCV*, since the *a* of the middle syllable should have become *e* by the regular sound changes. There are usually other clues that these forms were not simple stems in origin. They may lack the inflectional forms of normal kin term stems. There may be other supporting evidence that the original form of the stem was simply **aCe*. These forms are therefore interpreted as erstwhile reduplicated stems, whose creation was motivated by a preference for longer stems and facilitated by the prevalence of reduplicated forms of kin terms used to express affection, familiarity, and so on.[40]

The term for "elder brother" occurring in most Upper Arrernte lects is *kake* (it is only marginally present in Aly, where the normal term for eB is *awaye*). Its inflected forms, however, are built on a shorter stem, **ke-*. In ECAr these are *katye* 'first', *kangkwe* 'second', *kikwe* or *keyekwe* 'third', and *kenhenge* 'dyadic'. In Modern WAr *kake* is used only as a term of address; otherwise *kelye* is used (Breen 2000:23). The dyadic form *kenhenge* is based on the short stem *ke-*. The only suffix that *kake* takes is in the form *kakeye*, which is attested marginally in Ant and Aly, as well as in Anm and Kay, where for some speakers it is regarded as Baby Talk. Arandic *kakeye* has apparently been borrowed, via Pidgin English, into Warlpiri as *kakiyi*, a Baby Talk form for "brother" (for which, see Laughren 1984:86). It appears that *kake* has also been borrowed into Pintup/Luritja as *kaaka* eB, apparently from WAr.

I posit an earlier stem, **ake*, and a reduplicated stem,

**ak-ake*, which dropped the first vowel and became *kake*. This stem also occurs in LAr compounded with an alternative term for "brother," *akelye*, in *akely-ake*, and with a form I have interpreted as *werre* 'boy', in *werre-ake* eB (see section 2.2). The bare stem **ake* is actually attested in the earliest source for WAr, with the characteristic loss of the initial *a*, as *ke* (spelled *kā*), glossed as "brother" (Strehlow n.d.). The array of forms (WAr *ke*, LAr *-ake* in *akely. ake*, the inflected stem *[a]ke-*, and the reduplicated *kake* < **ak-ake*) combine to support the reconstruction to Proto-Arrernte of **ake* eB. No external cognates are obvious.

A corresponding term for eZ is *yaye*, which is found alongside *angkwere* in many lects. It is not found in Aly or Ant. In Kaytetye and for some Anmatyerr speakers it is considered to be a Baby Talk form. It has been borrowed into Warlpiri Baby Talk as *yayi*, with a generalized meaning of "sister," and into Pintupi/Luritja as *yayi* or *ayi*,[41] with a specific meaning of "female's elder sister."[42] The only inflected form is the WAr dyadic *yayenhenge*. Here too I propose that *yaye* originated as the reduplicated form **ay-aye* of a shorter stem, **aye*. This short form survives, in a stem that is compounded with the "girl" classifier *kwe-*, in WAr (including Pertame) *kwaye*. Hence the form **aye* is reconstructible to Proto-Arrernte.[43]

A third erstwhile reduplicated form, in my interpretation, is Kay *tyatye* MF. This word does not inflect for person or dyad. The corresponding inflected form is the longer stem *atyewaleye*, which I interpret as a historical compound involving *atye-* as its first member (see the next section). The form *tyatye* can be treated as a former reduplication, *aty-atye* of **atye*, which otherwise survives as the inflecting stem of *(a)tyemeye* in ECAr, WAr, and Anm (see the next section). Note that the first-person inflected form of the latter is *aty-atye*, where the second *-atye* is the person marker. This will not explain Kay *tyatye*, however, since the first-person suffix in Kaytetye is not *-atye* but *-ye*. There is a grandparental form, *jaju* in the Ngumpin-Yapa languages and *jaaju* in Warumungu (these would be *tyatyu* and *tyaatyu* in Arandic orthography), but they mean, rather, MM(B) and so could only be considered cognate if we assumed a semantic shift from MM(B) to MF. The form *tyatyi* occurs with the meaning MF in Kalkatungu at some distance to the east. The explanation of Kay *tyatye* as an erstwhile reduplicate is a more economical theory than borrowing at this distance without attestation in an intermediate language. These interpretations suggest that the form **atye* can be reconstructed back to pArc; this form has cognates with the shape *ngatyi* in other Pama-Nyungan languages (McConvell, chapter 10, this volume).

The term *nyanye* MM occurs in Kay, Anm, Aly, Ant, and ECAr. In Kay it lacks any inflection (which is supplied by the stem *aytnmenhe*). It is signaled as possibly a Baby Talk form of MM for Anm and ECAr. In most lects where it occurs (except Anm) it is limited to upper-generation senses (MM, MMZ, MMB) and is not used to refer to the corresponding lower-generation senses like fDC. One could suspect that in origin this was a reduplicated form of **anye*. There is, however, no other evidence in the Arandic languages for the short stem **anye*. On the other hand, *nyanye* is also a Baby Talk form for "vegetable food" in ECAr and Anm. This sense is also found in the Warlpiri Baby Talk *nyanya* (Laughren 1984:81).

3.6.3. Stems from Compounds

Arandic kin terms with known etymologies are at most three syllables long. Any longer form can be suspected of being bipartite in origin. This suspicion is reinforced if the stem contains the vowel *a* in a noninitial syllable (which should have changed to *e*) or a consonant cluster consisting of a nasal plus homorganic stop (which should have been reduced to just the nasal by the sound changes). Further support for a compound analysis is found where part of a long kin term stem recurs as part of another form—see the "recurrent partials" *atye-*, *-waleye*, and *arte-* discussed below.

MF has the form *atyemeye* in Anm, *atyemeye* or *ityemeye* in ECAr, and *tyemeye* in WAr. Given that the corresponding inflections are based on the short stem *(a)tye-*, the longer form can be analyzed as an erstwhile compound. The second element is apparently *meye* M and reinforces the maternal element of this grandparental term. Kay for MF has a different term, *atyewaleye*, which appears to share the same first element, *atye-*, combined with a different and not fully explained second element. That same first element, *atye-*, it was argued above (in section 3.6.2), is involved in *tyatye*, from the reduplicated **aty-atye*. We now have three or possibly four pieces of evidence that justify reconstructing back to pArc the form **atye* MF, which in turn is explicable as a reflex of the widespread Pama-Nyungan term **ngatyi*: the short inflected stem *atye-* of the Arrernte *(a)tyemeye*; the Kay reduplicated form *tyatye* (< **aty-atye*); the compound forms *atye-meye* in Arrernte and *atye-waleye* in Kaytetye; and possibly the Anm and Aly (former) compound *artart-etye* (see section 3.5).

Another Kay kin term, *artewaleye* 'female's child', appears to contain the same second element, *-waleye*, combined with a first element that recurs in *artemperre* 'man's child'. The *mp* in the latter form could have been preserved—according to the Arandic sound changes—only in a shorter word of the structure **CVmpVrrV*, where the consonant cluster follows the first syllable. Here I can posit a first element, **arte*, with a meaning something like "child,"[44] followed by a second element that distinguishes between the paternal and the maternal relation. The same element, *-waleye*, would have distinguished "maternal" from "paternal" in Kay *arte.waleye* 'female's child' and (redundantly) signaled the maternal component in the Kay "grandfather" (MF) term *atye.waleye*, as I claim *meye* did in the Arrernte complex form *atye.meye*.

The "father-in-law" term I have reconstructed for pArc as **ahenterre* is suspected of being originally a compound: *ahe-nterre*. The *h* probably reflects *k* after an original long vowel (cf. Koch 1997b), hence **CVVkV*. Semantically a WB is typically regarded as a kind of MB. So I suspect a MB term behind *ahe-*. The term *kaka* MB is widespread in the Pama-Nyungan languages: it is conceivable that behind **ahe-* is a variant with a long vowel, **kaaka*. The second element would go back to the form **CVntVrrV*, and we would expect an in-law meaning. A possible cognate is from Wakaya, the northeastern neighbor of Arandic: *mentirru* means "father-in-law"/"son-in-law." Its prehistorical form should have been something like **mantirrV*.[45]

The term *kamerne* MB occurs in all Arrernte lects except Aly and Ant (which, rather, have *apmarle*) and so is potentially reconstructible to pAr. The vowel *a*, however, is irregular if it descends from the pre-Arc form **CVkamVrnV*. Hence we can suspect that this was in origin a compound consisting of **ake* + *amerne*: both elements may have meant MB. The second element could be cognate with one of the forms beginning with *ngam-* and denoting MB that are found in other Pama-Nyungan languages (and hence possibly derived ultimately from **ngama* M): *ngamarna* in the Thura-Yura languages, *ngamirni* in the Ngumpin-Yapa languages and Warumungu, *ngamirn* in the Mayi languages. The first element may be cognate with the *kaka* MB found in the Karnic and Warluwarric languages to the east and languages of the far west (Nyangumarta, Kariyarra, Ngarluma). Then the Arrernte form may historically have compounded two separate terms for MB.

Kay *arrengkwe* M and Aly *arrwengke* fDDD, mentioned in section 3.4, look like erstwhile compounds because of the preservation of the *ngk* cluster and the rounding to the right of the first consonant. A plausible source would be the compound *arre* + *ngkwe*, the latter part from the earlier **ungke*—with the rounding anticipated on the earlier consonant *rr* in Aly. The first element might be cognate with the *arre-* in *arrere* eZ (section 3.6.4) and may have designated some kind of female.[46] Also reconstructible as compounds with one element that no longer occurs alone are WAr *kw.aye* and LAr *akely.ake* (section 3.6.2).

3.6.4. Stems Incorporating Incremental Syllables

A number of kin term stems contain a final syllable that recurs in other kin terms. Since these terms would otherwise have the phonotactic structure *VCe* (where C may be a single consonant or a cluster), the longer forms may be motivated partially by a preference for longer stems. The addition of increments with unknown negligible semantic function is fairly common in Australian kin terms. The increment *-rti* has been discussed by Nash (1992) and McConvell (2008); the latter also discusses *-ntyarr* and *-ny*. Since most of the relevant Arandic terms lack clear etymologies, an explanation in terms of a shorter stem plus an increment remains hypothetical. In a few instances, however, the case is strengthened by the presence of language-internal variants with a different increment or the existence of possible cognates without the extra syllable.

The MM term that I have reconstructed as **aylpmenhe* is reflected in Kaytetye as *aytnmenhe*, with the lateral replaced by a nasal. There is a variant Kay form, *aytnmerre* (*aypmerre* in Modern Kaytetye). This suggests that an original disyllabic stem received two different increments, *-nhe* and *-rre*. The first recurs in the Arrernte lects as an increment to short interrogative and demonstrative stems (see ECAr *iwe.nhe* 'what', *[a]ngwe.nhe* 'who', *nthe.nhe* 'which one', *nhe.nhe* 'this'—for which the existence of shorter stems justifies the conclusion that these extra syllables are historically increments [Koch 1995]). If *-nhe* is historically an increment in pArc **aylpmenhe* (reflected as *ipmenhe* in some lects), it may also be an increment in pAr **awenhe* FZ. Likewise, if *-rre* is an increment in Kay *aytnmerre*, it may also be an increment in Kay *atyerre* 'younger sibling'.

The pArc term for "male cousin," **a(t)nkele*, has a possible external cognate in the Ngumpin languages—*parnku*, which differs in having a retroflex *rn* in place of an apical *n* (not a huge difference) and in lacking a syllable corresponding to Arandic *le*. The Ngumpin term,

TABLE 8.11. Arandic kin terms possibly incorporating incremental syllables.

Kin Gloss	Language	Form	Pre-Arandic Form	Increment	Cognate
MM	pArc	**aylpmenhe*	**Calmi-*	*nhe/rre*	
FZ	pAr	**awenhe*	**CawV-*	*nhe*	
FZ	Kay	**akele*	**CakV-*	*le*	
MB	Kay	**awele*	**CawV-*	*le*	
mMBC	pArc	**atnkele*	**panku-*	*le*	Ngumpin *parnku*
fMBD	pArc	**altyele*	**CaltyV-*	*le*	
eB	Kay	*alkere*	**CalkV-*	*re*	cf. *alkenhe* 'big'
eZ	Kay	*arrere*	**CarrV-*	*re*	
mC	pAr	**alere*	**CalV-*	*re*	
yB/yZ	Kay	*atyerre*	**CatyV-*	*rre*	

Note: Kay = Kaytetye; pAr = Proto-Arrernte; pArc = Proto-Arandic.

however, is often found with an incremental syllable, usually *rti*. If the Arandic form is cognate, it has also had an increment added to an erstwhile stem, **panku*, which by sound changes would have developed into **a(t)nke*. It is conceivable that the same increment was then added to the corresponding "female cousin" term in pArc, **altyele*, and to the terms for the parents of cross-cousins in Kaytetye, **awele* MB and **akele* FZ—if these were originally disyllabic stems. Note that these four terms share a semantic component of parent's cross-sex sibling.

There is a possible language-internal cognate of Kaytetye *alkere* eB. If *alkenhe* 'big' contains the same original root, *alke-*, we have here the separate increments *re* and *nhe* being added.[47] If eB has absorbed the increment *re* into the stem, it is possible that *arrere* eZ did likewise. The pAr term **alere* 'man's child' may have incorporated the same increment—if it was originally disyllabic.[48] The pre-Arandic forms presupposed by these historical analyses are summarized in Table 8.11.

3.7. Language-Internal Chronology

Any study of etymology needs to take into consideration the chronological differences of the documentary sources.[49] Since Australian languages lack a written history, it might be thought that all sources represent the same era in a language's history. This is not so, since the documentation of Australian languages spans a period of nearly 200 years, depending on the area. For the Arandic languages written documentation began after Europeans entered their territory, with the building of the Overland Telegraph Line beginning in 1872 and the establishment of the Finke River Mission at Hermannsburg in 1877. The introduction of a European economy, consisting largely of cattle stations, with its towns, transport systems, and Aboriginal settlements, led to different patterns of Aboriginal residence and communicative interaction. This has had consequences for the languages, including language shift and lexical changes especially through borrowing. This complicates the task of reconstructing the linguistic history.

Data relevant to kinship terminology are available from early word lists published in compendiums (Curr 1886–87; Taplin 1879), the ethnographical studies by Spencer and Gillen (1899, 1904), and the large unpublished dictionary of Western Arrernte compiled by the Hermannsburg missionary Carl Strehlow by the 1920s (Strehlow n.d.). The imperfect transcription of Arandic words means that these have to be interpreted in the light of modern understandings of their phonology. And the absence of a kin term from a short word list does not necessarily indicate that it was lacking in the lect; nevertheless, the absence of a modern Western Arrernte word in the long dictionary by Strehlow can reasonably be interpreted as an indication that the word came into that lect more recently. Closer to the present, differences in kinship vocabulary between the Modern Kaytetye represented in Turpin and Ross (2012) and the data collected in the 1960s by Kenneth Hale and in the 1970s by me can be attributed to the fact that Modern Kaytetye is heavily influenced by Alyawarr and Anmatyerr, since many current Kaytetye speakers are bilingual in one of these. A few examples will be presented of instances where recent changes in kin terminology can be inferred by respecting the chronology of the documentation.

The term *artarte* MF, which I claimed above was a loanword from Karnic languages, is attested in modern Western Arrernte (as *tartarte*) but is absent from Strehlow's older dictionary. This appears to confirm the scenario that the term spread from the east, even if it has since diffused through WAr to Pintupi/Luritja.

The term *arrwempe*, which I claimed above was borrowed from Western Desert, is attested in all lects of Arandic except Alyawarr. Normally this would be sufficient basis to reconstruct it to Proto-Arandic. I have noted phonological aspects, however, that make such an origin impossible. Its absence from Kaytetye except for the modern version represented in Turpin and Ross (2012), however, shows that it was earlier restricted to the Arrernte lects, where it may well have spread after the dissolution of Proto-Arrernte.

The term *lamparre*, for "man's father-in-law" and the converse, is given in the Kaytetye dictionary (Turpin and Ross 2012). This term has spread widely in modern times, probably through the medium of Pidgin/Kriol/Aboriginal English (Patrick McConvell, personal communication, August 24, 2010). In fact it is indicated to be "Aboriginal English" in Turpin and Ross (2012). Another term that has spread through the same medium is *pantyeye*, occurring in Anm and Kay for "brother-in-law." A related form (sometimes given as *banji*) is found over a large area, including Queensland, as "sibling-in-law" or in some cases "partner" or "sweetheart." In fact, Green mentions its likely etymology: "probably from English 'fancyman'" (2009:465).

Some modern kin terms are obviously borrowed from English, for example, Anm *pape*: "[Baby Talk] dad (from English 'papa')" (Green 2009:465); and Anm *mame*: "[Baby Talk] mother (from English 'mum')" (Green 2009: 410).[50] Interestingly, the English-derived *pape* in WAr is extended to include FB, as is normal in Arandic kinship semantics. The reverse influence of English semantics on Arandic kin terms is also found; for example, the ECAr term for "elder brother," *kake*, can now be used for "brother (older or younger). This was probably only used with this meaning by young children originally but it is now common with many people under 40" (Henderson and Dobson 1994:436). It is important for purposes of reconstruction to distinguish between shared terms that reflect common inheritance from a protolanguage and those that reflect the fact that different lects have borrowed a term from the same source language or one lect has borrowed it and then passed it on to its sister lects in a chain of linguistic borrowing.

3.8. Outstanding Issues

The major portion of Arandic kinship terminology can be explained historically, as I have shown above. Nevertheless, the historical interpretation of a few kin terms remains unresolved. A form for "man's mother-in-law" (WM) and the converse (fDH) seems to be reconstructible as **mwere* at least to pAr on the basis of *mwere* in most Arrernte lects, plus the not unexpected forms (without rounding) *mare* in WAr and *mere* in LAr. The reduplicated form *mweremwere* occurs in Anm, which "may be a more affectionate or respectful way of talking than using *mwer*" (Green 2009:431). The reduplicated form *mweyemweye*, with *y* in place of *r*, occurs in ECAr and Anm and is described for ECAr as "a more casual form of *mwere*, probably from the 'baby talk' style of pronunciation used with babies and young children" (Henderson and Dobson 1994: 487). Anm *mweyemweye*, and its further variant *meyemeye*, "is particularly used when talking to children about people related to them as sons-in-law or mothers-in-law etc." (Green 2009:420). Kay also has the form *meyemeye*.

One issue is whether the Anm and Kay forms represent simplifications of *mweyemweye* (and ultimately *mweremwere*) or whether they were possibly borrowed from or influenced by Warumungu *miyimi*, which also occurs in its northwestern neighbor Warlmanpa. Or was the Warumungu form borrowed from the Arandic languages? The Arrernte form would normally justify a reconstruction to a pAr **mwere*, which would reflect an earlier **umere*. Now an apparent cognate occurs in Western Desert as *umari* or *yumari* (and *wumari* in Manjiljarra), a word for a taboo relative. A term for "taboo relative" in the Yolngu languages of northeast Arnhem Land, *rumaru*, is another apparent cognate.[51] Unfortunately, according to the established sound changes, Arandic *mwere* should, rather, be the reflex of a form whose initial consonant was a nasal; otherwise it should be **pmwere* with a prestopped nasal—barring an irregular loss of the prestopping. On the other hand, if Arandic has borrowed the term from the Western Desert languages, we would expect its form to be **mware*, with its middle vowel *a* preserved. I tentatively treat pAr **mwere* as resulting, via an irregular but not unprecedented loss of prestopping, from an inherited **pmwere*, which in turn is the reflex of the form **yumari* cognate with the Western Desert term.[52]

TABLE 8.12. Reconstructed Arandic kin terms, by generation.

Generation	Kin Gloss	Language	Form	Pre-Arandic Form
2	FF	pArc	**arrenge*	**CarrVng(k)V*
2	FM	pArc	**aperle*	**kaparli*
2	MM	pArc	**aylpmenhe*	**Calmi-*
2	MF	pArc	**atye*	**ngatyi*
+1	M	pArc	**ame-*	**ngama*
+1	MB	pArc	**amerne*	**ngamVrnV*
+1	FZ	pAr	**awenhe*	**CawV-*
+1	F	pAr	**akngeye*	**CangV-*
+1	F	pUpAr	**ayne-*	**Na(r)ni*[a]
0	cousin (m.)	pArc	**atnkele*	**panku-*
0	cousin (f.)	pArc	**altyele*	**CaltyV-*
0	eB	pAr	**ake-*	**CakV*
0	eZ	pAr	**aye*	**CayV*
0	yB/yZ	pAr	**ayteye*	**Ca(r)tiyV*
–1	mC	pAr	**alere*	**CalV-*
–1	fC	pAr	**ampe*	**CampV*
1af	HM	pArc	**anherre*	**ngunharri*
1af	WF	pArc	**ahenterre*	**CVVkV + *mantirrV*
1af	WF	pAr	**mwere*	**yumari*
0af	HZ	pArc	**arntenge*	**CarntOngV*[b]
0af	WB	pArc	**mpwerne*	**ngumparna*

Note: pAr = Proto-Arrernte; pArc = Proto-Arandic; pUpAr = Proto–Upper Arrernte.
[a] N indicates an unspecified nasal consonant.
[b] O indicates a vowel that must have been *u* or *a* but could not have been *i*.

4. Summary and Conclusions

My reconstruction has involved comparing forms of similar meaning across the Arandic lects and to other Pama-Nyungan languages. Taking into account their distribution across the lects, as well as the chronology of their attestation in the documentation, terms have been reconstructed to different chronological levels: Proto-Arandic, Proto-Arrernte, and Proto–Upper Arrernte. Some terms have been identified as innovations in restricted areas within the Arandic domain. Some have been found to be loanwords from languages to the west (Western Desert or Warlpiri) or from Karnic languages to the south and east. Some terms can be explained as having been built out of language-internal material, including compounding elements, reduplication of the stem, absorption of an inflectional suffix (especially the 1Sg *-ye*), or the addition of an incremental syllable of uncertain function. The positing of earlier compounds and reduplications is justified in a large measure by the fact that these patterns occur synchronically, as established in section 2.2.

In the process I have illustrated the methods of linguistic reconstruction, especially as they apply to the more formal aspects of kinship terminology. This exercise has involved much more intricate reasoning than is normal for Australian languages—because the drastic phonological changes undergone by the Arandic languages have resulted in much reworking of the relevant vocabulary, as many inherited words became too short and/or ambiguous to be viable lexemes without some kind of expansion. The formal aspects of this study are intended to complement the study of semantic aspects of kinship reconstruction and change, whether focused on individual kin terms

(McConvell, chapter 10, this volume) or whole systems (Keen, this volume).

The study of the Arandic *forms* of kin terms needs to be complemented by a study of the *semantics* of each kin term, especially the various extensions that are made from the basic sense of each. This can be done (and will be done within my project) using the copious data included in the AUSTKIN database, which has drawn on the comprehensive dictionaries of several lects. Green (1998) is another rich source on kinship usage that will be exploited in this endeavor.

The results of my Arandic reconstructions are summarized in Table 8.12. (The glosses are what are considered the most basic senses, and other senses are not indicated.) The forms are sorted according to generation and consanguineal versus affinal nature. Indications are given about which level of protolanguage each can be attributed to—Proto-Arandic, Proto-Arrernte, or Proto–Upper Arrernte. It emerges clearly from these results that a system of four separate grandparental terms, plus a set of cross-cousin terms separate from sibling-in-law terms, can be reconstructed to the highest level, that is, Proto-Arandic. This strongly supports the assertion made at the beginning of the chapter that the Proto-Arandic kinship system belonged to Radcliffe-Brown's "Aranda" type of Australian kinship classification—whose terminology distinguishes four grandparental terms and presupposes marriage between people classed as second cousins (cf. Scheffler 1978:42). From this we can conclude that this system was not a recent development within the culture of the Arandic-speaking peoples but was already in place among their Proto-Arandic-speaking ancestors.

Appendix: Supplementary Examples of Complex Kin Terms

TABLE 8.A1. Arandic phrasal kin terms including *big* and *little*.

Lect	Kin Gloss	Form	Literal Gloss
WAr	FeB	*kngeye kngerre*	father big
CAr	FeB	*akngeye akngerre*	father big
WAr	FeB	*karte kngerre*	father big
WAr	MeZ	*meye kngerre*	mother big
WAr	FeZ	*wenhe kngerre*	auntie big
WAr	WeZ/HeB	*newe kngerre*	spouse big
WAr	eZH	*mparne kngerre*	brother-in-law big
ECAr	eZ	*yaye akngerre*	sister big
WAr	FyB	*karte kweke*	father little
CAr	FyB	*akngeye akweke*	father little
NEAr	FyB	*akngeye akelye*	father little
WAr	MyZ	*meye kweke*	mother little
WAr	FyZ	*wenhe kweke*	auntie little
ECAr	yZ	*yaye akweke*	sister little
WArSt	FyB	*karte lere*	father *little
WArSt	MyZ	*meye lere*	mother *little
WArSt	WyZ/HyB	*newe lere*	spouse *little
WArSt	yZH	*mparne lere*	brother-in-law *little

Note: CAr = Central Arrernte; ECAr = Eastern and Central Arrernte; NEAr = Northeastern Arrernte; WAr = Western Arrernte; WArSt = Western Arrernte from Strehlow n.d.

TABLE 8.A2. Arandic phrases with *boy* and *girl* as modifiers.

Lect	Gloss	Form	Literal Gloss
ECAr	boy	*ampe urreye*	child + boy/male
ECAr	girl	*ampe marle*	child + girl/woman/female
WAr-B	D	*ketyeye kwarre*	(woman's) child + girl
WAr-B	S	*ketyeye werre*	(woman's) child + boy
WAr-B	fBC	*ketyeye lere*	(woman's) child + man's child

Note: ECAr = Eastern and Central Arrernte; WAr-B = Western Arrernte from Breen 2000.

TABLE 8.A3. Western Arrernte phrasal kin expressions with a "classifier" as the first member.

Kin Gloss	Form	Literal Gloss
MM, MMZ	*lyurre ipmenhe*	senior female + MM
FM, FMZ	*lyurre perle*	senior female + FM
WFM	*lyurre arrenge*	senior female + FF
WMF	*kngeye ipmenhe*	senior male + MM
WMF	*kngerretye ipmenhe*	senior male + MM
FMB, WFF	*kngeye perle*	senior male + FM
FMB, WFF	*kngerretye perle*	senior male + FM
MMB	*kelye ipmenhe*	male + MM
[f]DD[a]	*kweye ipmenhe*	junior female + MM
[f]SD, [Z]SD	*kweye perle*	junior female + FM
ZDS	*weye ipmenhe*	junior male + MM
[f]DS	*werre ipmenhe*	junior male + MM
[f]SS, [Z]SS	*weye perle*	junior male + FM
[BDS]	*weye tyemeye*	junior male + MF
[mSS]	*weye arrenge*	junior male + FF

Note: Not all combinations are attested, but those phrases and glosses that are listed in Strehlow n.d. are given in Table 8.A4. (Note that the system presupposes the following equivalences between one's own and one's spouse's grandparents: FF = SpFM, FM = SpFF, MM = SpMF, MF = SpMM.)

[a] Elements in brackets indicate semantic features inferred but not explicitly given in the source.

TABLE 8.A4. Compound kin terms in Lower Arrernte.

Term	Kin Gloss	First Element	Second Element
akely-irteye	yB	male	younger sibling
akely-ake	eB	male	*eB[a]
akely-ankele	cousin (m.)	male	male cross-cousin
akely-alere	mS	male	male's child
kwey-alere	D?	girl	male's child
kwey-irteye	yZ	girl	younger sibling
kw-irteye	yZ	girl	younger sibling
kwe-ltyele	cousin (f.)	girl	female cross-cousin
kw-ampe	ZD	girl	female's child
kungkere[b]	eZ	girl	eZ
kw-arntenge	fZil	girl	female sibling-in-law
wey-alere	mS	boy	male's child
awey-irteye	yB	boy	younger sibling
w-alere	fBS	boy	male's child
w-irteye	yB	boy	younger sibling
werre-irteye	yB	boy	younger sibling
werre-ake	eB	boy	*eB
akng-arrenge	FF	senior male	FF
aknge-rtarte	MF	senior male	MF
akng-ipmenhe	MMB	senior male	MM
aknge-mperne	WB	senior male	brother-in-law
alywe-rtarte	MFZ	senior female	MF

[a] See section 3.6.2 for the reconstruction of the stem **ake* eB.

[b] Interpreted as *kw-ungkere* (cf. section 3.5).

Notes

This research was supported by the Australian Research Council's Discovery Projects funding scheme (project number DP0878556), the Australian National University (ANU), and the Centre National de la Recherche Scientifique through the Centre de Recherche et de Documentation sur l'Océanie (CREDO). The software for this project was developed by Laurent Dousset of CREDO and uses a geospatial interface developed by the Research School of Humanities at ANU using the AUSTLANG (http://austlang.aiatsis.gov.au/disclaimer.php) coordinates and language list developed by Kazuko Obata of the Australian Institute of Aboriginal and Torres Strait Islander Studies. Original forms and glosses of terms cited in this chapter are found in the AustKin project database at http://austkin.pacific-credo.fr/. I thank Patrick McConvell, David Nash, and Jane Simpson for comments on an earlier draft of this chapter.

1. For more detailed discussion of the Arandic lects and a description of Arandic phonology, see Breen 2001.
2. Breen (2001) and Breen and Pensalfini (1999) analyze words as ending in a consonant and treat the final *e* as being predictable and hence not part of the phonological representation of the word. This analysis underlies the orthographical system of Alyawarr and Anmatyerr, where final vowels

are not indicated. In this chapter words from all the lects are standardized to an orthography that does employ final vowels.

3. See section 3.7 for more on the value of early sources.
4. While contemporary Western Arrernte lacks person inflection, first- and third-person forms are present in Carl Strehlow's (n.d.) dictionary. This shows that the inflection was given up within the last century.
5. For dyadic constructions in general, see Evans 2006. In Central Australian Aboriginal English, dyadic relationships are expressed by terms such as *father-gether*, with *-gether* (from the English *together*) rendering the Arandic suffix *-nhenge* (Koch 2000).
6. In WAr *kantyenye* 'younger' is also used as a modifier—to three terms for father: *karte*, *kngeye*, and *kngerretye*.
7. Here *auntie* is used—as is normal in Australian kinship terminologies—to denote "father's sister."
8. For "big brother-in-law" (eZH) in WAr the elder sibling is the linking relative: this kin term is given in Strehlow n.d.
9. Strehlow's earlier dictionary gives "child" as the only sense of *ketyeye* (spelled *katjia*). The same polysemy that Breen (2001) reports is found for the Warlpiri *kurdu* (David Nash and Jane Simpson, personal communication, August 8, 2010).
10. Elements in brackets indicate semantic features inferred but not explicitly given in the source.
11. The source says: "*woialirra* cf. alirra son, daughter; *woiambe* cf. amba (mother's son or daughter; nephew sr's son)" (Strehlow n.d.).
12. The *e* automatically drops before another vowel.
13. The tap/trill *rr* in *werre* was heard as *l*—which was not uncommon in early word lists recorded by linguistic amateurs.
14. One form, *akngepeye*, given by Breen (2001) as MM cannot be explained. It does not denote a male relative, and the second element *-peye* is unknown.
15. An alternative scenario, according to which *aperle* was borrowed separately into all the Arandic lects (presumably from Western Desert), appears to me to be much less likely; for instance, the middle vowel would be expected to be *a*.
16. Cf. Kay *atnnge* 'eye' beside the Arrernte *alknge*. The sound change is articulated by Breen (2001:58) for Northern Alyawarr, which is like Kaytetye in its phonology.
17. Cf. "drop of water," with its variants Aly *aylmerr*, *aypmerr*, *iypmerr* versus Anm *aypmerr*, *ipmerr*; and Anm *aylpmerr-* 'sleep a lot' versus Aly *iypmerr-* 'sleep all day'.
18. The form *pankula* recorded for Ngarinyman is liable to be rather a dyadic form, *parnku-rla* 'cousin-gether' (Patrick McConvell, personal communication, August 24, 2010).
19. "With bilabials...we have a regular loss of roundness from the WAr form, often with the change of the vowel from /e/ to /a/:...[Central Arrernte] *mpwerne* and [WAr] *mparne* 'brother-in-law'; *mwere* and *mare* 'mother-in-law'" (Breen 2001:65).
20. The form *karntiya* WB occurring in Ngumpin-Yapa languages, Ganggalida *karntiya* W, and the Nyikina dyadic *karnti-rangu* 'man plus W or WB' are unlikely to be cognate, because the *i* vowel following should have caused the *rnt* to become prepalatalized in Arandic.
21. For the changing usage of *ngunyarri* in Warumungu, including its present sense HM/fSW, see Simpson, this volume.
22. It is also found in Warlmanpa, the sister language of Warlpiri, as *wantiyi*.
23. Its resemblance to the widespread **mukul* FZ is suggestive. However, this etymon should have left a trace of *u* in the rounding of the following consonant: we would expect the Kay form to be **kwele* or **akwele*.
24. The Yandruwandha form *ngalari* 'sister's child' could be cognate on the basis of phonological correspondences, but the differences between the Arandic "male's child" or "son's child" and the Yandruwandha "sister's [and presumably female's] child" would have to be accounted for. The same semantic problem would hold for seeing a possible cognate in Jaru (Ngumpin) *ngalayi* fC (with a different third syllable). A better semantic fit is found in the Warlpiri and Warlmanpa *ngalapi* mC, which also fails to match the third syllable.
25. If a Proto–Upper Arrernte form has cognates from outside Arandic, it would have been present in Proto-Arrernte and perhaps Proto-Arandic as well (but lost in the other lects). It may therefore not have been a lexical innovation in Proto–Upper Arrernte—unless the innovation consisted in a semantic association with the kin term meaning "father."
26. "Female's child" in WAr; this information is not specified in the Breen (2001) LAr source.
27. Cf. Scheffler 1978:155–161 (on the "Mongkan" system on Cape York Peninsula).
28. In some lects this is considered a Baby Talk form (see section 3.6.2).
29. Cf. Breen: "The initial *k* probably results from prefixing of *kw-* which occurs with some kinship terms referring to females" (2001:67).
30. The term *makurnta* also occurs in Warlpiri, where it refers to in-laws in general (Hale [1995] glosses it as "opposite matrimoiety [from ego's]"), and in Warlmanpa, where it refers to the mother-in-law/son-in-law relation.
31. The same term was apparently borrowed into Warumungu, where it is a "special word...which emphasizes the respect that must be shown between two families related by marriage" (Simpson 2002:35).
32. It is also conceivable that it was borrowed after the main Arandic sound changes took place but was adapted by the normal truncation of the initial consonant and, in addition, by substituting *yl* for *l* before *i* in imitation of the historical sound changes—if the latter change could be supported by further examples (see Koch 1997a:32–36 for principles of loanword analysis between Warlpiri and Kaytetye).
33. Here the initial *u* suggests a regular change from the earlier form **nwewe* (cf. Breen 2001:67).
34. This term is found from the westernmost to the easternmost Pama-Nyungan languages.
35. Perhaps this adaptation was due in part to the rarity of initial consonants in pAr, since all inherited initial consonants were lost by sound change (Koch 1997b).

36. See Hendery and McConvell, this volume, for a discussion of Baby Talk forms in general.
37. Unless *ngartarta* was borrowed from Wangkangurru after the initial *ng* had already been lost in that language.
38. It is uncertain whether the direction of change with the Karnic languages was MF > FF in Pitta-Pitta and Wangka-Yutjurru or FF > MF in the rest of the languages. Note that *kami* has shifted from MM to FM in most Karnic languages (McConvell 2013).
39. *Meye* is not citable for Ant, which attests *matye, mangkwe, meyekwe*, and *menhenge*.
40. Note that some short terms for body parts have also been replaced by longer alternatives in Arrernte: ECAr *akaperte* 'head' (versus Kay *ake*) and *arrakerte* 'mouth' (versus Kay *arre*).
41. Variants with and without the initial *y* are common in the eastern varieties of the Western Desert language.
42. O'Grady and Fitzgerald (1997:353) wrongly reconstruct a Proto-Pama-Nyungan term for "elder sister" on the basis of a supposedly cognate relation between Pintupi *yayi* and Dyirbal *yayin* eZ. This mistake shows the necessity of identifying loanwords in the enterprise of reconstruction.
43. I assume that this form has been totally replaced in Aly by the (borrowed) term *angkwere*.
44. According to Patrick McConvell (personal communication, August 24, 2010), Gurindji has the term *karu* 'child', which derives by lenition from **kartu*; this could be a cognate.
45. An *i* vowel in the second syllable, however, should have caused the preceding *nt* to become prepalatized to *ynt*. So an etymology with a different second vowel would be preferable.
46. The Aly term for fDDS is *arraynge*, which looks like another compound with *arre-* as the first element.
47. For Aly *alkenh* a possible use of *big* is in the sense "eldest," e.g., *awey atyenh alkenh* 'my eldest boy', literally "boy my big" (Green 1992:24).
48. For example, if Warlpiri and Warlmanpa *ngalapi* mC is cognate, with a different increment added to the disyllabic stem **ngala*.
49. For a fuller discussion of the chronology of kin terms in an Australian language, see Simpson, this volume.
50. See Hendery and McConvell, this volume, on *papa* and *mama* in traditional Australian languages.
51. It remains to be established that the Western Desert *y-* corresponds to the Yolngu *r-*.
52. The Kaytetye form should have lost the rounding of the first vowel after an initial palatal, according to a sound change established in Koch 2007. So Kay *meyemeye* may represent a (Baby Talk) reduplication of the form **mere*, which in turn was a reflex, via **yimari* and loss of prestopping, of **yumari*.

References Cited

Bowern, C., B. Evans, G. Koch, and L. Miceli. 2008. Introduction. In *Morphology and Language History: In Honour of Harold Koch*. C. Bowern, B. Evans, and L. Miceli, eds. Pp. 1–11. Current Issues in Linguistic Theory, 298. Amsterdam: John Benjamins.

Bowern, C., and H. Koch, eds. 2004. *Australian Languages: Classification and the Comparative Method*. Current Issues in Linguistic Theory, 249. Amsterdam: John Benjamins.

Breen, G. 1997. Lower Arrernte wordlist. Typescript. Alice Springs, Australia: IAD Press.

Breen, G. 2000. *Introductory Dictionary of Western Arrernte*. Alice Springs, Australia: IAD Press.

Breen, G. 2001. The Wonders of Arandic Phonology. In *Forty Years On: Ken Hale and Australian Languages*. J. Simpson, D. Nash, M. Laughren, P. Austin, and B. Alpher, eds. Pp. 45–69. Pacific Linguistics, 512. Canberra: Australian National University.

Breen, G. 2002. Antekerrepenh wordlist. Electronic file, Institute for Aboriginal Development, Alice Springs, Australia.

Breen, G., and R. Pensalfini. 1999. Arrernte: A Language with No Syllable Onsets. *Linguistic Inquiry* 30:1–25.

Campbell, L., and W. J. Poser. 2008. *Language Classification: History and Method*. Cambridge: Cambridge University Press.

Curr, E. M. 1886–87. *The Australian Race: Its Origin, Languages, Customs, Place of Landing in Australia, and the Routes by which It Spread Itself over That Continent*. Melbourne: J. Ferres, Government Printer.

Dixon, R. 1997. *The Rise and Fall of Languages*. Cambridge: Cambridge University Press.

Dixon, R. 2001. The Australian Linguistic Area. In *Areal Diffusion and Genetic Inheritance: Problems in Comparative Linguistics*. A. Y. Aikhenvald and R. Dixon, eds. Pp. 64–104. Oxford: Oxford University Press.

Dixon, R. 2002. *The Australian Languages: Their Nature and Development*. Cambridge: Cambridge University Press.

Evans, N. 2006. Dyadic Constructions. In *Encyclopedia of Language and Linguistics*, vol. 4. K. Brown, ed. Pp. 24–28. Oxford: Elsevier.

Green, J. 1992. *Alyawarr to English Dictionary*. Alice Springs, Australia: Institute for Aboriginal Development.

Green, J. 1998. *Kin and Country: Aspects of the Use of Kin Terms in Arandic Languages*. Melbourne: University of Melbourne, Linguistics and Applied Linguistics.

Green, J. 2009. *Central and Eastern Anmatyerr to English Dictionary*. Alice Springs, Australia: IAD Press.

Hale, K. 1962. Internal Relationships in Arandic of Central Australia. In *Handbook of Australian Languages, pt. 2: Some Linguistic Types in Australia*. A. Capell, ed. Pp. 171–183. Oceania Linguistic Monographs, 7. Sydney: University of Sydney.

Hale, K. 1995. *An Elementary Warlpiri Dictionary*. Alice Springs, Australia: IAD Press.

Henderson, J., and V. Dobson. 1994. *Eastern and Central Arrernte to English Dictionary*. Alice Springs, Australia: Institute for Aboriginal Development.

Koch, H. 1995. The Creation of Morphological Zeroes. In *Yearbook of Morphology 1994*. G. Booij and J. van Marle, eds. Pp. 31–71. Dordrecht: Kluwer Academic.

Koch, H. 1996. Reconstruction in Morphology. In *The Comparative Method Reviewed: Regularity and Irregularity in Language Change*. M. Durie and M. Ross, eds. Pp. 218–263. New York: Oxford University Press.

Koch, H. 1997a. Comparative Linguistics and Australian Prehistory. In *Archaeology and Linguistics: Aboriginal Australia in Global Perspective*. P. McConvell and N. Evans, eds. Pp. 27–43. Melbourne: Oxford University Press.

Koch, H. 1997b. Pama-Nyungan Reflexes in the Arandic Languages. In *Boundary Rider: Essays in Honour of Geoffrey O'Grady*. D. Tryon and M. Walsh, eds. Pp. 271–302. Pacific Linguistics C-136. Canberra: Australian National University.

Koch, H. 2000. Central Australian Aboriginal English: In Comparison with the Morphosyntactic Categories of Kaytetye. *Asian Englishes: An International Journal of the Sociolinguistics of English in Asia/Pacific* 3(2):32–58.

Koch, H. 2001. Basic Vocabulary of the Arandic Languages: From Classification to Reconstruction. In *Forty Years On: Ken Hale and Australian Languages*. J. Simpson, D. Nash, M. Laughren, P. Austin, and B. Alpher, eds. Pp. 71–87. Pacific Linguistics, 512. Canberra: Australian National University.

Koch, H. 2003. Morphological Reconstruction as an Etymological Method. In *Historical Linguistics 2001: Selected Papers from the 15th International Conference on Historical Linguistics, Melbourne, 13–17 August 2001*. B. J. Blake and K. Burridge, eds. Pp. 271–291. Amsterdam: John Benjamins.

Koch, H. 2004. The Arandic Subgroup of Australian Languages. In *Australian Languages: Classification and the Comparative Method*. C. Bowern and H. Koch, eds. Pp. 127–150. Current Issues in Linguistic Theory, 249. Amsterdam: John Benjamins.

Koch, H. 2007. Divergent Regularity in Word-Initial Truncation in the Arandic Languages. In *Description, History and Development: Linguistic Indulgence in Memory of Terry Crowley*. D. Eades, J. Lynch, and J. Siegel, eds. Pp. 267–280. Amsterdam: John Benjamins.

Laughren, M. 1982. Warlpiri Kinship Structure. In *Languages of Kinship in Aboriginal Australia*. J. Heath, F. Merlan, and A. Rumsey, eds. Pp. 72–85. Oceania Linguistic Monographs, 24. Sydney: University of Sydney.

Laughren, M. 1984. Warlpiri Baby Talk. *Australian Journal of Linguistics* 4:73–88.

McConvell, P. 2008. Grand-Daddy Morphs: The Importance of Suffixes in Reconstructing Pama-Nyungan Kinship. In *Morphology and Language History: In Honour of Harold Koch*. C. Bowern, B. Evans, and L. Miceli, eds. Pp. 313–327. Current Issues in Linguistic Theory, 298. Amsterdam: John Benjamins.

McConvell, P. 2013. "Granny Got Cross": Semantic Change from "Mother's Mother" to "Father's Mother" in Pama-Nyungan. In *Lexical and Structural Etymology: Beyond Word Histories*. R. Mailhammer, ed. Studies in Language Change. Berlin: De Gruyter Mouton.

Meggitt, M. 1962. *Desert People: A Study of the Walbiri Aborigines of Central Australia*. Sydney: Angus and Robertson.

Nash, D. 1979. *Preliminary Vocabulary of the Warlmanpa Language*. Cambridge: Massachusetts Institute of Technology.

Nash, D. 1992. An Australian Kinship Affix *-rti*. *Australian Journal of Linguistics* 12:123–144.

O'Grady, G., and S. Fitzgerald. 1997. Cognate Search in the Pama-Nyungan Language Family. In *Archaeology and Linguistics: Aboriginal Australia in Global Perspective*. P. McConvell and N. Evans, eds. Pp. 341–355. Melbourne: Oxford University Press.

Scheffler, H. W. 1978. *Australian Kin Classification*. Cambridge: Cambridge University Press.

Simpson, J. 2002. *A Learner's Guide to Warumungu: Mirlamirlajinijiki Warumumunguku apparrka*. Alice Springs, Australia: IAD Press.

Spencer, B., and F. Gillen. 1899. *The Native Tribes of Central Australia*. London: Macmillan.

Spencer, B., and F. Gillen. 1904. *The Northern Tribes of Central Australia*. London: Macmillan.

Strehlow, C. N.d. Aranda–Loritja–English Dictionary. Unpublished MS, Australian Institute of Aboriginal and Torres Strait Islander Studies, Canberra.

Sutton, P., and H. Koch. 2008. Australian Languages: A Singular Vision. Review of R. M. W. Dixon, *Australian Languages: Their Nature and Development*, 2002. *Journal of Linguistics* 44:471–504.

Swan, C., and M. Cousins. 1993. *A Learner's Wordlist of Pertame*. Alice Springs, Australia: Institute for Aboriginal Development.

Taplin, G. 1879. *The Folklore, Manner, Customs, and Languages of the South Australian Aborigines*. Adelaide: Government Printer.

Turpin, M., and A. Ross. 2012. *Kaytetye to English Dictionary*. Alice Springs, Australia: IAD Press.

9

Desertification of an Arandic Dialect

Barry Alpher

Kinship terminologies classify types of relatives in ways appropriate to social understandings and arrangements, and changes in social circumstances can be reflected in changed kinship classifications. Population movement and language contact, bringing with them new marriage patterns, ideas of kinship group membership, and land-tenure beliefs and practices, can stimulate conflations and new distinctions among kin categories. This chapter considers a case of such change in Lower Arrernte (LA), an Arandic language of the southern end of the Northern Territory and northern South Australia, whose speakers have intermarried with speakers of dialects of the Western Desert (WD) language. Kinship terminological categorizations in the two languages are dissimilar.

Languages of the Arandic subfamily (of Pama-Nyungan, Australia) are spoken on the northern, western, and southern fringes of the Simpson Desert in Australia (Figure 9.1) and in good years were spoken far into its interior. The kinship terminological data reported on here, relating to the Lower Arrernte (also called Lower Southern Arrernte) language of this family, were gathered in 1984 and 1985 in Finke, Oodnadatta, Eringa, Hamilton, Dalhousie, and Kulgera in the course of preparing documentation of traditional attachment for the Simpson Desert land claim under the Aboriginal Land Rights (N.T.) Act of 1973.[1]

Kinship terminologies of the Aranda type have as one of their properties the distinction among four types of grandparents: father's father (and his sister), mother's father (and his sister), father's mother (and her brother), and mother's mother (and her brother). The terminology distinguishes the descent lines of the males of these four types, down to the second descending (grandchild) generation, for which the corresponding grandparental terms are, in the common Australian way, repeated (see Figure 9.2).[2]

Among Arandic-speaking peoples, an individual's affiliation to a given piece of land can come via the male line, involving ceremonial performance responsibilities; via the mother's patriline, involving ceremonial management; or through prolonged residence, birth, conception, or exceptional attention to ceremonial duties.[3] The town of Finke, Northern Territory, is in the country of Southern and Lower Arrernte speakers. Because it is located on the former route of (having come into being because of) the Port Augusta–Alice Springs railway line ("The Ghan")[4] and has been a source of railway-related employment, it has attracted Aboriginal migrants from country to the west. These people speak one or another Western Desert dialect, of which the most mentioned one is Yankuntjatjarra (see Figure 9.1).

The kinship terminology of the WD languages of this region is largely characterized by single terms (one for each gender). This system designates grandparents and grandchildren of all kin types under a single term for males and another single term for females: see the terms in the right-hand column of Table 9.1.[5]

In "Desertified" LA, certain aspects of the traditional kin terminology have been altered on the model of WD terminology. Although the grandparent terms are unmodified from the old system, the grandchild terms conflate categories in the WD way (*rtartarte* 'woman's daughter's child'/'man's sister's daughter's child' > *arrengarrenge*, originally only "man's son's child"). It is worth noting that the kinship terms in the Arandic languages of areas bordering varieties of the WD language reflect WD influence in making gender distinctions in certain kin types not made (or not made in a systematic way) in more conservative varieties of Arandic (Figure 9.3; and see Koch, this volume, especially Tables 8.6 and 8.7, for comprehensive lists of Western and Lower Arrernte terms). There are other influences from WD, such as (sporadic) first-syllable stress in vowel-initial words (the normal Arandic pattern

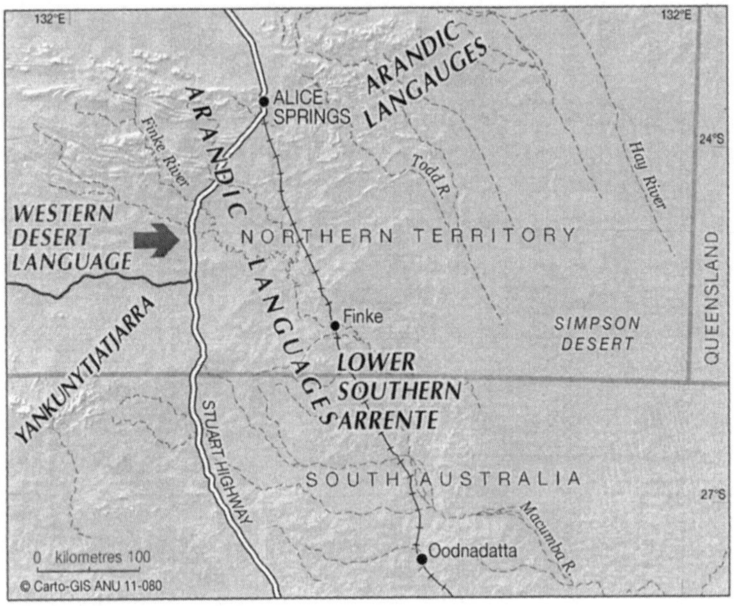

FIGURE 9.1. Languages of the Arandic subfamily.

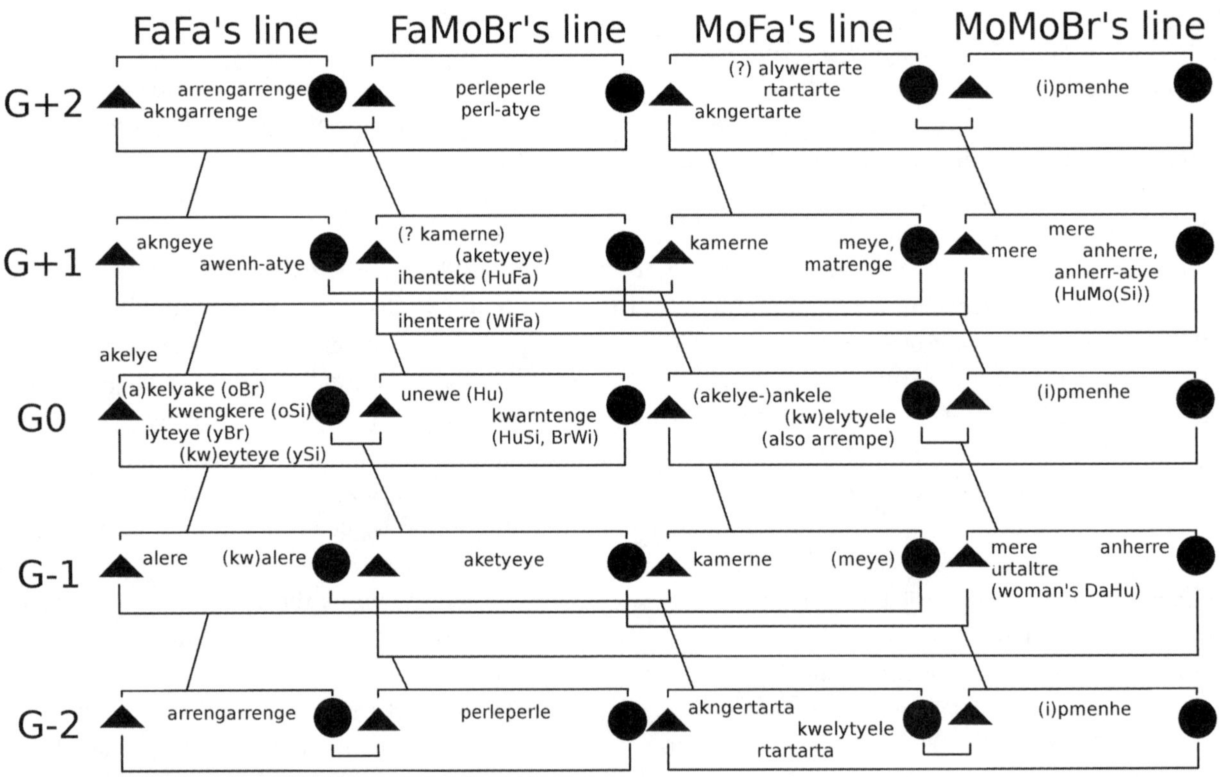

FIGURE 9.2. Lower Arrernte kinship terminology.

is to stress the first vowel after a consonant), for example, *Úrrempele* (an important dreaming) and *árrengàrrenge* (*~arréngarrènge*) 'father's father'.[6]

WD land tenure differs from that of Arrernte in placing much greater emphasis on birthplace and residence and little or no emphasis on patrilines and the differentiation of responsibilities according to patriline—as is consistent with the kinship terminology. It is easier to maintain, over generations, an affiliation to a distant and rarely visited place in the Arrernte system than it is

TABLE 9.1. Lower Arrernte (LA) GRAND (G+2, G–2) terms, conservative and Desertified, in comparison with Western Desert terms for the corresponding kin.

Standard LA Form	Kin Gloss	Desertified LA Form	Western Desert Form	
			Male	Female
arrengarrenge	FF, FFZ	*arrengarrenge*	*tjamu*	*kami*
arrengarrenge	mSC, (f)BSC	*arrengarrenge*	*tjamu*	*kami*
perl+	FM, FMB		*tjamu*	*kami*
perl+	wSC, (m)ZSC		*tjamu*	*kami*
rtartarte	MF, MFZ	*rtartarte*	*tjamu*	*kami*
rtartarte	mDC, (w)BDC	*arrengarrenge*	*tjamu*	*kami*
(i)pmenhe	MM, MMB		*tjamu*	*kami*
(i)pmenhe	wDC, (m)ZDC		*tjamu*	*kami*

Note: Where gaps stand in this table, the term is not recorded in my Finke genealogies. Koch (this volume), citing Breen 1997, has *perle-* and *ipmenhe*.

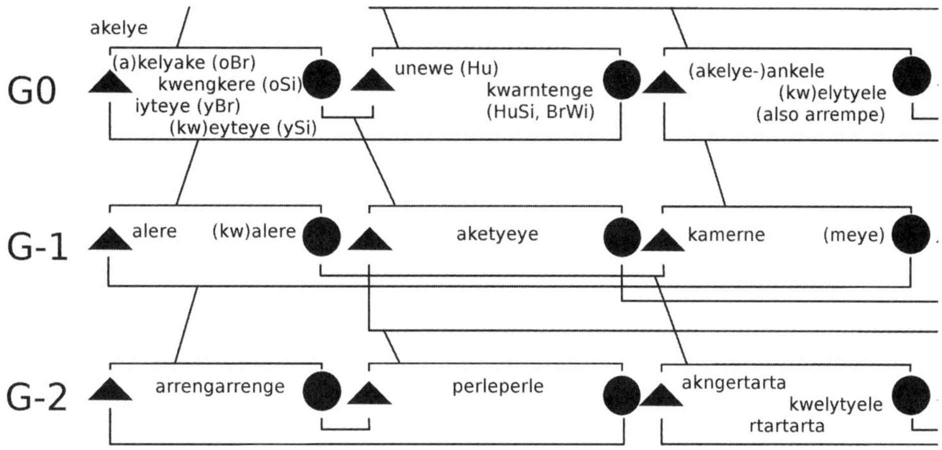

FIGURE 9.3. Lower Arrernte (conservative) G0, G–1, and G–2 terms: FF, FMB, and MF lines.

under the WD system. It is, then, possible to interpret the LA conflation of grandchild terms under the "man's son's children" (*arrengarrenge*) head as reflecting a subsuming of a man's daughter's children (no matter how distant the country of their WD parent) under his own patriline's (*arrengarrengekenhe*) country.

The interpretation of the first descending generation (G–1) terminology is, however, not so simple. Here kin of one's children's generation (at least, children of a male ego and children of a female ego) are subsumed, as in WD languages, under a single category, but the Arrernte term chosen is *aketyeye*, standardly used only of a woman's children and a man's sister's children.[7] The logic posited above (subsumption into ego's patriline) for the G–2 terms fails here, since under it the use of the "man's child"/"woman's brother's child" (*alere*) category would be expected (Figure 9.3 and Table 9.2). Note especially that a male ego's children are also *aketyeye*, not *alere*.

Arrernte of this area have a four-section ("skin") system (pairs displayed vertically are related as mother and child):

Penangke = Perrurle
Kemarre = Peltharre

An actual genealogy is shown in Figure 9.4.

Whereas ego's terminology (Figure 9.4) for relatives in generations above his own (not shown) is conservative, that for his own children and his grandchildren through his daughter is not, and his daughter's children's reciprocal usage toward him fluctuates. This man's use of *aketyeye* for his own children is not a matter of a wrong marriage, and the section terminology (Kemarre, children of a male Perrurle) is correct.

The kin term *aketyeye*, recorded only in this southwestern Arrernte-speaking area and meaning "woman's child" in the conservative varieties, appears to be a loanword from WD *katja* 'male child (from either parent's point of view)'.[8] The LA G–1 terms *alere* 'child [to male]' and *ampe* 'child [to female]' are reconstructed to the Proto-Arrernte (that is, Arandic minus Kaytetye) **alere* and **ampe*, respectively (Koch, this volume, Table 8.11).[9] A scenario for the importation of *katja* (as *aketyeye*, constructed according to one of the normal phonological Arandization processes)[10] would be its usage by an in-marrying WD woman toward her own children, taken by speakers of Arrernte as a first language as the exact equivalent of, and replacement for, the indigenous **ampe*.

The generalization of *aketyeye* to "man's child," recorded only for the extended family part of whose genealogy is shown in Figure 9.4,[11] can be seen as an extension of terminological patriline neutralization already manifested in the G–2 terms,[12] facilitated by bilinguals' consciousness that WD *katja* and Arrernte *aketyeye* are otherwise equivalent.

The system at the time of recording was evidently in flux toward a more thoroughly WD classification, but people were unwavering in their self-identification as Arrernte. The evident terminological changes seem to be more an accommodation of the old system to in-marrying newcomers than a WD "takeover."

TABLE 9.2. Gendered forms of certain Lower Arrernte kin terms.

Term	Kin Gloss
With *akng* from *akngeye* 'father'[a]	
akngertarte	MF, MBSSS
rtartarte	MF, MFZ, MBSSC
akngerrenge	FF
arengarrenge	FF, FFZ, mSC
With *kw* from *kweye* 'girl'[b]	
kweyteye	Z
iyteye	Z, B
kwalere	mD
alere	mS, mD

Note: See Koch, this volume, Table 8.7, for a more complete list.
[a] The presumed stimulus is WD *tjamu* 'male grandparent' versus *kami* 'female grandparent'.
[b] The presumed stimulus is WD *tjurtu* 'sister' and *kurta* 'brother'.

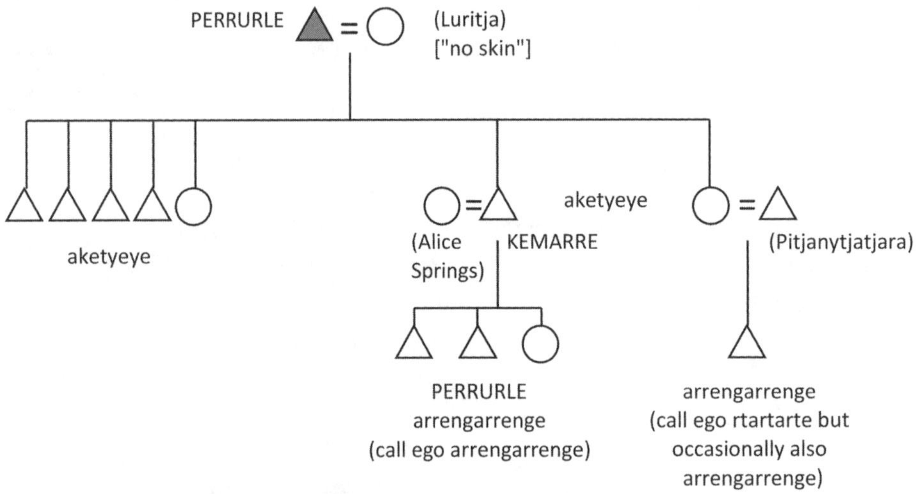

FIGURE 9.4. Terminology as used by a particular grandfather.

NOTES

This chapter originated as a presentation at the International Conference on Historical Linguistics (ICHL), Nijmegen, August 12, 2009. My thanks go to Claire Bowern for delivering the talk at ICHL and for her comments and insights and to Gavan Breen, Laurent Dousset, Ian Keen, Harold Koch, and Pat McConvell for their input.

1. This fieldwork was begun by Diane Bell in 1983 and continued by Bell and me. The nature of the claim changed over time, and in 1992 a High Court decision made claims possible under a different legal framework, that of Native Title.
2. The LA kin terms discussed in this chapter are from the corpus I collected in 1985.

3. This is an oversimplified statement. See Bell 2002:137–138, 140–141, and elsewhere for a detailed description of a system of this type, that of the Kaytej (Kaytetye).
4. The route of the railway was shifted roughly 100 kilometers to the west of Finke in 1980. The now-defunct route through Finke is known as the "Old Ghan."
5. My sources for WD kinship terms are L. Dousset, personal communication, September 2010; Glass et al. 2003; Goddard 1987; Hansen and Hansen 1992.
6. A possible model for this stress pattern is that of the WD language Pitjantjatjarra, with its loss of initial *y but retention of first-syllable stress. G. Breen (personal communication, November 2011), however, suggests that the consonant *rr* induces stress in a preceding initial syllable regardless of contact with non-Arandic languages.
7. *Aketyeye* has the polysemy of the indigenous Arrernte term *ampe*, both "child" (non-kin) and "child [to woman]"; see Henderson and Dobson 1994:119. Gavan Breen (personal communication, November 2011) believes, on the basis of his own fieldwork with LA, that *aketyeye* is basically the general (non-kinship) "child" term.
8. I thank Claire Bowern for this insight; Koch (this volume) has come independently to the same conclusion.
9. Koch (this volume, citing Breen 1997) gives the "child [to male]" term as *lere* (without an initial *a*). This variation is normal in Arandic languages (see, e.g., Henderson and Dobson 1994:1, rule ["trick"] 1) and has no effect on the validity of Koch's reconstruction. Note in this connection that I have recorded the LA "child"/"woman's child" term as both *aketyeye* and *ketyeye*.
10. See the discussion in Alpher and Nash 1999:14 of the adaptation of Warlpiri *kurdungurlu* 'group holding "managerial" responsibility for country' as Arrernte *akwertengerle*.
11. These data (from a single European-surname family) are incomplete as regards kinship terminology.
12. Following Dousset (2003), I recognize that there are likely two (or more) levels of usage and semantic inclusiveness of kinship terms here, and I am avoiding typological terms such as *Hawaiian* and *Hawaiianization*.

References Cited

Alpher, B., and D. Nash. 1999. Lexical Replacement and Cognate Equilibrium in Australia. *Australian Journal of Linguistics* 19(1):5–56.

Bell, D. 2002[1993]. *Daughters of the Dreaming*. Melbourne: McPhee Gribble.

Breen, G. 1997. Lower Arrernte Wordlist. Electronic file. Alice Springs, Australia: IAD.

Dousset, L. 2003. On the Misinterpretation of the Aluridja Kinship System Type (Australian Western Desert). *Social Anthropology* 11(1):43–61.

Glass, A., D. Hackett, and B. Newberry. 2003. *Ngaanyatjarra-Ngaatjatjarra to English Dictionary*. Alice Springs, Australia: IAD Press.

Goddard, C. 1987. *A Basic Pitjantjatjara/Yankunytjatjara to English Dictionary*. Alice Springs, Australia: IAD.

Hansen, K. C., and L. E. Hansen. 1992. *Pintupi/Luritja Dictionary*. Alice Springs, Australia: Institute for Aboriginal Development.

Henderson, J., and V. Dobson. 1994. *Eastern and Central Arrernte to English Dictionary*. Alice Springs, Australia: IAD Press.

10

Proto-Pama-Nyungan Kinship and the AustKin Project

Reconstructing Proto-terms for "Mother's Father" and Their Transformations

Patrick McConvell

This chapter presents work on a knotty problem in the reconstruction of kinship terms in Australian proto-languages, especially the very large Pama-Nyungan family. The problem concerns terms for grandparents: this is a significant issue for the discovery of ancient social systems in Australia, as explained below (see also McConvell 2012, 2013; McConvell and Hendery 2010).

The chapter also exemplifies a method of reconstructing kinship systems that relies heavily on linguistic reconstruction of individual terms and their meanings. When a set of roots and meanings has been reconstructed, this forms a *kinship system* as understood in anthropology, which would normally fall into one or another of the limited types recognized in ethnological typologies of kinship systems. This in turn has implications for other features of the social organization of the society of the protolanguage speakers.

After an introduction to language classification in Australia and methods of reconstruction of meaning in sections 1–3, in section 4, the particular problem at hand is introduced: how to deal with cases in which a proto-language at least initially looks as if it has two or more synonyms. In sections 4.1 and 4.2, the necessary background is discussed for the case at hand of the two widespread roots for "mother's father": the patterns of grand-kin terms in Australia and the Pama-Nyungan family. We need to probe behind the superficial appearance to see if, in fact, more than one protolanguage is involved and if the roots do both have the meaning "mother's father" in the relevant protolanguages.

The results of this investigation of the terms concerned, **ngatyi* and **tyam(p)V*, presented in sections 5–6 begin to point toward a more complex phylogeny for the higher-level groupings of languages in Australia, together with bursts of early diffusion of one of the terms (**tyam[p]V*). This paints a more nuanced picture of the early development of kinship systems in Australia, set out in sections 6.4–6.6, with conclusions in section 7.

1. The Pama-Nyungan Family

One of the tasks of the AustKin project (http://austkin.pacific-credo.fr) is to reconstruct the kinship system of Proto-Pama-Nyungan, the ancestral language of the Pama-Nyungan (PNy) family, which occupies the bulk of the Australian continent except for the central north (with 20 or so non-PNy families) and Tasmania (Alpher 2004; O'Grady et al. 1966; see Figure 10.1). The proposal of a Pama-Nyungan family was a key breakthrough in Australian linguistics made by Geoffrey O'Grady and Ken Hale. While the validity of the PNy family has been questioned (Dixon 2002), it is becoming increasingly clear that this is a family of languages of similar diversity to Indo-European, perhaps of similar age, and one that can be reconstructed in the same way as other protolanguages have been reconstructed, by the comparative method (McConvell and Bowern 2011).

2. The Comparative Method: Comparing and Reconstructing Forms

The comparative method proceeds by comparing forms of words and their meanings in different languages. The words are assembled into sets that are proposed to be historically related. The historical relationships are of two kinds: inheritance and borrowing. The words that are

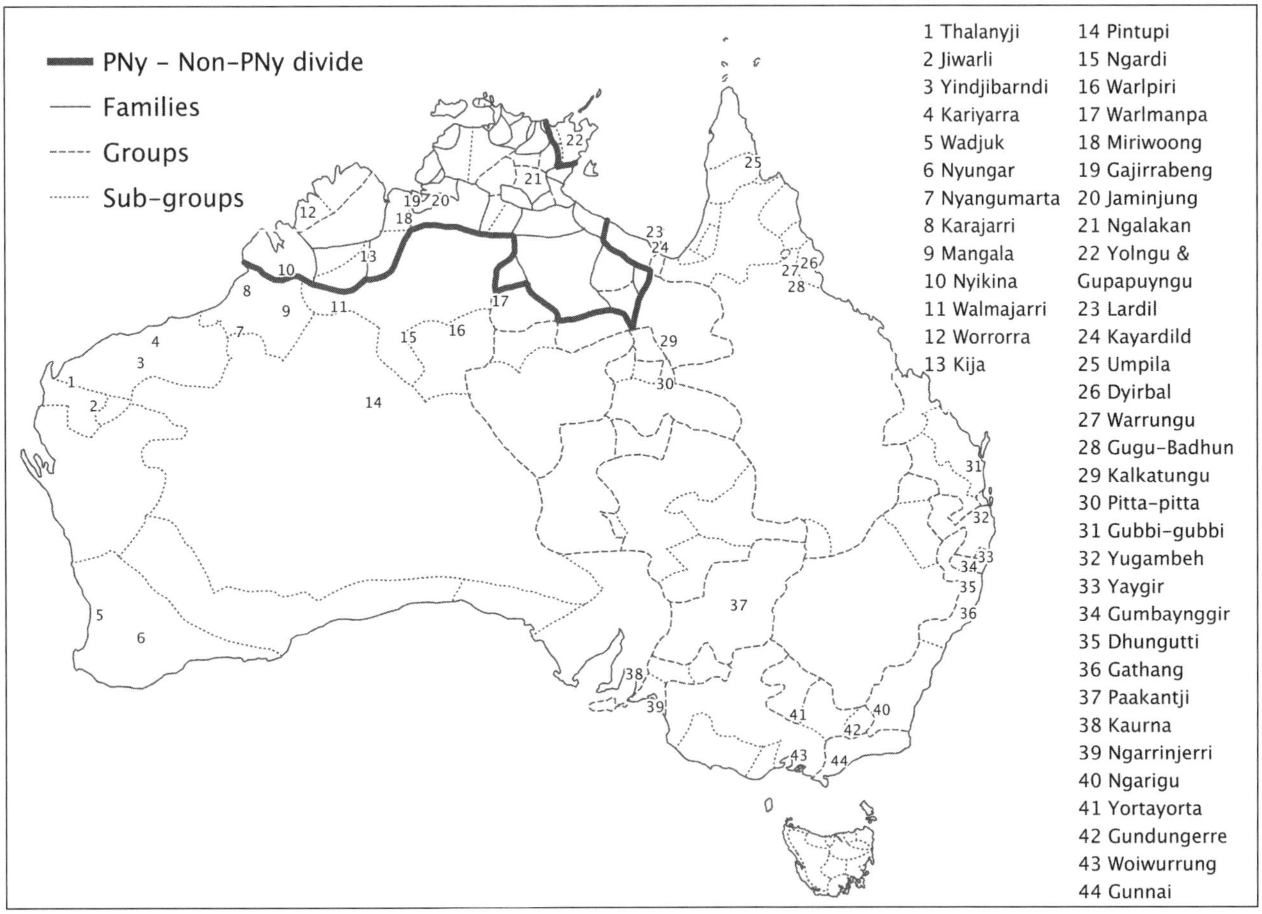

FIGURE 10.1. Pama-Nyungan languages.

inherited from the same proto-word in an ancestral language are said to be *cognates*. When these cognate words are compared, we can see that the sounds in them often bear regular relations to each other (regular sound correspondences). From looking at the different forms of the cognates we can form a hypothesis about what the original protoform of the word probably was: this is called *reconstruction*.

In Indo-European, kinship terms are often used as examples to show that the languages in the family are related and how they arose from a common protoform. Some of these are presented in Table 10.1, based on Clackson (2007).

We can see how similar some of these terms are to each other in the different branches. Some of them do not look particularly alike but can be related because they obey regular sound changes (or sound laws). In Armenian, for instance, a language notorious for bizarre but regular sound changes, *k'oyr* 'sister' is a descendant of the Proto-Indo-European **swesor* by means of a sequence of regular sound changes. First, the medial *s* is lost, and the initial *sw* becomes *hw*, yielding **hweur*; then the initial *hw* becomes *k'*, and with a change in the diphthong, *k'oyr* is the modern Armenian form.

Others in the table, however, are simply not related to the Proto-Indo-European form with the same meaning. This illustrates an important aspect of language change: words are not always inherited but can be replaced—by *loanwords* or new coinages. In Table 10.1 such replacements are written in bold. By and large, however, there is remarkable continuity and stability in kinship terms over the six millennia or so since Proto-Indo-European was spoken. Loanwords that are borrowed often do not display the regular changes found in inherited words, because they arrived in the recipient language after the sound change had stopped operating. This is one of a number of sources of evidence that enable us to distinguish between inherited items that can be reconstructed to a protolanguage and terms that are borrowed from another language.

TABLE 10.1. Indo-European kinship terms.

Language	F	M	B	Z	S	D
Germanic (English)	*father*	*mother*	*brother*	*sister*	*son*	*daughter*
Proto-Indo-European	**ph2ter*	**meh2ter*	**bhreh2ter*	**swesor*	**su:-nu-/*su:-yu-*	**dhugh2ter*
Indo-Iranian (Sanskrit)	*pitar-*	*ma:tar*	*bhra:tar*	*svasar-*	*su:nu-*	*duhitar-*
Greek	*pate:r*	*me:te:r*	*adelphos*	*adelphe*	***huios***	*thugate:r*
Latin	*pater*	*mater*	*fra:ter*	*soror*	***filius***	***filia***
Celtic (Old Irish)	*athir*	*mathir*	*brathir*	*siur*	***macc***	***ingen***
Baltic (Lithuanian)	***tevas***	*motnya*	*brolis*	*sesuo*	*sunus*	*dukte*
Slavic (Russian)	***otec***	*mat'*	*brat'*	*sestra*	*syn*	*doch'*
Armenian	***hayr***	*mayr*	*elbayr*	*k'oyr*	***ordi***	*dustr*

Note: Loanwords appear in bold.
Source: From Clackson 2007:202.

3. Comparing and Reconstructing Meaning

As well as reconstructing a protoform (a string of sounds), we must also reconstruct a protomeaning. For the Indo-European examples above, this is easy; all the cognate forms have the same meaning, so taking the simplest option, we reconstruct the same meaning for the protoform. However, this is not always the case: sometimes the meanings of the cognate forms are different, so there is a decision to be made about what to reconstruct as the protomeaning. As we shall see, we cannot always do this by reference to one term alone but, rather, must consider other meanings within the semantic field of the kinship system as a whole. For instance, if there are two roots that appear to be reconstructible with the same meaning in the same protolanguage (synonyms), we may need to think again about the reconstructions, as discussed further below.

While a great deal is understood about how regular sound change works, the study of semantic change is far less advanced. However, in the kinship realm there has been a great deal of research on semantics, which assists in the formulation of constraints and hypotheses about semantic change.

One particularly fruitful way of thinking about semantic change is to relate it to polysemy. In general, semantic change in a root from meaning A to meaning B proceeds by way of a stage of polysemy in which the root has both meanings A and B. Now it is known that there are strong constraints on polysemy in kinship (or what are known as "equations" in the field of kinship studies). Common patterns of equations have been classified into typologies with conventional names that are widely used in anthropology.

In modern European languages the equation FB = MB ≠ F ≠ M is found, that is, both father's brother and mother's brother are called by the same term, *uncle* (or equivalents in other languages), different from what father or mother is called. This is known as an Eskimo or lineal pattern. However, in Latin, for instance, the protolanguage of the Romance subgroup of languages, mother's brother was called *avunculus*, and father's brother was called by a different term, *patruus*; similarly MZ and FZ had different terms, in a pattern known as Sudanese. These are both relatively common patterns in some areas of the world, although very rare in other areas such as indigenous Australian societies, for instance.

If we now bring in the linguistic dimension of the form of words, we can see that the Latin term *avunculus* looks similar to the English word *uncle*. Indeed they are related: the French word *oncle* is directly inherited from the Latin *avunculus* and was then borrowed by English in the Middle Ages (see Kronenfeld, this volume, and McConvell, chapter 1, this volume, for possible reasons for this and other borrowings into English and other languages from French during that period). However, there has been a change of meaning of *avunculus* from MB to MB *and* FB—the development of a *polysemy* or *equation* that changes the Sudanese pattern to the Eskimo pattern.

The other type of transition we are concerned with here is the loss of a meaning in a polysemy so that only a single meaning remains. If we now look at another term in Latin, *nepos*, this had two meanings, "grandson" and "nephew." At some point in the development of French

TABLE 10.2. Common equations and paths of semantic change in Australian kinship terms.

Code	Name	Equation (Example)	System Type	Citation in Scheffler 1978 (no.:pp.)	Name in Scheffler 1978
A	Merger within parallel and within cross	FF = MMB ≠ MF = FMB	Kariera	4:226	Parallel/cross neutralization
				5:226	Parallel/cross status extension
B	Merger of same gender	FF = MF ≠ MM = FM	Aluridja		
C	Skewing	e.g., Omaha, M = cross-cousin, etc.	Ngarinyin	5:404	Omaha skewing (adjacent generation)
D	Alternate-generations equivalence	Sibling = parallel grandparent; cross-cousin = cross-grandparent		7:226, 376	Alternate generations agnatic
E	Consanguineal/affinal	FZ = WM		8:226	Spouse equation
F	Merger of opposite-sex siblings	MM = MMB			

the term *neveu* lost the "grandson" meaning and came to mean only "nephew" (and in this case, too, the French word was borrowed into English).

The equation of "child's son" and "sibling's son" in Latin represents a polysemy that joins members of adjacent generations, rather than the same generation, as in the example of FB = MB above. Such an adjacent-generation equation is known as *skewing*.[1]

Both these types of transitions can chain together in a sequence:

1. monosemy of a term as A to polysemy A and B
2. polysemy A and B to monosemy of B

Thus the entire sequence represents a semantic shift from A to B. For other similar transitions in fields other than kinship, see Evans 1992 and Wilkins 1996.

In relation to Omaha skewing in Australia (McConvell 2012; McConvell and Alpher 2002; McConvell and Keen 2011), linguistic evidence shows that this two-stage sequence is found quite commonly:

1. MB > MB and MBC; reciprocal ZS > ZS and FZC
2. MB and MBC > MBC; reciprocal ZS and FZC > FZC

Thus the probable Proto-Pama-Nyungan form **kaala-* MB in the northeast of the continent has reflexes meaning MBC or more generally "cross-cousin" or "spouse" (due to cross-cousin marriage) in the west, with some relics of the polysemous situation in between. In a parallel way **tyuwa-* ZC is reflected as FZC, "cross-cousin," or "spouse" in the west, also with polysemous cases in between.

This is a clear case of a two-stage semantic shift via polysemy, for the following reasons:

a. The linguistic forms are cognate.
b. The semantic change is in line with a known type of equation pattern on a world scale (Omaha skewing in this case).
c. The equation pattern is also found extant in the same region where the linguistic evidence shows it has occurred in the past.

These are the ingredients more generally for making a strong case for a meaning change in a root. The anthropological semantic components (b and c) are important in this procedure because they provide constraints on what can plausibly be asserted about earlier kinship semantics.

Apart from Omaha skewing (under C in Table 10.2) there are other polysemies that are also common, both on a world scale and in Australia, that can be legitimately used to justify such historical hypotheses. Such constraining polysemies or equation types include those listed in Table 10.2. Scheffler (1978) has a system of 11 "equivalence rules" that he used to create a typology of Australian kinship systems, which are partially similar to these common equations but are differently constituted within his theoretical model. Where the similarity is clear, reference to Scheffler's equivalence rules is included in the table. For fuller discussion, see McConvell and Hendery 2010.[2]

However, in addition to the equations that are the subject of Scheffler's rules, it is important to recognize other equations that are commonly found playing a role in semantic change. These include equation types D and F in Table 10.2.

On the other hand, other ad hoc hypotheses about polysemies lying behind a historical change would not be acceptable. If it were proposed that a term for "daughter" changed meaning to "grandfather," this would be greeted with skepticism, unless perhaps instead of a daughter/grandfather polysemy there was a chain of changes linking these two meanings, with evidence for each link in the chain, or if there were some evidence in this case of some otherwise unheard of cultural practice that justifies this improbable claim.

Any of the equation patterns in Table 10.2 could be involved in diachronic steps involving

a. the merger of two kin types under one term or
b. the split of a kin type into two terms, one continuing the former term and another term recruited (extended or borrowed) to do duty for the other, newly expressed kin type.

Both these steps could also be involved in a sequence that has the appearance of a change from one meaning to another distinct one but historically had an intermediate stage of polysemy.

For instance, the term **kami* fairly certainly had the meaning "mother's mother" in Proto-Pama-Nyungan, but in some regions it turns up meaning "father's mother" (McConvell 2013; Peterson et al. 2005:90). Now according to the preference of positing an intermediate stage of polysemy, rather than a direct transition between two distinct meanings, I would have to propose a hypothesis that the intermediate stage was **kami*, which spanned both meanings MM and FM. I would then ask three questions: (1) Is this a commonly found and plausible polysemy generally in world kinship systems? (2) Is there evidence for such polysemy in the relevant area of Australia? (3) Does a reflex of this term specifically display such polysemy in a relevant area of Australia?

In this case the answer to all three questions is yes. MM/FM polysemy is what we know in English as *grandmother* and is perhaps the most common way for the FM and MM meanings to be grouped in kinship systems around the world. While less common in Australia, this arrangement is found in several areas of Australia, including the "Aluridja" systems of the Western Desert. In relation to question (3) such polysemy is also found in Bandjalang relatively close to areas in which the full change to FM has been completed.

There do, however, exist cogent cases of kinship term roots changing meaning that do not fall in line with the constrained model of change via polysemy proposed above. Rather than either arbitrarily discounting such cases or being excessively liberal in allowing types of implausible and unattested polysemies, it is probably going to be necessary to recognize other types of semantic change in roots. I do not have the space to go into this in detail here, but see the introduction to this book (McConvell, chapter 1, this volume) for some discussion and note 8 below for a case where extensions of the meaning of one term narrow the meaning of another.

The above discussion has been about deciding what the meaning of a reconstructed proto-kinship term is when its reflexes differ in meaning in different languages. Much more could be said about this and is addressed in other work within the AustKin project already cited. However, we now turn instead to a different issue: What if two forms seem to be reconstructible with a single meaning in a single protolanguage?

4. The Problem of Reconstructed Synonyms

It is possible to have synonyms in languages, so since protolanguages are also languages like any others, we might expect to find synonyms in them too. But full synonyms are quite rare: apparent synonyms often have a difference in usage. For instance, *father* and *daddy* in English might refer to the same kin relation, but the latter is used mainly as an address term and usually implies a display of affection, rather than formality or respect.

This kind of distinction can be harder to retrieve in a reconstructed protolanguage than in a living language or one with extensive historical records. Different synonymous or near-synonymous forms may belong to different dialects or registers, and the evidence for this may be much weaker in reconstructed protolanguages than in living languages. Subtle meaning differences in the protolanguage may have been submerged in the daughter languages and become hard to retrieve without detailed etymological work or perhaps not possible at all.

Dyen and Aberle (1974:16), in discussing Proto-Athapaskan kinship, suggest that many such cases concern terms that would have had different usage (e.g., address versus reference) and/or have closely related

TABLE 10.3. Grandparent kinship term pattern equations in Australia.

Parity	Pattern "Kariera"	"Aranda"	"Karadjeri"	"Aluridja"
Parallel	MM = FFZ ≠ FM	MM ≠ FFZ ≠ FM	MM ≠ FFZ ≠ FM	MM = FM
	FF = MMB ≠ MF	FF ≠ MMB ≠ MF	FF ≠ MMB ≠ MF	FF = MF
Cross	FM = MFZ ≠ MM	FM ≠ MFZ ≠ MM	FM = MFZ ≠ MM	FM = MM
	MF = FMB ≠ FF	MF ≠ FMB ≠ FF	MF = FMB ≠ FF	MF = FF

meanings (e.g., generic sibling versus "brother" versus "brother—woman propositus") that have subsequently merged. The other possibility is that the two apparently synonymous forms actually belong to two different protolanguages, one a sister or daughter of the other, but the subgrouping at that time depth is not reliable enough to establish this.

We should therefore regard with some suspicion a reconstruction that ends up with two terms with exactly the same meaning and the same usage in a single protolanguage. Nevertheless, it is important for our task to negotiate these issues and attempt to establish which kinship terms existed with which meanings in which protolanguages and thus the kinship systems that characterized these different protolanguages.

4.1. Grandkin Patterns in Australia

The grandparental terms in Australia are particularly important since they are a prime indicator of what kind of system existed in Proto-Pama-Nyungan, in PNy subgroups, and in other groupings older than PNy and closer to Proto-Australian. The main typological system proposed for Australia (Elkin 1964; Radcliffe-Brown 1931; Scheffler 1978) has as its main diagnostic criterion the number of terms in the grandparental generation and their diagnostic equations.[3] These are listed in Table 10.3.

There are many systems in which the distinction between opposite-sex siblings is also neutralized, for example, MM = FF = FFZ in a Kariera system, but this is not diagnostic of main system types. Kariera equates parallel grandparents of the same sex or, as noted above, of either sex and similarly equates cross-grandparents under one term. Aranda systems distinguish cross and parallel but also distinguish paternal and maternal—so MM, FF, FM, and MF all have separate terms. Karadjeri is a kind of "halfway house" between Kariera and Aranda, with paternal and maternal distinguished for parallel grandkin but not for cross.[4] Aluridja is a less differentiated system without a cross/parallel distinction in grandkin and often a gendered grandfather versus grandmother distinction, as in European languages.

As can be seen from Figure 10.2, among Pama-Nyungan languages, Kariera systems are found in the eastern Pilbara of Western Australia (including the Kariyarra group from which the type is named), Cape York Peninsula and some way south of that in Queensland, and central New South Wales. In non-Pama-Nyungan languages they are found in the Daly River region. Karadjeri is found among the Karajarri northeast of the Kariyarra and among the Yolngu in northeast Arnhem Land. Aluridja covers a vast area of the west of the continent, mostly Western Desert dialects but also some other languages of the southwest and in some groups in South East Queensland. Outside these areas there is a predominance of Aranda systems.

One of the key questions for the AustKin project is: Which system can be reconstructed to Proto-Pama-Nyungan, and how did that system evolve into the other systems found in Pama-Nyungan? A preliminary hypothesis is that the Proto-PNy system was Kariera, as suggested by Elkin (1970) and others (not for PNy but some vague scope covering most of Australia). This is how the reconstructed grandkin terms cited in the next section have been interpreted.

A reconstruction of the system of Proto-Pama-Nyungan would provide further evidence for or against the idea that the protosystem of many language families (e.g., Hage 2003; Hage et al. 2004) or even the primeval world kinship system (e.g., Allen 1986, 1998) was Kariera/Dravidian. I return to this issue at the end of the chapter.

Here I am regarding Kariera as a form of Dravidian terminology. In Dravidian terminology, a cross-cousin is equated with ego's spouse, and the opposite-sex cross-cousin's children are classed as ego's sons and daughters. In addition to this, in a Kariera terminology this strict application of the cross/parallel division is extended to the grandparental generation. In terms of

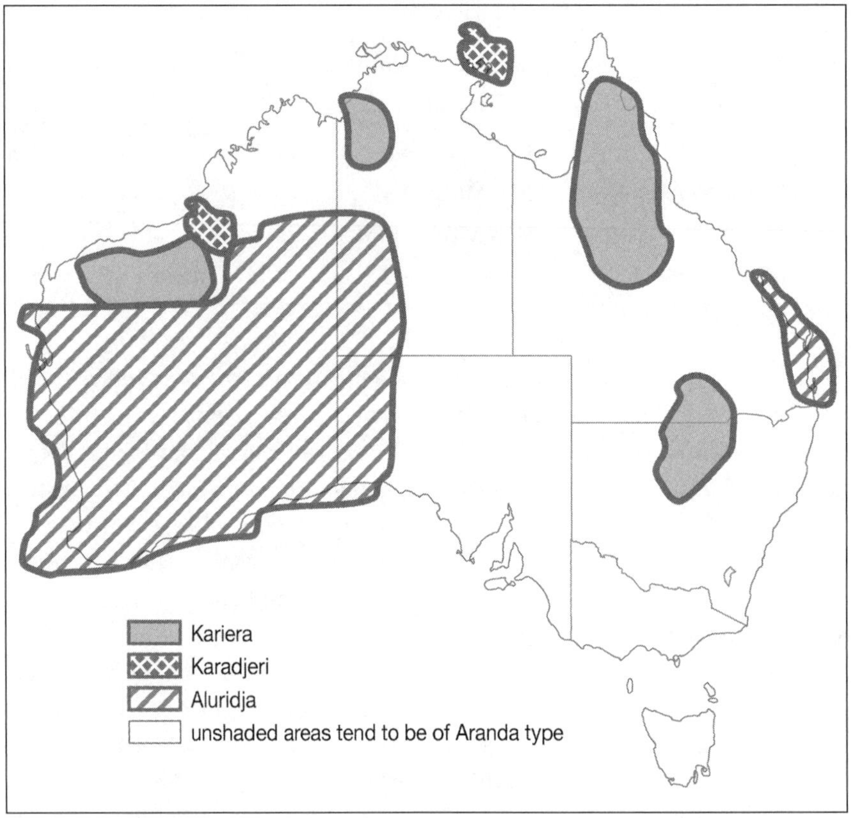

FIGURE 10.2. Distribution of main kinship systems in Australia (based on grandkin equations).

standard Dravidian affinal equations, which are usually linked to bilateral cross-cousin marriage, FFZ, for instance, is equivalent to FWM since FZ is mother-in-law. FW is M, so FFZ = MM, one of the Kariera diagnostic equations. Dravidian kinship systems elsewhere may not extend their principles so consistently to the +/–2 generation and may have a simple grandfather/grandmother pattern, for instance. Kariera systems in Australia do, however, regularly make this extension of the cross/parallel distinction to grandkin and the grandchild generation.[5]

4.2. Grandkin Terms in Proto-Pama-Nyungan

Four grandkin terms have been tentatively reconstructed (Table 10.4; McConvell 2008). This looks like a Kariera system with gender distinctions. The primary meaning is the first one, and the one in parentheses is the sibling of the same gender as the first one of the other grandparent in the set, parallel or cross. Such systems are found on Cape York Peninsula with reflexes of these terms with these meanings, for instance, in Umpila. However, there is more work to be done to confirm this hypothesis.

TABLE 10.4. Proto-Pama-Nyungan grandkin terms: Eastern set.

	Female		Male	
Parity	Form	Kin Gloss	Form	Kin Gloss
Parallel	**kami*	MM (/FFZ)	**pula*	FF (/MMB)
Cross	**papi*	FM (/MFZ)	**ngatyV*	MF (/FMB)

Note: The gloss in parentheses is the secondary meaning, the sibling of the other grandparent in the set, of the same gender as the first referent.

Alongside one of the prototerms, **ngatyV* MF/FMB, there is another term, **tyam(p)V*, which is also on the face of it reconstructible as MF. This duplication of meaning by two roots throws doubt on the reconstruction of one, the other, or both.

The geographical distributions of these two roots are distinct and seem to be complementary (see the next section and Figure 10.3). This applies also to other grandparent terms possibly reconstructible to Proto-Pama-Nyungan. I have named the set with **ngatyV* "Eastern" and the set in which **tyam(p)V* is found "Western" due to

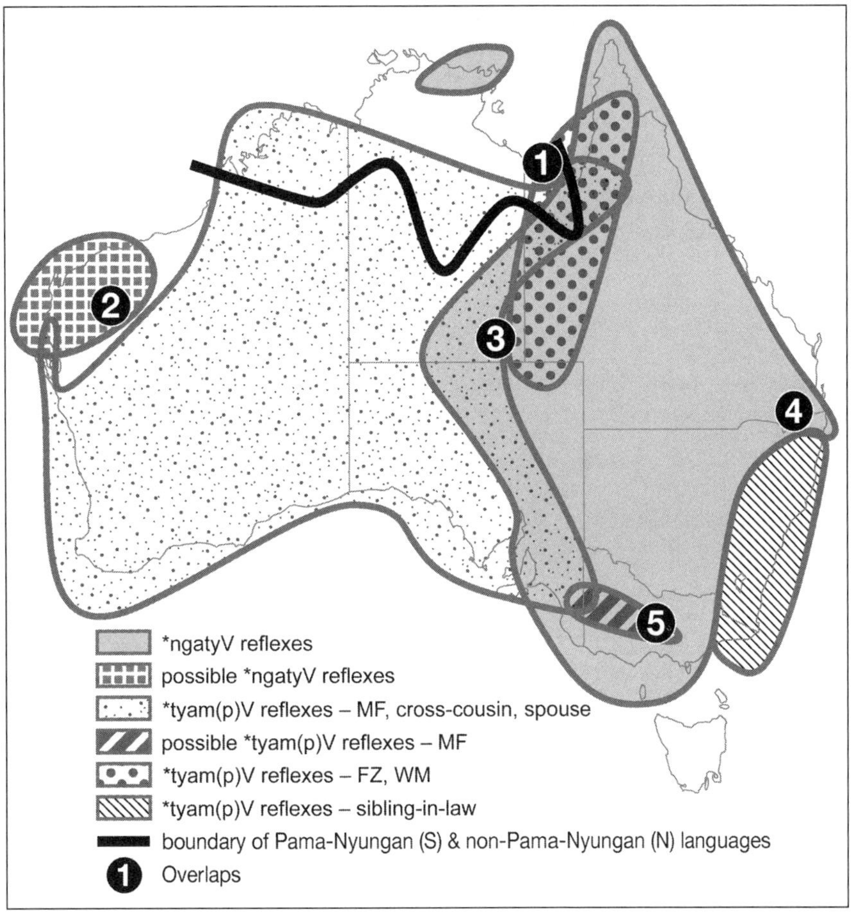

FIGURE 10.3. Geographical distribution of reflexes of the roots **ngatyV* and **tyam(p)V*.

their geographical distribution. Only the MF roots are to be discussed in detail in this chapter; for MM **kami* and **kanytyV*, see McConvell (2013).

The Western set to which **tyam(p)V* belongs is shown in Table 10.5.[6] Again it represents a Kariera system with gender distinctions, and exactly this type of system is found in Kariyarra, for instance, with reflexes of all these roots in these meanings.

**NgatyV* (primarily *ngatyi*) MF is a Pama-Nyungan innovation not found in non-Pama-Nyungan. However, *ngatyi* with other meanings, primarily "mother," exists in several non-PNy and some PNy groups, so that there is a possibility of some kind of Omaha skewing (Lounsbury's Type 3) being at work in a meaning change between MF and M(B). However, at this stage there is no strong evidence against the possibility that this resemblance is coincidental, so this is not discussed further in this chapter, although more research on this question is warranted.

The **tyam(p)V* root is also found in some non-Pama-Nyungan families, meaning MF and "cross-cousin"/"spouse." Mother's father and cross-cousin are commonly equated through alternate-generations equation—polysemy type C in Table 10.2; the further polysemy with and shift to "spouse" and "spouse's sibling" result from Type D, linked to cross-cousin marriage.

TABLE 10.5. Proto-Pama-Nyungan grandkin terms: Western set.

Parity	Female		Male	
	Form	Kin Gloss	Form	Kin Gloss
Parallel	**kanytyV*	MM (/FFZ)	**mayi-*	FF (/MMB)
Cross	**ngapV*	FM (/MFZ)	**tyam(p)V*	MF (/FMB)

Note: The gloss in parentheses is the secondary meaning, the sibling of the other grandparent in the set, of the same gender as the first referent.

I (1997b) have proposed that **tyam(p)V* was borrowed into a branch or area of PNy languages from non-Pama-Nyungan. However, further research on the distribution of this root, particularly in the southeast of the continent and in the non-PNy languages in the north, by the AustKin project is leading to a reassessment of this proposal. An alternative is that it was inherited into Proto-Pama-Nyungan from some protolanguage somewhat higher on the tree of Australian languages than Proto-PNy in the narrow sense and then diffused from some PNy subgroup in the west through a number of non-PNy families. This alternative is examined in this chapter.

The chapter works through various issues of sound change, meaning change, and morphological complexity as dealt with in the comparative method, to arrive at an answer to our question of how these roots fit into a hypothesis of Proto-Pama-Nyungan grandparent terminology and how this affects our understanding of the Proto-PNy kinship system and social organization. This pair of apparently synonymous roots, **ngatyi* and **tyam(p)V*, will be the focus of this discussion. The question of the two sets of apparently synonymous grandkin roots (also mentioned in McConvell 2008) as a whole is briefly discussed at the end of the chapter.

5. **NGATYV* AND **TYAM(P)V*

5.1. Geographical Distribution of Reflexes of the Roots

Figure 10.3 shows the broad distribution of the two roots with the meaning MF and meanings that clearly seem to be related by regular semantic change via polysemy as described in section 2 (Table 10.2): "cross-cousin" (via change Type D) and "spouse" and "sibling-in-law" (via additionally change Type E). More detail is given for **ngatyi* and **tyam(p)V* separately in the following sections and figures, including other meanings of the terms and discussion of whether they are in fact related.

The general pattern is as follows:

- Each of the two grandparent sets has a near-complementary geographical distribution, the "Eastern" one (**ngatyi*) centered in Queensland and the "Western" one (**tyam[p]V*) elsewhere.
- The Eastern set's **ngatyV* also has outliers on the western periphery, in Yolngu in northeast Arnhem Land and probably on the extreme northwestern periphery in the western Pilbara, beyond the distribution of **tyam(p)V* reflexes.[7]
- There are a few languages on the boundary of the two sets that have an *overlap*—reflexes of a root from both sets. These are marked in Figure 10.3:

1. Kayardild and other Tangkic languages at the northern end of the boundary of the Queensland distribution of *ngatyi* and the distribution of *tyam(p)V* west of there.
2. Jiwarli and other languages in the western Pilbara that have *thami-*, a reflex of **tyam(p)V* for MF and a form related to **ngatyV* as "cross-cousin."
3. Pitta-Pitta in Central Queensland, farther south along this boundary, with *tyami/yami/yampi* meaning FZ and so on and *ngathanha* meaning MF/FM.[8] This is in fact part of a much larger "overlap" of the two roots in languages of North Queensland, but the **tyam(p)V* reflexes do not have the MF meaning.
4. Bandjalangic in northern New South Wales where there are *ngatyang* 'grandfather' and so forth at the southern end of the Queensland distribution of **ngatyV* reflexes and in some languages also *tyampang* 'in-law' (Yugambeh; meaning not precisely recorded; cf. also *tyapangkan* 'wife') and in the north of the New South Wales distribution of *tyampV(ng)* terms for "brother-in-law" and so on.
5. Ngarigu and Gundungerre in far southeastern New South Wales, which provide possible cases of overlap with *tyamukang* 'husband's sister's husband' and *ngakun* MF. Both of these are problematic as descendants of **tyam(p)V* and **ngatyV*, respectively, for reasons to be explored below. *Thamala* MF in Yortayorta is a probable cognate of other **tyam(p)V* reflexes in the west, with the *-la* a possible old suffix.

In each case only one of the terms has the MF meaning, and the other one is different ("cross-cousin"/"sibling-in-law" or "father's sister"). In cases 1 and 2, the **tya(m)pV* reflex is the MF form, and the **ngatyV* reflex is a "cross-cousin" term. In cases 3, 4, and 5 the position is reversed: The **ngatyV* reflexes are MF (originally where there has been some extension), and the **tyam(p)V* forms have other meanings—"cross-cousin," "spouse," and "in-law" and, less tractably in terms of my method, "father's sister"/"mother-in-law" in case 3 and adjacent areas in the north. The following sections go into more detail about the distribution of reflexes of the two roots under discussion.

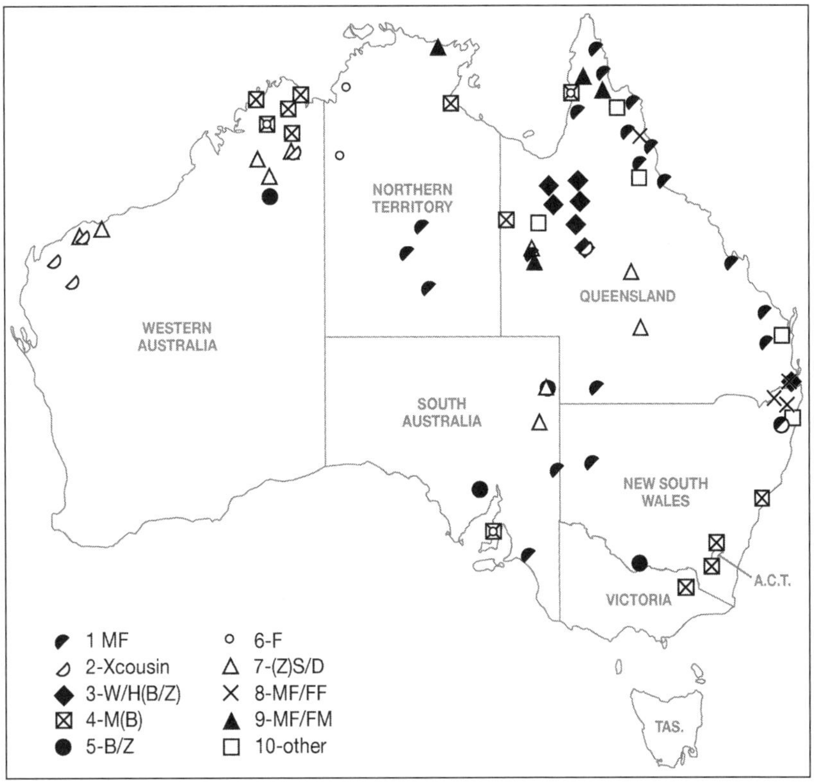

FIGURE 10.4. Reflexes of **ngatyi*.

5.2. *NgatyV

**NgatyV* is a very solid Proto-Pama-Nyungan reconstruction in the "mother's father" meaning. Alpher (2004) gives a comprehensive listing of cognates; Hale (1976:46) reconstructs it for Proto-Paman. It is found in a large number of languages in that meaning, especially in the Paman, Maric, Waka-Kabic, Bandjalangic, and Gumbaynggirr subgroups throughout most of Queensland and northern New South Wales. It is also in Arandic in Central Australia, although many of the forms are old compounds with *atye-* as the reflex of **ngatyi* (Koch, this volume), and in Paakanji and neighboring languages on the Upper Murray River. It is also found in western outliers, in the Yolngu subgroup in northeast Arnhem Land, far to the west in Kanyara-Mantharda and Ngayardic in the Pilbara (mainly in a "cross-cousin" meaning), and in Yaraldi of South Australia in the MF meaning. With this kind of wide distribution with little change in meaning—and where there is a meaning change, it is of the regular expected types discussed—it passes the test for a "gold-standard" Proto-PNy reconstruction. Its absence from large areas of Australia where a reflex of **tyam(p)V* is the dominant instantiation of MF is an issue to be addressed, however.

Figure 10.4 shows the distribution of reflexes of **ngatyi* together with some of the meaning changes this root has undergone in Pama-Nyungan languages:

1. "Cross-cousin" (MBC/FZC) and "spouse" as a secondary meaning in Gumbaynggirr, via polysemies D and E. Polysemy between MF and "cross-cousin" terms is very widespread in Australia, related to the general tendency toward equivalence of alternate generations—in this case between cross-relations in the +2 and 0 generations.
2. "Cross-cousin" as a primary meaning in Mayi languages south of the central Gulf of Carpentaria in Queensland and in Kanyara-Mantharda and Ngayardic languages in the western Pilbara (presumably via polysemy D, as in 1).
3. "Grandfather" (MF/FF) in some Bandjalangic dialects by polysemy B.
4. Some instances of the root showing up as FF in Queensland, which may be mediated through polysemy B as in 3 above: these include Kalkatungu, Gubbi-gubbi (a Waka-Kabic language), Yaygir, and Warrungu and Gugu-Badhun, two closely related languages north of Townsville.[9]

TABLE 10.6. Patterns of polysemy and meaning change in **ngatyV* reflexes.

Language	Form	Original/Basic Kin Gloss	Kin Gloss via Polysemy Type				
			A	B	D	E	F
Arandic	*atye-*	MF					
Yaraldi	*ngatyanu*	MF					
Umpila	*ngatyi*	MF	FMB				
Pitta-Pitta	*ngathanha*	MF	(*FMB)				FM
Bundjalung	*ngatyang*	MF		FF			
Gugu Badhun	*ngatyi*	(*MF)		FF			
Jiwarli	*ngathal*	(*MF)			MBS		
Gumbaynggir	*ngatyi*	MF			MBS	Spouse	
Mayi	*ngathiya*				(*MBS)	Spouse	

Note: Polysemy types are based on the alphabetical coding from Table 10.2. Kin types in parentheses with an asterisk indicate a polysemy hypothesized to have occurred earlier in the transition to a meaning change.

5. Kariera equations (polysemy A) found with this root in several Paman languages, Pitta-Pitta in Central Queensland, and Yolngu; this is assumed to be a polysemy preserved from the protolanguage: MF/FMB but extended by neutralizing gender distinctions in some languages to produce MF = FM (polysemy F). No case of a full sequence culminating in *ngatyi* meaning only FM has been found.

Table 10.6 shows changes in some of the languages, to exemplify the polysemies and transitions involved. In the top row the relevant polysemies (based on the alphabetical coding from Table 10.2) are shown. If the kin type is in parentheses with an asterisk, this indicates a polysemy hypothesized to have occurred earlier in the transition to a meaning change; if it is a current or recently recorded polysemy, there are no asterisks or parentheses. Type C is omitted from the table as there is no relevant case of skewing with this root as far as is known. Figure 10.4 shows the geographical distribution of the **ngatyV* reflexes and their different meanings.

Apart from the examples in Table 10.6 and Figure 10.4, showing reasonably clear evidence of semantic shift from an original meaning, MF, there are a number of cases of kinship roots of the form *ngatyi* or *ngatya* whose connection with **ngatyV* MF is more debatable. There are a number of terms that bear some similarity (not, however, very close) in Karnic and other eastern-central languages that are sibling terms. A transition to "sibling" from MF is not a plausible scenario in terms of the constraints on semantic change discussed above. Sibling terms of the form *ngatya-* in Kimberley Pama-Nyungan languages may be borrowed from Bunuban non-PNy neighbors that also have such terms.

Ngatyi and related forms are fairly widespread in non-Pama-Nyungan languages (e.g., Worrorran, Marra) with the meaning "mother" (sometimes MB, with some evidence in Tangkic that MB might have been an earlier meaning). There are also a few PNy languages that have a similar root with the meaning "mother" very far away in Ngarrinjerri in South Australia and in southern New South Wales. The inclination would be to class these as unrelated to each other or to the major MF and so on set of cognates. Again, making a connection between M and MF within the constraints is not plain sailing. There is a form of Omaha skewing that equates MB and MF—Lounsbury's Type 3. This type is very rare in Australia, but it is found in Worrorran and Marra. It is interesting, however, that the distribution of the *ngatyV* M forms in southern Australia is quite similar to the distribution of the *tyampV* "spouse"/"sibling-in-law" term (see the following section and Figure 10.5).

5.3. *Tyam(p)V

The other widespread MF form in Pama-Nyungan and contender for reconstruction in Proto-PNy is **tyam(p)V*. As shown in Figure 10.5, this has a relatively western distribution as compared with **ngatyi*, but it also has probable cognates in the southeast. There are very similar and almost certainly related forms in a number of languages across the non-PNy languages in the north with MF and "cross-cousin"/"spouse" meanings.

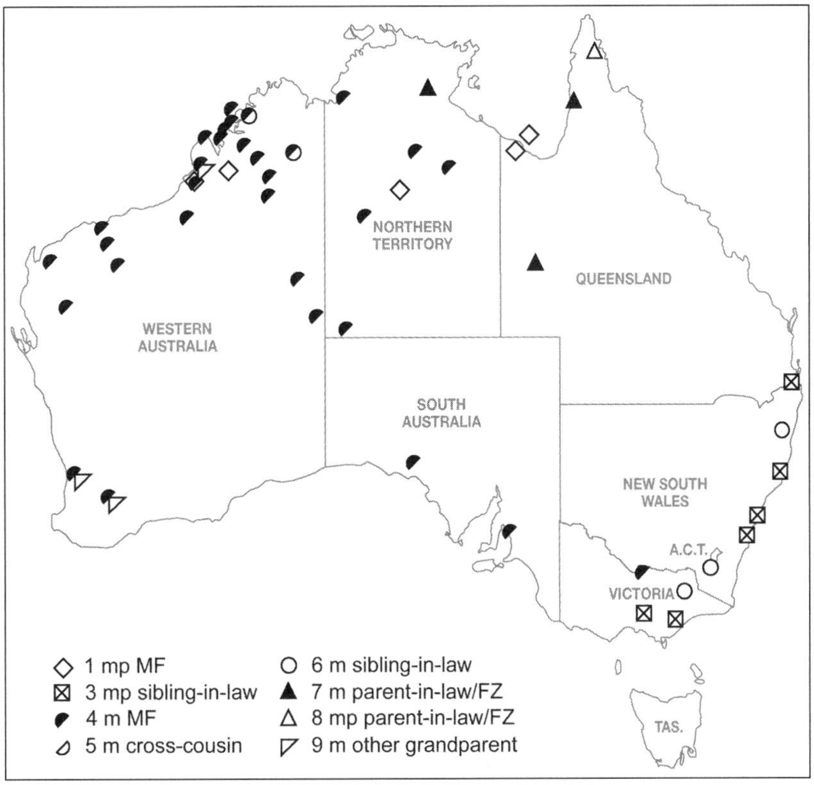

FIGURE 10.5. Reflexes of **tyam(p)V.*

I have used the representation with the parenthetical *p* advisedly to represent both **tyamV* and **tyampV.* Forms without *p* are found most commonly throughout Pama-Nyungan and non-Pama-Nyungan forms. A form with *p*, *tyampa-thu*, is found in Tangkic, a non-PNy family, regarded as part of Macro-Pama-Nyungan by Evans (2003; for details, see the next section).[10] In the Ngumpin-Yapa subgroup, Warlpiri has *tyami-rdi* MF, and its sister in the Yapa branch, Warlmanpa, has *tyampi-rti*. In the Pilbara Karajarri has *tyampa-thu* (also in Nyikina). The alternation between *m* and *mp* in this root does seem to be partially understandable in terms of linguistic subgroups but not entirely: this is discussed together with consideration of *tyap(V)* below.

There are also forms, mainly in southeast Pama-Nyungan, with the *mp* alternant, for example, the Gathang *tyampang* WB and the Sydney, Gunnai, and Woiwurrung *tyampi* WB; the Dhangatti form *thapuny* is no doubt a cognate also.[11] A solution to the meaning difference from MF in this case would be to assume that MF shifted to "cross-cousin" via polysemy D and then to "brother-in-law" via polysemy E, as applied to cases of meaning change for **ngatyi* above. Gumbaynggirr just to the north has a MF = "cross-cousin" = "spouse" polysemy for the reflex of **ngatyV* (Muurrbay Aboriginal Language and Cultural Co-operative 2001).

In the remainder of this section I present what Geoffrey O'Grady and Barry Alpher had to say about this root. In most cases they did not consider the *mp* alternants as part of the same etymon, as I have done. I also look at the significant non-Pama-Nyungan distribution of related forms, which was also not considered by O'Grady or Alpher.

Geoffrey O'Grady passed away in 2009. He made a great contribution to Australian linguistics, especially by elaborating on the idea of the Pama-Nyungan family. He assembled etymologies and notes for etymologies for many years. He admitted himself that he was prone to "throwing caution to the winds," and therefore some of his etymologies involve some doubtful meaning and sound changes.

In relation to the root under discussion, O'Grady (1990:88) reconstructs **jaami* 'mother's father' as a Proto-Pama-Nyungan root, which he says is not found reflected in Bandjalangic (Yugambeh has *tyampang* DH, but O'Grady probably excluded this because of the *p* and the aberrant meaning). O'Grady lists as cognates the following:

1. Nyangumarta *jamu.ji* 'mother's father' (*-ji* < *+*ju* 'my'...)
2. Warlpiri *jami-rdi* 'mother's father'...
3. Pintupi *tjamu* MF, FF
4. Kaurna *tama.mmu(.ta)* 'grandfather on mother's side [*thamamu*]'
5. Kaurna *tammu(.tta)* 'grandson of *tamammu* [*thamu*]'
6. Wadjuk *tammin* 'grandfather, grandmother'
7. Yindjibarndi *thami.i* MF (*.i* < **ju*, cf. Nyangumarta)
8. Proto-Mantharta **thami* MF (> Warriyangka, Tharrgari *thami*)
9. Nyungar *tem* 'cousin'
10. possibly Gupapuyngu *dhumu.n-gur* FZDDC
11. probably Lardil *jembe* MF...
12. probably also Lardil *thama.rr.ka* 'bereaved brother'...
13. Umpila *yaami* 'wife's mother'
14. Dyirbal *jami.ya.n* 'younger sister'

Items 1–8 are unproblematic. Of interest is the partial reduplication of the Kaurna grandparent term MF *thamamu* as compared with the root form used for the junior reciprocal mDC *thamu*. I have suggested that this may continue an ancient, perhaps Proto-Pama-Nyungan pattern (McConvell 2007b, 2008:326).

Item 9 is presumably drawn from Douglas (1976:75), but it does not occur in Bindon and Chadwick's compilation of old Nyungar sources, although they (1992:159–160) do list *tam*, *tammin*, and *temmen*, all glossed "grandfather." Item 10, the term from Gupapuyngu (Yolngu), is far removed from the source, with different vowels and a meaning that might conceivably be linked to MF but is testing credibility.[12] Item 11 is a cognate I believe, and in this case it is a form with *mp* from a Tangkic language, but item 12 is very doubtful as a cognate. The Umpila form in item 13 has an unexplained sound correspondence of the initial *ty* to *y*, as well as an unexplained meaning difference (but see below for Alpher's approach to this and other similar items from North Queensland, where there are also doublets with the initial *ty* and initial *y* in some languages such as Pitta-Pitta). The meaning of the Dyirbal form in item 14 seems unrelated to the original MF meaning or to the other North Queensland FZ/WM(B) meanings.

Alpher (2004) suggests that the protoform **tyaami* may have the meaning "wife's mother's brother" not "mother's father." He holds out the possibility that this may be the same etymon as **tyamu*, a term found in the west, but is not categorical about that. The correspondence in meaning between WMB and MF is unusual, implying if anything Crow skewing (if WMB is MFZD/MMBD), as Alpher suggests. Crow skewing is unexpected in this region and usually associated with matrilineal institutions, which are rare in Australia and only in isolated pockets and weakly in Cape York Peninsula.

The method being advocated here raises strong doubts about this proposed meaning transition, in either direction: MF > WM(B) or WM(B) > MF. Alpher also brings in the FZ form in Pitta-Pitta, outside Cape York Peninsula, and some distance into west-central Queensland. WM is commonly equated with FZ in systems with cross-cousin marriage (polysemy type E), and Pitta-Pitta has the Kariera equation MF = FM (polysemy type A), which correlates with such marriage. Again FZ can only be linked to cross-cousin (FZC) by Crow skewing and thence to MF by alternate-generations equivalence, and the Crow skewing step is problematic.[13]

There is an absence of similar forms that could be related to his root, **tyaami*, or the current proposal, **tyam(p)V*, with the meaning MF in Queensland. Alpher (2004), as noted, has proposed that there are cognates with different meanings in North Queensland and that possibly the other proposed meanings such as WMB and FZ were earlier. This could be a useful solution for the question to be answered by this chapter, since it could provide a different meaning for the Proto-PNy term—we would no longer be faced by problematic synonymy. Moreover, this solution would be in line with what we have been finding in other cases, that the oldest meanings of kinship roots are found in North Queensland (McConvell and Alpher 2002; McConvell and Keen 2011).

Another conjecture that could offer a solution might rely on the fact that in some areas (north and southeast Cape York Peninsula) there is an unusual form of "oblique" marriage with a cross-cousin's child (Dixon 1989; McConnel 1950–51).[14] In such a case the cross-cousin is the mother-in-law, so if a group had been through such a stage, it is feasible that a "cross-cousin" term would end up meaning WM/FZ or vice versa. Cross-cousin/MF is one of the common types of polysemy (D).

Linguistic evidence for this mechanism of change would be welcome, in particular showing that forms of the **tyam(p)V* root were involved in polysemy and change reflecting this marriage arrangement. Such evidence, discussed briefly in the accompanying note, remains weak at present.[15]

Returning to the proposals of McConvell 1997b, the solution of borrowing of **tyam(p)V* from non-Pama-

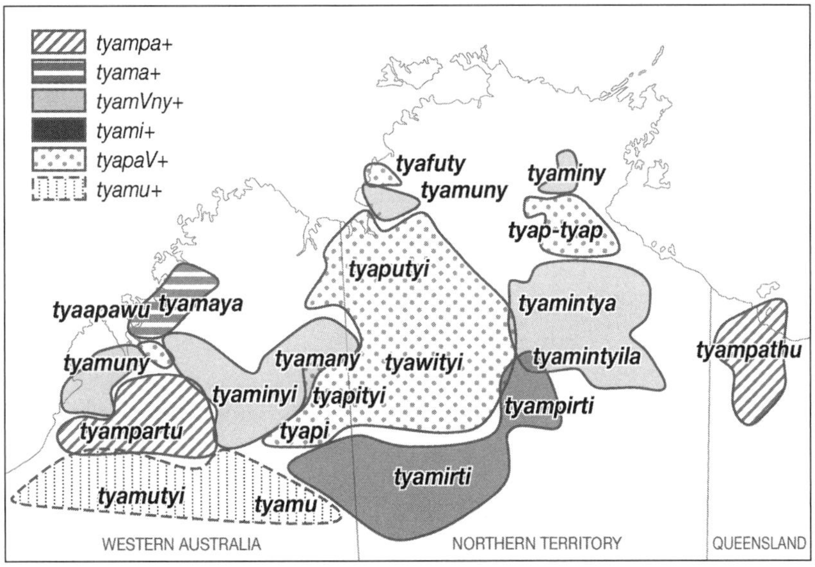

FIGURE 10.6. Distribution of **tyam(p)V* reflexes in north-central Australia.

Nyungan has turned out to be unsustainable. Rather, the evidence is quite strong that the root was borrowed in the opposite direction, from Pama-Nyungan into non-PNy, at least for the swathe of non-PNy languages from the west Kimberleys almost to the Gulf of Carpentaria where related forms are found. The Tangkic family, which has the root *tyampa+* MF, is a different case: initially classified as PNy, it has more recently been regarded as non-PNy but as perhaps a sister or first cousin of PNy. Questions of classification in non-PNy or its relationship to PNy are discussed in the next section, but first we need to look at the distribution of apparent cognates of **tyam(p)V* in non-PNy. Neither O'Grady nor Alpher looked at the non-PNy forms since they were concerned with PNy. In the case of this root, however, the non-PNy forms are extensive and clearly related to PNy forms.

Figure 10.6 shows the distribution of various reflexes of **tyam(p)V*, all with the meaning MF, except in Ngalakgan, where it is "spouse." The forms shown in the figure can be divided into six major variants:

1. *tyampa+*: This is found in the extreme east in the Tangkic family of languages in the central Gulf of Carpentaria and in the extreme west in the Marrngu subgroup of Pama-Nyungan (Karajarri and Mangala). These have common PNy kinship suffixes, *-thu* and *-rtu*, respectively (McConvell 2008). The form *tyampartu* was borrowed into eastern Nyulnyulan (Nyikina—non-PNy), and the form in the third Marrngu language, Nyangumarta, *tyamu+tyi*, is no doubt borrowed from a PNy language to the south and west where *tyamu* is the widespread form.
2. *tyamVny+*: These forms with the third consonant being *ny* (a lamino-palatal nasal) are the most frequent in non-PNy, stretching from the western (and Proto-) Nyulnyulan *tyamuny*, through *tyaminyi* (Bunuban and encroaching into Worrorran) and *thamany* (Kija, southern Jarragan), to western Mirndi in the Barkly Tableland (*tyaminy*, with the suffix *-tya* or *-tyila*). To the north *tyaminy* is also found with the meaning "spouse" in Ngalakgan, and *thamuny* appears in the Daly languages as MF.
3. *tyapV+*: Forms are found in the central part of the distribution. The bare form *tyapi* is found in Walmajarri, and *tyapiy* appears in Bunuba alternative to *tyaminyi* There is also a form with the common PNy kinship suffix *-tyi* in northern Jarragan (Gajirrabeng) and Jaru. The Miriwoong form *tyawityi*, produced by the regular intervocalic lenition *p* > *w*, was borrowed into Jaminjungan (western Mirndi, non-PNy) with the Miriwoong suffix *-ng* and into the eastern Ngumpin languages (PNy) without the *-ng*, as *tyawityi* (McConvell 1997a).[16]
4. *tyamaya*: The form (meaning MF and "cross-cousin") is found in Worrorra and a couple of other western Worrorran languages but not in southern or eastern Worrorran. It is not clear at this stage of research if the *-ya* suffix developed from the third consonant *ny* or is an added suffix.
5. *tyami*: Roots without the *ny* and with the common PNy kinship suffix *-rti* appear in Ngumpin-Yapa (as an alternative to *tyapi* in Walmajarri and in Warlpiri and Ngardi). Warlmanpa, the sister language of Warlpiri

in Yapa, has *tyampirti*, with an *mp* cluster, discussed below.

6. *tyamu*: Roots without *ny* appear in Nyangumarta and other PNy languages to the south and west with the meaning MF and with a broader "grandfather" meaning throughout the Western Desert.

The *tyampa+* roots in Tangkic and in Marrngu may well be connected despite the great geographical distance between them. This would involve either a western spread of this form, which has subsequently been overlaid by spreads of other variants, or contiguity of Marrngu and Tangkic at some point in prehistory, which has been suggested (McConvell 1996).

It is possible that the variant with *p* as the second consonant (set 3 above) might come from an *mp* form. It is likely that the **tyapi* form originated in Ngumpin-Yapa, where it is attested in the western languages. In one of the Yapa languages, Warlmanpa, *mp* is found, and this could be a relic of a **tyampi-* protoform.[17] Even so there is no evident motivation for the change *mp* > *p* in this account.

Another possible explanation for the set 3 terms with *p* as the second consonant is that they descend from either **tyampiny+tyV* or **tyaminy+tyV* and the denasalization is a result of regressive nasal cluster dissimilation (the progressive form of this change/constraint is mostly in focus in McConvell 1988). The forms without the suffix, then, as in Walmajarri and Bunuba, might have to be the result of the removal of the suffix *-tyV* after the nasal cluster dissimilation change had occurred.

It is likely that the *p* forms originate in Ngumpin-Yapa and are borrowed from there into Jarragan and thence into western Mirndi, after the medial lenition *p* > *w* in Miriwoong and closely related (now extinct) Jarragan languages. The Ngumpin-Yapa origins can be seen in the PNy kinship suffix *-tyi* (the form *-tyi*, rather than *-tyu*, being a distinctive innovation in Ngumpin-Yapa). The fact that the western Mirndi loans came via Jarragan is clear from the *-ng* suffix, distinctive of northern Jarragan. The Kija form *thamany*, on this account, reflects a different, perhaps earlier, stratum of the diffusion of these variant forms of **tyam(p)V*.

**Tyaminy+tyV* MF is perhaps reconstructible for Proto–Eastern Mirndi (not in Harvey's 2008 list) but could also be an early loan into the family, especially if the *-tya* and *-tyila* suffixes reflect the Pama-Nyungan **tyV*. The western Mirndi form *tyawitying* is clearly a later loan from Jarragan, probably replacing an earlier *tyaminytya* or *tyaminytyi*. The ethnonym Jaminyjung, the major language group of western Mirndi, is part of an ethnonymic paradigm zone (McConvell 2006), with ethnonyms made up of a typical word of the language of the group concerned plus a Jarragan suffix, *-pung* or *-wung*. It may possibly contain the word *tyaminytyV*, the putative earlier pan-Mirndi form of the MF kinship term before it was replaced by *tyawityi*. This is a speculation, however, and it begs the question of why this kinship term should be salient enough to form an ethnonym.

This is related to the question of why this kinship term diffused so widely in this zone. Other examples of wide diffusion of kinship terms seem to involve terms with affinal senses and be motivated by changes in marriage systems (McConvell 2010a). In this case, for instance, in Nyulnyulan the term for "father-in-law," **tyamunyarri* (Stokes and McGregor 2003:62), is analyzable as "associated with MF," and in Nyul-nyul WF can be termed "MB associated with MF" (Scheffler 1978:183); it seems likely that **tyamunyarri* is a contraction of such a phrase. Now, as we have seen, MF is often extended to mean "cross-cousin" and "spouse" in a cross-cousin marriage regime, especially where there is a preference for matrilateral marriage of a man to his MBD. A new marriage rule and authority structure could lie behind this diffusion.

As for Ngalakgan, where *tyaminy* means "spouse," it is a Gunwinyguan language, but the root **tya(m)pi* MF or similar is not reconstructed for this family (Harvey 2003), so it could well be a loanword in Ngalakgan. The form looks related to those far to the west, but the meaning is different. It can be linked via the polysemy chain D–E, as has been discussed previously, but the current marriage rule is not with a first cross-cousin but, rather, a MMBDC (an Aranda system), and the term *tyaminy* designates this kin type as well as "spouse." This indicates the fact that once an affinal extension is consolidated—presumably in this case based on cross-cousin marriage—the actual consanguineal/classificatory kin designation can change to the new preferred marriageable kin type.

At this early stage of investigation, it appears that the *tyamVny* MF form spans at least five non-Pama-Nyungan families stretching throughout the Kimberley and across parts of the Northern Territory as far as the Queensland border, with some intrusion into southeast Arnhem Land. The eastern limit of the distribution of *tyamVny* is not far from the occurrence of *tyampa+* (*tyampa-thu*) in the Tangkic family (non-PNy but classed as close to PNy); and *tyampa+* (*tyampa-rtu*) is also to the immediate west

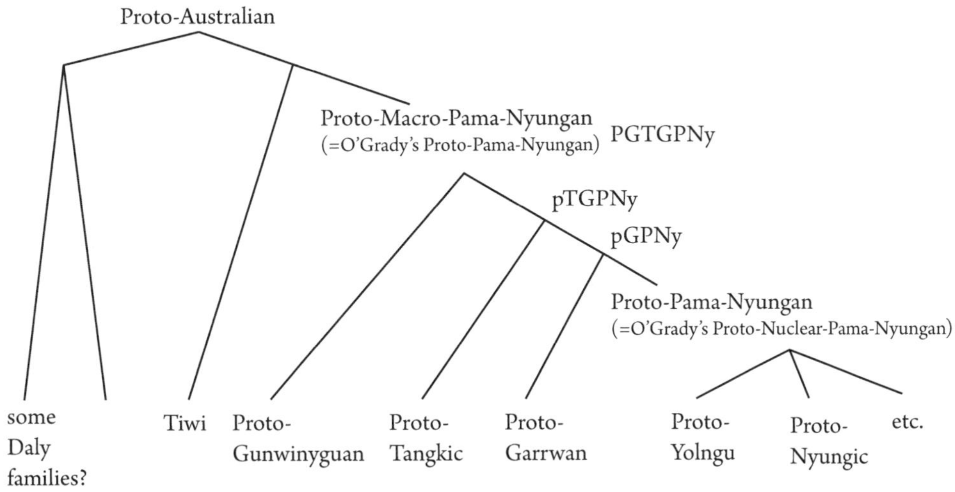

FIGURE 10.7. Phylogeny of Australian languages. pGPNy = Proto-Garrwan-Pama-Nyungan; pTGPNy = Proto-Tangkic-Garrwan-Pama-Nyungan; pGTGPNy = Proto-Guwinyguan-Tangkic-Garrwan-Pama-Nyungan. From Evans 2003.

of the *tyamVny* distribution in Marrngu (Karajarri and Mangala), and probably **tyampi* in the Ngumpin proto-language, giving rise to *tyapi+* and *tyawi+* forms.

The very wide distribution of a very similar form and meaning across a number of different families that have little in common lexically indicates strongly that this is a diffusion, a chain of borrowing. Since the root is very widespread in Pama-Nyungan as a result of inheritance, the most favored hypothesis would be that the root was borrowed into some non-Pama-Nyungan languages and spread from there mainly by diffusion. A number of questions remain to be answered more fully than has been possible here:

1. What is the Pama-Nyungan loan source?
2. What was the primary non-Pama-Nyungan recipient?
3. What is the reason behind this unusual wide diffusion of a kinship term?

6. Split between the Two Roots

6.1. A More Articulated Tree

Figure 10.7 reproduces the phylogeny for Australian languages in Evans 2003 together with some labeling of nodes that I have added: Proto-Garrwan-Pama-Nyungan, Proto-Tangkic-Garrwan-Pama-Nyungan, and Proto-Gunwinyguan-Tangkic-Garrwan-Pama-Nyungan, which Evans calls Proto-Macro-Pama-Nyungan. While I cannot give any definitive answer as to whether this phylogeny is correct, I will use it here as a working hypothesis and attempt to fit the phylogeny of the two kinship roots under discussion into this framework. The following sections review some key pieces of evidence that need to be accounted for in doing this; then I present a hypothesis about the evolution of the terms including their meanings at various stages. This is followed by a section that briefly discusses the implications of this for the reconstruction of the kinship systems at various stages in indigenous Australian prehistory.

6.2. Overlap of the Two Terms

One of the pieces of evidence we need to review here is the co-occurrence of the two different roots in single languages at the overlaps of the geographical distributions of each term. As noted, there is no case of full synonymy of the two terms in these cases. Clearly if this situation existed in a relevant protolanguage from which both descended (whether Proto-PNy or some other node such as those in Figure 10.7), then our dilemma over proto-language synonymy might be solved.

Let us look at the overlap of *tyampathu* (MF and MBS) and *ngathityu* (MBS [Evans 1995:554]) in Kayardild (case 1, above, regarding overlapping geographic distribution patterns; see Figure 10.3). Much the same is found in other Tangkic languages (Figure 10.8).

In Kayardild, a reflex of **tyampa* with *p* has the core meaning MF. It has the suffix *-thu*, which is clearly a form of the first-person possessive enclitic that has lost this meaning in kin terms (as also found in *ngama-thu* M and *ngathi-ju* MBS [McConvell 2008]).

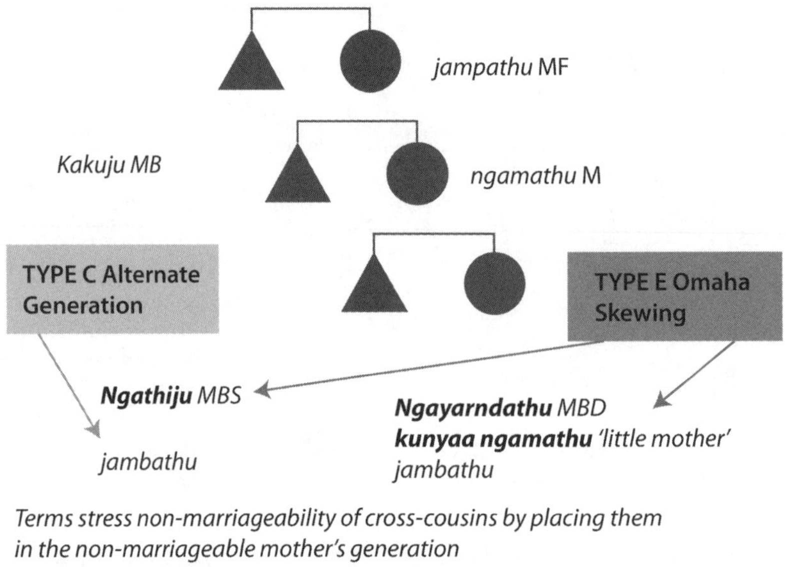

FIGURE 10.8. Co-occurrence of **ngatyV* and **tyam(p)V* in Tangkic. Kayardid, in the northern overlap of the roots, has a reflex of both terms (Evans 1995: 554).

Importantly, though, *jampathu* also has the meaning of "cross-cousin" (MBC). This is due to the alternate-generations agnatic principle (polysemy Type D in Table 10.2), which is found operating to assign the MF terms to cross-cousins in many languages.

In Kayardild, however, there are other terms for cross-cousins, *ngayarnda-thu* MBD and *ngathi-ju* MBS, the latter no doubt reflecting the Proto-PNy root **ngatyi* under discussion in this chapter. It is possible that the *ngathi* in this case descends from MF in the protolanguage, has been extended to MBS by the alternate-generations agnatic principle, and then has had the MF meaning overlain by the *tyampa* root. Alternatively one might argue that the term **ngathi/*ngatyi* only had the meaning MBS in the protolanguage (presumably Proto-Tangkic-Garrwan-Pama-Nyungan) and was extended to mean MF in subsequent protolanguages such as Proto-PNy. This goes some way toward removing the difficulty associated with having reconstructed synonyms but causes problems of its own, which are discussed further in the next section.

A similar pattern is found in the western Pilbara on the other side of the continent. In Thalanyji *thami* is MF (< **tyam[p]V*), and *ngathal* is "cross-cousin" (presumably < **ngatyV* + some suffix). Again this might be taken as pointing toward a protolanguage with a similar arrangement without synonymy. Both this and the previous example are at opposite ends of the very large western segment of the continent where **tyam(p)V* reflexes are dominant.

The other examples cited earlier have the opposite pattern, where the **ngatyV* reflex is MF and the **tyam(p)V* reflex is something else: "spouse," "sibling-in-law," "mother-in-law"/"father's sister" or "mother-in-law's brother." These are found on the eastern side of the continent in the north and far south. One way to make this compatible with the tentative proposal about the meanings in a protolanguage in the western case, discussed previously, would be to propose that, in this case too, there is no synonymy in the relevant protolanguage: that **ngatyV* means MF, and **tyam(p)V* is some affinal term, perhaps "sibling-in-law," perhaps descending from "cross-cousin," shifting to the +1 generation terms by some mechanism that needs to be worked out in more detail, perhaps involving a form of marriage to a cross-cousin's child. The identity of the protolanguage in this case could be Proto-PNy.

6.3. M/MP/P *Alternation in* *Tyam(p)V

As well as systematic meaning differences that can be interpreted as resulting from specific changes, there are also differences in the sounds of the words concerned, which have sound changes, presumably regular, as their cause. There are a number of these that could be investigated, but one that is especially salient is the alternation between *m* and *mp* in the middle of the root. Some issues surrounding these proposed alternatives and patterns of change, and another related alternant with *p* alone in the C2 position, were discussed in relation to a subset of languages in the central north.

While looking for systematic semantic change in comparative linguistics, one usually looks for regular sound change to justify linking one form to another. I have already mentioned instances where the change *mp* > *m* is regular in some Pama-Nyungan languages but not evident in exactly the languages we are dealing with here. Alternation between *m* and *mp* in **tyam(p)V* in closely related languages has been mentioned.

The distribution is shown in Figures 10.5 and 10.6. In addition to cases discussed in relation to Figure 10.6, in the south the *mp* forms are found in coastal New South Wales and parts of Victoria.

The following suggests itself as a scenario: the protoform in Proto-Tangkic-Pama-Nyungan was **tyampV-ny*. The form retaining the *p* and the nasal is found in the southeast. Forms retaining the *p* but dropping the final nasal descended into Proto-Ngumpin-Yapa and Proto-Marrngu or a combined protolanguage, Proto-Ngumpin-Yapa-Marrngu, not yet justified. In the rest of Pama-Nyungan the *mp* has become *m*, as it has in the non-PNy forms, which are dealt with next.

This scenario does not constitute a claim that there are three major subgroups in Tangkic-Pama-Nyungan (TPNy) based on this single change in a single root, of course. It is more likely that the *mp* forms were borrowed from Tangkic into Ngumpin-Yapa-Marrngu, for instance, implying that they were perhaps geographically much closer at one time than they are today, perhaps on or close to the Gulf of Carpentaria.[18]

6.4. **Tyam(p)V* in Non-Pama-Nyungan

The non-Pama-Nyungan families in which reflexes of **tyam(p)V* are found are in a continuous block throughout the Kimberley and across the savanna belt of the Northern Territory. The Warluwarric and Garrwan subgroups intervene between the eastern end of this block (eastern Mirndi) and Tangkic to the east.

All these languages have forms with *m*, not *mp*, and have a final nasal *-ny* (with added augments in some languages). As already noted, there is strong similarity in these forms between language families that are not relatable at this stage of research and have small numbers of reconstructible lexemes even within the families. This strongly points to diffusion (borrowing) having had a hand in spreading the forms, although inheritance might have had some role after a burst of diffusion. The fact that some families have more than one distinctive root form (e.g., *thamany* and *tyapV+* in Jarragan) also suggests borrowing and possibly stratification of loans.

The wide-scale diffusion of a kinship term like this is a fairly rare and striking phenomenon and calls for some explanation. Other examples of widespread diffusion of kinship terms investigated in AustKin seem to be all affinal terms, like *spouse* or *parent-in-law* (McConvell 2010b). Only one of the related forms in non-Pama-Nyungan is an affinal term—the Ngalakgan *tyaminy* 'spouse'. We have already encountered several times the semantic change sequence "mother's father" > "cross-cousin" > "spouse"/"sibling-in-law," with polysemies to hand justifying each step. However, in this case the spread has clearly been of the root with the meaning MF (with the secondary meaning "cross-cousin" in a number of languages). The final step to "spouse" only plausibly takes place in societies with cross-cousin marriage.

Possible other causes for a wide diffusion of a MF term have to be sought. In a Kariera system without gender distinctions (MF = FM) certain social changes may have warranted the addition of a term that distinguishes FM from MF, and the addition of a MF term by borrowing is one way to achieve this.

One such change is the transition from Kariera (or Karadjeri) to an Aranda system. This may often coincide with a change from cross-cousin to second-cousin marriage. In many systems the MF(Z) is equivalent to a cross-cousin and the FM(B) is equivalent to one's spouse in the new marriage system. The subsection system also represents this split and could at least in some cases go along with the change in marriage and kinship terminology—although it may also be a later development, for subsections have not spread through the entire area where the terms like **tyamV-ny* have spread.

The most likely source for the spread of the non-PNy form **tyamV-ny* is a Pama-Nyungan or Tangkic-Pama-Nyungan language after the loss of *p*—the same source as that of the majority of PNy forms. The final nasal may be a remnant of an old final consonant or a suffix added in the group from which the root was borrowed or in an early non-PNy recipient.

6.5. Hypothesis

The root **ngatyV* is reconstructed as MF in Proto-Pama-Nyungan in this proposal. In Proto-Tangkic-Pama-Nyungan it had the meaning of "cross-cousin," as discussed for Kayardild.[19] Possibly this descends from an earlier term for "mother"/"mother's brother" that changed to "cross-cousin" by Omaha skewing, but this is not an essential part of my hypothesis here, although it might be possible to explain the occurrence of some

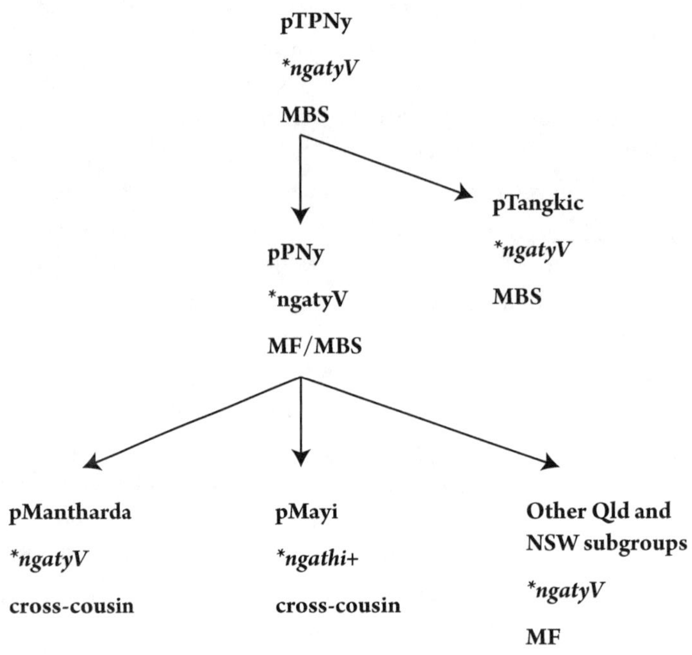

FIGURE 10.9. Phylogeny of **ngatyV.* NSW = New South Wales; p = Proto-; pPNy = Proto-Pama-Nyungan; pTPNy = Proto-Tangkic-Pama-Nyungan; Qld = Queensland.

ngatyi terms for "mother" in southeastern Pama-Nyungan in light of this ancestry.

In Pama-Nyungan the former "cross-cousin" term extends to MF. In this hypothesis the "cross-cousin" meaning is retained in the western Pilbara languages and in some of the Mayi languages of Queensland. On the phylogeny in Figure 10.9, these are not shown as linked to a common daughter node of PNy, since I am not aware of any other evidence for this. One possibility for the west is that the term was present on the western periphery with a polysemy between MF and "cross-cousin," and the other term, **tyam(p)V,* took over the MF meaning (Figure 10.10).

As for **tyam(p)V,* the hypothesis is that this had the meaning MF in Proto-TPNy with extension to "cross-cousin." The form with *p* was carried far south in the expansion of TPNy, and its meaning changed to "spouse"/ "sibling-in-law" based on the "cross-cousin" meaning in the context of cross-cousin marriage. The *mp* form also ended up in the western PNy subgroups Ngumpin-Yapa and Marrngu, possibly by borrowing when these groups were closer to Tangkic.

The form without *p* spread very widely in the western languages that we know as Pama-Nyungan, mostly with the meaning MF. This distribution spreads as far as Victoria, where it overlaps with *mp* forms with the meaning of an affine.

In the northeast, overlapping with **ngatyV* forms is a scattered distribution of **tyamV* forms with the meaning WMB and FZ. These two meanings can be linked by the affinal polysemy, but it is harder to link either of them to the general MF, "cross-cousin," or "spouse" meanings. As discussed earlier, one possibility is that the unusual "oblique" pattern of marriage to one's cross-cousin's child on Cape York Peninsula may have lain behind this change. It is concluded that this was a regional change in the direction "cross-cousin" to "wife's mother"—and subsequently to "father's sister" in the (usually Kariera) systems where this is the regular equation. This scenario rules out reconstructing the term as meaning WM(B) and/or FZ in Proto-Pama-Nyungan. Reconstructing the WM(B)/FZ meaning to Proto-PNy would dispose of the synonymy problem, but it is problematic on other grounds. Finally, in the savanna belt of non-Pama-Nyungan languages a solid distribution of *tyamV-ny* forms (with a couple of *tyap-* forms) is identified as a diffusional phenomenon initiated by a loan from PNy or Tangkic-Pama-Nyungan.

6.6. Implications for the Reconstruction of Australian Kinship Systems

The hypothesis presented above splits the question of the original meaning of the two roots into two successive stages: Proto-TPNy and Proto-PNy. At the Proto-TPNy stage, there is a distinct "cross-cousin" term (**ngatyV*)

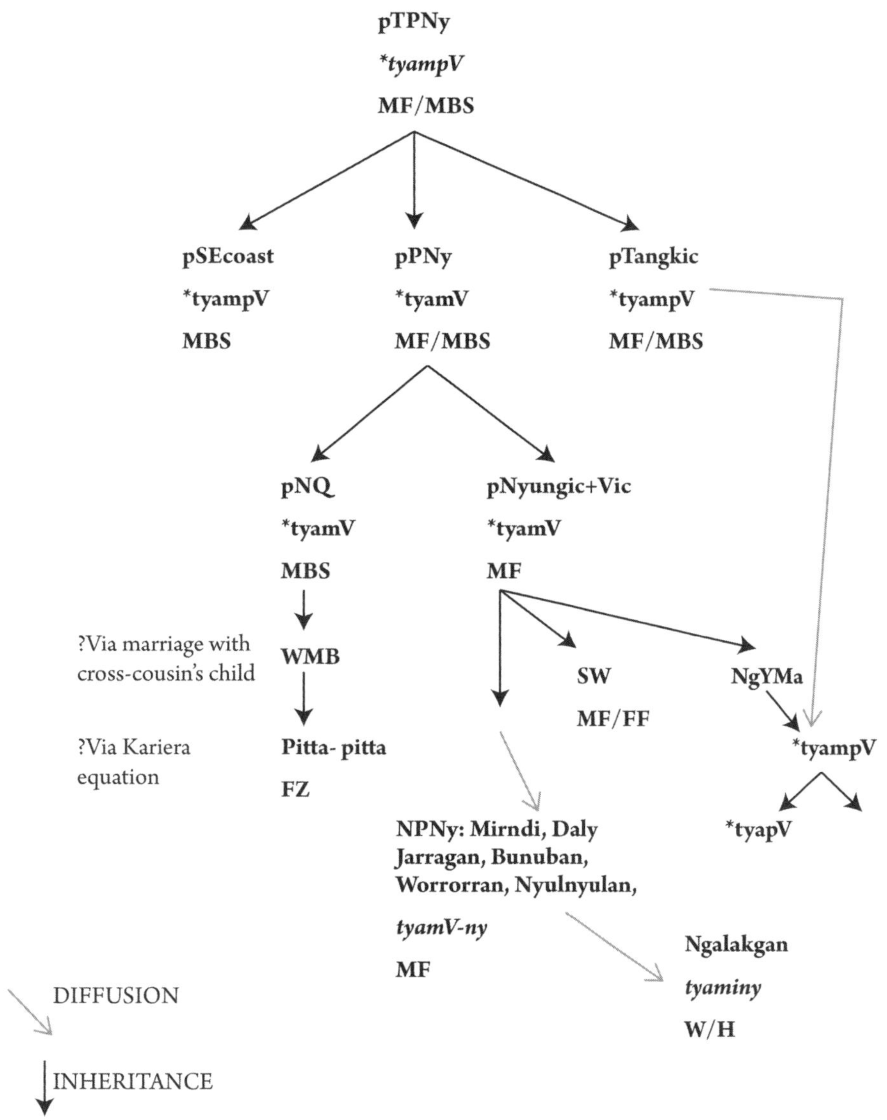

FIGURE 10.10. Phylogeny and diffusion of **tyam(p)V*. NPNy = non-Pama-Nyungan; p = Proto-; pPNy = Proto-Pama-Nyungan; pTPNy = Proto-Tangkic-Pama-Nyungan; Vic = Victorian.

and a MF term that has a "cross-cousin" extension resulting from the alternate-generations equivalence agnatic principle. This type of principle implies fairly strong patrilineality at this stage. If the "cross-cousin" term results from Omaha skewing, this also points toward patrilineality. At the Proto-PNy stage, the cross-cousin MBS term of Proto-TPNy has been extended to MF and taken over in that role.

One of the prime questions one might want to ask of grandparental terms at different stages in the phylogeny is whether or not they patterned in the Kariera way. For the terms under consideration, Kariera would mean that the MF term also covers FMB and, in some cases of sibling gender neutralization, FM.

Kariera is a form of Dravidian kinship that has a strong implication that bilateral marriage of (at least classificatory) cross-cousins was the rule. As we see in Figure 10.1, this type of system is found in significant patches in recent times in Queensland and parts of New South Wales and in the eastern Pilbara of Western Australia in Pama-Nyungan languages, as well as in some non-Pama-Nyungan regions such as the Daly River.

We cannot be sure, on the basis of the investigation carried out here alone, if the Proto-TPNy and/or Proto-PNy systems were Kariera. An important step toward answering this question would be to submit the widespread FM terms (Eastern **papi* and Western **ngapi*) to a similar distributional and semantic examination.

It seems significant, however, that the occurrence of the Kariera equations for cross-grandparent coincides with other Kariera/Dravidian equations being implicated in the history of the meaning change of other kin terms, particularly the affinal equations. The term *tyami* FZ in Pitta-Pitta is connected to WMB in its history, and Pitta-Pitta has the MF = FM equation. The Mayi languages (e.g., Mayi-Kulan) have *ngatyi*, with the meaning "cross-cousin"/"spouse," along with the Kariera/Dravidian link to cross-cousin marriage, and Mayi also has MF = FM. Further research in the AustKin project will pursue these correlations in other areas.

A suggestion made here is that the unusual meanings of **tyam(p)V* reflexes in the northeast may be connected with the oblique form of marriage practiced in some peripheral areas in recent times but possibly more widespread in the past. Although these unusual meanings and the oblique marriage systems were not in the end reconstructed to Proto-PNy, it is still important to understand this, because these occur in areas close by and perhaps overlapping those with Kariera systems. Such systems do not have the characteristics of Kariera/Dravidian bilateral cross-cousin marriage, and the kinds of kinship equations associated with that kind of oblique marriage warrant investigation.

One of the other significant findings of this examination is the burst of diffusion of the *tyamV-ny* term through a number of non-Pama-Nyungan families in the north. The proposal is being made that this event may have been due to the need for a new term in order to change *from* a Kariera or Karadjeri system to a new Aranda system, which requires a distinction between MF and FM(B). Some of the terminological relations also suggest, however, that new emphasis on the mother's brother as father-in-law of a bride was also involved with this diffusion, and this is, rather, something one might expect from a change to an asymmetrical matrilateral "Karadjeri" system.

7. Conclusions

This chapter has introduced and used a method for reconstructing kinship that combines the comparative method in linguistics with ethnological work on the typology of kinship interpreted as constraints on possible systems. Key to the method is the idea that semantic change occurs most often via a stage of transitional polysemy, so that changes can only normally be entertained if they are between different senses of a polysemy known to occur generally in world kinship systems and specifically in the region where the change is proposed.

This constrained approach to semantic change can help us to reconstruct the meanings of kinship terms and then put these reconstructions together to reconstruct proto-kinship systems. This framework allows us to say that, for kinship at least, meaning change is highly predictable, and it brings a notion of regularity to our research akin to that used for sound change in comparative linguistics.

Specifically I have investigated two widespread kinship roots in Australia, found mostly meaning "mother's father" and mostly in the Pama-Nyungan family—entirely, in one case, and spilling over into non-Pama-Nyungan, in the other. It has been shown that the latter case is due to a burst of diffusion into the north, and we have been pursuing the reasons why such a diffusion should take place, with some interesting possibilities emerging of linking the diffusion with changing marriage and kinship systems in prehistory.

This kind of diffusion offers a case of change that differs from the model of change via polysemy. A term has been borrowed from neighboring languages to effectively split a previously polysemous term and add a new, more distinctive "mother's father" term, interpreted here as part of a broad change from a Kariera to another (Aranda or Karadjeri) system of kinship and marriage in an area of northern Australia.

Further research on the stratigraphy of the sound changes and associated morphology of this diffusion could determine its geographical trajectory and, under favorable circumstances, its chronology. If this can be carried out, it will be a notable achievement for the historical method of reconstructing kinship systems and changes in them.

This brings us back again to the question of synonymy in the protolanguage. I have reconstructed different but overlapping meanings for **ngatyi* and **tyampV* in Proto-Tangkic-Pama-Nyungan, a node above Proto-Pama-Nyungan—MBS and MF/MBS, respectively. However, the reconstruction to Proto-Pama-Nyungan favors polysemy with synonymy: MF/MBS for both roots, although the core or prototype of each may have been different. The fact that these roots have such a distinct and almost complementary distribution geographically therefore seems to point to the idea that the two forms belonged to two dialects of Proto-PNy—one western (**tyam[p]V*) and one eastern (**ngatyi*).

This situation begs the question of whether these dialects were in fact the separate protolanguages for distinct subgroups of Pama-Nyungan at the highest level. This would take us beyond the current chapter and beyond what current research can support. However, it is important to bear in mind, as mentioned earlier, that the pair of terms considered in this chapter are not the only ones that have a roughly east/west split in their geographical distribution. All the tentatively proposed Proto-Pama-Nyungan grandkin terms are similar in this respect. The broader significance of this for the structure of the Pama-Nyungan family and for the reconstruction of the kinship systems of ancient Australia will surely emerge more clearly as we continue to work using the methods illustrated in this chapter.

Notes

1. Two relatively common types of skewing are Omaha (in which people in a male line are equated) and Crow (in which people in a female line are equated). There are several subtypes of skewing (Lounsbury 1964). The type in Latin appears not to be tied exclusively to patriline in the later period, but some authorities cite the earlier meaning of *nepos* as "sister's son," the reciprocal of "mother's brother." Now MB, as has been noted, is *avunculus*, which is a diminutive of *avus* 'grandfather'. There is not a strong indication that the Latin *avus* designated exclusively or prototypically "mother's father." However, one strong hypothesis about Proto-Indo-European is that it was of the Omaha type, with equation of MB and MF or grandfather and polysemy of **nepots* (from which the Latin *nepos* descends) between "grandson" and "sister's son" (Mallory and Adams 1997, 2006:212). This is Lounsbury's Omaha Type 3. Omaha systems in Australia are by contrast generally of Type 1 (McConvell 2012).
2. Some of Scheffler's (1978:106, 145, 419) equivalence rules (half-sibling merging, step-kin merging, same-sex sibling merging) are found in all or most Australian systems and so are not considered here as they do not play a part in the paths of change to be discussed. Cross-step-kin (Scheffler 1978:6:226) and alternate-generations uterine equivalences (Scheffler 1978:6:376) are also omitted from the table as not relevant to the present discussion. These are numbered 1–3 in Scheffler's scheme. The numbers used in the table are found in Scheffler most often, but they are not used consistently to label rules, since they signify the ordering of rules in a system. The equivalence of the equations here and Scheffler's rules is compromised by his use of the notion of "superclass" particularly for type A.
3. Other criteria are included in Radcliffe-Brown's scheme, including types of marriage, but the importance of grandparental-generation terms distinguishes this scheme from other typologies introduced and widely used internationally that can also be applied in Australia but have not been (McConvell and Hendery 2010).
4. This is said to be related to asymmetrical marriage, but there is not a good fit between such systems and marriage patterns (see Keen, this volume). There is another logical possibility in which paternal and maternal are distinguished in cross, but not parallel, grandkin, but this seems rare.
5. The formulation used here follows Radcliffe-Brown (1931). However, others (e.g., Hage) have used the term *Kariera* in a nonstandard way to refer to systems that have alternate-generations equivalence, e.g., where FF = B = mSC. Alternate-generations equivalence is associated with some Kariera systems but is really an independent variable (cf. McConvell and Hendery 2010).
6. V in these forms represents a vowel of uncertain quality. Reflexes of these terms most commonly have *i* as the second vowel, but *a* is also common and, in the case of **tyam(p)V*, also *u* in some areas. The *p* in parentheses represents the fact that both *m* and *mp* are found in reflexes in different regions, and a judgment as to which was in the protoform may be difficult. My own preference is for reconstruction of **tyampV*, since there are a number of cases of a regular sound change *mp* > *m* in Australia and no clear examples of a change in the opposite direction. There are also reflexes of the form *tyapV* probably descended from **tyampV*. A cautious approach might split **tyamV* and **tyampV* into two unconnected roots. In view of the identity of meaning and substantial other evidence, such as the existence of *m/mp* variants in some subgroups including in the same language (e.g., the Pitta-Pitta *tyami/yampi/yami* FZ/WM/MBW), I have chosen to regard them as variants of the same root. Full proof of these and motivations of the changes in *mp* and the vowels would require more space than I have available to examine phonological reconstructions and their relations with subgrouping, as in Harold Koch's chapter (this volume).
7. The *probably* is added here because the form *ngathal* 'cross-cousin' in this area has a final *-l* that cannot be fully explained at present. Many of the reflexes of **ngatyV* do have a second *a* vowel and a suffix. The *-l* is one of the suffixes mentioned in McConvell 2008 (and further elaborated on in McConvell 2007a), where it is proposed that it may descend from a junior reciprocal suffix. In this case it could be interpreted perhaps as a junior alternate-generation suffix deriving "cross-cousin" from MF.
8. Roth (1897) gives this polysemous meaning, but later work (Blake 1979) identifies the meaning as FM only. The most likely interpretation of this is that there was a narrowing of the meaning during the 20th century. The recent source gives *tyanka/yanka* as meaning MF, encroaching on the former scope of the general cross-term *ngathanha*. *Tyanka/yanka* is glossed by Roth as FF, not MF, and there are cognates for *yanku* FF in other languages in the same subgroup, Karnic. The recent form given for FF in Pitta-Pitta is *ngartarta*. This form is widespread in Karnic languages in the meaning MF but also has an extension to FF in some such

as Yarluyandi. It is likely that the original FF term *tyanka/yanka* was extended to mean MF, narrowing *ngathanha* to FM.

9. Warrungu is also reported to have a shift in the meaning of *kami*, normally MM, to FM, like a number of other languages farther south on the east coast. If FM was polysemous in the Kariera fashion (FM = MF), then loss of the MF element in a MF = FF polysemy could have been caused by this change: this is speculation. Yaygir is also affected by a switch in meaning of *kami* MM > FM and *papi* FM > MM (McConvell 2013).
10. The *-thu/-tyu* is a suffix originating in a first-person possessive enclitic and is found on many of the terms formed from *tyam(p)V* MF in Pama-Nyungan, as is the kinship suffix *-rti/-rtu* (McConvell 2008). A transitional polysemy in this process appears in Jiwarli: *thami-ju* 'my MF' *and* junior reciprocal mDC.
11. In the Sydney region there is an alternation between homorganic nasal cluster (NC) in most dialects and just nasal (N) in others (Nash 2010). However, no record of the WB term was collected, so we do not know if the predicted alternant *tyami* existed in the latter dialects. A similar sound change, NC > N, also characterizes the Yolngu languages (Heath 1981:336), but there is no reflex of **tyam(p)V* MF in them, as far as is known. *Mp* also becomes *p* in some languages, such as Dhangatti (mentioned here), Ngumpin, and others.
12. This term is about the only Yolngu kinship term that does not have a traceable genealogy in terms of inheritance or borrowing (McConvell and Keen 2011), but unfortunately O'Grady's idea is not the answer.
13. There are clearly demonstrated examples of an MB root shifting meaning to FZ, as in the case of **mukur* (McConvell and Alpher 2002) as the root moved out of Cape York Peninsula. Despite being well supported by linguistic evidence, it does not follow any of the common polysemy paths so far discussed and had to be justified in terms of the affinal roles of these kin (both being wife-bestowers). For the case being discussed, of **tyaami* WM(B)/FZ in Queensland, we might therefore conjecture that MF might have become MB by some form of Omaha skewing and thence FZ. Or if the original meaning was FZ/WM, this could have become MB and thence MF by Omaha skewing (Type 3, not commonly found in Australia). These solutions are implausible.
14. A less rare form of oblique marriage, not attested in Australia, is "avuncular" marriage where a woman marries a cross-uncle, yielding most often the equation FZC = ZC, which is also an Omaha skewing equation, but also others that are not Omaha (Shapiro 1966).
15. The Dyirbal WM/"cross-cousin" form *waymin* does not look like a cognate of *tya(a)mi*. In north Cape York Peninsula McConnel (1950–51:132ff.) reports oblique marriages as the norm, primarily FyZDD marriage for a man.
16. Two other forms have been included in this set as they have *p* rather than *mp*: the Warrwa *tyapawu* and Mangarrayi/Alawa *tyap-tyap*. Mangarrayi has a synchronic alternation between oral stops and nasals (Merlan 1982:205–206) and diachronic nasal > oral change in codas, e.g., **pam > pap* 'head' (Harvey 2003:224), which could explain *tyaptyap* as < **tyamtyam*. Mangarrayi also has a reciprocal of MF that retains *m* in a non-coda position: *tyamanywa* mDC. This *tyamVny-* root could be the conduit to the Ngalakgan form *tyaminy* to the north.
17. Harold Koch has pointed out to me that Warlmanpa also has the term *pimpirdi* FZ (cf. the Warlpiri *pimirdi*), which is clearly descended from the Proto-PNy root **pimV* FZ (Alpher 2004), and thus that there is perhaps a local *p > mp* change in Warlmanpa. However, it is still possible that **tyampi-rti* is the Proto-Ngumpin-Yapa form and *pimpirti* was constructed analogically.
18. The other possibility arising from this, though, is that Tangkic and the southeastern group of Pama-Nyungan (or of Tangkic-Pama-Nyungan) might be joint members of a subgroup. On the face of it that sounds unlikely, but the evidence has not been collected.
19. I have omitted the node Garrwan from this label for simplicity. Neither of the roots **ngatyV* and **tyam(p)V* occurs in Garrwan. Garrwan has *mimi* for MF, which is found in the neighboring Warluwarric subgroup of Pama-Nyungan with the meaning MF and in neighboring non-PNy languages as FM(B). If this is a loan into Garrwan, it may have replaced a cognate of one of the roots under discussion here.

References Cited

Allen, N. 1986. Tetradic Theory: An Approach to Kinship. *Journal of the Anthropological Society of Oxford* 17(2):89–109.

Allen, N. 1998. The Prehistory of Dravidian-Type Terminologies. In *Transformations of Kinship*. M. Godelier, T. B. Trautmann, and F. E. Tjon Sie Fat, eds. Pp. 314–331. Washington, DC: Smithsonian.

Alpher, B. 2004. Pama-Nyungan Etyma. On CD-ROM accompanying *Australian Languages: Classification and the Comparative Method*. C. Bowern and H. Koch, eds. Amsterdam: John Benjamins.

Bindon, P., and R. Chadwick, eds. 1992. *A Nyoongar Wordlist from the South West of Western Australia*. Perth: Anthropology Department, Western Australian Museum.

Blake, B. J. 1979. Pitta-Pitta. In *Handbook of Australian Languages*, vol. 1. R. Dixon and B. J. Blake, eds. Pp. 182–242. Canberra: Australian National University Press.

Clackson, J. 2007. *Indo-European Linguistics: An Introduction*. Cambridge: Cambridge University Press.

Dixon, R. 1989. The Dyirbal Kinship System. *Oceania* 59:245–268.

Dixon, R. 2002. *The Australian Languages: Their Nature and Development*. Cambridge: Cambridge University Press.

Douglas, W. H. 1976. *The Aboriginal Languages of the South-West of Australia*. Canberra: Australian Institute of Aboriginal Studies.

Dyen, I., and D. F. Aberle. 1974. *Lexical Reconstruction: The Case of the Proto-Athapaskan Kinship System*. London: Cambridge University Press.

Elkin, A. P. 1964. *The Australian Aborigines: How to Understand Them*. Sydney: Angus and Robertson.

Elkin, A. P. 1970. The Aborigines of Australia: "One in Thought, Word and Deed." In *Pacific Linguistic Studies in Honour of Arthur Capell*. S. Wurm and D. Laycock, eds. Pp. 697–716. Pacific Linguistics, C-13. Canberra: Australian National University.

Evans, N. 1992. Multiple Semiotic Systems, Hyperpolysemy and the Reconstruction of Semantic Change in Australian Languages. In *Diachrony within Synchrony: Language History and Cognition*. G. Kellermann and M. D. Morrissey, eds. Pp. 475–508. Duisburger Arbeiten zur Sprach- und Kulturwissenschaft/Duisburg Papers on Research in Language and Culture, 14. Frankfurt: Peter Lang.

Evans, N. 1995. *A Grammar of Kayardild: With Historical-Comparative Notes on Tangkic*. Berlin: Mouton de Gruyter.

Evans, N. 2003. Introduction: Comparative Non-Pama-Nyungan and Australian Historical Linguistics. In *The Non-Pama-Nyungan Languages of Northern Australia: Comparative Studies of the Continent's Most Linguistically Complex Region*. N. Evans, ed. Pp. 2–25. Pacific Linguistics, 552. Canberra: Australian National University.

Hage, P. 2003. The Ancient Maya Kinship System. *Journal of Anthropological Research* 59(1):5–21.

Hage, P., B. Milicic, M. Mixco, and M. Nichols. 2004. The Proto-Numic Kinship System. *Journal of Anthropological Research* 60(3):359–377.

Hale, K. 1976. Phonological Developments in a Northern Paman Language: Uradhi. In *Languages of Cape York*. P. Sutton, ed. Pp. 41–49. Canberra: Australian Institute of Aboriginal Studies.

Harvey, M. 2003. An Initial Reconstruction of Proto Gunwinyguan Phonology. In *The Non-Pama-Nyungan Languages of Northern Australia: Comparative Studies of the Continent's Most Linguistically Complex Region*. N. Evans, ed. Pp. 205–268. Pacific Linguistics, 552. Canberra: Australian National University.

Harvey, M. 2008. *Proto-Mirndi: A Discontinuous Language Family in Northern Australia*. Canberra: Pacific Linguistics.

Heath, J. 1981. A Case of Intensive Lexical Diffusion: Arnhem Land, Australia. *Language* 57:335–367.

Lounsbury, F. G. 1964. The Formal Analysis of Crow- and Omaha-Type Kinship Terminologies. In *Explorations in Cultural Anthropology: Essays in Honor of George Peter Murdock*. W. H. Goodenough, ed. Pp. 351–393. New York: McGraw-Hill Book Co.

Mallory, J., and D. Q. Adams. 1997. *The Encyclopaedia of Indo-European Culture*. London: Fitzroy Dearborn.

Mallory, J. P., and D. Q. Adams. 2006. *The Oxford Introduction to Proto-Indo-European and the Proto-Indo-European World*. Oxford: Oxford University Press, USA.

McConnel, U. 1950–51. Junior Marriage Systems: Comparative Survey. *Oceania* 21:107–145.

McConvell, P. 1988. Nasal Cluster Dissimilation and Constraints on Phonological Variables in Gurindji and Related Languages. In *Aboriginal Linguistics 1*. N. Evans and S. Johnson, eds. Pp. 135–165. Armidale, Australia: Department of Linguistics, University of New England.

McConvell, P. 1996. Backtracking to Babel: The Chronology of Pama-Nyungan Expansion in Australia. *Archaeology in Oceania* 31:125–144.

McConvell, P. 1997a. Long-Lost Relations: Pama-Nyungan and Northern Kinship. In *Archaeology and Linguistics: Aboriginal Australia in Global Perspective*. P. McConvell and N. Evans, eds. Pp. 207–235. Melbourne: Oxford University Press.

McConvell, P. 1997b. Semantic Shifts between Fish and Meat and the Prehistory of Pama-Nyungan. In *Boundary Rider: Essays in Honour of Geoffrey O'Grady*. D. Tryon and M. Walsh, eds. Pp. 303–325. Pacific Linguistics, C-136. Canberra: Australian National University.

McConvell, P. 2006. Shibbolethnonyms, Ex-exonyms and Eco-ethnonyms. Theme issue, "Name Theory—Théorie des noms—Namentheorie." R. Coates, ed. *ONOMA* 41:186–214.

McConvell, P. 2007a. The Pama-Nyungan Kin Suffix *-li/-lu*. Electronic document, http://wiki.pacific-credo.fr/index.php?title=AustKin_Publications.

McConvell, P. 2007b. Reduplication in Proto-PNy Kinterms. Electronic document, http://wiki.pacific-credo.fr/index.php?title=AustKin_Publications.

McConvell, P. 2008. Grand-Daddy Morphs: The Importance of Suffixes in Reconstructing Pama-Nyungan Kinship. In *Morphology and Language History: In Honour of Harold Koch*. C. Bowern, B. Evans, and L. Miceli, eds. Pp. 313–327. Current Issues in Linguistic Theory, 298. Amsterdam: John Benjamins.

McConvell, P. 2010a. The Archaeolinguistics of Migration. In *Migration History in World History: Multidisciplinary Approaches*. J. Lucassen, P. McConvell, and L. Lucassen, eds. Pp. 155–190. Leiden: Brill.

McConvell, P. 2010b. The Diffusion of a Parent-in-Law Term from the Kimberleys through the Northern Territory. Seminar paper presented at the Centre for Research in Language Change, Australian National University, Canberra.

McConvell, P. 2012. Omaha Skewing in Australia: Overlays, Dynamism and Change. In *Crow-Omaha: New Light on a Classic Problem of Kinship Analysis*. Thomas Trautmann and Peter M. Whiteley, eds. Pp. 243–260. Amerind Foundation Advanced Seminar Series. Tucson: University of Arizona Press

McConvell, P. 2013. Granny Got Cross: Semantic Change of *Kami* 'Mother's Mother' to 'Father's Mother' in Pama-Nyungan. In *Lexical and Structural Etymology: Beyond Word Histories*. Robert Mailhammer, ed. Pp. 147–184. Studies in Language Change. Berlin: de Gruyter.

McConvell, P., and B. Alpher. 2002. The Omaha Trail in Australia: Tracking Skewing from East to West. *Anthropological Forum* 12(2):159–176.

McConvell, P., and C. Bowern. 2011. The Prehistory and Internal Relationships of Australian Languages. *Languages and Linguistics* 5(1):19–32.

McConvell, P., and R. Hendery. 2010. Investigating the Multiple Meanings of "Kariera System" with AUSTKIN Database Queries. Unpublished MS, Australian National University, Canberra.

McConvell, P., and I. Keen. 2011. The Transition from Kariera to an Asymmetrical System: Cape York Peninsula to North-East Arnhemland. In *Kinship, Language and Prehistory: Per Hage and the Renaissance in Kinship Studies*. D. Jones and B. Milicic, eds. Pp. 99–132. Salt Lake City: University of Utah Press.

Merlan, F. 1982. *Mangarayi*. Amsterdam: North-Holland.

Muurrbay Aboriginal Language and Cultural Co-operative. 2001. *A Gumbaynggir Language Dictionary/Gumbaynggir Bijaarr Jandaygam*. Nambucca Heads, Australia: Muurrbay Aboriginal Language and Cultural Co-operative.

Nash, D. 2010. Dawes' Law Generalized: Cluster Simplification in the Coastal Dialect of the Sydney Language. In *Indigenous Language and Social Identity: Papers in Honour of Michael Walsh*. B. Baker, I. Mushin, M. Harvey, and R. Gardner, eds. Pp. 169–190. Canberra: Pacific Linguistics.

O'Grady, G. N. 1990. Pama-Nyungan **m-*, **j-* and **k-*. In *Studies in Comparative Pama-Nyungan*. G. N. O'Grady and D. Tryon, eds. Pp. 79–103. Pacific Linguistics, C-111. Canberra: Australian National University.

O'Grady, G. N., C. Voegelin, and F. Voegelin. 1966. Languages of the World: Indo-Pacific Fascicle 6. *Anthropological Linguistics* 8(2):1–199.

Peterson, N., P. McConvell, H. McDonald, F. Morphy, and B. Arthur. 2005. Social and Cultural Life. In *Macquarie Atlas of Indigenous Australia*. B. Arthur and F. Morphy, eds. Pp. 88–107. Sydney: Ryde.

Radcliffe-Brown, A. R. 1931. *The Social Organization of Australian Tribes*. Melbourne: Macmillan.

Roth, W. E. 1897. *Ethnological Studies among the North-West-Central Queensland Aborigines*. Brisbane: Government Printer.

Scheffler, H. W. 1978. *Australian Kin Classification*. Cambridge: Cambridge University Press.

Shapiro, W. 1966. Secondary Unions and Kinship Terminology: The Case of Avuncular Marriage. *Bijdragen tot de Taal-, Land- en Volkenkunde* 122(1):82–89.

Stokes, B., and W. McGregor. 2003. Classification and Subclassification of the Nyulnyulan Languages. In *The Non-Pama-Nyungan Languages of Northern Australia: Comparative Studies of the Continent's Most Linguistically Complex Region*. N. Evans, ed. Pp. 29–74. Pacific Linguistics, 552. Canberra: Australian National University.

Wilkins, D. 1996. From Part to Person: Natural Tendencies of Semantic Change and the Search for Cognates. In *The Comparative Method Reviewed: Regularity and Irregularity in Language Change*. M. Durie and M. Ross, eds. Pp. 264–304. New York: Oxford University Press.

11

Mama and *Papa* in Indigenous Australia

Rachel Hendery and Patrick McConvell

Background

Anthropologists and linguists following Murdock (1959) and Jakobson (1960) have explained the high frequency of words like *mama* and *papa*, respectively, for "mother" and "father" around the world as spontaneously recurring inventions, in the case of *mama* related to sounds made by an infant while breast-feeding. This type of explanation has tended to make linguists generally suspicious of finding deep etymologies for such words or reconstructing them to protolanguages. At the other extreme there are linguists of the "long-range comparison" school who believe that they can reconstruct a number of "Proto-World" or "Proto-Sapiens" kinship terms and include **mama* and **papa* among this set (Bancel et al. 2011; Matthey de l'Etang and Bancel 2002, 2005; Matthey de l'Etang et al. 2011).

As a corrective to both these approaches we closely examine the kinship roots *mama* and *papa*, which are widespread in Australian indigenous languages. In investigating the distribution and varying meanings of these roots we use the online database of Australian kinship terms AUSTKIN, compiled as part of an Australian Research Council Discovery grant based at the Australian National University.

Contrary to some versions of both the "Baby Talk" and "Proto-World" approaches, *mama* in Australia is mostly found as "father," not "mother," and *papa* is found as "mother" in some areas. *Mama* is a possible candidate for Proto-Pama-Nyungan "father," but its distribution is mainly in the west of the continent and Victoria and in central and northern New South Wales with the meaning "father." In the north of Western Australia, it shifts meaning to "elder brother"; in other places there are shifts of meaning to be discussed below. Elsewhere versions of *papa* are found sporadically for "father" and also for "(elder) brother." *Pap(a)* is also found as "mother," mainly in Victoria. Other kinship roots (for grandparents) have been shown to have a split distribution, with one root dominating in the east and one in the west for what is apparently a single protomeaning (McConvell 2008, and chapter 10, this volume). The distribution of *mama* and *papa* is not so clear-cut, but we outline how it can be accounted for without resorting either to recurrent invention or to inheritance from some putative proto-world ancestral language.

Mama *and* Papa *around the World*

The common existence across the world's languages of the terms *mama*, *papa*, and similar-sounding kinship terms (including *tata* or *dada* and *kaka*, which will not be discussed in this chapter) has long been known (Gheorgov 1911; Jakobson 1960). A sample of languages showing the similarity of these terms is reproduced in Table 11.1. Explanations for this phenomenon usually fall into one of two camps: the "Proto-World" theory or the "Baby Talk" hypothesis. The Baby Talk hypothesis in its best-known form was first proposed by Jakobson (1960:542–543), where he notes that nasals are the only sounds that can be produced while suckling and, therefore, are used to signal desire for food and come to be a name for the prime dispenser, one's mother. The vowel [a] is the "default" sound made by an unrestricted airstream, so that the sequence *NaNa* (where N represents any nasal) is a natural symbol a baby would develop for "food." The association between suckling/food and "mother," while strong, is a later development, reinforced by the parents' desire to see their child asking for and referring to them. It is true that not just *mama* but also *nana* and *nganga* are found as words for "mother" in the languages of the world.

A weaker version of the Baby Talk hypothesis is simply that, just as [a] is the simplest vowel to acquire, the sounds [m], [p/b], and [t/d] are among the first learned by babies, and as such, their babbling often contains the sequences *mama*, *baba*, *tata*, *dada*, *papa*, and so on. It is also the case that reduplication is a common feature of "nursery forms," not only in the kinship semantic field but also beyond (cf. Bavin 1993:93; Sandefur 1986:59). Again, it is the parents, with their desire to see the child communicate with them, who assign the meaning of "parent" to these sound sequences, and this is gradually reinforced until the child him- or herself comes to associate the meaning and sound. Well-known proponents of various versions of this Baby Talk hypothesis include Murdock (1959) and Campbell and Poser (2008:198ff.).

The other widely publicized explanation for the frequency of *mama* and *papa* is the "Proto-World" hypothesis, whereby they are said to be retentions from the ancestor language from which all modern languages are descended. The existence of Proto-World is not accepted by most mainstream linguists, and the idea that any cognates from Proto-World in modern languages would still be recognizably similar in form would surprise Indo-Europeanists or any other practitioners of the comparative method, who are used to cognates with less than 10,000 years of divergence being undetectable until painstaking reconstruction of etymology has taken place and those of greater age being largely irretrievable, so that the ability to prove a relationship between languages disappears. Even those who say that they have techniques that push this boundary back tend not to claim to penetrate the past more than around 20,000 years. The idea that we might still be using words that are hundreds of thousands of years old appeals, however, to the popular media, and so this hypothesis is as widely known as the more mainstream Baby Talk theory. The main proponents of the Proto-World explanation for *mama* and *papa* are Matthey de l'Etang, Bancel, Bengtson, and Ruhlen (Bancel et al. 2011; Bengtson and Ruhlen 1994; Matthey de l'Etang and Bancel 2005, 2008; Ruhlen 1994).

Bancel et al. concede that 26 percent of the *mama* words in their world languages database mean "father" or F = FB, as opposed to 43 percent meaning "mother" or M = MZ. Nevertheless they select "mother" as the "Proto-Sapiens" meaning, explaining:

> Many of the numerous *mama* words meaning "father"–"father + father's brother" occur in clusters in the same language family. Such clusters must have resulted from a single erratic language shift early in the history of the family, whose result was then transmitted with the usual fidelity to the descendant languages. (2011:42)

Austronesian is singled out as one such family that has a preponderance of *mama* words for "father" resulting from a supposed "erratic meaning shift."

This type of argument is seriously flawed. There is no evidence for such a meaning shift, which is vanishingly rare in the annals of semantic change—presumably this is why it is described as "erratic." This leads us to question whether there was a meaning shift at all—perhaps such *mama* F forms are simply *different etyma* from those meaning M and other kin types and cannot be connected.

Bancel et al. also point out that 136 out of 166 occurrences (81 percent) in their database of *mama* F are from Austronesian. While this figure may be cited to minimize the perception that *mama* F is common, in fact it raises further doubts about their method. It is not clear what steps

TABLE 11.1. Partial list of *mama* and *papa* terms.

Language	Mother	Father
Swahili	*mama*	*baba*
Kikuyu (East Africa)	*nana*	*baba*
Xhosa (South Africa)	*-mama*	*-tata*
Tagalog (Philippines)	*nanay*	*tatay*
Malay	*emak*	*bapa*
Romanian	*mama*	*tata*
Welsh	*mam*	*tad*
Urdu	*mang*	*bap*
Turkish	*ana, anne*	*baba*
Pipil (El Salvador)	*naan*	*tatah*
Kobon (New Guinea)	*amy*	*bap*
Basque	*ama*	*aita*
Hungarian	*anya*	*apa*
Dakota (U.S.)	*ena*	*ate*
Nahuatl (Mexico)	*naan*	*ta'*
Luo (Kenya	*mama*	*baba*
Apalai (Amazon)	*aya*	*papa*
Chechen (Caucasus)	*naana*	*daa*
Cree (Canada)	*-mama*	*-papa*
Quechua (Ecuador)	*mama*	*tayta*
Mandarin Chinese	*mama*	*baba*

Source: From Trask 2004.

they took to deal with Galton's problem, that is, to adjust their sample so that connected sets like languages in the same family are not overrepresented. The actual listing of languages in their database is not made available. Presumably it includes at least some Australian languages, and in light of the large number of *mama* F forms in Australia discussed later in this chapter, some of the residue (30 apart from the Austronesian examples) are likely to be Australian. As we argue, the dominance of *mama* F in Australia may well be due to this form/meaning pair being Proto-Pama-Nyungan, but there is no evidence for an "erratic meaning shift" from an earlier *mama* M.

The two hypotheses make different predictions about the distribution, meaning, and historical behavior of *mama* and *papa*. Under the Baby Talk hypothesis, *mama/papa* forms will be randomly scattered among languages, will have no great time-depth and few sound changes since they are regularly replaced, and will not be reconstructible to protolanguages; and according to the "strong" version of this hypothesis, *mama* or a similar nasal word will mean "mother." One of the main points made by the Baby Talk proponents is that these forms should never be used for reconstruction: "Such nursery words are not considered viable evidence in proposals of distant genetic relationships" (Campbell and Poser 2008:199). Because of this, linguists have generally ignored nursery forms entirely. Among Australianists, for instance, Heath recommends not making any judgment about the etymology of the Pama-Nyungan Yolngu *ba:pa* and the non-Pama-Nyungan neighbor Wubuy *baba*—both "father"—because of the "possibility of coincidental sharing" (1981:347).[1]

It seems odd that Campbell and Poser abrogate the use of the comparative method, which can surely show that some forms are indeed descended from protoforms of some age, as they show changes and regular correspondences with cognates in a geographically and historically coherent group of languages, or that others are borrowed from particular source languages. If this kind of evidence is absent, then one might indeed look for an explanation in terms of recurrent invention, but surely not before looking at the evidence. That is what we intend to do in Australia for *mama* and *papa* forms.

Ruhlen (2000:521) argues against this resistance to reconstructing such forms to protolanguages and indeed proposes that such forms are among the best evidence for the notion of Proto-World put forward by him and others of the long-range comparison school. He suggests that other kinship terms are found very commonly among the world languages and that Jakobson's explanations cannot apply to them. One of these is *kaka*, which is found with a range of meanings including both older male and older female relatives. Campbell (1997:299) and Campbell and Poser (2008:199–200) show that Ruhlen misinterprets Jakobson and in fact his explanation does extend to other forms such as *tata*, *nana*, and *kaka*. However, it is by no means clear that such "baby talk" recurrent invention explanations are well grounded or that this hypothesis alone is enough to exclude all such forms from consideration in comparative reconstruction as Campbell and Poser propose.

If the Proto-World explanation were correct, on the other hand, we would expect *mama/papa* terms to have a great time depth, display regular sound changes, and be reconstructible (if reconstruction were possible beyond the generally accepted ~15,000-year limit). This condition is not a credible proposition, and we would not necessarily expect an association of *NaNa* with the meaning "mother" since the number of sound changes and meaning changes over that immense period of time would have changed the lexical items so profoundly. The Proto-World hypothesis does not necessarily make predictions about the distribution of terms, other than that they would be widespread among the world's languages (suspending judgment for the time being about whether cognates could actually be recognized). It would not be surprising to find that enough languages had lost the terms that the current distribution would appear fairly "random." On the other hand, some clusters of occurrence in related languages might also be expected.

What we will show for the Australian data, at least, is that the Proto-World hypothesis is unnecessary and the baby talk explanation is not the whole story. It is possible that *mama* and *papa* terms might be reconstructible to some protolanguages, without us having to reconstruct them back to "Proto-World." Their existence in multiple unrelated protolanguages can then be attributed to the baby talk explanation and/or random chance. The advantage of this sort of "middle ground" explanation, if correct, is that it means that "baby talk" kinship terms are not as useless for historical, comparative, or typological studies as has usually been claimed. If these terms are inherited and not regularly replaced, we would expect that the patterns of distributions of their forms, lexical and

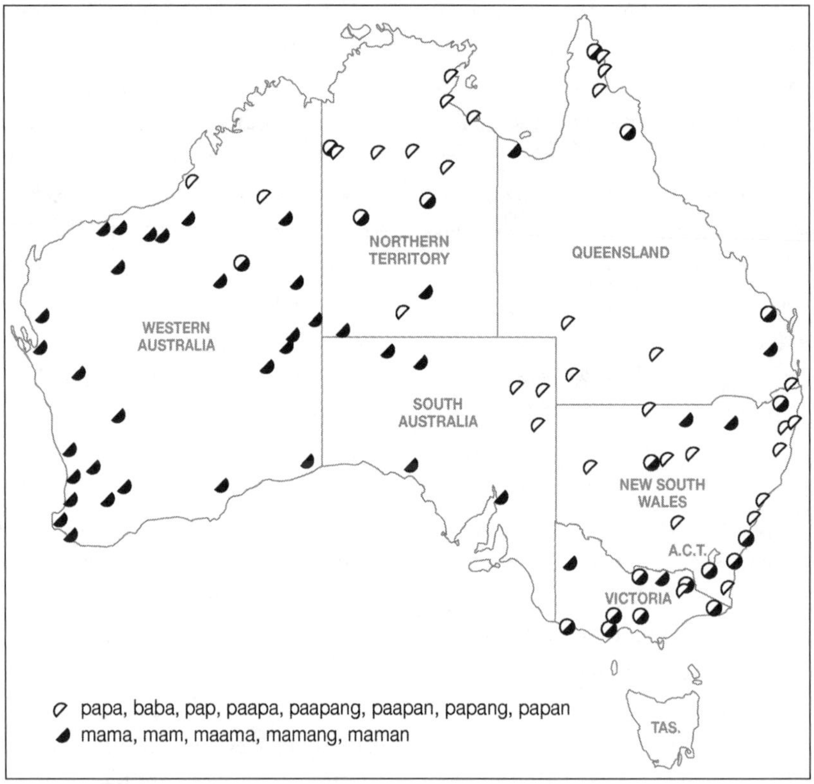

FIGURE 11.1. *Mama* and *papa* forms across Australia.

morphological correspondences, patterns of polysemy, and other semantic matters would yield useful information that can contribute to our understanding of language relatedness, borrowing patterns, and semantic change. We will show in this chapter that this is actually the case: the distribution of *mama* and *papa* forms and meanings in Australian languages clusters in interesting ways that should not be ignored just because the terms belong to the so-called nursery words set.

Mama *and* Papa *in Australia*

Our data for this chapter, and the mapping software, come from the "AustKin project," described in detail in Dousset et al. 2010. The AUSTKIN database contains more than 600 lists of kinship terms from 304 Australian languages (where we count as separate languages all those that are considered separate by the Australian Institute of Aboriginal and Torres Strait Islander Studies AUSTLANG database). These lists are taken from 427 different sources (dictionaries, grammars, field note manuscripts, etc.). In total the database contains more than 80,000 words. It is fully searchable, and the results of queries can be displayed on a Google Maps interface.

Figure 11.1 shows the distribution of *mama*- and *papa*-like terms in our database. Under "*mama*-like" and "*papa*-like" terms we include *mama*, *papa*, *mam*, *pap*, variants with one or more long vowels, variants with a final nasal, and the voiced equivalents of the *papa* forms. Each of these variant forms will be considered in more detail below, as will the forms *ama*, *ngama*, *mami*, *mamu*, *papi*, and *papu*, which are not shown on the map, as we will argue that they (in the case of *ama* at least sometimes) represent different roots.[2]

It is immediately apparent from the map that *mama* and *papa* have very different—almost complementary—distributions, although there is a cluster of languages on the southeast coast that have both terms.[3] What are not shown in Figure 11.1, but will be discussed in more detail below, are the meanings of the terms. The most common meaning for *mama* in Australian languages is, in fact, "father," and *papa* is usually "mother." This is the opposite from what we find in most other languages in the world (with a few well-known exceptions such as Georgian) and is a fact not accounted for by either of the two best-known hypotheses. The proponents of the Proto-World hypothesis ignore forms in which *pap(a)* means "mother"

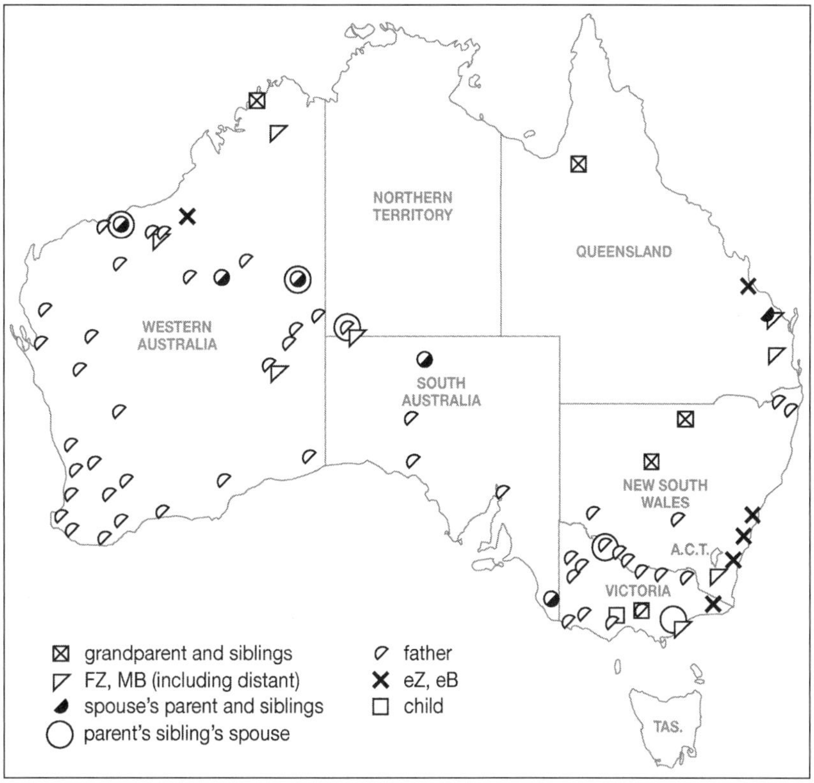

FIGURE 11.2. Meanings of *mam(a)N.*

(cf. Matthey de l'Etang and Bancel 2005: app. A), and while they account for most other meaning changes by reconstructing a generic "elder male" or "elder female" meaning, that makes a gender shift problematic. Some Jakobson-style baby talk explanations predict that the nasal form is the one associated with the mother, since she is the provider of food to the infant, although this aspect of the explanation is not strictly necessary.

In the following sections we will first discuss the distributions of *mama* and *papa* with their associated meanings, including semantic changes the terms have undergone in some language groups, and then we will show that there are regular sound correspondences that apply to the formal variants found. It will be seen that *mama* and *papa* are reconstructible to protolanguages in Australia but that it cannot be ruled out that "nursery words" have played a role in some forms or at some point in time.

The Term *Mam(a)(N)* 'Father', 'Mother'

As seen in Figure 11.2, the term *mama(a)(N)* is found across Australia, although less commonly in the northeast than elsewhere. It is found most commonly with the meaning "father" across the Western Australian, South Australian, and Victorian Pama-Nyungan languages, with occurrences also in central New South Wales (NSW) and on the NSW/Queensland border (Bandjalangic). This root is also found with a number of other meanings, most of which can easily be seen to be extensions of "father" or "mother."[4] The important changed meanings include the following:

1. "elder sibling" ("elder brother" in Nyangumarta in the Pilbara and in Bayali in North Queensland; "elder sister" in Bidawal, Dharawal, Dhurga, and Eora in southeastern NSW);
2. "parent's opposite-sex sibling" (FZ in Noongar and Ngarigu in southern NSW; MB in Waka Waka and Gureng Gureng);
3. "child" (Wathawurrung, Kukatja, Malngin), "great-grandchild" (Ngaanyatjara);
4. "spouse's parent" or "spouse's parent's sibling" (Gureng Gureng, Kariyarra, Pintupi, Martu Wangka);
5. "distant cousin" (Mandjindja, Nyamal, Pintupi), "spouse"/"wife" (Wangaaypuwan), and "grandparent"/"father's mother" (Wangaaypuwan, Yuwaalayaay) in central New South Wales, alongside languages with the meaning "father."

The most frequent of these meanings are shown on the map in Figure 11.2.

The following meaning differences are clearly more normal polysemies rather than radical meaning changes:

- "child" (the reciprocal of "father") in Wathawurrung;
- "great-grandchild" (in Ngaanyatjarra in the Western Desert) equates with "father" by the alternate-generations agnatic principle—four generations apart (see McConvell, chapter 10, this volume);
- MZH regularly = F, as in Nyamal and Kariyarra, as a father's classificatory brother marries a mother's classificatory or actual sister in most systems; and
- in at least some of these cases, the spouse's father's sister is likewise referred to as *mother*—this extension is quite unsurprising.

The equation of "wife" and FM as in #5 above is also a common polysemy in many groups also reflecting the alternate-generations agnatic principle (FF = "self"/"brother"). However, the primary shift from "father" to FM/"spouse" is not so easy to account for—see below.

The meanings not shown on the map have been left off for the sake of simplicity: those that only occur in one or two languages ("spouse," "great-grandchild," and "cousin"). We have also left off the "mother" meanings, as these are most likely a borrowing from English or Kriol, a matter that will be discussed further later on. The meaning "father" is also understood to cover "father's brother" as well, as this polysemy is almost ubiquitous in Australian languages.

It is clear from Figure 11.2 that the distribution of the various meanings is not arbitrary. The "father" meanings are concentrated across the west and south of the country. The non-"father" meanings are most common along the boundary of this "core" *mama* region. Several of them (spouse's parents and their siblings, parent's siblings' spouses) even seem to form a line along this boundary.

Elder Sibling, Uncle, Aunt

The "elder sibling" meanings are clustered in the southeast, along the coast. Even in this cluster, however, three different language families are represented: Yuin, Ioric, and Kurnic. (Yuin and Ioric are thought to be related but only distantly.) It seems likely that this group represents a regional phenomenon where *mama* with the sense of elder sibling was borrowed.

There are two more occurrences of *mama* meaning "elder sibling"—namely, "elder brother" in Bayali and Nyangumarta. The extreme distance of these from the southeast languages and each other, and their genetic unrelatedness, suggests that these were independent innovations.

Interestingly, in all of the cases where *mama* means "elder sibling" there is also at least one nearby language in which *mama* means "aunt" or "uncle." The probable explanation is as follows:

a. In the case of the meaning shift from "father" to "elder brother," this may be a case of altercentricity (see McConvell, chapter 1, this volume) in which the point of view of the child is adopted (filiocentricity). Thus the father's brother is called *brother*, following what the father calls this relation. As noted, FB = F.
b. In the case of the meaning "elder sister" a similar filiocentric extension is involved from FZ. This implies that there had been a prior shift of the *mam(a)(N)* root from F to FZ. Indeed, in the languages close to and related to those where the "older sister" meaning is found (Ngarigu, Gunnai) there has been a shift in gender of the root, with different roots taking over the "father" meaning (mainly *mungkan* in Gunnai and *papang* in Ngarigu).[5]

The polysemies "aunt" = "elder sister" and "uncle" = "elder brother" are found elsewhere in Australia (Dunghutti, Wirangu, Wajarri, Kattang). It is therefore possible that one of these two meanings is an extension from the other. This hypothesis is strengthened by the genders of the kin involved: in the southeast languages, *mama* means "elder sister," and the nearby languages (Ngarigu and Gunnai) have *mama* as "father's sister." In Bayali, *mama* means "elder brother," and the nearby languages Waka Waka and Gureng Gureng have *mama* meaning "mother's brother." In Nyangumarta, *mama* means "elder brother," and Nyamal has it meaning "distant uncle." If it is the case that one sense was extended to the other, the most likely explanation would be that "uncle" or "aunt" was extended to "elder sibling," not the other way around. This is probable for several reasons: first, the original extension from "father" or "mother" to "parent's sibling" seems more likely than a direct extension to "elder sibling." Second, the meaning "elder sibling" for *mama* is only found in regions where there is also the meaning "parent's sibling," while the latter is found elsewhere without this polysemy as well.

Returning to the southeastern languages that have the term *mama* meaning "elder sibling," we can now reconstruct a likely development for the spread of this meaning across the various language families. The extension would have originated in the Yuin family, since we have examples of both meanings in languages of this family (Dhurga and Dharawal with "elder sister" and Ngarigu with "father's sister"). The association of the meaning "elder sister" with *mama* then spread to other, unrelated families in the region: Bidhawal and Eora.

Spouse's Parent and Sibling

The use of *mama* for "spouse's parent" and "spouse's parent's sibling" is found in a few of the Western Desert languages in our database but also in Buandig on the Victoria/South Australia border, Gureng Gureng, and Kariyarra. The pathways of change involved here are as follows:

a. In cross-cousin marriage systems, which are widespread in Australia, FZ has an affinal equation, FZ = WM 'mother-in-law'. In conformity with that, the mother-in-law's brother will be designated *father*—so the appearance of F with the extension WMB is unsurprising.
b. In cross-cousin marriage, especially those varieties that have a "matrilateral" preference for a man to marry his MBD, the mother's brother is the man's father-in-law. Now MB would not normally fall into the same category as "father" in Australian Aboriginal systems, which generally rigorously divide cross- from parallel relations, so the term *father* would not normally be used for "father-in-law." However, it seems that there are two small groups of languages that show this kind of polysemy, which is reminiscent of English and other European practices of calling "in-laws" by consanguineal terms, for example, a father-in-law called *father* in address and so on. Buandig is a current polysemy, with F being the main meaning of *mam*, which is also recorded as being used for "husband's father." In Gureng Gureng, F is no longer a meaning, but there has been a shift to WF by way of the unusual equation of F = WF and thence MB by the regular equivalence mentioned above. In neighboring and related Waka Waka the meaning is apparently only MB.

It seems likely, then, that this polysemy has been independently innovated more than once. The equation of one's parents with one's spouse's parents is not unusual in Australia (it is found, e.g., in some languages of Cape York, in Warlpiri, and in Buandig). Even more common is the equation of "mother" and "father" with one's spouse's aunts and uncles. And it is this that seems to be the case for these *mama* terms, which all refer to men, either to the spouse's father (Buandig, Gureng Gureng), or to the spouse's mother's brother, or to both. In at least some of these cases, the spouse's father's sister is likewise referred to as *mother.* If cross-cousin marriage is the norm, one's wife is one's FZ, which makes her MB one's F; that is, the term for "father" would also be the term for "wife's mother's brother," so this extension is quite unsurprising.

Parent's Sibling's Spouse

The use of *mama* for "parent's sibling's spouse" seems like a natural extension from its use for "parent's sibling" ("aunt," "uncle," as discussed above). The meaning "parent's sibling's spouse" is found in five languages in our database, and in three of these *mama* also simply means "parent's sibling." In the other two languages, Kariyarra and Wadi Wadi, the polysemy "parent's sibling" = "parent's sibling's spouse" also exists, but *mama* does not participate in it (Kariyarra *thuwa*, *yumani*, *yuro*, all meaning FZ, MBW; Wadi Wadi *ninik*- FZ, MBW and *kaka* MB, FZH). In Wadi Wadi, *mama* means "mother's sister's husband," which is easily derived from "father." A mother's sister is considered equivalent to a mother in most Australian languages, and so it makes sense that her husband would be considered terminologically equivalent to a father.

Son

The use of *mama* for "son" is a little more surprising. It is not common in our database, being found only in Woiwurrung and Wathawurrung and not in exactly the same form as the *mama* that means "father." In Woiwurrung *mama* and *maman* are attested with the meaning "father," and *mam* and *mam-mam* are attested as the words for "son" (Blake 1991). In Wathawurrung, we only find *mamam* 'son'. A father/son or mother/daughter polysemy is not uncommon in our database, being found in nine languages, but if we consider the Woiwurrung and Wathawurrung cases to be examples of such a polysemy (at least historically), they are the only such examples found in Victoria.

Grandparent and Grandparent's Sibling

The examples of *mama* meaning "grandparent" or "grandparent's sibling" are not frequent and do not follow any genetic or geographical boundaries. They appear in Yuwaalayaay and Wangaaypuwan, related languages of New South Wales. The occurrence in the north Kimberley

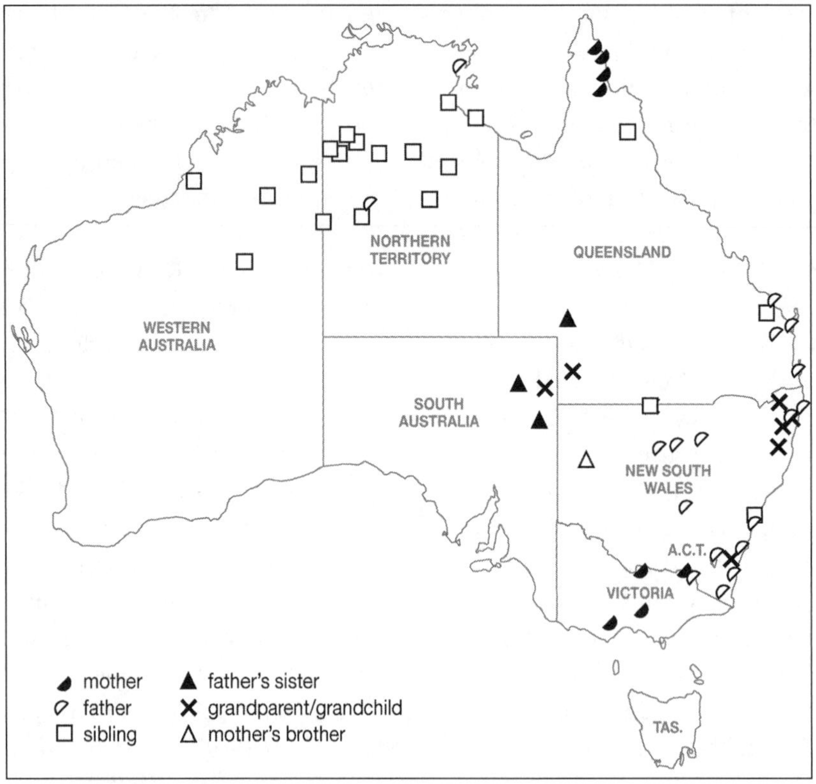

FIGURE 11.3. Meanings of *papa*.

non-Pama-Nyungan (Worrorran) language Wunambul is most likely not a cognate. In Walangama, in northwest-central Queensland, *mama* is MM, unlike the forms in NSW to be discussed below, where the meaning is usually "father's mother." It seems possible to us that this form is related to forms such as *mimi*, *mumu*, *memem*, and so on for MM along the Gulf of Carpentaria and in Arnhem Land, with *mimi* also found in Wangaaypuwan as MM/FFZ, rather than that it is an extension from *mama* 'father' (cf. Nichols 2003 for some principles of "closed class sound symbolism" that could explain the development of a pair such as *mama* and *mimi*).

The Yuwalaayaay and Wangaypuwan FM/W forms have a better chance of being related to **mama* 'father' (FM extending to "wife" is unproblematic, as mentioned previously). The neighboring and closely related language Wiradjuri has *mam* 'father', and none of these are very far away from the southern block of languages with this meaning or the Bandjalangic block to the northeast. The presence of what could be an older root for FM (*ngaki*, related to the Proto-Pama-Nyungan **ngatyi* MF [McConvell, chapter 10, this volume]) might point to a later extension of **mama* to this meaning. However, the mechanism involved in the putative change F > FM is unclear.

Other (Great-Grandchild, Spouse, Cousin)

The remaining senses of *mama* are also infrequently attested. The meaning of "great-grandchild" is a natural extension in languages that follow a principle of alternate-generations equivalence: if "grandparent" equals "grandchild," then "parent" equals "great-grandchild." It is possible that this polysemy exists more widely than our database attests: most of the word lists used as sources to populate the database do not include terms for great-grandchildren at all. The meanings of "spouse" and "cousin," on the other hand, are hard to explain through semantic change. *Mama* is found with these meanings only in two languages, however (Yiningay and Wangaaypuwan), which do not have *mama* meaning "father" or any of the other core meanings discussed. It is probable, therefore, that this is not a matter of extension but, rather, an independent development that just coincidentally has the same form as the *mama* found elsewhere. This hypothesis is strengthened by the fact that both languages are well outside the "core" region of Australia that has the typical *mama* term—that is, the southwest half shown in Figures 11.2 and 11.3.

So, in general, the examination of *mama* shows that it is an old root for "father" (not "mother") in Pama-

Nyungan and that it has undergone various systematic meaning changes in various subgroups and areas, another indication of its age and variability. There is no evidence for regular reinvention as one might expect from the "Baby Talk theory."

The Term *Pap(a)(n)* 'Mother'

The most common meanings for *papa* are "sibling" and "father." The meaning "mother" is the most widespread sense, as it is found both in the north and in the south, but it is not as frequent purely in terms of the number of languages it is found in. In Paakantyi *papa* means "mother's brother," and in Wangaaypuwan it means "son." In Yandruwandha and Awabakal it means "wife." Because these latter two meanings are only found in one or two languages each, we have left them off the map in Figure 11.3. We have left in "mother's brother," because it is conceivable that this is the result of a semantic change from "father's sister," which is the meaning in three nearby languages.

It is possible that the cases of *papa* with the meaning "father" are borrowings from English, but we will show later that this is not necessarily the case. When it means "sibling," it always means either "brother" alone or both "brother" and "sister" but never only "sister." Usually it means "elder sibling," and it never means "younger sibling." For the sibling terms, then, it seems like "elder brother" must be the original meaning, with extension to other types of siblings in some cases. *Papa* forms are also found in a number of non-Pama-Nyungan languages in the north, which are not all in the database as we have concentrated on Pama-Nyungan languages: These may be loans from Pama-Nyungan, but further research is needed.

When it comes to grandparents, the term usually means "mother's mother." But in Muruwari it also refers to "father's father," and in Yandruwandha "elder sister" (*papa*) seems to provide the root for "parallel grandparent" (*papatu*), with the addition of the common grandparental kin suffix *-tu* (McConvell 2008). Polysemy between sibling terms and parallel grandparents arises in a number of Australian languages due to alternate-generations equivalence polysemy, which Scheffler (1978) divides into agnatic (B/Z = FF[Z]) and uterine (B/Z = MM[B]) (see also McConvell, chapter 10, this volume).

It is not impossible that some of these meanings are the result of semantic shifts. Our database shows that, though rare, polysemy between "mother's brother" and "elder brother" or "father's sister" and "elder sister" does exist. Dhungutti and Kattang, already commented on, represent an overlap between Omaha and cross/parallel neutralization polysemies. (Yir Yoront, Mayi-Thakurti, Diyari, Ngatjumaya, Wilyakali, Wangaaypuwan, Yuwaalayaay, Gumbaynggir, and Darumbal require further investigation.) Polysemy between "parent" and "grandparent" is quite rare but can be found (Wirangu, Anmatyerre, Guugu Yimidhirr), as can polysemy between "mother's brother" and "grandfather" (Jagara, Ungarinyin—resulting from Omaha skewing Type 3—and Guugu Yimidhirr). Any or all of these polysemies could have provided a "bridge" between the various meanings, but if this is the case, it is odd that so few languages currently have more than one of the *papa* meanings and that the geographic clustering of the meanings is so distinct. This suggests that if we are talking about a process of semantic shift, it happened a long time ago, and the modern "clusters" are descendants of a protolanguage that had already lost the polysemies.

To check this hypothesis, we can compare the distribution of each "meaning cluster" on the map with the extent of known language families. While the clusters in Figure 11.3 do coincide with some families, generally they go beyond the extent of a single genetic group. For example, the cases of *papa* with the meaning "father" on the east coast include the Waka-Kabi languages, the Wiradjuric languages, Gumbaynggir-Yaygir, Ngiyaampaa, the Yuin languages, and at least one Kurnic (Gippsland) language. The only cluster on the map in which all languages belong to the same family is the group in which *papa* means "father's sister." These are all Karnic languages, but as there are only three of them in the database, it is hardly conclusive. In all other cases, the semantic cluster extends beyond genetic boundaries, even in the very tight-knit group at the top of Cape York. This suggests that the clusters may be the result of borrowing rather than inheritance.

Coincidence cannot, of course, be ruled out, especially when we are dealing with short reduplicated words that are learned early in a child's language acquisition (thereby narrowing the number of sounds to those that children master early on). The clustering of meanings, however, suggests that more than coincidence is needed to explain all of the forms. The fact that all the meanings involved can also be found as polysemies in other languages (using other forms besides *papa*) also suggests that we may not need to propose multiple independent origins but, rather, that a combination of semantic extension and areal dissemination is sufficient to account for these

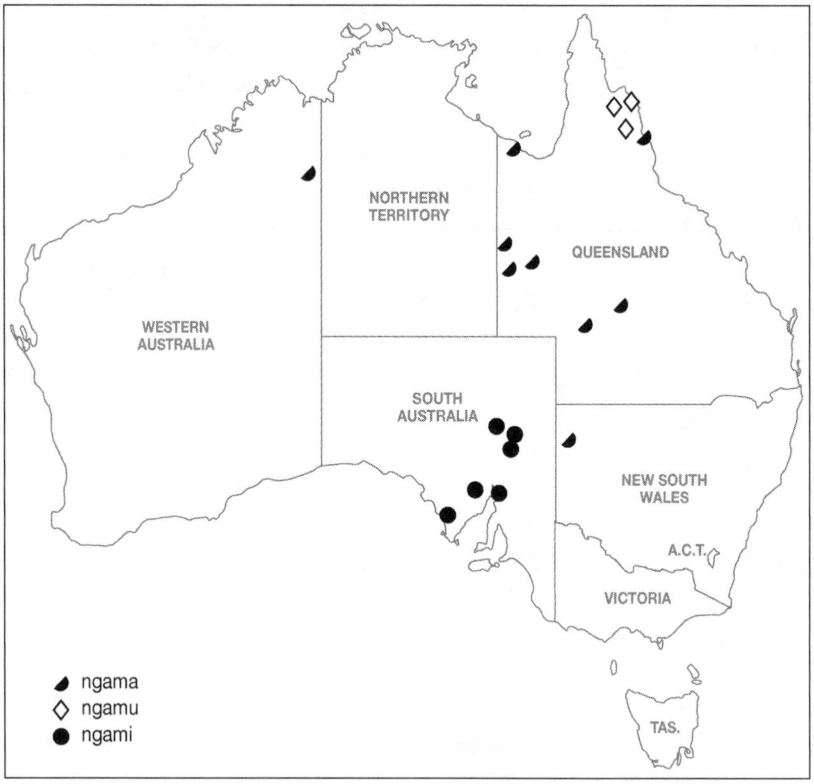

FIGURE 11.4. Distribution of *ngama*, *ngami*, and *ngamu* (mother).

patterns. In any case, since the meanings of the root go beyond "parent" and there is at least some semantic change involved, a "baby talk" recurrent invention scenario is not the correct explanation.

The Term *Ngama* 'Mother'

It could well be argued that in Australian indigenous languages the nasal *ng* is at least as unmarked as the *m* that features in "baby talk" explanations more generally. The terms *ngama*, *ngamu*, perhaps also *ngami*, and in some cases *ama*, on the other hand, are likely to be continuations of the Proto-Pama-Nyungan **ngama* 'mother'/'breast' (cf. Alpher et al. 2008). An alternation between *ngama* and *ngamu* is reconstructed already for Proto-Paman (cf. Hale 1976), and there are also shifts in both these variants from this meaning to "cross-cousin" on Cape York Peninsula, due to prior Omaha skewing and loss of the original meaning (McConvell and Alpher 2002). It is highly unlikely that there is a connection between *ngama/ngami/ngamu* and *mama/mami/mamu*, as *ngama* and *ngamu* usually mean "mother" and *mama* and *mamu* usually mean "father." Neither do *ngami* and *mami* seem likely to be related, as there are only a few cases of each that mean "mother," and the other meanings each form has are not shared. *Ngami* and *mami* also co-occur in some languages, specifically Yiningay, Djabwurrung, and Buandig, and if *ngamirni* is considered part of the same set, they also co-occur in Mayi-Yapi and Mayi-Thakurti. Co-occurrence in a single language of the two forms with unrelated meanings is particularly strong evidence that the terms are not related.

The use of the same term, **ngama* and its reflexes, for "mother" and "breast" (or in some languages "milk") supports the Jakobson theory that there is an association among suckling (and nasal sounds made during suckling), food provision, and ultimately the "mother" kin term. However, the long life cycle of this term, if it has survived from Proto-Pama-Nyungan, speaks against the supposed "uselessness" of nursery forms for reconstruction. Sound changes and semantic changes do seem to have taken place, which suggests that the term is not regularly renewed or replaced in every generation, as one might expect on the basis of the Baby Talk hypothesis.

This distribution of the three forms *ngama*, *ngami*, and *ngamu* is also interesting. Figure 11.4 shows the distribution for those cases in which these terms mean "mother."

The forms *ngamu* and *ngami* in particular form very strong geographical clusters. None of the three co-occurs in the same language as variants. (The one case on the map that looks like a co-occurrence is simply nearby languages: *ngama* in Djabugay and *ngamu* in Kuku Yalanji, Guugu Yimidhirr, and Gugu Yawa.) The clusters are also, in each case, thought to be genetically related languages: The three languages with *ngamu* are all Yalanjic languages, according to the classifications of Wurm (1972) and Oates (1975), and all of the languages with *ngami* are Yura languages (Oates 1975; Walsh 1981; Wurm 1972). The final vowel is therefore likely to be the result of shared sound changes.

As for a relationship between *ngama* and the cases of *mama* that do mean "mother," there is at least one example where the two forms are related by regular sound change. According to Sommer (2006), Oykangand has the root *ama* for "mother," which is derived from **ngama* through regular sound change. This form appears in, for example, the reference form *amangarr* and the respect form *amandarr*. The vocative in Oykangand is formed by reduplication of the root and the addition of a final *-ng*. This means that the address form for "mother" is *amamang*. Utterance initially, the first vowel is always dropped, which results in *mamang* as an utterance-initial vocative form, historically derived from **ngama*. The sound changes involved here are not uncommon in Australian languages: Initial dropping is also found, for example, in Arrernte, and reduplication of short roots is common in various contexts and languages (cf. Koch 2010), although their combination in just this way would have low probability. It is therefore just possible that some other cases of *mama* meaning "mother" may be related historically to **ngama* as well.

Sound Changes

As has just been shown for *ngama/ngami/ngamu*, there exist various forms that resemble *mama* or *papa* closely enough that they are worth examining to see whether they are only accidentally similar in form or whether they are the result of sound change. We will show that most of these variants show regularity in the way they pattern geographically, genetically, and/or semantically, such that we would argue that they are cases of sound change. The existence of regular sound change acting on *mama* and *papa* forms is, then, further evidence that such "nursery forms" can be reflexes of old forms, not regularly renewed, and should therefore not be excluded from historical linguistic investigation.

Final Vowel Apocope

Besides *mama* and *papa*, we also frequently find the forms *mam* and *pap* (with long vowels in some cases, which will be discussed separately below). We find the form *pap* mainly in the languages of Victoria: Wemba Wemba, Waywurru, Wergaia, Weadjali, Mardidjali, Dhauwurd Wurrung, and Djabwurrung, as well as Buandig. Knenknenwurrung has *papap*. The only language it is found in besides this cluster is Yawuru, in the north of Western Australia, which is a non-Pama-Nyungan language and in which it has a different meaning. It is therefore no doubt a separate etymon.

Mam is found in Noongar, Wardandi, Waka Waka, and Woiwurrung. In eastern Noongar dialects final vowel apocope is part of a suite of regular changes (cf. **kata* > *kaat* 'head' [Dench 1994:177]), so **mama* > *maam/mam* is entirely regular. In Woiwurrung, *mama(n)* means "father," while *mam* and *mam-mam* are given as the terms for "son" (the latter two each by different sources). This is a little harder to explain. Since some languages in the region have *mama* for "father" and some have *mam* or *maam*, it is possible that Woiwurrung has borrowed one of the two, creating a doublet. This theory is supported by the existence of another word for "son" as well: *pupukurt*. The semantic change is a little problematic. There are five languages in our database in which the words for "father" and "son" are the same, so if Woiwurrung originally borrowed the new term to mean "father" and then it spread to "son," this would not be unheard of, although it is fairly uncommon. The fact that it now *only* means "son," however, would require us to postulate yet another step, where the doublet terms were reorganized semantically, for example, such that *mama(n)* fully took over the "father" meaning, narrowing the borrowed term to "son." All of this is possible, yet perhaps not very likely. Another possible explanation is that there is confusion of dialects or mistakes in the sources (see Blake 1991 for a list of these sources) or that both *maam* and *mama(n)* are inherited and are each from different protoforms. This latter also seems unlikely, given the existence of the alternative form for "son," *pupukurt*. Moreover, final vowel apocope as well as partial reduplication are common processes affecting kinship terms in the Victorian languages, as will be shown for *pap* and *papap* below. As Woiwurrung is the

TABLE 11.2. List of mainly Victorian kinship terms that have undergone apocope or semi-reduplication.

Victorian Term	(Victorian) Language(s)	Cognate Found Elsewhere
mamam 'father'	Dhauwurd Wurrung Wathawurrung	*mama*
mimim 'mother's brother'	Dhauwurd Wurrung	*mimi*
ngap 'mother's father'	Dhauwurd Wurrung Bewadjali	*ngapu, ngapa, ngapi*
ngart 'daughter'	Dhauwurd Wurrung Knenknenwurrung	*ngartu, ngartang?*
yaat '(step)father'	Dhauwurd Wurrung	*yathu*
mam 'father'	Almost all Victorian languages	*mama*
mim 'paternal grandparent'	Yitha Yitha Wemba Wemba Wergaia Bewadjali	*mimi*
waw 'elder brother'	Almost all Victorian languages	*wawa*
kut 'younger brother'	Wergaia Djadjala	*kuta*
tyat(y) 'elder sister'	Wergaia Buandig Mardidjali Wemba Wemba Barababaraba Djabwurrung	*tyatya*

only problematic case for the hypothesis that *mama* and *ma(a)m* are the result of sound change rather than being derived from separate protoforms, and since the Woiwurrung data are not impossible to explain, we will continue to assume the identity of *mama* with *ma(a)m* here.

In all of the Victorian languages in which it occurs, *pap* means "mother," "mother's sister," or both (the default polysemy in most Aboriginal languages). In Dhauwurd Wurrung *pap* and *papap* mean "mother's sister" and "man's mother's sibling's daughter," the latter meaning involving some kind of skewing. This could have come from either *papi* or *papa*, as both of these are common in Victoria with the meaning "mother." The apocope of the final vowel and the semi-reduplication found in *papap* are regular processes in these languages found in other kinship terms as well: some examples are shown in Table 11.2.

The Victorian languages, therefore, show a clear-cut case of regular sound change affecting *papa*. Note that in Yawuru *pap* means "son" or "daughter." There is no obvious explanation for the Yawuru term (the five other languages in which a *papa*-like term means "son" or "daughter" are all on the other side of the country), so it is possible that it arose independently from any of the other forms.

Alternation in Final Vowel

Besides *mama* and *papa*, our database also attests the forms *mami*, *mamu*, *papi*, and *papu*. The same is true for *ngama* (*ngami*, *ngamu*), as was shown above. These alternations also exist for *ama* (*ami*, *amu*) and for some other kinship terms as well (e.g., *tyatya/tyatyi/tyatyu*, *wawa/wawi/wawu*, and *ngapa/ngapi/ngapu*, which will not be discussed in detail here). We will argue that most of these are probably reflexes of different terms historically. We will briefly outline three sorts of evidence for this: evidence from semantics, evidence from regional distributions, and evidence from patterns of co-occurrence.

Mami almost always means either "mother" (Waalubal, Bundjalung, Dhungutti, Dhurga, Mandjiljarra, Gureng Gureng), "cross-cousin" (Yiningay), or "in-law" (Mayi-Thakurti, Mayi-Yapi). The "mother" meanings are probably borrowings from the English *mummy* or from

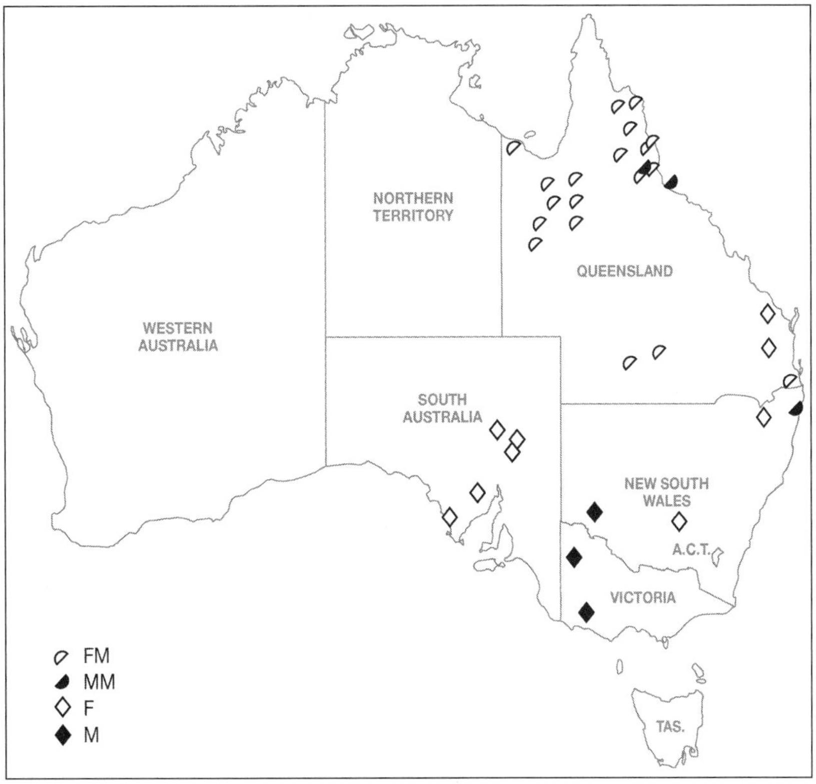

FIGURE 11.5. Semantics of *papi*.

Kriol, as all of these languages have alternative unrelated terms for "mother" as well. None of the others are terms that would be likely semantic extensions from "father." The only cases in which *mami* means "father" are in Djabwurrung, Madhi Madhi, and Buandig (where it alternates with *ma[a]m*). These three languages form a cluster geographically and to some extent genetically (all are in the Kulinic subgroup of Pama-Nyungan according to Oates 1975 and the West Victorian Areal Group according to Dixon 2002). The term *mami* is the only word for "father" in Djabwurrung and Madhi Madhi, while Buandig has the alternative form *wayti* or *wayati*. Madhi Madhi often has nouns (including non-kinship terms) ending in *-i* that correspond to no final vowel in related languages, said to be from the nominative ending *-i* (Blake and Reid 1998:3.1.1), but this does not explain the forms in Djabwurrung or Buandig.

As is the case for *papa*, the semantics of *papi* are a mixture of parental and grandparental terms, which are shown in Figure 11.5. The form **papi* is the proposed Proto-Pama-Nyungan root for FM/MFZ (McConvell 2008), shifting to MF in Gumbaynggirr. Unlike for *papa*, we only very rarely find sibling meanings for *papi* (only in Bardi and Darkinyung, where in both cases it means "brother"). There are a couple of other occurrences of *papi* with rare meanings: "mother's brother" in Waka Waka and Tulua, for example. These languages are part of a complex found in southeast and to some extent central Queensland, where there are several meaning changes in major Proto-Pama-Nyungan roots that still need dedicated research to fully explain. "Mother's father" in Kuku Yalanji is part of a Kariera system in which FM = MF, and "father's sister" in Djinang may be a loan from non-Pama-Nyungan. Most frequently *papi* means "father's mother," the inherited meaning: with this latter meaning it forms a clear geographical and genetic grouping. *Papi* has also been reconstructed for Proto-Paman by Hale (Sommer 1969) with the general meaning "grandparent." It is not clear why he reconstructs "father's father" when this never occurs at all and "mother's father" when this only occurs in one language. The cases of *papi* with the meaning "mother's mother" could possibly be extensions or shifts from "father's mother." For discussion of the few "grandparent" *papi* forms in northern New South Wales, see McConvell (2013).

The meaning "mother" is confined to three languages of the Kulin subgroup. The meaning "father" is more widespread but especially found in South Australia and on the east coast. The distributions here, as well as the clear distinction between the "grandparent" cluster and the "father" cluster, suggest that we may be dealing with two different etymologies: the northern cluster being a reflex of the Proto-Paman **papi* FM and the southern cases being related to **papa* 'father' by sound change. For further evidence for such a sound change, see the discussion above and Figure 11.4 for the distribution of the *ngama/ngami* forms: this indicates that **ngama* became *ngami* in the same South Australian region that we find many of the *papi* forms.

The term *mamu* is not common in the AUSTKIN database, but it does occur. The only place we find an unambiguous *mamu* is in Curr's Wiradjuri list, in which he (1886) spells it *mamoo* and gives the meaning as "father." We also find *mamurung* (original spelling: *manmorong*) in Taungurung, meaning "father"/"father's brother"; *mamuna* in Eora, meaning "sister"; *mampu* in Kuuku Ya'u, meaning "elder sister's child"; and *mamuk* in a few languages of Victoria, with the meaning "father." The Victorian *mamuk* can be excluded from this "set," since the *-uk* can be analyzed not as part of the stem but as a possessive inflection (cf. *mamik* 'my father', *mamuk* 'your father' in Djadjala). These could therefore equally well have come from *mama*. The form *mamuna* could conceivably be a mistranscription for *mamana*, as *u* is often used in old manuscripts to represent an [a] sound. If this were the case, that would fit with other languages from the region: we have *mama(ng)* in Dhurga, Dharawal, and Birdhawal, meaning "elder sister." The terms *mamurung* and *mamu* in Wiradjuri and Taungurung, respectively, are harder to explain, but the database contains several word lists for each of these languages and for nearby related languages, and in each case the *mamu(-)* forms only occur in one list, so perhaps not too much weight should be placed on it. Semantic extension between "father" and "sister" is hard to explain, given that no languages in our database have the same term for both "father" and "sister."

The most common meaning for *papu* is, by far, "father" (in 14 of the 19 languages in which *papu* occurs). In particular, a cluster of four languages in Western Australia have *papu* with this meaning, and there are no other occurrences of *papu* (in our database) for the rest of the western side of the continent. These four languages are Martuthunira, Yindjibarndi, Thalanyji, and Banyjima. Three of these four belong to the Ngayarda subgroup of Southwest Pama-Nyungan, while Thalanyji does not (it is a Kanyara language, but this is also one of the Southwest Pama-Nyungan languages). As we have seen for the other terms discussed here, genetic grouping is not the only factor in the distribution of the form/meaning pair.

In Ganula there is the form *papuri* with the meaning "younger brother," but since *papu* is not found with a sibling meaning elsewhere, we will assume that this is unrelated. In Yindjibarndi, as well as *papu* 'father', we find *papuyi* with the meaning "brother's child" or "child-in-law." This could presumably be derived from *papu*, by derivation from a reciprocal ("father's brother"/"brother's child"), and if so, seems likely to be a recent development, as it is not found in any other languages in our database. In Gattang and Gubbi Gubbi, we find *papu* and *papun*, respectively, with the meaning "father's father." In Gubbi Gubbi it also means "father," so it could be the result of a (rather unusual) semantic extension. In the nearby language Yugambeh, we find *paapuny* with the meanings "father's mother" and "mother's mother," but by other sources this was given as *paapiny*, which seems more likely given the usual meanings of *papi*, as discussed above. A mistranscription of *papu* for *papi* is unlikely to explain the Gattang or Gubbi Gubbi cases, however, as *papu* for "father's father" is documented for each of these in multiple old sources. There is one other language in the database that has *papu* as a grandparent term, in this case "father's mother," and which is geographically very distant from the others, namely, Yalarngga. Yalarngga also has *papipi* and *pawiri* with the same meanings, however, so perhaps *papu* here is a variant of one of these, unrelated to the *papu* found elsewhere. Yalarngga and related languages utilize partial reduplication in senior grandkin terms, as do other scattered Pama-Nyungan languages, a trait perhaps to be reconstructed to Proto-Pama-Nyungan (McConvell 2008).

The final meanings found for *papu* are "mother's brother" (Butchulla and Taungurung) and "father's sister" (Tulua, Yorta Yorta, and Waka Waka). In two of these latter three, this meaning co-occurs with the meaning "father" and so is presumably an extension of this. The "mother's brother" meanings do not co-occur with "father" and are less likely to have arisen through this semantic extension, as "mother's brother" = "father" is a relatively rare polysemy; these occurrences probably demand explanation as the results of a longer chain of changes, yet to be explored.

It is possible that *papu* and *papa* are related, in that each is frequently found with the meaning "father," particularly (in both cases) on the east coast. For some languages (e.g., Waka Waka, Kabi Kabi), a *papu* form is given for "father" in one word list and a *papa* form is given in another, or they are both given in the same list as variants (Gureng Gureng). For Waka Waka, Holmer notes that *papu* is "esp. of a deceased father" (1983:44), so it is possible that in some of these languages at least, a doublet has been created for avoidance purposes, perhaps by borrowing from a language that had a sound change.

Looking at regional distributions of all of the *-a/-i/-u* "variants" in our database's mapping system, there does not seem to be the sort of clear clustering pattern that we found with *ngama/ngami/ngamu* above. For each of the individual terms (apart from the *ngam-* forms), there are some small geographical clusters of forms but also regions where two or even all three variants are found, sometimes in the same language. Overall, the geographical distribution of each "type" does not line up; that is, there is no region in which *ngam-*, *mam-*, *pap-*, *ngap-*, *tyaty-*, *waw-*, and *am-* all end in *-i* and another where they all end in *-u* or any such patterning. The only distributions that pattern like that are for the set *ngapa*, *papa*, *tyatya*, and *wawa* and the pair *ngami* and *papi*, which are found roughly in the same regions. Even the other "variants" of these terms, however (*papu*, *tyatyu*, *wawu*, and *ngapu*; *tyatyi*, *papi*, *ngapi*, and *wawi*; or the pair *ngamu* and *papu*, for example), do not align. This is evidence that we are not dealing with regular sound change rules in this instance but perhaps with historically independent forms.

Finally, the co-occurrence of the various forms should be factored into any conclusions about their relatedness. The term *mamu* does not co-occur with *mama* or *mami*. The forms *mami* and *mama*, on the other hand, do co-occur: in Ungarinyin, Kartujarra, Manjiljarra, Gureng Gureng, and Dhurga. This supports the idea that *mama* and *mami* represent historically different terms. The terms *papa* and *papi* co-occur in Kuyani, Woiwurrung, Wiradjuri, Waka Waka, and Gugu Yawa. The forms *papu* and *papi* co-occur in Barunggam and Tulua, and *papu* and *papa* co-occur in Yorta Yorta. These facts would seem to suggest that all three forms—*papa*, *papi*, and *papu*—must be historically unrelated. We cannot completely rule out a relationship, however, as looking more closely at the co-occurrences shows that they are not all clear-cut. In one case, Waka Waka, the terms *papa* and *papi* never actually appear in the same word list: Holmer (1983) is the only source to record *baba* for "father." Earlier sources list only *babu* 'father' (Curr 1886; Mathew 1910; Roth and the Australian Museum 1984[1907–10]) and *babi* 'mother's brother' (Roth and the Australian Museum 1984[1907–10]). As Holmer is such a late salvage study, it seems likely that *papa* is only a recent borrowing of an alternative to *babu*. Borrowing of this kind can create doublets with slight differences.

In Wiradjuri, the co-occurrence of *papa* and *papi* is simply variation: both mean "father." The co-occurrence of *papa* and *papi* in Gugu Yawa is not relevant here, as it is in the region where we are suggesting *papi* is from a different source, unrelated to *papa*. This leaves Kuyani and Woiwurrung as the only examples of "problematic" co-occurrence. In Kuyani, we find *papi* for "father" and *papa* for "younger sibling." As both "father" and "younger sibling" are common senses of *papa* (see Figure 11.3), it is possible that this is a matter of a doublet created by later borrowing of one or the other. For Woiwurrung, we have *baba(n)* meaning "mother" and *babi* meaning "niece," according to Blake (1991). If by *niece* he means a man's sister's child, this could be a semantic extension from "mother," via "woman's child" (reciprocal of "mother"), and "man's sister's child" (= *niece* in English). The marking of "mother" and its reciprocal with the same term is not all that common, but it does appear in six languages in our database. This could derive *babi* 'niece' from *papi* 'mother', but it does not explain why we find *papa* in Woiwurrung as well. The cases of Woiwurrung and Kuyani remain problematic if we want to relate *papa* and *papi* in the south.

All in all, it seems likely that *mama* and *mami*, and possibly *papa* and *papi* (at least in Cape York), represent historically independent forms. The *papi* forms may represent two different sources: the NSW and Victorian examples may be from *papa* 'father', while the forms in Cape York could be from a different protoform with a grandparent meaning. The form *mamu* is not strongly attested and so may not actually exist; the form *papu* may be related to *papa*, although the evidence for this is not especially strong. We will return to *ama*, *ami*, and *amu* in the next section.

Initial Dropping

Unlike for *ngama/ngami/ngama*, but similar to the case for other *-a/-i/-u* "variants" discussed above, there is no clear pattern in the distribution of *ama/ami/amu*, although all three terms do exist. The form *ama* is by far the most frequently occurring, and the other two forms generally have grandparent meanings and so perhaps can be explained as **kami* > *ami* and **tyamu* > *amu* (the only exceptions in these semantics being Nhanda, where *ami* means "brother-in-law," and Wulguru, where it means "mother"). The form *ama*, on the other hand, usually means "mother" or sometimes "father". In both

Yawarrawarrka and Yandruwandha it means "mother's brother" and "wife's father"; and in both Gugu Warra and Gugu Rarmul it means "brother." It seems likely that the *ama* forms with the nonparent meanings derive from other protoforms, rather than from *ngama* or *mama*, while the "father" forms are good candidates for **mama*, and the "mother" ones are good candidates for **ngama*. (See Alpher et al. 2008 for a discussion of **ngama* > *ama* on Cape York Peninsula.) The "mother's brother" meaning, on the other hand, could be an extension from "mother" or "father."

Final Nasals

In almost all of the sets of words discussed in this chapter, there are variants that end in a final nasal. No matter the word involved, the distribution of these variants is similar: all along the east coast, final nasals are common. As well as this, however, there is a cluster of *papiN* in Queensland, a cluster of *ngamaN* in South Australia, and a cluster of *mamaN* in the south corner of Western Australia. These final nasal forms therefore look very much like the result of regular change. If the final nasal is the fusion of now-opaque morphology, this is evidence that the forms affected by this change have been around for a long time and are not renewed each generation, as the proponents of a "Baby Talk" hypothesis like to argue.

Long Vowels

The languages that use long vowels in these terms tend also to be the same, no matter whether the term in question is *maamaa*, *paapaa*, *maami*, or *papii*. Again, most of these languages are on the east coast, but there are also a few inland in New South Wales and a large cluster in Cape York. Once again, this is an example of regular sound change affecting terms in a way that a true "baby talk" scenario would not predict.

Homorganic Stops

In many languages we find the forms *mampa* and *pampa*, which at first glance look as though they might be related to *mama* and *papa* with the insertion of a homorganic nasal before the second consonant. This is the sort of rule that might be involved in regular sound change. None of the cases of *mampa* or *pampa* (or *mampu*, *pampu*, *mampil*, *mampari*, *mampar*, *mampado*, etc.) in our database means "mother" or "father," however. The meanings range instead from "son" and "daughter" (also "sister's son/daughter," "in-law's son/daughter," "cross-cousin's son/daughter") to "great-grandparent" and various sibling types. The term *mampil*, meaning "husband," seems to be unrelated to the others. Thus only the "son" and "great-grandfather" terms are serious contenders for a relationship with the *mama* (father) terms, and these are the *ma(a)mpa* terms in Kuuku Ya'u and Umpila. Neither of these languages have any of the other *mama*-like terms. The semantics would already be a little bit unusual, even if the meanings were exactly "son." As mentioned above, it is not unheard of for "son" and "father" to be represented by the same term, and it is also not unusual for fieldworkers to accidentally "reverse" terms like this when eliciting them. (For example, the fieldworker points to a man's father and asks, "What do you call him?" and the answer given is, "He calls me X," or vice versa.) In the case of Umpila, either this or semantic change would be a possible explanation, as *mampa* specifically refers to a man's child. However, in the case of Kuuku Ya'u, *maampa* is a woman's child. Such a reversal, therefore, or a semantic extension to the reciprocal of "father," cannot account for this example. It thus seems likely that *mamp-* forms are not the result of sound changes from *mama* but, rather, are from a different source entirely.

The *pamp-* forms do not seem to constitute a coherent group. There are no two cases with the same meaning, and the forms are slightly different for each as well. If, on the other hand, the /mp/ is the result of a sound change from /p/, it would not be surprising that, for example, *pampa* and *pampu* have different meanings, as they would originally belong to the sets *papa* and *papu*, respectively. This hypothesis makes sense for Woiwurrung *pampu* (father's sister), Wangaaypuwan *pampu* (father), and perhaps Gamilaraay *pampuy* (father-in-law), as the former two at least are near other languages with *papu* with similar semantics. Gamilaraay's "father-in-law" could be an extension or shift from "mother's brother," as this is commonly polysemous with "wife's father." We also find *bamba* for "mother" and "sister" in Dhangu, a Yolngu language. This is geographically distant from any of the languages in which *papa* means "mother," but it is in a region where *papa* commonly means "sibling," sometimes specifically "sister," so that is presumably the source of the *bamba* term here. Yolngu languages have lost the oral stops in homorganic nasal + oral stop clusters (cf. Alpher 2004:112), so *bamba* cannot be an old form, in any case. *Bambay* in Yolngu (related to *bamba* in some dialects) has a set of senses, including "mother" and "sister" but also "old woman" and "blind" (Zorc 1986:9), with the kinship

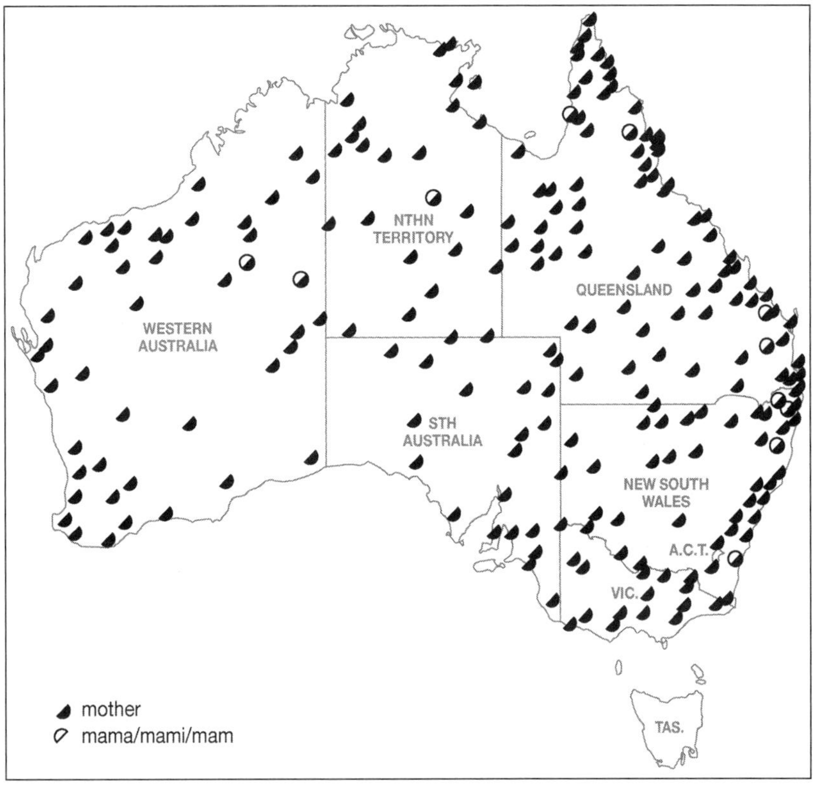

FIGURE 11.6. Terms for "mother."

senses clearly developing from the "old woman" sense. This alerts us to the fact that kinship terms can have their source outside kinship and in such cases the derived kinship senses can be disparate and may not be found among normal kinship polysemies.

The one final occurrence of a *pamp-* form is *pampa* 'mother's brother' in Dyirbal. While there are very few instances of *papa* nearby, and *papa* almost never means "mother's brother" in any case, there is an already existing polysemy between "mother" and "mother's brother" in Dyirbal, as *wayupurr* is used for both. It is possible therefore that *pampa* was borrowed from the Cape York languages, in which *papa* means "mother," and that it was equated with *wayupurr* and so came to be used for "mother's brother." It thus seems that all of the *pamp-* terms can be accounted for by counting them in the *papa* or *papu* set and assuming a change from /*p/ to /mp/. However, this is not a common type of sound change and should not be assumed without further evidence.

Elimination of English Loan Forms

The "elephant in the room" with any discussion of terms like *mama* and *papa* in a country with a large English-speaking population is whether they were simply borrowed from English. In Australia a second possibility exists, namely, that the originally English terms could have been diffused into parts of Australian before English was widely spoken there via Aboriginal Pidgin or Kriol. Obviously it is unlikely that *mama* meaning "father" or that *papa* meaning "mother" came from English, but it would not be surprising if English and/or Kriol proved to be the source of *mama*, *mami*, or *ma(a)m* when these mean "mother." As the word *papa* for "father" is not especially common in Australian English, this is perhaps less likely to have been borrowed, but it is not impossible, particularly since there may have been immigrants from other European countries in the early days of settlement who used this term within their families.

One piece of evidence that we can take into account when weighing this possibility is the existence of other words for "mother" in the same language. That is not to say that we can be 100 percent certain of borrowing when two or more words for "mother" exist, but it is much less likely that (recent) borrowing is the source of a word if it is the *only* word in the language with that meaning, particularly in the case of "core" vocabulary such as *mother* or *father*. In Figure 11.6 we mark the words *mama*, *mami*, and *mam* meaning "mother" with empty half circles and use

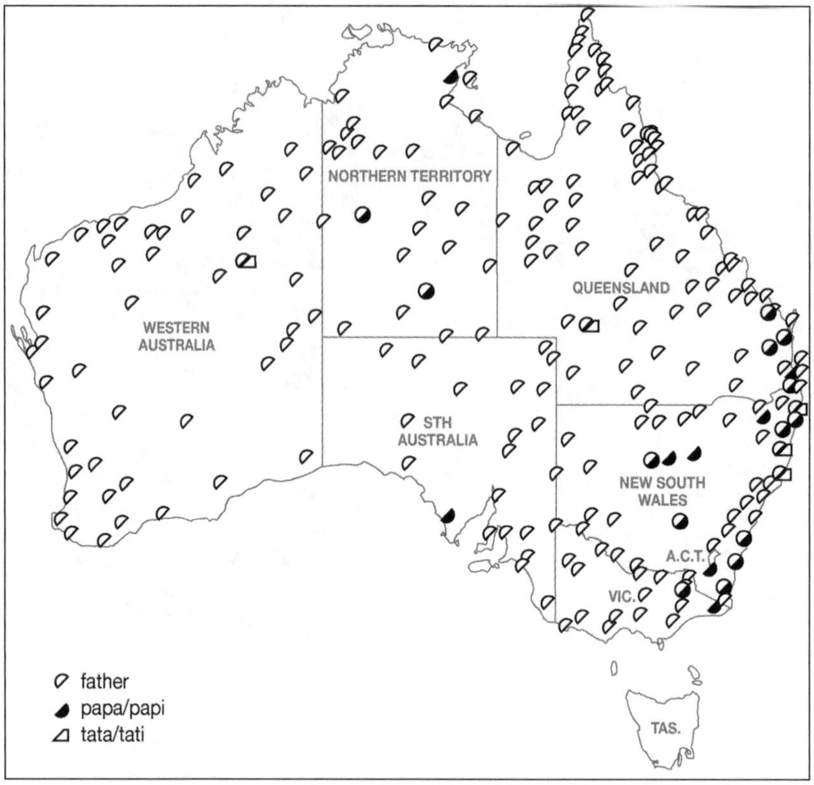

FIGURE 11.7. Multiple terms for "father."

filled half circles to mark all other words with the meaning "mother." It can be seen that in every case where the word *mama*, *mami*, or *mam* exists meaning "mother," the language also has at least one other word for "mother" as well. This means that it is at least *not unlikely* that these *mama* terms are borrowed.

In Figure 11.7 we mark all the *pap-* terms (i.e., *papa*, *pap*, *papi*) with filled half circles; the terms *tata*, *tat*, *dada*, *dad*, and so on with empty triangles; and all the other terms for "father" with empty half circles. In contrast to the situation apparent on the *mama* map, many of the languages in which *papa* or similar is used for "father" have no other word for this relationship. This makes it unlikely that the word is a recent borrowing and thus unlikely that it came from English or Kriol. The *dada/dad/tata* forms, on the other hand, all co-occur with other words for "father," so these are most likely borrowed from English. Given the prevalence of *dad* over *papa* in Australian English, this is not surprising.

Reconstruction Depth of Protoforms

The existence of regular sound changes, opaque morphology, and semantic changes, as argued for in the preceding sections, all suggest a greater time depth for *mama* and *papa* terms in Australia than proponents of a "nursery word" hypothesis would expect. On the other hand, many of the forms, and especially the form/meaning pairs, are geographically constrained, and a few are constrained to a single genetic group. Even if we were believers in a "Proto-World" language, we would not find evidence for it here. Instead it seems that we need to appeal to a middle ground: *mama* and *papa* in Australia are old terms that can be reconstructed for certain protolanguages but not for Australia as a whole. *Mama* is possibly the Proto-Pama-Nyungan root for "father."

The form *papa* with the meaning "father's sister" is the only one that is found only in a single subgroup, and that is only in three (Karnic) languages. Otherwise distributions usually span multiple subgroups. Nevertheless this might be useful if we find that the same sets of subgroups are involved in more than one pattern—this could point to so far unrecognized higher-level linguo-genetic groupings or areal diffusion zones. This can be investigated by drawing the patterns found above as "isoglosses" and looking for isogloss bundles.

A map showing all of the possible "isoglosses" is overwhelming, but in Figure 11.8 we show only those boundaries that mark the distribution of multiple features, that

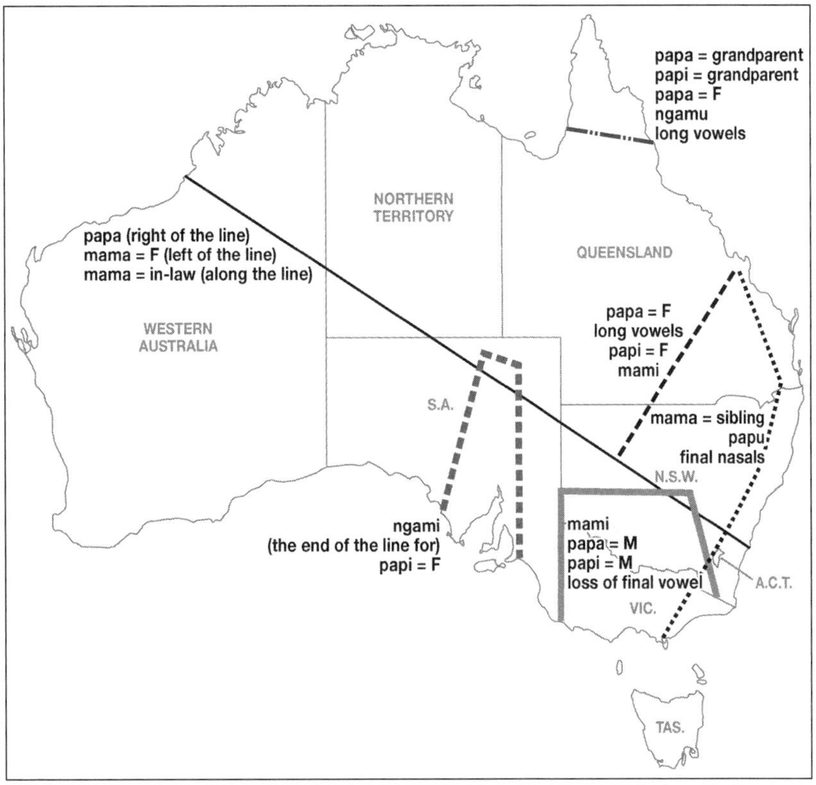

FIGURE 11.8. Summary of the distribution of features and lexemes.

is, "isogloss bundles." These have been approximated to straight lines for ease of drawing and display. This map shows some interesting patterns. The South Australian and Victorian languages are clearly delineated, as is Cape York (some of the features counted here seem perhaps to be limited to Northern or Middle Paman, while others affect the whole region). The east coast of the country is distinct from other regions. The diagonal line across Queensland and part of New South Wales ends where three features that followed the same boundary that far diverge and their isoglosses "fan out" (not shown on the map). Finally, a strong diagonal line across the whole country can be drawn.

Conclusions

In summary there appear to be several independent lexemes in Australian languages that have the canonical "nursery" form *NVNV* or *pVpV* and a meaning that refers to an immediate family member. On the basis of their distributions, including co-occurrence patterns, and semantics, we have to distinguish at least the following terms: *mama* 'father', *ngama* 'mother', *papa* 'mother', *papi* 'grandparent, usually father's mother', *mami* 'cross-cousin'/'in-law', and *mamp-* (various meanings, perhaps various unrelated lexemes). The form *ama* seems likely to be related to *mama* in some cases and *ngama* in others. The form *mamu*, if it exists at all, seems likely to be a variant form of *mama*. The form *ma(a)m* appears to be a variant of *mama* as well, although sometimes this may be the English- or Kriol-derived *mama* that means "mother" rather than the inherited form with the meaning "father."

Having investigated each of the *mama-* and *papa-*like terms in detail, we are now in a position to return to the question of whether these apparent "nursery forms" in Australian languages really are the result of baby talk creations, whether they are inheritances from some sort of Proto-World (or more realistically, perhaps a sort of Proto-Australian), or whether there is another explanation. The only evidence in support of the "Baby Talk hypothesis" is the shape of the forms. In descriptions of baby talk in Warlpiri, for example, it is noted (among other features) that the shape of words is simplified to CVCV, consonants are often "harmonised" (e.g., *jarntu* 'dog' > *tutu* [Bavin 1993:93]), initial consonants are often dropped, and /-i/ is sometimes substituted for /-a/ (Bavin 1993:91). For Kriol, Sandefur (1986:59) notes that baby talk forms often involve reduplication. The *mama* and *papa* forms discussed here do tend to have the CVCV form, have the same consonant in both slots, and look like reduplication could have been involved. The *ami/ama/amu* forms have presumably undergone initial consonant-dropping. The *mami* and *papi* forms could, on formal considerations alone, be forms of *mama* and *papa* with /-i/ substituted for /-a/ (but see the discussion of semantics and distribution above for reasons why this is probably not the case). In other words, if the Warlpiri and Kriol baby talk features are also common to other Australian languages, they can explain the shapes of the *mama* and *papa* forms. Baby talk as described by Bavin (1993), Laughren (1984), and Sandefur (1986) is not necessarily speech as *produced* by children but, rather, that used to address infants, both by adults and by older children. However, it is supposedly based on sound substitutions and morphological simplifications that are used by young children themselves when acquiring language, so it could still fit with the Jakobson-style "nursery language" source for *mama* and *papa*.

The evidence against such a hypothesis as the sole explanation for the Australian data, however, is strong. As noted at the outset of this chapter, the Baby Talk hypothesis predicts not only that *mama* is likely to mean "mother" but also that forms will be randomly scattered among languages, will have no great time depth and few sound or meaning changes because they are regularly replaced, and will not be reconstructible to protolanguages. None of these are the case in Australia. The various maps presented in this chapter clearly show that the forms are not randomly scattered but, rather, show clear geographical clusters, but in terms of phonological forms and the meanings that these are associated with. Some of these clusters appear to correlate with known subgroups of Australian languages, and some show common sound changes, such as vowel lengthening or the addition/loss of a final nasal. Some of the especially widespread forms can probably be reconstructed to Proto-Pama-Nyungan.

On the other hand, there is also strong evidence against a "Proto-World"–style explanation for the data. The fact that *mama*, *mami*, *ngama*, and so on have such diverse "core" meanings and so little semantic overlap makes it quite implausible to reconstruct a shared origin, even within Australia. Conversely, the *lack* of diversity of *forms* means that even if these lexemes did have a shared origin, we would hardly want to place it many tens of thousands of years ago. Even within well-known language families like Indo-European, words that have undergone probably less than 10,000 years of divergence are already unrecognizable as cognates.

Instead of either of these extreme explanations, we would suggest that terms like *mama*, *papa*, and the others discussed in this chapter and identified as separate lexemes are reflexes of earlier protoforms, therefore explaining their distribution throughout certain language groups, but that they also spread areally beyond genetic boundaries. This is supported by the fact that many of the languages discussed have multiple terms for "mother" and "father." We would not rule out that the form of some of these words may have been influenced by "baby talk" (either when originally created or in later incarnations) or that the constraints of children's phonological inventories may have caused or retarded particular sound changes. This does not mean that the forms were constantly renewed or independently innovated in each generation: the patterns in the data strongly suggest that this is not the case.

No matter what the specific historical scenarios involved might be, the most important point we wish to make here is methodological. The distribution of *mama* and *papa* forms in Australia is not random, and it is therefore not useless for reconstruction. We have been able to draw conclusions about inheritance, borrowing patterns, and specifically the influence of English or Kriol. The traditional advice to ignore "nursery forms" in historical linguistics is misguided, particularly in the case of sparsely documented languages where only small word lists are available and therefore the comparative method is difficult to implement. In such cases exploring the distribution of those words that are available, so-called nursery forms included, is perhaps the only option, and as we have shown here, this approach can yield valuable insights.

Notes

This research was supported under the Australian Research Council's Discovery Projects funding scheme (project number DP0878556); the Australian National University (ANU), and the Centre National de la Recherche Scientifique (CNRS) through the Centre de Recherche et de Documentation sur l'Océanie (CREDO). The software for this project was developed by Laurent Dousset of CREDO and uses a geo-spatial-interface developed by the Research School of Humanities (RSH) at ANU using the AUSTLANG (http://austlang.aiatsis.gov.au/disclaimer.php) coordinates and language list developed by Kazuko Obata of the Australian Institute of Aboriginal and Torres Strait Islander Studies (AIATSIS).

1. As we will see, *papa~baba* forms for "father" are rare in Pama-Nyungan but more common in non-Pama-Nyungan, so borrowing from Wubuy into Yolngu is likely. Zorc (1986:13) claims that the Yolngu word is a loan from the Makassarese *bapa'* (Austronesian). While making judgments about loan sources and directions can be difficult, it is not an enterprise to be abandoned simply because the item is a "nursery word."
2. Other terms common in Australian languages that seem to follow the typical "nursery form" template include *mimi* and *pipi*. The term *mimi* most commonly has a grandparent meaning, including MF and MM in different groupings, and frequently co-occurs in the same languages as *mama*. The vowel differences cannot be ascribed to any known processes of sound change. Therefore it seems certain that *mimi* and *mama* represent historically different roots. The term *pipi* is mainly found in Pama-Nyungan languages on Cape York Peninsula as well as in some non-Pama-Nyungan languages with the meaning "father" and in Western Australia with the meaning "mother." The distributions of *pipi* and *papa* overlap on Cape York Peninsula, where the same languages tend to have *pipi* for "father" and *papa* for "mother." If there is any historical relationship between *pipi* and *papa*, it would have to be in the languages of Western Australia, but the forms are different enough that more evidence would be needed before this could be seriously proposed. The terms *mimi* and *pipi* might be interesting to explore from a similar perspective as that taken here, but this is beyond the scope of this chapter.
3. One difficulty with these maps that should be mentioned at this point is the implication of how "a language" is defined. The AustKin project has chosen to follow the Australian Institute of Aboriginal and Torres Strait Islander Studies AUSTLANG database in its definition of individual languages, mainly for purposes of interoperability and for ease of updating. AUSTLANG tends to split where some linguists would group, for example, treating Yuwaalayaay, Yuwaalaraay, and Gamilaraay as three separate languages. This extreme distinction of dialects has the consequence for our mapping interface that sometimes two or three markers will appear on the map where one might expect one to suffice. It also means that apparent small "clusters" of meanings or forms are not necessarily as significant as one might expect at first glance. They are not completely insignificant either, but the time depth of any associated reconstruction would not be great. The larger such a cluster is, on the map, however, the more significant it is likely to be historically.
4. There are several *mam(a)(N)* forms recorded in the meaning "mother." Some of these are borrowed from the English *mum*, *mama*, etc. (see section on detection of English loans below).
5. The polysemy "uncle (MB)" = "elder brother" is found on the NSW Central Coast in Dunghutti and Kattang with a different root, *piyang*. However, this root also has a cross-cousin meaning (MBS) and can be better analyzed as involving an overlap of two types of polysemy, Omaha skewing and cross/parallel neutralization (McConvell and Hendery 2010).

References Cited

Alpher, B. 2004. Pama-Nyungan: Phonological Reconstruction and Status as a Phylogenetic Group. In *Australian Languages: Classification and the Comparative Method.* C. Bowern and H. Koch, eds. Pp. 93–126. Current Issues in Linguistic Theory, 249. Amsterdam: John Benjamins.

Alpher, B., G. O'Grady, and C. Bowern. 2008. Western Torres Strait Language Classification and Development. In *Morphology and Language History: In Honour of Harold Koch.* C. Bowern, B. Evans, and L. Miceli, eds. Pp. 15–30. Current Issues in Linguistic Theory, 298. Amsterdam: John Benjamins.

Bancel, P. J., A. Matthey de l'Etang, and J. D. Bengston. 2011. Back to Proto-Sapiens (pt. 2): The Global Kinship Terms *Mama, Papa,* and *Kaka.* In *Kinship, Language, and Prehistory: Per Hage and the Renaissance in Kinship Studies.* D. Jones and B. Milicic, eds. Pp. 38–45. Salt Lake City: University of Utah Press.

Bavin, E. 1993. Language and Culture: Socialisation in a Warlpiri Community. In *Language and Culture in Aboriginal Australia.* M. Walsh and C. Yallop, eds. Pp. 85–96. Canberra: Aboriginal Studies Press.

Bengtson, J. D., and M. Ruhlen. 1994. Global Etymologies. In *On the Origin of Languages: Studies in Linguistic Taxonomy.* M. Ruhlen, ed. Pp. 277–336. Stanford: Stanford University Press.

Blake, B. 1991. Woiwurrung, the Melbourne Language. In *Handbook of Australian Languages, vol. 4: The Aboriginal Language of Melbourne and Other Grammatical Sketches.* R. Dixon and B. J. Blake, eds. Pp. 30–122. Melbourne: Oxford University Press.

Blake, B. J., and J. Reid. 1998. Classifying Victorian Languages. In *Wathawurrung and the Colac Language of Southern Victoria.* B. J. Blake, ed. Pp. 1–58. Pacific Linguistics, C-147. Canberra: Australian National University.

Campbell, L. 1997. *American Indian Languages: The Historical Linguistics of Native America.* Oxford: Oxford University Press.

Campbell, L., and W. J. Poser. 2008. *Language Classification: History and Method.* Cambridge: Cambridge University Press.

Curr, E. M. 1886. *The Australian Race: Its Origin, Languages, Customs, Place of Landing in Australia, and the Routes by which It Spread Itself over That Continent.* Melbourne: J. Ferres, Government Printer.

Dench, A. C. 1994. Nyungar. In *Macquarie Aboriginal Words: Words from Australian Aboriginal and Torres Strait Islander Languages.* N. Thieberger and W. McGregor, eds. Pp. 173–192. Melbourne: Macquarie Library.

Dixon, R. 2002. *The Australian Languages: Their Nature and Development.* Cambridge: Cambridge University Press.

Dousset, L., R. Hendery, C. Bowern, H. Koch, and P. McConvell. 2010. Developing a Database for Australian Indigenous Kinship Terminology: The AustKin Project. *Australian Aboriginal Studies* 1:42–56.

Gheorgov, I. 1911. Le développement du langage chez l'enfant. In *Premier Congrès International de Pédologie*. Pp. 201–218. Premier Congrès International de Pédologie. Brussels: Librairie Misch and Thron.

Hale, K. 1976. Phonological Developments in a Northern Paman Language: Uradhi. In *Languages of Cape York*. P. Sutton, ed. Pp. 41–49. Canberra: Australian Institute of Aboriginal Studies.

Heath, J. 1981. A Case of Intensive Lexical Diffusion: Arnhem Land, Australia. *Language* 57:335–367.

Holmer, N. M. 1983. *Linguistic Survey of South-Eastern Queensland*. Canberra: Australian National University.

Jakobson, R. 1960. Why "Mama" and "Papa"? In *Selected Writings: Phonological Studies*. Pp. 538–545. The Hague: Walter de Gruyter.

Koch, H. 2010. Etymologies of Some Australian Kinterms. Paper presented at the Australian Languages Workshop, Kioloa, March.

Laughren, M. 1984. Warlpiri Baby Talk. *Australian Journal of Linguistics* 4:73–88.

Mathew, J. 1910. *Two Representative Tribes of Queensland*. London: T. Fisher Unwin.

Matthey de l'Etang, A., and P. J. Bancel. 2002. Tracing the Ancestral Kinship System: The Global Etymon "KAKA": Pt. II: An Anthropological Study. *Mother Tongue* 7:245–258.

Matthey de l'Etang, A., and P. J. Bancel. 2005. The Global Distribution of (P)APA and (T)ATA and Their Original Meaning. *Mother Tongue* 9:133–169.

Matthey de l'Etang, A., and P. J. Bancel. 2008. The Age of Mama and Papa. In *In Hot Pursuit of Language in Prehistory: Essays in the Four Fields of Anthropology—In Honor of Harold Crane Fleming*. J. D. Bengtson, ed. Pp. 417–438. Amsterdam: John Benjamins.

Matthey de l'Etang, A., P. J. Bancel, and M. Ruhlen. 2011. Back to Proto-Sapiens (pt. 1): The Global Kinship Terms *Mama*, *Papa*, and *Kaka*. In *Kinship, Language, and Prehistory: Per Hage and the Renaissance in Kinship Studies*. D. Jones and B. Milicic, eds. Pp. 29–37. Salt Lake City: University of Utah Press.

McConvell, P. 2008. Grand-Daddy Morphs: The Importance of Suffixes in Reconstructing Pama-Nyungan Kinship. In *Morphology and Language History: In Honour of Harold Koch*. C. Bowern, B. Evans, and L. Miceli, eds. Pp. 313–327. Current Issues in Linguistic Theory, 298. Amsterdam: John Benjamins.

McConvell, P. 2013. Granny Got Cross: Semantic Change of *Kami* 'Mother's Mother' to 'Father's Mother' in Pama-Nyungan. In *Lexical and Structural Etymology: Beyond Word Histories*. R. Mailhammer, ed. Pp. 147–184. Studies in Language Change. Berlin: de Gruyter.

McConvell, P., and B. Alpher. 2002. The Omaha Trail in Australia: Tracking Skewing from East to West. *Anthropological Forum* 12(2):159–176.

McConvell, P., and R. Hendery. 2010. Investigating the Multiple Meanings of "Kariera System" with AUSTKIN Database Queries. Unpublished MS, Australian National University, Canberra.

Murdock, G. P. 1959. Cross-Language Parallels in Parental Kin Terms. *Anthropological Linguistics* 1(9):1–5.

Nichols, J. 2003. Diversity and Stability in Language. In *The Handbook of Historical Linguistics*. B. D. Joseph and R. D. Janda, eds. Pp. 283–310. Malden, MA: Blackwell.

Oates, L. 1975. *The 1973 Supplement to a Revised Linguistic Survey of Australia*. Armidale, Australia: Armidale Christian Book Centre.

Roth, W. E., and the Australian Museum. 1984[1907–10]. *The Queensland Aborigines: Vol. III Being Bulletins 9–18, "North Queensland Ethnography." Records of the Australian Museum Sydney*. K. F. MacIntyre, ed. Carlisle, Australia: Hesperian Press.

Ruhlen, M. 1994. *On the Origin of Languages: Studies in Linguistic Taxonomy*. Stanford: Stanford University Press.

Ruhlen, M. 2000. Why *Kaka* and *Aya*? In *Functional Approaches to Language, Culture and Cognition*. D. G. Lockwood, P. H. Fries, and J. E. Copeland, eds. Pp. 521–525. Amsterdam: John Benjamins.

Sandefur, J. 1986. Kriol of North Australia: A Language Coming of Age. M.A. thesis, SIL.

Scheffler, Harold W. 1978. *Australian Kin Classification*. Cambridge Studies in Social Anthropology, 23. Cambridge: Cambridge University Press.

Sommer, B. A. 1969. *Kunjen Phonology: Synchronic and Diachronic*. Canberra: Australian National University.

Sommer, B. A. 2006. *Speaking Kunjen: An Ethnography of Oykangand Kinship and Communication*. Canberra: Australian National University.

Trask, L. 2004. Where Do *Mama/Papa* Words Come From? Electronic document, http://www.sussex.ac.uk/english/documents/where-do-mama2.pdf.

Walsh, M. 1981. The Languages of Australia. In *Language Atlas of the Pacific Area*, pt. 1. S. A. Wurm and S. Hattori, eds. Pp. 20–23. Canberra: Australian Academy of the Humanities.

Wurm, S. A. 1972. *Languages of Australia and Tasmania*. The Hague: Mouton.

Zorc, R. D. 1986. Yolngu-Matha Dictionary. Batchelor: School of Australian Linguistics.

12

Warumungu Kinship Over Time

Jane Simpson

Lexical semanticists have long been attracted by the terms used by groups of people to refer to and address members of their families. Such terms often appear to form an interrelated and internally consistent set, or kinship system, unlike most other terminology sets. These terms often provide clear examples of differences among "reference": a particular person called "Anna"; "denotation": "the set of female people who are the children of someone's sister or someone's brother" (the set of kin relations denoted by the kin term); "connotation": how nieces and their aunts and uncles are expected to act toward one another; and "sense," the hardest aspect of meaning to define: what it is to be someone's "niece."[1] Under "sense" I will also include knowledge about word use that is not cancelable, that is, is true of the term's use in any context. An example of such uncancelable information would be the designation of relations by trirelational kin terms that "simultaneously relate the designated referent to the speaker and to another person, commonly the addressee, so that three (rather than just one) relationships are indexed by a single term (speaker–referent, address–referent, speaker–addressee)" (Heath 1982:11).[2]

To some extent the idea of "a" kinship system is an idealization. In fact, each member of a group may use a slightly different set of kin terms and relationships between the terms. But they will be similar enough for the members of the group to understand who is being talked about or addressed. For example, Anna may refer to her mother's mother (MM) and father's mother (FM) as *grandmother* but actually address her MM as "Gran" and her FM as "Grandma." Sally, Anna's mother's brother's daughter (MBD), may also address their shared grandmother (Sally's FM) as "Gran" but call her MM "Granny." "Gran," "Granny," and "Grandma" are variants of *grandmother*, which can become the normal way in which someone addresses a particular relative (FM or MM). That is, they can be used as semiproper names.[3] "Gran," "Granny," "Grandma," and *grandmother* are instances of the same relationship being described by different terms by different individuals; that is, different terms have the same denotation. The reverse is possible; one term may have overlapping denotations. For example, most Australian English speakers would describe the sister of their spouse (WZ, HZ) or the wife of their brother (BW) as their "sister-in-law." But they will vary as to whether they can also describe as "sister-in-law" the wife of the brother of their spouse (WBW, HBW). Another example is what to call the child of one's first cousin—*cousin*, *first cousin once removed*, or *second cousin*. The result of such speaker variation is a range of closely related kinship systems, rather than one single Australian English kinship system.

The desire and pressure for simple communication mean that many speakers do not recognize that there is variation; they feel that there must be a single definition of *sister-in-law* or *second cousin*. They would have little hesitation in telling a visiting ethnographer what a sister-in-law is, and so the visiting ethnographer would get two definitions. Over *sister-in-law*, the temptation for the ethnographer is to take the larger denotation (WZ, HZ, BW, WBW, HBW) as *the* denotation and to assume that the speakers who did not include WBW and HBW would have done so had they been asked. Over the term for "cousin's child," the temptation is to take the most systematic-looking term, *first cousin once removed*, as the "right" term (especially when the speaker goes on to explain how *second cousin* and *first cousin twice removed* fit into the system) and to assume that the speakers who give *cousin* or *second cousin* do not know the system well. Even greater variation in kinship systems is likely to be found in communities where speakers are shifting languages. We must think in terms of kinship system terminology sets, rather than seeking a single kinship system terminology set.

Over time, groups of people change the terms they use to refer to and address members of their families. The connotations, denotations, and senses of these terms change (e.g., greater overlap or differentiation of denotations, change of connotation from neutral to formal, change of connotation from being just an implication to being part of the sense). But since the terms used for kinship relations are interrelated, a change in the connotations, denotations, or senses of one term may cause changes in relationships to other terms; consequently an overlap of denotation between two terms may result in one becoming narrower. Thus a change in one term may start a chain reaction of changes in the connotations, denotations, and senses of other terms. A kinship system may evolve into one that looks quite different.

Any account of a change of denotation, connotation, or sense needs to propose some kind of bridging context that can account for the shift. An example comes from the shift of semiproper names to common nouns. Anna may start using "Gran" as a way not only of addressing but also of referring to her MM, "my Gran." She may start extending this term to using it as a common noun: "your gran," "their grans." She may do the same with "my Grandma." That is, she starts using it with the same denotation as *grandmother* (and, perhaps, sense) but with connotations of intimacy and low formality. Sally and Anna also know the word *grandmother* and know that they can apply it to the people they call "Gran," "Granny," and "Grandma," whether FM or MM. This is everyday practice among many English speakers. Whether semiproper names like "Gran" eventually replace terms like *grandmother* as the normal way of describing MM or FM will depend on the practices in a particular community as to how one addresses particular relatives. If group members do not normally address relations by the name of their relationship (e.g., calling mothers and fathers by their first names instead of "Mum" or "Dad"), then it is unlikely that a rarely used address term will take the place of other descriptive terms. Such semiproper names can become the normal term—for example, in Afrikaans *ouma* is the normal word for "grandmother," whereas in Dutch both *grootmoeder* 'grandmother' and *oma* 'granny' occur. But there is no shift in denotation here. While a young child might split off *gran* as MM generally and *grandma* as FM, as Anna gets older she is less likely to do this because she hears her MBD Sally calling Sally's FM (their shared grandmother) "Gran".

It is easy to see how a shift of denotation could occur in multilingual communities. Suppose Anna lives in a multilingual community in which other people she is friendly with make the distinction between MM and FM. She already uses "Gran" to and about her MM and "Grandma" to and about her FM, and she hears her parents using these names too and making the same distinction. In this case, the pressure to have a distinction between MM and FM may outweigh the knowledge that her cousin Sally uses "Gran" for her FM. Then Anna may generalize the terms so that *gran* means MM and *grandma* means FM. Thus a shift of denotation has occurred.

Multilingual communities or families are common in Aboriginal Australia and have been noted since early settlement (e.g., Schürmann 1846:28). Since that time, there has been great dislocation of residence, and many groups have been forced into living together. So, change in kinship systems over time can be examined in Australia by comparing the kinship systems of Indigenous peoples recorded by anthropologists in the 19th century and the kinship systems used by the descendants of the people recorded by those anthropologists. This will be most effective in those areas where the descendants still speak the language of the people recorded by the early anthropologists. An obvious source of case studies are the systems recorded by the anthropologists Baldwin Spencer and Francis Gillen in the late 19th and early 20th century over the course of their travels in central and northern Australia.

In undertaking such a case study of possible change in kinship systems from time t to time $t+1$, we need to be alert to the likelihood that we are tracking change, not from one system to another system but from one set of similar kinship systems to another set. Older sources have to be considered in the light of this. How did the older recorder gather information? Was it from eliciting terms ("What do you call your mother's sister?"), or from referents ("What do you call X? How is X related to you?"), or from both? Was there more than one consultant? How old were the consultants, and what were their sexes? How internally consistent is the original source? Does the apparent internal consistency result from the researcher filling in the gaps, or from genuine internal variation that the researcher blurred over by collapsing several systems or because people vary considerably in their ability to talk consistently about their kinship systems? So, where possible, it is important to consider who gave the recorders the information.

If the source is deemed to be internally consistent, then it is possible to compare the system proposed in, or inferable from, the original source with present-day systems used by the same group. This then allows us to consider how kinship systems change over a specified period of time, given the pressures and influences on their speakers. Research questions following from this include the following:

Are some parts of kinship systems more likely to undergo change than others?
What kinds of changes are made?
Are there correlations between types of change and other factors?

In comparing the different recordings of kinship systems at different times, we need to explain the following differences:

- If in the modern record two form/denotation pairs exist that have the same denotation and no difference in sense (e.g., not trirelational counterparts) and one of them has clearly been borrowed. I shall suggest that, while borrowing can reflect a change in the system, it need not do so. Indeed it may argue for the stability of the system if the borrowed form has a different denotation from its original denotation in the source language.
- If a form is present in the record from an earlier time but is not present in the most modern record.
- If a form is present in an early record with a different denotation from the denotation in the most modern record. A difference in denotation does not entail the absence of the form/denotation pairing at the earlier time because of the possibility of recorder error. Circumstantial evidence for a change of denotation would arise from another form being used in the earlier record with the missing denotation but for that second form/denotation pairing to be absent in the most recent record. For example,

earlier time:	Form F1 Denotation D1;	Form F2 Denotation D2
later time:	Form F1 Denotation D2;	Form F2 absent

- If a form is present in the earlier records but is recorded with a different sense in modern records. These are hard to argue for, but if my claim is accepted that the speaker/addressee information contained in trirelational terms is part of the sense of a word, then a change of a kinship term to or from a trirelational kinship term is a change in sense.
- If a form is present in the modern record but absent in earlier records. The absence in the early records does not entail the absence of the form at the earlier time. However, if another form is used with the denotation of the missing form, and if the second form is not found in the most recent record, then this is circumstantial evidence for the form not having been present at the earlier time.

In this chapter, I make a start on analyzing such differences between the Warumungu data recorded by Gillen and Spencer and later recordings made by anthropologists and linguists. Establishing plausible bridging contexts for changes in denotation will be discussed. A comparison with forms and systems in neighboring languages leads to a suggestion about a change in marriage patterns and its consequences for the Warumungu kinship system. The chapter ends with a discussion of why affinal terms are likely to change.

Recordings of Warumungu Kinship Terms

In 1901 Frank Gillen and Baldwin Spencer spent several months with the Warumungu around the Tennant Creek Telegraph Station. Subsequently, Warumungu kinship data have been recorded at roughly 30-year intervals (Chakravarti 1967; Hale 1959; Heath 1977; Stanner 1979), most recently in the context of genealogical research for the land claims over Warumungu country (Office of the Aboriginal Land Commissioner 1988). This allows some fine-grained checking of vocabulary and systems.

Gillen and Spencer worked with a large group of people at the Tennant Creek Telegraph Station, which had been established in the late 19th century in the heart of Warumungu country near a major water source and acted as a ration depot:

> We spent two months amongst the Warramunga and got to know them well and also to like them. We had previously known some of them for many

> years, which made our work amongst them much easier than it would otherwise have been....
>
> We fortunately visited the Warramunga during a comparatively good season, when it was possible for a large number of them to gather together. News of our coming had been sent on ahead of us from Barrow Creek, and when we arrived at Tennant Creek we met with a very warm welcome from those who had known us before.... There were altogether at least two hundred natives in camp. (Spencer and Gillen 1912:364–365)

It was a time of intense ceremonial activity, and there were visitors from other countries (Kaytetye, Wakaya, "Wulmalla," and Warlpiri [Spencer and Gillen 1912:200]). A Wakaya man played a major role in some ceremonies.

In terms of methods of eliciting kinship terms, Gillen and Spencer were undoubtedly influenced by the work of Lewis Morgan and, later, of Fison and Howitt (Gardner 2008, 2009) in collecting terms and in their interest in marriage systems. They probably had more data from men than women, since they went on trips with men, and seem to have collected more information generally about men's activities:

> We called in the assistance of one of the few women who are not under the ban of silence and we had a long tussle with her as to the different names she gives to different members of the tribe. It was a severe mental effort for her and I don't think we have them all right yet but she is now resting after her work and we shall try and settle the matter finally tomorrow. (Spencer 1997:346)

They give a clear account of Warumungu kinship, but it is one that does not admit of much variation, something noted by the next anthropologist to visit the Warumungu, William Stanner, who writes of "Spencer and Gillen's tendency to record the ideal system and disregard the irregularities" (1979:28).

Stanner visited in 1934, after the discovery of gold near the telegraph station in the early 1930s. His visit had two purposes:

> 1. to study and report upon the problem of the aboriginal reservation at Tennant's Creek, which it was proposed to throw open to mining occupation....
> 2. to re-examine several tribes studied by Spencer and Gillen in order to obtain, if possible, more exact information of the local organization, totemic systems, and kinship systems of these tribes, and to extend as much as possible the general sociological knowledge of tribes in this big area. (1979:1)

He failed in his efforts to support Warumungu people (in particular Zulu Jappangarti, traditional owner of the Tennant Creek area, and King Charlie Jampin, whose country was in the south of Warumungu country) in retaining their reserve. But he did collect some genealogical information and compiled meanings for kinship terms in his field notes and his report on his field trip.

The Warumungu then endured many changes (Nash 1984), as they were dispossessed of their land and were moved from settlement to settlement. People from other groups (Alyawarr, Warlmanpa, Warlpiri, Kaytetye, Wakaya, Wambaya, Mudburra, and Jingili) began to congregate on Warumungu country, resulting in new alliances, marriages, and a more complex linguistic landscape.

The next recorders of Warumungu kinship terms were linguists: in 1952 Arthur Capell worked with Nat Juppurla at Phillip Creek north of Tennant Creek (see Capell 1953). In 1959 Ken Hale worked with two men, Sandy Nandy Juppurla (born ca. 1917, according to Hale) and George Booth Juppurla (born ca. 1932, according to Hale), whose traditional countries were to the northwest of Tennant Creek and who were living out of Warumungu country at Amoonguna, near Alice Springs. Hale recorded 79 pages of field notes, which included some kinship vocabulary. Between July and December 1966 Prithvindra Chakravarti undertook linguistic fieldwork in the Tennant Creek area and recorded many tapes of texts, vocabulary, and ethnographic information (see Chakravarti 1967) from a range of Warumungu people. In April–June 1977 Jeffrey Heath carried out fieldwork in Tennant Creek and recorded vocabulary and texts from speakers such as William Fitz Juppurla (born around 1900, who lived much of his life at Banka Banka station in the extreme north of Warumungu country), including some specifically relating to family relationships from Albert Murphy Jappaljarri (probably born around 1913 and from country to the south of Tennant Creek).[4]

In 1979 I visited Tennant Creek and continued to do linguistic fieldwork, which moved into investigating kin terms as part of helping to develop the claimants' case for the Warumungu land claim. Initially my major

TABLE 12.1. Terms for grandparents and grandchildren.

Source	MM(B)	(Z)DC	FF(B/Z)/Reciprocal	MF(Z)/Reciprocal	FM(B)/Reciprocal
Spencer and Gillen (1904)	*turtundi*	*nuralli*	*kangwia*	*tapertapu*	♀SC *tapa-tapu*
Stanner (1979 [collected in 1934])		*ngurali*		*tabutabu*	*tabutabu*
Hale (1959)	*tjúṭanti*	*ŋúraḷi* ♀DC	*káŋkuya* FF(Z), ♂SC	*ṭápṭap* (*ṭápuṭapu*) FM, MBC, ♂DC	*ṭápṭap* (*ṭápuṭapu*) MF, MBC
Modern Warumungu	*jurttanti*	*ngurrarli*	*kangkuya*	*tapu-tapu*	*tapu-tapu*

consultants were Mary Morphett Narrurlu (born around 1900, sister of William Fitz Juppurla) and Bunny Narrurlu (born around 1940, sister of George Booth Juppurla), followed by Peggy Dawson Naljarri (born 1954, granddaughter of King Charlie Jampin). As I began working in language programs for children, I worked with more people, including the family of Nat Juppurla and Zulu Jappangarti. Thus there was continuity of family at least as far back as Stanner's work. What I shall call "Modern Warumungu" here describes the variety of Warumungu and the uses of kinship terms that emerged in the course of the Warumungu land claims, that is, 1980s Warumungu. The loss of many older speakers, pressure from English, and general language shift to a creole have resulted in considerable changes in how Warumungu is spoken since 1990. Thus the case study involves a spread of data over time, recorded from people affiliated with places across Warumungu country and related to each other.

The Data

Figure 12.1 is a family tree on which I have put the terms provided by Gillen and Spencer (in plain text) and the modern (1980s) terms (in italics). Most of the terms recorded by Gillen and Spencer have denotations consistent with at least subsets of the modern denotations that I have recorded. Larger aspects of the modern system that they do not discuss include trirelational terms, obligatory skewing of MMB and MMBC, and contextual skewing of MB and MBC.

Stability: Extra Forms with the Same Denotation Present in Modern Records

Perhaps the greatest evidence of stability comes from the continuity of the three-grandparent-term system in Warumungu. This system is attested by Gillen and Spencer, then in Stanner's records, and on into Modern Warumungu. The terms for cross-grandparent/grandchild (self-reciprocal), FF/grandchild (self-reciprocal), and MM (separate term for grandchild) are all attested in Gillen and Spencer, as in Table 12.1.[5] (Note, in the table ♀ and ♂ denote the sex of the propositus, thus ♀C is the child of a woman or a man's sister's child, [Z]C.)

Warumungu's neighbor Wakaya appears to have a similar system (with different terms), according to Gillen and Spencer.[6] However, the neighboring Ngumbin-Yapa and Arandic languages all have four-grandparent-term systems. Despite the long-term contacts with these other groups, the Warumungu system remained stable into the 1980s. Even when terms from neighboring languages were borrowed, they appear to have been assimilated into the system. Thus, the concept of having a three-term system with *tapu-tapu* as the cross-grandparent term is fairly stable, since, while Hale recorded two cross-grandparent terms, Warumungu *tapu-tapu* as well as *yápaḷa* (Warlmanpa and Warlpiri) and *yápiḷi* (Kaytetye), this has not resulted in a four-term system. Instead *appirli* has extended its denotation in line with *tapu-tapu* and has in addition gained a connotation of endearment; both *apurtu* and *appirli* are used by children in different families to address cross-grandparents, as shown in Table 12.2.

I now examine the differences between earlier recordings and later recordings. These include

- Form plus denotation present in the earlier records but absent in modern records
- Forms present in the earlier records but with different denotations in modern records
- More forms present in the modern record than in earlier records
- Forms present in the earlier records but with different senses in modern records
- Forms absent in the earlier records

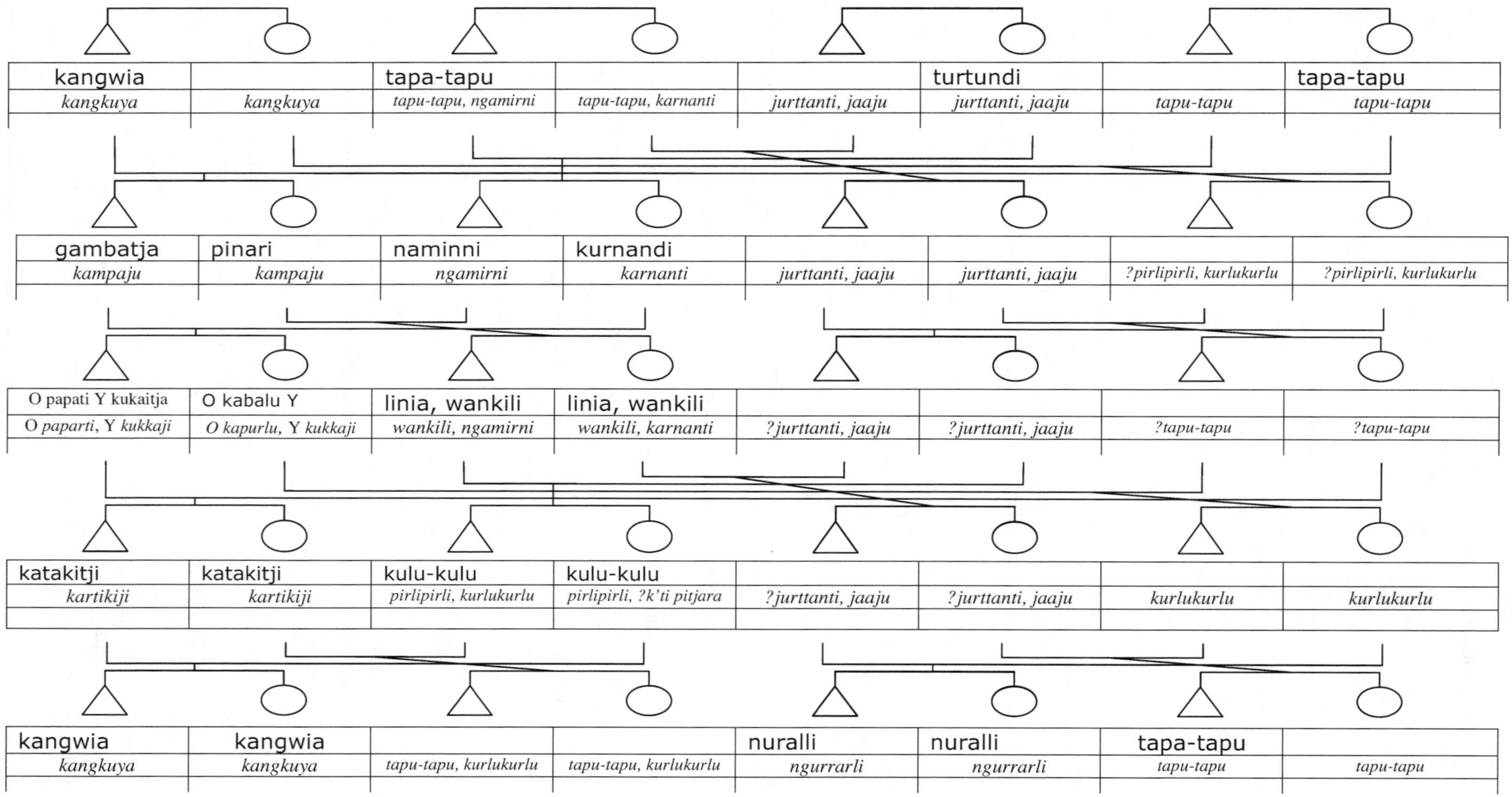

FIGURE 12.1. Some of Gillen and Spencer's Warumungu terms and their modern counterparts. Plain font = Gillen and Spencer; italics = modern counterpart. Template provided by Mark Harvey, from his work in progress on Top End kinship.

TABLE 12.2. Later attested terms for grandparents and grandchildren.

Source	MM(B)	(Z)DC	FF(B/Z)/ Reciprocal	MF(Z)/ Reciprocal	FM(B)/Reciprocal	Cf.
Hale (1959)	*tjúṭanti*	*ŋúraḷi* ♀*DC*	*káŋkuya* FF(Z), ♂SC	*ṭápṭap* (*ṭápuṭapu*) FM, MBC, ♂DC *yápaḷa* FM, ♀SS *yápiḷi* FFW, FFZH	*ṭápṭap* (*ṭápuṭapu*) MF, MBC	Arandic *aperl* FM(B), (Z)SC Kaytetye *aperleye* FM
Modern Warumungu	*jurttanti*	*ngurrarli*	*kangkuya*	*tapu-tapu*	*tapu-tapu*	
	jaaju					Warlpiri *jaja* MM(B) Gurindji *jaju*
Ultramodern Warumungu	*jaaju*		*kangku*	*apurtu*	*apurtu*	
				appirli	*appirli*	Kaytetye *aperle* FM[a]

[a] With regard to the Arandic *aperl*, in Anmatyerr *aperl* FM(B/Z) and its reciprocal are also glossed as "the husband or wife of someone who is not in the same generation moiety as oneself, for example, this would include a person's children's or nephew's and niece's husbands and wives, and a person's aunt's and uncle's husbands and wives. One's own parent could be referred to as *aperl-nheng*" (Green 2009:447).

Source: Kaytetye kin terms come from Turpin 2000. Gurindji kin terms come from McConvell 1982.

TABLE 12.3. Forms denoting "father's sister."

Source	F	FZ	Trirelational
Spencer and Gillen (1904)	*gampatja*[a]	*pinari*	
Stanner (1979 [collected in 1934])	*kambaju*	*kambaju*	*pinari* "used for ? Narrulu + Tjupula by Tjambin. . . . Nalyeri by Thapanungga"
Hale (1959)	*kámpatju*	*kámpatju*	
Modern Warumungu	*kampaju*	*kampaju*	*panara* talking to one's F/B about one's B/F (also in Warlmanpa)
Wakaya (Spencer and Gillen 1904)	*wakathua*	*pinauara*	
Wakaya (Breen 1974)	*uku-thu*	*pern'awurr*	

[a] The difference in the final vowel in *gampatja* is in line with common variation in final vowels in Gillen and Spencer's recordings of Warumungu.

Form Plus Denotation Present in the Earlier Records but Absent in Modern Records

There is only one clear example of a form plus denotation present in the earlier records but absent in modern records. A term for "father's sister," *pinari*, appears in Gillen and Spencer, whereas from Stanner onward there is no specific term for FZ—the same term is used as for "father." Table 12.3 shows the relevant forms for F and FZ. I have given for comparison relevant forms from Wakaya and trirelational terms.

The use of *kampaju* for F and FZ seemed robust in the 1980s, despite the fact that Warumungu speakers were living with speakers of Arandic languages and Ngumbin-Yapa languages that make a terminological distinction between "father" and "father's sister." This makes it somewhat doubtful that in the 1900s Warumungu speakers used the term *pinari* with the denotation FZ but had lost this denotation by 1934. So where did *pinari* come from? Gillen knew Arrernte and had worked for years with Arrernte speakers. The Arandic languages make a distinction between F (Spencer and Gillen *okinia*, Modern Arandic *akngey*)[7] and FZ (Spencer and Gillen *uwinna*, Modern Arandic *awenh*), and this would have predisposed Gillen to looking for two terms reflecting the differences in denotation.[8] The term *pinari* for FZ does not

TABLE 12.4. Terms for "mother" and "mother's sister."

Source	M	MeZ	(Z)DDD Reciprocal/MMM	MyZ	Young Mother
Spencer and Gillen (1904)	*kurnandi*	*kurnandi bilibili* (compound)		*kurnandi pithara* (compound)	
Stanner (1979 [collected in 1934])	*kanandi*				
Hale (1959)	*káṇanti*				
Modern Warumungu	*karnanti*	*karnanti*	*pirlipirli*		*pijjara*

appear to be cognate with either of the Arandic terms, but it seems to be cognate with a Wakaya form that Gillen and Spencer, and later Breen, recorded for FZ.

The presence of the form *pinari* in Stanner's notebook suggests that he sought to understand what the denotation of Spencer and Gillen's *pinari* was. He received an answer, which he marked with a question mark: the term appeared to be used of someone (male or female) in the subsection of one's MMF or MMBC, that is, the subsection from which one's mother-in-law is drawn. Stanner does not mention this term in his published report, which suggests that he was unsure of the denotation.

A somewhat similar form, *panara*,[9] was given to me by Bunny Narrurlu for talking to one's father or brother about one's brother, father, or brother's son.[10] The term and its denotation are shared with Warlmanpa (which she gave as her first language) and, as *parnara*, with Warlpiri and Gurindji. Trirelational terms were not much used by the oldest speaker who taught me (Mary Morphett Narrurlu, born ca. 1900), and the more unusual ones have mostly been recorded from speakers who also speak Warlmanpa.

For this difference caused by the absence of a term in the record, there is little to decide between

- a scenario in which Warumungu did not have the term (or another term) for the FZ denotation but Gillen and Spencer were led to believe that Warumungu used the Wakaya form for the same FZ denotation as in Wakaya, perhaps as a result of discussion with the senior Wakaya man in the Warumungu group they mention, and
- a scenario in which the Warumungu did use the trirelational term *panara*, which could denote FZ among other denotata, but Gillen and Spencer mistook this as primarily denoting FZ.

As to why Stanner recorded *pinari* as used of people in the MMF subsection, I note that many Warumungu have people in the subsection of MM(B) whom they call *sister* or *brother* and whose parents they may consequently call F(Z). It is possible that in such cases, the trirelational term used would be *panara*, rather than *wururru*, a term used to MM(B) about her (or his) father's or brother's children. This may have led to Stanner's note.

Forms Present in the Earlier Records but with Different Denotations in Modern Records

A clear example of different denotations being provided for the same form is *bilibili*, which is given as part of a compound term used for "mother's elder sister" (MeZ) by Gillen and Spencer, as in Table 12.4. In Modern Warumungu, *pirlipirli* is used as a great-grandparent/child term, often for mother's mother's mother (MMM[B/Z]), a relation that is important for many children given that their MMM is more likely to be alive and involved in their upbringing than their other great-grandparents. Warumungu great-grandparent terms are not well understood, a problem Green (1998:29) notes also for Alyawarr. Spencer and Gillen do not record great-grandparent terms.

In Modern Warumungu, a mother's older and younger sisters (MyZ) are also called *karnanti*, and this is carried over into contemporary Wumpurrarni English (a local creole [Disbray 2008]), where a mother's sisters may be called "Mum [Proper Name]," for example, "Mum Rosemary." However, young women who might be classificatory mothers can be called "young mothers," *(karnanti) pijjara*. Exactly what determines someone's designation as "young" is not clear,[11] although in the neighboring Arandic languages terms for "mother" and "father" combine with terms for "big" and "small" to denote older or younger siblings of parents (Koch, this volume). Thus the denotation of *kurnandi pithara* is partly consistent with that of *pijjara* as "young mother."

At first glance, the denotation of *kurnandi bilibili* as MeZ is quite different from the modern denotation as

TABLE 12.5. Terms for cross-cousins.

Source	MBC	FZC	Trirelational
Spencer and Gillen (1904)	*linea?* *lina* (♀ speaker)	*wankilli*	*wankilli*
Stanner (1979 [collected in 1934])		*wangili* (FZD)	
Hale (1959)	*ṭápuṭapu* ("mobro and káṭikiji's ch.")	*wánkili* ("mobro and kampaju's ch.") FZC	
Modern Warumungu	*wankili*	*wankili*	*linya* talking to MM about one's "sister-in-law" = MM's cross-cousin

MMM(B/Z), but in fact, the modern term *pirlipirli* is used reciprocally for a woman's DDC (great-grandchild), who is in the subsection of the woman's mother. Thus Gillen and Spencer's denotation is subsumed by that of the modern term. The possibility that there was a distinction specifically between MeZ and MyZ and that *kurnandi bilibili* was used to denote MeZ is not implausible, given that the distinction is made in Wambaya (Nordlinger 1998), in Garrwa the term for M and MeZ (in contrast with MyZ) is *bili-ki* (Furby and Furby n.d.), and *pileku* is used for MB in Wakaya (Breen 1986). But given how strong the contemporary use of *pirlipirli* as a great-grandparent term is, it may well have been a presumption that Gillen and Spencer made, based on hearing *pirlipirli* used for older women and *pijjara* used for younger women.

But this still leaves the meaning of *pijjara* unclear. Looking at cognates in neighboring languages does not help, as there are no obvious cognates for *pijjara*, although there are for *pirlipirli*, discussed further in the concluding section.

Forms Present in the Earlier Records but with Different Senses in Modern Records

Terms for MBC and FZC provide an instance of one form being recorded with different senses at different times. (See Table 12.5.) Gillen and Spencer have two terms and indicate at one point that the sex of the speaker is important for *linya*. *Linya* does not seem to have cognates in neighboring languages, and in Modern Warumungu it is a trirelational term denoting the cross-cousin of one's MM (I have heard it used of female cross-cousins). In Modern Warumungu *wankili* is used for cross-cousins regardless of the sex of the speaker or of whether the referent is MBC or FZC. *Wankili* is a widespread word and can be involved in a sex distinction:[12] with the Arandic *ankel* 'male cross-cousin' contrasting with *altyel* 'female cross-cousin' and *arrwemp* 'cross-cousin' and the Warlpiri *wankili* 'male child of maternal uncle' contrasting with *jukana* 'female child of maternal uncle'.

I have no evidence to decide between, on the one hand, possible misinterpretation by Gillen and Spencer of a trirelational term (perhaps from preferred conversation usage of "your cross-cousin" rather than "my cross-cousin") and, on the other, the possibility that the denotations of *wankili* and *linya* have changed, that is, that one was for female cross-cousins and the other was for male cross-cousins, or that one was used by female speakers and the other was used by male speakers, or that they once denoted MBC versus FZC.

Forms Absent in the Earlier Records

The absence of forms in Gillen and Spencer is mostly important if the absences concern easily definable sections of the kinship system. I discuss here absences relating to affinal terms.

The Warumungu marriage system, as described during the Warumungu land claim (Office of the Aboriginal Land Commissioner 1988), involved men marrying as their first choice someone in the subsection corresponding to their MMBDC/FMBSC (which is also the subsection of ZSC and FM, *tapu-tapu*) and as their second choice someone in the subsection corresponding to MBC/FZC (which is also the subsection of BDC *wankili* and MF *tapu-tapu*).[13] Genealogies showed both patterns occurring. Some marriages involved brothers and sisters marrying into the same country. While there were many marriages that were not "straight," given the disruptions and pressure to assimilate that the Warumungu had faced and

TABLE 12.6. Woman's perspective on affinal terms.

Source	HF	HM	DH	SW	BDH	BSW
Spencer and Gillen (1904)	*kulukulu* (ZC)		*tjurtalia*			
	auiniari	*auiniari* *unnyari*		*auiniari*		
Hale (1959)			*kúṇṭaŋa*			
Modern Warumungu	*lamparra*	*ngunyarri*	*miyimi*	*ngunyarri*	*lamparra*	*lamparra*
	jurṯalja	*jurṯalja*	*(kúrṇṭaŋa jurṯalja)*	*jurṯalja*		

TABLE 12.7. Man's perspective on affinal terms.

Source	WF	WM	DH	SW
Spencer and Gillen (1904)	*kulukulu*		*(naminni)* (MB)	
	auiniari (also ZS)	*unnyari*		
Stanner (1979 [collected in 1934])	*ngunyara* (if MMBDD)	*tjudaldZa*[a]		
	kulngulu (if ZSD)			
	lambarra			
Hale (1959)	*kúḷukúḷu*, also MMBC's spouse	*kúṇṭaŋa*, also MMBC	*ŋámiṇi*	*káṇanti*
Heath (1977)	*jud̲alja*	*jud̲alja*		
Modern Warumungu	*lamparra*	*miyimi*	*lamparra*	*lamparra*

[a] The Z in *tjudaldZa* appears to represent a lamino-palatal stop.

were facing, the number of straight (first- or second-choice) marriages was impressive.[14]

Gillen and Spencer show three types of affinal terms: a term for the kinship relationship involved, *kulukulu* (the modern *kurlukurlu* 'a woman's child', which is the subsection of a woman's HF or a man's WF); a term that in modern use focuses on the avoidance and respect relationship involved, *jurtalja*; and a term that in modern use seems more purely an affinal term, *ngunyarri*. One difference between Modern Warumungu and what Gillen and Spencer describe is their broader denotation of the term *ngunyarri*, which includes HF. Forms from a woman's and a man's perspectives are given in Tables 12.6 and 12.7. Note that I am assuming that both *auiniari* and *unnyari* are transcriptions of the term *ngunyarri*.

The terms from the man's point of view make the kinship relationships involved clear. From the father-in-law's point of view, his daughter would marry as first choice his *ngamirni* MB, that is, the child of the man's *tapu-tapu* (MF) and *jurttanti* (MM). This explains Gillen and Spencer's recording of *ngamirni* for DH and the reciprocal *kurlukurlu* for WF. The correspondent Anmatyerr *kamern* MB is also given as BDH.

Stanner (1979) adds a distinction between whether the man is marrying his MMBDD (WF *ngunyara*) or his ZSD (WF *lambara* or *kulngulu*) and observes that the latter pattern is found in the north among the Jingili and Mudburra.[15] I have no evidence as to whether this distinction was observed during the 1980s. As for Stanner's term *kulngulu*, it is not clear whether *kulngulu* is the kinship term *kurlukurlu* (woman's child) or the Warlpiri landowning term *kurdungurlu* for the "manager" relation of people in the opposite patri-moiety. Either would fit the denotation associated with the subsection of HF.

In the 1980s, consultants gave the avoidance terms *kurntanga* and *jurtalja* or the general affine terms *miyimi*, *lamparra*, and *ngunyarri* in preference to kin terms. They rarely used kin terms of actual relations by marriage and did not use them when talking of relations by marriage who were distant classificatory kin.

Thus we are left with three types of words for affines: specific affine terms, general avoidance terms, and the terms for kin relationships that have been discussed. The general avoidance terms are shared with several neighboring languages: correspondents of *jurtalja* are found in Gillen and Spencer, in Stanner, and also in Warlpiri

TABLE 12.8. Changing record of the denotation of *ngunyarri*.

Language	Referent of *Ngunyarri*	Kin Gloss	WF	HF	WM	HM	*Lamparra* Attested
1900s Warumungu	Either	ZS	WF	HF	WM	HM, ♀SW	—
1930s Warumungu			father of W (W = MMBDD)				*lamparra* 'father of W' (W = ZSD)
1980s Warumungu	Female					HM, ♀SW	*lamparra* HF, WF, ♂SW, ♀SW

and Arandic as terms for various categories of in-laws.[16] Correspondents of *kurntanga* are found in Warlpiri and Warlmanpa, and the term is etymologically analyzable in Warlmanpa (*kurnta* 'shame') but not in Warumungu. This suggests borrowing.

Of the specific affine terms, *miyimi* (WM, woman's SW) is probably cognate with Wambaya *mimayi* 'daughter's husband' and *mimayirna* 'mother-in-law', 'son's wife (female ego)', 'son's wife', and Garrwa *mimi* MF (Nordlinger 1998).[17] *Lamparra* is a widespread *Wanderwort* used for categories of in-laws. It is found in Warlpiri, Walmajarri, and Gurindji and farther afield. While Gillen and Spencer do not record it for Warumungu,[18] it has been around for some time—Stanner recorded it for Mudburra as well as Warumungu in 1934.

Ngunyarri is an early term. Assuming that the identification of it with both *auiniari* and *unnyari* is correct, it has a much broader denotation in Gillen and Spencer than it does in contemporary usage, where it is predominately used by women for HM and ♀SW. By including ZS, it probably includes a man's father-in-law when a man marries his sister's son's daughter. In 1980s Warumungu the terms *miyimi* and *lamparra* have taken over part of the denotation of Gillen and Spencer's *ngunyarri* correspondent, so that the latter now has a narrower denotation, as shown in Table 12.8. *Lamparra* has taken over the HF/reciprocal part of the denotation and has extended to include WF—it has become a general affinal term used with respect to men's children and their in-laws by women and men, while *ngunyarri* is mostly used by women of their sons' wives (and reciprocally), and *miyimi* is used by women of their sons-in-law (and reciprocally).

Comparisons and Historical Speculations

In this section I set the Warumungu terms in an areal context. This leads to some suggestions as to changes in kin term denotations and finally to the proposal that traces of an earlier FZC marriage pattern can be seen in Modern Warumungu kin terms.

Starting with the term *ngunyarri*, the same restriction to HM/♀SW is seen in the form *anherre*, an old word in Arandic, which, as Koch (this volume) argues, can be reconstructed as the pre-Arandic **ngunharri* (HM). The presence of *lamparra* is probably not the source of this restriction, since *lamparre* appears in the northern Arandic language Kaytetye but is not recorded for Anmatyerr (unless *ampaty-ampaty* HF is distantly related). In addition, the Kaytetye form appears to be HF but is not extended to WF. Instead the MMM(B) kin term *ahenterre* is retained for WF. (See Table 12.9.)

However, in contrast with *anherr*, the term *ngwenyarr* is also found as a "respectful word for sons-in-law (closely related young or old ones), MMF, FMM, woman's MMBS" (Green 2009:447). This is a switch of kin denotation (from MMM[B] to MMF or FMM) and a corresponding switch of in-law referent from female referents (HM, BSW) to male referents (♀DH). The form,[19] the change of denotation, and the special connotation make *ngwenyarr* a candidate for borrowing into Central and Eastern Anmatyerr. The likely source is Warlpiri, which has a similar denotation for *ngunyarri* as MMF, and the definition suggests a male referent. This is not characteristic of other Ngumbin-Yapa languages—the neighboring Gurindji has *ngunyarri* with a different denotation, as the kin term MMM(B). And the westernmost Ngumbin-Yapa language, Walmajarri, has *ngunyarri* as HM, as do several Western Desert languages, as well as Wakaya to the east.

Table 12.10 suggests that the 1980s Warumungu use of *ngunyarri* with female referents and mostly as HM and its reciprocal is consonant with the use of this form elsewhere in Western Desert, Arandic, and Ngumbin-Yapa languages, with some exceptions—the great-grandparent usage in Bilinarra, the HF use in Martu Wangka, and most strikingly, the WMB use in Warlpiri and Anmatyerr. The generalized Bilinarra use of *ngunyarri* as a great-grandparent term is partly consonant with the generalized 1900s Warumungu recording of *ngunyarri* as a general in-law term, since HF and WM structurally include several

TABLE 12.9. Comparison of the denotations of affinal terms in Arandic languages.

Language	WF(Z)/♂DH	HF(Z)/♂SW	WM(B)/♀DH	HM/♀SW
Modern Warumungu, Affine Terms	*lamparra*	*lamparra*	*miyimi jurdalja* *kurntanga*	*ngunyarri*
Modern Warumungu, Relation Terms	*kurlukurlu* ZC (*pirlipirli* reciprocal MMM)	*pirlipirli* reciprocal MMM (*kurlukurlu* ZC)	*jurttanti* (reciprocal *ngurrali*) MMBC/FMM skewed	*jurttanti* (reciprocal *ngurrali*) MMBC/ FMM skewed
Kaytetye	*ahenterre*	*lamparre*	*rtwaltye* *meye-meye* *ayletyeye*	*atnherre* 'mother-in-law', WM, ♀DH
Eastern and Central Anmatyerr	*arnemerr* (E, T) *maly* (*maly-maly* [E], child-directed speech; MMM[B]) *ahenterr, ahenterr-ahenterr* (E; MMM[B])	*ampaty-ampaty*	*rtwalty* *mwer* *mey-mey* *ateyarrp*	*anherr* (*nhey-nhey*, child-directed speech) Cf. Arandic *anherr* WM, HF, ♀SW

Note: Close relations in the MMBF/C or FMM class are called MM(B) *jurttanti* or its reciprocal, *ngurrali*. For *lamparre*, see Koch, this volume. With regard to the Arandic *anherr* WM in the final column, Green (1998: app. 1) cites Gillen and Spencer's *quaia-nurra* for this. Kin term denotations are included if in the source: E = Eastern Anmatyerr; T = Ti-tree Anmatyerr.

TABLE 12.10. Denotations of *ngunyarri* in Central Australian languages.

Language	Referent of *Ngunyarri*	Kin	Affinal HF	WM	HM	*Lamparra* Attested
1980s Warumungu	Female				HM, ♀SW	*lamparra* HF, WF, ♂SW, ♀SW
Arandic	Arandic *anherre* pre-Arandic **ngunharri*				HM, ♀SW	Kaytetye *lamparre* HF
Anmatyerr	*ngwenyarr*, mostly male	MMF, FMM, fMMBS		"respectful word for sons-in-law (closely related)"		
Wakaya	*winara*, female				HM	
Warlpiri		MMF		WMB		*lamparra* WF, HF, ZC
Walmajarri	Mostly female	"Aunty"			HM, ♀SW	*lamparr* 'father in-law'
Bilinarra, Gurindji	Either (general great-grandparent term)	Bilinarra: MM(F/M), MF(F/M), FF(F/M), FM(F/M) Gurindji: MMM(B/Z)				Gurindji *lamparra* WF(B/Z), ♂DH
Kukatja	Female				HM	*lamparrpa* WF
Western Desert	Female?	Niece and other relatives			♀SW	—
Martu Wangka	Either		♂SW, HF			—

Note: For pre-Arandic **ngunharri*, cf. Koch, this volume. Wakaya is from Spencer and Gillen 1904:81. Walmajarri is from Richards and Hudson 1990. *Aunty* in Walmajarri is probably FZ. In Martu Wangka *umari* is "mother-in-law, son-in-law, FZ in avoidance relation," and in Western Desert *yumari* is WM/"taboo person." This suggests that in Walmajarri *ngunyarri* may have connotations of being a respect word. Bilinarra is from Felicity Meakins—in the AUSTKIN database. McConvell (1982) has Gurindji *ngunyarri* as MMM. Kukatja is from Valiquette 1993. Form found in English finder-list only. *Waputju* WF, *yumari* WM. Western Desert is from Douglas and the Western Australian College of Advanced Education, Institute of Applied Language Studies 1988: *mingkayi* SW, *yurntalpa* SW, *waputju* WF, *yumari* WM/'taboo person'. Martu Wangka is from Burgman et al. 2005: *marruku* WM, fDH; *umari* WM, fDH, FZ avoidance relation.

TABLE 12.11. Correspondents to *pirlipirli* in Central Australian languages.

Language	Pirlipirli	Cognates with Pirlipirli	Ngunyarri
1980s Warumungu	MMM(B), ♀DDC		HM, ♀SW
Warlmanpa	Actual MMBD, FMM	Also *pirlipina*	
Warlpiri	FMM (WM) (Lajamanu, Yuendumu dialect)	*pirlipina* MMF (Hanson River dialect) *yapirliyi* (Willowra dialect) Trirelational "spouse": ♀ talking to BS/BSW of the other. BSW is equivalent (dialect not noted) to ♀DD	*ngunyarri* MMF, WMB
Gurindji		*pilirli* trirelational (speaking about MM[B]/♀DC to B/Z/ MM[B]/WM[B]/ MM[B], F[Z] and reciprocals; or talking to F about WM/♀DH)	*ngunyarri* MMM(B)
Central and Eastern Anmatyerr		*aperl, aperley* FM *aperl-aperl* 'future spouse' (child-directed talk)	*anherr, anherrey* HM, ♀SW *ngwenyarr* 'son-in-law' (respect), MMF, FFM
Kaytetye		*aperleye* FM	*anherreye* HM, ♀SW
Wakaya		*pileku* MB (Breen 1986) *bilaku* MBS (Spencer and Gillen 1904)	
Garrwa		*biliki* M, MeZ (Furby and Furby n.d.)	

great-grandparent terms in many Central Australian languages (MMF, FMM, MMM, FMF).

The divergence of the denotation of the Warlpiri term and the recent borrowing in Arandic from the denotation of the equivalent terms in most other languages needs explanation. It may be due to the presence in Warlpiri of the terms *pirlipirli* and *pirlipina*, neither of which are apparently found in Western Desert languages or Walmajarri. These terms denote FMM or MMF in Warlpiri, contrasting with MMM in Warumungu. Thus the denotation of these terms in Warlpiri overlaps with the denotation of *ngunyarri* (or *anherr*) in other languages. (See Table 12.11.)

Thus there is an apparent flip between having *ngunyarri* as WMB (MMF) and *pirlipirli* as WM (FMM [Warlpiri]) and having *ngunyarri* as HM and *pirlipirli* as MMM(B) and possibly WF (Warumungu). Both sets of great-grandparent denotations are consonant with the generalized Bilinarra use of *ngunyarri* as a general great-grandparent term.

This comparison with other languages gives rise to a further speculation that leads to possible sources for the lack of an FZ term in Warumungu and to sources for the three-grandparent-term system. The implication that *ngunyarri* in Walmajarri is FZ suggests an earlier marriage pattern of marrying FZD. This in turn could explain the absence of a special term for FZ in Warumungu—if the marriage pattern had been to call F *kampaju* and FZ *ngunyarri* 'mother of spouse' and then the pattern changed to favor FZDDC as spouse, then one's spouse's mother would be FZDD, and so there could be a consequent shift of denotation to FZDD as *ngunyarri*. This would have left FZ without a term, which was subsequently filled by extending *kampaju* to cover FZ as well as F.

Another consequence of this FZD marriage pattern would be that FM and MF could be structurally siblings, as opposed to the structural sibling set of FF and MM. The pairing of FM and MF is kept in the term *tapu-tapu* in Modern Warumungu. How distinct terms for FF (*kangkuya*) and MM (structurally the same as *spouse*; *jurttanti/ngurrali*) evolved is beyond the scope of this chapter, but we note the use of correspondents to *kangku* and *kangkuya* for FF in Wambaya (Nordlinger 1998) and Jingilu (Spencer and Gillen 1904) and the form *jurtu* in Ngaatjatjarra (Dousset 2003) for MM, FM, and HZ. The MM and HZ denotations of *jurtu* would fit well with an earlier FZD marriage pattern in Warumungu and perhaps the use of *tapu-tapu* for MF and FF.

Conclusion

The data in this chapter suggest that the ways Warumungu people talked about kinship remained reasonably stable from 1901 until the mid-1980s. Perhaps this is not surprising, since one of the main contributors to the analysis in the mid-1980s was born around 1900. But that her account was supported by younger people suggests some resilience in the kinship systems. Unusual features have remained stable, such as the lack of an FZ term and the presence of the three-grandparent-term system (the latter is indeed supported by borrowing). These features may have arisen out of a change from an FZC marriage pattern to an FZDDC pattern, but this would have predated Gillen and Spencer's visit.

Where change is most noticeable is in the system of affine terms, as borrowing appears to have affected the denotations of earlier terms. This may be due to the social emotions and responsibilities bound up in marriage, as well as to language loss and changes in marriage patterns. The emotions ("shame") and social responsibilities involved with marriage relations may have made it easier to borrow words as general polite terms for these respectful relationships. Once a word has come into the system, then there may be an unstable situation resulting from overlapping denotations. Terms may have their denotations narrowed, or they may become polite trirelational terms. The use of affinal terms like *lamparra* and *miyimi* (and the very widespread word *panji* for "brother-in-law"), which make no commitment to blood relationship, may have been encouraged by loss of language and marriage patterns involving more outsiders without clear kinship relations to the parents of children's spouses. In general, this suggests that words for in-laws are more likely be borrowed or replaced. This could also result in turn in shifts in the denotations of words for kin relations that are structurally equivalent to in-law terms.

Notes

Earlier versions of this chapter were presented at the Kinship Workshop, Kioloa, 2009, and the Australian Languages Workshop, Kioloa, 2010. I thank the attendees for helpful discussion as well as Mark Harvey, Patrick McConvell, Harold Koch, David Nash, and an anonymous referee. Data sources are as follows: Western Desert: Douglas and the Western Australian College of Advanced Education, Institute of Applied Language Studies 1988. Warlpiri: Laughren et al. 2000. Warlmanpa: Nash 1979. Wambaya: Nordlinger 1998. Walmatjarri: Richards and Hudson 1990. Wakaya: Breen 1986. Martu Wangka: Burgman et al. 2005. Kukatja: Valiquette 1993. Kaytetye: Turpin 2000; Turpin and Ross 2004; Koch, this volume. Gurindji: McConvell 1982. Central and Eastern Anmatyerr: Green 2009. Bilinarra: Felicity Meakins, contribution to the AustKin Project. Sources of Warumungu data are discussed in the text.

1. Green (1998) describes problems with identifying senses, comparing speakers' folk definitions of terms and dictionary definitions.
2. I realize that information about the speaker and the addressee is usually considered part of pragmatic information, rather than semantic information. However, it is an inherent property of the meaning of the trirelational terms that one uses a different term to identify, say, the child of one's mother's mother's brother (MMB) when talking to one's MMB from that used to identify that same person when talking with one's father. The property cannot be canceled, and so I treat it as part of the sense and not as a connotation or as something that is purely pragmatic.
3. The use of kin terms as semiproper names allows them to be extended. So Anna's mother can, when talking about her own mother to Anna or Sally, call her "Gran," and she may use "Grandma" of her husband's mother.
4. "Albert" was recorded in 1938 by T. Strehlow as aged about 25 and working for a butcher at Tennant Creek.
5. See the handwritten note by Hale on the typescript page 39: "mobro and káṭikiji's ch." (1959:39).
6. Breen (1974) has the same or similar terms with an odd set of denotations that do not look internally consistent and which involve a shift to a single grandmother term.
7. Unless otherwise specified, Arandic terms come from the discussion in Green 1998.
8. The influence of their experience with speakers of Arandic languages is noted by Stanner: "One has the impression also that Spencer and Gillen, coming straight from an intensive study of the Aranda and Kaititj to the Warramunga, who bear many striking resemblances to the former, may not have been quite prepared for these differences" (1979:10).
9. For relating this form to *pinari/pernawurr*, note that while the [a]/[i] difference in the first vowel is problematic, if the nasal is retroflex, a preceding [a] or [e] vowel is often heard as quite high.
10. The term can probably be used of their female counterparts (as the Warlpiri term can), but I did not check this.
11. Green notes the Anmatyerr term *amey* with the denotations M(Z), woman's DDC, "male cross-cousin's daughter," and "young mother"/"little mother," which seems parallel to *pijjara*.
12. See Koch, this volume, for the suggestion that the Arandic term is prior and its appearance in other languages is due to borrowing.
13. In the 1980s Warumungu people often talked about marriage in terms of subsections: Nangali marries Jungurrayi. This is obviously a simplification, and Stanner argues that "Warramunga marriage is thus primarily governed by

kinship and totemic affiliations, and not by sub-sections or moieties, though these do give a conventional form to marriage" (1979:14). Genealogies prepared for the land claim are not reliable enough at the great-grandparent level to determine actual genealogical relationships between marriage partners, especially since adoptions and fostering may lead to someone having several parents.

14. Stanner (1979:30) indicates that Warumungu disliked marriages that resulted in children having a different moiety from their father and that such marriages were infrequent at the time of his visit.
15. Stanner writes:

    The father of one's wife (if mother's mother's brother's daughter's daughter) is *ngunyara*; if sister's son's daughter, is *lambara* or *kulngulu*; but in both cases the wife's mother is *tjudaldZa* (Spencer and Gillen's *tjurtalia*). Because of the avoidances which in the Warramungu, as in other Australian tribes, impose a strict prohibition upon the use of the names of the wife's parents, and particularly the wife's mother, it is often only with the greatest difficulty that these can be obtained. (1979:10)

    Note, the Z in *tjudaldZa* appears to represent a lamino-palatal stop.
16. *Jurdalja* is discussed in the *Warlpiri Dictionary* as follows:

    We call our mother-in-laws *jurdalja*. And one's *juka* (i.e. sister's husband), and one's *jaja* (i.e. mother's mother's brother). Our own *mirntirdi* (i.e. sister's daughter's children) we call them *jurdalja*. We call *jurdalja* our *jaja* and *mirntirdi* who provide us with our *juka*. We only call *jurdalja* those who actually give us a *juka*. But we call our mother-in-law *jurdalja*. That is the ones who give us their young daughters (in marriage). And our sister's husband, our *juka* too. The one we give our sisters to. These are all the ones that we call *jurdalja* as they are one mob. (Laughren et al. 2000)

17. It is perhaps more distantly correlated with the Wakaya *mimimo* recorded by Gillen and Spencer as MF, FM, SWF, and DHF (i.e., the subsections of H or W, or of a woman's child's spouse's mother or a man's child's spouse's father, or of one's children's spouses' parents) and the Kaytetye *meyemeye* FZH (i.e., the subsection of a man's children's spouses); for the latter, see Koch, this volume. Note that MF is in the subsection of second-choice spouses and is also the father-in-law of a man's children.
18. They do record *limpa-ri-ntha* as DH for Jingulu, but whether this is related remains to be proved.
19. That is, the failure to undergo regular sound changes.

References Cited

Breen, G. 1974. Wakaya Vocabulary and Preliminary Grammar. Unpublished MS, Australian Institute of Aboriginal Studies, Canberra.

Breen, J. G. 1986. Wakaya Vocabulary. Unpublished MS, Aboriginal Studies Electronic Data Archive, Australian Institute of Aboriginal and Torres Strait Islander Studies, Canberra.

Burgman, A., J. Marsh, K. Hansen, and J. Booth. 2005. *Martu Wangka Dictionary and Topical Finder Lists*. South Hedland, Australia: Wangka Maya Pilbara Aboriginal Language Centre.

Capell, A. 1953. Notes on the Waramunga Language, Central Australia. *Oceania* 23(4):296–311.

Chakravarti, P. 1967. A Report on WaRumuŋu. Unpublished MS, Australian Institute of Aboriginal Studies, Canberra.

Disbray, S. 2008. More Than One Way to Catch a Frog: A Study of Children's Discourse in an Australian Contact Language. Ph.D. dissertation, University of Melbourne, Melbourne. Electronic document, http://repository.unimelb.edu.au/10187/8533.

Douglas, W. H., and the Western Australian College of Advanced Education, Institute of Applied Language Studies. 1988. *An Introductory Dictionary of the Western Desert Language*. Perth: Institute of Applied Language Studies, Western Australian College of Advanced Education.

Dousset, L. 2003. On the Misinterpretation of the Aluridja Kinship System Type (Australian Western Desert). *Social Anthropology* 11:43–61.

Furby, C. E., and E. S. Furby. N.d. Garawa Dictionary. MS, item 471. Aboriginal Studies Electronic Data Archive, Australian Institute of Aboriginal and Torres Strait Islander Studies, Canberra.

Gardner, H. 2008. The Origin of Kinship in Oceania: Lewis Henry Morgan and Lorimer Fison. *Oceania* 78(2):137–150.

Gardner, H. 2009. "By the Facts We Add to Our Store": Lorimer Fison, Lewis Henry Morgan and the Spread of Kinship Studies in Australia. *Oceania* 79(3):280–292.

Green, J. 1998. *Kin and Country: Aspects of the Use of Kinterms in Arandic Languages*. Melbourne: University of Melbourne, Linguistics and Applied Linguistics.

Green, J. 2009. *Central and Eastern Anmatyerr to English Dictionary*. Alice Springs, Australia: IAD Press.

Hale, K. L. 1959. Waṛumuŋu Notes. Unpublished MS, Australian Institute of Aboriginal and Torres Strait Islander Studies, Canberra.

Heath, J. 1977. Warramunga Grammatical Notes. Warramunga–English Wordlist. Warramunga Texts. Copy at Australian Institute of Aboriginal and Torres Strait Islander Studies, Canberra.

Heath, J. 1982. Introduction. In *Languages of Kinship in Aboriginal Australia*. J. Heath, F. Merlan, and A. Rumsey, eds. Pp. 1–18. Oceania Linguistic Monographs, 24. Sydney: University of Sydney.

Laughren, M., K. Hale, and R. Hoogenraad. 2000. *Warlpiri Dictionary: Electronic Datafiles*. Brisbane: University of Queensland.

McConvell, P. 1982. Neutralisation and Degrees of Respect

in Gurindji. In *Languages of Kinship in Aboriginal Australia*. J. Heath, F. Merlan, and A. Rumsey, eds. Pp. 86–106. Oceania Linguistic Monographs, 24. Sydney: University of Sydney.

Nash, D. 1979. *Preliminary Vocabulary of the Warlmanpa Language*. Cambridge: Massachusetts Institute of Technology.

Nash, D. 1984. The Warumungu's Reserves 1892–1962: A Case Study in Dispossession. *Australian Aboriginal Studies* 1: 2–16.

Nordlinger, R. 1998. *A Grammar of Wambaya, Northern Territory*. Canberra: Australian National University.

Office of the Aboriginal Land Commissioner. 1988. *Warumungu Land Claim/Report by the Aboriginal Land Commissioner, Mr. Justice Maurice, to the Minister for Aboriginal Affairs and to the Administrator of the Northern Territory*. Canberra: Australian Government Publishing Service. Electronic document, http://nla.gov.au/nla.cat-vn1259459.

Richards, E., and J. Hudson. 1990. *Walmajarri–English Dictionary with English Finder List*. Darwin: Summer Institute of Linguistics.

Schürmann, C. W. 1846. *The Aboriginal Tribes of Port Lincoln, in South Australia: Their Mode of Life, Manners, Customs, Etc.* Adelaide: George Dehane. Electronic document, http://nla.gov.au/nla.aus-f4378, accessed October 13, 2010.

Spencer, B. 1997. Journal Entry August 23rd 1901 Camp 39 Tennants Creek. In *My Dear Spencer: The Letters of F. J. Gillen to Baldwin Spencer*. H. Morphy, D. J. Mulvaney, and A. Petch, eds. P. 346. Flemington, Australia: Hyland House.

Spencer, B., and F. Gillen. 1904. *The Northern Tribes of Central Australia*. London: Macmillan.

Spencer, B., and F. J. Gillen. 1912. *Across Australia*, vol. 2. London: Macmillan and Co.

Stanner, W. E. H. 1979. *Report on Field Work in North Central and Northern Australia 1934–35*. Canberra: Australian Institute of Aboriginal and Torres Strait Islander Studies.

Strehlow, T. G. H. 1938. Aboriginals at Tennant's Creek, October 15, 1938. Australian Archives N.T. Region: CA 1115 Patrol Officer, Alice Springs and Jay Creek, Darwin.

Turpin, M. 2000. *A Learner's Guide to Kaytetye*. Alice Springs, Australia: IAD Press.

Turpin, M., and A. Ross. 2004. *Kaytetye Picture Dictionary*. Alice Springs, Australia: IAD Press.

Valiquette, H. 1993. *A Basic Kukatja to English Dictionary*. Balgo, Australia: Luurnpa Catholic School.

List of Contributors

Barry Alpher
Independent researcher

Eve Danziger
Department of Anthropology
University of Virginia

Rachel Hendery
Linguistics
School of Culture, History and Language
Australian National University

Alf Hornborg
Human Ecology Division
Lund University

Fiona M. Jordan
Department of Archaeology and Anthropology
University of Bristol

Ian Keen
School of Archaeology and Anthropology
Australian National University

Harold Koch
School of Language Studies
Australian National University

David B. Kronenfeld
Department of Anthropology
University of California, Riverside

Patrick McConvell
School of Language Studies
Australian National University

Dwight Read
Department of Anthropology
University of California, Los Angeles

Jane Simpson
School of Language Studies
Australian National University

Index